THE GUINNESS BOOK OF NUMBER ONE HITS

Paul Gambaccini
Tim Rice
Jonathan Rice

GRR Editorial Associate: Tony Brown

GUINNESS PUBLISHING

First edition 1982, Second edition 1988, Third edition 1994
Published in Great Britain by Guinness Publishing Ltd, 33 London Road, Enfield, Middlesex
Printed and bound in Great Britain by The Bath Press, Bath, Avon

A catalogue record for this book is available from the British Library

ISBN 0-85112-769-X

Editor: David Roberts
Deputy Editor/Picture Researcher: Paola Simoneschi
Page make-up and typesetting: Sallie Collins
Additional editorial support: Mandy Sedge, Sarah Silvé and Kelly Hopwood
Computer Systems Manager: Alex Reid

ACKNOWLEDGEMENTS

The three authors would like to thank all those who have helped in the production of this book, in particular Tony Brown, Mark Clements, Jan Rice and Eileen Heinink. We would also like to thank all those record company press officers who have provided the answers to the strange questions we asked, as well as many of the artists who feature in the book. We also thank *Music Week* and *New Musical Express*. The first best-selling record chart was published in the *New Musical Express* on 14 November 1952, consisting of just 15 singles. The *NME* chart increased over the years to a Top 30, but on 10 March 1960 the trade publication *Record Retailer* (now *Music Week*) published the first UK Top 50 singles chart. The *Music Week* chart, now the copyright of CIN and compiled by Millward Brown, but previously compiled by Gallup and BMRB, is used by the BBC and is accepted as the country's premier chart. In keeping with our *Guinness Book Of British Hit Singles*, this book uses the *NME* chart until 10 March 1960 (the first 96 number ones), and the *RR/MW* chart thereafter.

We have consulted many other rock books, notably those by Joel Whitburn on American chart history, and the *Guinness Encyclopedia Of Popular Music*, edited by Colin Larkin. We have also checked facts with the *Guinness Book Of Rock Stars*, edited by Dafydd Rees and Luke Crampton; the *Billboard Book Of Number One Hits*, by Fred Bronson; the *Penguin Encyclopaedia Of Popular Music*, edited by Donald Clarke; the *Book Of Golden Discs*, compiled by Joseph Murrells; and the *Big Book Of The Blues*, by Robert Santelli. We have also consulted many magazines, of which *Record Collector* and *In Tune* have been particularly helpful. Any mistakes, however, are our own.

Finally, we would like to thank David Roberts, Paola Simoneschi and Sallie Collins at Guinness Publishing for their help, coffee and expert skills which enabled us to get the book together roughly on schedule.

CONTENTS

1

Section One: The full story of each hit, listed chronologically, with artist details. Information includes songwriter and producer, catalogue number, plus the date the record reached the top and the number of weeks at number one. **Page 7**

2

Section Two: The number ones listed alphabetically by artist, with chronological title list showing the date a record reached number one and the weeks spent on top of the chart. **Page 401**

3

Section Three: The number ones listed alphabetically by record title, showing the name of the artist and the chronological reference number.

THE DEFINITION OF SUCCESS

Since November 1952, when Elvis Presley was 17 years old, Cliff was 12, Elton John just five and Madonna minus six, there have been over 700 records that can justly claim the title of Britain's best-selling single, for at least one week of their lives. There have been probably almost another 700 that have falsely claimed the title of chart-topper, because having a number one hit has, for over four decades, been the definition of success in the record industry.

As the 1990s slip away into the new millenium, we seem to hear almost 700 voices a week proclaiming the death of the single, but we beg to differ. Certainly the nature of the singles chart has changed dramatically since the 1950s, but even in those early days the conflict between different things to spend your money on, differing record technologies and various musical styles, which are the reasons now cited for the impending death of the single, were as pronounced as they are today. When the record charts were launched, the single-play record was made of easily breakable shellac. It played at 78 rpm, and the quality of sound reproduction compared to the record players of the day was poor. People did not buy records - they spent their spare money on books, on films, on going to football matches and on drinking in pubs. The competition for the leisure pounds, shillings and pence was as intense then as it is now, and perhaps even more so in that there was much less spare cash in the average household in those austere post-war years. Today's dilemma is whether to buy a computer game or a video or a record, or whether to buy all three.

As far as musical tastes are concerned, there is no doubt that there appears to be a greater diversity of music in the charts today than ever before, and that fans of one genre rarely buy the music of another genre. Heavy metal acts do not 'cross over' into the general market, and rap remains a minority pleasure despite its many chart successes. There is no one universally popular act or musical style that masks differences in musical tastes as there was when the Beatles and the Stones were at their peak, or when disco conquered all in the late 1970s. But is the contrast between, say, 'I Will Always Love You', 'No Limit' and 'Oh Carolina' as consecutive number ones in the 1990s greater than the contrast between 'Smoke Gets In Your Eyes', 'Side Saddle' and 'It Doesn't Matter Anymore' in the 1950s? Or 'Let The Heartaches Begin', 'Hello Goodbye' and 'The

Ballad Of Bonnie And Clyde' in the 60s? The whole point of a hit single is that it is unpredictable, that it does not necessarily follow a trend, and that all types of song can be popular at the same time. And, of course, some songs can be popular over a very long period of time.

Since the previous edition of this book came out, we have seen over one hundred more number ones, including the first record ever to go back to number one on a totally separate occasion, Queen's 'Bohemian Rhapsody'. We have also seen the first record since 1969 to bounce back to number one a week after falling off the top - Mr. Blobby's eponymous Christmas 1993 blockbuster - and we have seen the first instrumental to top the charts since 1973, Doop's eponymous 1994 hit. These two, incidentally, were the first number one singles ever in which the song and the act had identical names. We have seen old hits reach the very top, records such as the Clash's 'Should I Stay Or Should I Go?' and the Bluebells' 'Young At Heart' (which were both used in TV commercials – the former in a Levi's jeans ad and the latter in an ad for the Volkswagen Golf); we have seen old songs revamped for another spell at the top, like 'Can't Help Falling In Love' and 'Dizzy'; and we have seen both phenomena at once with the Righteous Brothers' 'Unchained Melody'. We have seen the longest-running number one of all time, Bryan Adams' '(Everything I Do) I Do It For You', and the longest-running and biggest-selling number one by a woman, Whitney Houston's 'I Will Always Love You'. Take That have broken all records by crashing straight on to the charts at number one with four consecutive releases, and there are further entries for the man with more Top 10 hits than anybody else, Cliff Richard, as well as new additions to the one-hit-wonder list, Partners In Kryme and Robin Beck to mention but two.

There are still those names that fail to break into this book. Since the last edition, Prince, U2 and Elton John (on his own) have all topped the charts for the first time, but there is still no room for Bruce Springsteen, R.E.M. or Simply Red. Perhaps next time. And there will be a next time. If there is one thing about recording the movements of hit singles that we can be sure of, it is that the hit single refuses to die.

PAUL GAMBACCINI   TIM RICE   JONATHAN RICE

THE AUTHORS

Jonathan Rice now owns every number one hit single except two (nos. 137 and 389). He has several on 10-inch 78 rpm shellac, most on 7-inch 45 rpm plastic, some on 12-inch 45 rpm plastic and a few on 4¾ inch CD. He has the Japanese version of no. 275, the French version of no. 329 and the American version of no. 554. He has advance promotion versions of nos. 188 and 310, and at least 12 versions, on single, EP, LP and CD, of number 135. He was in Hong Kong for no. 220's one week of glory, in Canada when no. 236 hit the top, and in Australia when no. 604 ruled the roost. He loves them all (except possibly no. 374).

Tim Rice (lyrics) has here continued his tradition of adding one UK number one to his personal list with every new edition of this book. Represented in the first edition by only no. 400, 'Don't Cry For Me Argentina', he was part of no. 545, 'I Know Him So Well', that debuted in edition two, and for this latest tome he has come in at an ominous 666 with 'Any Dream Will Do' The gap between the knighted Tim's number ones has thus come down from 145 hits to 121, which indicates that his fourth moment of glory should be number 763 of all time, if he and the singles chart survive that long. Don't hold your breath.

Paul Gambaccini anticipates a blockbuster number one on 2 April 1999, his 50th birthday. This is because 'I Heard It Through The Grapevine' was number one when he was 20, 'I Will Survive' aptly led the list when he was 30, and 'Like A Prayer' was on top when he turned 40. If Paul had a landmark birthday each week, every number one would be a classic.

Section One

The Number Ones Listed Chronologically: The Full Story

1

HERE IN MY HEART

AL MARTINO

14 November 1952, for 9 weeks

●●●●●●●●●●

CAPITOL CL 13779

Writers: Pat Genaro, Lou Levinson and Bill Borelli
Producer: Voyle Gilmore

Al Martino's first single release was selling very well when the *New Musical Express* established the first-ever record sales chart, on 14 November 1952. 'Here In My Heart' was the song at the top for the first nine weeks of the new chart, setting a record for the longest continuous run at number one which, even after 40 years, has been beaten only four times. By staying at number one until 1953, Martino secured for himself for all time the record of being the only performer to have a number one hit in 1952. Needless to say, no subsequent act has ever dominated the top spot so entirely in any year since. All the same, Martino was not the top chart act of 1952. That honour fell to Vera Lynn, who clocked up four Top 10 hits against

We will never know how long 'Here In My Heart' by AL MARTINO was Britain's best-selling single, since it was already number one when the chart began. (Pictorial Press)

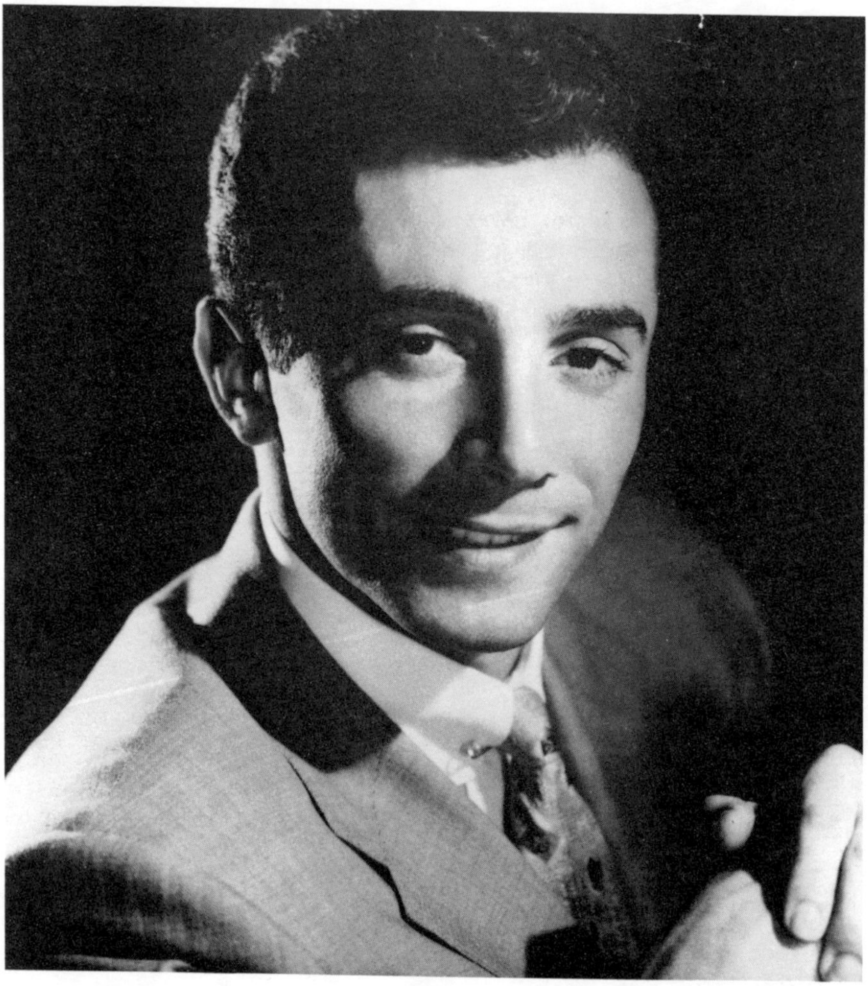

Martino's two in the short period of the first chart year.

Al Martino, born Alfred Cini in Philadelphia on 7 October 1927, faded from the charts after his version of 'The Man From Laramie' made the Top 20 briefly, late in 1955. After many fallow years, he came back into the limelight with a strong performance as the Mafia-owned nightclub singer in *The Godfather*, and had a Top 5 hit in 1973 with 'Spanish Eyes', his second million seller.

On 25 November 1952, 11 days after the British singles chart was instituted, another British cultural phenomenon began. Agatha Christie's play *The Mousetrap* opened in London, destined to become the longest-running show in the world.

2

YOU BELONG TO ME

JO STAFFORD

16 January 1953, for 1 week

•

COLUMBIA DB 3152

Writers: PeeWee King, Red Stewart and Chilton Price
Producer: Paul Weston

'You Belong To Me' came on the chart on 14 November 1952, two days after Jo Stafford's 32nd birthday, and made number one in its tenth week on the chart. This is no longer the slowest climb to the top, however, the record having been broken, finally, by Jennifer Rush (see no. 558), who took 16 weeks to climb the Top 75 in 1985. But as the chart in 1952 and 1953 was only a Top 12, Miss Stafford certainly took her time to climb up the final few rungs of the ladder.

In her one week at the top, Stafford claimed for herself for all time the title of first female performer at number one, but her claim to pop music fame is based on far more than this statistical quirk. She began her career as a member of Tommy Dorsey's Pied Pipers in 1940, making many recordings with another Dorsey vocalist, Frank Sinatra. She hit number one in America in 1945 with Johnny Mercer's orchestra, and had hits with Frankie Laine, Liberace and Gordon Macrae, as well as many solo successes. 'You Belong To Me' was also an American number one, and the biggest- selling record of Stafford's career.

Paul Weston, who produced the record and whose orchestra backed Jo Stafford on this and practically all of her records from the time she left the Tommy Dorsey Orchestra in 1942, was also her husband, so 'You Belong To Me' became the first chart-topping single whose singer and producer were husband and wife.

Stafford's only other Top 10 hit in Britain was also her final US chart-topper, 'Make Love To Me', in 1954. Her final week on the British charts was from 3 February, 1956, 14 weeks before Elvis first hit the charts. By being the first woman at number one, Stafford's place in British chart history is secure.

3

COMES A-LONG A-LOVE

KAY STARR

23 January 1953, for 1 week

•

CAPITOL CL 13876

Writer: Al Sherman
Producer: Mitch Miller

Starr shares with Marvin Rainwater (see no. 70) the distinction of being the only full-blooded American Indians to have reached number one in Britain. Johnnie Ray and Cher also have Indian blood flowing through their veins, but not as many pints of it as Kay or Marvin.

Kay Starr was born Katherine Starks on 21 July 1922 on an Oklahoman Indian reservation, and began her career in the 1940s singing with the Glenn Miller, Bob Crosby and Charlie Barnet big bands before launching her successful solo career. She moved away from the big band sound towards a more countrified approach by recording a few titles with Tennessee Ernie Ford in the early 50s. One of their duets, 'I'll Never Be Free', reached number three on the US charts, but that was in 1950, before the British charts began. Her biggest American hit came in

1952 with the million-selling 'Wheel Of Fortune', a Stateside number one, and by then her music had become more middle of the road. 'Comes A-Long A-Love' only reached number nine in her home country, but it gave both Starr and 50s super-producer Mitch Miller their first number one on this side of the Atlantic. Before Starr's final hit (see no. 44), her other British chart entries were the standard 'Side By Side' and two new songs, 'Changing Partners' and 'Am I A Toy Or A Treasure'.

4

OUTSIDE OF HEAVEN

EDDIE FISHER

30 January 1953, for 1 week

●

HMV B 10362

Writers: Sammy Gallop and Chester Conn
Producer: Hugo Winterhalter

The chart was just getting into its stride as January drew to a close, and after Al Martino's nine-week run at the top, Eddie Fisher's first number one became the third consecutive chart-topper to stay only one week at the top. This meant that for five consecutive weeks, there was a different record at the top. In subsequent chart history, this has never been repeated.

Edwin Jack Fisher was born on 10 August 1928, in Philadelphia and, although he is better known now as an ex-husband of Elizabeth Taylor, he was – at the time of his first UK chart-topper – a single man and had yet to meet his first wife, Debbie Reynolds, whom he married in 1955. Their daughter, Carrie Fisher, went on to star as Princess Leia in the *Star Wars* movies and later married (and divorced) Paul Simon (see no. 283).

Fisher first appeared on radio in 1940, as a member of the cast of The Magic Lady Slipper Club on station WFIL in Philadelphia. Eddie Cantor took him under his wing, and by the time he was 21 he had signed a recording contract with RCA Victor. His army call-up came only a short time later and he spent much of his army career entertaining the troops in Korea. He was still in the army when 'Outside Of Heaven' hit the top, for he was not discharged until 10 April 1953. In June that year, he performed at the Savoy, where Princess Margaret sent a message backstage to request her favourite song of the time, 'Outside Of Heaven'.

5

DON'T LET THE STARS GET IN YOUR EYES

PERRY COMO

6 February 1953, for 5 weeks

●●●●●

HMV B 10400

Writer: Slim Willet
Producer: Eli Oberstein

Born on 18 May 1912, in Pennsylvania, the Singing Barber, as Perry Como became known, is one of the most enduring of all performers on the British charts. He began his singing career in the 1930s with the Freddie Carlone Band, but his first major success was singing 'Deep In The Heart Of Texas' with Ted Weems and his orchestra, in 1942. After the war, he began to generate big hits, starting with 'Till The End Of Time', his first US number one, in 1945. 'Don't Let The Stars Get In Your Eyes' had originally been a country hit for its composer, Slim Willet, as well as for Pat Boone's father-in-law Red Foley, Skeets McDonald and Ray Price. Gisele McKenzie and Eileen Barton also hit with the song on the pop charts in the States, as did Como and Foley.

Como hit a barren chart period in Britain for over a year after this first hit dropped off the charts in April 1953, but three more hits in the latter half of 1954 re-established him as a chart star. By the time of his second number one hit, 'Magic Moments' (see no. 69), he had become the world's highest-paid television star in succession to the man he took over from at the top of the British charts, Eddie Fisher.

6

SHE WEARS RED FEATHERS

GUY MITCHELL

13 March 1953, for 4 weeks

●●●●

COLUMBIA DB 3238

Writer: Bob Merrill
Producer: Mitch Miller

The inexhaustibly successful early-50s team of Bob Merrill, Mitch Miller and Guy Mitchell came up with an astonishing run of chart successes in the first years of the chart. 'She Wears Red Feathers' was their first number one. Of Mitchell's first eight hits in the UK, six were written by Bob Merrill and all were produced by Mitch Miller and his production team at Columbia (CBS) in America.

Guy Mitchell was born on 22 February 1927, his real name being Al Cernik. His parents had emigrated from Yugoslavia, and Mitchell made a name for himself as a child actor before the war. By the 1950s, he had given up acting for singing, and was hugely popular all over the world. 'She Wears Red Feathers' was his second success in the UK, following the number two hit 'Feet Up (Pat Him On The Po-Po)', which set the pattern of bouncy sentimentality for which Merrill, Miller and Mitchell became rich and famous. 'She Wears Red Feathers' was a bizarre tale of an English banker's love for a hula-hula girl, a storyline which may explain why the record did so much better in Britain than in the USA, where it peaked at number 19. The formula was repeated with less success in a later song, 'Chick-A-Boom', which extolled the virtues of a rich Eskimo lady and which Mitchell took to number four in Britain early in 1954.

7

BROKEN WINGS

THE STARGAZERS

10 April 1953, for 1 week

●

DECCA F 10047

Writers: John Jerome and Bernard Gunn
Producer: Dick Rowe

Twenty-one weeks after the chart was established, a British act hit the number one position for the first time. This period of British weakness does not compare with the dominance of American acts from July 1957 to November 1958, when only two weeks of Michael Holliday (see no. 68) interrupted 70 weeks of American number ones, but it was long enough to make the emergence of the first British number one an important day in chart history. The group in question was the Stargazers, in the early 50s the most popular of Britain's few vocal groups.

Three versions of 'Broken Wings' made the charts in UK, although no version hit the pop charts in the song's homeland America. The Stargazers' version was the first cover version of any song to hit the top, but the original by Art and Dotty Todd, as well as another cover by Dickie Valentine, both hit the charts. A song of the same title gave a big hit to the US band Mr. Mister, in 1986, but it was not the same song.

Art and Dotty Todd suffered from cover versions just as badly as Ray Peterson, the original recorder of both 'Tell Laura I Love Her' and 'The Wonder Of You'. Art and Dotty were first with 'Broken Wings' and with another song that they took into the Top 20 of both soul and pop charts in America, 'Chanson D'Amour' (no. 402).

8

(HOW MUCH IS) THAT DOGGIE IN THE WINDOW

LITA ROZA

17 April 1953, for 1 week

●

DECCA F 10070

Writer: Bob Merrill
Producer: Dick Rowe

The first question to be asked from the number one spot was also probably the silliest. Many other questions have been asked over the years by number ones – deep philosophical questions like 'Da Ya Think I'm Sexy?' and 'Are 'Friends' Electric?' (the answer to both questions being not unless turned on), but nobody else has asked how much anything is. For an industry in which money is the Holy Grail, it is surprising how unsuccessful money songs have been. Abba and the Bay City Rollers both failed to hit number one with money songs when they were at the peaks of their careers, and apart from this burning question, only a handful of songs, including 'Can't Buy Me Love' and 'Sixteen Tons', have dealt with money in any way and still made it to the very top. There must be a moral there somewhere.

For 27-year-old Liverpudlian Lita Roza, whose record was a cover of Patti Page's original, this was the peak of her recording career. Producer Dick Rowe became the first of 11 producers or production teams to achieve two consecutive number ones, and Bob Merrill became the first writer to come up with two number ones. On 19 April, the first *New Musical Express* Poll Winners' Concert took place at the Royal Albert Hall. Lita Roza, as Top Female Vocalist, was there, as was her employer Ted Heath, leader of the Dance Band Of The Year.

With his total of 18 weeks at number one from three separate turns at the top for 'I Believe', FRANKIE LAINE is the only chart-topper who can justifiably still look down on Bryan Adams' 16 consecutive weeks. (Pictorial Press)

9

I BELIEVE

FRANKIE LAINE

24 April 1953, for 9 weeks

●●●●●●●●●

and 3 July 1953, for 6 weeks

●●●●●●

and 21 August 1953, for 3 weeks

●●●

PHILIPS PB 117

Writers: Erwin Drake, Irvin Graham, Jimmy Shirl and Al Stillman
Producer: Mitch Miller

Frankie Laine's quasi-religious hit 'I Believe' broke all number one longevity records and, after around 700 successors in the top slot, still holds the record for most weeks on top. Although four records subsequently stayed at number one for longer than nine consecutive weeks, no record has come within two weeks of the 18 weeks in total for which this record stayed at number one. During those weeks, Queen Elizabeth was crowned, Mount Everest was climbed for

the first time, Sir Gordon Richards won his only Derby and the England cricket team won back the Ashes from Australia after 19 years.

No disc has quite matched the achievement of 'I Believe' in having three separate runs at number one, although Guy Mitchell's 'Singing The Blues' (see no. 53) almost did.

No artist has matched Laine's 27 weeks at number one in 1953, a year in which his discs notched up a total of 66 weeks on the chart, more than any of his rivals. His success was mainly responsible for a run from 24 April 1953 to 1 January 1954, during which time the Philips label retained the top spot for 34 out of 37 weeks, a label domination that has never been equalled.

'I Believe' was revived by David Whitfield in 1960 and by the Bachelors in 1964, to give the song a total of 54 weeks on the chart, making it the 14th most successful song in British chart history.

EDDIE FISHER had no more number ones after 1953, but he won a greater prize – the hand of Elizabeth Taylor in marriage. (Pictorial Press)

10

I'M WALKING BEHIND YOU

EDDIE FISHER featuring SALLY SWEETLAND

26 June 1953, for 1 week

•

HMV B 10489

Writer: Billy Reid
Producer: Hugo Winterhalter

Eddie Fisher became the first performer to achieve a second British number one hit when 'I'm Walking Behind You' ousted 'I Believe' for one week. Like

'Outside Of Heaven', the song dealt with lost love. In this lyric, British-born Billy Reid pictured Mr. Fisher walking behind his love down the aisle as she prepares to marry somebody else. Soprano Sally Sweetland shares vocal credit with Fisher, but there is no doubt that it was his name on the label that made the song a hit.

This was to be Fisher's last number one hit, although he had four more Top 10 entries stretching to early 1957, when 'Cindy Oh Cindy' dropped off the charts. By that time Tommy Steele had reached the top with 'Singing The Blues' (see no. 54) and British pop music was changing irreversibly.

'I'm Walking Behind You' gave Dorothy Squires one week of chart glory with her cover version, but it was to be 16 years before she would reappear as a solo act in the charts. Fisher's version also reached number one in the States, and became his fifth million-selling single. He was at this time hosting the American TV show *Coke Time*, and, on his own admission, making around $25,000 a week. He had a network of 65,000 fan clubs around the world, and for a while could do no wrong.

11

MOULIN ROUGE

MANTOVANI AND HIS ORCHESTRA

14 August 1953, for 1 week

●

DECCA F 10094

Writer: Georges Auric
Producer: Frank Lee

The first instrumental to top the charts was the theme tune from the film *Moulin Rouge*, subtitled 'Where Is Your Heart?', by the legendary British orchestra of Mantovani. Only 26 other instrumentals have reached the number one spot in the history of the charts, making barely one in 30 of all number ones.

Annunzio Paolo Mantovani was born in Venice, Italy, on 15 November 1905, and moved to England with his parents in 1921. By the 1930s he had formed his own orchestra, which became known for its

GUY MITCHELL had eight British Top 10 hits that missed the American Top 10, in seven cases the entire chart, until 'Singing The Blues' was an international number one. (Pictorial Press)

'cascading strings', and in the 1940s he began recording with the Decca label. He immediately became as immensely popular on record as he had long been on radio, and in 1951 recorded a stereo album aimed at the American market. It was a huge hit, and a single from the LP, 'Charmaine', reached the US Top 10 and sold over one million copies.

Two years later, with no sign of his popularity fading, Mantovani took the theme from *Moulin Rouge*, the film which starred José Ferrer on his knees as the French painter Henri de Toulouse Lautrec, to number one in Britain. Percy Faith had the biggest hit version in the States, but Mantovani hit the Top 10 once again and both versions sold over the million. Mantovani, who also backed David Whitfield on virtually all of his recordings, died on 31 March 1981.

12

LOOK AT THAT GIRL

GUY MITCHELL

11 September 1953, for 6 weeks

●●●●●●

PHILIPS PB 162

Writer: Bob Merrill
Producer: Mitch Miller

When Frankie Laine's 'I Believe' finally relinquished the top spot, in moved Guy

Mitchell for his second number one hit. Mitchell's first four chart singles produced two number two hits and two number ones, and his chart career rolled on with staggering success from 14 November 1952 until July 1957 when, for the first time, a Guy Mitchell single failed to make the Top 20. By then he had scored four number ones and seven other Top 10 hits, a track record almost as good as that of his labelmate Frankie Laine.

Once again, it was the team of Merrill, Miller and Mitchell (try saying that three times quickly) that created the record, but this was to be the last chart-topper for this particular team. Interestingly, the record failed to chart at all in the United States.

One girl that much of America was looking at during the autumn of 1953 was Jacqueline Bouvier, who, on 12 September, became Mrs John Fitzgerald Kennedy.

13

HEY JOE

FRANKIE LAINE

23 October 1953, for 2 weeks

●●

PHILIPS PB 172

Writer: Boudleaux Bryant
Producer: Mitch Miller

Frankie Laine's second number one hit, in direct contrast to his amazingly longlasting 'I Believe', only stayed in the chart for eight weeks, having reached the number one position in its second week on the chart. That week Frankie Laine had three singles on the chart, which was only a Top 12 at the time. 'I Believe' was in its 31st week of chart action, 'Where The Wind Blows' (a number two hit) was in its eighth week, and 'Hey Joe' was at the top of the heap. The next week, on 30 October 1953, Frankie Laine's third number one hit, 'Answer Me' (see no. 15) entered the chart, and for the next three weeks Frankie Laine singles occupied four of the top 12 chart positions, giving the Chicagoan one third of all the records on the chart, a feat that is never likely to be equalled in these days of a Top 75.

Needless to say, 'Hey Joe' is not the same song as the one that gave Jimi Hendrix his first hit, in 1967. It is a country-tinged song in which the singer gives somebody called Joe due warning that he intends to steal his girlfriend away from him. It is most unlike many Mitch Miller productions, featuring a lead guitar which, if it is not played by Les Paul, is certainly a very good imitation of his style. It was also the first number one to be written by Boudleaux Bryant, whose main success was to come a few years later, writing songs with his wife, Felice, for the Everly Brothers.

14

ANSWER ME

DAVID WHITFIELD

6 November 1953, for 1 week

●

and 11 December 1953, top equal for 1 week

●

DECCA F 10192

Writers: Gerhard Winkler and Fred Rauch; English lyrics by Carl Sigman
Producer: Bunny Lewis

The late David Whitfield, the biggest-selling British vocalist of the mid-50s, began his chart career at the beginning of October 1953 with a ballad called 'Bridge Of Sighs'. Two weeks later, his version of 'Answer Me' hit the chart, two weeks ahead of Frankie Laine's recording, and within three weeks David Whitfield had his first number one. On 13 November, for the first, but not the only, time in chart history, a song was knocked off the top by another version of the same song. Four weeks later, for the only time in British chart history, the two versions of the same song were at number one together.

Eighteen songs have made number one in two different versions: ('Answer Me', 'Can't Help Falling In Love', 'Cherry Pink And Apple Blossom White', 'Dizzy', 'Do They Know It's Christmas', 'Everything I Own', 'I Got You Babe', 'Living Doll', 'Mary's Boy Child', 'Singing The Blues', 'Spirit In The Sky', 'Take A Chance On

Me', 'This Ole House', 'Unchained Melody', 'With A Little Help From My Friends', 'You'll Never Walk Alone', 'Young Love', 'Without You'), but only 'Can't Help Falling In Love' and 'Unchained Melody' beat 'Answer Me''s total chart success. Ray Peterson, this time covering an original rather than vice versa, hit the chart with 'Answer Me' in 1960, and Barbara Dickson gave the song its third Top 10 outing, in 1976.

15

ANSWER ME

FRANKIE LAINE

13 November 1953, for 8 weeks (11 December 1953 top equal)

●●●●●●●●

PHILIPS PB 196

Writers: Gerhard Winkler and Fred Rauch; English lyrics by Carl Sigman
Producer: Mitch Miller

Frankie Laine rounded off an astonishing year of undiluted chart success by becoming the first act to have three number one hits, the first act to hit number one with consecutive releases, and still the only man in chart history to have spent as many as 27 weeks of calendar year in the top slot. Nobody else has ever managed more than 18 weeks at number one in a year, which Elvis Presley achieved in 1961.

Frankie Laine was born Frank LoVecchio in Chicago on 30 March 1913. Early publicity handouts talk of his holding the all-time marathon dance record of 145 days, set in 1932. However, his hold on that record must have been much shorter than his strangehold on the top of the British charts in 1953, because according to our sister publication, *The Guinness Book Of Records*, the marathon dancing record was set at 173 days on 30 November 1932, by two dancers – neither of whom were Frank LoVecchio! However, it may have been marathon dancing that ruined his clothes. On one trip to Britain, a reviewer criticised Laine's clothing, which led him to reply from the stage that, "They can criticise my voice, but not my tailor."

'Answer Me' was known in its original German as 'Mutterlein', and the feat of placing top equal with itself on the British charts is all the more amazing for the fact that the BBC banned the English-language version because of its semi-religious lyric (a fate which had not befallen the equally semi-religious 'I Believe'). Nat 'King' Cole brought out a version which changed the lyric from "Answer me, oh my Lord" to "Answer me, oh my love", and his version was much more successful than Laine's in the United States. In Britain, however, Cole missed out altogether.

16

OH MEIN PAPA

EDDIE CALVERT

8 January 1954, for 9 weeks

●●●●●●●●●

COLUMBIA DB 3337

Writers: Paul Burkhard; English lyrics by John Turner and Geoffrey Parsons
Producer: Norrie Paramor

The Man With The Golden Trumpet, British trumpeter Eddie Calvert, scored his first – and biggest – hit with the sentimental Swiss tune 'Oh Mein Papa', from which most of the lyrics had been excised. A girl chorus wistfully sang the title intermittently behind Calvert's vigorous trumpet style, but listeners who could not stomach the full treacle of the lyrics in Eddie Fisher's vocal version could keep their emotions in check by buying the Calvert arrangement.

Fisher, who decided to record the song as soon as he heard the title, took the record to number one in the United States, while Calvert had to be content with climbing only as far as number six. On this side of the Atlantic, the positions were reversed, with Fisher reaching number nine and Calvert reaching the very top. The lyrics, originally in German for the Swiss musical film *Fireworks*, were described by Fisher as "pure schmaltz, but somehow they touched everyone". The Calvert version being almost lyricless, we can only

Right: EDDIE CALVERT is caught in mid-mouthful on a trip to Italy. (Pictorial Press)

assume that the great British public preferred to remain untouched.

The record has a further claim to fame as the first number one hit recorded at the most successful of all British studios, Abbey Road. At least 75 of Britain's number ones have been recorded there, representing 40 years of artistic and technical excellence from the EMI studio not a cricket ball's throw from Lord's Cricket Ground.

17

I SEE THE MOON

THE STARGAZERS

12 March 1954, for 5 weeks

●●●●●

and 23 April 1954, for 1 week

●

DECCA F 10213

Writer: Meredith Wilson
Producer: Dick Rowe

In taking 'I See The Moon' to number one, the Stargazers became the first act in British chart history to reach number one with their first two chart hits. Like three other acts (Tennessee Ernie Ford, Art Garfunkel and the man that the Stargazers replaced at the top, Eddie Calvert), the Stargazers' number ones were not with consecutive releases, but all the singles between 'Broken Wings' and 'I See The Moon' missed the charts.

The Stargazers were led by Cliff Adams, the man who, a few years later, had a small hit with the theme from the Strand cigarettes TV advertisement, 'The Lonely Man Theme'. At the time, Cliff Adams became the top act alphabetically in British chart history, taking over from Alfi and Harry, who had been the first on the list for four years. Adams retained the title at the head of the alphabetical list of chart acts for 14 years until the current champions, Abba, hit the chart with 'Waterloo' (see no. 348).

Cliff Adams is also famous for years of *Sing Something Simple* with his Cliff Adams Singers on BBC Radio. The other Stargazers at this time were Marie Benson, Fred Datchler (father of Clark Datchler of Johnny Hates Jazz), Bob Brown and Dave Carey.

'I See The Moon' was at the top of the chart when, on March 31 1954, the Soviet Union made one of its more bizarre post-war attempts to reduce tension in Europe by offering to become a member of NATO. The offer was refused.

18

SECRET LOVE

DORIS DAY

16 April 1954, for 1 week

●

and 7 May 1954, for 8 weeks

●●●●●●●●

PHILIPS PB 230

Writers: Paul Francis Webster and Sammy Fain
Producer: Ray Heindorf

Doris Day, born Doris Von Kappelhoff on 3 April 1922, was by far the most successful female vocalist of the early 1950s. Her two number ones remain two of the best-known songs of the pre-rock era (see also no. 49), although some of her sillier songs from the Mitch Miller production line, such as 'Ooh Bang Jiggily Jang', failed to prise open the purse strings of the record-buying public.

'Secret Love' came from the film *Calamity Jane*, starring Day and Howard Keel, and won an Oscar for Best Song Of 1953. The film was an enormous box-office success, justifying Day's belief that the producers of *Annie Get Your Gun* had been wrong not to cast her in the title role. The success of the film owed much to Howard Keel, who was then one of the top Hollywood musical stars, with hits including *Seven Brides For Seven Brothers* to his credit, and in the 1980s he found further fame and fortune playing Miss Ellie's second husband, Clayton Farlowe, in the long-running TV megasoap *Dallas*.

Doris Day, who had first hit the American charts in the late 40s, continued a recording and film career throughout the 50s and early 60s, which earned her the title of Top Box Office Star as a result of her light comedies with the late Rock Hudson. One of the theme songs of a

Day/Hudson film, 'Move Over Darling', which had originally been a Top 10 hit in 1964, reappeared in the British charts in 1987 as a result of being featured in a television commercial for tights.

19

SUCH A NIGHT

JOHNNIE RAY

30 April 1954, for 1 week

●

PHILIPS PB 244

Writer: Lincoln Chase
Producer: Mitch Miller

Johnnie Ray, born in Dallas, Oregon, on 10 January 1927, was partially deafened in an accident at the age of nine but, like Beethoven before him, he did not allow hearing problems to interfere with a musical career. At 15 he appeared on a child talent radio show in nearby Portland, Oregon, and at 17 worked his way south to Los Angeles, where he became a soda fountain assistant and a movie extra. He was numbered among the millions who failed to be discovered and, at the age of 24, moved eastwards to Detroit to sing at the Flame Club.

By the end of 1951 he had moved to Cleveland and made his first hit record, the classic double-sided hit for the Okeh record label, 'Cry', and 'The Little White Cloud That Cried'. The Prince Of Wails was on his way.

'Such A Night' was not a major hit for Ray in the USA, partly, no doubt, because it was refused airplay on many radio stations there. Nevertheless, it was a hit for the Drifters (number five on the Rhythm And Blues charts) in 1954, and in 1964 the song was a hit for Elvis Presley both in the UK (number 13) and the USA (number 16).

There was 'such a night' for world athletics that week. On the evening of 6 May 1954, Roger Bannister completed four laps of the Iffley Road track in Oxford in 3 minutes 59.4 seconds, to become the first man to break four minutes for the mile.

20

CARA MIA

DAVID WHITFIELD, with chorus and Mantovani and his orchestra

2 July 1954, for 10 weeks

● ● ● ● ● ● ● ● ● ●

DECCA F 10327

Writers: Lee Lange and Tulio Trapani
Producer: Bunny Lewis

David Whitfield's second number one was one of the biggest-selling British records of the pre-rock era. It sold well over a million copies, and Whitfield joined Dame Vera Lynn in the ranks of British stars who had achieved a Top 10 hit in America. In Britain, the ten-week run at the top was then the longest-ever run of consecutive weeks at the top and, nearly 700 hits later, Whitfield still takes equal third place, after Slim Whitman (see no. 36) and Bryan Adams (see no. 667).

The writers of 'Cara Mia', Lee Lange and Tulio Trapani, were actually David Whitfield's producer, Bunny Lewis, and his arranger, Mantovani. On this record Mantovani's orchestra is given full label credit, and there is no doubt that the lush strings of the Mantovani sound were a major contribution to the phenomenal success of this record.

Although David Whitfield (born in Hull on 2 February 1925) never topped the charts again, his light operatic tenor tones were a regular fixture in the charts until the end of 1956, when he, like many others, was swept away by the tidal wave of rock and roll. He never managed to make the sort of money that his success would have brought him if it had happened ten years later, although it was said that his voice was insured for the sum of £18,000.

When David Whitfield died, on 15 January 1980, he left only £3,000, but was accorded a four-column obituary notice in *The Times*.

21

LITTLE THINGS MEAN A LOT

KITTY KALLEN

10 September 1954, for 1 week

●

BRUNSWICK 05287

Writers: Carl Stutz and Edith Lindemann
Producer: Milt Gabler, musical arrangement by Jack Pleis

Kitty Kallen is the first of the one-hit wonders, the recording acts whose only chart hit has reached number one. Nobody would pretend that Kitty Kallen or the Floaters have made a greater contribution to British popular music than the Who, Depeche Mode or Billy Fury, but whereas none of those last three acts has had a lone number one hit in the UK, Kitty Kallen has done.

Kallen's career in her native America was not nearly so meteoric. Born on 25 May 1923, she began as a big band singer with Jack Teagarden, Jimmy Dorsey and Harry James, with whom she hit the very top of the American charts in 1945 with 'I'm Beginning To See The Light'. Her first solo hit was in 1949 and, apart from 'Little Things Mean A Lot', her biggest hit on both sides of the Atlantic, she made sporadic chart entries in the States until early 1963, when her last hit, a Top 20 version of 'My Coloring Book', dropped off the charts. 'Little Things Mean A Lot' was written by disc jockey Carl Stutz from Richmond, Virginia, and the leisure editor of the *Richmond Times-Despatch*, Edith Lindemann, who had worked on the newspaper since 1933 and was 56 years old when her only hit composition charted.

DON CORNELL never had a number one at home in America. 'Hold My Hand' was a US number two, but his longest stay in the runner-up position was as vocalist on the 1950 smash 'It Isn't Fair' by Sammy Kaye and his Orchestra. (Pictorial Press)

22

THREE COINS IN THE FOUNTAIN

FRANK SINATRA

17 September 1954, for 3 weeks

●●●

CAPITOL CL 14120

Writers: Sammy Cahn and Jule Styne
Producer: Voyle Gilmore; musical arrangement by Nelson Riddle

The Academy Award-winning Best Original Song Of 1954 was Frank Sinatra's first number one hit. Written by the prolific team of Sammy Cahn and Jule Styne for a lightweight film of the same name, 'Three Coins In The Fountain' was Sinatra's first major chart hit in Britain. It actually entered the charts one week after Sinatra's version of 'Young At Heart' had given him his first hit in Britain, but that song lasted only one week and disappeared as 'Three Coins In The Fountain' arrived.

Francis Albert Sinatra, possibly the most famous popular singer of all time, was born in Hoboken, New Jersey, on 12 December 1915. By the early 1940s he was creating scenes of hysteria among the 'bobbysoxers' which would be equalled only by the rise of Elvis Presley in 1956 and the Beatles in 1963. In the 1990s, still performing and still selling records, Frank Sinatra is Ol' Blue Eyes to record company executives and his fans alike.

Twenty-five numbers songs have reached the top, of which this was the first. Five of those songs have included the number three in the title ('Three Coins In The Fountain', 'Three Steps To Heaven', 'Knock Three Times','Three Times A Lady', and '3 a.m. Eternal'), which is one more than the number two, which has hit four times ('Two Little Boys', 'Goody Two Shoes', 'Two Tribes' and 'Nothing Compares 2 U').

23

HOLD MY HAND

DON CORNELL

8 October 1954, for 4 weeks

●●●●

and 19 November 1954, for 1 week

●

VOGUE Q 2013

Writers: Jack Lawrence and Richard Myers
Producer: Bob Thiele

Don Cornell, one of the least-known number one hitmakers of the 50s, at least as far as British audiences are concerned, had two coincidental links with the rock music which overtook him and many other big band singers a year or two later. He recorded on the same label as Buddy Holly and the Crickets, who gave the label their only other British number ones, and he also put out a single of the song 'Mailman Bring Me No More Blues', which Buddy Holly heard, liked and subsequently recorded.

Don Cornell was born in New York City, reputedly in 1924, although from the late 1930s he worked as a vocalist/guitarist with a number of American bands, when he would only have been around 15 years old. He served briefly in the army, but in 1946 came back to the Sammy Kaye Band that he had left in 1942, and recorded a number of major chart hits with them. Beginning with 'That's My Desire' in 1947, Cornell's vocals took the Sammy Kaye Band into the American Top 10 eight times, the biggest hit being his final single with Kaye, 'It Isn't Fair', which spent six weeks at number two in early 1950. Cornell did not hit the American Top 10 as a soloist until 1952, when his first two records on the Coral label (Vogue in the UK) brought him firmly back into the limelight. In that year he also charted with what is still the shortest title ever to hit the American, or any, charts, 'I'.

'Hold My Hand' was featured in *Susan Slept Here*, a 1954 film starring Dick Powell and Debbie Reynolds (at that time Eddie Fisher's wife). The musical accompaniment for this hit was by Jerry Carr's Orchestra. In Britain, Cornell's only other hit was his version of 'Stranger In Paradise'. In America, he continued to hit the Hot 100 until 1957, once with a cover version of Lonnie Donegan's hit, 'Rock Island Line', but his big days ended with 'Hold My Hand'.

24

MY SON MY SON

VERA LYNN

5 November 1954, for 2 weeks

●●

DECCA F 10372

Writers: Bob Howard, Melville Farley and Eddie Calvert
Producer: Frank Lee

Dame Vera Lynn, born Vera Welsh on 20 March 1919 in East Ham, had already sung with Joe Loss and the Ambrose Orchestra by the time she began her wartime radio series, *Sincerely Yours*, which quickly earned her such popularity that she became known as the Forces' Sweetheart. She then spent the remaining war years touring and entertaining the troops to become, by the end of the war, one of the most famous voices in Europe. However, her popularity was not limited to Europe, because the American troops had heard her and liked her too.

In 1952, her recording of 'Auf Wiederseh'n Sweetheart' climbed to the very top of the American charts, and stayed there throughout the summer months. She would no doubt have repeated the feat in Britain had there been a chart here at that time, but in the event she had to wait until the ballad 'My Son My Son' hit the number one spot over two years later. On the record, she sang with the Frank Weir Orchestra. Eddie Calvert, who co-wrote the song, joined Mantovani as the second number one hit recording star to write a number one hit for somebody else.

Into the 1990s, Dame Vera is still singing 'The White Cliffs Of Dover' and 'Auf Wiederseh'n Sweetheart', to full houses of all ages. She remains one of popular music's most enduring and well-loved legends.

25

THIS OLE HOUSE

ROSEMARY CLOONEY

26 November 1954, for 1 week

●

PHILIPS PB 336

Writer: Stuart Hamblen
Producer: Mitch Miller

Stuart Hamblen was apparently on a hunting expedition when he and his fellow hunters came across a tumbledown hut in the mountains, many miles from civilisation. They went into the hut and there, lying amongst the rubbish and rubble, was the body of an old man. Most of us would have made our excuses and left, but not Mr. Hamblen. He sat down and wrote this song, which Rosemary Clooney (and later Shakin' Stevens, see no. 477) treated as a bouncy novelty number rather than the epitaph for a mountain man that it was meant to be.

Rosemary Clooney, born on 23 May 1928, began her singing career in the late 1940s with her sister Betty, singing with the Tony Pastor Band. Together they provided the vocals for one of Pastor's biggest hits, 'A You're Adorable'.

Clooney married José Ferrer, star of the film *Moulin Rouge*, which gave Mantovani his chart-topping hit. Her first number one hit in America was 'Come On-A My House', written by author William Saroyan and his cousin Ross Bagdasarian, but it preceded the launch of British charts. Bagdasarian is the man who scored hits under the pseudonyms of David Seville, Alfi and Harry, and the Chipmunks, making him the only man to hit the charts as a soloist, both halves of a duo and all three of a trio. Miss Clooney was possibly less versatile, but, in British chart terms, far more successful.

26

LET'S HAVE ANOTHER PARTY

WINIFRED ATWELL

3 December 1954, for 5 weeks

●●●●●

PHILIPS PB 268

Medley of the following songs: 'Another Little Drink Wouldn't Do Us Any Harm', by Nat D. Ayer and Clifford Grey; 'Broken Doll' by James W. Tate; 'Bye Bye Blackbird' by Ray Henderson and Mort Dixon; 'Honeysuckle And The Bee' by Albert Fitz and William Penn; 'I Wonder Where My Baby Is Tonight' by Gus Cahn and Walter Donaldson; 'Lily Of Laguna', by Leslie Stuart; 'Nellie Dean' by Harry Armstrong; 'Sheik Of Araby' by Ted Snyder; 'Somebody Stole My Gal' by Leo Wood; 'When The Red Red Robin (Comes Bob Bob Bobbin' Along)' by Harry Woods.
Producer: Johnny Franz

Despite the almost total blanketing of the upper reaches of the chart by medley discs in the summer of 1981, Winifred Atwell's Christmas chart-topper of 1954 remained the only medley of over two songs to reach the number one slot until Jive Bunny managed it three times in the second half of 1989.

Winifred Atwell, the vast West Indian with the smile and the 'other piano', was the first black person to have a number one hit in Britain, and is still the only female instrumental soloist to have hit the top. Her hit, the third instrumental disc at number one, was the first piano instrumental to top the list and, after 40 years, only Russ Conway, Floyd Cramer, B.Bumble and Lieutenant Pigeon have matched Atwell's success.

This was Atwell's sixth hit single, and her second medley hit after the success of 'Let's Have A Party' the previous Christmas. That record had climbed to number two, and in subsequent festive seasons she treated us to 'Let's Have A Ding Dong' (1955 - number three), 'Make It A Party '(1956 - number seven), 'Let's

Have A Ball' (1957 - number four) and 'Piano Party' (1959 - number ten). In 1958 it was Russ Conway's 'More Party Pops' (a number ten hit) that won the Christmas singalong race.

27

FINGER OF SUSPICION

DICKIE VALENTINE

7 January 1955, for 1 week

●

and 21 January 1955, for 2 weeks

●●

DECCA F 10394

Writers: Al Lewis and Paul Mann
Producer: Dick Rowe

Dickie Valentine, born Richard Bryce in London on 4 November 1929, was given his big break by Ted Heath in 1951 when he invited him to become vocalist with his Band, the most successful of all British big bands. By 1952, Valentine was voted Britain's Most Popular Singer, a title he retained for years beyond his chart heyday, which began early in 1953. His first number one hit came only two months after his marriage at Caxton Hall to Elizabeth Flynn, which caused scenes of crowd hysteria and which was reliably expected to sound the death knell to his chart career. In fact, 1955 was by far his best chart year, with two number ones and three other Top 10 hits.

But even when the hits stopped coming, Valentine kept working as hard as ever. There was a publicity story that reported that he had once been a pageboy at the London Palladium, but had been sacked for some undisclosed misdemeanour. "I'll be back," vowed the determined young Master Bryce, "I'll be back at the top of the bill." And so he was, time and again throughout the 50s.

'Finger Of Suspicion' by DICKIE VALENTINE was the first number one to be pushed off the perch twice by the same record – in its case, 'Mambo Italiano' by Rosemary Clooney. (Pictorial Press)

28

MAMBO ITALIANO

ROSEMARY CLOONEY

14 January 1955, for 1 week

●

and 4 February 1955, for 2 weeks

●●

PHILIPS PB 382

Writer: Bob Merrill
Producer: Mitch Miller

Only 12 of the songs that have reached number one have had foreign-language titles, and of these, five were instrumentals. Rosemary Clooney's second consecutive number one hit was the fourth of the foreign-language titles to reach the top. It was the last vocal chart-topper with a foreign title until Jane Birkin and Serge Gainsbourg's excessively vocal 'Je T'Aime....Moi Non Plus' (see no. 277) made the top 14 years 235 days (and 249 number ones) later. Miss Clooney was the first lady to hit the top of the British charts twice, a record that has been equalled many times, but was not beaten until Sandie Shaw scored her third number one (see no. 232) 12 years and 103 days later.

There is a story that around the time of 'Mambo Italiano''s success a visitor came to dinner at the home of José Ferrer and Rosemary Clooney. On seeing a child or two, the guest enquired how many children the Ferrers had. "Seven", was the reply. "And what are their ages?" asked the polite guest. "Seven, six, five, four, three, two and one", said Miss Clooney. "Oh, I do hope I'm not interrupting anything", replied the guest, tucking into the fish. Perhaps it was not surprising that Clooney's next Top 10 hit, in May 1955, was 'Where Will The Baby's Dimple Be?'

29

SOFTLY SOFTLY

RUBY MURRAY

18 February 1955, for 3 weeks

●●●

COLUMBIA DB 3558

Writers: Mark Paul and Pierre Dudan; English lyrics by Paddy Roberts
Producer: Norrie Paramor

The tenth female artist to top the charts was Ruby Murray, the shy 19-year-old from Belfast, who was easily the most successful singer on the British charts in 1955. However, her total of 80 weeks on the charts in that year stood as the record for only one year, because Bill Haley clocked up the as yet unmatched total of 110 weeks in 1956, but it was not until 1985 that another female vocalist, Madonna, passed Murray's 1955 total.

Ruby Murray's first chart entry had been on 3 February 1954 with the song 'Heartbeat', which was destined to rise to number three. At the end of January 1955, her second hit, 'Softly Softly', entered the hit parade and within a month was number one. By the end of the year, Murray had taken seven songs into the British Top 10, including both sides of her third hit single, 'Happy Days And Lonely Nights' (which reached number 6), backed by 'Let Me Go Lover' (which climbed one rung higher to number five). Yet just as suddenly as her success had begun, it stopped again. 'I'll Come When You Call', her sixth Top 10 record, dropped off the chart at the end of November 1955, and no Ruby Murray record hit the chart after that until the end of August 1956, when 'You Are My First Love' tottered up to number 16.

In 1957 she was hitless. Her last brief spell of chart success came when 'Real Love' hit the Top 20 over Christmas 1958, and a few months later 'Goodbye Jimmy Goodbye' gave Murray her final Top 10 hit. Then it was goodbye, Ruby, goodbye, at least as far as the record buyers were concerned. She is still performing, however, touring regularly – and to great acclaim – with 50s revival shows.

30

GIVE ME YOUR WORD

TENNESSEE ERNIE FORD

11 March 1955, for 7 weeks

●●●●●●●

CAPITOL CL 14005

Writers: George Wyle and Irving Taylor
Producer: Lee Gillette

Ernest Jennings Ford was born on a farm near Bristol, Tennessee, on 13 February 1919, a background not so different from the hero of his final hit, Davy Crockett, who was "born on a mountain top in Tennessee". At school he played the trombone, and on graduation joined the local radio station as an announcer. He studied music in Cincinnati and, by the end of 1941, he was working for a radio station in Knoxville, Tennessee. He served in the US Air Force during the war, and in 1945 moved to Pasadena, California, with his wife Betty. It was while he was working on KXLA Pasadena that he was heard singing along to a record by Capitol producer Lee Gillette and, in 1949, he was signed to an exclusive recording contract. His first hit followed at the very end of 1949, a Top 10 hit in the States, 'Mule Train'.

'Give Me Your Word' was Ford's first hit on this side of the Atlantic. He is perhaps best known here for his deep-voiced country-tinged songs, including his own composition 'Shotgun Boogie', and his biggest hit of all, 'Sixteen Tons' (see no. 41), but his biggest-selling album was a religious compilation called 'Hymns'.

That arose because he was the regular host of a television show in America for five years or so from the mid-50s, and he ended each show with a gospel song.

31

CHERRY PINK AND APPLE BLOSSOM WHITE

PEREZ PRADO

29 April 1955, for 2 weeks

●●

HMV B 10833

Writer: Louis Guiglielmi Louiguy
Producer: Herman Diaz

Originally a French tune (by a Spanish composer!), and therefore not surprisingly called, in the original, 'Cerisiers Rouges Et Pommiers Blancs', 'Cherry Pink And Apple Blossom White' was used as the theme tune for the 1955 film *Underwater*, starring Jane Russell, for whom Howard Hughes reinvented the bra.

Damaso Perez Prado was born in Cuba on 11 December 1916, and began playing in those pre-Castro days in Havana with Orquestra Casino de la Playa. In 1951, he first recorded 'Cherry Pink', but when the producers of *Underwater* decided to use the tune as their theme, the King Of The Mambo was asked to re-record it. The new recording spent ten weeks at the top of the American charts, before being knocked off the top by Bill Haley and another film theme, 'Rock Around The Clock'. In Britain, its success was less long-lived, but Prado helped to establish two very minor chart records. Firstly, the title was the longest number one title at the time, equalling the record set by Lita Roza's 'Doggie' two years earlier. Secondly, 'Cherry Pink' joined 'Answer Me' as the second song to hit number one in two different versions when Eddie Calvert's recording took over the top slot at the end of May, and it is still the only instrumental on that particular list.

English lyrics to the song were written by Mack David, but, as the lyrics were not used in either hit version, perhaps David's efforts went unappreciated. Perez Prado, who died on 14 September 1989, at the age of 72, hit number one again in America, with 'Patricia' in 1958, a record which climbed as high as number eight in Britain. Prado was not the featured trumpeter on either hit - the lead trumpeter on 'Cherry Pink' was Billy Regis.

32

STRANGER IN PARADISE

TONY BENNETT

13 May 1955, for 2 weeks

●●

PHILIPS PB 420

Writers: Robert Wright and George Forrest, based on a theme by Aleksandr Borodin
Producer: Mitch Miller

Anthony Dominick Benedetto was born on 13 August 1926 in Queen's, New York City. His first public appearance was at the age of seven in a church minstrel show, but his climb from there to the top was interrupted by World War II, by the end of which Benedetto was an infantryman in Europe. After the war, an appearance on Arthur Godfrey's *Talent Show* led to a concert engagement with Bob Hope, and Bennett's career was under way. In 1951 he topped the American charts twice, with 'Because Of You' and then the Hank Williams song 'Cold Cold Heart', and in 1953 he recorded 'Stranger In Paradise', with backing, as usual, from Percy Faith's Orchestra.

The show *Kismet* opened on Broadway in 1953, the hit song based on a theme from the Polovetsian Dances in Borodin's 1888 opera, *Prince Igor*. The first recording of that theme had been by Sir Thomas Beecham in 1915, but clearly its popularity was timeless. *Kismet* came to London in 1955, and in that year no fewer than six versions of 'Stranger In Paradise' hit the British charts.

In America in 1953, Bennett had stopped at number two with the song (although this was no disgrace, as the other side of his single, 'Rags To Riches', hit number one), but in Britain two years later he climbed to the very top. Not only did it prove to be his only chart-topper, but also his only Top 10 hit in Britain. Even his most famous recording, 'I Left My Heart In San Francisco', only peaked at number 19 in America and at number 25 in Britain. Yet, despite a comparative lack of chart success over the years, Bennett has long been acknowledged as one of the great jazz balladeers of his time.

33

CHERRY PINK AND APPLE BLOSSOM WHITE

EDDIE CALVERT

27 May 1955, for 4 weeks

●●●●

COLUMBIA DB 3581

Writer: Louis Guiglielmi Louiguy
Producer: Norrie Paramor

The day after Sir Anthony Eden's General Election victory as leader of the Conservative Party, Eddie Calvert moved his version of 'Cherry Pink' into the top position, giving him his second number one. He was the first instrumentalist to achieve this feat.

Eddie Calvert was born in Preston, Lancashire, on 15 March 1922. His father was an amateur musician in a brass band, and it was he who taught Calvert to play the cornet. No wonder Eddie's first million seller was 'Oh Mein Papa'.

During the war, Calvert was a despatch rider and played part time with various bands, graduating from Jimmy McMurray's Band at the Birmingham Casino, past Billy Ternent's Band at BBC Wales and finally, by now fully professional, touring Europe at the end of the war with Geraldo. By this time, he was beginning to take centre stage during performances, playing his solos in a dramatic spotlight, while the rest of the orchestra accompanied him from a darkened stage.

Calvert's chart career, which had begun with two widely spaced number one hits, then faded a little. He reached the Top 20 with an instrumental version of the song he replaced at the top, 'Stranger In Paradise', and still had enough of a following in 1958 to score a Top 10 hit with 'Mandy'. By mid-1958, his chart successes had finished, but his simple style had showed the way for later chartbound trumpeters such as Herb Alpert, Al Hirt and Nini Rosso.

Calvert died in South Africa on 8 August 1978.

34

UNCHAINED MELODY

JIMMY YOUNG

24 June 1955, for 3 weeks

●●●

DECCA F 10502

Writers: Alex North and Hy Zaret
Producer: Dick Rowe

A cheap and instantly forgettable American B-movie called *Unchained* had one redeeming feature, its theme tune. Those who went to see the film could be forgiven for thinking that any film with a tune as strong as 'Unchained Melody' behind the opening credits would be worth sitting through. In fact, anybody who walked out of the cinema as soon as he had heard the tune missed nothing else of any merit. The original version was by the American singer Todd Duncan, but Dick Rowe at Decca decided it was right for a singer they had recently signed, whose career was then as far down as it had been up when his version of Nat 'King' Cole's American chart-topper, 'Too Young', had been a major hit on the tiny Polygon label in pre-chart days.

So Jimmy Young got the song and the mighty Decca publicity machine was rolled out to support it. The American Al Hibbler's version took off first and seemed to be winning the race, but, as more versions flooded on to the market (14 different recordings of the song were available that summer), it was the British singer who started picking up the airplay and the sales. By the end of June, he was at number one, and Hibbler had to be content with taking his only British hit to number two. Suddenly, Jimmy Young was an overnight sensation again.

'Unchained Melody' is one of only two songs that have been a hit in seven different versions. Apart from Jimmy Young and Al Hibbler, Les Baxter and Liberace reached the charts with it in 1955, and then Jimmy Young re-recorded his hit in 1964 and took it back into the Top 50. The following year, the Righteous Brothers made the sixth hit version of the song and, in 1986, Leo Sayer brought the song back into the lists after a 21-year absence. The Righteous Brothers' version recharted in 1990, to become the 653rd number one. Only 'White Christmas', which has never hit the very top of the charts, can match these seven hit versions, and no other number one can beat the total of 79 weeks that the different versions of 'Unchained Melody' have spent on the British charts.

35

DREAMBOAT

ALMA COGAN

15 July 1955, for 2 weeks

●●

HMV B 10872

Writer: Al Hoffman
Producer: Walter Ridley

Throughout the mid-50s, the most consistently successful singer in Britain, in chart terms, was Alma Cogan, who was born in London on 19 May 1932. From March 1954, when her first hit, 'Bell Bottom Blues', came on to the chart, until 1959, she was rarely out of the charts. She never matched the huge record sales that Ruby Murray achieved in the same year that Cogan had her only chart-topper, nor the volume that Shirley Bassey managed when she was enjoying simultaneous Top 10 hits in early 1959, but Cogan's 18 hit records made a list longer than any other female star could boast by the time her last hit, 'Cowboy Jimmy Joe', dropped off the charts in May 1961. Only four of those hits reached the Top 10, but her versions of the big hits of the day always gave the original artists a run for their money. Apart from her own number one, she hit the charts with her versions of three other chart-toppers: 'Little Things Mean A Lot' (number 11), 'Why Do Fools Fall In Love' (number 22) and 'The Story Of My Life' (number 25).

Alma Cogan was known for her chuckle and her extravagant dresses, which all seemed to feature yards of tulle petticoat. Yet her musical image was not just lightweight and happy-go-lucky. Shortly before her tragic death from cancer on 26 October 1966, she recorded a few titles with Andrew Loog Oldham, then the manager and producer of the Rolling Stones. The tracks were never released, but the mere fact that the Stones' mastermind wanted to record her shows that her range was far greater than bubbly songs such as 'Never Do A Tango With An Eskimo' and 'Dreamboat'. The latter, incidentally, provided an American Top 20 hit in 1961 for another major female star of the 50s, Connie Francis.

36

ROSE MARIE

SLIM WHITMAN

29 July 1955, for 11 weeks

●●●●●●●●●●●

LONDON HL 8061

Writers: Rudolf Friml, Otto Harbach and Oscar Hammerstein II
Producer: Lew Chudd

The song that was number one in Britain when James Dean died was sung by Otis Dewey Whitman Jr, who was born on 20 January 1924, the same year that the musical *Rose Marie* was first produced. Like many other country singers before and since (of whom Charley Pride is perhaps the best-known example), Slim Whitman was an excellent baseball player, and it was only the intervention of war, which resulted in his enlistment in the US Navy, that steered him to a singing rather than baseball career.

Whitman's recording career began to flourish at Imperial Records, which was one of America's fastest-growing independent labels, thanks largely to the success of Fats Domino. Whitman's career hit the very peak when he recorded a 30-year-old love song which proceeded to break all records for sustained chart success in Britain. Not until Bryan Adams rewrote the record books with '(Everything I Do) I Do It For You' in 1991

Left: Among the odd aspects of the success of 'Rose Marie' by SLIM WHITMAN is the fact that it fell short of the Top 20 in America, but did so a year before it charted at all in Britain. (Pictorial Press)

did any record beat Rose Marie's record of 11 consecutive weeks at number one. It was actually the second song from the musical that Whitman had turned into a million seller. In 1951, before the existence of the British charts, he hit the American Top 10 with 'Indian Love Call'.

After 'Rose Marie', there were no more number ones for Slim Whitman. Nevertheless, he came back so strongly in the mid-70s that two of his albums topped the British charts, and a single, 'Happy Anniversary', reached number 14 at the end of 1974, almost 20 years since the success of 'Rose Marie'. Whitman's other claim to fame is that of being the first left-handed guitarist to hit the top spot, many years before Paul McCartney or Jimi Hendrix joined that select category.

37

THE MAN FROM LARAMIE

JIMMY YOUNG

14 October 1955, for 4 weeks

●●●●

DECCA F 10597

Writers: Lester Lee and Ned Washington
Producer: Dick Rowe

On Harry Webb's 15th birthday, Jimmy Young established a new record which Cliff Richard was to equal but never beat - he became the first British solo star to place two consecutive single releases at number one. Once again, Young relied on the team of producer Dick Rowe, musical director Bob Sharples and a song from a Hollywood film. This song was the theme from a big-budget Western starring James Stewart, rather than the theme to a B-film prison drama like his previous single, 'Unchained Melody'. Ten versions of 'The Man From Laramie' were released in Britain, and the *Daily Mirror*, in reviewing the records, wrote: "It might just as well be 'The Man From The Coal Board' for all the fire some get into it." Only two of the ten versions hit the British charts, the Al Martino version, which climbed to number 19, and Young's triumphant single.

The main immediate result of the success of 'The Man From Laramie' was that Jimmy Young won a starring role opposite Hylda Baker in the Christmas pantomime *Robinson Crusoe* at the Grand Theatre, Wolverhampton. Success does not come much bigger than that, but more was to follow for JY. The *New Musical Express* listed him as the second-biggest selling artist of 1955 (after Ruby Murray, of course), and in the *NME Annual*, that latterday bible of pop orthodoxy, Young (born Leslie Ronald Young on 21 September 1923) was described as "the success of the year. One name above all others deserves to shine forth in letters of gold. The name, of course, is Jimmy Young". The *Record Mirror* agreed, and called him "Mr. Comeback 1955 - Jimmy Young, the man they said was finished, the man who hasn't had a hit for years".

That was not the only comeback that JY has made during his long, and ultimately highly successful, showbiz career. Now, nearly 40 years after his second – and last – chart-topping single, he is one of Britain's most famous radio voices, with an OBE to boot. As the man himself would say, "TTFN."

38

HERNANDO'S HIDEAWAY

THE JOHNSTON BROTHERS

11 November 1955, for 2 weeks

●●

DECCA F 10608

Writers: Richard Adler and Jerry Ross
Producer: Hugh Mendl

The musical *The Pajama Game* was the source of this much-recorded song, which provided the British Johnston Brothers with their only number one hit. Sadly, it reached number one in Britain in the week that one of the composers, Jerry

Ross, died in New York. It was the second big hit from the musical, after 'Hey There', which had been a Top 20 hit in no less than four versions - by Rosemary Clooney (number 4), Johnny Ray (number 5), Lita Roza (number 17) and Sammy Davis Jr. (number 19). Johnnie Ray's version included 'Hernando's Hideaway' on the B-side, and that track climbed to number 11. In America, Rosemary Clooney hit number one with 'Hey There', but it was the Everly Brothers' mentor, Archie Bleyer, who had the biggest hit with 'Hernando's Hideaway'. His version on his own Cadence label climbed to number two, thanks to Maria Alba's castanet solo.

The Johnston Brothers were, like the Righteous Brothers, not brothers at all. They were Johnny Johnston, Miff King, Eddie Lester and Frank Holmes, with a vocal style very much in the Stargazers mould. To complicate matters, the Johnston Brothers often included Jean Campbell in their line-up, and then they were known as the Keynotes, although they never hit the charts under that name. Two of the Johnston Brothers' hits were vocal versions of Winifred Atwell's Christmas medleys - tracks called 'Join In And Sing Again' and 'Join In And Sing No. 3'. The original 'Join In And Sing' had failed to hit the charts, but the Brothers' ability to come up with hit versions of middle-of-the-road tunes continued until May 1957, when their 'Heart' lost the chart race to Max Bygraves by nine lengths.

39

ROCK AROUND THE CLOCK

BILL HALEY AND HIS COMETS

25 November 1955, for 3 weeks

●●●

and 6 January 1956, for 2 weeks

●●

BRUNSWICK 05317

Writers: Jimmy de Knight (James Myers) and Max C. Freedman. Producer: Milt Gabler

On 12 April 1954, a 28-year-old country-and-western bandleader went into Decca's Pythian Table studios in New York to record, as a favour to his manager Jim Myers, a song which had been part of his stage act for almost a year, but which his previous recording company, Essex, had been unwilling for him to record. When first released, the record was a small hit for Bill Haley (born William John Clifton Haley in Highland Park, Michigan, on 6 July 1925) and his Comets, who, for this session, were Danny Cedrone, Billy Williamson, John Grande, Marshall Lytle and session drummer Billy Guesack.

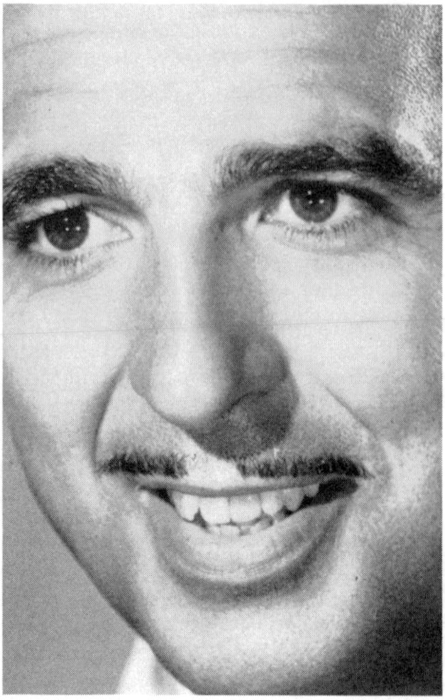

'Sixteen Tons' by TENNESSEE ERNIE FORD was one of Princess Margaret's Desert Island Discs. (Pictorial Press)

It was not until 'Rock Around The Clock' was featured in a 1955 Glenn Ford movie called *Blackboard Jungle* that the record became perhaps the single most significant recording in popular music history. Nine months after the song had briefly entered the British charts, it reappeared and within six weeks, it was at number one. Eventually, it sold over a million copies in Britain alone, and changed popular music for ever. Not bad for a song co-written by a man (Max Freedman) born in 1893! In 1956, Bill Haley had more chart success in one year than any other act before or since, but his tour of Britain early in 1957 marked the beginning of the end. In the flesh, the twice-married Haley was not every teenage girl's dream, and Elvis Presley took over and built on Haley's amazing success.

It is impossible to analyse the reasons for Haley's success with 'Rock Around The Clock'. It reached the Top 20 in Britain twice more, in 1968 and 1974, and, in chart longevity terms, is the second most successful number one record of all time. But what did this lively number have about it that transformed the musical heritage of Western youth? Bill Haley, who died on 9 February 1981, never knew.

40

CHRISTMAS ALPHABET

DICKIE VALENTINE

16 December 1955, for 3 weeks

●●●

DECCA F 10628

Writers: Buddy Kaye and Jules Loman
Producer: Dick Rowe

For three weeks at Christmas, Dickie Valentine played King Canute to Bill Haley's incoming tide of rock and roll. More than that, this record marked the first time that a song created specifically for the Christmas market had hit number one, showing that his astute management had learnt from Winifred Atwell's singalong successes of previous Christmas seasons.

'Christmas Alphabet' was the first of the big Christmas hits, apart from 'White Christmas', which first hit the chart (in Mantovani's version) for three weeks in 1952, and its chart career was almost as brief as the season of goodwill itself. It spent only seven weeks on the chart in total, three of which were at number one, and it held the undisputed title of Shortest-Lived Number One Hit until Ferry Aid's 'Let It Be' (see no. 589) equalled its seven-week chart run in 1987. It was not until two more seasonal hits, 'Let's Party 'and 'Do They Know It's Christmas?' (see nos. 637 and 638), spent only six weeks on the chart that Valentine's unenviable record was finally broken.

Dickie Valentine was busy that Christmas, not only because of his chart hit, but also with playing the part of Wishee Washee in the pantomime *Aladdin*. He was also preparing for the birth of his first child, a daughter, Kim, who was born in January 1956. His next, and final, Top 10 hit did not come until a year later, with a song called 'Christmas Island', but even so, he remained year in and year out Britain's Most Popular Male Vocalist until Cliff Richard appeared on the scene. Valentine never lost his popularity, and continued to play to full houses until he lost his life in a car crash on 6 May 1971.

41

SIXTEEN TONS

TENNESSEE ERNIE FORD

20 January 1956, for 4 weeks

●●●●

CAPITOL CL 14500

Writer: Merle Travis
Producer: Lee Gillette

Eleven days before Sex Pistol Johnny Rotten was born, the song that ushered in rock and roll dropped off the top of the charts, to be replaced by Tennessee Ernie Ford's second number one hit. Country and western star Merle Travis wrote the coal-mining song 'Sixteen Tons', and first recorded it in 1947. Travis' father was a coal miner in Beech Creek, Kentucky, and the chorus was based on a saying of his father, "Another day older and deeper in debt."

'Sixteen Tons' was the biggest hit of Ford's career. In America, it was one of the fastest-selling records in pop history, and it stayed at the top of the charts for seven weeks from late November 1955. The week before it climbed to number one in Britain, it was knocked from the top in America by the same record that was to topple it in Britain five weeks later, Dean Martin's 'Memories Are Made Of This'.

'Sixteen Tons' was Tennessee Ernie Ford's

second consecutive number one hit in Britain, although, like Eddie Calvert and the Stargazers before him, he had released records between his number ones that had missed the chart altogether. His follow-up to 'Sixteen Tons' was 'The Ballad Of Davy Crockett', a record that had been a hit for him in America before 'Sixteen Tons', but which had been kept under wraps for the British market until the film from which it was taken, starring Fess Parker, was released. 'Davy Crockett' made number three in the charts, but was kept off the top spot not only by Bill Hayes' original version of the song, but also by 'Sixteen Tons'. On 27 January 1956, Ford had two of the top three chart placings, a feat that – 650 number ones later – has been equalled only by Guy Mitchell, Frankie Laine, Elvis Presley, Shirley Bassey, the Beatles, John Lennon, Frankie Goes To Hollywood and Madonna.

42

MEMORIES ARE MADE OF THIS

DEAN MARTIN

17 February 1956, for 4 weeks

●●●●

CAPITOL CL 14523

Writers: Terry Gilkyson, Richard Dehr and Frank Miller
Producer: Lee Gillette

Dean Martin, born Dino Paul Crocetti on 7 June 1917, in Steubenville, Ohio, had, in true show business tradition, been a petrol pump attendant, a steelworker, a dealer in a casino and even a prizefighter (under the name Kid Crochet) before he switched to singing in the mid-40s. By 1946, he was vocalist with the Cleveland-based Sammy Watkins Band, and during a spell at a club in Atlantic City, he met a young comedian called Jerry Lewis. Within a few months they had become one of the most popular comedy duos in the nation.

Dean Martin's biggest-selling single of his career, a number one hit on both sides of the Atlantic, hit the top just a few months before the Martin/Lewis partnership broke up. 'Memories Are Made Of This' came from the film *The Seven Hills Of Rome*, in which it was sung by Mario Lanza, but it was Martin who had the big hit. The backing voices, singing "Sweet, sweet, the memories you gave to me", belonged to the three co-writers of the song, under the name of the Easyriders, who went on to have a Stateside Top 10 hit of their own, 'Marianne', as well as featuring on Frankie Laine's final American Top 10 hit, 'Love Is A Golden Ring', in 1957.

Dean Martin's chart career extended until 1969, when his last hit, 'Gentle On My Mind', became his fourth number two. Even without Jerry Lewis, his film and stage career continued successfully, with starring roles in such films as *Airport*, *Rio Bravo* and *Kiss Me, Stupid* to his credit. Well known as a heavy drinker, by 1994 Martin was a virtual recluse in failing health.

43

IT'S ALMOST TOMORROW

THE DREAMWEAVERS

16 March 1956, for 2 weeks

●●

and 6 April 1956, for 1 week

●

BRUNSWICK 05515

Writers: Wade Buff and Eugene Adkinson
Producers: Wade Buff, Eugene Adkinson and Milt Gabler

Gene Adkinson and Wade Buff, from Miami in Florida, wrote 'It's Almost Tomorrow', but could find nobody to record it. So, being resourceful people, they formed their own group and made the record. Milt Gabler at American Decca picked it up for national distribution and, in November 1955, the session group hit the Hot 100. It was a Top 10 hit in their own country, but in Britain things went even better. By climbing to number one, the Dreamweavers established two rather minor chart records. Firstly, they became the first studio band to hit the top, heading a list that now includes the Archies,

Edison Lighthouse, Spitting Image and others. Secondly, by having no more chart success at all, they joined the one-hit-wonder club, which at the time included only Kitty Kallen (see no. 21), and they remained the only one-hit wonders to have climbed back to number one after being ousted from the top, until the feat was matched by Mr. Blobby.

In America, the Dreamweavers fared slightly better. After 'It's Almost Tomorrow', they managed two more hit singles, both sides of which hit the chart. However, only one of those tracks, 'A Little Love Can Go A Long Long Way', hit the Top 40 and (at the end of June 1956) the Dreamweavers dropped off the British and American charts simultaneously, never to return. 'It's Almost Tomorrow' made a comeback, though. David Whitfield sang the song on 'All Star Hit Parade', which reached number two in July 1956, and Mark Wynter's version climbed to number 12 at the very end of 1963, to give him his last but one hit.

44

ROCK AND ROLL WALTZ

KAY STARR with the HUGO WINTERHALTER ORCHESTRA

30 March 1956, for 1 week

●

HMV POP 168

Writers: Dick Ware and Shorty Allen
Producer: Joe Carlton

Kay Starr's 'Rock And Roll Waltz', the only number one with the words rock and roll in the title, put her on the list of female performers with two number one hits to their credit. At that time it was a short list, with just Starr and Rosemary Clooney, but two weeks later Winifred Atwell added her name to it. Even now, only four female performers have managed more than two solo number ones: Madonna (seven), Whitney Houston (four), Kylie Minogue (three) and Sandie Shaw (three).

Kay Starr's other number one (see no. 3) had been her first British hit, so, as she failed to hit the charts again after 'Rock And Roll Waltz', she established a weird – and ultimately unique – record of starting and finishing her British chart life with a number one.

Starr had recorded for Capitol until 1955, when she switched to RCA (released on HMV in England). At her first recording session for RCA, she was given 'Rock And Roll Waltz' and, to begin with, did not like it at all. However, her new producer Joe Carlton was right to insist, and the song, which brilliantly combined modernity with the more conservative sound of the 1940s, reached the summit both in Britain and in the United States.

In America, Kay Starr hit the charts several more times, but even a change back to Capitol in the early 60s failed to return her to the charts over here. Her achievement of hitting number one on two different labels did not remain unique for long either. Winifred Atwell equalled that feat just two weeks later.

45

THE POOR PEOPLE OF PARIS

WINIFRED ATWELL

13 April 1956, for 3 weeks

●●●

DECCA F 10681

Writers: Marguerite Monnot and René Rouzaud
Producer: Hugh Mendl

The second chart-topper for the girl from Tunapuna, Trinidad, was the second 'French' instrumental, after Mantovani's 'Moulin Rouge', to top the hit parade. Winifred Atwell, a qualified chemist, began playing for charity in Trinidad before going first to New York and then to London to study the piano. She hit the big time when she realised that boogie piano was more lucrative than classical piano, and by 1951 she had a recording contract. It was a happy 42nd birthday for her in 1956, for on that day, 27 April, she was at number one, and the rest of the year proved good for her as well. She did not win on the Premium Bonds, which were introduced in that year's budget on 17 April, but she had big hits with two more French-sounding tunes, 'Port Au Prince' (which is, of course, in the French-speaking island of Haiti) and 'Left Bank' (also written by Marguerite Monnot). And all this on that 'other piano' which reportedly cost Miss Atwell 50 shillings (£2.50) in a Battersea junk shop.

'Poor People Of Paris' was a genuine French tune, written by composer Marguerite Monnot and with lyrics by René Rouzaud, which had been made popular in France by the legendary Edith Piaf. The original title was 'La Goualante Du Pauvre Jean', which translates as 'The Ballad Of Poor John'. However, a mistake in a cable from Paris to Capitol Records in Hollywood meant that when Les Baxter recorded his instrumental version that became a number one hit in America, he was told that the song was about Pauvres Gens (Poor People), not Pauvre Jean. Thus, his hit became 'The Poor People Of Paris', and Atwell's cover version followed. It is possible, perhaps, that the title refers to those not super-rich or super-chic enough to be invited to the wedding of the year in Monte Carlo, where Prince Rainier married Grace Kelly on 19 April 1956.

Winifred Atwell died in Sydney, Australia, on 12 February 1983.

46

NO OTHER LOVE

RONNIE HILTON

4 May 1956, for 6 weeks

●●●●●●

HMV POP 198

Writers: Richard Rodgers and Oscar Hammerstein II
Producer: Walter Ridley

From the comparatively unsuccessful Rodgers and Hammerstein musical *Me And Juliet*, Ronnie Hilton took the song 'No Other Love', and scored his one and only number one hit. The song had already been a number one hit in America in 1953 for Perry Como, but in 1956, Hilton's opposition came only from Canadian-born Edmund Hockridge and Britain's Johnston Brothers. No American versions of this song ever hit the British charts, the Perry Como version never being released as a single over here because HMV, who held the British rights to the Como recording, decided to promote the Hilton single rather than the Como import.

Hilton's light operatic style, which first saw the professional light of day at the Hippodrome Theatre, Dudley, was already, by mid-1956, being overtaken by major changes in public tastes. Elvis Presley's British chart career began in the second week of Hilton's six-week run at the top, when 'Heartbreak Hotel' entered the *NME* Top 30. By the time 'No Other Love' dropped off the charts, Elvis had also introduced 'Blue Suede Shoes' and 'I Want You I Need You I Love You' to the charts. 1956 was the year in which Bill Haley clocked up an all-time record of 110 chart weeks, so the chart-topping efforts of the British stars such as Ronnie Hilton and the late Winifred Atwell were entirely against the run of play. Nevertheless, Hilton continued to hit the charts until 1965, and remains in the 1990s a popular performer and disc jockey on BBC Radio Two.

47

I'LL BE HOME

PAT BOONE

15 June 1956, for 5 weeks

●●●●●

LONDON HLD 8253

Writers: Ferdinand Washington and Stan Lewis
Producer: Randy Wood

Charles Eugene 'Pat' Boone, born 1 June 1934, was the clean-cut all American boy of popular music. A descendant of the American frontiersman Daniel Boone, Pat was raised in Tennessee, and it was winning a talent contest in Nashville that drew him to the attention of Randy Wood at Dot Records. His first American hit was a song called 'Two Hearts', but the British record-buying public were introduced to him through his version of Fats Domino's 'Ain't That A Shame', which hit number seven at the beginning of 1956. His follow-up was his version of another rhythm and blues hit, the Flamingos' 'I'll Be Home', and it gave him his first chart-topping single on either side of the

Atlantic, and his only British number one. The Flamingos also made the first US chart version of Art Garfunkel's number one hit 'I Only Have Eyes For You' (see no. 379), but their only British chart entry was a minor skirmish with the lower reaches of the Top 40 late in 1969, with the forgettable 'Boogaloo Party'.

Boone's chart career has been far more distinguished. Hits such as 'Friendly Persuasion', 'Don't Forbid Me', 'April Love' and his biggest worldwide hit, 'Love Letters In The Sand', established him as the acceptable alternative to the rebellious Elvis Presley. His British chart career continued for seven years, until 1962, but 30 years on, he still ranks as one of the 30 most successful chart acts of all time.

Boone is married to country star Red Foley's daughter Shirley. The eldest of their four daughters, Debbie Boone, had the biggest hit of the 1970s in the United States, with her multi-million-selling smash, 'You Light Up My Life'.

FRANKIE LYMON stands on a ladder behind THE TEENAGERS (left to right: Sherman Garnes, Joe Negroni, Herman Santiago and Jimmy Merchant). (Pictorial Press)

48

WHY DO FOOLS FALL IN LOVE?

THE TEENAGERS featuring FRANKIE LYMON

20 July 1956, for 3 weeks

●●●

COLUMBIA DB 3772

Writers: Frankie Lymon and George Goldner
Producer: Richard Barrett

Rarely has a star shone so brightly so soon and gone out more quickly than in the case of Frankie Lymon. Discovered singing gospel songs in the hallway of a

New York apartment block, Lymon and the Teenagers had a hit with their very first attempt. 'Why Do Fools Fall In Love' entered the US Top 100 in the first week of February 1956, ultimately reaching number six. It got to the top of the rhythm and blues list in the first week of March, and remained there for five weeks. By summertime, the record had reached the UK, and began a three-week run at the summit in July. It was the first R&B side to go to number one in Britain.

In the time-honoured tradition of overnight sensations, it was all so nearly very different. The song had been written as 'Why Do The Birds Sing So Gay', based on some love letters received by a friend of the group. The group was called the Premiers, and the lead singer was one Herman Santiago. George Goldner, the head of Gee Records, persuaded the group to rework the lyrics, but before the session Herman Santiago fell ill, so 13-year-old Frankie Lymon stood in for him. The leader of the backing band on the session, Jimmy Wright, also came up with the name the Teenagers, and the rest is history.

In 1957, 14-year-old Lymon went on to become the youngest act to top the bill at the London Palladium. In that year the group scored three more chart hits, including the immortal 'I'm Not A Juvenile Delinquent', the Top 10 hit 'Baby Baby' and the evergreen 'Goody Goody'. Lymon's career went downhill from then on. Diana Ross took his song to the Top 10 a quarter of a century later, but Lymon was not alive to see it. He had died of a drug overdose on 28 February 1968, aged 25, one of the very first rock drug casualties.

49

WHATEVER WILL BE WILL BE

DORIS DAY

10 August 1956, for 6 weeks

●●●●●●

PHILIPS PB 586

Writers: Ray Evans and Jay Livingston
Producer: Mitch Miller

'Whatever Will Be Will Be (Que Sera Sera)' was the Oscar-winning song from the 1956 film *The Man Who Knew Too Much*, directed by Alfred Hitchcock and starring James Stewart and Doris Day, with a supporting cast of well-known British actors of the 50s including Bernard Miles, Richard Wattis and Brenda de Banzie. It was the second time within a year that a song from a James Stewart movie had hit number one in Britain, coming only 12 hits after Jimmy Young's 'The Man From Laramie'. It was also the second time that Doris Day had taken an Oscar-winning song to number one in Britain, an achievement that is still unequalled. Irene Cara, who took the 1980 Oscar-winning song to number one (see no. 505) and the 1983 winner, 'Flashdance - What A Feeling', to number two, is the only person to get near to Doris Day's double.

Ray Evans and Jay Livingston wrote many movie songs and even featured as themselves in the film *Sunset Boulevard*. 'Whatever Will Be Will Be' was inspired by the family motto of the character played by Rossano Brazzi in the 1954 film *The Barefoot Contessa*. The motto in the film was in Italian, "Che Sera Sera", but Evans and Livingston switched it to the Spanish "Que Sera Sera", on the sound principle that more people speak Spanish than Italian, especially in the world's biggest record-buying market, the United States. The song was not written particularly for Hitchcock's film, but when the producers asked for a song that could be sung in the film by Miss Day to her young son, and which had a key role in the plot when her son was kidnapped, the half-written 'Que Sera Sera' seemed to fit the bill perfectly. The legal department at

Paramount studios objected to the title 'Que Sera Sera', so the song became officially known as 'Whatever Will Be Will Be'. At first, Doris Day did not think that the song would become a hit, thus proving the lyrics of the song correct - the future's not ours to see.

50

LAY DOWN YOUR ARMS

ANNE SHELTON

21 September 1956, for 4 weeks

●●●●

PHILIPS PB 616

Writers: Leon Land and Ake Gerhard; English lyrics by Paddy Roberts
Producer: Johnny Franz

Paddy Roberts, the humorist and songwriter who had put English lyrics to Ruby Murray's 'Softly Softly' (see no. 29), found a Swedish song called 'Ann-Caroline' and turned it into the saga of a returning soldier, 'Lay Down Your Arms'. He showed it to the popular band vocalist Anne Shelton, who liked it enough to record it. Shelton (born Pat Sibley on 10 November 1923) had been the vocalist with the Ambrose Orchestra since the age of 14 and was the only serious rival in popularity to Vera Lynn during the war years, so it was shrewd of Shelton to record a song which harked back to her great years a decade earlier. Messrs. Land and Gerhard thus became the only nationals of Sweden, a neutral country during World War II, to write a British number one, until Andersson, Anderson and Ulvaeus almost 20 years later. Previously, Anne Shelton had had happy experiences of recording a European song with English lyrics, when her version of Tommy Connor's adaptation of 'Lilli Marlene' gave her a hit in 1946. In 1949, she recorded 'The Wedding Of Lilli Marlene', and her version became the biggest-selling record of a song that topped the British sheet-music charts for seven weeks, from June to August that year. Anne Shelton died 31st July 1994.

In America, the Chordettes recorded 'Lay Down Your Arms' in a reverse of the usual route for cover versions in the 50s, and took it to number 16 on the Top 100. Britain had its revenge when the Mudlarks covered the Chordettes' 'Lollipop' and took it to number two in Britain, leaving the Chordettes trailing at number six.

51

A WOMAN IN LOVE

FRANKIE LAINE

19 October 1956, for 4 weeks

●●●●

PHILIPS PB 617

Writer: Frank Loesser
Producer: Mitch Miller

'A Woman In Love' has been the title of two different number ones. Frankie Laine's song and Barbra Streisand's song (see no. 468) have nothing in common except their title. The same can be said for the other titles used twice for chart-topping songs, 'Forever And Ever' (no. 384 by Slik and no. 392 by Demis Roussos), 'The Power Of Love' (no. 542 by Frankie Goes To Hollywood and no. 558 by Jennifer Rush) and 'Tears On My Pillow' (no. 373 by Johnny Nash and no. 640 by Kylie Minogue). Laine's 'A Woman In Love' was written by Frank Loesser, composer of many popular songs of the 40s and 50s, including, for example, 'Slow Boat To China', which Emile Ford turned into a Top 10 hit in 1960.

This was Laine's fourth and, as it turned out, final number one. His total of four chart-toppers established a record which was equalled just over six months later, on 17 May 1957, by Guy Mitchell. Laine and Mitchell then shared the lead until they were joined by Elvis Presley on 15 May 1959 and finally overtaken by him on 3 November 1960, when 'It's Now Or Never' crashed into the charts at number one. By that time, Laine had held, or shared, the record for most number ones since 'Hey Joe' hit the top seven years and 11 days earlier.

During 'A Woman In Love''s run at the top, many people had their minds on other things. The British Prime Minister Sir Anthony Eden stated that there were 'very grave issues at stake', and on 31

Aviation buffs will note the period features as JOHNNY RAY prepares to fly from America to Britain. (Pictorial Press)

October 1956, the Anglo-French invasion of the Suez canal area began. This action was not supported by President Eisenhower of the United States, and for some time there was a rift in the special relationship between Britain and America, which not even the lungs of Mr. Laine could repair.

52

JUST WALKIN' IN THE RAIN

JOHNNIE RAY

16 November 1956, for 7 weeks

●●●●●●●

PHILIPS PB 624

Writers: Johnny Bragg and Robert S. Riley
Producer: Mitch Miller

Two and a half years after his previous number one, at a time when the gathering tide of rock and roll was preparing to sweep the crooners of the early 50s into obscurity, both Johnnie Ray and Guy Mitchell came back with a pair of number one hits apiece. By this time, Johnnie Ray was already a show business institution, but many people considered him to be nothing more than a gimmick. The Sultan Of Sob, the Cry Guy, the Tearleader and the Prince Of Wails were all nicknames given by the cynical critics who recognised but scorned Ray's ability to play on the emotions of his audience. To that, one can only reply in the words of the sleevenotes of one of his albums: "Johnnie's tears were always real, induced by the sadness of the songs he sang, and did not originate in some carefully concealed artificial tear duct devised by some James Bondian genius of refined gadgetry. He didn't hide his feelings, which meant he was the centre of controversy around the world, particularly here in Britain, where our upper lips retain much of their traditional stiffness and we are often embarrassed by public displays of emotion." We may have been embarrassed, but not enough to stop buying his records.

'Just Walkin' In The Rain' was a song first recorded by The Prisonaires, inmates at Tennessee State Prison, in 1954. In America it gave Johnnie Ray his biggest hit since his only chart-topper, 'Cry', by climbing up to number two, only to be stopped by Elvis Presley's 'Love Me Tender'.

53

SINGING THE BLUES

GUY MITCHELL

4 January 1957, for 1 week,

●

18 January 1957, for 1 week

●

and 1 February 1957, for 1 week (top equal)

●

PHILIPS PB 650

Writer: Melvin Endsley
Producer: Mitch Miller

Guy Mitchell's third number one, and the fourth song to hit number one in two different versions, was written in 1954 by

Melvin Endsley, who had been paralysed since contracting polio at the age of three, in 1937. It was number one in America for ten consecutive weeks from early December 1956, beating the Marty Robbins original, which peaked at number 17. Mitchell repeated his success in Britain, although the local competition proved rather stronger than in the United States. The backing that the Ray Conniff Orchestra gave to Guy Mitchell's version of 'Singing The Blues' made it a very different sound from the slap-happy skiffle-rock of the Steelmen, who, perversely, may well have come closer to the sound that Melvin Endsley was looking for than the men under the technical precision of Mr. Conniff's baton.

Mitchell's 'Singing The Blues' all but equalled the record of 'I Believe' in returning twice to the number one spot, but the second time it had to share the top ranking with Frankie Vaughan (see no. 55). Mitchell's run of 22 weeks on the chart with the song gave him the longest chart run of any of his 14 hits.

Dave Edmunds revived 'Singing The Blues' in 1980, and when Daniel O'Donnell also charted the song in 1994, he pushed the total number of weeks the song has spent on the chart towards 50, making it one of the most successful songs in British chart history.

At the time, Steele was managed by John Kennedy, who had discovered him playing at the 2 I's coffee bar during a period of shore leave, and at about this time, Larry Parnes, the legendary promoter known as Mr. Parnes Shillings and Pence, also took an interest. Despite Parnes' subsequent stableful of pop stars (including Marty Wilde, Duffy Power, Georgie Fame, Dickie Pride, Vince Eager and Billy Fury), Tommy Steele was the only Parnes act ever to have a number one hit. Marty Wilde, Billy Fury and the eccentrically named Joe Brown all reached number two, but Georgie Fame's number ones came only after he left the Parnes fold. (Incidentally, when Kim Wilde followed her father to number two in 1981, they became the only case of two generations of a family reaching number two without making number one. Kim Wilde did, however, reach the very top in America early in 1987, with her revival of the Supremes' 'You Keep Me Hanging On'.)

Lionel Bart was writing for Tommy Steele at this time, although both 'Singing The Blues' and the follow-up, 'Knee Deep In The Blues', were Guy Mitchell covers and written by Melvin Endsley. Two and a half years later, Lionel Bart wrote his first number one hit, 'Living Doll', which, like 'Singing The Blues', went on to become a chart-topper in two different versions.

54

SINGING THE BLUES

TOMMY STEELE AND THE STEELMEN

11 January 1957, for 1 week

●

DECCA F 10819

Writer: Melvin Endsley
Producer: Hugh Mendl

The story of Tommy Hicks, the merchant seaman from Bermondsey who became Tommy Steele - Britain's answer to Elvis Presley - is too well known to bear repetition here. Steele was never really a rock and roller, despite a first hit called 'Rock With The Caveman', but all the same he hit number one six months and a day before Elvis first hit the top in Britain.

55

THE GARDEN OF EDEN

FRANKIE VAUGHAN

25 January 1957, for 4 weeks
(1 week top equal)

●●●●

PHILIPS PB 660

Writer: Denise Norwood
Producer: Johnny Franz

Frankie Vaughan was only the second Liverpool act to top the charts, but his style is very different from his famous successors like the Beatles and Frankie Goes To Hollywood. Vaughan was an extension of the music-hall tradition, and his high-kicking top-hatted routine of "Give me the moonlight, give me the girl and leave the rest to me" remains instantly recognisable, to the British public, some four decades on.

In the late 50s, Frankie Vaughan was established as one of Britain's most popular male vocalists, and one of the main pillars of his success was his recording of 'Garden Of Eden'. The original version of the song was by the American Joe Valino, who scored his only chart success on either side of the Atlantic, and it was covered for the British market by Dick James, later to achieve fame and fortune as music publisher for the Beatles and Elton John, by Gary Miller and by Frankie Vaughan. Vaughan won the chart battle easily, and began a string of hits with cover versions of songs by acts as varied as Charlie Gracie, Jimmy Rodgers, Edith Piaf and Perry Como, over the next four and a half years before he topped the charts again (see no. 130).

'The Garden Of Eden' featured lyrics including the line "A voice in the Garden tells you she is forbidden", which attracted censure from oversensitive religious circles at the time, and even gave rise to a partial broadcast ban on the song. There was no long-term effect on Frankie Vaughan's reputation, however, and the singer went on to gain a much-deserved OBE for his charity work.

56

YOUNG LOVE

TAB HUNTER

22 February 1957, for 7 weeks

●●●●●●●

LONDON HLD 8380

Writers: Carole Joyner and Ric Cartey
Producer: Billy Vaughn

Tab Hunter was born Arthur Kelm on 11 July 1931 in New York, but was known by his mother's maiden name, Gelien, until he was discovered working at a stable by talent scout Dick Clayton. The surname Hunter came from the connection with horses, and legend has it that Hollywood agent Henry Wilson, who gave Rock Hudson his name, said, "We have to tab you with something," and a star was born. Tab Hunter made his debut in the 1948 film *The Lawless*, and soon landed his first starring role, opposite Linda Darnell in *Island Of Desire*.

'Young Love' was written by two close friends from Atlanta, Georgia, but the first recorded version, by co-writer Ric Cartey, failed to set the charts alight. However, Sonny James was given the song to record, and in December 1956 his version entered the charts. Randy Wood, president of Pat Boone's label Dot, had the idea of asking film idol Tab Hunter to record the song, and by early January of 1957, Hunter's rival version was in the American record stores. In America, Hunter and James chased each other right to the top of the charts, with Hunter eventually edging out James, whose record peaked at number two. In Britain, James only reached number 11, despite a total lack of British cover versions of the song.

Tab Hunter had one more chart hit, '99 Ways', on Dot before Warner Brothers, to whom he was under contract for virtually everything, formed their own record label and signed him. The first Warner Brothers single to be released in Britain hit number one (see no. 101), but Hunter never hit the charts again. He has continued his acting career in films and on television, however, including a starring role with the late Divine in the Western *Lust In The Dust*.

57

CUMBERLAND GAP

LONNIE DONEGAN

12 April 1957, for 5 weeks

●●●●●

PYE NIXA B 15087

Writers: Traditional, arranged by Lonnie Donegan
Producer: Alan Freeman

Lonnie Donegan, born Anthony Donegan in Glasgow on 29 April 1931, was the most successful British act in our own charts up to the arrival of Cliff Richard. He was the King Of Skiffle, the craze that swept the world in the early 50s and which enabled anybody with a tea chest, a broomhandle and a washboard to perform popular songs. After completing national service in 1951, he joined Ken Colyer's Jazzmen, where he took the name Lonnie after his hero, the blues guitarist Lonnie Johnson. Donegan played guitar in Ken Colyer's skiffle group, along with Chris Barber, and when Barber formed his own jazz band, Donegan went with him as banjoist.

In 1954, Barber's band recorded Leadbelly's 'Rock Island Line' as a skiffle record, with Donegan on vocals. Originally included on an album, it was not released as a single until the beginning of 1956, when it rose quickly to the British Top 10, and, more amazingly, up to number eight in the American charts. Donegan left Barber, somewhat reluctantly, and the hits rolled out with a consistency that had never before been achieved, even by the likes of Frankie Laine and Guy Mitchell. 'Cumberland Gap' was Donegan's fifth single. The previous four had all reached the Top 10. In fact he was so popular in 1956 that an EP, 'Skiffle Session', and an album, *Lonnie Donegan Showcase*, also reached the singles Top 30.

58

ROCK-A-BILLY

GUY MITCHELL

17 May 1957, for 1 week

●

PHILIPS PB 685

Writers: Woody Harris and Eddie V. Deane
Producer: Mitch Miller

Mitch Miller's 15th number one production was also Guy Mitchell's fourth – and final – number one hit in Britain, and it was as near as Mitch Miller would ever get to acknowledging the existence of rock and roll, skiffle or the blues. The title of the song became the name for a whole style of music, a cross between rock and hillbilly country music, and Guy Mitchell's version was far closer to what we think of as rockabilly music than his previous recording career would have us suspect. The tempo of the song is much brisker than anything else that Mitchell took into the charts and, despite the jangling piano which sounds more like Winifred Atwell than Floyd Cramer, the mood is unlike any other Mitchell or Miller hit. It also predates Rocky Burnette's claim that rockabilly was invented by his father, the late Johnny Burnette, and his uncle Dorsey Burnette, and that they named their music after Rocky and his cousin, Dorsey's son Billy.

'Rock-A-Billy' just scraped into the American Top 10, and proved to be Mitchell's last major hit for almost three years. During that time, the rockers completed their conquest of the charts of the world and left the disciples of Mitch Miller out in the cold. Mitchell's comeback hit, his last hit in Britain, was called 'Heartaches By The Number' and it reached number one in America. In Britain it climbed as high as number five, making it the most successful of the comeback hits of the three 50s superstars who were all briefly back on the charts at the same time at the end of 1959. Frankie Laine's TV theme, 'Rawhide', reached number six, Johnnie Ray's 'I'll Never Fall In Love Again' made number 26, and then the three cornerstones of Philips' success faded into the sunset.

59

BUTTERFLY

ANDY WILLIAMS

24 May 1957 for 2 weeks

●●

LONDON HLA 8399

Writer: Anthony September
(aka Kal Mann and Bernie Lowe)
Producer: Archie Bleyer

Howard Andrew Williams was born on 3 December 1928, in the town of Wall Lake, Iowa, one of four brothers who sang in the local church choir, and a little later performed regularly, together with their parents, on their own radio show. The Williams Brothers made their first recording in 1944, when Andy was 15. That session was with Bing Crosby, and the record they made hit number one in the States for nine weeks. It was 'Swinging On A Star', the song that was revived by Big Dee Irwin and Little Eva in 1963. In 1952, Andy Williams began his solo career, featuring regularly on Steve Allen's *Tonight* television show until 1955.

His first solo hit in the States was 'Walk Hand In Hand' in April 1956, a song which gave Tony Martin a Top 10 hit on both sides of the Atlantic. The next year, Williams released the only record that has ever given him a number one hit, 'Butterfly'. The song was written by Kal Mann and Bernie Lowe, under the pseudonym Anthony September. Mann and Lowe were the writers of Elvis Presley's 'Teddy Bear' and founders of the Cameo-Parkway label, which gave us Chubby Checker, Bobby Rydell and the Orlons. It also produced Charlie Gracie, who recorded the original version of 'Butterfly', but who failed to beat the Andy Williams version, despite hitting the Top 20 with his record both in Britain (number 12) and America (number 7).

Since that early success, Andy Williams has established himself as one of the most popular of all American ballad singers, with an immensely successful and long-running television show of his own, and a long list of Top 10 hits, including 'Can't

ANDY WILLIAMS dials a phone that now looks so antiquated he could be calling Alexander Graham Bell. (Pictorial Press)

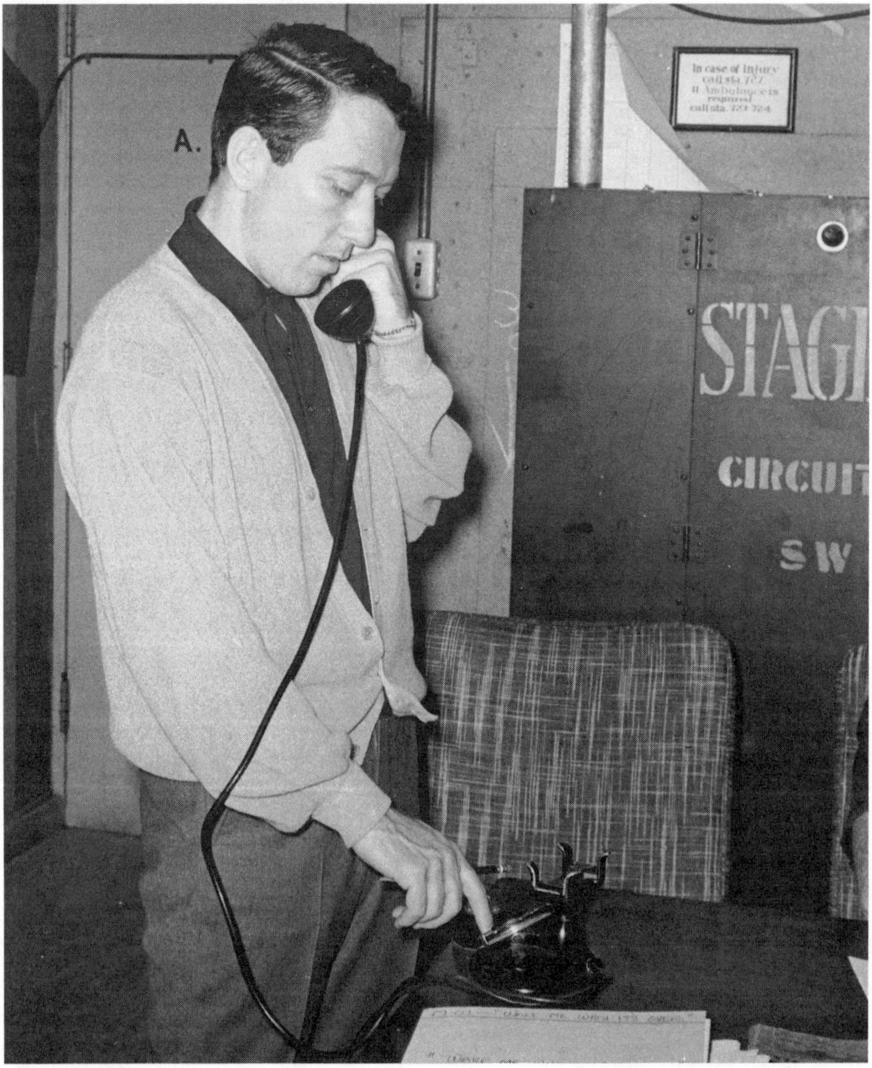

Get Used To Losing You', 'Almost There', 'Where Do I Begin? (Love Story)' and 'Can't Take My Eyes Off You'. 'Butterfly', however, remains Williams' only number one record on either side of the Atlantic.

60

YES TONIGHT JOSEPHINE

JOHNNIE RAY

7 June 1957, for 3 weeks

●●●

PHILIPS PB 686

Writers: Winfield Scott and Dorothy Goodman
Producer: Mitch Miller

Johnnie Ray's third and final number one was one of the few happy songs he recorded. It was an uptempo number, and, like stablemate Guy Mitchell's 'Rock-A-Billy' (see no. 58), it involved producer Mitch Miller in something closer to rock and roll than his usual, unquenchably bouncy style usually did. That is not to say that 'Yes Tonight Josephine' was a rock song, as it was more in the tradition of 'Green Door' and 'Rock And Roll Waltz' than 'Hound Dog' or even 'Why Do Fools Fall In Love'. The song was revived by producer Stuart Colman in 1981 for the Jets, but it was not as successful as his revamping of 'This Ole House' or 'Green Door' with Shakin' Stevens.

On 14 June, the second week that 'Yes Tonight Josephine' topped the charts, Elvis Presley's 'All Shook Up' came in at number 24 and then dropped off the chart again. This false start for the first number one by the King was just a hiccup in the revolution that was to sweep all the big Columbia acts under Mitch Miller's control out of the number one positions of the world for ever. From then on, it was the nostalgia market that guaranteed record sales for the early 50s balladeers, and not the pop fans. For producer Mitch Miller it was the end of his British successes. Only one more of his productions was to make the top, and that was a song (see no. 72) recorded in 1956.

Miller had fought against rock. He had condemned it and ignored it, but it still wouldn't go away. On 25 February 1990, in Los Angeles, California, Johnnie Ray died aged 63.

61

GAMBLIN' MAN/ PUTTING ON THE STYLE

LONNIE DONEGAN

28 June 1957, for 2 weeks

●●

PYE NIXA N15093

Writers: 'Gamblin' Man' – Woody Guthrie and Lonnie Donegan; 'Putting On The Style' – traditional, arranged by Norman Cazden
Producers: Alan Freeman and Michael Barclay
(recorded live at the London Palladium)

Lonnie Donegan's second consecutive number one, his sixth consecutive Top 10 hit, was also Britain's first live chart-topper and the first double-sided number one. Of all the double-sided number ones since this trailblazer, few have been so genuinely split in sales between the two sides as this classic skiffle single.

'Gamblin' Man' is a Woody Guthrie tune, adapted by Donegan, just as he later adapted Guthrie's 'Grand Coolie Dam' for yet another Top 10 hit a year later. Guthrie, whose son Arlo has charted in America with such hits as 'Alice's Restaurant' and 'Coming Into Los Angeles', was the major influence on Bob Dylan and other folk artists of the early 60s. But by the time Lonnie Donegan was at number one with the only Woody Guthrie song that ever reached the very top in Britain, the writer had given up performing as a result of his increasing disability caused by a rare nerve disease, Huntington's Chorea. He died on 3 October 1967.

'Putting On The Style' hit the charts twice more after its ultimate success in the summer of 1957. In August and September of that year, a version by Billy Cotton roamed around the lower reaches of the Top 20 as part of the 'All Star Hit Parade No. 2' charity hit single. At Christmas in 1958, Donegan brought it back into the charts as part of his medley single, 'Lonnie's Skiffle Party', which peaked at number 23. Donegan is thus on the short list of those who have had hits with re-recorded versions of their own number ones - along with Elvis Presley, Jimmy Young, Slade and Cliff Richard.

62

ALL SHOOK UP

ELVIS PRESLEY

12 July 1957, for 7 weeks

●●●●●●●

HMV POP 359

Writers: Otis Blackwell and Elvis Presley
Producer: Steve Sholes

After two number two hits and seven other hits in the first year of his chart career, Elvis Presley finally hit number one with his tenth British hit single. It was to be his only number one on the HMV label, and is the only one of his 17 number ones on which he shares a writing credit.

Otis Blackwell had written the classic 'Don't Be Cruel' (which was not released as an A-side in Britain until 1978, despite topping the US charts for 11 weeks in 1956), and he was looking for another song for Elvis. A publishing colleague, Al Stanton, suggested the title and, within a few days, Blackwell came up with another classic. Elvis, however, was not entirely satisfied with the song and so, with Blackwell's consent, he rewrote some of the words. The rest is history.

Born in Tupelo, Mississippi, on 8 January 1935, Elvis Aron Presley was to prove to be the King, the man who defined rock'n'roll and who was responsible for creating the demand for rock music on which a mammoth industry has been built. He once said, "Rhythm is something you either have or you don't have, but when you have it, you have it all over." He had it so much that when TV host Ed Sullivan announced that he would only show Elvis performing on his show from the waist up, it was front-page news in the *New York Times*.

63

DIANA

PAUL ANKA

30 August 1957, for 9 weeks

●●●●●●●●●

COLUMBIA DB 3980

Writer: Paul Anka
Producer: Don Costa

Canadian-born Paul Anka was 16 years and 31 days old when his self-penned single reached the number one spot in Britain, and he was not much older by the time his paean to young love had become one of the biggest-selling records of all time. Its total sales of over eight million copies made it the biggest hit his American label ABC-Paramount had ever had, and it made Anka a world star.

Diana was a real girl, Diana Ayoub, who used to babysit for Anka's younger brother and sister. She was 20, Anka was 15, and his heartache over the age gap was poured into the song. In April 1957, Anka borrowed $100 from his father, travelled to New York and, in true show business tradition, persuaded ABC staff producer Don Costa to listen to his limited repertoire. Costa, one of the great producers of the rock era, knew a hit when he heard it, and promptly arranged Anka's father to be flown to New York to sign a contract on behalf of his son. The next day, 'Diana' was recorded - in one take.

Paul Anka never had another number one hit in Britain, although his chart career included six more Top 10 hits and lasted well into the 1970s. He also wrote 'It Doesn't Matter Any More' for Buddy

Holly (see no. 84), and thus became the first person ever to write a British chart-topper for himself and for somebody else. His 'Puppy Love' (see no. 316), became a number one hit for Donny Osmond in 1972 (also produced by Don Costa), but his main claim to composing fame must now be his English lyrics to the only song that has been a hit for Elvis Presley, Frank Sinatra and the Sex Pistols - 'My Way'.

64

THAT'LL BE THE DAY

THE CRICKETS

1 November 1957, for 3 weeks

●●●

VOGUE CORAL Q 72279

Writers: Buddy Holly, Jerry Allison and Norman Petty
Producer: Norman Petty

'That'll Be The Day' was the phrase used by John Wayne, playing the role of ex-Confederate soldier Ethan Edwards, in the classic 1956 John Ford Western, *The Searchers* (a film which also gave the 'Needles And Pins' group their name). A group of high-school boys from Lubbock, Texas, led by Charles 'Buddy' Holley, saw the film and remembered the phrase. Holly (the 'e' was dropped for artistic reasons) and his friend and drummer Jerry Allison created a song around it and took it to Decca. The song was recorded, but this first release by the Crickets flopped. However, lead singer Holly still had faith in the song, so the Crickets (Holly, Allison, Larry Wellborn and Niki Sullivan) drove to Norman Petty's studios in Clovis, New Mexico, and re-recorded it in a very different style.

The Crickets' contract with Decca meant that they could not sell the recording elsewhere, but eventually Bob Thiele, A&R manager at the Decca subsidiary, Coral Records, decided he wanted to release the track, so Decca dissolved the contract with the parent label and bound the Crickets to another one with Coral.

'That'll Be The Day' was released in the States in June 1957, but moved very slowly at first. By the end of July it had crept onto the lower reaches of the national chart. From then on, it rose rapidly to the top – Buddy Holly and the Crickets had arrived.

65

MARY'S BOY CHILD

HARRY BELAFONTE

22 November 1957, for 7 weeks

●●●●●●●

RCA 1022

Writer: Jester Hairston
Producer: René Farnon

Harry Belafonte, whose record label in the UK had changed from HMV to RCA when the American giant formed its own UK subsidiary in the summer of 1957, gave his employers their first British number one with one of the most famous Christmas hits of all time. It was the first record to sell a million copies in Britain alone, reaching the top over a month before Christmas. Its seven-week run at number one is the longest by a song with a Christmas theme, and it became the first Christmas song to hit number one in two different versions when Boney M took it back to the top in 1978 (see no. 430).

Harold George Belafonte was born in New York on 1 March 1927. He spent three years in the US Navy and then enrolled at the American Negro Theatre Workshop. His singing came to the attention of manager Marty Kaye, and eventually a recording contract with RCA followed. He starred in a series of films, including *Carmen Jones*, *The World The Flesh And The Devil* and *Island In The Sun*. It was the latter, together with his 1957 albums *Calypso* and *Belafonte Sings Of The Caribbean*, that gave him the nickname King Of Calypso, and hits like the self-penned 'Banana Boat Song', 'Scarlet Ribbons' and 'Mary's Boy Child'. 'Island In The Sun' was also the inspiration for the name of Chris Blackwell's record company, Island Records.

Writer Jester Hairston was seen ten years later acting in the Sidney Poitier/Rod Steiger film *In The Heat Of The Night*, and Belafonte himself returned to number one 28 years later when he and one of his most ardent admirers in the late 50s, Bob Dylan, both participated in USA For

Africa's 'We Are The World' get together during April 1985. (see no. 548).

66

GREAT BALLS OF FIRE

JERRY LEE LEWIS

10 January 1958, for 2 weeks

●●

LONDON HLS 8529

Writers: Otis Blackwell and Jack Hammer
Producer: Sam Phillips

Jerry Lee Lewis, born in Ferriday, Louisiana, on 29 September 1935, is one of the great originals of rock. Like Elvis Presley, Roy Orbison and Johnny Cash, he began his career at Sam Phillips' Sun record label in Memphis, and he became the only white rock'n'roller of real note to use a piano rather than a guitar as his main weapon.

'Great Balls Of Fire', co-written by Otis Blackwell of 'All Shook Up' fame, is one of the wildest rock records ever to top the British charts. Lewis lived as frantic a life as the music he played, and his first music career came to an end when it was disclosed that he had married his 14-year-old cousin, Myra Gale Brown. Three years later he was back in the Top 10 with what is still the only version of Ray Charles' classic 'What'd I Say' to reach the British charts. Then a move back to his country roots, coupled with further personal problems, pushed his career into obscurity as far as Britain was concerned.

Despite health problems throughout the 80s, Lewis has survived to continue recording and performing into the 90s. The 1989 biopic of his life, starring Dennis Quaid as Jerry Lee, was – inevitably – called *Great Balls Of Fire*, and brought him further acclaim, reminding rock fans 30 years on that Jerry Lee Lewis has always performed as he has lived, to the edge of self-destruction.

Right: ELVIS PRESLEY devised his own choreography for the film *Jailhouse Rock*. (Pictorial Press)

67

JAILHOUSE ROCK

ELVIS PRESLEY

24 January 1958, for 3 weeks

●●●

RCA 1028

Writers: Jerry Lieber and Mike Stoller
Producer: Steve Sholes

For the first time since the chart had begun over five years earlier, a record entered the hit parade at number one. Needless to say, it was Elvis Presley who achieved this unbelievable feat, with the title tune from his third film, *Jailhouse Rock*. Most Elvis fans would list *Jailhouse Rock* as his best movie; his four pre-Army films seem, in hindsight, to be in a completely different class from the increasingly insipid post-demobilization efforts.

Written by Jerry Lieber and Mike Stoller, whose hit songs for the Coasters and others had made them one of the most successful of rock writing teams, 'Jailhouse Rock' showed Elvis' talent at its very best. Initially discovering their work through a lounge group's version of Willie Mae Thornton's original R&B hit 'Hound Dog', Elvis cut over 20 Lieber/Stoller songs during his career, but this was the only UK chart-topper written solely by these two songwriting giants. The recording was made at MGM's studio in Culver City on 2 May 1957, with the following line-up: Elvis (vocals and guitar), Scotty Moore (guitar), Mike Stoller and Elvis (piano), Bill Black (bass), D. J. Fontana (drums) and the Jordanaires (backing vocals).

For five weeks, one of the records in the Top 20 trying to outsell 'Jailhouse Rock' was an EP containing five songs from the

6240

film, including 'Jailhouse Rock' itself. No other number one A-side had ever appeared in the Top 20 in two different positions in the same week, but many fans were buying both the single and the EP, needing both to get all six songs from the movie, as the flip side of the single, 'Treat Me Nice' (another Lieber/Stoller song), was not on the EP.

68

THE STORY OF MY LIFE

MICHAEL HOLLIDAY

14 February 1958, for 2 weeks

●●

COLUMBIA DB 4058

Writers: Burt Bacharach and Hal David
Producer: Norrie Paramor

The story of Michael Holliday's life was tragic. Born Michael Milne in Liverpool, on 26 November 1925 (possibly 1928), he used his mother's maiden name for his musical career. By the beginning of 1956 he was breaking through the ranks of British hopefuls and into the charts, basing his style on the casual phrasing and delivery of Perry Como and Bing Crosby. In 1956 he had three chart singles (the highest of which climbed to number 13) and was given his own TV show, *Relax with Mike*. However, Holliday lacked self-confidence and was unable to cope with the success he found. All the same, his popularity continued beyond the end of the decade, and in 1960 he scored his second chart-topper (see no. 95). He committed suicide the following year.

'The Story Of My Life' was the first of six Bacharach/David number one hits, and had first been recorded by Marty Robbins. In Britain, Michael Holliday also faced competition from Alma Cogan, Dave King and Gary Miller, but Holliday's version won easily. This was not the first time that Marty Robbins had missed out on the British market, because his first major American pop hit, 'A White Sport Coat', was covered by Terry Dene, who took the song into the British Top 20. Robbins had also been the major hitmaker on the American country charts with 'Singing The Blues' and 'Knee Deep In The Blues', UK hits for Guy Mitchell. However, Robbins did not finally hit the UK charts until 1960, when 'El Paso', a single which ran for what was then the amazing length of over four minutes, climbed to number 19 - 18 places lower than its peak in Robbins' homeland.

69

MAGIC MOMENTS

PERRY COMO

28 February 1958, for 8 weeks

●●●●●●●●

RCA 1036

Writers: Burt Bacharach and Hal David
Producer: Joe Reisman

For the first time in chart history, consecutive number ones were written by the same team, a feat that was not to be repeated for over five years, when Bruce Welch co-wrote both 'Summer Holiday' and 'Foot Tapper' (see nos. 148 and 149). Burt Bacharach and Hal David were never firmly linked with any act (although they wrote a great deal for Dionne Warwick in the 60s) and their immense success is based entirely on the brilliance of their songs rather than the popularity of the performer.

Having said that, in 1958 Perry Como was a very popular singer indeed. His *Perry Como Show* was the most successful television variety show of the time in America, Britain and many other countries, and he was the highest-paid performer of that period, a title he had taken over from Eddie Fisher. 'Magic Moments', and the flip side, 'Catch A Falling Star', were both sung by Como on his show early in January 1958, and both sides immediately took up separate chart positions on both sides of the Atlantic. In America it was 'Catch A Falling Star' that climbed all the way to the top, while 'Magic Moments' just scraped into the Top 30. In Britain the roles were reversed: 'Catch A Falling Star' climbed to number nine, but 'Magic Moments' held on to the number one slot for eight weeks.

At this time, a major event in rock history occurred. Elvis Presley was drafted into the US Army on 24 March 1958.

70

WHOLE LOTTA WOMAN

MARVIN RAINWATER

25 April 1958, for 3 weeks

●●●

MGM 974

Writer: Marvin Rainwater
Producer: Jim Vinneau

With a name like Marvin Rainwater, you either had to succeed outrageously or sink without trace. He actually did both, in that order. Born on 2 July 1925, Cherokee Indian Marvin Percy took his mother's maiden name to become a country singer.

He first scored on the national charts in America in the summer of 1957 with 'Gonna Find Me A Bluebird'. That reached number three on the American country charts, and number 22 on the pop charts, and the combination of Marvin Rainwater and the hot MGM label seemed certain to carry on succeeding. His follow-up was 'Majesty Of Love', a duet with the girl destined to be MGM's hottest star of the late 50s, Connie Francis, which also sold a million. Then came 'Whole Lotta Woman', which, for no apparent reason (it made only number 60 on the *Billboard* pop charts), was released in the UK, and starting picking up airplay action, what little of it there was in 1958. In a year which featured 'Great Balls Of Fire', 'Jailhouse Rock' and 'It's Only Make Believe' at the top of the British charts, 'Whole Lotta Woman' stands comparison with those greats as a fine rock and roll record, typical of the era when country and rock were still blood brothers.

Marvin Rainwater's follow-up was a lesser hit called 'I Dig You Baby'. Thereafter, chart obscurity reclaimed him almost as quickly as he had found fame. In 1992, Bear Family records issued an exhaustive collection of his work, which proved that Rainwater had a great deal of talent.

71

WHO'S SORRY NOW?

CONNIE FRANCIS

16 May 1958, for 6 weeks

●●●●●●

MGM 975

Writers: Ted Snyder, Bert Kalmar and Herman Ruby
Producer: Harry Myerson; orchestra and chorus arranged by Joe Lippman

For one last attempt at a solo hit before her recording contract at MGM lapsed, Concetta Franconero was persuaded by her father to revive his favourite standard from the 1920s, 'Who's Sorry Now?' The answer? The acts she kept away from the top of the charts for six weeks in the early summer of 1958.

Concetta Rosa Maria Franconero found fame as CONNIE FRANCIS but still sought her father's opinion of her intended repetoire. (Pictorial Press)

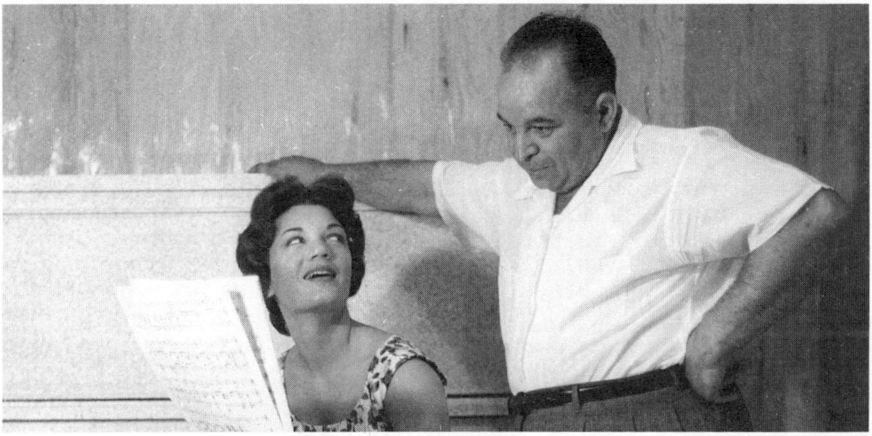

Born on 12 December 1938, Connie Francis left university in New York before graduating, to concentrate on a musical career. At first, her decision seemed misguided. Apart from her hit duet with Marvin Rainwater, all her recordings failed totally. Then she recorded a song from 1923. With a very straightforward arrangement her luck changed, and she took it to the top of the British charts. Contrary to popular belief, 'Who's Sorry Now?' did not make number one in the States, peaking at number four. Her other British number one, 'Stupid Cupid', coupled with 'Carolina Moon' (see no. 75), made only number 17 in America, while her three American number ones all failed to reach the very top in Britain. Generally speaking, her successful songs in Britain were the uptempo numbers like 'Stupid Cupid', 'Robot Man' and 'Lipstick On Your Collar'. 'Who's Sorry Now?' was the exception that launched her career.

72

ON THE STREET WHERE YOU LIVE

VIC DAMONE

27 June 1958, for 2 weeks (one week top equal with no. 73)

●●

PHILIPS PB 819

Writers: Alan Jay Lerner and Frederick Loewe
Producer: Mitch Miller

My Fair Lady is probably the best known of all 50s musicals. It launched the career of Julie Andrews, while Rex Harrison gave non-singers new career prospects with his expert and much-imitated style, of talking to music. When the show opened on Broadway, the producers went to great lengths to ensure that the music was not exported, so that the show could open in markets such as Britain in front of audiences to whom it would be completely new. The formula worked.

Vic Damone (born Vito Farinola on 12 June 1928, in Brooklyn, New York) was the lucky man with the British hit version of the hit song 'On The Street Where You Live'. Damone had the advantage of having already had an American Top 10 hit with the song, even though this occurred two years earlier, in the spring of 1956. Thus it was that Mitch Miller's final British number one production, his 17th, was actually recorded before his 16th, Johnnie Ray's 'Yes Tonight Josephine' (see no. 60), not to mention the 15th, 14th, 13th, 12th, and 11th (see nos. 58, 53, 52, 51 and 49). Such was the time lag in musicals between Broadway and London that by the time 'On The Street Where You Live' reached number one in Britain, Damone's version of the title tune from Lerner and Loewe's next musical, *Gigi*, had been and gone from the American charts. Many years later, during a BBC Radio Two interview, Damone claimed that if this single, recorded while *My Fair Lady* was in an out-of-town preview, had not been a hit, 'On The Street Where You Live' would have been cut from the Broadway production.

Although it is 30 years since Vic Damone was in the British charts, he remains a popular performer in cabaret and on television on both sides of the Atlantic.

73

ALL I HAVE TO DO IS DREAM/CLAUDETTE

THE EVERLY BROTHERS

4 July 1958, for 7 weeks

●●●●●●●

LONDON HLA 8618

Writers: 'All I Have To Do Is Dream' – Felice and Boudleaux Bryant; 'Claudette' – Roy Orbison
Producer: Archie Bleyer; arranged by Don Everly

Don (born 1 February 1937) and Phil (born 19 January 1939) Everly launched their careers as the most successful vocal group in pre-Beatles history with the classic 'Bye Bye Love'. That was written for them by the husband and wife team of Boudleaux and Felice Bryant, so when – a year later – the same writers came up with 'All I Have To Do Is Dream', it was to the Everly Brothers that they took their song.

Don and Phil hailed from Brownie, Kentucky, but soon moved to Shenandoah, Iowa, where their parents

Ike and Margaret began hosting their own country radio show on the local station, KMA. When Phil was six and Don eight, they made their debut on their parents' show, and from then on they kept on singing. 'All I Have To Do Is Dream' was their fourth American single. The Bryants claim they wrote it in 15 minutes. If so, it was one of the most profitable quarter-hours ever spent, because the song has become a standard, with hundreds of different versions recorded over the years. Bobbie Gentry and Glen Campbell took their version to number three in 1969, but nobody has quite matched the plaintive harmonies of the Everly Brothers, with whom the song will always be associated.

The flip side, which was listed with the A-side for 20 of the record's 21 weeks of chart action, was written by the then unknown Roy Orbison as a rocking tribute to his wife Claudette. It was the first of two number ones for the Everlys with a girl's name in the title - 'Cathy's Clown' (see no. 101) was to follow. All in all, Don and Phil charted with songs about Suzie, Claudette, Mary, Jenny, Cathy, Lucille and Ebony Eyes, who were only seven of the millions of girls who worshipped the Everlys when they were at their peak.

74

WHEN

THE KALIN TWINS

22 August 1958, for 5 weeks

●●●●●

BRUNSWICK 05751

Writers: Jack Reardon and Paul Evans
Producer: Jack Pleis

For the only time in chart history, a pair of brothers succeeded a pair of brothers at number one. Harold and Herbie Kalin were born on 16 February 1939, making them one day older than John Leyton (see no. 124). They were discovered by Clint Ballard Jr., the writer of many hits, including 'Good Timin'' for Jimmy Jones and 'I'm Alive' for the Hollies. Harold and Herbie were the first set of twins to make it to number one in Britain. There were twins in the Bee Gees, the Equals and Bros to name but three other chart-topping groups, but the Kalins remain the only twins to hit the top as a duo.

The Kalin Twins proved to be one-hit wonders, the third on the list. The plea of their follow-up, 'Forget Me Not', was not heeded, and the fans quickly forgot them. Even the song, co-written by 'Seven Little Girls Sitting In The Back Seat' hitmaker Paul Evans, had a longer chart life than its originators, for Showaddywaddy took it to number three as the follow-up to their number one, 'Under The Moon Of Love' (see no. 397). However, that was not quite the end of the Kalin Twins' chart-topping career. The flip side of Cliff Richard's number one at Christmas in 1990, 'Saviour's Day', was the 'Oh Boy Medley', recorded live. Singing with Cliff on 'Oh Boy', 'Bird Dog', 'C'Mon Everybody' and 'Whole Lotta Shakin' Going On' were the Kalin Twins, 32 years after their greatest triumph but still rocking with the best of them.

75

CAROLINA MOON/ STUPID CUPID

CONNIE FRANCIS

26 September 1958, for 6 weeks

●●●●●●

MGM 985

Writers: 'Carolina Moon' – Benny Davis and Joe Burke; 'Stupid Cupid' – Neil Sedaka and Howard Greenfield
Producers: Connie Francis and Leroy Holmes; arranged and conducted by Leroy Holmes

The combination of a revival of an American 20s standard and a brand new teenybop rocker by Neil Sedaka and Howard Greenfield gave Connie Francis her second number one in three releases. It also meant that she spent 12 weeks of 1958 at the very top of the charts, which at the time was second only to Frankie Laine's unbeatable total of 27 weeks on top in 1953. She has subsequently been overtaken by Elvis Presley (18 weeks at the top in 1961 and 15 weeks in 1962), the Beatles (16 weeks in 1963), John Travolta and Olivia Newton-John (16 weeks in 1978), Frankie Goes To Hollywood (15 weeks in 1984) and Bryan Adams (16 weeks in 1991).

After 1958, Connie Francis never hit number one again in the UK. Top 10 hits, eight more in all, continued until 1962, and she remains, after Madonna, Donna Summer and Diana Ross, the fourth most successful American female vocalist in British chart history, despite having not charted since 1966. Perhaps more surprisingly, 'Stupid Cupid' is the only Neil Sedaka song ever to hit the top in the UK. Sedaka himself scored his first hit with 'I Go Ape', some six months after 'Stupid Cupid' dropped from the summit, but in a career spanning 18 hits between 1959 and 1975, Neil Sedaka never climbed higher than number three, a position claimed by both 'Oh Carol' and 'Happy Birthday Sweet Sixteen'.

76

IT'S ALL IN THE GAME

TOMMY EDWARDS

7 November 1958, for 3 weeks

MGM 989

Writers: Charles Gates Dawes and Carl Sigman
Producer: Harry Myerson

In 1951, Tommy Edwards (born in Richmond, Virginia, on 17 February 1922) hit the American charts with two singles, 'Morning Side Of The Mountain' and 'It's All In The Game'. The latter tune had been written in 1912, by a Chicago banker who went on to become Vice President of the United States from 1925 to 1929. He called the tune 'Melody In A Major' and, almost 40 years later, Carl Sigman added the lyrics that turned the tune into a standard.

After Edwards' successes in 1951 he failed to chart again. MGM were about to release him from his contract when they decided to ask him to re-record some of his early hits to demonstrate the new technological breakthrough - stereo. To everybody's astonishment, 'It's All In The Game' became a massive hit once again, selling over three million copies worldwide and topping the charts in both Britain and America. Five years later, Cliff Richard took the song to number two in Britain and to number 25 in America, his US biggest hit until the mid-70s. The Four Tops' version reached number five in Britain in 1970. By then, Tommy Edwards was no more, having died at the age of 47, on 22 October 1969.

Early 50s minor American hits by TOMMY EDWARDS included his own future number one, 'It's All In The Game', the would-be chart-topper for Elvis Presley, 'A Fool Such As I', and the about-to-be long-running champ as recorded by Doris Day, 'Secret Love'. (Pictorial Press)

77

HOOTS MON

LORD ROCKINGHAM'S XI

28 November 1958, for 3 weeks

DECCA F 11059

Writer: Harry Robinson
Producers: Hugh Mendl and Jack Good; arranged by Harry Robinson

The stomping party hit 'Hoots Mon' was based on a traditional Scottish folk song called 'One Hundred Pipers', and adapted by Lord Rockingham's XI's leader, Harry Robinson. The record owed its popularity to constant plugging on Jack Good's television show *Oh Boy!*, on which Lord Rockingham's XI were the house band. The music featured the rasping saxophone of Red Price, who retired from the music business a short while after the zenith of 'Hoots Mon'. It is not known if the two events were connected. He then spent the rest of his days happily pulling pints in his own pub, until his death in the mid-70s. Lord Rockingham's XI also included author and critic Benny Green, who has vowed not to rest until rock and roll is slain.

The track was recorded at Decca's studios in West Hampstead and, despite sales of over half a million copies, the musicians were paid only £6 each for their part in the first number one band to feature Roman numerals in their name (predating Soul II Soul and Boyz II Men). The record made a fleeting reappearance in the charts late in 1993, climbing to number 60 as a result of being featured in an advertisement for Maynard's Wine Gums.

78

IT'S ONLY MAKE BELIEVE

CONWAY TWITTY

19 December 1958, for 5 weeks

●●●●●

MGM 992

Writers: Conway Twitty and Jack Nance
Producer: Jim Vinneau

Conway Twitty, born Harold Jenkins in Mariana, Arkansas, on 1 September 1933, is reputed to have chosen his stage name from the names of two towns he passed through on one of his early tours as a back-up musician in a country band. The name was certainly memorable and it gave Peter Sellers the inspiration for his parody of a pop star of the late 50s, Twit Conway.

Even in 1956 and 1957, record companies knew that Elvis imitators could strike lucky. Twitty was signed to Mercury until 1957, making a stream of unsuccessful country singles and almost equally unsuccessful rock singles, based on his ability to sound like Elvis. It was his switch to MGM that changed everything. Perhaps it was knowing that any company that already had Marvin Rainwater on its roster would not find anything odd about the name Conway Twitty, but whatever the reason, Twitty came up with a massive worldwide hit with his first single for his new employer.

'It's Only Make Believe' became the first song to reach the British Top 10 in four different years when Billy Fury in 1964, Glen Campbell in 1970 and Child in 1978 all took the song back to the higher reaches. Only 'Unchained Melody' and 'Can't Help Falling In Love' can match the feat of four different Top 10 versions.

Conway Twitty, who went on to become one of country music's biggest stars, with over 40 number one country singles, died after collapsing in a tour bus on 5 June 1993.

79

THE DAY THE RAINS CAME

JANE MORGAN

23 January 1959, for 1 week

●

LONDON HLR 8751

Writers: Gilbert Becaud; English lyrics by Carl Sigman
Producer: Vic Schoen

Jane Morgan, born Jane Currier in Boston, Massachusetts, was trained as a lyric soprano at the Julliard School Of Music in New York. To work her way through school, she sang blues in nightclubs, and was noticed there by French impresario Bernard Hilda, who offered her a contract to sing in Paris. What happened to her lyric soprano training is veiled in the mists of time, but within weeks of Miss Morgan's arrival in the French capital she had taken the city by storm. For the next few years she made appearances all over Europe, establishing a fine reputation and a growing following. In 1958 she recorded a song by Gilbert Becaud in French, called 'Le Jour Où La Pluie Viendra', which she

decided to record in English as well. It climbed only to number 21 in the States, but in Britain her European reputation helped to push this melodramatic ballad to the very top. The French version, incidentally, was on the B-side of the British release.

Jane Morgan subsequently married Jerry Weintraub, the man who put Elvis back on the road in 1970, and who managed John Denver among others.

80

ONE NIGHT/ I GOT STUNG

ELVIS PRESLEY

30 January 1959, for 3 weeks

●●●

RCA 1100

Writers: 'One Night' – Dave Bartholomew and Pearl King; 'I Got Stung' – Aaron Schroeder and David Hill
Producers: Steve Sholes and Chet Atkins

Elvis', third UK number one was his first to reach the top after he went into the US Army in March 1958, and was his first double-sided UK chart-topper. 'One Night' was co-written by Dave Bartholomew, responsible for many of Fats Domino's hits, including the song that Bitty McLean took to number two in 1993, 'It Keeps Rainin'', and recorded – without great commercial success – by Smiley Lewis in 1956. Elvis got to grips with it in Radio Recorders Studio in Hollywood in February 1957, his vocal and guitar being supported by Scotty Moore (guitar), Dudley Brooks (piano), Bill Black (bass), D. J. Fontana (drums) and the backing vocals of the Jordanaires. It thus remained unissued for two years, to become one of many tracks that kept Elvis' name in the chart while he was a guest of Uncle Sam in Germany and unable to make many new recordings.

'I Got Stung' was actually cut shortly after Elvis' induction into the Army, at RCA in Nashville in June 1958, his last sessions

SHIRLEY BASSEY is shown in her first television appearance, in 1958. (Pictorial Press)

for nearly two years. By this point in Elvis' career, his recording output was controlled by music publisher Freddy Bienstock, who acted as a clearing house for the enormous number of songs that were submitted to Elvis, together with Steve Sholes and Chet Atkins. Atkins played guitar on 'I Got Stung', the rest of the line-up comprising Floyd Cramer on piano, Bob Moore on bass, D. J. Fontana on drums, Murray Harmon bashing the bongoes, and, of course, the Jordanaires backing Presley's vocals.

81

AS I LOVE YOU

SHIRLEY BASSEY

20 February 1959, for 4 weeks

●●●●

PHILIPS PB 845

Writers: Jay Livingston and Ray Evans
Producer: Johnny Franz

Shirley Veronica Bassey, born in Cardiff on 8 January 1937 was, for over a quarter of a century, the most successful female vocalist on the British charts, holding the title until the early 90s, when she was eclipsed by both Madonna and Diana Ross. Bassey's chart career began a month after her 20th birthday, when her version of Harry Belafonte's 'Banana Boat Song' entered the charts. Although outsold by the original version, it nevertheless secured Bassey her first of 12 Top 10 hits. Two more minor hits followed, but 1958 was a blank year, chartwise, for the girl from Tiger Bay until TV exposure broke 'As I Love You'.

'As I Love You', written by the same American team that had come up with 'Whatever Will Be Will Be' for Doris Day (see no. 49), reached number one nine weeks after its first chart placing, and at the same time her next single, 'Kiss Me Honey Honey Kiss Me', was racing into the Top 10, to peak at number three. For one week, the two singles shared the number three position on the charts, making Bassey one of only nine acts to have had two hits in the Top 3 in the same week.

After that, Shirley Bassey's chart career just kept on rolling. No fewer than four of her hits have enjoyed chart runs of more than 20 weeks, the longest-running of all being her 1960 recording of the hit song from Lionel Bart's *Oliver*, 'As Long As He Needs Me' – which enjoyed 30 weeks of chart action, but only climbed to number two.

82

SMOKE GETS IN YOUR EYES

THE PLATTERS

20 March 1959, for 1 week

●

MERCURY AMT 1016

Writers: Jerome Kern and Otto Harbach
Producer: Buck Ram

The Platters were formed in 1953 and, by the time 'Smoke Gets In Your Eyes' hit number one, the line-up was lead vocalist Tony Williams (born 5 April 1928), David Lynch, Herb Reed, Paul Robi and Zola Taylor. But the mastermind behind the group was their manager and producer, Buck Ram.

At the end of 1955, the Platters kicked off their American chart career with a Top 10 million seller, 'Only You', a Buck Ram song which has subsequently hit the British chart in five different versions. The follow-up in America was 'The Great Pretender', a Stateside number one, but nothing was released in Britain until late in 1956, shortly after the Platters' fourth American single had given them their second US number one. Their first British single was possibly the greatest double-sided pop single ever released, at least until the Beatles' 'Penny Lane'/'Strawberry Fields Forever'. It was 'Only You'/'The Great Pretender' which eventually climbed to number five.

The British public was a little unsure of the Platters, and their first four singles bobbed in and out of the chart no fewer than 12 times between them. In 1958, the Platters switched to recording oldies, a decision which met with great approval. 'Twilight Time', written in 1944, climbed to number three and the follow-up,

'Smoke Gets In Your Eyes', from the 1933 musical *Roberta*, hit the very top.

83

SIDE SADDLE

RUSS CONWAY

27 March 1959, for 4 weeks

●●●●

COLUMBIA DB 4256

Writer: Trevor Stanford
Producer: Norman Newell

Trevor Stanford was born in Bristol on 2 September 1927, and joined the Merchant Navy at the age of 15 in 1942. Two years later, he joined the Royal Navy and almost immediately cut off the top of the third finger of his right hand in mortal combat with a bread slicer. It was not for this action that he won the Distinguished Service Medal, but by the time he left the Navy in 1955, he was Trevor Stanford DSM.

His 'transformation' into Russ Conway was rapid. Stanford had taught himself piano during his seafaring years, and on demobilization he began playing in clubs. There he was heard by dancer Irving Davies, who recommended him to producer Norman Newell.

Conway's recording career began on the well-worn lines of Winifred Atwell, with a medley, 'Party Pops', at Christmas 1957, and 'More Party Pops', his first Top 10 hit, at Christmas 1958. Then he wrote and recorded 'Side Saddle', which hit number one, sold a million and stayed on the chart for 30 consecutive weeks, a run which, at the time, was second only to Frankie Laine's 'I Believe'.

'Side Saddle' still holds the record for the longest-running instrumental number one, but its chart longevity pales into insignificance beside the 55-week run of Mr. Acker Bilk's 1962 clarinet instrumental, 'Stranger On The Shore', which peaked at number two.

'It Doesn't Matter Anymore' by BUDDY HOLLY was the first posthumous number one. (Pictorial Press)

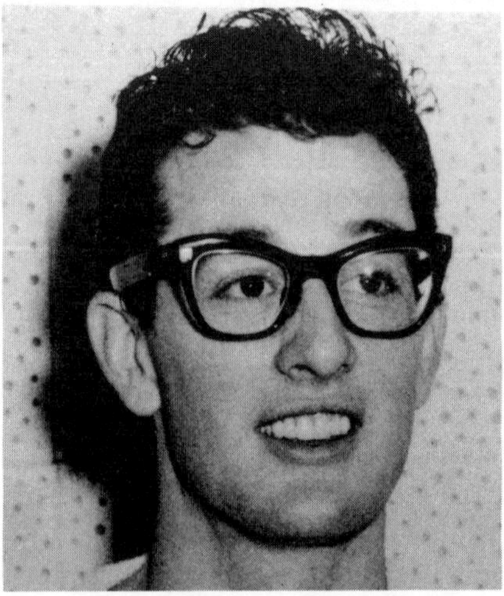

84

IT DOESN'T MATTER ANYMORE

BUDDY HOLLY

24 April 1959, for 3 weeks

●●●

CORAL Q 72360

Writer: Paul Anka
Producer: Dick Jacobs

The death of Buddy Holly in an air crash near Clear Lake, Iowa, on 3 February 1959, is one of the major events of rock history. Holly, already established as a major force in pop music through his work with the Crickets, was beginning a solo career which, judging by the tapes made just before he died, would have been even more spectacular than his time with the Crickets. Since his death, it is possible that he has been the biggest single influence on the development of British pop music. The Beatles and the Rolling Stones recorded his songs, the Hollies named themselves after him, Adam Faith copied the pizzicato string section that featured so heavily in 'It Doesn't Matter Anymore', and numerous acts have taken Holly songs into the charts in the 30-plus years since his death.

'It Doesn't Matter Anymore' was Holly's only solo number one, and it was the first of 11 records that have hit number one after the singer's death. It was written by Paul Anka and recorded almost without rehearsal at the Coral Records Studios at Pythian Temple, New York City, on the evening of 21 October 1958. Al Caiola's guitar was the mainstay of the backing band, but a line-up of eight violins, two violas and two cellos was also in the studio to give the effect for which Holly and Coral producer Dick Jacobs were looking.

The flip side of 'It Doesn't Matter Anymore' was recorded at the same session. It was the Felice and Boudleaux Bryant composition 'Raining In My Heart', so this single was the only one released in Holly's lifetime on which he had no hand in the writing of either side.

85

A FOOL SUCH AS I/ I NEED YOUR LOVE TONIGHT

ELVIS PRESLEY

15 May 1959, for 5 weeks

●●●●●

RCA 1113

Writers: 'A Fool Such As I' – William Trader; 'I Need Your Love Tonight' – Sid Wayne and Bix Reichner
Producers: Steve Sholes and Chet Atkins

Elvis' fourth number one in Britain not only put him level with Guy Mitchell and Frankie Laine in the list of most number one hits, but also provided him with his first instance of number ones with consecutive releases, this double-sider following on directly after 'One Night'/'I Got Stung' (see no. 80).

'A Fool Such As I' had been a favourite of Elvis' since 1953, when it had reached number four in the American country charts as recorded by Hank Snow, an artist at one time handled by Elvis' manager, Colonel Tom Parker. The first number one ballad hit for Elvis, it had been written by Bill Trader in 1952 and also provided a fair-sized pop hit in the States for Jo Stafford in 1953.

'I Need Your Love Tonight' was a new song written by Sid Wayne and Bix Reichner, and both titles were recorded in Nashville at the same sessions that produced 'I Got Stung'. Almost certainly, none of Elvis' number ones featured *all* the legendary musicians who regularly backed him - Chet Atkins, Floyd Cramer, D. J. Fontana and Bill Black. These tracks featured the first three, but not Bill Black or even Scotty Moore, who had both been on 'One Night'.

86

ROULETTE

RUSS CONWAY

19 June 1959, for 2 weeks

●●

COLUMBIA DB 4298

Writer: Trevor Stanford
Producer: Norman Newell

The only solo instrumentalist ever to achieve consecutive number one hits is Russ Conway. He managed this feat with ridiculous ease as his second self-penned composition glided up to the top spot only eight weeks after 'Side Saddle' had dropped from number one. 'Roulette' was not as memorable a tune as 'Side Saddle', which is still earning Russ Conway a crust or two, but it was still good enough to beat all opposition for two weeks.

After 'Roulette', Conway never topped the charts again, but racked up four more Top 10 hits and a succession of smaller chart entries up to 1963. 'More And More Party Pops' and 'Even More Party Pops' gave Conway two more Christmas medley hits, bringing his total up to four, a good number but still a long way short of Winifred Atwell's seven medley hits, the most by any act until Jive Bunny.

The hits stopped in the mid-60s, and although Russ went on working almost as busily as ever, he subsequently suffered a nervous breakdown and went into retirement for several years. Now happily restored to health, his breezy smile and nine-and-a-half-finger playing style can still, from time to time, be seen and heard on radio and television, even if your collection of Russ Conway 78s has long since been confined to the attic.

Neil Sedaka played piano on 'Dream Lover' by BOBBY DARIN. (Pictorial Press)

87

DREAM LOVER

BOBBY DARIN

3 July 1959, for 4 weeks

●●●●

LONDON HLE 8867

Writer: Bobby Darin
Producer: Ahmet Ertegun

The first record produced on Atlantic Records' new 8-track machine was cut on 19 May 1958. The producer was Ahmet Ertegun, the song was 'Splish Splash' and the singer was Bobby Darin. 'Splish Splash' was Darin's first hit (covered in the UK by Charlie Drake). His second, 'Queen Of The Hop', climbed to number 24 in Britain, but it was his third consecutive self-penned single, 'Dream Lover', which turned him into a major star by climbing to number one on both sides of the Atlantic. Walden Robert Cassotto (born 14 May 1936) had made it. It was his last teenybop single, though, for his next release turned him into a major jazz-oriented star, and thus began the odyssey through different styles which proved that Darin was a great singer who never quite found a unique sound. If he had settled on one style, he would probably have been far more successful. But 'Dream Lover', 'Mack The Knife', 'Things', 'Multiplication' and 'If I Were A Carpenter', five of Darin's biggest hits, were in five quite different styles, so as he picked up one set of fans, he was constantly losing others.

Darin suffered from heart problems for most of his career, which limited his output, and he died from a heart attack at the age of 37, on 20 December 1973. Two number ones and seven other Top 10 hits is not the record of an unsuccessful performer, but he was vastly underrated, even at the peak of his popularity.

88

LIVING DOLL

CLIFF RICHARD AND THE DRIFTERS

31 July 1959, for 6 weeks

●●●●●●

COLUMBIA DB 4306

Writer: Lionel Bart
Producer: Norrie Paramor

After Elvis Presley and the Beatles, Cliff Richard has had more number one singles than any other act. He is the only artist to have number one hits in each of four decades, and he has had by far the longest active chart career of any British chart-topper.

Cliff was born Harry Roger Webb in Lucknow, India, on 14 October 1940. He moved to England, his native country, with his parents and his sister in 1948. After playing in various local groups in Cheshunt, Hertfordshire, he signed a long-term contract with Columbia on 9 August 1958, and made his television debut on ABC TV's *Oh Boy* just four weeks later.

The beginning of 1959 saw Cliff with his first permanent backing group: they were still called the Drifters when they played on his first chart-topper, 'Living Doll'. The song was written by Lionel Bart for the Anthony Quayle-starring film *Serious Charge*, in which Cliff had a small part, and, although initially conceived by the composer as an uptempo rock'n'roll song, it was the Drifters' rhythm guitarist Bruce Welch who suggested the slower country feel that was eventually adopted.

'Living Doll' won an Ivor Novello award and became Cliff Richard's first million seller, earning him the first of many gold discs. In 1986 he re-recorded the song with the TV comedy quartet the Young Ones (see no. 567), in aid of Comic Relief, and once again the song climbed to the very top, almost 27 years after its first victory.

89

ONLY SIXTEEN

CRAIG DOUGLAS

11 September 1959, for 4 weeks

●●●●

TOP RANK JAR 159

Writer: Barbara Campbell (aka Lou Adler, Herb Alpert and Sam Cooke)
Producer: Bunny Lewis

'Only Sixteen' was Sam Cooke's eighth American hit but, like six of its seven predecessors, it peaked outside the Top 20. In Britain it gave Cooke his second of eight hits, four of which eventually reached the Top 10. 'Only Sixteen' was not one of them, mainly because of local competition from an Isle of Wight milkman called Terence Perkins. Perkins had transformed himself into Craig Douglas a few months earlier and first brushed the charts with his rendition of Dion and the Belmonts' immortal piece of 50s punk, 'Teenager In Love'. That song had taken Marty Wilde, father of Kim, to his highest-ever chart placing, at number two, but Craig Douglas, who had stopped at number 13, was undaunted. Picking up another American hit, Douglas and his cover version climbed to the summit and gazed down on Sam Cooke's and Al Saxon's versions far below.

Craig Douglas starred in the 1961 film *It's Trad Dad* with Helen Shapiro, which did not really set up a permanent acting career for either of them. He also achieved the quite ridiculous, and almost impossible, feat of four consecutive hits which all peaked at number nine. Shortly after his final hit, 'Town Crier', lost its voice in March 1963, Douglas signed to do commercials for a well-known brand of washing powder. This proved very lucrative for some years, and Craig Douglas has never had to go back to his milk round.

90

HERE COMES SUMMER

JERRY KELLER

9 October 1959, for 1 week

●

LONDON HLR 8890

Writer: Jerry Keller
Producer: Richard Wolf

Jerry Keller, born on 20 June 1937 in Arkansas, moved with his family to Tulsa, Oklahoma, at the age of six. His first group, which went under the zippy name of The Lads Of Note, was formed in Tulsa in the early 50s. From there he progressed to the Tulsa Boy Singers and then won a talent contest which led to a job with Jack Dalton's Orchestra in the mid-West. That was short lived, however, and Keller then became a disc jockey back in Tulsa for nine months from mid-1955, before moving to New York in 1956, still only 19 years old, to try to hit the big time as a singer.

Sometimes being good pays off, as it did for Jerry Keller. Another regular member of the congregation at Keller's church in New York was Pat Boone, and he gave Keller the introductions that led to his being signed by Kapp Records. His first single was 'Here Comes Summer', which hit the British charts at the end of August. Either summer was even shorter than usual in 1959 or else the record company's timing was about as good as Wizzard's, whose 'Rock And Roll Winter' was released in April 1974. Not that it mattered, as 'Here Comes Summer' became the ultimate high school summer song, and it soared to number one, Keller's only hit in Britain and America.

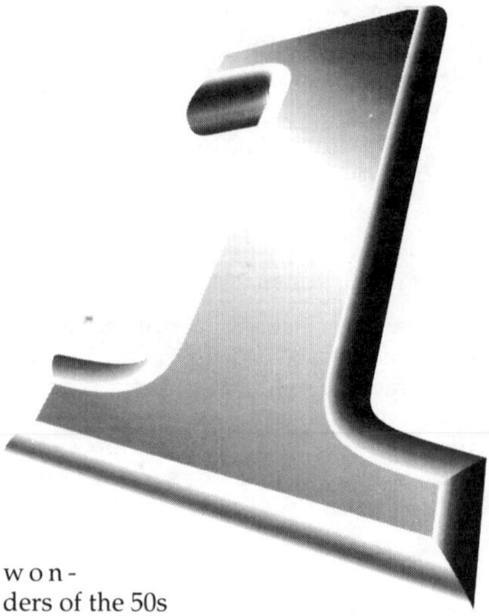

That meant that three of the four one-hit wonders of the 50s had surnames beginning with K (Kallen, Kalin and Keller). In fact no K act really became established in the charts until the Kinks in 1965.

91

MACK THE KNIFE

BOBBY DARIN

16 October 1959 for 2 weeks

●●

LONDON HLE 8939

Writers: Bertolt Brecht and Kurt Weill; English lyrics by Marc Blitzstein
Producer: Ahmet Ertegun

One of the biggest hits in history would never have been made had not the artist insisted. A teen rock and roll favourite, Bobby Darin longed to be a respectable mass-audience artist. He recorded an album of adult-oriented material, including Brecht and Weill's 'Moritat' from *The Threepenny Opera*, translated into English by Marc Blitzstein and called 'Mack The Knife'. The inclusion of the song was not as odd as it may sound, since at one point in early 1956, there had been five versions in the American Top 40, the greatest cover battle in chart history. Even more confusingly, the competing artists included the almost identically named Dick Hyman and Richard Hayman.

However, it was Louis Armstrong's version that inspired Darin, and the young rocker gave the song a hip jazz-flavoured treatment. Darin phoned the television disc jockey Dick Clark, a personal friend, and informed him that he would debut the record on Clark's Saturday night ABC network show. The host told him he was crazy, and the programme's producer said, "If he wants to turn his career into chopped liver, so be it." It was Darin who was proved right. 'Mack The Knife' was his second consecutive number one, America's list leader for nine weeks and Atlantic's best-selling single to that date. Bobby Darin had a new career and never returned to rock and roll.

92

TRAVELLIN' LIGHT

CLIFF RICHARD AND THE SHADOWS

30 October 1959, for 5 weeks

●●●●●

COLUMBIA DB 4351

Writers: Sid Tepper and Roy C. Bennett
Producer: Norrie Paramor

'Living Doll' was the only record that ever topped the charts for Cliff Richard and the Drifters, as the name was changed to Cliff Richard and the Shadows for the follow-up, 'Travellin' Light'. The change was to avoid confusion with the American Drifters, as Cliff's singles began to be released in the States.

Cliff's first four singles had all been uptempo, all in the fashionable rock-and-roll vein and all sung with a hint of surliness in the voice, but it was not until the success of the easy-paced 'Living Doll', his fifth single, that Cliff actually topped the charts.

The same winning format was used for 'Travellin' Light', which topped the singles charts for five weeks from October to December 1959, and reappeared in December 1960 on 'Cliff's Silver Discs' EP. The B-side, 'Dynamite', was so popular that it charted for four weeks in its own right, reaching number 16.

'Travellin' Light' was an aptly titled song to be at the top when the first sections of the M1 motorway were opened. The motorway system has done at least as much for live gigs as the invention of the synthesizer.

93

WHAT DO YOU WANT

ADAM FAITH

4 December 1959, for 3 weeks
(1 week top equal)

●●●

PARLOPHONE R 4591

Writer: Les Vandyke
Producer: John Burgess; arranged by John Barry

Few people watching BBC TV's *Drumbeat* in the summer of 1959 would have expected the blond, moody Adam Faith to become one of Britain's most successful acts of the early 60s. His first few singles, including a version of Thurston Harris' 'Runk Bunk', deservedly failed to sell, and it was Faith's good fortune that a member of the Raindrops vocal group who also featured on *Drumbeat*, Johnny Worth, decided that Faith was the person to interpret his songs, songs written under the name Les Vandyke. Worth took the name Vandyke from his telephone exchange in London, having decided it was a better name for a songwriter than either Johnny Worth or his real name, Yani Skordalides.

Adam Faith, born Terence Nelhams on 23 June 1940, was taken into the Parlophone studios, and, despite his uninspiring track record, produced one of the pop classics of the pre-Beatles era. The last line, "Wish you wanted my love, bay-bee", gave Adam a catch phrase that lasted well beyond his first hit. It was also the first ever number one for Parlophone, Faith being, at the time, the only pop act recording on the label.

Before George Martin signed the Beatles to Parlophone and turned it into the most successful record label of all time, Faith's stable mates were acts such as the Temperance Seven, Mike Sarne (both of whom subsequently reached number one) and Peter Sellers. Long on talent, short on rock and roll.

94

WHAT DO YOU WANT TO MAKE THOSE EYES AT ME FOR?

EMILE FORD AND THE CHECKMATES

18 December 1959, for 6 weeks (1 week top equal)

●●●●●●●

PYE NIXA 7N 15225

Writers: Joseph McCarthy, Howard Johnson and Jimmy Monaco
Producer: Michael Barclay

Emile Ford was born Emile Sweetman in Nassau, in the Bahamas, on 16 October 1937, and as a young boy he moved to Britain with his family. His first single was a revival of a song first recorded way back in 1917 by Ada Jones and Billy Murray, and revived in 1945 by Betty Hutton for her film, *Incendiary Blonde*.

MICHAEL HOLLIDAY was the first British male soloist to have two number ones with at least one intervening year. (Pictorial Press)

Emile Ford was the first black man based in Britain to have a major hit, although Winifred Atwell and Shirley Bassey, two black women based in Britain, had hit number one before him.

Ford owed his success to the song's arrangement and his gentle delivery of lyrics like "I'll get you alone some night, and baby you'll find you're messing with dynamite". It was a happy, friendly singalong version of the old favourite, which made it perfect for the Christmas season, as Shakin' Stevens realised when he took the song back into the Top 10 at Christmas 1987.

Ford's follow-up was a more modern song, Frank Loesser's 1948 composition 'Slow Boat To China', which reached number three early in 1960, but apart from the upbeat 'Counting Teardrops' at the end of that year, there were no more Top 10 hits. Ford later moved to Sweden, where he enjoyed several more years of success. He is remembered in Britain not only for the length of the title of his number one hit, but also because, for the week ending 18 December 1959, he shared the top slot with Adam Faith's 'What Do You Want', the last time that two records were placed equal top on the British charts.

95

STARRY EYED

MICHAEL HOLLIDAY

29 January 1960, for 1 week

●

COLUMBIA DB 4378

Writers: Earl Shuman and Mort Garson
Producer: Norrie Paramor

Michael Holliday had been out of the charts for 18 months since the last of three consecutive 'Love' hits ('In Love', 'Stairway Of Love' and 'I'll Always Be In Love With You') disappeared in mid-July 1958. However, at the end of 1959, his producer Norrie Paramor found a song by Mort Garson and Earl Shuman (neither of whom were related to Mort Shuman, who wrote hits for Elvis with Doc Pomus), which fitted Holliday's style perfectly. The American version, by a singer almost as unknown then as he is now, by the name of Gary Stites, had stopped at number 77 on the *Billboard* charts, but Paramor and Holliday's confidence in the song paid off in Britain. On the first day of the new decade, the single entered the charts, and four weeks later it was at the very top.

The hit was not enough to give Michael Holliday's career a real boost. After 'Starry Eyed' he enjoyed two more minor hits, but neither of them would have featured on the chart had it not expanded from a Top 30 (courtesy of *New Musical Express*) to a Top 50 (published by *Record Retailer*) while 'Starry Eyed' was still on the charts. His last, and aptly-titled, chart single was 'Little Boy Lost', which achieved the minimum ranking of number 50 for one week in September that year.

'Starry Eyed' is one thing that Michael Holliday never was about his life in show business. He was the first Liverpudlian to achieve two number ones, but in the week that this record was broken by the Liverpool group Gerry and the Pacemakers in October 1963, Michael Holliday died, a probable suicide at the age of 37.

96

WHY

ANTHONY NEWLEY

5 February 1960, for 4 weeks

●●●●

DECCA F 11194

Writers: Bob Marcucci and Peter de Angelis
Producer: Ray Horricks

Like John Leyton and David Soul after him, Anthony Newley was an actor who became a pop star almost by accident. He had appeared in such films as *Oliver Twist*, in which he played the part of the Artful Dodger, and Peter Ustinov's *Vice Versa*, in which one of his co-stars was another child star turned pop singer, Petula Clark.

The film *Idle On Parade*, a hastily made movie about a pop star called up for national service inspired by the brief, but highly publicised, army career of Terry Dene, gave Newley his first chance to be a pop singer, and the EP of songs from the film reached number 13 in mid-1959. A single from the film, 'I've Waited So Long', was also released, and despite the fact that the song was included on the 'Idle On Parade' EP, it climbed to number three. The only man to do better than that was a man whose US Army career ended during the weeks that 'Why' topped the charts - Acting Sergeant US 53310761 Presley, EA - whose 'Jailhouse Rock' single had been at number one while the EP from the film also made the Top 20 (see no. 67).

'Why' was a cover version of Frankie Avalon's American number one, and it became the seventh question to reach number one in Britain, the third in four chart-toppers. At the time, it was also the shortest title ever to reach number one, a record it has subsequently surrendered to Telly Savalas' 'If' (see no. 367).

97

POOR ME

ADAM FAITH

10 March 1960, for 1 week

●

PARLOPHONE R 4623

Writer: Les Vandyke
Producer: John Burgess; arranged by John Barry

The first number one on the *Record Retailer* chart, which was Britain's first record-industry chart and the first Top 50 chart, was Adam Faith's second consecutive chart-topper, written, produced and arranged by the same team that had been responsible for 'What Do You Want' (see no. 93). A very similar construction, with pizzicato strings and hiccuping delivery of the lovelorn lyrics, made it a formula number one. Faith was close to a hat-trick but, like Cliff Richard a few weeks earlier, he failed in his attempt at a third chart-topper in a row when his follow-up, 'Someone Else's Baby', stopped at number two. Unlike Cliff, Faith never had another number one, but by the time his final hit dropped off the charts six and a half years later, he had clocked up two number ones, nine other Top 10 hits and a total of 251 weeks on the chart.

He also played a big part in bringing Sandie Shaw and Leo Sayer to the public. A rare example of a pop singer with a talent for acting, Faith's subsequent career in films and television has won him even more praise than his long string of record smashes. After the success of his TV series with Zoe Wanamaker, *Love Hurts*, Faith went back into the recording studios in 1993 to make his first album in over two decades. *Midnight Postcards* went straight into the album charts, where, in December 1993, it found itself up against competition from other 50s hitmakers Frank Sinatra, Shirley Bassey and Doris Day.

98

RUNNING BEAR

JOHNNY PRESTON

17 March 1960, for 2 weeks

●●

MERCURY AMT 1079

Writer: J.P. Richardson
Producer: J.P. Richardson

John Preston Courville was born on 28 August 1939 in Port Arthur, Texas. He formed a high-school band called the Shades and became very popular in Southern Texas. Late in 1958 a local disc jockey from radio station KTRM approached him during a gig and asked him if he would like to record a few songs. The disc jockey was J.P. Richardson, better known as the Big Bopper.

The first attempts at coming up with a hit single were unsuccessful, but one winter's morning in Houston they cut 'Running Bear', the Romeo and Juliet saga of the Indian brave and Little White Dove, whose warring tribes ensured their love could never be. Singing backing vocals on the disc ("ook-a-chunka, ook-a-chunka") are the Big Bopper himself and, among others, country star and erstwhile husband of Tammy Wynette, George Jones. Shortly after the record was cut, the Big Bopper died with Buddy Holly and Richie Valens in the plane crash in Iowa, and Mercury decided not to put the record out for over six months. It was finally released in America in October 1959, and it climbed all the way to the top.

The 'ook-a-chunka' vocal style was copied years later by Jonathan King on his inventive version of B.J. Thomas' 'Hooked On A Feeling'. That arrangement was in turn lifted in its entirety by a Swede called Bjorn Skifs, who led a band called Blue Swede and took his version of 'Hooked On A Feeling' to number one in America in 1974. In the 1980s Skifs took the role of the Arbiter in the Andersson/Rice/Ulvaeus musical *Chess*. Tim Rice had won an album from the pop newspaper *Disc* in 1960 by writing a letter headlined "I Tip Johnny Preston For Number One Hat-Trick". He proved to be a better lyricist than clairvoyant, and it was to be a year and a week before anybody managed the elusive hat-trick. It was not Johnny Preston who did it, but the rather more consistent Elvis Presley.

99

MY OLD MAN'S A DUSTMAN

LONNIE DONEGAN

31 March 1960, for 4 weeks

●●●●

PYE NIXA 7N 15256

Writers: Traditional; new lyrics by Lonnie Donegan, Peter Buchanan and Beverly Thorn
Producers: Michael Barclay and Alan Freeman
(recorded live at the Gaumont, Doncaster)

Lonnie Donegan's third number one reached the summit in only its second week of chart action, making him the third act, after Adam Faith and Michael Holliday, to have a number one in two different decades. It also affected his musical output for the rest of his career. Having had two number ones and eight Top 10 hits with his nasal bluesy style of skiffle, he switched his priorities away from the American tradition to the British music-hall type of skiffle, which had already provided him with one Top 10 hit, 'Does Your Chewing Gum Lose Its Flavour?', a year earlier.

'My Old Man's A Dustman', complete with dreadful jokes ("My dustbin's full of toadstools" - "How do you know it's full?" - "because there's not mushroom inside"), was a cleaned-up version of the old pub song, 'What Do You Think About That?', and gave Donegan his biggest hit of all.

In 1985 Donegan underwent heart surgery, from which he happily recovered, but news of his illness had a surprising effect on the Japanese stock market. As the tickertapes announced the fact that Lonnie Donegan had undergone heart surgery, the Nikkei index plunged. The reason was not that Lonnie was particularly well known in Japan, in fact quite the opposite. The first Japanese interpreters of the news thought the patient was Ronnie Reagan, then President of the United States, rather than Lonnie Donegan. The market recovered almost as quickly as the patient himself.

100

DO YOU MIND

ANTHONY NEWLEY

28 April 1960, for 1 week

●

DECCA F 11220

Writer: Lionel Bart
Producer: Ray Horricks

The 100th number one hit single in British chart history was the second number one for both the singer, Anthony Newley, and the composer, Lionel Bart. Both went on to greater fame in the musical theatre, but for Newley it was his last dose of chart supremacy. After consecutive number ones with question songs, Newley's chart career gradually faded, although his personal fortune was assured by writing, with Leslie Bricusse, another question song, 'What Kind Of Fool Am I?', which became the hit of the show which he wrote and in which he starred, *Stop The World - I Want To Get Off*.

It is not often remembered that before the success of *Stop The World*, Newley played the title role in the unusual TV series *The World Of Gurney Slade*. The theme tune of the series, by Max Harris, reached number 11 in the last chart of 1960, on 29 December.

For Lionel Bart, *Oliver* was imminent. By the end of 1960, it had become the most successful British musical in history, and was well set on a run in London that would not be eclipsed until *Jesus Christ Superstar* broke all previous box-office records in the late 70s. But the biggest hit recording of a song from *Oliver*, Shirley Bassey's version of 'As Long As He Needs Me', reached only number two, despite a 30-week run on the charts. Bart's career has been down and up since *Oliver*, but nobody can deny his leading place among British popular composers of this century.

101

CATHY'S CLOWN

EVERLY BROTHERS

5 May 1960, for 7 weeks

●●●●●●●

WARNER BROTHERS WB 1

Writers: Don and Phil Everly
Producer: Wesley Rose

The day before Princess Margaret married Antony Armstrong Jones, Don and Phil Everly took over the number one spot, which they held on to until well after the 'Caribbean Honeymoon' (a number 42 hit for the Frank Weir Orchestra) was over.

The Everly Brothers had recently signed a million-dollar contract with the newly-formed Warner Brothers label, but the industry felt that splitting Don and Phil from the Cadence label and its owner Archie Bleyer, as well as from writers Felice and Boudleaux Bryant, was a considerable risk. The Brothers responded with 'Cathy's Clown', the biggest hit of their career as the first single on the Warner Brothers label. If Warner Brothers had been able to ship enough copies in the week of its release, it may well have entered the charts at number one. As it was, it enjoyed five weeks at the top of the American charts and seven weeks at the head of the British lists, a longer run at number one than any record since their own 'All I Have To Do Is Dream'/ 'Claudette' (see no. 73), which had spent

The EVERLY BROTHERS take the Coasters' advice and go 'shoppin' for clothes'. (Pictorial Press)

seven weeks at number one in July and August 1958.

'Cathy's Clown' remains one of the greatest of all pop records of its era, capturing in less than three minutes all the excitement, harmonies and emotion of the Everlys at their best. As far as the mid-90s, no duo has ever had a more successful chart career than the Everly Brothers.

102

THREE STEPS TO HEAVEN

EDDIE COCHRAN

23 June 1960, for 2 weeks

●●

LONDON HLG 9115

Writers: Eddie and Bob Cochran
Producers: Jerry Capehart and Eddie Cochran

Eddie Cochran, born 3 October 1938, was killed in a car crash at Chippenham, Wiltshire, on his way from Bristol to London airport on 17 April 1960, shortly after recording the prophetically titled 'Three Steps To Heaven'. It became his only number one hit single and the second posthumous number one on the British charts.

Since his death at the age of 21, Cochran has become a legend for his astonishing guitar work and the songs he wrote, some of which can rank with the best of Chuck Berry and Buddy Holly as rock classics. 'Three Steps To Heaven', written with his brother Bob and revived with great success in the 1970s by Showaddywaddy, was not his greatest composition, however. 'C'mon Everybody' and 'Summertime Blues' remain the songs for which he is best remembered. Cochran's great influence on those that followed him was not his writing, but his guitar style. Listen to his playing on 'Hallelujah I Love Her So' or 'Don't Ever Let me Go' and you will hear the roots of the styles of many of the great rock guitarists of the 60s and 70s.

103

GOOD TIMIN'

JIMMY JONES

7 July 1960, for 3 weeks

●●●

MGM 1078

Writers: Fred Tobias and Clint Ballard Jr.
Producer: Otis Blackwell

Jimmy Jones, born on 2 June 1937, began his career with an all-time classic single that failed to make number one. That song was 'Handy Man', a number three hit which introduced rock falsetto to the British charts, and subsequently gave hits to Del Shannon and James Taylor. Following that up ought to have been impossible, but Jones came up with a song as different as possible from 'Handy Man' and reached the very top. 'Good Timin'', a simply structured verse/chorus/verse/chorus song about what Carl Jung called synchronicity, was really nowhere as good as the free-running 'Handy Man' but it nevertheless hit the top.

There it stopped. Jones' follow-up was the underrated 'I Just Go For You'/'That's When I Cried', which, like Jones' next two singles, hit the charts but failed to make the Top 30. 'Good Timin'' was also the last record at the top in a long while for MGM. After four number ones on the yellow label in 1958, 'Good Timin'' was their only chart-topper until the Osmonds between them gave MGM five more number ones and 18 more weeks at the top between 1972 and 1974.

In 1982, 'Good Timin'' was revived by who else but Showaddywaddy, proving it is still remembered by the rock fans.

104

PLEASE DON'T TEASE

CLIFF RICHARD AND THE SHADOWS

28 July 1960, for 1 week

•

and 11 August 1960, for 2 weeks

••

COLUMBIA DB 4479

Writers: Pete Chester and Bruce Welch
Producer: Norrie Paramor

Cliff's third chart-topper held the unique distinction of having been chosen by members of the public.

A cross section of people were played a selection of songs and, over tea and biscuits, were asked to choose their favourite. The majority went for a song written by the Shadows' rhythm guitarist Bruce Welch and Pete Chester, son of Charlie Chester the comedian. The song was 'Please Don't Tease', which Cliff re-recorded in a slower vein in 1978. It was subsequently released as the B-side of 'Please Remember Me' in July of that year.

After two consecutive number two hits, it was no doubt a great pleasure for Cliff to be back on top. He has never achieved a hat-trick of number one hits, despite the fact that all 19 single releases between 'Living Doll' and 'Don't Talk To Him' at the end of 1963 reached the Top 4. In that period, he had seven number ones, six numbers twos, four number threes and two number four hits, but never more than two consecutive number ones. Twice he issued five consecutive singles which gave him three number ones and two number twos.

105

SHAKIN' ALL OVER

JOHNNY KIDD AND THE PIRATES

4 August 1960, for 1 week

•

HMV POP 753

Writers: Frederick Heath and Gus Robinson
Producer: Walter Ridley

Johnny Kidd was born Frederick Heath in Willesden, London, on 23 November 1939. He learned to play both the guitar and banjo, forming the group Freddie Heath and the Nutters in 1958. The group was rechristened Johnny Kidd and the Pirates in 1959, and appearances on BBC Radio's *Saturday Club* led to a recording contract with HMV.

The Pirates, appropriately dressed in the garb of swashbucklers, released their first single, 'Please Don't Touch', in May 1959. Both this and their cover version of Marv Johnson's US hit, 'You Got What It Takes', struggled to number 25 in the charts. Then came their fourth release, 'Shakin' All Over', which Kidd wrote with Pirates' manager Gus Robinson and which ranks with Cliff Richard's 'Move It' as one of the few original rock and roll sounds to be produced by a British act before 1963.

The Pirates on this single were guitarist Alan Caddy, bassist Brian Gregg and drummer Clem Cattini, although the distinctive guitar riff was not played by a Pirate at all but by session man Joe Moretti. Two lesser hits followed until Caddy, Gregg and Cattini left the Pirates to join the Tornados (see no. 141) at the end of 1961. New Pirates were taken on board and Johnny Kidd set sail again, scoring another Top 10 hit in 1963 with 'I'll Never Get Over You', a song with a definite Merseybeat flavour.

Kidd was returning from a gig on 7 October 1966 when he was killed in a car accident just outside Bury, Lancashire. The Pirates continued to perform into the 70s as a tribute to the underrated Kidd, who was a true pioneer of British rock.

106

APACHE

THE SHADOWS

25 August 1960, for 5 weeks

●●●●●

COLUMBIA DB 4484

Writer: Jerry Lordan
Producer: Norrie Paramor

In 1960 the Shadows were Hank B. Marvin on lead guitar, Bruce Welch on rhythm guitar, Jet Harris on bass and Tony Meehan on drums. As well as backing Cliff Richard, they had issued three records in their own right before the success of 'Apache'. Two of these discs were issued under the name the Drifters, a name which they changed after the American Drifters ('Save The Last Dance For Me', etc.) issued an injuction over the name duplication.

The Shadows first heard 'Apache' while they were on tour around Britain and when a fellow artiste on the bill, singer Jerry Lordan, played them the tune on his ukelele. Bert Weedon had already recorded the song, but seemingly had no plans to release it. The Shadows recorded the tune, released it and swiftly knocked their boss (see no. 104) off the top. In America they were beaten by a cover version by the Danish guitarist Jorgen Ingmann, who three years later won the Eurovision Song Contest with his sister Grethe.

The Shadows won many accolades in the polls of 1960, including being voted Britain's Top Instrumental Group Of The Year and 'Apache' being voted Top Record Of 1960 in the prestigious *New Musical Express* Readers' Poll.

107

TELL LAURA I LOVE HER

RICKY VALANCE

29 September 1960, for 3 weeks

●●●

COLUMBIA DB 4493

Writers: Jeff Barry and Ben Raleigh
Producer: Norrie Paramor

In the 1950s and early 60s the BBC was the only national source of broadcast music in Britain, and almost invariably it refused to play any song that mentioned death in any way. This unusual 'moral' attitude meant that several American hit records were not even released by record companies in Britain, or that the hits sank without trace, a fate that befell Mark Dinning's massive American smash, 'Teen Angel'. Most of these songs were tasteless ('Tell Laura I Love Her' most certainly is), but they were not immoral nor likely to exert a bad influence on the listener. After all, who would go out and kill himself in a stock car race as a result of listening to the sad story of Laura and Tommy?

Because of its restrictive pop music 'needle-time' agreements with the Musicians Union, the BBC Light Programme was scarcely more important to the pop fans of Britain than Radio Luxembourg, which never banned records just because they featured a grisly death or two. So, when RCA decided not to release Ray Peterson's original verison of 'Tell Laura I Love Her' in England, EMI decided to go ahead with a cover by a Welsh singer called David Spencer, who had nothing to lose.

Spencer changed his name to Ricky Valance, and the great Norrie Paramor produced the record. The BBC banned it,

The SHADOWS were the first part of a number one act to go on to have its own number one. (Pictorial Press)

Radio Luxembourg did not, and it climbed quickly to the top of the charts. Ricky Valance, however, could not find the right follow-up, and – after 16 weeks of chart action – became just another name on the list of one-hit wonders. He has not left the business, however, and still performs regularly today, although he has not yet found his way back into the charts.

108

ONLY THE LONELY

ROY ORBISON

20 October 1960, for 2 weeks

●●

LONDON HLU 9149

Writer: Roy Orbison
Producer: Fred Foster

The first song that six-year-old Roy Kelton Orbison (born Vernon, Texas, 23 April 1936) learned to pick out on his guitar was 'You Are My Sunshine'. By the age of 13 he'd put together a band, the Wink Westerners, and by the time his education had progressed to the North Texas State College, where he was a contemporary of Pat Boone, he had formed his third group, the Teen Kings.

In 1956 Orbison cut his first single, 'Ooby Dooby', which he financed himself. This became a minor US hit when he re-recorded it on Sun Records in Memphis. However, he was signed to that legendary label for only a brief period before moving on to Nashville and Fred Foster's Monument Records.

As a songwriter Orbison was never comfortable with rock and roll. His forte was the rock ballad. Jerry Lee Lewis and Buddy Holly recorded his material, and the Everly Brothers had taken his song 'Claudette' to the top in 1958 (see no. 73). In 1960 he set out from his Texas home to record his third single for Monument. Having already released two flops,

Orbison decided to try to sell his new song to an established star. Stopping off in Memphis he called in on Elvis Presley to see if he was interested, but the King was asleep. Getting back in his car he continued to Nashville and played his song to the Everly Brothers. They liked it but had just recorded their latest single and didn't need a new song, so Orbison was forced to record it himself. Released on the London label in the UK, the single became the first of 33 hits for the Big O, reaching the summit 12 weeks after it had first appeared on the chart. In the US it peaked at number two.

109

IT'S NOW OR NEVER

ELVIS PRESLEY

3 November 1960, for 8 weeks

●●●●●●●●

RCA 1207

Writers: Eduardo di Capua, Aaron Schroeder and Wally Gold
Producers: Steve Sholes and Chet Atkins

As soon as Elvis left the army in March 1960, he rushed back to the recording studios at RCA in Nashville. Sessions there in March and April produced some of his most famous and successful work, including the entire *Elvis Is Back* album, 'It's Now Or Never' and 'Are You Lonesome Tonight?'.

It's Now Or Never was Elvis' fifth single to reach number one in Britain, but for quite some time it seemed possible that it would never be issued over here at all. Instead of being Elvis' second post-army single ('Stuck On You', which reached number three, was the first), it was delayed by copyright problems arising from the fact that the song was an adaptation of the 1901 Italian song, 'O Sole Mio'. The song had been popularized by Elvis' favourite Italian tenor, Mario Lanza, and Presley's music publisher Freddie Bienstock had asked the American writers, Aaron Schroeder and Wally Gold, to put new words to Eduardo di Capua's tune.

No copyright problems existed in America, where the single became the biggest hit of Elvis Presley's career during the summer of 1960. To keep his British

CLIFF RICHARD AND THE SHADOWS appear on Sunday Night At The London Palladium. (Pictorial Press)

fans happy, RCA released the American B-side, 'A Mess Of Blues', as an A-side, and even that made number two thanks, in part, to the enormously popular song put onto the British flip-side, 'The Girl Of My Best Friend'. When 'It's Now Or Never' was finally cleared for UK release in November, interest had built up to such a level that a second straight-in-at-number-one single for Elvis was a foregone conclusion. Recorded on 3/4 April 1960, 'It's Now Or Never' gave the King a new adult audience to add to his millions of younger fans. It featured Scotty Moore (guitar), Hank Garland (guitar), Floyd Cramer (piano), Bob Moore (bass), Murray Harmon (drums) and the Jordanaires (backing vocals). No other Elvis single spent as many as 'It's Now or Never''s eight weeks at the top of the UK charts.

'O Sole Mio' had been a major American pop hit in 1949 for singer Tony Martin, under the title 'There's No Tomorrow'. It is more widely known today as the tune for the Cornetto advertisement.

110

I LOVE YOU

CLIFF RICHARD AND THE SHADOWS

29 December 1960, for 2 weeks

●●

COLUMBIA DB 4547

Writer: Bruce Welch
Producer: Norrie Paramor

Cliff's fourth number one saw him reverting to the easy-paced style of his first two chart-toppers, 'Living Doll' and 'Travellin' Light'.

For the first time, Cliff took over from Elvis at number one, a feat that was to be repeated exactly three years later when 'Return To Sender' was displaced by Cliff's 'The Next Time'/'Bachelor Boy' (see nos. 143 and 144). Elvis only displaced Cliff at the top once, when his double-sided hit 'Rock-A-Hula Baby'/ 'Can't Help Falling In Love' knocked Cliff's biggest British hit, 'The Young Ones' (see nos. 132 and 133), from the top slot. Written by Bruce Welch, 'I Love You' stayed in pole position for a fortnight over New Year 1961.

It was now apparent that Cliff and his group were fast becoming a self-contained unit thanks to the songwriting talents of Shadows Hank Marvin and Bruce Welch. 'I Love You' was Cliff's 11th single in just over two years, and only one of those, his third single, 'Livin' Lovin' Doll', had failed to reach the Top 10. Cliff's 26 consecutive Top 10 hits, of which 'I Love You' was the eighth, constituted a record that remained unbeaten until Madonna overtook him in the 90s.

'I Love You' must be the most unimaginative title of all the number ones. Nevertheless, it was the first song with this title to enter the British charts, and it was not until 1977 that a second song called 'I Love You', this time by Donna Summer, hit the UK charts. In 1983 the Swiss band Yello used the title for their chart debut single, and Vanilla Ice used the title a fourth time in 1992. Four songs of this name are nothing compared to the ten different songs called 'Tonight' which have become British hit singles.

111

POETRY IN MOTION

JOHNNY TILLOTSON

12 January 1961, for 2 weeks

●●

LONDON HLA 9231

Writers: Paul Kauffman and Mike Anthony
Producer: Archie Bleyer

Johnny Tillotson was born on 20 April 1939 in Jacksonville, Florida, and before the age of 20 had been signed to Cadence Records, the label that built the careers of the Everly Brothers, the Chordettes and Andy Williams.

Basically a country singer, Tillotson's biggest UK hit was written by two New Yorkers who gave it to Cadence chief Archie Bleyer. Bleyer recorded Tillotson twice with the song, once in New York, where the result was not quite right, and once in Nashville, where Tillotson's performance was enough to make the record a number one hit in many countries around the world. Tillotson's other singles were more countrified, which may explain their relative lack of success in Britain, but in America he is still as well known for songs such as 'It Keeps Right On A-Hurting' and 'Talk Back Trembling Lips' as for his British number one.

When the Everly Brothers moved from Cadence to Warner Brothers in 1960, it was not long before Archie Bleyer wound up his record company, incidentally selling many of his masters to Andy Williams. Tillotson moved to MGM, where his country hits continued in the States for many years. He is still an active country singer, even though the hits in Britain have long since dried up.

112

ARE YOU LONESOME TONIGHT?

ELVIS PRESLEY

26 January 1961, for 4 weeks

●●●●

Writers: Roy Turk and Lou Handman
Producers: Steve Sholes and Chet Atkins

For his sixth number one hit, Elvis revamped a song from 1926 and shot to number one, mainly thanks to the inclusion of a long spoken passage beginning with the immortal line based loosely on Jaques' speech in Act II Scene VII of Shakespeare's *As You Like It* - "You know, someone said that all the world's a stage." Elvis hardly ever seemed to be able to remember this long recitation or to want to recite it accurately at his concerts in the 70s. RCA even released a live version of 'Are You Lonesome Tonight?' in the UK in 1982 in which Elvis sings incorrect (and unfunny) lyrics and laughs all the way through the spoken-word section of the number. Not a worthy release. The 1960 version, however, was deservedly one of Elvis' most popular recordings of all. Recorded in Nashville at the 'It's Now Or Never' sessions of April 1960 (see no. 109), the track did nearly as well as its predecessor on both sides of the Atlantic.

By the beginning of 1961, Elvis was at his peak of popularity with the record-buying public. 'Are You Lonesome Tonight?' was the second of a run of a dozen successive Presley single releases in the UK, of which ten made number one. From this point until the emergence of the Beatles, Elvis had no challenger to his position as the most popular recording act in the world.

113

SAILOR

PETULA CLARK

23 February 1961, for 1 week

●

PYE 7N 15324

Writers: Fini Busch and Werner Scharfenburger;
English lyrics by David West
Producer: Alan Freeman

Petula Clark first came to public attention immediately after the war in a radio series called *Meet The Huggetts,* in which she played Jack Warner's daughter. She was born in Epsom on 15 November 1933, and was only in her mid-teens when stardom struck. By the mid-50s, she was well established, not only as an actress but also a bouncy singer, a British derivation of the all-conquering Mitch Miller style, and she managed four Top 10 hits before 1958.

Her first number one was a song written by two Austrians, Fini Busch and Werner Scharfenburger, and titled 'Seemann'. A German girl called Lolita turned it into a monster European smash. English lyrics were then added by EMI producer Norman Newell, under the pseudonym David West, and Lolita re-recorded the song in English.

five in the *Billboard* charts, but on home ground Petula Clark not only annihilated Lolita, who failed to make the Top 50, but also beat Anne Shelton (see no. 50), who was hoping for a second number one with a European song but had to be content with a Top 10 hit.

114

WALK RIGHT BACK/ EBONY EYES

THE EVERLY BROTHERS

2 March 1961, for 3 weeks

●●●

WARNER BROTHERS WB 33

Writer: 'Walk Right Back' – Sonny Curtis; 'Ebony Eyes' – John D. Loudermilk. Producer: Wesley Rose

The Everly Brothers' third number one hit, and their second for the new Warner Brothers label, was their second double-sided number one. There have been 24 double-sided number ones altogether, including four by Elvis and two by the Beatles, as well as four EPs at the very top. The most played side was written by Sonny Curtis of the Crickets. The other side was 'Ebony Eyes', and was less played because it was a song about death, a classic to rank alongside 'Tell Laura I Love Her' and 'Leader Of The Pack'. The writer, John D. Loudermilk, has, over the years, come up with a wide range of highly original songs, but 'Ebony Eyes' is probably his best known. 'Indian Reservation' for Don Fardon, 'Tobacco Road' for the Nashville Teens and 'Language Of Love', which he performed himself, are all Loudermilk compositions and were all Top 20 hits in Britain.

The sad saga of Flight 1203 ("And then came the announcement over the loud-speaker; Will all those having relatives and friends on Flight 1203 please report to the chapel across the street") made 'Ebony Eyes' one of the most parodied songs in pop history. Despite its title, 'Walk Right Back' was not a song about the sending off of a football defender, and thus does not rank with nos. 286, 646 and 708 as a football number one.

115

WOODEN HEART

ELVIS PRESLEY

23 March 1961, for 6 weeks

●●●●●●

RCA 1226

Writers: Bert Kaempfert, Kay Twomey, Fred Wise and Ben Weisman Producer: Steve Sholes

Elvis' seventh UK number one was unique in that it was not released as a single in the US at the time of its enormous success in Britain and Europe. The most popular song from Elvis' first post-army movie, *GI Blues*, it made Elvis the first artist to score three number one hits with consecutive British releases (see also nos. 109 and 112). It was an adaptation of a German folk song, 'Muss I Denn', by Fred Wise, Kay Twomey, Ben Weisman and Bert Kaempfert, the latter being the German bandleader who recorded the Beatles in Hamburg in 1961, and had his own US number one that year with 'Wonderland By Night', which knocked Presley's 'Are You Lonesome Tonight?' off the top. Bert Kaempfert also wrote 'Strangers In The Night' for Frank Sinatra, and thus has close connections with three of the top five chart acts of all time. RCA's baffling decision not to release 'Wooden Heart' as an American single allowed unknown singer Joe Dowell to take his version to number one in America in the summer of 1961. The 27 weeks that Elvis Presley's 'Wooden Heart' spent in the UK Top 50 was the longest consecutive run by any of Presley's 100-plus hit singles.

116

BLUE MOON

THE MARCELS

4 May 1961, for 2 weeks

●●

PYE INTERNATIONAL 7N 25073

Writers: Richard Rodgers and Lorenz Hart Producer: Stu Phillips

One of the only songs that Rodgers and

Hart wrote outside a musical, 'Blue Moon' was published in 1934 as a 'slow foxtrot ballad'. It had survived most recorded versions over the next 27 years (including a straight version by Elvis Presley), but the Marcels brought a new meaning to the song with their astonishing arrangement, featuring vocals not in the original version, and ending each chorus with the unanswerable "dang-a-dang-dang, ding-a-dong-ding Blue Moon".

In 1957, the obscure Wimley label issued a record called 'Zoom Zoom Zoom' by the Collegians. It failed to do anything on any chart, but it has been mentioned as an inspiration for the Marcels' 'Blue Moon'. Listening to the two records clarifies the issue - 'Blue Moon' was not so much inspired by 'Zoom Zoom Zoom', it was virtually a direct copy of the arrangement.

The MARCELS were the second group to have a number one version of 'Blue Moon', Glen Gray and the Casa Loma Orchestra having led the American list in 1935. (Pictorial Press)

There is some confusion as to exactly who the Marcels were on the record. The probable line-up of the lads from Philadelphia is Cornelius Harp (lead vocals), Ronald Mundy, Fred Johnson, Dick Knauss and Gene Bricker. Anyway, five Marcels appeared in the Chubby Checker movie *Twist Around The Clock,* which still holds the world record as the quickest-made feature film of all time - 28 days from the day producer Sam Katzman got the idea to release of the film. Not much shorter than the Marcels' career!

117

ON THE REBOUND

FLOYD CRAMER

18 May 1961, for 1 week

•

RCA 1231

Writer: Floyd Cramer
Producer: Chet Atkins

Floyd Cramer, born in Shreveport, Louisiana, on 27 November 1933, was Elvis Presley's pianist on many of the early RCA hits. The Nashville sound of the late 50s and early 60s was built around the guitar style of Chet Atkins and Les Paul, the bass of Bill Black, the drums of D.J. Fontana and the piano of Floyd Cramer. Elvis was never a pure country singer, even though he regularly used many of these musicians on his sessions, but just as he influenced a thousand pure country singers, so his musicians were more versatile than their country- style imitators.

Cramer's biggest hit, a number two in America, demonstrates this perfectly. It was called 'Last Date' and failed to register in Britain, but it was more than just country piano. It had traces of jazz, rock, and rhythm and blues which crop up again on the records of people as diverse as Alan Price, Roger Williams and Elton John. If 'Last Date' was Floyd Cramer's masterpiece, 'On The Rebound' was not far behind. It climbed to number four in America as the follow up to 'Last Date', and in Britain it gave Cramer the first of three hits over the next 18 months.

118

YOU'RE DRIVING ME CRAZY

THE TEMPERANCE SEVEN

25 May 1961, for 1 week

•

PARLOPHONE R 4757

Writer: Walter Donaldson
Producer: George Martin

The Temperance Seven was formed, so their publicity said, in 1906 for a season at the Pasadena Coca Rooms in the Balls Pond Road. The personnel were: Captain Cephas Howard (trumpet and euphonium), leader of the gang, Sheikh Haroun Wadi el John R. T. Davies (trombone and alto sax), Frank Paverty (sousaphone), Mr Philip 'Fingers' Harrison (alto and baritone sax), Alan Swainston-Cooper (clarinet, soprano sax, phonofiddle, swanee whistle and pedal clarinet), Canon Colin Bowles (piano and harmonium), Brain Innes (drums), Dr John Gieves-Watson (banjo), with vocal refrain by Whispering Paul McDowell. 'You're Driving Me Crazy' was written in 1930 by Walter Donaldson, whose 'I Wonder Where My Baby Is Tonight' was one of the tunes on 'Let's Have Another Party' (see no. 26). Perhaps the group's most important contribution to pop music history is the fact that 'You're Driving Me Crazy' was producer George Martin's first number one hit single.

The Temperance Seven, so named because they were always one over the eight, were a dance band rather than a jazz band in the style of Kenny Ball or Acker Bilk, and their brief spell of glory inspired such acts as the Bonzo Dog Doo Dah Band and the New Vaudeville Band in the years that followed. They broke up not long after their hits ended less than a year later, although in the early 1970s Ted Wood, brother of Face and Stone Ron Wood, briefly re-formed the band. Little success ensued.

119

SURRENDER

ELVIS PRESLEY

1 June 1961, for 4 weeks

●●●●

RCA 1227

Writers: Ernesto and B.G. de Curtis; English lyrics by Doc Pomus and Mort Shuman
Producer: Steve Sholes

For his eighth British number one, Elvis revamped another old Italian song, using the 'It's Now Or Never' formula with almost equal success. This time it was 'Torna A Sorrento' (Return To Sorrento), written in 1911 by Ernesto and B.G. de Curtis, who sound no more Italian than Doc Pomus and Mort Shuman, who provided the English lyrics. The song gave Elvis his fifth US number one with successive releases and his fourth on the trot in the UK.

'Surrender' was recorded in Nashville on 30 and 31 October 1960, the only non-spiritual song laid down at those sessions. Elvis recorded *His Hand In Mine*, his highly successful gospel album, as well as 'Crying In The Chapel', which was not on the album but which was to hit number one in Britain four years later.

The Jordanaires sang on the single but there is no accurate record of the musicians who played on the tracks, which were all produced, as usual, by Steve Sholes.

120

RUNAWAY

DEL SHANNON

29 June 1961, for 3 weeks

●●●

LONDON HLX 9317

Writers: Del Shannon and Max Crook
Producers: Harry Balk and Irving Micahnik

Del Shannon, born Charles Westover in Coopersville, Michigan, on 30 December 1934, began his recording career with one of the most influential records in pop history, a disc that used the organ for the first time in a really commercial way. The organ (or more correctly, the 'musitron') was played by Max Crook, who co-wrote 'Runaway' with Shannon, and his solo in the middle of the record has become one of the best-known instrumental breaks of all time.

Del Shannon built a successful four-year chart career on the strength of 'Runaway'. He had no other number ones, but his seven other Top 10 hits included two number two hits, 'Hey Little Girl' and 'The Swiss Maid', a song written by the then unknown Roger Miller (see no. 194). Shannon also recorded 'From Me To You' for the American market in 1963, when the Beatles were unheard of in the United States, and with that record became the first person to take a Lennon/McCartney song into the Hot 100. He also wrote Peter and Gordon's big American hit, 'I Go To Pieces', and produced Brian Hyland's comeback hit, 'Gypsy Woman', which also featured Max Crook on organ. When Roy Orbison died in December 1988, there were discussions about Shannon taking his place in the Traveling Wilburys, but nothing came of it. On 8 February 1990 Shannon died by his own hand.

121

TEMPTATION

THE EVERLY BROTHERS

20 July 1961, for 2 weeks

●●

WARNER BROTHERS WB 42

Writers: Nacio Herb Brown and Arthur Freed
Producer: Wesley Rose

The Everly Brothers' fourth and final chart-topper was a drum-dominated reworking of 'Temptation', a song originally performed by Bing Crosby in the 1933 film *Going Hollywood*. Twenty-one records reached number one in 1961, of which five were old songs ('Are You Lonesome Tonight?', 'Blue Moon', 'You're Driving Me Crazy', 'Temptation' and 'Michael') and a further two ('Wooden Heart' and 'Surrender') were old tunes with new lyrics. There has never been – before or since – such a dominance of the top of the charts by old songs, even at the peak of charity-disc mania in the mid-80s. With hindsight it is clear that the pop world was ready for something new, something which would fill the void in musical imagination which was in 1961 being filled by reworkings of old songs. A little over a year later, the something new emerged when 'Love Me Do' entered the charts.

The Beatles were destined to take over the Everly Brothers' title as the world's top vocal group, but the decline in Don and Phil's popularity was not connected with the Beatles' rise. It may have been their stint in the US marines from mid-1962 which kept the Brothers out of the limelight at a crucial time and which contributed to their fall from the top of the charts.

In 1984 their reunion gave them more chart action. Sixteen years and 96 days after their previous chart hit, the Everly Brothers came back into the British Top 50 with a song written by ex-Beatle Paul McCartney, 'On The Wings Of A Nightingale'.

122

WELL I ASK YOU

EDEN KANE

3 August 1961, for 1 week

●

DECCA F 11353

Writer: Les Vandyke
Producer: Bunny Lewis

Almost two years after Johnny Worth (alias Les Vandyke) wrote 'What Do You Want?' and 'Poor Me' for Adam Faith, he came up with his third and final chart-topping song for another newcomer, with a name taken from Genesis, chapter one, Eden Kane.

Eden Kane began life on 29 March 1942 as Richard Sarstedt. Like Cliff Richard and Engelbert Humperdinck, he was born in India and came to Britain as a child. He first created interest with an advertising jingle for Cadbury's called 'Hot Chocolate Crazy', which was played almost as often as Horace Batchelor's football pools advertisement on Radio Luxembourg. 'Well I Ask You' followed, and then came further Top 10 hits, 'Get Lost', 'Forget Me Not' and 'I Don't Know Why'.

A couple of flops, financial problems and a change in labels finished Kane's chart career. One comeback hit, 'Boys Cry', on Fontana in 1964, failed to re-establish him permanently in the charts, and he was left with a list of five hits to his name, all of which made the Top 10. Of all the other 5000 or so chart acts over 40 years, none has had more than Eden Kane's five chart hits, all of which were Top 10 hits. Everybody else either failed to reach the Top 10 at least once in their chart career, or else had fewer hits in total than Kane.

In 1969 Kane's brother, Peter Sarstedt, hit number one with 'Where Do You Go To, My Lovely?' (see no. 267), and in 1976

himself Robin Sarstedt, reached number three with his rendition of Hoagy Carmichael's 'My Resistance Is Low'.

'Well I Ask You' by EDEN KANE and 'Genius + Soul = Jazz' by Ray Charles were popular in the same year, 1961. (Pictorial Press)

123

YOU DON'T KNOW

HELEN SHAPIRO

10 August 1961, for 3 weeks

●●●

COLUMBIA DB 4670

Writers: John Schroeder and Mike Hawker
Producer: Norrie Paramor

By reaching number one with her second single while still at school, Helen Shapiro became a national celebrity, the schoolgirl with the grown-up voice. Helen was 14 years and 316 days old when she hit the top, thus becoming the youngest British artiste to get to number one. But she was still a year older than Frankie Lymon had been when 'Why Do Fools Fall In Love' hit number one in 1956 (see no. 48).

Born in Bethnal Green on 28 September 1946, Helen Shapiro was a protégée of the well-known singing coach Maurice Burman, who introduced her to John Schroeder, then an assistant to Norrie Paramor at Columbia. Her first single was a Schroeder song, 'Please Don't Treat Me Like A Child', which cruised happily into the Top 10. For the follow-up, Schroeder and Mike Hawker wrote a ballad, and it took over the number one spot on 10 August 1961. Three days later, in a move apparently unconnected with Miss Shapiro's success, the East Germans began building the Berlin Wall.

124

JOHNNY REMEMBER ME

JOHN LEYTON

31 August 1961, for 3 weeks

●●●

and 28 September1961, for 1 week

●

TOP RANK JAR 577

Writer: Geoff Goddard. Producer: Joe Meek

John Leyton, born on 17 February 1939, was a TV actor previously known for his portrayal of Ginger in the BBC TV children's serial *Biggles* when he landed the part of a pop singer called Johnny St. Cyr (pronounced Sincere) in a weekly series, *Harpers West One*. Leyton's manager at the time was a young Australian, who was called Robert Stigwood on his way to his first million. Stigwood realised the importance of television exposure and managed to arrange for Leyton to feature his latest single on the show. The song, written by Geoff Goddard and produced by the first great British independent producer, Joe Meek, was a minor-key, agony-laden song about a dead love: "Singing in the sighing of the wind, blowing in the treetops, Johnny Remember Me". It couldn't miss and it didn't.

John Leyton went on to clock up one more Top 10 hit and seven other lesser chart entries over the next two and a half years. He also landed his biggest film part, appearing with Charles Bronson, Steven McQueen and James Garner in the prisoner-of-war classic *The Great Escape*. His song went on to feature in the medley of 'I Feel Love' (see no. 409), 'Love To Love You Baby' and 'Johnny Remember Me' which Bronski Beat and Marc Almond took to number three in 1985. Not surprisingly, their version bore very little resemblance to the original.

125

REACH FOR THE STARS/CLIMB EV'RY MOUNTAIN

SHIRLEY BASSEY

21 September 1961, for 1 week

●

COLUMBIA DB 4685

Writers: 'Reach For The Stars' – Udo Jurgens; English lyrics by David West; 'Climb Ev'ry Mountain' – Richard Rodgers and Oscar Hammerstein II
Producer: Norman Newell, with musical direction by Geoff Love

Shirley Bassey, the most successful British solo female artiste in British chart history, is one of many ladies who have hit the top twice, but she could be said to be a little ahead of the pack because she took three titles to number one with two hits.

Her second number one featured on one side a song written by the man who won the 1966 Eurovision Song Contest for Austria, with English lyrics by Bassey's producer Norman Newell under the pseudonym David West. The other side was a song from *The Sound Of Music*. Despite its fabulous success in album form and on stage and celluloid, *The Sound Of Music* has not supplied as many hits to the single charts as some other, less successful shows. The only other hit of a song from the show was Vince Hill's 'Edelweiss', which climbed to number two in 1967.

From 14 September to 19 October 1961, the British charts had a new number one each week. There were actually only five records involved in those six weeks of musical chairs, as 'Johnny Remember Me' hit the top twice, but there has never in the history of the British charts been a longer run than this one: six weeks of new number ones. The record was equalled in 1968, when again one record ('Mony Mony' - see no. 254) featured twice.

126

KON-TIKI

THE SHADOWS

5 October 1961, for 1 week

•

COLUMBIA DB 4698

Writer: Michael Carr
Producer: Norrie Paramor

The Shadows' fifth hit was their second to top the chart. It was written by Michael Carr, who had also penned their follow-up to 'Apache' (see no. 106), the number five hit 'Man Of Mystery', which also served as the theme for a series of black and white B-movies based on the stories of Edgar Wallace. Carr was born in Leeds in 1904, but moved to Dublin at a tender age and took to the sea at the age of 18. He became a windjammer seaman, film stuntman, cowboy and globetrotter, experiences which no doubt inspired him to write such hits as 'South Of The Border', 'The Wheel Of The Wagon Is Broken' and 'Hang Out The Washing On The Siegfried Line'.

The line-up for this record was still the original Shadows line-up, but by the time the tune was at number one, drummer Tony Meehan had left the Shadows and had been replaced by the drummer from Marty Wilde's Wildcats, Brian Bennett. For Bennett this was a wise move. Marty Wilde had scored his final Top 10 hit at the beginning of 1961, but the Shadows were still creating Top 10 hit albums in 1990.

127

MICHAEL

THE HIGHWAYMEN

12 October 1961, for 1 week

•

HMV POP 910

Writer: Traditional, arranged by Dave Fisher
Producer: Dave Fisher

Lonnie Donegan covered four American hits in his chart heyday, but the only time he lost out to the original version was when he took on the Highwaymen and their version of the traditional Negro spiritual, 'Michael'.

The Highwaymen were five students from the Wesleyan University at Middletown, Connecticut, who got together to put on a show for their fellow students in 1959, and were so well received that they decided to carry on performing together. The leader was Dave Fisher who, apart from singing lead tenor, also arranged their songs and played banjo. Bob Burnett, who, when not singing or studying, was the university pole vault champion, sang and provided the exotic percussion. Steve Butts, crippled as a result of childhood polio, played guitar and sang bass. Steve Trott played guitar, and baritone Chan Daniels specialized in an instrument called a charango, made from an armadillo shell.

A visit to New York in November 1960 resulted in a contract with United Artists and a first album, from which the title track, 'Michael', was released as a single in America at the beginning of 1961. It was six months before it started to sell well, but by September it was number one in the States. It duly repeated its success in Britain, leaving Lonnie Donegan floundering at number six.

Despite another big American hit, 'Cottonfields', in 1962, the Highwaymen broke up when they graduated that year and never really consolidated their success. Dave Fisher was the only Highwayman who stayed in the music business and Steve Trott became prominent in American legal affairs. In the late 70s the group got back together to re-record 'Michael', but it was not a hit.

128

WALKIN' BACK TO HAPPINESS

HELEN SHAPIRO

19 October 1961, for 3 weeks

●●●

COLUMBIA DB 4715

Writers: John Schroeder and Mike Hawker
Producer: Norrie Paramor

Helen Shapiro was still at school when her third single became her second consecutive number one. Another hit from what were rapidly becoming the prolific pens of John Schroeder and Mike Hawker, 'Walkin' Back To Happiness' was a lively song in the style of 'Don't Treat Me Like A Child', and would have been perfect Eurovision material. It has always seemed odd that while singers like Lulu, Sandie Shaw, Mary Hopkin and Sonia have all sung Britain's Song For Europe, Helen Shapiro was never given the opportunity.

She did have the opportunity to make a film, though, and left school early at the end of 1961 to begin filming *It's Trad, Dad*. The film was successful, making good profits for the producers, but it did not further the careers of its two main stars, Shapiro and Craig Douglas.

At the beginning of 1963, six months after her fifth and final Top 10 hit, Shapiro headlined a nationwide tour on which the Beatles were the main supporting act. Nobody could have coped with that, least of all a 16-year-old girl. Her pop career never recovered from the impact of that tour, so successful for the Beatles and so disastrous for the girl from Bethnal Green. However, she has successfully moved her career in other directions and she remains very much in demand as an actress and singer.

129

LITTLE SISTER/ HIS LATEST FLAME

ELVIS PRESLEY

9 November 1961, for 4 weeks

●●●●

RCA 1258

Writers: Doc Pomus and Mort Shuman
Producers: Steve Sholes and Chet Atkins

Elvis recorded both sides of his ninth UK number one at sessions in Nashville on 25 and 26 June 1961, while his eighth UK number one was still at the top of the charts. Both sides of the new single were written by Doc Pomus and Mort Shuman, who had also written the English lyrics for that eighth number one, 'Surrender' (see no. 119). Between that single and this one, RCA had released the title song to Elvis' newest film, *Wild In The Country*, backed by the first Elvis single ever to feature saxophone, 'I Feel So Bad'. Surprisingly, it peaked at number four, becoming the only Elvis single in ten issued between November 1960 and November 1962 not to hit the very top. However, RCA were quick to cover its

comparative failure. Only nine weeks after 'Wild In The Country' hit the charts its follow-up, 'Little Sister/His Latest Flame', was at number one. It proved to be the first of his longest stretch of successive chart-toppers (five). 'His Latest Flame' is sometimes known as '(Marie's The Name) His Latest Flame', and is a fairly gentle country-flavoured rock number. 'Little Sister' was Elvis' first genuine rock number one since 'I Need Your Love Tonight' in 1959 (see no. 85), and subsequent cover versions ran the range from Ry Cooder to Robert Plant.

130

TOWER OF STRENGTH

FRANKIE VAUGHAN

7 December 1961, for 3 weeks

●●●

PHILIPS PB 1195

Writers: Burt Bacharach and Bob Hilliard
Producer: Johnny Franz

A number five hit in America for Gene McDaniels was turned into a number one hit in Britain by Frankie Vaughan. It was yet another number one for Burt Bacharach, the only one not co-written with Hal David. Co-author of this song was Bob Hilliard, who wrote various hits, such as 'Seven Little Girls Sitting In The Back Seat', 'Dear Hearts And Gentle People' and 'In My Little Corner Of The World', with other partners. He died on 1 February 1971.

Frankie Vaughan's career had been in some considerable lull when he recorded 'Tower Of Strength'. His previous hit had dropped off the charts almost a year earlier, and his previous Top 10 hit, 'The Heart Of Man', was a summer 1959 release. However, 'Tower Of Strength' was perfect for Vaughan's vigorous style and he quickly cornered the airplay to find himself with his second number one. After this hit, he was never to be a major chart force again, although he had further Top 10 hits in 1963 and 1967, bringing his total to nine.

Another cover version of 'Tower Of Strength' that Frankie swamped was by Paul Raven, who had to change his name to Gary Glitter a decade later to find Vaughan-type chart fame for himself.

As a cabaret performer Frankie Vaughan has retained his pulling power for many years and has never had to wonder where the money to pay the gas bill was coming from.

131

MOON RIVER

DANNY WILLIAMS

28 December 1961, for 2 weeks

●●

HMV POP 932

Writers: Henry Mancini and Johnny Mercer
Producer: Norman Newell

The fourth Oscar-winning song to top the British charts out of a total of seven was the theme from the Audrey Hepburn film 'Breakfast At Tiffany's'. It gave Danny Williams his third chart hit and his only number one. In America the hit versions, both of which climbed to number 11 in the *Billboard* charts, were by composer Henry Mancini and sung by Jerry Butler, who must be the most successful and influential rock-era singer never to have had a hit single in Britain. Apart from 'Moon River', Butler also recorded the original version of the Walker Brothers' first number one, 'Make It Easy On Yourself' (see no. 203), and many of his other songs, including 'For Your Precious Love', 'He Will Break Your Heart' and 'Only The Strong Survive', are now soul standards. In Britain Danny Williams' only competition was from Henry Mancini, whose version peaked at number 44.

Williams (born 7 January 1942 in Port Elizabeth, South Africa) was, for a couple of years, Britain's answer to Johnny Mathis, with a smooth-as-silk delivery and a choice of material by his experienced producer Norman Newell which accentuated his talents. All the same, for 14 years after his seventh hit, 'My Own True Love', dropped off the charts, Danny Williams disappeared from the chart-watcher's view. He re-emerged in 1977 with 'Dancing Easy', a song that began life as an advertising jingle for Martini.

132

THE YOUNG ONES

CLIFF RICHARD AND THE SHADOWS

11 January 1962, for 6 weeks

●●●●●●

COLUMBIA DB 4761

Writers: Sid Tepper and Roy C. Bennett
Producer: Norrie Paramor

'The Young Ones' was not only Cliff's second million-selling single but the fourth single in history to enter the charts at number one, the first by a British artist. By the day of its release 'The Young Ones' had amassed record advance orders for a single to date (524,000 copies), an achievement that paled into insignificance two years later when 'Can't Buy Me Love' (see no. 166) clocked up advance orders of over one million.

'The Young Ones' was written by Sid Tepper and Roy Bennett, the Americans who had also written 'Travellin' Light' (see no. 92) for Cliff. It was not just Cliff's fifth number one, it was – more importantly – the title song of his first starring film, which also cast Robert Morley, Carole Gray, Grazina Frame, the Shadows and budding actors Melvyn Hayes and Richard O'Sullivan. In America the film was released as *It's Great To Be Young* so the title tune became an ex-title tune and flopped accordingly.

'The Young Ones' remained on the charts for 21 weeks, equalling 'Living Doll' as Cliff's longest continuous chart runner. Twenty-four years later, when Cliff topped the charts with the comedy quartet the Young Ones, they became the first act named after a number one hit to hit the number one spot themselves.

133

ROCK-A-HULA BABY/CAN'T HELP FALLING IN LOVE

ELVIS PRESLEY

22 February 1962, for 4 weeks

●●●●

RCA 1270

Writers: 'Rock-A-Hula Baby' – Fred Wise, Ben Weisman and Dolores Fuller; 'Can't Help Falling In Love' – George David Weiss, Hugo Peretti and Luigi Creatore
Producer: Steve Sholes

The third consecutive number one to come from the movies was Elvis Presley's tenth number one and his fourth double-sided number one hit. The film in question was the King's eighth and most money-spinning film, *Blue Hawaii*. It was possibly not one of Presley's best films but it had a very strong soundtrack, and crops up on television with monotonous regularity. 'Can't Help Falling In Love', written by George David Weiss and 'Plume De Ma Tante' hitmakers Hugo and Luigi, was an integral part of the film from the outset, subsequently becoming one of Elvis' most popular recordings and the closing number in his Las Vegas stage act. 'Rock-A-Hula Baby', on the other hand, was inserted in the film after regular filming had been completed, to help the film cash in on the twist boom. The *Blue Hawaii* album, recorded at Paramount in Hollywood in September 1961, became Presley's biggest-selling soundtrack album of all.

'Can't Help Falling In Love', based on the old French tune 'Plaisir D'Amour', has subsequently been a British hit for Andy Williams (number three in 1970), the Stylistics (number four in 1976) and UB40 (see no. 690), making it only the third song in British chart history to have been a Top 10 hit in four versions. The other two are 'It's Only Make Believe' and 'Unchained Melody'.

134

WONDERFUL LAND

THE SHADOWS

22 March 1962, for 8 weeks

●●●●●●●●

COLUMBIA DB 4790

Writer: Jerry Lordan
Producer: Norrie Paramor

The Shadows' third number one was the second from the pen of Jerry Lordan, who has proved the most successful writer of instrumentals in the history of the British charts. Lordan had three hits as a singer in 1960, 'I'll Stay Single', 'Who Could Be Bluer' and 'Sing Like An Angel'. But his voice was very lightweight, and his talents clearly lay in writing rather than performing.

'Wonderful Land' had a horn section added to the basic lead/rhythm/ bass/drums line-up, an example of the adventurous production style of Norrie Paramor which brought him his 16th number one, to put him, at that stage, only one behind Mitch Miller's total. 'Wonderful Land' stayed at the top for eight weeks, a record for an instrumental second only to Eddie Calvert's 'Oh Mein Papa' (see no. 16), which held the top for nine weeks in 1954 and which was another Paramor production.

While the Shadows' third chart-topper was still riding high, bass guitarist Jet Harris left the group to concentrate on a solo career. He was replaced by another musician from the rapidly thinning ranks of Marty Wilde's Wildcats, Brian 'Licorice' Locking.

Michael Scheur found fame as MIKE SARNE, shown here outside but without WENDY RICHARD. (Pictorial Press)

135

NUT ROCKER

B BUMBLE AND THE STINGERS

17 May 1962, for 1 week

●

TOP RANK JAR 611

Writer: Pyotr Ilyich Tchaikovsky, arranged by Kim Fowley. Producer: Kim Fowley

For the first time, an instrumental took over from another instrumental at number one. B Bumble and the Stingers - the first instrumental one-hit wonder - revamped Tchaikovsky's 'Nutcracker Suite' and created a classic from a classic.

Mastermind of this hit was Kim Fowley, born in Los Angeles on 27 July 1942, who had already produced another one-hit wonder in America, the Hollywood Argyles (who hit with 'Alley-Oop'). In Britain, 'Nut Rocker' was the zenith of his achievement, but his influence on, and involvement with, chart acts like P. J. Proby, the Rockin' Berries, Emerson Lake and Palmer and REO Speedwagon has kept his name in the rock press and cash in his pocket. Fowley's reputation is that of a rather weirder American version of Jonathan King, brilliant at producing hit singles but incapable of creating a long-lasting successful chart act. But at least, unlike Jonathan King, he has one number one hit to his credit. 'Nut Rocker' stayed on the charts for 15 weeks in 1962, and when re-issued on the Stateside label in 1972, spent another 11 weeks on the chart.

136

GOOD LUCK CHARM

ELVIS PRESLEY

24 May 1962, for 5 weeks

●●●●●

RCA 1280

Writers: Aaron Schroeder and Wally Gold
Producers: Chet Atkins and Steve Sholes

Number 11 in the staggering list of Presley number ones is a gentle rock ballad recorded in Nashville on 15 and 16 October 1961. The exact line-up of musicians on this track is unknown, but the Jordanaires were there and are in fact featured even more than usual on this particular cut. The song was written by Aaron Schroeder and Wally Gold, who had already provided Elvis with a UK number one with their adaptation of 'O Sole Mio', 'It's Now Or Never', in 1960. Aaron Schroeder also co-wrote 'I Got Stung' for the King in 1959 (see no. 80).

Every single Presley released in 1962 went to the top of the charts, and he was thus at number one for 15 weeks of the year, a record surpassed only by Frankie Laine (27 weeks in 1953), the Beatles (16 weeks in 1963), John Travolta and Olivia Newton-John (16 weeks in 1978), Bryan Adams (16 weeks in 1991) and by Elvis himself (18 weeks in the previous year, 1961, when not all of his singles made number one). Elvis' tally of 15 weeks was matched by Frankie Goes To Hollywood in 1984, but what has still never been equalled is his total of 33 weeks at number one in a two-year period (1961 and 1962). The nearest rival to that record is not Frankie Laine, who did not hit the top either in 1952 or 1954, but the Beatles, with 28 weeks at number one in 1963 and 1964.

'Good Luck Charm' also completed Elvis' second hat-trick of number ones, a unique achievement at the time and since matched only by the Beatles and Abba.

137

COME OUTSIDE

MIKE SARNE with WENDY RICHARD

28 June 1962, for 2 weeks

●●

PARLOPHONE R 4902

Writer: Charles Blackwell
Producer: Charles Blackwell

Mike Sarne was born Michael Scheur in 1939 of German extraction. Wendy Richard was just beginning as an actress specializing in the not-so-dumb-blonde roles that were still coming her way 20 years later, especially after her success as Miss Brahms in the long-running BBC television series *Are You Being Served?*. 'Come Outside' was the saga of an optimistic boy at a Saturday-night dance trying to persuade his date to step into the moonlight with him. It was only the second comedy record (Lonnie Donegan's 'My Old Man's A Dustman' was the first) to reach number one, and since 1962 only 13 comedy records have hit the top.

Mike Sarne followed up 'Come Outside' with 'Will I What?' (with Billie Davis) and other less original variations on the theme. When he turned his hand to film directing he succeeded, with *Myra Breckinridge* (starring Raquel Welch), in creating what many eminent critics consider the worst film of all time. Wendy Richard now plays Pauline Fowler in *Eastenders* and until her screen nephew Wicksy (actor Nick Berry) hit the top in 1986, was the only member of the cast with a number one hit. She even re-recorded 'Come Outside' at that time with a replacement for Mike Sarne, but it failed to attract the record-buying public the second time around.

138

I CAN'T STOP LOVING YOU

RAY CHARLES

12 July 1962, for 2 weeks

●●

HMV POP 1034

Writer: Don Gibson
Producer: Sid Feller; orchestra and chorus conducted by Marty Paich

One of the most influential albums of all time was Ray Charles' 1962 LP *Modern Sounds In Country And Western Music*. For the first time there was acknowledged crossover from rhythm and blues to country and western, meeting pop in the middle. The highlight of the album was Don Gibson's 1957 country ballad, completely reworked by Ray Charles to give him his biggest worldwide hit.

Ray Charles Robinson was born in Albany, Georgia, on 23 September 1930. He was blinded by glaucoma at the age of six and orphaned by the age of 14. In the early 50s, after working with a hillbilly band called the Florida Playboys, Charles formed his own trio based on the successful Nat 'King' Cole formula. He dropped his surname to avoid confusion with boxer Sugar Ray Robinson and by 1952 had a recording contract with Atlantic. His career at Atlantic produced two classics, 'I Got A Woman' and 'What'd I Say?', neither of which hit the British charts, but it was not until he moved to ABC Paramount at the end of 1959 that he really began turning out the hits.

'I Can't Stop Loving You' has been Charles' only number one in Britain, partly because of a long – and ultimately successful – fight against drug addiction, which severely restricted his career in the late 60s and 70s. In 1985 he was back at the very top as part of USA For Africa (see no. 548).

139

I REMEMBER YOU

FRANK IFIELD

26 July 1962, for 7 weeks

●●●●●●●

COLUMBIA DB 4856

Writers: Johnny Mercer and Victor Scherzinger
Producer: Norrie Paramor

Frank Ifield was born in Coventry on 30 November 1936, but emigrated from that much-bombed city to Australia with his parents shortly after the war. He began his singing career in Australia, and returned to Britain in 1959 to try to break through in his homeland. Almost immediately, he had a minor hit with a song called 'Lucky Devil', covering the American hit by Carl Dobkins Jr. After that, the success which had seemed so near drifted away, and Ifield looked destined to join the ranks of not-quite-stars such as Dickie Pride, Mike Preston and Nelson Keene.

Then, in the middle of 1962, Norrie Paramor and Ifield decided to give it one more shot. Like Connie Francis, four years earlier, they went through the box of old sheet music and came up with 'I

Remember You', a song from the 1942 Dorothy Lamour movie *The Fleet's In*. What made the song stand out was the yodelling that Ifield put into 'I Remember Yoo-hoo'. Suddenly he was a big star, with a record that stayed at number one for seven weeks and which eventually sold a million copies in Britain alone.

140

SHE'S NOT YOU

ELVIS PRESLEY

13 September 1962, for 3 weeks

●●●

RCA 1303

Writers: Doc Pomus, Jerry Lieber and Mike Stoller
Producers: Chet Atkins and Steve Sholes

Elvis completed a round dozen of UK number ones with his fourth chart-topper in as many releases, equalling his own record set 15 months earlier. The song was not linked to any movie and was one of a dozen or so titles recorded in Nashville (RCA studios) on 19 March 1962. The majority of the titles recorded that day found their way onto the *Pot Luck* album (including 'Suspicion', which, like 'Wooden Heart', was 'lost' by RCA as a possible single and became instead a huge hit for unknown Terry Stafford in 1964, at a time when Elvis was running short of strong material).

Pot Luck was a healthy album seller for Presley in the last half of 1962. Jerry Lieber and Mike Stoller had been asked by Elvis' publisher, Freddy Bienstock, to come up with some new country-flavoured material for this session, and they produced 'She's Not You', together with Doc Pomus, and the song that became its flip, 'Just Tell Her Jim Said Hello', on their own. 'She's Not You' thus became the second Elvis number one for Lieber and Stoller and the fourth for Doc Pomus, who had co-written both sides of Elvis' ninth number one, 'Little Sister'/ 'His Latest Flame' (see no. 129), and was partly responsible for his eighth, 'Surrender' (see no. 119).

141

TELSTAR

THE TORNADOS

4 October 1962, for 5 weeks

●●●●●

DECCA F 11494

Writer: Joe Meek
Producer: Joe Meek

The third instrumental number one of 1962 was one of the better and more significant records of the early 60s. It was written, produced and arranged by Joe Meek, the man who had previously hit the top with John Leyton and who had used the five men who made up the Tornados as session musicians since before Leyton's success. The Tornados (Alan Caddy, Heinz Burt, Roger Jackson, George Bellamy and Clem Cattini) were officially Billy Fury's backing group, but their relationship with Fury was short-lived. 'Telstar', named after the American communications satellite launched earlier in the year, was an organ-dominated instrumental that not only reached number one in Britain, but went right up to the top of the American charts as well.

'Telstar' was the first major British hit in America for years and, apart from novelties such as Lonnie Donegan's 'Does Your

Chewing Gum Lose Its Flavour' and Laurie London's 'He's Got The Whole World In His Hands', was about the only straight pop hit from Britain since the days of Vera Lynn and David Whitfield. It prepared the way for the Liverpool invasion a year later.

Accidentally adding to the significance of the record, it was during 'Telstar's' weeks on top that the first Beatles hit, 'Love Me Do', entered the British charts, and the world of popular music was on the verge of being changed forever.

142

LOVESICK BLUES

FRANK IFIELD

8 November 1962, for 5 weeks

●●●●●

COLUMBIA DB 4913

Writers: Irving Mills and Cliff Friend
Producer: Norrie Paramor

Following up a monster hit such as 'I Remember You' is not easy. Frank Ifield, the man with the yodel gimmick, looked a racing certainty for obscurity as rapid as his fame. In the event, not so. Ifield and Paramor came up with the country and western standard 'Lovesick Blues', which had given Hank Williams one of his biggest successes over ten years earlier. Originally, the song had been recorded by Emmett Miller in 1928, but despite the many hit versions that have been recorded since, nobody has sold as many copies of 'Lovesick Blues' as Ifield.

Ifield was now following in the well-worn footsteps of Cliff Richard, Adam Faith, the Shadows and others in achieving two consecutive number one hits. Only Elvis Presley had completed a hat-trick of number ones (see no. 115), and in retrospect it is amazing to think that the Aussie from Coventry could even have had a chance of completing the hat-trick, for the Liverpool bombshell was on the point of exploding.

143

RETURN TO SENDER

ELVIS PRESLEY

13 December 1962, for 3 weeks

●●●

RCA 1320

Writers: Otis Blackwell and Winfield Scott
Producers: Chet Atkins and Steve Sholes

'Return To Sender' was Elvis Presley's fifth consecutive number one, a record for consecutive chart-toppers that lasted only one year and 363 days, until 10 December 1964, when the Beatles' sixth consecutive number one, 'I Feel Fine', hit the top. 'Return To Sender' was from Elvis' 11th film, the uninspiring *Girls! Girls! Girls!*. The main interest in the film is the ineptness of the title as there were actually only two girls featured in the film, played by Stella Stevens and Laurel Goodwin, although in addition to this number one smash, the score included the attractive ballad 'Because Of Love' covered on a single by Billy Fury, himself perhaps the greatest British pop singer never to have a number one.

Otis Blackwell, author of such classics as 'All Shook Up' and 'Great Balls Of Fire', did not extend himself in concocting, with Winfield Scott, this lightweight gentle rocker for the abdicating King to churn off the production line. Amazing to relate,

'Return To Sender' was the first Elvis UK number one to feature the saxophone. The track was recorded late in 1962 at Paramount Studios in Hollywood, but the line-up of musicians at the session, apart from the Jordanaires on backing vocals as usual, is not certain.

144

THE NEXT TIME/ BACHELOR BOY

CLIFF RICHARD AND THE SHADOWS

3 January 1963, for 3 weeks

●●●

COLUMBIA DB 4950

Writers:'The Next Time' – Buddy Kaye and Philip Springer; 'Bachelor Boy' – Bruce Welch and Cliff Richard.
Producer: Norrie Paramor

Between 8 November 1962 and 10 April 1963, Norrie Paramor produced six of the eight number ones, taking the top spot for 16 of those 22 weeks. The only two chart-topping records in that period that he did not produce were by Elvis (no. 143), and by Jet Harris and Tony Meehan (no. 146), who owed their start in the music business to their time as Shadows.

The second of those six Paramor hits was the only Cliff double-A-side single which topped the charts. The two songs both came from Cliff's second very successful musical film, *Summer Holiday*. 'The Next Time' was a slow romantic ballad performed in Greece against the exotic setting of the Acropolis, with Cliff sporting a rather unflattering string vest. 'Bachelor Boy', on the other hand, was very much an afterthought. It was written by Cliff – his only number one as a writer – and Bruce Welch after it was discovered that the film was a few minutes too short, and was shot at Pinewood studios as a semi-dance routine with the Shadows, rather than incurring the extra cost of taking the film crew back to Greece for just one sequence. The ultimate success of the record would have perhaps justified the cost, but few of the hundreds of thousands of fans who saw the film spotted the difference.

145

DANCE ON!

THE SHADOWS

24 January 1963, for 1 week

●

COLUMBIA DB 4948

Writers: Valerie and Eileen Murtagh and Ray Adams
Producer: Norrie Paramor

'Dance On!' was a tune found by the manager of Cliff Richard and the Shadows, Peter Gormley, who was listening to the pile of tapes that were always being sent in to his office, and looking for a potential single. It had been written by the three members of the vocal group the Avons, who had hit the Top 3 over Christmas 1959 with their cover version of Paul Evans and the Curls' American Top 10 hit, 'Seven Little Girls Sitting In The Back Seat'. Their fourth and final hit had come early in 1961 with their version of Bobby Vee's American smash, 'Rubber Ball'. The Avons reached only number 30 with that song, beaten outright by Bobby Vee, who reached number four, and by Marty Wilde, who reached number nine. Playing on the Marty Wilde single were then Wildcats Brian Bennett and 'Licorice' Locking, so perhaps it was apt that the Avons' only connection with a number one hit should come with the help of two of the people whose 'Rubber Ball' had bounced higher than theirs.

As well as being a chart-topping instrumental for the Shadows, Kathy Kirby reached number 11 with her vocal version of 'Dance On!' in 1963. 'Dance On!' thus just failed to join the ranks of songs that have been Top 10 hits in both vocal and instrumental versions - songs such as 'Oh Mein Papa', 'Annie's Song', 'Amazing Grace' and 'Don't Cry For Me Argentina', the last of which, instrumentally, was also a hit for the Shadows.

146

DIAMONDS

JET HARRIS and TONY MEEHAN

31 January 1963, for 3 weeks

●●●

DECCA F 11563

Writer: Jerry Lordan
Producer: Dick Rowe

Terence 'Jet' Harris was born on 6 July 1939 in Kingsbury, Middlesex, and David Joseph Anthony Meehan was born in Hampstead on 2 March 1943. After both had played with assorted groups during 1958, Cliff Richard enlisted them on bass and drums respectively for his backing group the Drifters. They subsequently became the Shadows and had notched up five Top 10 hits by the time that Tony vacated the drumstool in October 1961. Jet Harris remained with the group until March 1962, when he left to pursue a solo career.

After a couple of hits, 'Besame Mucho' and 'Main Title Theme From *The Man With The Golden Arm*', Jet teamed up with Tony, who had since become involved in production work for Decca, and they released the six string bass-dominated 'Diamonds' at the tail end of 1962.

The tune had been written by singer/songwriter Jerry Lordan, who had already supplied the Shadows with 'Apache' and 'Wonderful Land'. As 'Diamonds' hit number one, ironically deposing the Shadows' 'Dance On!' from the top spot, Jet and Tony spoke out about each other. Jet said, "As a musician, Tony is one of the best: I have learned musical terms and ways that I never knew existed. He's a wizard and impresses me a great deal." And Tony's thoughts on Jet:- "I have learned a great deal from Jet about stage-work, self-confidence and how to present myself." After just two more big hits, 'Scarlett O'Hara' and 'Applejack', both in 1963, the duo split up.

147

WAYWARD WIND

FRANK IFIELD

21 February 1963, for 3 weeks

●●●

COLUMBIA DB 4960

Writers: Stan Labowsky and Herb Newman
Producer: Norrie Paramor

On 21 February 1963, Frank Ifield succeeded in completing the first hat-trick of number one hits by a British-born artist when his version of Gogi Grant's 1956 hit, 'Wayward Wind', reached the very top. It was Ifield's third successive revival of a country song, and in reaching number one with three consecutive singles he joined Elvis Presley on what was then (and still is) a very select list.

The song had been written by Newman and Labowsky while they were students at UCLA, but it was not until many years later, when Newman owned a small record label called Era, that it was recorded. Era's first big success was a record called 'Suddenly There's A Valley', released in 1955 by Audrey Brown, who renamed herself Gogi Grant for show-business purposes. In searching for a follow-up, 'The Wayward Wind' was pulled out of Herb Newman's drawer. The song sold millions and topped the American charts for six weeks in 1956, between Elvis Presley's 'Heartbreak Hotel' and 'I Want You I Need You I Love You'.

'Wayward Wind' - originally written for a male voice - had climbed to number nine in Britain in 1956, but Norrie Paramor and Frank Ifield felt the song was ripe for a revival. They went into the Abbey Road studios and recorded the song. It became not only Ifield's third consecutive number one but also the first of seven consecutive number ones over a period of 23 weeks

recorded at Abbey Road, by far the most successful run by any studio in the years since the charts began.

ELSTREE DISTRIBUTORS LIMITED present
CLIFF RICHARD · LAURI PETERS
in "SUMMER HOLIDAY" Ⓤ
with DAVID KOSSOFF
Guest Star RON MOODY and THE SHADOWS
A CINEMASCOPE PICTURE IN TECHNICOLOR
Produced by Kenneth Harper
Released through Warner-Pathe Distributors Ltd

CLIFF RICHARD and pals get ready to board the bus in the film *Summer Holiday*. (Cinema Bookshop)

148

SUMMER HOLIDAY

CLIFF RICHARD AND THE SHADOWS

14 March 1963, for 2 weeks

●●

and 4 April 1963, for 1 week

●

COLUMBIA DB 4977

Writers: Bruce Welch and Brian Bennett
Producer: Norrie Paramor

The title song from the film *Summer Holiday* was written by Bruce Welch and the Shadows' drummer Brian Bennett while they were on a tour of Britain. The idea came to them while they were rehearsing in the orchestra pit of an empty theatre: Bruce just started singing "We're all going on a summer holiday, no more working for a week or two", and Brian immediately came up with the 'middle-eight', "We're going where the sun shines brightly, we're going where the sea is blue . . ."

Over the past 30 years it has almost become a traditional song to sing in coaches and cars on the way to the annual holiday. It was the song that the Young Ones (see no. 567) were singing in the double-decker bus in the last episode of their notorious TV series as the bus toppled over the edge of the cliff, thus ensuring that no further episodes of the series were possible.

Cliff Richard is the only act in British chart history to have had more than one chart-topper that has fallen from the top and then climbed back. 'Please Don't Tease' (see no. 104) was the first; 'Summer Holiday' was the second.

149

FOOT TAPPER

THE SHADOWS

29 March 1963, for 1 week

●

COLUMBIA DB 4984

Writers: Hank B. Marvin and Bruce Welch
Producer: Norrie Paramor

Norrie Paramor's third consecutive production at the top of the charts is now probably best known for being the signature tune of Radio 2's Saturday morning show, *Sounds Of The Sixties*. It was Bruce Welch's second consecutive number one as a writer (he co-wrote 'Summer Holiday', see no. 148, with Brian Bennett), to make him only the third person, after Burt Bacharach and Hal David, to achieve this feat. It was also his second consecutive number one as a performer as for the second time the Shadows knocked Cliff Richard and the Shadows off the top. A week later, Cliff Richard and the Shadows reclaimed pole position. Although Welch had already written or co-written four of Cliff's number ones, this was the only one of his compositions that the Shadows took to the top.

'Foot Tapper' featured in the film *Summer Holiday* and so another chart record was established by consecutive number ones coming from the same film. Other films, such as *Grease* and *Saturday Night Fever*, have been more successful in total chart terms, but no other film has provided two number ones in a row, nor three number ones in total (see also no. 144). Two other tunes were featured by the Shadows in *Summer Holiday*. These were 'Round And Round' and 'Les Girls', but neither was released as the A-side of a single.

'Foot Tapper' was the last of five number ones for the Shadows, although they hit the Top 10 with both of their next two hits, giving them a round dozen of consecutive Top 10s. They have a tally of 16 Top 10 hits, and remain, by a very long way, the most successful instrumental act in British chart history.

150

HOW DO YOU DO IT?

GERRY AND THE PACEMAKERS

11 April 1963, for 3 weeks

●●●

COLUMBIA DB 4987

Writer: Mitch Murray
Producer: George Martin

Gerry and the Pacemakers may have been the second Merseybeat act to be signed by

GERRY AND THE PACEMAKERS got their first number one before the Beatles' first, their second before the Fab Four's second, and their third before John, Paul, George and Ringo's third. (Pictorial Press)

manager Brian Epstein, but they were the first of his Liverpool protégés to score a number one. Vocalist/guitarist Gerry Marsden, an ex-British Railways employee (born 24 September 1942), had been singing with his drummer brother Fred (born 23 November 1940) as the Mars Bars for some years. The Pacemakers were created by adding bassist Les McGuire (born 27 December 1941) and pianist John 'Les' Chadwick (born 11 May 1943) to the line-up. Like countless other Liverpool acts, they too had made the trek to Germany to play in Hamburg's Top Ten Club.

Once the Pacemakers had been signed up, producer George Martin began the search for suitable material for a first single. The Beatles had written their own debut disc, 'Love Me Do', which had cracked the Top 20 in October 1962, but Martin was not convinced that McCartney and Lennon had the ability to compose big hits, so as a follow-up to 'Love Me Do' he suggested they record a song written by Mitch Murray, called 'How Do You Do It?'. This they did but their version was never released. Instead the Beatles insisted that their self-penned song 'Please Please Me' be issued, proving their point by climbing to number two. Thus, 'How Do You Do It?' was handed down to the Pacemakers, who showed the Beatles exactly how to do it!

151

FROM ME TO YOU

THE BEATLES

2 May 1963, for 7 weeks

●●●●●●●

PARLOPHONE R 5015

Writers: John Lennon and Paul McCartney
Producer: George Martin

When the Beatles' first single, 'Love Me Do', crept into the Top 50 on 11 October 1962, few people could possibly have guessed that by the end of the next year these four unknown lads from somewhere north of Watford would have sold more records in Britain more quickly than anybody in the world before or since, including two singles which, at the time, were the two biggest-selling singles in British history.

'From Me To You', the Beatles' third single, was the first of 11 consecutive number one hits for the Fab Four, a record unlikely ever to be broken. This first number one was on top for seven weeks, which was to be their longest run at the top, equalled only by 'Hello Goodbye' (see no. 241) four and a half years later. The Beatles were John Lennon (born 9 October 1940, died 8 December 1980), Paul McCartney (born 18 June 1942), George Harrison (born 25 February 1943), and Ringo Starr (born Richard Starkey on 7 July 1940), who joined the group just weeks before the Beatles bonanza got under way.

Everything was ready for the Beatles. The mediocre quality of pop music in 1962 had created a vacuum that had to be filled from somewhere, and the somewhere turned out to be Liverpool. Even before 1963, Liverpool had provided more than its fair share of musical talent (Frankie Vaughan, Michael Holliday and Billy Fury, for example), but during the 'beat group' explosion of 1963/4, Liverpool became the centre of world-popular music.

152

I LIKE IT

GERRY AND THE PACEMAKERS

20 June 1963, for 4 weeks

●●●●

COLUMBIA DB 7041

Writer: Mitch Murray
Producer: George Martin

When Gerry and the Pacemakers took over at the top with their second single, they became the first act to score number ones with their first two releases. The Stargazers, Eddie Calvert, Tennessee Ernie Ford and Adam Faith had all reached the summit with their first two hits, but by getting to number one with the only records they had ever released the Pacemakers achieved a feat that was unique at that time.

Like their previous hit, 'I Like It' was

recorded at EMI's Abbey Road studios, where the group were to produce their debut album, *How Do You Like It?*. When released in October the album climbed to number two, impeded by the Beatles' *Please Please Me* LP. 'I Like It' also became writer Mitch Murray's second number one in two months.

The phenomenon of Merseybeat and the hysteria which had begun to occur, particularly at Beatles' concerts, was by now beginning to catch the attention of the British press.

153

CONFESSIN' (THAT I LOVE YOU)

FRANK IFIELD

18 July 1963, for 2 weeks

●●

COLUMBIA DB 7062

Writers: Al J. Neiburg, Doc Daugherty and Ellis Reynolds
Producer: Norrie Paramor

After 'Wayward Wind', Frank Ifield's attempt to score a fourth consecutive number one failed when April 1963's 'Nobody's Darlin' But Mine' peaked at number four. By then Britain's charts were in the grip of the Liverpool sound and pundits wrote off Ifield as somebody who had better start working out his routine for singing his old hits in the clubs, for that was all the future held in store.

However, Ifield refused to be written off so quickly. Picking up a song written in 1930 and originally titled 'Lookin' For Another Sweetie', he yodelled his way back to the very top of the chart. But when Elvis eased him out on 1 August, it was indeed the end of the chart-toppers for Frank Ifield. More hits followed, but only one more record, a revival of 'Don't Blame Me', reached the Top 10.

Ifield's career is unusual in that he had four number one hits and two Top 10 hits in the space of seven releases in 18 months, but he never reached the Top 20 before or since, despite another nine singles that reached the charts. In December 1991, a remixed version of the original B-side of 'I Remember You' was released after much airplay on the Simon Mayo show on Radio One, and it climbed to number 40, giving Ifield his first taste of chart success for 25 years.

154

(YOU'RE THE) DEVIL IN DISGUISE

ELVIS PRESLEY

1 August 1963, for 1 week

●

RCA 1355

Writers: Bill Giant, Bernie Baum and Florence Kaye
Producers: Chet Atkins and Steve Sholes

At the end of February 1963, Elvis released what was, at that time, probably his worst, and definitely his shortest, single at considerably less than two minutes, 'One Broken Heart For Sale'. Despite the fact that it would not have sold more than ten copies if it had not had the magic Presley name on the label, it was considered a sensation when it peaked at number 12 – Elvis had failed to reach the British Top 10 for the first time since the switch to RCA in 1957.

The follow-up to this disaster was eagerly anticipated, and the song that was chosen from those recorded at a Nashville session at the end of May 1963 had one important difference from 'One Broken Heart For Sale'. The Jordanaires reappeared, having been usurped by the Mello-Men on the previous single. '(You're The) Devil In Disguise' did make number one for one week, but it was already the end of an era. Never again would Elvis be able to claim the top spot as his by right. In fact, of the eight releases between '(You're The) Devil In Disguise' and his next number one, 'Crying In The Chapel', 2 years later, only one reached the Top 10.

Elvis was not the only American in decline. Such was the domination of the Liverpool groups and British pop at this time that from 26 July 1962 to 25 June 1964, Elvis was the only non-British act to top our charts. Between 3 January 1963 and 25 June 1964, a period of 77 weeks, this one week in August 1963 was the only week when a British record was not top of the pops.

155

SWEETS FOR MY SWEET

THE SEARCHERS

8 August 1963, for 2 weeks

●●

PYE 7N 15533

Writers: Doc Pomus and Mort Shuman
Producer: Tony Hatch

The Searchers was the title of the 1956 John Wayne movie from which Buddy Holly had extracted the line 'That'll By The Day' (see no. 64). The group of the same name were the biggest Merseybeat band not to be managed by Brian Epstein. Their manager was the entrepreneur Tito Burns, who, like other showbiz bosses, had been quick to scour Merseyside for the talent that Epstein had missed.

The group line-up on this cover version of the Drifters' original was vocalist/lead guitarist Mike Pender (born Mike Prendergast, Bootle, Liverpool, 3 March 1942), vocalist/rhythm guitarist John McNally (born Walton, Liverpool, 30 August 1941), vocalist/bassist Tony Jackson (born Dingwall, Liverpool, 16 July 1940) and drummer Chris Curtis (born Christopher Crummey, Oldham, 16 August 1941). Having formed in 1962, the group signed to Pye in 1963. They were put in the hands of staff producer Tony Hatch, and this hit proved to be the first of the six number ones he has produced to date.

8 August 1963 was also the day of the Great Train Robbery. One member of the gang who committed that crime, Ronald Biggs, became a chart star himself when he appeared on the Sex Pistols single 'No One Is Innocent', a Top 10 hit in 1978. 'Sweets For My Sweet' returned to the Top 10 in 1994 when a reggae version by C.J. Lewis climbed to number three.

156

BAD TO ME

BILLY J. KRAMER AND THE DAKOTAS

22 August 1963, for 3 weeks

●●●

PARLOPHONE R 5049

Writers: John Lennon and Paul McCartney
Producer: George Martin

Billy J. Kramer and the Dakotas were the first act other than the Beatles to score a number one hit with a Lennon and McCartney composition. Furthermore, the song was one which the Beatles had not released on a single, album or EP. George Martin, by now aware of the phenomenal songwriting abilities of Lennon and McCartney, proceeded to build Billy J.'s career around their music. His first single, a cover version of 'Do You Want To Know A Secret', a track from the Beatles' *Please Please Me* album, had climbed to number two. Kramer could also thank Lennon for providing him with something else – a middle initial which stood for nothing whatsoever!

Kramer (born William Howard Ashton in Liverpool, 19 August 1943) had been a guitarist with a number of bands while still working for British Railways. Having become the singer with Liverpool group the Coasters, he signed a contract with manager Brian Epstein. Epstein immediately replaced the Coasters with Manchester backing band the Dakotas, having first sacked the Dakotas' vocalist Peter MacLain. The Dakotas were lead guitarist Mike Maxfield, rhythm guitarist Robin MacDonald, bassist Ray Jones and drummer Tony Mansfield, who was the brother of future chart star Elkie Brooks.

157

SHE LOVES YOU

THE BEATLES

12 September 1963, for 4 weeks

●●●●

and 28 November 1963, for 2 weeks

●●

PARLOPHONE R 5055

Writers: John Lennon and Paul McCartney
Producer: George Martin

In chart terms, this was the Beatles' biggest hit, staying in the Top 50 for 33 weeks (36, if you add its brief re-entry in 1983). It sold over a million copies in Britain alone, and until the follow-up, 'I Want To Hold Your Hand' (see no. 160), sold even more, it was the biggest-selling record ever in Britian. It is also one of only two records to come back to the top of the charts after two other songs had reached number one, the other one being Doris Day's 'Secret Love' (see no. 18). Only 21 records have ever regained the top spot, mostly after only one week in a lower position. However, the seven-week period while Brain Poole's 'Do You Love Me' and 'You'll Never Walk Alone' by Gerry and the Pacemakers were on top of the charts is the longest period ever between spells at number one by the same record, with the exception of the re-released 'Bohemian Rhapsody'.

'She Loves You' was the record that changed a generation. When 'From Me To You' was number one for seven weeks, Beatlemania was rising, but it was no greater than the fan worship that surrounded Cliff Richard earlier or the Bay City Rollers or Bros later. But 'She Loves You' was something else – the trigger for the swinging 60s. "She loves you, yeah, yeah, yeah" was the message and the lovable mop-tops were the medium. After over 30 years the record still sounds outstanding, with the driving rhythm section of John and Ringo, the simple lead of George and the hard-edged vocals of John and Paul. The message was happy, positive, upbeat; the doubts of 'Help', 'We Can Work It Out' and 'Eleanor Rigby' were years ahead. 'She Loves You' and 'I Want To Hold Your Hand' were the peak of the Beatles' achievements, the songs which most created their image. The only way from there should have been down, but it never happened.

158

DO YOU LOVE ME

BRIAN POOLE AND THE TREMELOES

10 October 1963, for 3 weeks

●●●

DECCA F 11739

Writer: Berry Gordy Jr.
Producer: Mike Smith

In 1959 Brian Poole, son of a Dagenham butcher, formed a group with school-friends in Barking, Essex. Two years later the line-up was basically the same, but instrumental responsibilities had changed. Alan Howard had swapped sax for bass, Alan Blakely had moved to rhythm guitar, replaced on drums by Dave Munden, and Ricky West, a trained classical musician, joined to become lead guitarist, allowing Poole to concentrate solely on singing. The BBC Light Programme's *Saturday Club* producer Jimmy Grant saw them at Southend and booked them for several appearances. They turned professional at the end of 1961, following a successful holiday-camp season at Butlins in Ayr.

On 1 January 1962, both Brian Poole and the Tremeloes and the Beatles underwent a Decca audition with Mike Smith from the company's A&R team. Head of the department, Dick Rower, would sign only one band and, having listerned to both tapes, he chose the one based eight miles from his London office, rejecting the Beatles and securing for himself an everlasting, if undeserved, place in rock history.

The band's recording career started with session work; for example, providing the backing for the Vernon Girls' version of 'The Locomotion'. Their first four singles all flopped, though their appearance in the film *Just For Fun*, with Bobby Vee and the Crickets, did give them exposure

The BEATLES are shown after recording *Juke Box Jury* on 11 December 1963. (Pictorial Press)

which helped bring their cover of the Isley Brothers' 'Twist And Shout' into the charts. No doubt it would have climbed higher than number four were it not for the competiton of the Beatles' EP version. They followed this with a group favourite, 'Do You Love Me', a song penned by Tamla Motown's Berry Gordy and an American smash for the Contours in 1962. The song gave Brian and the Tremeloes a number one in 16 countries. The Contours' version climbed back into the US Top 20 25 years later in 1988 as a result of its use in the smash-hit movie *Dirty Dancing*.

159

YOU'LL NEVER WALK ALONE

GERRY AND THE PACEMAKERS

31 October 1963, for 4 weeks

●●●●

COLUMBIA DB 7126

Writers: Richard Rodgers and Oscar Hammerstein II
Producer: George Martin

'You'll Never Walk Alone' came from Rodgers and Hammerstein's show *Carousel* (first performed in New York in 1945, although it arrived in London in 1950). In the show it was an inspirational number designed to give courage to the heroine, Jan Clayton, after the death of her husband, and it was reprised at the end of the show at a high school graduation. All this seems a very long way from the top of the British pop charts, but that is where the record went, to give Gerry and the Pacemakers the then unique record of three consecutive number ones with their first three releases. Another Liverpool band, Frankie Goes To Hollywood, equalled the feat in 1984 as did Rotherham-based Jive Bunny in 1989.

Perhaps the strangest part of the story is the way the song was adopted by the faithful home supporters at the Kop End of Anfield, the home of Liverpool Football Club. (The Kop was named after Spion Kop in South Africa, where many local men had lost their lives in the Boer War). The song didn't coincide with any specific success for Liverpool FC – it was two years since promotion from the Second Division, and it was not until April 1964 that the club next won the championship; it seemed to be taken up for no particular reason. Ultimately, the song would be sung by many different sets of fans, although it 'belongs' to the Reds.

The song's connection with football was strengthened further in 1985 when the Crowd (with lead vocalist Gerry Marsden) took it back to number one with a record whose proceeds all went to the Bradford City Disaster Fund (see no. 551).

While Gerry and the Pacemakers' version was at number one on 22 November 1963, Lee Harvey Oswald fired the shots from the Texas Book Depository Building in Dallas that killed President John F. Kennedy.

The SEARCHERS were number one in the UK the week the Beatles first reached the top of the *Billboard* Hot 100, opening the American charts to British groups like the Searchers. (Pictorial Press)

160

I WANT TO HOLD YOUR HAND

THE BEATLES

12 December 1963, for 5 weeks

●●●●●

PARLOPHONE R 5084

Writers: John Lennon and Paul McCartney
Producer: George Martin

When 'I Want To Hold Your Hand' took over from 'She Loves You' at number one, the Beatles completed a hat-trick of number one hits, to equal the achievements of Elvis Presley, Frank Ifield and Gerry and the Pacemakers. 'I Want To Hold Your Hand' also took over from 'She Loves You' as the biggest-selling single in British history, a record it kept until Paul McCartney's Wings sold over two million copies of 'Mull Of Kintyre' (see no. 416). It was also the first time an act had succeeded itself at number one, a record the Beatles kept until John Lennon equalled the feat with 'Imagine' and 'Woman' in 1981 (see nos. 473 and 474).

However, the main significance of 'I Want To Hold Your Hand' is that it is the record that conquered America. On 18 January 1964, two days after the record had dropped off the top of the British charts, it entered the *Billboard* Hot 100 and soared to the top. By the end of 1964 the Beatles had achieved six number one hits in

America, five more Top 10 hits and no less than 19 other charted sides, on a total of six different labels. Even 'Love Me Do', on the now defunct Tollie label, reached number one, while its B-side, 'P.S. I Love You', climbed as high as number ten. In more recent years the Bee Gees, Whitney Houston and Mariah Carey have equalled the Beatles' record of six consecutive number ones in America, but nobody has ever dominated world-popular music like the Beatles did in 1964.

161

GLAD ALL OVER

THE DAVE CLARK FIVE

16 January 1964, for 2 weeks

●●

COLUMBIA DB 7154

Writers: Dave Clark and Mike Smith
Producer: Dave Clark

The Dave Clark Five, purveyors of the brash, big-beat 'Tottenham Sound', knocked the Fab Four off the top. This was all that journalists needed to begin writing stories proclaiming that the end of the Beatles was nigh, and for a while some people believed what they read.

Formed in 1958, the group line-up in '64 was drummer, manager and former film stunt man Dave Clark (born 15 December 1942), vocalist/keyboard player Mike Smith (born 6 December 1943), guitarist Lenny Davidson (born 30 May 1944), bassist Rick Huxley (born 5 August 1942) and saxophonist Denis Payton (born 11 August 1943). They had released five singles on three labels before 'Glad All Over'. Their version of 'Do You Love Me' (see no. 158) reached number 30 in the charts, paving the way for the big breakthrough. In 1964 the USA caught Dave Clark Five fever and on Christmas Day 1965 the group grabbed one week at the top of the American charts with their minor UK hit, 'Over and Over'. Their surprisingly good film vehicle, *Catch Us If You Can* (directed by John Boorman), led to further successes but by 1970 the hits had stopped on both sides of the Atlantic.

Clark invested his earnings wisely. He bought the rights to the 60s pop show *Ready, Steady, Go,* which was released on video cassette and repeated on TV in the mid-80s. In 1986 the musical *Time,* which Clark had been working on as writer and producer since 1980, began a long run at London's Dominion Theatre. The leading role of the Rock Star was taken first by Cliff Richard and then by David Cassidy, both number one hitmakers themselves.

162

NEEDLES AND PINS

THE SEARCHERS

30 January 1964, for 3 weeks

●●●

PYE 7N 15594

Writers: Sonny Bono and Jack Nitzsche
Producer: Tony Hatch

The Searchers' second number one was their third single on Pye. It was another old song which, like 'Sweets For My Sweet', had not made any dent on the British charts when originally recorded. In fact, Jackie de Shannon had reached only number 84 in America, so putting it out as a single was a bit of a risk for the Searchers. However, their faith in the song was justified as it became their biggest hit and the song that even today people scream for at Searchers gigs.

Written by Jack Nitzsche and Sonny Bono, destined to achieve stardom 18 months later with his wife Cher (see no. 201), 'Needles and Pins' was a perfect example of supreme production transforming a minor song into a brilliant record. The producer in question, Tony Hatch, actually wrote the Searchers' second single, 'Sugar and Spice', which reached number two.

Had it not been for the domination of the charts at the end of 1963 by the Beatles, the Searchers would have started their chart career with four consecutive number ones. Hatch, thanks largely to his entertaining but blunt comments as a judge on TV talent shows, has come in for occasional ill-informed criticism during his career as a writer, producer and performer, but his production of records like this one, or 'Downtown' by Petula Clark, shows that he has been one of the most

Left: CILLA BLACK was the second British female vocalist to have two consecutive number ones, Helen Shapiro having been the first. (Pictorial Press)

imaginative and influential record makers in Britain.

163

DIANE

THE BACHELORS

20 February 1964, for 1 week

●

DECCA F 11799

Writers: Erno Rapee and Lew Pollack
Producer: Michael Barclay

Totally against the overwhelming Liverpool tidal wave, the Bachelors, three married men from Dublin, built up a highly lucrative career based on sweet-harmony versions of old favourites. Starting with 'Charmaine in 1963, they had Top 10 hits with, 'I Believe', 'Ramona' and 'Marie' among others, but 'Diane' was their only number one hit. The song was written in 1927 and originally featured in the film *Seventh Heaven*, performed by an off-screen, unidentified female vocalist.

Originally formed as a novelty instrumental trio called the Harmonichords, the Bachelors were Con Clusky (born 18 November 1941), his brother Declan (born 12 December 1942) and John Stokes (born Sean Stokes on 13 August 1940). Their clean, smiling image and highly professional stage presence made them particular favourites with TV producers. They were only the second Irish act to top the British charts, after Ruby Murray. The next Irish groups to do so were the Boomtown Rats (see nos. 428 and 440) and U2 (see nos. 616 and 668), with whom the Bachelors have only their Irishness in common.

164

ANYONE WHO HAD A HEART

CILLA BLACK

27 February 1964, for 3 weeks

●●●

PARLOPHONE R 5101

Writers: Burt Bacharach and Hal David
Producer: George Martin

Cilla Black (born Priscilla White on 27 May 1943) was a cloakroom attendant at the famous Cavern Club in Liverpool. She was signed by the Beatles' manager Brian Epstein, and was therefore provided with a Lennon-McCartney song for her first single, entitled 'Love Of The Loved', produced by George Martin. This reached number 35. The follow-up was a cover of Dionne Warwick's first US Top 10 single, and in Great Britian Cilla clobbered Dionne.

Cilla was thus launched on one of the most impressive recording careers enjoyed by any British female. Her next single was another number one (see no. 170) and the following 15 were all hits, two of them Top 10s. In the mid-70s, the hits stopped coming, but Cilla's popularity never waned. Her mastery of TV kept her in the eye of an adoring public and in the 1990s she was one of the country's biggest stars in any branch of entertainment. Indeed, many of her more recent fans probably do not realize what a powerful and dramatic singing voice the hostess of *Surprise, Surprise* and *Blind Date* possesses.

'Anyone Who Had A Heart' was the first number one by a female soloist since Helen Shaprio at the end of 1961.

165

LITTLE CHILDREN

BILLY J. KRAMER AND THE DAKOTAS

19 March 1964, for 2 weeks

●●

PARLOPHONE R 5105

Writers: Mort Shuman and John Leslie McFarland
Producer: George Martin

Billy J. Kramer and the Dakotas' first three hits had been written by Lennon and McCartney. For their fourth they turned to an American songwriting team containing Mort Shuman, who, along with Doc Pomus, had already penned two number ones for Elvis Presley. Shuman's talent also triumphed for Billy J. In the Merseybeat days there was often no time to rehearse material before it was put onto tape. Kramer claims that 'Do You Want To Know A Secret' and 'Little Children' were the only numbers he ever rehearsed before stepping into the studio.

'Little Children' was followed by another Top 10 hit, the Lennon and McCartney composition 'From A Window'. Feeling he needed a spell away from the break-neck pace, Kramer and the band spent four months at the North Pier, Blackpool, sharing the bill with comedian Tommy Trinder. Instead of rejuvenating the group, it kept them out of the public eye.

The next single, 'It's Gotta Last Forever', failed completely. Kramer returned to the charts with the Bacharach and David song 'Trains and Boats and Planes' in 1965, but he and the Dakotas, who in 1963 had had an instrumental hit of their own, 'The Cruel Sea', went their separate ways as soon as the hits began to dry up.

Billy J. continues to record occasionally and can still be found performing in clubs and theatres throughout Britain and Europe.

166

CAN'T BUY ME LOVE

THE BEATLES

2 April 1964, for 3 weeks

●●●

PARLOPHONE R 5114

Writers: John Lennon and Paul McCartney
Producer: George Martin

The Beatles' fourth number one was from their first film, *A Hard Day's Night*, and it gave George Martin the unique honour of having produced three consecutive number ones for the second time in 12 months.

Shooting on the film began in March 1964, after the Beatles got back from their first American visit, but much of the music had been recorded earlier. 'Can't Buy Me Love' set a (still unbeaten) record in Britian by achieving advance sales of over one million copies, and yet it still failed to reach the top in its week of release. It took two weeks to get there, as did every Beatles' number one from 'I Want To Hold Your Hand' to 'Hey Jude'. It was, in retro-spect, a slight disappointment compared with the two previous releases, which had been the supreme achievements of the Beatlemania days. All the same, 'Can't Buy Me Love' gave the Beatles yet more gold records and their third American number one.

The flip-side was a John Lennon song, 'You Can't Do That'. He described it as his attempt to be Wilson Pickett. Wilson Pickett's last British hit in the 60s was 'Hey Jude', his attempt to be John Lennon.

167

A WORLD WITHOUT LOVE

PETER AND GORDON

23 April 1964, for 2 weeks

●●

COLUMBIA DB 7225

Writers: John Lennon and Paul McCartney
Producer: Norman Newell

Peter and Gordon's first and most successful hit was a song that Billy J. Kramer had turned down, thus allowing two ex-Westminster School boys to be the second act, after Billy J., to top the charts with a Lennon and McCartney composition which the Beatles had not recorded themselves.

Peter Asher (born London, 22 June 1944) and Gordon Waller (born Braemar, Scotland, 4 June 1945) were spotted by Norman Newell at London's Pickwick Club. At that time Peter's actress sister, Jane, had become friends with Paul McCartney and he had begun using the Asher family home as a London base. Once Newell had signed the duo to EMI, the source of possible songs to record was literally on Asher's doorstep.

In 1967, after seven Top 30 hits, including 'Woman', a song that McCartney wrote under the pseudonym Bernard Webb, Peter and Gordon went their separate ways. Asher became producer and head of A&R with the Beatles' Apple label, where he produced James Taylor's debut album, *Sweet Baby James*. He subsequently became Taylor's manager and also producer and manager of another major American star, Linda Ronstadt. 27 years later, Asher returned to number one as producer of 'The Shoop Shoop Song' for Cher (see no. 664). Gordon, on the other hand, has left the entertainment industry. Soon after the duo split, he recorded several solo singles and one solo album, and appeared as Pharaoh in the West End production of 'Joseph And The Amazing Technicolour Dreamcoat', but by the end of the 70s he had settled down to a world without show business.

168

DON'T THROW YOUR LOVE AWAY

THE SEARCHERS

7 May 1964, for 2 weeks

●●

PYE 7N 15630

Writers: Jimmy Wisner and Billy Jackson
Producer: Tony Hatch

By the time the Searchers had recorded the Orlons' 'Don't Throw Your Love Away', a rift had opened within the group. Tony Jackson left to form his own band, the Vibrations, whose subsequent career consisted of little more than one minor hit, 'Bye Bye Baby', at number 38 in October 1964.

While Jackson was fading out, Frank Allen from Cliff Bennett and the Rebel Rousers was being brought in. The Searchers' success continued unabated for another 12 months through classic songs like 'When You Walk In The Room' and 'Goodbye My Love'. During 1966, their last year of chart success, Chris Curtis vacated the drum seat, which was kept warm by Johnny Blunt until the arrival of Billy Adamson in 1969. In the meantime, Curtis had formed the ill-fated Roundabout, a group which failed, despite the inclusion of future Deep Purple members Jon Lord and Ritchie Blackmore.

The Searchers' line-up of Pender, McNally, Allen and Adamson remained unchanged for nearly 20 years, but in 1986 the act split into two rival camps. Mike Pender formed a new group called Mike Pender's Searchers, while the remaining three veterans plus Spencer James continue as the Searchers that ever was.

169

JULIET

THE FOUR PENNIES

21 May 1964, for 1 week

●

PHILIPS BF 1322

Writers: Mike Wilsh, Fritz Fryer and Lionel Morton
Producer: Johnny Franz

In October 1963 Marie Reidy of 'Reidy's Home Of Music' in Blackburn, Lancashire (the place where they had to count all the four thousand rather small holes, according to the Beatles' 'Day In The Life'), telephoned Johnny Franz to ask whether he might be interested in a local group, the Lionel Morton Four. "Send a tape," replied Mr Franz, and according to his later recollections, "the tape was so good they were immediately signed to a contract". The first session produced 'Do You Want Me To?', which crept into the charts at the beginning of 1964, and 'Juliet', the second single, which climbed all the way to number one. It had originally been selected as B-side to 'Tell Me Girl'.

Lead singer Lionel Morton (born 14 August 1942) had been a choirboy at his local church in Blackburn for seven years, which may have helped him when he played the title role in *Jesus Christ Superstar* for a year of the show's lengthy West End run. He was at one time married to the actress Julia Foster. Co-writers of 'Juliet' with Morton were Fritz Fryer (guitar, born 6 December 1944) and Mike Wilsh (keyboards, born 21 July 1945). The fourth Penny in the group was Alan Buck (born 7 April 1943), who had drummed for both Joe Brown's Bruvvers and Johnny Kidd's Pirates before joining the Four Pennies.

'Juliet' proved to be the group's only Top 20 hit. One of those singles was 'Until It's Time For You To Go', a song that Elvis Presley took to number five in 1972.

170

YOU'RE MY WORLD

CILLA BLACK

28 May 1964, for 4 weeks

●●●●

PARLOPHONE R5133

Writers: Umberto Bindi and Gino Paoli;
English lyrics by Carl Sigman
Producer: George Martin

'You're My World' followed hot on the heels of 'Anyone Who Had A Heart' and gave Cilla Black her second consecutive number one, and one that would prove to be her last chart-topper. The song was an adaptation of an Italian tune by the versatile translator Carl Sigman, whose previous adaptations included 'Answer Me', 'The Day The Rains Came' and 'It's All In The Game'. 'You're My World' was Cilla's only US Top 40 hit and was revived there successfully in 1977 by Helen Reddy.

Among the many smashes Cilla enjoyed in the later 60s were her interpretation of the Bacharach-David classic 'Alfie' and a Paul McCartney theme tune for one of her TV series, 'Step Inside Love'. Her only major error was to compete with the Righteous Brothers' 'You've Lost That Lovin' Feelin'. Her version reached number two but it still looked like a failure when it was overtaken by the unknown Americans (see no. 186).

The late Brian Epstein would have been delighted by the sustained success of his only solo female signing, although possibly slightly baffled by her apparent reluctance to sing more than occasionally during her numerous TV appearances. Cilla has long been happily married to her second manager but first husband, Bobby Willis.

Right: ROY ORBISON was the only American to top the British chart in 1964. (Pictorial Press)

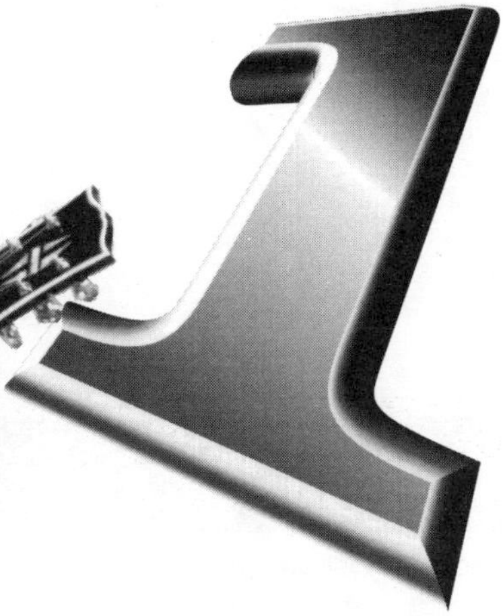

171

IT'S OVER

ROY ORBISON

25 June 1964, for 2 weeks

●●

LONDON HLU 9882

Writers: Roy Orbison and Bill Dees
Producer: Wesley Rose

'It's Over' became The Big O's second number one single four years after 'Only The Lonely' glided to the top in November 1960. Like most of his songs, 'It's Over' had a highly orchestrated arrangement that helped display Orbison's marvellous soaring voice to best effect. His tunes were often referred to as 'pop arias'.

Orbison attained even greater popularity in Great Britain than in his homeland, and during his second British tour in 1963 topped the bill over no less than Gerry and the Pacemakers and the Beatles. His motionless stage persona, with the dark glasses, black outfit and, occasionally, motorcycle leathers, hid a man who was in fact terribly shy. Offstage Orbison underwent a traumatic three years between 1966 and 1968. First a motorbike accident claimed his wife Claudette (she was the inspiration for the Orbison song 'Claudette' that the Everly Brothers had taken to number one). Two years later, two of his three children died in a fire at his home in Nashville.

'It's Over' was the first American number one hit in the UK for 47 weeks. Strange to relate, it is probably now not as well remembered as most of the lesser hits he scored in the previous four years – items such as 'Running Scared', 'Crying' and 'In Dreams' – now all standards.

172

THE HOUSE OF THE RISING SUN

THE ANIMALS

9 July 1964, for 1 week

•

COLUMBIA DB 7301

Writer: Traditional, arranged by Alan Price
Producer: Mickie Most

The Animals were keyboard player Alan Price (born 19 April 1942), bass player Chas Chandler (born 18 December 1938), guitarist Hilton Valentine (born 2 May 1943), drummer John Steel (born 4 February 1941) and vocalist Eric Burdon (born 19 May 1941). They started in 1962, doing all-nighters at the Downbeat Club near the Newcastle docks, but when their popularity increased they moved towards the centre of town, graduating to the more up market Club-A-Go-Go. They became Newcastle's finest live band, performing a varied set ranging from blues standards like 'Pretty Thing' to rock 'n' roll favourites such as 'Shake Rattle And Roll'.

At the end of 1963 the group had 500 EPs pressed, highlighting a selection from their club set. Mickie Most, a freelance record producer in London, obtained a copy and liked it so much he went north to see them live. His belief in the band was reaffirmed. He quickly signed them to Columbia and persuaded them to move to London.

In March the following year the group released their first single, 'Baby Let Me Take You Home', a song Bob Dylan had re-worked for his debut LP and which had started life as a blues number titled 'Baby Don't You Tear My Clothes'. The follow-up, 'The House Of The Rising Sun', had been taped at Most's first session with the group and was a traditional piece previously recorded by Josh White and, again, by Dylan for his debut LP. At over four minutes long the record company didn't think 'The House Of The Rising Sun ' was a wise choice, but the success of the first single gave Most the casting vote and the track, which had been recorded at a Kingsway studio in just two takes, was released. The official playing time printed on the label of promotional copies, however, was under three minutes, so as not to discourage airplay.

In the UK it entered at number 31, shot to number six, then to number one. In America it fared just as well, becoming the first UK record not penned by Lennon/McCartney to make number one in the States since the Beatles instigated the British invasion. Success in America was no longer a Merseyside prerogative.

173

IT'S ALL OVER NOW

THE ROLLING STONES

16 July 1964, for 1week

•

DECCA F 11934

Writers: Bobby and Shirley Womack
Producer: Andrew Loog Oldham

The first number one by the only group that could ever stand comparison in popularity with the Beatles was a Bobby and Shirley Womack song that was, at the same time, a small American hit for the Valentinos. It held the top spot for only one week, but with their fourth single the Stones had finally made the big time.

Their first single was Chuck Berry's 'Come On', which gave them their first hit, and like the first single of many acts who were to become major chart powers, it hung around the lower reaches of the charts for some time without ever getting as high as the Top 10. That single was followed by a Lennon/McCartney tune which Ringo had sung on the *With The Beatles* album, 'I Wanna Be Your Man'. This was the first time that the Stones had to put up with the 'Beatles copiers' tag, which dogged them throughout their career and which John Lennon acidly commented on in his interviews with the magazine that took its name from Mick Jagger and co., *Rolling Stone*.

The group's third single was a magnificent version of the Crickets B-side 'Not Fade Away', and to prove the title prophetic they scored the first of five consecutive number ones with their fourth single, 'It's All Over Now'. It wasn't; it was only just beginning.

174

A HARD DAY'S NIGHT

THE BEATLES

23 July 1964, for 3 weeks

●●●

PARLOPHONE R 5160

Writers: John Lennon and Paul McCartney
Producer: George Martin

The title song from the Beatles' first film was their fifth consecutive number one, equalling the record for consecutive chart-toppers held by Elvis Presley. It was their second number one hit from the film, after 'Can't Buy Me Love', which had not been written specifically for the movie.

Dick Lester directed *A Hard Day's Night*, which starred Wilfred Brambell as Paul's Irish grandfather and featured Patti Boyd as a schoolgirl on the train. It is considered one of the best pop films to come out of Britain, and justified its inevitable massive success.

The soundtrack was one of the strongest collections of Beatles songs ever put together. Only seven songs were actually in the film, but these included 'And I Love Her' and 'If I Fell', as well as the two number one hits. *A Hard Day's Night* was chosen as the title for the film after Ringo, at the end of one long session on the set, quoted from John Lennon's book *In His Own Write* with the comment, "That was a hard day's night, that was." Appropriately, Lennon sang lead.

The late Peter Sellers took his version of the song, recorded as an imitation of Laurence Olivier playing Richard III, into the Top 20 a year later. It was the first cover version of a Beatles single to hit the British charts.

175

DO WAH DIDDY DIDDY

MANFRED MANN

13 August 1964, for 2 weeks

●●

HMV POP 1320

Writers: Jeff Barry and Ellie Greenwich
Producer: John Burgess

'Do Wah Diddy Diddy' was the first number one to bear a nonsense title. If you met a girl walking down the street singing "do wah diddy diddy dum diddy do", you'd be far more likely to refer her to a psychiatrist than marry her as vocalist Paul Jones did in the song.

Jones (born Paul Pond, 24 February 1942) was the central attraction of the group, but the backbone of the band was Johannesburg-born keyboard player, Manfred Mann (born Manfred Liebowitz, 21 October 1940). Mann had moved to London in 1961, having studied music at the Vienna State Academy and the Juilliard School Of Music, New York. In 1962 Mann joined with drummer Mike Hugg (born 11 March 1940) to form the Mann-Hugg Blues Brothers, a jazz/blues instrumental outfit. With the addition of guitarist Mike Vickers (born 18 April

1941), bassist Dave Richmond and Paul Jones, Manfred Mann came into being. Richmond quit after their first two singles flopped, replaced by Tom McGuinness (born 3 December 1941). Their third record, '5-4-3-2-1', the signature tune to ITV's new pop show, *Ready Steady, Go*, hit big in January 1964. Two releases later

The KINKS spanned the mid-60s with three number ones in three different calendar years. (Pictorial Press)

Manfred Mann were sitting at the top of the chart with this cover version of a US flop by the Exciters.

176

HAVE I THE RIGHT

THE HONEYCOMBS

27 August 1964, for 2 weeks

●●

PYE 7N 15664

Writers: Ken Howard and Alan Blaikley
Producer: Joe Meek

The Honeycombs had a female drummer, so in 1964 they were news. There was nothing else very exciting about the group except that they were the first act to be taken over and marketed by Ken Howard and Alan Blaikley, who later achieved massive success with Dave Dee, Dozy, Beaky, Mick and Tich (see no. 246) and who wrote 'I've Lost You', a number nine hit for Elvis Presley in 1970.

The Honeycombs were Dennis D'Ell (born Dennis Dalziel on 10 October 1943) on lead vocals, Martin Murray (born 7 October 1941) on lead guitar, Alan Ward (born 12 December 1945) on rhythm, John Lantree (born 20 August 1940) on bass and his sister, Ann 'Honey' Lantree (born 28 August 1943), bashing out a rhythm every bit as subtle as Dave Clark's on drums. Martin Murray owned a hairdressing salon where Honey Lantree worked, which was the way the group got together and the origin of the group's name. The fact that Miss Lantree boasted a beehive hairdo was probably coincidental.

The Honeycombs' smash repeated its success in many other countries, including America (where it reached number five), Australia and New Zealand. Follow-ups, alas, were less spectacular and a number 12 placing with 'That's The Way' a year after their promising start proved to be their swan song.

177

YOU REALLY GOT ME

THE KINKS

10 September 1964, for 2 weeks

●●

PYE 7N 15673

Writer: Ray Davies
Producer: Shel Talmy

The Kinks in 1964 consisted of Ray Davies (born 21 June 1944) on lead guitar and vocals, his brother Dave (born 3 February 1947) on rhythm, Pete Quaife (born 27 December 1943) on bass, and Mick Avory (born 15 February 1945), a drummer from Devon who was the band's only non-Londoner. Their first single was the only one with an A-side not written by Ray Davies. It was a version of Little Richard's 'Long Tall Sally' and it flopped. Single number two, 'You Still Want Me', also disappeared down the plughole, but single number three was to be a classic of British rock, 'You Really Got Me', as was the fourth, 'All Day And All Of The Night', a re-working of 'You Really Got Me' that made number two three months later.

Jimmy Page, of the Yardbirds and later Led Zeppelin, is persistently rumoured to have played lead guitar on both this single and Herman's Hermits' 'I'm Into Something Good'. Even if these rumours are untrue, Page certainly played lead on Joe Cocker's 'With A Little Help From My Friends' (see no. 260), so he got to number one eventually.

178

I'M INTO SOMETHING GOOD

HERMAN'S HERMITS

24 September 1964, for 2 weeks

●●

COLUMBIA DB 7338

Writers: Gerry Goffin and Carole King
Producer: Mickie Most

Mickie Most, hot from his success with the Animals, saw the actor Peter Noone (born 5 November 1947) on *Coronation Street* in 1964 and decided he looked like John F. Kennedy. Noone was leader of a group called the Heartbeats in Manchester when Most contacted him. Soon Herman's Hermits and 'Hermania' were born, the Hermits being Derek 'Lek' Leckenby (born 14 May 1946), Keith Hopwood (born 26 October 1946), Karl Green (born 31 July 1946) and Barry Whitwam on drums (born 21 July 1946).

Most provided them with 'I'm Into Something Good', which is, amazingly enough, the only Goffin/King song ever to top the British charts. It had been a minor hit in the States for a lady named Earl-Jean. The Hermits recorded it (with a little help from session men) and the disc moved rapidly to the top of the charts. It also established them in America, where their bouncy, unsophisticated style gave them many more hits than in their homeland and where 'Mrs Brown You've Got A Lovely Daughter' (originally written for a TV play starring Tom Courtenay) and 'I'm Henry VIII I Am' were the biggest of 12 consecutive Top 20 hits. When the Hermits broke up in 1971, Herman had one hit under his real name, Peter Noone, before disappearing from the charts. He emerged at the 1979 World Popular Song Festival in Tokyo singing an Elton John song called 'I'll Stop Living If You Stop Loving Me', and in 1982 released a solo album after a brief spell fronting a new wave group called the Tremblers. He has also appeared in many musical theatre productions around the world, such as *The Pirates Of Penzance*, in which he starred in London and on Broadway in 1982 and 1983.

Some of the Hermits, notably Lek Leckenby and Barry Whitwam, are still performing on the 60s nostalgia circuit, but without Noone, who lives in California.

179

OH PRETTY WOMAN

ROY ORBISON

8 October 1964, for 2 weeks

●●

LONDON HLU 9919

Writer: Roy Orbison
Producer: Wesley Rose

In the middle of the British domination of the number one position during 1963 and 1964, Roy Orbison managed two chart-toppers and was virtually the only American act whose records were guaranteed to sell in vast quantities at this time.

This was Orbison's final chart-topper, although the hits continued throughout the 60s. After 'Penny Arcade' dropped off our charts in the final week of the 60s, Orbison had no more hits until 1988, when the first of three small hits by the Traveling Wilburys, of which Orbison was a distinctive member, hit our charts. Don McLean's version of 'Crying'(see no. 460) had topped the charts in the interim, to give Orbison the accolade of having written number ones in the 50s ('Claudette', see no. 73), the 60s and the 80s, but contractual disputes over the ownership of the copyright of many of his greatest recordings had kept Orbison out of the studio for many years.

Speaking at Orbison's induction to the Rock & Roll Hall Of Fame in 1987, Bruce Springsteen commented, "In '75 I went into the studio to make 'Born To Run'... and most of all I wanted to sing like Roy Orbison. Now everybody knows nobody sings like Roy Orbison."

In 1988, Orbison's solo comeback was confirmed by his new album, *Mystery Girl*, his biggest-ever album apart from hits packages, and at the beginning of 1989 there was the first Orbison Top 10 hit single for 23 years, 'You Got It'. But by then it was too late. Orbison, who had

had a history of heart problems, had collapsed and died in Nashville on 7 December 1988.

180

(THERE'S) ALWAYS SOMETHING THERE TO REMIND ME

SANDIE SHAW

22 October 1964, for 3 weeks

●●●

PYE 7N 15704

Writers: Burt Bacharach and Hal David
Producer: Tony Hatch

Sandra Goodrich was born in Dagenham, Essex, on 26 February 1947. Rather than become a Girl Piper or a Ford factory worker, young Miss Goodrich made her way to Adam's Faith's dressing room and sang for the great man. He was impressed and the 17 year old landed a recording contract. She changed her name to Sandie Shaw, and her second single was a cover version of a small Lou Johnson hit in the USA, written by Burt Bacharach and Hal David. It gave her her first hit and her first number one in only its third week on the chart.

Sandie then proceeded to cut a string of hit singles with the writer/producer Chris Andrews which included her second number one, 'Long Live Love' (see no. 196). She became the first, and to date only, British female soloist to have three chart-toppers when her Eurovision winner, 'Puppet On A String', went all the way in 1967 (see no. 232). Madonna, two decades later, was the first female to equal (and then surpass) Sandie's achievement.

The short-sighted Miss Shaw drew further attention to herself in the early days of her career by never wearing shoes on stage.

SANDIE SHAW was the first woman to achieve three number ones. (Pictorial Press)

The ROLLING STONES perform on a 1964 television show. (Pictorial Press)

181

BABY LOVE

THE SUPREMES

19 November 1964, for 2 weeks

●●

STATESIDE SS 350

Writers: Brian Holland, Lamont Dozier and Eddie Holland
Producers: Brian Holland, Lamont Dozier and Eddie Holland

The Supremes were the first black act to top the UK singles list in nearly four years. 'Baby Love' served notice that a new form of rhythm and blues had arrived, a pop-orientated music that was heavy on beat and strong on melody. It became known as 'The Motown Sound' after the label formed by Berry Gordy Jr, and it provided one of the lasting styles of the 60s.

Florence Ballard (born 30 June 1943), Diana Ross (born 26 March 1944) and Mary Wilson (born 4 March 1944) were the Supremes who made the group's first successful recordings, though when they had started as the Primettes there had been five of them and Ross used her real name, Diane Earl. Ballard was the original lead vocalist of the group and chose the name the Supremes, but she was gradually phased out for the more glamorous and charismatic Ross, a personal favourite of Gordy. Both he and Smokey Robinson had tried fruitlessly to write and produce for the group. The trio of Holland-Dozier-Holland had better results, providing the Supremes with four years of hits.

The breakthrough came with 'Where Did Our Love Go', an American number one and a British number three. Lyricist Eddie Holland battled with himself for weeks before putting 'Baby Love' on paper, considering the song trite. He need not have felt embarrassed. This single was the second of five consecutive American number ones for the group.

182

LITTLE RED ROOSTER

THE ROLLING STONES

3 December 1964, for 1 week

●

DECCA F 12014

Writer: Willie Dixon
Producer: Andrew Loog Oldham

Originally a US soul hit in 1951 for the Griffin Brothers featuring Margie Day, the Willie Dixon song 'Little Red Rooster' was covered by Sam Cooke 12 years later. It was this recording, which reportedly featured Billy Preston on keyboards, that brought the song to the attention of the Stones.

The Rolling Stones hold many all-time chart records, and among the countless groups of the early and mid-60s, their consistency and longevity is second to none. They were formed in 1962 and played regularly at London clubs like Wardour Street's Marquee and Giorgio Gomelsky's Crawdaddy Club in Richmond. There they quickly acquired a following and a manager, Andrew Loog Oldham. He juggled the line-up so that by the time they signed with Decca and cut their first single they were five Londoners, Mick Jagger (born on 26 July 1943) on vocals, lead guitarist Keith Richards (born on 18 December 1943), who dropped the 's' from his surname in imitation of Cliff Richard, drummer Charlie Watts (born 2 June 1941), Bill Wyman (born 24 October 1936) on bass and Brian Jones (born 26 February 1942, died 3 July 1969) on rhythm guitar. This was the line-up on all their number one hits except 'Honky Tonk Women' (see no. 274).

The Stones owed their record contract to George Harrison of the Beatles. Despite the fact that Decca had turned down the Beatles, when George met Decca's A&R chief Dick Rower as a fellow judge at a music contest in Liverpool, he told Rower of the brilliance of the Rolling Stones, and recommended he go and see them at the Crawdaddy Club. Rowe raced down from Liverpool to Richmond and liked what he saw. This time, a major rock act did not slip through Decca's fingers.

183

I FEEL FINE

THE BEATLES

10 December 1964, for 5 weeks

●●●●●

PARLOPHONE R 5200

Writers: John Lennon and Paul McCartney
Producer: George Martin

Brian Epstein understood the importance of release dates. In the first five years of Beatlemania, from 1963 to 1967 inclusive, the only year the Beatles did not have the Christmas number one was 1966, when they were too involved in the making of *Sgt Pepper* to release a single. The second of these Christmas hits was 'I Feel Fine'. This was the single that put the Beatles one step ahead of Elvis in the successive number one stakes. 'I Feel Fine' was six out of six for the mop-tops – Elvis' greatest run had been five.

The fourth Beatles album, *Beatles For Sale,* was also released that Christmas, and for the first time it was admitted that not all Lennon/McCartney tunes were co-operative efforts. In his liner notes, Beatles publicist Tony Barrow says that various tracks on the LP were considered as potential singles "until John Lennon came up with 'I Feel Fine'". Lennon also sang lead on the single, but perhaps the most arresting feature of it was his feed-back guitar work. By the end of their second year as the biggest thing ever to hit British show business, the Beatles were beginning to be recognized as musicians and not as just pretty faces. George Harrison was the first to attract approving remarks from the critics, having always been considered the group's best musician. Before long he was being called one of the best rock guitarists in the world.

184

YEH YEH

GEORGIE FAME AND THE BLUE FLAMES

14 January 1965, for 2 weeks

●●

COLUMBIA DB 7428

Writers: Rodgers Grant, Pat Patrick and Jon Hendricks
Producer: Tony Palmer

Georgie Fame began life as Clive Powell on 26 June 1943 at Leigh in Lancashire. He sang in his local church choir and learnt the harmonica and piano by ear, joining his first group, the Dominoes, when aged 14. In the summer of 1959, he played at Butlins holiday camp in Pwllheli and was seen by drummer Rory Blackwell, who invited him to London to join his band as pianist and vocalist.

Lionel Bart heard Powell play and recommended him to impresario Larry Parnes. It was Parnes who changed the youngster's name to Georgie Fame, and used his talents on package tours backing stars like Billy Fury and Marty Wilde. He also tried, unsuccessfully, to launch Fame on a solo career as a rock and roll pianist.

In mid-1962, Fame left rock and roll behind and formed the five-man Blue Flames, a rhythm and blues/jazz band. The Blue Flames were Colin Green on guitar, Tony Makins on bass, Peter Coe on sax, Bill Eyden on drums and Ghanaian Speedy Acquaye on congas. Within a short time Fame earned a residency at London's Flamingo Club, whose owner, Rik Gunnell, became Fame's new manager and secured him a recording deal with Columbia.

The band's Flamingo appearances became so popular that Fame was persuaded to release a live album early in 1964, *Rhythm And Blues At The Flamingo*, before he had a hit single. Although this first album was not a chart hit, his second LP, *Fame At Last* charted some three months before 'Yeh Yeh', his fourth single with the Blue Flames, climbed to number one, and even reached number 21 in the States. At the end of 1985, the song climbed back to number 13 when recorded by Matt Bianco.

On 20 January 1965, American DJ Alan Freed, the man who coined the phrase 'rock and roll', died of uremia in Palm Springs, aged 42.

185

GO NOW

THE MOODY BLUES

28 January 1965, for 1 week

●

DECCA F 12022

Writers: Larry Banks and Milton Bennett
Producer: Denny Cordell

The Avengers and the Diplomats were two Birmingham-based groups that spawned several chart-topping stars. The former included Roy Wood and Graeme Edge (born 30 March 1942), the latter Bev Bevan and Denny Laine (born Brian Hines, 29 October 1944). Wood and Bevan went on to form the Move and ELO. Edge and Laine joined Mike Pinder (born 19 December 1942), Ray Thomas (born 29 December 1942) and Clint Warwick (born 25 June 1940) to form the Moody Blues.

This line-up played extensively on the Midland circuit and gave their first performance at Birmingham's Carlton Ballroom in May 1964. They soon signed with a London manager, Tony Secunda, and secured a deal with Decca. Their first single was the totally unsuccessful 'Lose Your Money' but the second release, a cover version of Bessie Banks' soul classic, 'Go Now', gave them a UK smash and an American Top 10 hit.

The next few releases did not fare as well, and in August 1966 Warwick gave up music and Laine left to set up his own Electric String Band. He later joined forces with Paul McCartney in Wings (see no. 416). Replacements John Lodge (born 20 July 1943) and Justin Hayward (born 14 October 1946) helped change the Moody Blues' musical style from white R&B to orchestrated rock.

Three decades later, with 40 million-plus album sales for the Moody Blues Mark II worldwide, this appears to have been a wise move.

186

YOU'VE LOST THAT LOVIN' FEELIN'

THE RIGHTEOUS BROTHERS

4 February 1965, for 2 weeks

●●

LONDON HLU 9943

Writers: Phil Spector, Barry Mann and Cynthia Weil
Producer: Phil Spector

Mickie Most's favourite record is one of the best-known records of all time, and the most spectacular production of Phil Spector's long and influential career. The tiny Californian label Moonglow Records is where the story starts. They put out the first Righteous Brothers single in the spring of 1963, a song called 'Little Latin Lupe Lu', which reached number 49 on the Hot Hundred, but it then took luck as much as the soulful voices of the two white and unrelated brothers to lead them to Phil Spector.

The RIGHTEOUS BROTHERS (Bill Medley, left, and Bobby Hatfield) are shown in their happy mid-60s days, before they lost their own lovin' feelin'. (Pictorial Press)

Bill Medley was born on 19 September 1940 in Santa Ana, near Los Angeles. Bobby Hatfield was born on 10 April 1940 in Beaver Dam, Wisconsin, but grew up in Anaheim, in the same Orange County of southern California as Medley. They played with a group called the Paramours, but left in 1962 to go out as a duo, and soon they were big in California. Their big break came in 1963 when they performed on the same bill as Phil Spector's top act of the time, the Ronettes. In 1964, they toured the States opening the show for the Beatles, and towards the end of that year, TV producer Jack Good signed them as regulars on his rock show *Shindig*. Spector saw them, remembered them from the previous year and took them into his studio. By February 1965, 'You've Lost That Lovin' Feelin'' was number one in both Britain and America.

The single was also the first record that Jonathan King chose to re-issue when he became personal assistant to the head of Decca, Sir Edward Lewis, in the late 60s. The success of the re-issue (it reached number ten in the spring of 1969) encouraged other companies to re-activate past hits, setting a trend that has revolutionized the value of catalogue material as a source of new chart hits.

All in all, 'You've Lost That Lovin' Feelin'' has been re-issued three times, twice hitting the Top 10 again, but it was the re-issue of their follow-up, 'Unchained Melody', which created chart records by going all the way to number one in 1990 (see no. 653).

187

TIRED OF WAITING FOR YOU

THE KINKS

18 February 1965, for 1 week

●

PYE 7N 15759

Writer: Ray Davies
Producer: Shel Talmy

'Tired Of Waiting For You' was the second Kinks number one and their third consecutive hit single. Its predecessor, 'All Day And All Of The Night', had only missed the very top by a whisker, but in early 1988 became the first song of the three to return to the Top 10, via the Stranglers.

'Tired Of Waiting For You' was a gentler item than the first two offerings had been, and it can now be seen as the beginning of a long spell of more subtle Ray Davies songs that were to bring the Kinks a most impressive run of 60s and early 70s recording success. Apart from one or two singles, such as the comparatively unsuccessful 'Everybody's Gonna Be Happy' and 'Till The End Of The Day', their singles became quieter and the lyrical content often outstanding, a vital factor in the songs' appeal. In between their second number one and their third, 'Sunny Afternoon' (see no. 218), were Davies gems such as the raga rocker 'See My Friend' and the witty assaults on the narcissism of Carnaby Street ('Dedicated Follower Of Fashion'), and hypocritical pillars of society ('Well Respected Man').

Around the time of their second chart-topper the group ditched the pink hunting jackets that manager Robert Wace had originally suggested for them. Wace had been in the band in their early days as the Bo-Weevils and the Ravens at the time they were studying at the Croydon School Of Art.

TOM JONES meets Louis Armstrong on 2 December 1965. Both would reach number one (again, in Jones' case) before the end of the decade.

188

I'LL NEVER FIND ANOTHER YOU

THE SEEKERS

25 February 1965, for 2 weeks

●●

COLUMBIA DB 7431

Writer: Tom Springfield
Producer: Tom Springfield

'I'll Never Find Another You' was written and produced by Tom Springfield and launched the career of the group that filled the gap in the market when Tom's own group broke up in 1963. Named The Springfields, they featured Tom's sister Dusty as lead vocalist (see no. 213), and without becoming a huge international attraction, the trio had achieved considerable success with a series of pop-folk songs, including two British Top 10 entries and one, 'Silver Threads And Golden Needles', that did well in America.

The Seekers were a combination of three Australians and a Sri Lankan, who got together in Melbourne in the early 60s. Arriving in England via a singing engagement on an ocean liner, they were introduced to Tom Springfield almost immediately after they had disembarked. He promptly gave them 'I'll Never Find Another You'. It was their first release and it appeared on the charts in the first week of 1965. Seven weeks later it was at number one, which marked the beginning of a two-year association with Columbia that was to bring great success and profit to all concerned.

It was also the third consecutive number one to feature 'You' in its title, since it had knocked 'Tired Of Waiting For You' off the top, which in turn had displaced the Righteous Brothers' classic 'You've Lost That Lovin' Feelin''.

189

IT'S NOT UNUSUAL

TOM JONES

11 March 1965, for 1 week

●

DECCA F 12062

Writers: Les Reed and Gordon Mills
Producer: Peter Sullivan

'It's Not Unusual' was originally intended for Sandie Shaw but she turned it down as unsuitable, so Gordon Mills offered it to an unknown Welshman, Tom Jones (born Thomas Jones Woodward on 7 June 1940). Jones' voice and the powerful orchestral arrangement made the song sound so unlike anything Sandie Shaw might have sung that it is hard to understand how it could have been written with her in mind. Still, her loss was Tom Jones' gain and a major career was launched.

The song was played on *Juke Box Jury* with Tom Jones behind the screen, listening to the comments of the jury. His appearance on that show probably made the difference – the macho Welsh miner's son (if he wasn't a miner's son, he ought to have been) with the tight trousers and the rabbit's foot swinging from this belt was what the female population of Britain from eight to 80 had been waiting for. He became the most sophisticated, most sexy and most imitated British singer in pop history and his career was made. With the help of minor surgical alterations to the state of his nose and his tonsils, Tom Jones eventually conquered the whole world to become the all-round entertainer that he remains to this day.

190

THE LAST TIME

THE ROLLING STONES

18 March 1965, for 3 weeks

●●●

DECCA F 12104

Writers: Mick Jagger and Keith Richard
Producer: Andrew Loog Oldham

'The Last Time' gave the Rolling Stones a hat-trick of number ones, to make them the fifth act on that rapidly expanding list. More importantly for them, it marked not the last time but the first time a Rolling Stones A-side had been written by the duo that was to become one of the most creative in rock music, Mick Jagger and Keith Richard. At this stage the pair were uncertain about their writing abilities, and when every newspaper was comparing the Stones with the Beatles, it is perhaps not surprising that Jagger and Richard were not confident of standing comparison with Lennon and McCartney. The B-side, 'Play With Fire', was credited to Nanker and Phelge, a pseudonym Mick and Keith used on many early sides. This was not the first Jagger/Richard composition to hit the UK Top 10. Both Marianne Faithfull, with 'As Tears Go By', and Gene Pitney, with 'That Girl Belongs To Yesterday', had taken Jagger/Richard songs into the Top 10 in 1964.

'The Last Time' gave the Stones their second Top 10 hit in America, as the follow-up to 'Time Is On My Side'. They had to wait for their first number one in the States until the next single (see no. 202), which was recorded in America.

The TV go-go dancers are mystified at how to move to the country music of ROGER MILLER. (Pictorial Press)

191

CONCRETE AND CLAY

UNIT FOUR PLUS TWO

8 April 1965, for 1 week

●

DECCA F 12071

Writers: Brian Parker and Tommy Moeller
Producer: John L. Barker

Unit Four Plus Two's brilliantly original number one hit 'Concrete And Clay' was, surprisingly, one of the few big British hits of 1965 not to be an equal smash in America, where it climbed only to number 28. A cover version, by American Eddie Rambeau, climbed to number 35 at the same time, so perhaps combined sales of the two versions were not far short of the successes enjoyed by other British hits of that year.

Unit Four Plus Two was a six-man band, as the name suggests. They took their name from the very popular Alan Freeman radio show *Pick Of The Pops* which was divided into four units, Unit Four being the section in which Freeman played the Top 10. The group started out as Unit Four, but then added two more members, and so adapted the name. The six members were Rod Garwood, Hugh Halliday, Howard Lubin, Buster Miekle, Tommy Moeller and Pete Moules.

Russ Ballard, later to compose 'So You Win Again' for Hot Chocolate (see no. 408), played on the record but did not join the group full time until 1967 when its best days were past. In fact, their last chart hit, their fourth, was 'Baby Never Say Goodbye', which lurched onto the chart for one week at number 49 from 17 March 1966, less than a year after 'Concrete And Clay' had been at the top of the charts.

This was the third consecutive number one on the Decca label, a feat that had only been achieved by three other labels (Philips in 1953 and in 1956/57, Columbia in 1960 and 1963 and Parlophone in 1964). It would not happen again until 1989, when three chart-toppers running were on the PWL label.

192

THE MINUTE YOU'RE GONE

CLIFF RICHARD

15 April 1965, for 1 week

●

COLUMBIA DB 7496

Writer: Jimmy Gately
Producer: Norrie Paramor

The first Cliff Richard number one hit that did not feature the Shadows was Cliff's eighth number one, and his sixth single release without his long-time backing group. 'The Minute You're Gone' was also the second British number one, after 'Young Love' (see no. 56), to have been recorded earlier by American country superstar Sonny James. His version had reached number nine on the American country charts in the summer of 1963. Cliff's version was recorded in Nashville, Tennessee, in the summer of 1964, but its release, as his 29th single, was delayed by almost a year.

At the time of its eventual release, Cliff and the Shadows were coming to the end of their three-month stint at the London Palladium in the pantomime *Aladdin*. Cliff took the title role, the Shads were cast as Wishee, Washee, Noshee and Toshee, Una Stubbs was the romantic interest Princess Balroubadour, and the late Arthur Askey played Widow Twankey.

'The Minute You're Gone' was Cliff's 26th consecutive Top 10 hit, and although it was the last in this run of consecutive top 10ers, he was still at the peak of his career (a statement that is equally true almost 30 years later). Nevertheless, Cliff was quoted in the daily papers as saying that he still drew just £10 a week pocket money, despite press insistence that he was a millionaire.

193

TICKET TO RIDE

THE BEATLES

22 April 1965, for 3 weeks

●●●

PARLOPHONE R 5265

Writers: John Lennon and Paul McCartney
Producer: George Martin

The Beatles extended their record string of number one hits with consecutive releases to seven with the first offering on single from their second feature film, *Help!*. The song, 'Ticket To Ride', featured John Lennon on lead vocal, which was not unusual, but unexpectedly, Paul McCartney played lead guitar rather than George Harrison. Brian Epstein, the Beatles' manager, won an album in the music weekly *Melody Maker* for one of the best letters of the week when he wrote pointing out this temporary change in Beatle musical duties.

The *Help* album not only introduced 'Ticket To Ride', and the eighth Beatles' chart-topper (see no. 200), but also the song that within ten years became the most covered Beatles composition and one of the most performed and most recorded songs in the history of popular music, Paul McCartney's beautiful ballad 'Yesterday'. This was released as a single in 1965 in the United States (number one, of course), but not in the UK until 1976, six years after the Beatles had broken up. It still made the Top 10.

'Yesterday' was not actually featured in the movie, which was another wacky Dick Lester comedy, co-starring Leo McKern, Eleanor Bron and Victor Spinetti. The film was inevitably a major box-office attraction, but it lacked some of the fresh and unforced magic of *A Hard Day's Night*.

194

KING OF THE ROAD

ROGER MILLER

13 May 1965, for 1 week

●

PHILIPS BF 1397

Writer: Roger Miller
Producer: Jerry Kennedy

Texan Roger Miller, born on 2 January 1936, was a country singer and composer whose songs embraced comedy ('You Can't Roller Skate In A Buffalo Herd') and extreme sentimentality (e.g. his version of 'Little Green Apples'), but not often both simultaneously. After a period in the US Army, he moved to Nashville in order to hawk his songs around various record companies, and it was as a songwriter that he found fame. Country singers Ernest Tubb, George Jones and Ray Price and pop stars such as Andy Williams all recorded Miller material before he began having American country hits of his own in 1960. His biggest UK success before 'King Of The Road' was as the writer of Del Shannon's 1962 number two hit, 'The Swiss Maid'.

Miller scored two US pop hits, 'Dang Me' and 'Chug-A-Lug', in 1964. Then came 'King Of The Road', a gently swaying saga of a train hobo, the 'road' referred to being the railroad. It was to be a worldwide hit, proving that Peter and Gordon's enthusiasm for the singer they'd seen while touring America was well founded. Four further UK hits followed, including the song that took London as its theme, 'England Swings'. Miller's career in the US continued, albeit unevenly, through the 70s. In 1985, *Big River*, a Miller musical that he had based on Mark Twain's *Huckleberry Finn*, opened on Broadway. It won the Tony Award for Best Musical Of The Year.

Roger Miller died of cancer in 1993.

195

WHERE ARE YOU NOW (MY LOVE)

JACKIE TRENT

20 May 1965, for 1 week

●

PYE 7N 15776

Writers: Tony Hatch and Jackie Trent
Producer: Tony Hatch

The fifth number one to be produced by Tony Hatch was the first hit for the woman who was later to take Mr Hatch to be her lawful wedded husband. Trent's singing talent had become well known through regular appearances on radio and television, and Hatch, as well as being staff producer at Pye, was building a reputation as a songwriter, having penned 'Sugar And Spice' for the Searchers and 'Downtown' for Petula Clark. He had also managed to score an instrumental hit of his own, 'Out Of This World', which had enjoyed one week at number 50 in 1962.

One of Hatch's best-known compositions was the theme to the long-running ITV soap opera *Crossroads*, which was first broadcast on 2 November 1964. His original theme was rearranged in the 80s but it's unlikely that this was the sole cause for the series' demise in 1988. The tune even popped up as the last track on Paul McCartney and Wing's 1975 number one album, *Venus And Mars*, and the producers of *Crossroads* occasionally substituted this version at the end of particularly emotional episodes.

Two more Top 40 hits followed for Jackie Trent (born 6 September 1940 in Staffordshire). In 1988 the answer to Trent's musical question of 1965 was Australia, for in the mid-80s she and her husband moved Down Under. Tony Hatch continues to compose; the theme to the Australian soap opera *Neighbours* is one of his.

196

LONG LIVE LOVE

SANDIE SHAW

27 May 1965, for 3 weeks

●●●

PYE 7N 15841

Writer: Chris Andrews
Producer: Chris Andrews

Most of Sandie Shaw's biggest hit singles were written and produced by Chris Andrews, the man who wrote 'The First Time' for Adam Faith, to give him his final Top 10 hit. He gave Sandie Shaw hits like 'I'll Stop At Nothing', 'Message Understood', 'Nothing Comes Easy' and 'How Can You Tell'. He also wrote and sang 'Yesterday Man', which climbed to number three at the end of 1965, but the only one of Miss Shaw's three number ones that he wrote was 'Long Live Love', which has turned out to be the only Chris Andrews song ever to top the charts.

Shaw's underrated achievement in being the first, and for almost two decades the only, solo female singer to manage three number one British hits is only partly explained by her voice, original and strong though it is. Lulu, for example, recorded songs by Bowie, Neil Diamond and Marty Wilde, and yet her biggest solo chart success in Britain was her Eurovision song 'Boom Bang-A-Bang', which reached number two. Sandie

Right: JACKIE TRENT enjoyed her own number one single but today earns more royalties for having penned several Petula Clark hits with husband Tony Hatch. (Pictorial Press)

Shaw's choice of writers was always more conservative than Lulu's, and over the years Lulu has had the benefit of far more TV exposure than Sandie. So how did Miss Shaw manage three chart-toppers? It must have been the bare feet.

197

CRYING IN THE CHAPEL

ELVIS PRESLEY

17 June 1965, for 1 week

•

and 1 July 1965, for 1 week

•

RCA 1455

Writer: Artie Glenn
Producer: Steve Sholes

The world of popular music had been turned upside down for the first time since the advent of Elvis himself between the King's 14th and 15th number one successes in the UK. The Beatles, of course, were responsible.

Elvis' record sales, while still good by most artists' standards, had taken a major dive and no longer could he rely on his records hitting even the Top 10 every time out. The advent of the British groups was not solely responsible for Elvis' decline, however. His own career had been artistically off the rails anyway, consisting mainly of feeble movies and weak songs from undistinguished soundtracks which would have sunk completely any performer other than Elvis. But he still retained a devoted following despite his output and the fans rallied round in extremely healthy numbers to make 'Crying In The Chapel' his first number one for two years. It was, in fact, recorded five years before its release, at the sessions that produced 'Surrender' (see no. 119) and his sacred LP *His Hand In Mine*. The song was written in 1952 by Artie Glenn, whose son Darrell and Rex Allen had separate country hits with it in 1953. The same year, 'Crying In The Chapel' was an R&B and pop hit in the US for the Orioles.

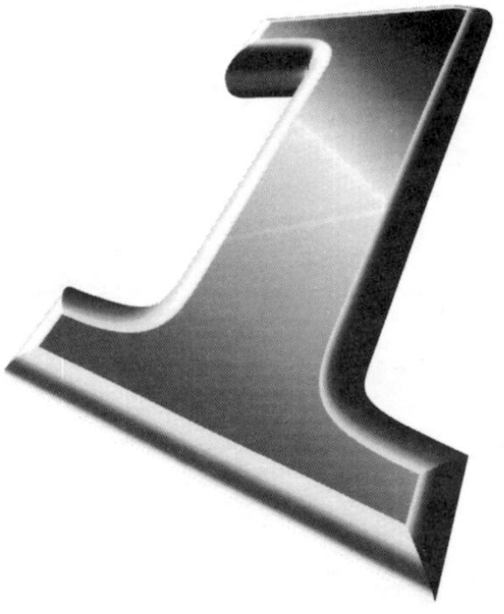

198

I'M ALIVE

THE HOLLIES

24 June 1965, for 1 week

•

and 8 July 1965, for 2 weeks

••

PARLOPHONE R 5287

Writer: Clint Ballard Jr.
Producer: Ron Richards

Graham Nash (born 2 February 1942) and Allan Clarke (born 5 April 1942) first sang together at their Salford primary school. Later, as The Two Teens, they performed hits by Lonnie Donegan, Cliff Richard and the Everly Brothers for the Manchester cabaret circuit. A name change turned them into the Guytones, and doubling their numbers forced them to become the Fourtones. Then a return to the original pairing found them performing as Rikki and Dane. In 1961 bass guitarist Eric Haydock and drummer Donald Rathbone joined and this foursome became the Deltas, a title that stayed until Christmas 1962, when they became the Hollies, in tribute to Buddy Holly.

In 1963, apprentice electrician and guitarist Tony Hicks (born 16 December 1943) joined on a freelance basis. EMI staff producer Ron Richards, having been told about this Manchester group, travelled to the famous Cavern in Liverpool to see them perform, and signed them to Parlophone. Their first single, a remake of the Drifters' 'Just Like Me', did reasonably well, halting at number 25, but not well enough to stop drummer Rathbone leaving and being replaced by former Fentone Bobby Elliott (born 8 December 1942). The Hollies recorded a string of reworked American rhythm and blues hits, including Maurice Williams' 'Stay', Doris Troy's 'Just One Look' and the Coasters' 'Searchin'', but by 1965 Ron Richards was beginning to find good original songs for them. Several were by Graham Gouldman, who went on to write three number ones with 10 C.C., while 'I'm Alive' was by the American who also wrote 'Good Timin'' for Jimmy Jones and 'The Game Of Love' for Wayne Fontana and the Mindbenders, Clint Ballard.

Despite the departure of Haydock, Nash and Clarke (who came back again) in the days since 'I'm Alive' topped the charts, the Hollies remain one of Britain's most successful groups, with 17 Top 10 hits, over 300 weeks on the chart and another taste of life at the top in 1988 (see no. 615).

199

MR. TAMBOURINE MAN

THE BYRDS

22 July 1965, for 2 weeks

●●

CBS 201765

Writer: Bob Dylan
Producer: Terry Melcher

In the summer of 1965 folk rock stormed the world. Producer Terry Melcher, the son of 1950s chart-topper Doris Day, took the Bob Dylan song 'Mr. Tambourine Man' from the album *Bringing It All Back Home* and electrified the jingle-jangle.

The Byrds were Roger McGuinn, a Chicagoan born on 14 July 1942, Gene Clark, David Crosby, Chris Hillman and Michael Clarke. However, on the 'Mr. Tambourine Man' single only Roger McGuinn actually performed. The rest of the musicians were session men Leon Russell, Larry Knechtel and Hal Blaine. Blaine has drummed on so many major hits that he could be the most successful chart performer of all time. Hits like 'Strangers In The Night', 'Bridge Over Troubled Water' and 'You've Lost That Lovin' Feelin'' all feature his drumming, as do many of Elvis Presley's later hits.

All the Byrds composed and played on their albums, but after a short while individual feelings replaced group harmonies and the Byrds began to disintegrate. David Crosby left to be part of Crosby, Stills and Nash. The late Gram Parsons, who became the major influence on Emmylou Harris and her pure country-rock style, joined the Byrds but left shortly afterwards with Chris Hillman, to form the Flying Burrito Brothers. Soon McGuinn was the only Byrd left, just as he had been on 'Mr. Tambourine Man'.

200

HELP!

THE BEATLES

5 August 1965, for 3 weeks

●●●

PARLOPHONE R 5305

Writers: John Lennon and Paul McCartney
Producer: George Martin

The title song from their second film gave the Beatles their eighth number one, putting them at the time equal second with Cliff Richard on the list of most chart-toppers in Britain. The Beatles' eight were uniquely consecutive and achieved within a period of just 2 years and 95 days. The other acts to have had eight or more number ones before or since (Elvis, Cliff, Abba and the Rolling Stones) never crammed any eight into so brief a span.

The film *Help!* was originally to be called *Eight Arms To Hold You*, which would have made an interesting title for a love song, possibly breaking lyrical ground that was not actually achieved until 'Je T'Aime' in 1969. The Beatles, however, did have another go at writing a song featuring a similar number of limbs when Ringo came up with 'Octopus's Garden' on the *Abbey Road* LP.

Help! was not as successful a film as *A Hard Day's Night*. It was shot in colour, had a much larger budget and made plenty of money, but the Beatles were not happy with it. They gave up films (apart from the self-produced *Magical Mystery Tour* TV film and the *Let It Be* documentary) and got back to what they knew best, composing and recording.

201

I GOT YOU BABE

SONNY AND CHER

26 August 1965, for 2 weeks

●●

ATLANTIC AT 4035

Writer: Sonny Bono
Producer: Sonny Bono

Sonny and Cher - she was the one with the deeper voice and the slightly longer hair - burst onto the British summer of 1965 with the ultimate hippie anthem, a full two years before hippiedom took over the youth of Europe and America. "Let them say your hair's too long, I don't care, with you I can't go wrong" became the compulsive theme of all young lovers of the mid-60s.

Not that Sonny, at least, was all that young. He was born on 16 February 1935 and had been writing and performing for some years. He wrote 'Needles And Pins' with Jack Nitzsche, which became the 162nd British number one when recorded by the Searchers. He thus joined the select group who have written number ones for themselves and for another act, at the same time proving convincingly that he was a better writer than singer.

Sonny and Cher (born Cherilyn LaPier on 20 May 1946) divorced in 1974, and Cher began a hectic period as the gossip columnists' delight, her name being linked with many men, both eligible and ineligible. She gave up recording for a while to concentrate on the movies and by the 1980s, her film career had blossomed, with an Oscar nomination for her role in the 1983 film *Silkwood*, followed by an Oscar for Best Actress in the 1987 movie *Moonstruck*.

'I Got You Babe' returned to the number one spot exactly 20 years later, as performed by UB40 with guest vocals by Pretender Chrissie Hynde (see no. 555). Cher's return to the top took even longer, but 25 years and 239 days after 'I Got You Babe' finished its run at the top, she climbed back with her version of a song written before 'I Got You Babe' (see no. 664). In 1994, she re-recorded 'I Got You Babe' with MTV cartoon antiheroes Beavis and Butt-head, and climbed to number 35.

202

(I CAN'T GET NO) SATISFACTION

THE ROLLING STONES

9 September 1965, for 2 weeks

●●

DECCA F 12220

Writers: Mick Jagger and Keith Richard
Producer: Andrew Loog Oldham

1965 was the single most important year in the breakthrough of the Rolling Stones. They began writing their own hits with 'The Last Time' (see no. 190), they passed the million mark in sales for the first time, achieving this with several discs, and they scaled the summit of the American chart for the first time, with '(I Can't Get No) Satisfaction'. This latter title, recorded in Hollywood, remains their calling card. It stated eloquently and forcefully the Stones' unhappiness with the conventions of society, and in its power suggested the restrained aggression that was part of the group's image at the time. Many American radio stations edited out the last verse, which they believed referred to menstruation.

Keith Richard composed the introductory riff. Though it became one of the most famous in rock history, Richard at one point thought it might have suited a horn section rather than a guitar. He was thus pleased when Otis Redding used brass to begin his version on his album *Otis Blue*.

Not only is '(I Can't Get No) Satisfaction' the definitive Rolling Stones track, it is one of only two songs to have been a hit in as many as six different years, with charted cover versions by Redding (1966), Aretha Franklin (1967), Bubblerock (Jonathan King under a pseudonym, 1974), Devo (1978) and Vanilla Ice (1991).

The other much-charted title is 'White Christmas', which has hit the lists over six different Christmasses since 1952.

203

MAKE IT EASY ON YOURSELF

THE WALKER BROTHERS

23 September 1965, for 1 week

•

PHILIPS BF 1428

Writers: Burt Bacharach and Hal David
Producer: Johnny Franz

The Walker Brothers were not brothers and none of them was called Walker. They were bassist Scott Walker (born Noel Scott Engel, 9 January 1944), guitarist John Walker (born John Maus, 12 November 1943) and drummer Gary Walker (born Gary Leeds, 3 September 1944). It was Gary who, having come across his future partners singing in Gazzari's, a Los Angeles club, persuaded them that their fortunes were to be made in Britain. Scott had already appeared solo on several of Eddie Fisher's TV shows (see nos. 4 and 10), and had worked with Sonny Bono (see no. 201). John was a TV soap star, playing Betty Hutton's son in *Hallo Mom.*

At the time, Gary was not the world's greatest drummer, although he had drummed on one tour of England with P.J. Proby. His musicianship was not to be heard on the Walker Brothers' early records, and even on stage a second drummer would be hidden in the wings to cover for him. This mattered not, for on arriving in London in 1965, the Walker boys cracked the chart with their second single, 'Love Her', a Top 20 hit in April. Then came their first number one, a US Top 20 tune for Jerry Butler in 1962. It was the fifth UK chart-topper to be written by Bacharach and David. The Walker Brothers' treatment featured lush orchestration and the rich baritone of Scott.

204

TEARS

KEN DODD

30 September 1965, for 5 weeks

•••••

COLUMBIA DB 7659

Writers: Billy Uhr and Frank Capano
Producer: Norman Newell

In 40 years of chart history, only about 20 acts have hit number one and had a chart career lasting for more than 20 years. Most people would immediately be able to guess some of those names - Elvis, Cliff, the Rolling Stones, the Bee Gees, the Shadows and Frank Sinatra, but they would probably get stuck before they came up with the name of the only Liverpudlian on this illustrious list - Ken Dodd.

The chief of the Diddymen, born on 8 November 1932, had his first hit in the summer of 1960, when 'Love Is Like A Violin' reached the Top 10. His final chart record so far hit the chart 21 and a half years later, when 'Hold My Hand' enjoyed a five-week listing over the Christmas period of 1981. A few days later, he joined the even more select band of number one hitmakers to have been honoured by the Queen, when his OBE was announced in the 1982 New Year's Honours List.

Ken Dodd's singing career has given him a completely different image from the wild-haired purveyor of the tickling stick that we all know and Lady Thatcher loves. He has scored 19 hits, four of which including his million-selling 'Tears', reached the Top 10. None of his hits has been a comedy record. In fact, only 'Happiness' (number 31 in 1964) and 'Hold My Hand' were even cheerful. The Ken Dodd of the pop charts is a tragic soul, singing songs with titles like 'Tears', 'Let Me Cry On Your Shoulder', 'Tears Won't Wash Away My Heartache' and 'Broken Hearted'. As a comedian and singer, he does not seem to know whether to laugh or cry - all the way to the bank.

205

GET OFF OF MY CLOUD

THE ROLLING STONES

4 November 1965, for 3 weeks

●●●

DECCA F 12263

Writers: Mick Jagger and Keith Richard
Producer: Andrew Loog Oldham

The fifth consecutive number one hit for the Stones was their second successive number one to be recorded in Hollywood. It lasted at the top for one week more than '(I Can't Get No) Satisfaction', even though global sales of 'Get Off Of My Cloud' were lower.

By the end of 1965, the Rolling Stones were probably at the peak of their popularity. They had achieved five number ones in a row, a total previously reached by only Elvis and the Beatles; they had toured America, Australia and Scandinavia with massive success; and they had yet to alienate any section of their fans through their problems with the laws of drug abuse. Certainly their image was non-conformist and anti-establishment, but at the end of 1965, the Rolling Stones were close to achieving conventional acceptance, something they managed to avoid at the last minute by living up to the rebellious, orgiastic image they had been made to project. In this, Jagger, Richard and the late Brian Jones were the main protagonists. Charlie Watts and Bill Wyman, the two oldest members of the band, were always just two cricket-loving guys who happened to play drums and bass in the best rock band in the world.

206

THE CARNIVAL IS OVER

THE SEEKERS

25 November 1965, for 3 weeks

●●●

COLUMBIA DB 7711

Writer: Tom Springfield
Producer: Tom Springfield

The Seekers were three Melbournians - Judith Durham (born 3 July 1943), Athol Guy (born 5 January 1940) and Bruce Woodley (born 25 July 1942) - and the Sri Lankan Keith Potger, who was born in Colombo on 2 March 1941. 'The Carnival

It is February 1965, and the SEEKERS are enjoying their first number one. (Pictorial Press)

Is Over' gave the band their second number one in three singles. The one that missed out after 'I'll Never Find Another You' (see no. 188) was another Tom Springfield song, 'A World Of Our Own', which peaked at number three.

The Seekers never had another number one, although their popularity and hits continued for some time. 'Morningtown Ride' climbed to number two at Christmas 1966, but 'Georgy Girl', written by Tom Springfield and Jim Dale for the James Mason/Lynn Redgrave film of the same name, was their biggest worldwide hit after 'The Carnival Is Over', reaching number three in 1967. In America, it reached number two.

By the time the Seekers broke up, they had notched up three more Top 10 hits and a couple of number 11s in the 18 months between March 1966 and September 1967. A measure of their success is that their final charting single, 'Emerald City', which made only number 50 for a week in December 1967, was the only one of their nine 45s not to crack the Top 20.

They re-formed briefly in 1994 but their re-recorded version of 'A World Of Our Own' peaked at number 76.

207

DAY TRIPPER/WE CAN WORK IT OUT

THE BEATLES

16 December 1965, for 5 weeks

●●●●●

PARLOPHONE R 5389

Writers: John Lennon and Paul McCartney
Producer: George Martin

The first of four Beatles singles to be officially released as a double A-side duly became their ninth consecutive number one the week after it entered the charts, and it gave them the Christmas number one for the third year in a row.

Both sides became immediate Beatles favourites, and attracted many cover versions. 'Day Tripper' hit the charts again in 1967, recorded by Otis Redding, and 'We Can Work It Out' came back to chart life twice in the 70s, once when Stevie Wonder took his version to number 27 in 1971, and again five years later when the Four Seasons followed up four consecutive Top 10 hits with their rendition, which stopped at number 34. A different song of the same title was a very minor chart hit for Brass Construction in 1983.

A group called the Vontastics took for themselves a share in the title of Least Successful Chart Act In America when their recording of 'Day Tripper' (a Top 10 soul hit) made number 100 for one week only, from 3 September 1966. Thus it was that the most successful and the least successful chart acts in US chart history both hit with the same song.

208

KEEP ON RUNNING

THE SPENCER DAVIS GROUP

20 January 1966, for 1 week

●

FONTANA TF 632

Writer: Jackie Edwards
Producer: Chris Blackwell

Chris Blackwell was on the lookout for black talent for his fledgling Island label when he came across the exceptional voice of Stevie Winwood at Birmingham's Golden Eagle pub. He immediately signed Winwood and the group he was performing with to Fontana. A year later they were at number one.

Vocalist, guitarist and keyboard player Steve (born 12 May 1948) and his bassist brother Muff (born 15 June 1945) had joined drummer Peter York (born 15 August 1942) and guitarist Spencer Davis (born 17 July 1942) in 1963 to form the Rhythm And Blues Quartet, playing material by the likes of Muddy Waters and Sonny Boy Williamson. On signing a recording contract they changed their name and turned professional, releasing a John Lee Hooker song, 'Dimples', as their first single. It flopped but the follow-ups, 'Every Little Bit Hurts' and 'I Can't Stand It', fared better. Then, with a piece of inspired musical cross-fertilization, producer Blackwell introduced the group to

Wilfred 'Jackie' Edwards, a Jamaican ska artist whom he'd discovered during his Island research. Winwood and Davis were off and running.

209

MICHELLE

THE OVERLANDERS

27 January 1966, for 3 weeks

●●●

PYE 7N 17034

Writers: John Lennon and Paul McCartney. Producer: Tony Hatch

The Overlanders were discovered and managed by top rock photographer Harry Hammond. Initially they were a three - part harmony group consisting of lead vocalist Laurie Mason, Paul Arnold and Pete Bartholomew. This line-up was extended in 1965 when Terry Widlake and David Walsh joined. The group signed to Tony Hatch at Pye.

Their first eight releases in the UK all failed, but they registered in the States with 'Yesterday's Gone', which climbed to number 75 there, while fellow Englishmen Chad and Jeremy took the song to number 21. Despite their total lack of chart success at home, their folk-beat sound became a popular club attraction, most notably in the northern cabaret clubs and ballrooms where they were always in demand. They even toured as support to the Rolling Stones.

The Overlanders' one and only triumph on disc came when Hatch and Hammond decided to raid the outstanding recently released Beatles' album, *Rubber Soul*. None of the tracks had been released as singles by the Beatles themselves, so a host of lesser acts descended on the 14 titles with an eye on instant chartdom.

'Michelle', a Paul McCartney ballad sung partly in French, was nabbed by both the Overlanders and by vocal duo David and Jonathan, in reality songwriters Roger Cook and Roger Greenaway (see no. 308). Both versions charted, but the Overlanders peaked ten places higher than David and Jonathan. Their follow-ups, however, all sank without trace and by the end of the year the group had disbanded. They are now remembered only as the first act to take a cover of a Beatles album track to number one.

210

THESE BOOTS ARE MADE FOR WALKING

NANCY SINATRA

17 February 1966, for 4 weeks

●●●●

REPRISE R 20432

Writer: Lee Hazelwood. Producer: Lee Hazelwood

Frank Sinatra's eldest daughter, Nancy, to whom one of her father's greatest hits, 'Nancy (With The Laughing Face)', was dedicated in 1944, was born in her distinguished father's home on 8 June 1940. She made her national TV debut in 1960 with her dad and Elvis Presley, which is a pretty good line-up of co-stars for a new girl's first television appearance. 1960 was also the year in which she married singer/actor Tommy Sands, whose own record career was in decline after a storming start with 'Teenage Crush' in 1957.

Nancy was one of the first signings to her father's own Reprise label in 1961, but for five years a series of forgettable recordings of ballads and show tunes advanced her no further than being known as Frank Sinatra's daughter or Mrs. Tommy Sands. She eliminated the latter problem by divorcing Sands in 1965. Then, in 1966, Lee Hazelwood, who had supervised twangy guitar man Duane Eddy's recording career in the late 50s and early 60s, gave her the aggressive and witty 'Boots' (his own composition) to record. The result was a number one hit for Nancy on both sides of the Atlantic.

The smash set Nancy off on a healthy string of hits, masterminded by Hazelwood. The next single was really 'Boots 2', entitled, 'How Does That Grab You Darlin'?', but it made the Top 10 in the US and Top 20 in Britain. More distinguished was her third hit, the whimsical 'Sugar Town', which peaked at number five, just before she hit the jackpot again in conjunction with her famous parent (see no. 231).

The SPENCER DAVIS GROUP rehearse for an appearance on *Ready Steady Go*. (Pictorial Press)

211

THE SUN AIN'T GONNA SHINE ANYMORE

THE WALKER BROTHERS

17 March 1966, for 4 weeks

●●●●

PHILIPS BF 1473

Writers: Bob Crewe and Bob Gaudio
Producer: Johnny Franz

After 'Make It Easy On Yourself' (see no. 203), the Walker Brothers put out another heavily emotional ballad as the follow-up. They made the mistake, however, of choosing the basically optimistic song 'My Ship Is Coming In', which did not match the fragile and tortured image that Scott Walker had been moulded into, so it reached only number three.

No such mistakes on the next single. A title as bleak as any that has reached number one, 'The Sun Ain't Gonna Shine Anymore', written by the Four Seasons' masterminds Bob Crewe and Bob Gaudio, gave the Walkers a second number one.

By the spring of 1966, Scott Walker was certainly the most popular male vocalist among the female teenage population of Britain, and his looks and voice seemed destined to keep him at the top for as long as he wished. But signs of disintegration within the group were already beginning to appear by this time, and when the inevitable parting of the ways took place, not even Scott Walker found sustained success easy to achieve. Maybe he never wanted it, but after several powerful and big-selling albums, some TV shows and a couple of hit singles, he faded.

Nothing of great importance was heard from any Walker Brother until 1976, when they suddenly reunited out of nowhere, made an album and one excellent Top 10 single, 'No Regrets', before another lengthy spell of mysterious inactivity. Yet their impact remains. In 1992, a greatest hits album featuring the best of the Walker Brothers and Scott's solo work, entitled *No Regrets*, climbed to number four in the albums chart over 25 years after they first set teenybop hearts on fire.

212

SOMEBODY HELP ME

THE SPENCER DAVIS GROUP

14 April 1966, for 2 weeks

●●

FONTANA TF 679

Writer: Jackie Edwards
Producer: Chris Blackwell

The Spencer Davis Group's second number one was, like their first (see no. 208), written by Jackie Edwards. So was their next hit, 'When I Come Home', but this was nothing like as successful as the first two, and from then on, the band began to write more and more of their own material. The high chart positions of the next two singles, 'Gimme Some Lovin'' and 'I'm A Man' (the latter also a hit for Chicago in 1970) proved the wisdom of this change of policy.

By the spring of 1967, it had become clear that the prodigious talents of Steve Winwood could not be contained within the confines of the Spencer Davis Group, and he left to form Traffic. This move spelt the beginning of the end for the Davis band. Steve's brother Muff also departed, to a behind-the-scenes role at Chris Blackwell's Island Records. Spencer soldiered on for a while with a variety of replacements, but never came up with a combination that captured the magic of the days with the Winwood brothers.

Traffic rapidly became an international success. Their biggest hit single was 'Hole In My Shoe', a piece of hippie daftness that was less than seriously revived by *Young Ones* hippie neil in 1984. They survived various comings and goings (including Steve's short-lived stint with Eric Clapton and Rick Grech as Blind Faith in 1969) until the mid-1970s. Winwood lay low for the rest of the decade, but came back with a vengeance in the 80s with seven hit albums and two American number one hit singles, 'Higher Love' in 1986 and 'Roll With It' in 1988.

213

YOU DON'T HAVE TO SAY YOU LOVE ME

DUSTY SPRINGFIELD

28 April 1966, for 1 week

●

PHILIPS BF 1482

Writers: Pino Donaggio, Vito Pallavicini; English lyrics by Vicki Wickham and Simon Napier-Bell
Producer: Johnny Franz

Dusty Springfield (born Mary O'Brien on 16 April 1939 in Hampstead, London) spent the early part of her career with her brother Tom and Tim Field in the folk group the Springfields. When this group split in September 1963, she began a solo career that got off to a tremendous start four months later with a number four hit, 'I Only Want To Be With You'. Then Dusty shed the constraints of the Springfields style and moved towards a more soulful Tamla Motown sound. She notched up four more Top 10 hits between July 1964 and September 1965, before achieving her only number one hit in April 1966 with an adaptation of an Italian song originally titled 'Io Che No Vivo Senza Te'.

Often making use of such top class writing teams as Bacharach and David or Goffin and King, Dusty's finest hour arrived with her *Dusty In Memphis* album, which was produced by Jerry Wexler and housed the classic single 'Son Of A Preacher Man', which made number nine in December 1968. In time she came to be seen as perhaps the finest British female vocalist of the 1960s, and still a strong enough commercial and artistic name in the 1980s to share a number two hit with the Pet Shop Boys late in 1987 - 'What Have I Done To Deserve This?' That year she also recorded with Richard Carpenter, who obviously considered Dusty one of the few vocalists with whom he could work after the death of his sister Karen.

214

PRETTY FLAMINGO

MANFRED MANN

5 May 1966, for 3 weeks

●●●

HMV POP 1523

Writer: Mark Barkan
Producer: John Burgess

The second Manfred Mann chart-topper came five singles and nearly two years after their first, but in the meantime the group had been consolidating its position as one of the most popular in the country. Personnel changes were always a feature of Manfred Mann, and by the time 'Pretty Flamingo' was recorded, Mike Vickers had left, to be replaced by Jack Bruce (born 14 May 1943), who played bass, with Tom McGuinness switching to lead guitar. It was the only occasion in the amazingly varied career of Jack Bruce (Cream, John Mayall, Graham Bond, even the Hollies) when he played on a number one hit single.

This was also the last big Manfred Mann hit featuring Paul Jones as lead singer. A single featuring Jones, 'You Gave Me Somebody To Love', was released after he had left the group that summer, but it climbed no higher than number 36. It is remembered now only as the answer to the trick question, "What was the last Manfred Mann single to feature Paul Jones?" The first single featuring the new lead singer hit the charts the week after 'You Gave Me Somebody To Love' disappeared. The new singer was Mike d'Abo (born 1 March 1944) and the single was the second Bob Dylan composition that Manfred Mann had released as a single, 'Just Like A Woman'. Their third Dylan-composed single was to give Manfred Mann their biggest hit of all.

215

PAINT IT, BLACK

THE ROLLING STONES

26 May 1966, for 1 week

●

DECCA F 12395

Writers: Mick Jagger and Keith Richard
Producer: Andrew Loog Oldham

After 'Get Off Of My Cloud', the Rolling Stones slipped. Their next single, 'Nineteenth Nervous Breakdown', was the first Stones single in two years not to hit number one, although it still reached number two both in the US and in the UK. The UK flip-side, 'As Tears Go By' (which had been a hit for Mick Jagger's girlfriend, Marianne Faithfull, two years earlier), had been a US Top 10 entry in its own right, but still the follow-up single was crucial. The song chosen was 'Paint It, Black', written during the Stones' tour of Australia, recorded in Hollywood and featuring Brian Jones on sitar. Once again there was criticism of the Stones as mere imitators of the Beatles, whose 1965 album, *Rubber Soul,* had first included George Harrison playing sitar, but the Beatles had never put out a death disc as a single. 'Paint It, Black' was a death disc.

After 'Paint It, Black', the Stones went off the boil a bit. Perhaps it was the prosecution of Jagger, Richard and Jones for the use of drugs that caused their standards to drop, but late 1966 and '67 were not good times for the group, artistically or commercially. Mick Jagger sang on the Beatles' number one hit 'All You Need Is Love' (see no. 235), but the next three Stones' singles, 'Have You Seen Your Mother Baby Standing In The Shadow', 'We Love You' and 'Let's Spend The Night Together', gave them Top 10 placings but nothing more.

216

STRANGERS IN THE NIGHT

FRANK SINATRA

2 June 1966, for 3 weeks

●●●

REPRISE RS 23052

Writers: Bert Kaempfert, Charlie Singleton and Eddie Snyder
Producers: Jimmy Bowen, with orchestral arrangement by Ernie Freeman

Frank Sinatra's second number one hit came 11 years and 244 days after his first, at that time the longest gap in British

FRANK SINATRA enjoyed seven American number ones in the 1940s, three singing with Tommy Dorsey's orchestra, one with Harry James' band and three as a soloist. (Pictorial Press)

chart history between number one hits by the same artist. It came from the most unlikely source, an extremely forgettable James Garner spy film called *A Man Could Get Killed*. Bert Kaempfert, who had also been involved in Elvis Presley's 'Wooden Heart' (see no.115), wrote the complete score for the film, the first Hollywood score he had been asked to compose. The song, thanks to Ol' Blue Eyes' impeccable performance, became far more successful than the film and won four Grammy Awards in 1966. In fact, 1966 was a very good year for the Sinatra family, as daughter Nancy had recently racked up her first number one (see no. 210), but by the end of the 1960s even more success was to be achieved by both generations of the family.

Together Frank and Nancy hit the top with 'Something Stupid' (see no. 231), while Frank Sinatra broke all British chart records with his amazingly longlasting hit 'My Way'. It set up a record 124 weeks of chart life, selling over a million copies in Britain alone. The song, with English lyrics by Paul Anka, was acknowledged as the most recorded composition of all time, ahead of 'Yesterday' and 'Tie A Yellow Ribbon Round The Old Oak Tree' (see no. 329).

217

PAPERBACK WRITER

THE BEATLES

23 June 1966, for 2 weeks

●●

PARLOPHONE R 5452

Writers: John Lennon and Paul McCartney
Producer: George Martin

The tenth consecutive number one for the Beatles was a Paul McCartney song featuring Paul double-tracked singing lead. The song was the first Beatles' A-side that could not be interpreted as a love song. This may explain why its initial acceptance was not quite as ecstatic as was usual for a new Fab Four platter.

Nonetheless, 'Paperback Writer', like its seven immediate predecessors in the triumphant line of Beatles' releases, reached number one in its second week on the chart. True, it held the top spot for only two weeks, which is the shortest run by any Beatles single at number one (equal with 'Hey Jude', see no. 258), but some of their very best work was still to come. Two months later, the *Revolver* album silenced the doubters. In 1967, the 'Penny Lane'/'Strawberry Fields Forever' single (which, for all its brilliance, became the first Beatles single since 'Please Please Me' in early 1963 not to make number one) and the masterpiece *Sergeant Pepper's Lonely Hearts Club Band* album turned the doubters into believers.

The B-side of 'Paperback Writer' was the John Lennon song 'Rain'. Possibly no other Beatles single highlights the difference between the styles of Lennon and McCartney as much as this, their twelfth single and tenth number one.

218

SUNNY AFTERNOON

THE KINKS

7 July 1966, for 2 weeks

●●

PYE 7N 17125

Writer: Ray Davies
Producer: Shel Talmy

It was the same writing and production team from the first two Kinks chart-toppers that gave the Davies brothers and their two co-Kinks their third and final number one single in the summer of 1966. Since the heady heights of the mid-1960s the Kinks have tended to appear only sporadically in the charts. The three singles immediately following 'Sunny Afternoon' went into the Top 10, but since 1967 only two more Top 10ers and a brace of number 12s have been added to the list of Kinks hits. Ray Davies' fascination with the English continued in work such as his *Village Green Preservation Society* album and his *Muswell Hillbillies* LP in 1971. Ironically, the Kinks now have a greater following in America than in their homeland.

With hindsight, Ray Davies is seen as one of the most talented songwriters of the 60s, and his idiosyncratic style is partially the result of Lonnie Donegan's acknowledged influence. An interesting footnote to the Kinks story is that Jam and Style Council singer-songwriter Paul Weller was influenced by Davies, who in turn was influenced by Donegan. Between them, they have achieved ten number ones.

219

GET AWAY

GEORGIE FAME WITH THE BLUE FLAMES

21 July 1966, for 1 week

•

COLUMBIA DB 7946

Writer: Clive Powell
Producer: Tony Palmer

Originally written and performed by Georgie Fame as a commercial jingle for petrol, 'Get Away' turned out to be so popular with all those who didn't leave the room to make a cup of tea during the advertisements that Fame decided to 'decommercialize' the song for general release. It became his second number one smash in five outings, three less substantial chart singles having hit the shops between 'Get Away' and 'Yeh Yeh' (see no. 184).

Fame's final album with the original Blue Flames was the 1966 package *Sweet Things,* which consisted mainly of covers of American soul songs. In September Fame disbanded the Blue Flames and devoted more time to working with the Harry South Big Band. The first of three albums on which Fame and South collaborated was released in September 1966, entitled *Sound Venture*. This unusual combination of a blues/pop singer with a big band was a brave and successful project that followed *Sweet Things* into the album charts Top 10.

Fame's single follow-up to 'Get Away' (featuring neither the Blue Flames nor Harry South) was a cover of the Bobby Hebb hit 'Sunny', which became a three-way fight when Cher also entered the fray with her version. The final score read Hebb at number 12, Fame at number 13 and Cher with the bronze at number 32. Fame's next single, the last before he left Columbia, was pulled from the *Sweet Things* album - Billy Stewart's 'Sitting In The Park'. This sat at number 12.

220

OUT OF TIME

CHRIS FARLOWE

28 July 1966, for 1 week

•

IMMEDIATE IM 035

Writers: Mick Jagger and Keith Richard
Producer: Mick Jagger

Chris Farlowe (born John Henry Deighton on 13 October 1940) found early musical success when his own John Henry Skiffle Group won the English Skiffle Group Contest at Tottenham's Mecca Club in 1957. By 1962 he was lead vocalist with a semi-professional beat group called the Thunderbirds. That same year, following a month-long tour of Germany, Farlowe met up with Rik Gunnell, the manager of London's Flamingo and Ram Jam Clubs. Gunnell became the group's manager and they turned pro when the first single, 'Air Travel', was released by Decca in June 1963.

Despite the Thunderbirds being favourites on the London club circuit, a hit single proved elusive. A cover of 'Just A Dream', Jimmy Clanton's US Top 5 smash from 1958, failed, as did 'Buzz With The Fuzz', a song which looked set to break the run of failures until it was withdrawn by EMI as soon as they worked out the meaning of the mod lyrics.

At the end of 1965 Farlowe moved to the Immediate label, run by the Rolling Stones' manager, Andrew Loog Oldham. Here Farlowe found the freedom to record what he wanted, coupled with people who believed in his talents. His second single for Immediate, 'Think', was a track from the Stones' LP *Aftermath,* and it crept into the charts. Farlowe had a hit at last, at his tenth attempt.

The follow-up was another song from *Aftermath*, called 'Out Of Time'. It made number one in the week that England won the World Cup, giving Jagger and Richard their only chart-topper as writers for another act. Farlowe's rendition differed greatly from the Stones version on *Aftermath*, but as the 1970 Stones' compilation album *Metamorphosis* shows, Jagger had previously recorded a demo of the song with the same backing track as Farlowe. On the number one hit, Farlowe's voice merely replaced Jagger's.

221

WITH A GIRL LIKE YOU

THE TROGGS

4 August 1966, for 2 weeks

●●

FONTANA TF 717

Writer: Reg Presley
Producer: Larry Page

The Andover-based Troggs were vocalist Reg Ball (born 12 June 1943), who modestly changed his name to Reg Presley, lead guitarist Chris Britton (born 21 January 1945), bass guitarist Pete Staples (born 3 May 1944) and drummer Ronnie Bond (né Ronald Bultis, born 4 May 1943, died 1993). Originally called the Troglodytes, they were spotted by performer-turned-producer Larry Page, who many years before had been billed as Larry Page The Teenage Rage. They signed to CBS, for whom they released one flop single, a Reg Presley composition.

Fontana were luckier. Page took the band to the Philips subsidiary and the first time out they struck gold. The song was by American Chip Taylor (the brother of screen actor Jon Voigt), and called 'Wild Thing'. Although not a number one, this earthy and extremely basic stomper remains the Troggs' most famous recording. The number one arrived next time out via a new Reg Presley effort, 'With A Girl Like You', sophisticated only in comparison with 'Wild Thing', but similarly irresistible.

The band were chart regulars until 1968, but their fame in later years rested on the bootleg but widely available *Troggs Tapes*, which come from a totally unsuccessful session and consist mainly of a stream of arguments and obscenities. In 1992, they suddenly reappeared with the album *Athens Andover*, masterminded by R.E.M's Peter Buck and Mike Mills. Suddenly, the Troggs were hip again.

222

YELLOW SUBMARINE/ELEANOR RIGBY

THE BEATLES

18 August 1966, for 4 weeks

●●●●

PARLOPHONE R 5493

Writers: John Lennon and Paul McCartney
Producer: George Martin

The first single that the Beatles released to coincide with the release of the album from which the tracks came was the double-sided hit 'Eleanor Rigby'/'Yellow Submarine'. The LP was *Revolver*. It was said at the time that the Beatles issued the single to prevent others from covering songs from their LPs, as had happened, for example, with 'Michelle' (see no. 209) and 'Girl' from *Rubber Soul*, and was later to happen with 'Ob-La-Di Ob-La-Da' (see no. 263) from the white album.

'Yellow Submarine' was the first Beatles single to feature Ringo singing lead. The enchanting children's singalong number was in stark contrast to 'Eleanor Rigby', an extraordinarily sophisticated song of loneliness that quickly became one of their most covered songs. Although sung by Paul accompanied only by a string quartet, John Lennon later revealed that he had made a major writing contribution to the song.

While this single was at number one, the Beatles played their final live date, at Candlestick Park in San Francisco on 29 August 1966.

223

ALL OR NOTHING

THE SMALL FACES

15 September 1966, for 1 week

●

DECCA F 12470

Writers: Steve Marriott and Ronnie Lane
Producers: Steve Marriott and Ronnie Lane

The nattily dressed Small Faces were led by former child actor Steve Marriott (born 30 January 1947). Marriott was later to admit that he could barely play guitar in the early days of the group, but despite that he and his fellow Small Faces, Ronnie Lane (born 1 April 1946), Ian MacLagan (born 12 May 1946) and Kenny Jones (born 16 September 1948), provided the only real competition to the Who in the mid-60s. Both groups came out of the mod scene in London. The Small Faces had five Top 10 hits between February 1966 and April 1968 with numbers such as 'Sha La La La Lee', 'Itchycoo Park' and 'Lazy Sunday', but the only number one was 'All Or Nothing', which dislodged the Beatles at the end of the summer.

In 1969 Marriott left the Small Faces to form Humble Pie with Peter Frampton from the Herd, while Lane and the others joined forces with Rod Stewart and Ronnie Wood to form the Faces. Later, Wood went on to become a Rolling Stone. While mainly a singles band, the Small Faces did make an impact in the albums arena when their 1968 album, *Ogden's Nut Gone Flake*, was issued with a revolutionary circular cover, becoming a minor classic.

Steve Marriott died in a fire at his Essex home in 1991.

224

DISTANT DRUMS

JIM REEVES

22 September 1966, for 5 weeks

●●●●●

RCA 1537

Writer: Cindy Walker
Producer: Chet Atkins

On 31 July 1964 Jim Reeves was flying to Nashville when his single-engined plane encountered a storm. Two days later his body was found in the wrecked aircraft. The country music world had lost one of its greatest performers, but a legend was born as a result of the singer's death.

James Travis Reeves (born 20 August 1923 in Galloway, Texas) made his first radio broadcast at the age of nine. An accident had prevented him from following his chosen career as a baseball professional, so he turned to broadcasting. It was as a DJ on radio station KGRI in Henderson, Texas, that he first made his mark. In November 1952 Reeves landed an announcer's job at KWKH in Shreveport, Louisiana, where his duties included announcing the famous country showcase *Louisiana Hayride* every Saturday night. Hank Williams failed to arrive one evening and Reeves' bosses asked him to fill in with some songs. A contract with Abbott Records and two US country numbers ones, 'Mexican Joe' and 'Bimbo', followed.

In 1955 Reeves moved to RCA, where he managed nine UK hits before his death, including the 1964 winners 'I Love You Because' and 'I Won't Forget You'. A further 17 hits, including 'Distant Drums', were amassed posthumously between 1964 and 1972. In the US, the success continued into the 1980s by the adding of new arrangements to original vocal tracks and by the electronic creation of duets with the living singer Deborah Allen. Record bosses may have overstepped the bounds of good taste in 1981, when an album of duets was produced by mixing Reeves' voice with that of Patsy Cline, who had herself died in a plane crash in 1963. This produced another Top 10 country hit, 'Have You Ever Been Lonely?'.

The FOUR TOPS (left to right: Levi Stubbs, Renaldo Benson, Abdul Fakir and Lawrence Payton) appear on *Ready Steady Go* in 1966, the year of their number one. (Pictorial Press)

225

REACH OUT I'LL BE THERE

THE FOUR TOPS

27 October 1966, for 3 weeks

●●●

TAMLA MOTOWN TMG 579

Writers: Brian Holland, Lamont Dozier and Eddie Holland
Producers: Brian Holland and Lamont Dozier

The day after the Beatles reached out for their MBEs at Buckingham Palace, the Four Tops made it to number one. It was the second song penned by Holland, Dozier and Holland to climb to the top (see no. 181) and became Motown's biggest seller up to that time.

The Four Tops, who had originally formed in Detroit as the Four Aims in 1953/'54, had their first UK hit with a song that had provided them with their first US number one, 'I Can't Help Myself', in the summer of 1965. Unlike most Tamla Motown groups, and indeed unlike most groups, the Four Tops' line-up has remained unchanged throughout four decades, with Levi Stubbs on lead vocals, supported by Renaldo Benson, Abdul 'Duke' Fakir and Lawrence Payton. Far more of a pop outfit than their more socially aware labelmates the Temptations, the Four Tops eventually left Motown in 1972 and, after a mediocre spell with Dunhill, signed to Casablanca Records, a move which resulted in a 1981 return to the Top 10 with 'When She Was My Girl'.

In 1986, Levi Stubbs supplied the voice of the man-eating plant Audrey II in the film version of *Little Shop Of Horrors*, and in 1988, 'Reach Out I'll Be There' returned to the Top 20 in a remixed version. At the end of that year, a song created for the Phil Collins movie *Buster*, 'Loco In Acapulco', gave the Four Tops their 11th Top 10 hit, 22 years after their first foray into the upper reaches.

226

GOOD VIBRATIONS

THE BEACH BOYS

17 November 1966, for 2 weeks

●●

CAPITOL CL 15475

Writers: Brian Wilson and Mike Love
Producer: Brian Wilson

For a few months in 1966 the Beach Boys (in the UK at least) were bracketed with the Beatles as progressive music innovators, and Brian Wilson was ranked with Lennon and McCartney as a songwriter of genius; their album *Pet Sounds* and the single 'Good Vibrations' were two of the principal reasons for this. The Beach Boys at the time of 'Good Vibrations' were brothers Brian (born 20 June 1942), Dennis (born 4 December 1944) and Carl Wilson (born 21 December 1946), along with their cousin Mike Love (born 15 March 1941), and Al Jardine (born 3 September 1942) and Bruce Johnston (born 27 June 1944).

The Beach Boys were formed in Hawthorne, California, in 1961. At high school they were successively Kenny and the Cadets, Carl and the Passions, and the Rendletones. They first recorded in 1961 and broke through in the States a year later with the first of many Brian Wilson surfing songs that paid tribute to a life in and around California's rolling waves. Their career took longer to break in Britain's colder climes, but they managed it in 1964 with 'I Get Around'.

The principal themes of early Beach Boy songs - surfing, girls, cars and more girls - were less in evidence by 1966. 'Good Vibrations' was recorded over six months during 17 sessions in four studios. Although the production was difficult and intricate, the extreme length between first session and final mix has to be put down to the talented yet erratic Brian Wilson.

227

GREEN GREEN GRASS OF HOME

TOM JONES

1 December 1966, for 7 weeks

●●●●●●●

DECCA F 22511

Writer: Claude 'Curly' Putnam Jr.
Producer: Peter Sullivan

Tom Jones' second – and so far final – number one was a country song about a condemned prisoner, which writer Curly Putnam (see also 381) was inspired to write after seeing the 1950 crime classic movie *The Asphalt Jungle*. In that film, which, incidentally, marked the big-screen film debut of Marilyn Monroe, Sterling Hayden plays a gangster from Kentucky who dreams one day of going back home to the farm. He finally dies of gunshot wounds, having made it back to the green, green grass of home.

For Tom Jones, the grass in America had long seemed greener than at home, but as his chart career in the States faltered slightly in 1967 and '68, everything started going right for him in the UK. 'Green Green Grass Of Home' was only Jones' second Top 10 hit in Britain, but over the next three and a half years, the lad from Treforest chalked up nine more Top 10 hits, including three consecutive number two hits in 1967 and '68. Not only that, he signed with ATV a contract to do 17 one-man shows a year for 5 years, for a total of £9 million, which at that time was by far the most lucrative TV contract ever signed in Britain.

In 1971 and '72, Jones had two more Top 10 hits, but after that he had to wait for almost 15 years until he crashed back into the UK Top 10 in the spring of 1987 with 'A Boy From Nowhere', which gave him his fifth number two hit. Further hits with Prince's 'Kiss' and Phyllis Nelson's 'Move Closer', among others, prove that Tom Jones as a grandfather in the 90s is as popular and successful as he ever was as a sex symbol in the 60s.

228

I'M A BELIEVER

THE MONKEES

19 January 1967, for 4 weeks

●●●●

RCA 1560

Writer: Neil Diamond
Producer: Jeff Barry

On 5 September 1966, America's NBC television network previewed two new series which it hoped would do well, *Star Trek* and *The Monkees*. The Monkees were Mike Nesmith (born 30 December 1942 in Houston, Texas), Peter Tork (born Peter Thorkelson on 13 February 1944 in Washington, DC), Mickey Dolenz (born 8 March 1945 in Tarzana, California) and

Davy Jones (born 30 December 1946 in Manchester, England). They had been brought together by the Screen Gems television company. Nesmith and Tork were musicians, Dolenz and Jones primarily actors. Many famous names reportedly auditioned for the parts, including, for example, Stephen Stills, but over the years it seems more people have claimed to have been turned down for a part in *The Monkees* than there were hopeful actors in California at the time.

The lucky four were given songs to perform that had been commissioned from such major songwriting names as Goffin and King, Mann and Weil, Boyce and Hart, Harry Nilsson and Neil Diamond. As soon as the series began airing in Britain, the Monkees repeated the success they had begun to achieve in the USA two months earlier. Initially, Screen Gems allowed them only to sing, not play, on their records, which upset Tork and Nesmith especially. It was the company's strict control of its stars' careers that finally led to the departure of first Tork and then Nesmith in 1969, but not before the group had come up with a run of excellent hit singles which proved that their ability was not merely manufactured.

A second generation of *Star Trek* television episodes was still in production in the mid-1990s, and the string of *Star Trek* films was threatening to break into double figures. In 1989, a Monkees greatest hits package broke into the albums chart Top 20, and episodes of the TV series first broadcast over 25 years previously can still be seen on television channels around the world.

229

THIS IS MY SONG

PETULA CLARK

16 February 1967, for 2 weeks

●●

PYE 7N 17258

Writer: Charles Chaplin
Producer: Ernie Freeman

Petula Clark, whose only other British number one had been 'Sailor' (see no. 113) in 1961, returned to the top almost six years later with this theme tune of the film *A Countess From Hong Kong*, starring Marlon Brando and Sophia Loren, and directed by the man who played a cameo role as a seasick waiter, Charlie Chaplin. Chaplin also wrote the theme song, which has sold more copies worldwide than even his famous theme from *Limelight*, which spent a record eight weeks at number two in 1953, Frank Chacksfield's version being held off the top by Frankie Laine in his *annus mirabilis*. 'This Is My Song' was also recorded by Harry Secombe, who, like Petula Clark, enjoyed his biggest-ever hit with the song, reaching number two five weeks after Miss Clark's version had tumbled from the very top. Neither version was actually used in the film.

Clark first recorded 'This Is My Song' in French, Italian and German for the European market. Then she made an English version, and thus managed to top the charts virtually all the way across Europe in four different languages.

Clark's biggest hit worldwide was not 'This Is My Song', which reached only number three in America. In 1964, her version of the Tony Hatch composition 'Downtown' had topped the charts in America and in most countries of the world. In Britain, it spent three weeks at number two, kept off the top by the Beatles' 'I Feel Fine'.

230

RELEASE ME

ENGELBERT HUMPERDINCK

2 March 1967, for 6 weeks

●●●●●●

DECCA F 12541

Writers: Eddie Miller and Dub Wilson
Producer: Charles Blackwell

The transformation of Gerry Dorsey into Engelbert Humperdinck is one of the most famous if-at-first-you-don't-succeed stories in show business. Arnold George Dorsey was born in Madras, India, on 2 May 1936, and moved with his family to England shortly after the end of the war.

After completing his national service in 1956, he began a show business career as Gerry Dorsey, which lasted for nine years and covered occasional recording contracts, sporadic TV and radio spots and endless shows in provincial theatres on pop package tours. There was also a great deal of resting between engagements.

In 1965, he met one of his former roommates, Gordon Mills, who was by then managing Tom Jones. Mills took Dorsey onto his management roster and changed his named to Engelbert Humperdinck, which was the name of the German composer (1854-1921) who wrote the opera *Hansel And Gretel*. Humperdinck recorded a couple of almost-successful singles, one of which, 'Dommage Dommage', was a big hit in Europe. Then he was asked to stand in for Dickie Valentine, who was ill, on *Sunday Night At The London Palladium*, and he sang his latest single, 'Release Me'. Over a year later it finally dropped off the chart, having achieved the longest-ever stay in the Top 50 by any single in Britain.

231

SOMETHING STUPID

NANCY SINATRA AND FRANK SINATRA

13 April 1967, for two weeks

●●

REPRISE RS 23166

Writer: C. Carson Parks
Producers: Jimmy Bowen and Lee Hazelwood

For the first time ever, two acts who had already achieved a number one hit in their own right combined to record yet another number one. The act was a father and daughter combination, a combination which has never topped the charts before or since, and by taking their only single to the summit, they became the first act to be one-hit wonders on both sides of the Atlantic.

Nancy Sinatra's producer Lee Hazelwood found the tune, and it was Nancy who showed it to her father. Frank Sinatra was the one who suggested they record it as a duet. The session turned out to be not only an artistic duet, but also a production duet, which went remarkably smoothly considering that both producers are known for their strong individual style, and it was the first time either of them had come up against eight-track studio equipment. Despite reservations by some executives that the lyrics were unsuitable for close relatives to sing to each other, nobody mentioned their doubts to Frank Sinatra, who after all owned the Reprise company. So the record was released and sold millions at a rate that would have been very impressive for Sinatra Sr. in his bobbysoxer heyday. In the mid-60s it was remarkable.

FRANK AND NANCY SINATRA remain the only father and daughter act to record a number one single. (Pictorial Press)

232

PUPPET ON A STRING

SANDIE SHAW

27 April 1967, for 3 weeks

●●●

PYE 7N 17272

Writers: Bill Martin and Phil Coulter
Producer: Ken Woodman

Sandie Shaw's third number one hit was

the song with which she won the Eurovision Song Contest in 1967. It made her the first, and for almost 20 years the only, female solo singer to top the British charts three times. Not until October 1986 did Madonna match Shaw with three number ones. Of course, Miss Ciccone has gone on to rack up her fourth, fifth, sixth and seventh number ones but before the advent of Madonna, Sandie Shaw had held a one-hit lead over 12 different ladies, all of whom clocked up two chart-toppers.

'Puppet On A String' was in itself an excellent and immediately memorable song, much more in the style of 'Long Live Love' (see no. 196) than '(There's) Always Something There To Remind Me' (see no.180). Unfortunately, it inspired so many inferior imitations from so many nations in subsequent Eurovision Song Contests (including the unspeakable 'Boom Bang-A-Bang' from Lulu in 1969) that the contest plumbed artistic depths in the late 60s and early 70s until revived temporarily by Abba's 'Waterloo' (see no. 348) in 1974. By then Sandie Shaw was spending less time in a recording scene that she admitted no longer interested her. Her comeback in the 80s, almost 15 years after her previous chart entry, matched the simultaneous chart revivals of 60s stars Shirley Bassey and Dusty Springfield. For a while it looked as though a fourth number one from Sandie was not an impossibility.

233

SILENCE IS GOLDEN

THE TREMELOES

18 May 1967, for 3 weeks

●●●

CBS 2723

Writers: Bob Gaudio and Bob Crewe
Producer: Mike Smith

Without lead vocalist Brian Poole, the Tremeloes could well have faded into musical obscurity. Instead, an astute image change launched them into a chart career that outdid anything they achieved backing Brian Poole: they even managed to claim three American hits in the process. Alan Howard had left the band before Brian Poole did, and his replacement, Mick Clark, lasted only a short while before moving aside for the group's new lead singer, Len 'Chip' Hawkes (born 11 November 1946).

Their first release, still on Decca, was a Paul Simon composition, 'Blessed', and it sank without a trace. So they grew their hair, wore trendier clothes and put out their favourite track from the Beatles' *Revolver* album, 'Good Day Sunshine'. Another miss. They switched labels to CBS and there they found the Cat Stevens song 'Here Comes My Baby'. Their up-tempo cover entered the Top 10 as its author's own 'Matthew And Son' slipped down to number five.

Their follow-up was the flip of the Four Seasons' big smash 'Rag Doll', a plaintive ballad called 'Silence Is Golden'. The Tremeloes version, featuring some beautiful tight harmonies, entered at 29 and three weeks later was at number one, outselling such classics as the Kinks' 'Waterloo Sunset' and 'Dedicated To The One I Love' by the Mamas and the Papas, both of which had to make do with the runner-up slot. Yet another Top 10 hit, 'Even The Bad Times Are Good', followed before the summer was gone. No bad times for the Tremeloes in 1967.

234

A WHITER SHADE OF PALE

PROCOL HARUM

8 June 1967, for 6 weeks

●●●●●●

DERAM DM 126

Writers: Keith Reid and Gary Brooker.
Producer: Denny Cordell

From June to September the number one spot was occupied by three songs which together sum up the summer of 1967, the Summer Of Love. Flower power, peace and love, together with many exotic substances, were in the air. 'A Whiter Shade Of Pale', with its tantalizingly meaningless lyrics and haunting melody lifted from Bach, matched the mood of the era perfectly.

Procol Harum was created to record the songs of lyricist Keith Reid and vocalist/keyboard player Gary Brooker (born 29 May 1945). Brooker was a former member of the respected Southend R&B quartet the Paramounts, who had received bad publicity when it was alleged that their 1964 Top 40 version of 'Poison Ivy' had been hyped into the charts. The other musicians who appeared on the number one were organist Matthew Fisher (born 7 March 1946), guitarist Ray Royer (born 8 October 1945), drummer Bobby Harrison (born 28 June 1943) and bassist Dave Knights (born 28 June 1945). By the time that the band's debut album had been recorded, Royer and Harrison had been replaced by two former Paramounts, B.J. Wilson on drums and Robin Trower. In March 1969 Knights and Fisher quit and in came the fourth Paramount, Chris Copping. Until 1971, when Trower left, Procol Harum were the Paramounts in all but name.

Procol Harum scored only five hit singles and five hit albums in their ten-year existence. Their last hit single, 'Pandora's Box' in 1975, neatly rounded off their chart career, for it was produced by the writers of 'Poison Ivy', Jerry Lieber and Mike Stoller.

235

ALL YOU NEED IS LOVE

THE BEATLES

19 July 1967, for 3 weeks

●●●

PARLOPHONE R 5620

Writers: John Lennon and Paul McCartney
Producer: George Martin

1 June 1967 was the day of the release in Britain of the *Sergeant Pepper's Lonely Hearts Club Band* LP, the album that completed the process of transformation of the Beatles from a group who prided themselves on their ability to reproduce on stage any sound they had put down on record, into a group who had given up live perfromances in favour of the sophistication of recording techniques to produce brilliant popular music. *Sergeant Pepper's Lonely Hearts Club Band* not only led the way for groups to spend more time in the studios exploring new ideas in sound, but it was also one of the first 'concept' albums. This was a long way from 11 January 1963, when the Beatles had completed ten tracks for their first album in just nine hours and 45 minutes.

Only 24 days after the release of *Sergeant Pepper's Lonely Hearts Club Band*, the Beatles appeared on a BBC TV show, *Our World*, that was beamed live by satellite to all five continents. They sang 'All You Need Is Love' in the Abbey Road studios, and within two weeks it became their next single and their 12th number one.

236

SAN FRANCISCO (BE SURE TO WEAR SOME FLOWERS IN YOUR HAIR)

SCOTT MCKENZIE

9 August 1967, for 4 weeks

●●●●

CBS 2816

Writer: John Phillips
Producers: Lou Adler and John Phillips

'San Francisco' is the best-remembered dippy hippie anthem of that dopey era. It is, however, a popular oldie to this day, not just as a wacky slice of social history but because the melody is one of the best ever crafted by the leader of the Mamas and the Papas, John Phillips. Scott MaKenzie's gentle vocal refrain and the production skills of Philips and Lou Adler (the Mamas and the Papas producer, still three years away from his remarkably successful association with Carole King) stand up well over the years.

Scott McKenzie (born Philip Blondheim on 1 October 1939, in Arlington, Virginia) sang with Phillips in the early 60s as two thirds of a folk group called the Journeymen. When that outfit broke up, Phillips formed the Mamas and the Papas with his wife-to-be Michelle Gilliam, Denny Doherty and Cass Elliott. This quartet took off early in 1966 with the first of a line of hit singles, a Phillips composition called 'California Dreamin''. The follow-up, 'Monday Monday', was the song that broke them big in England. McKenzie, in the meantime, had got no closer to international acclaim than an audition to be a Monkee (see no. 228), but this changed when his old mate handed him the tribute to San Francisco.

The hit bears the longest title of any song to have reached number one in Britain. McKenzie followed it up with another Phillips number, 'Like An Old Time Movie', which did just enough (one week at number 50) to keep McKenzie off the one-hit wonder list. After that, chart silence from the Voice Of Scott McKenzie (as he was billed on his second hit), but 20 years later he found himself back on the road as a fully fledged member of a reconstituted Mamas and Papas, and in 1988 he co-wrote (with John Phillips, Mike Love and Doris Day's son Terry Melcher) the Beach Boys' US number one hit, 'Kokomo'. Scott McKenzie proves there is life after chart extinction.

237

THE LAST WALTZ

ENGELBERT HUMPERDINCK

6 September 1967, for 5 weeks

●●●●●

DECCA F 12655

Writers: Les Reed and Barry Mason
Producer: Peter Sullivan

After 'Release Me' (see no. 230), Engelbert Humperdinck found a country standard called 'There Goes My Everything', which had been a country smash for Jack Greene in 1966. That climbed to number three. Next, he chose a song by the highly successful British songwriters Les Reed and Barry Mason, called 'The Last Waltz'. Within weeks it became the standard closing tune for every dance in every disco and church hall up and down the country, and Humperdinck had a hit that eventually sold even more copies worldwide than 'Release Me'. It was a monster hit in Europe too, where Mireille Mathieu recorded a French version, 'La Dernière Valse', which even reached the British Top 50. Of all the late-60s ballads which seemed to dominate world markets as the Liverpool tide receded, 'The Last Waltz' is probably the best known, probably the biggest seller and certainly the biggest hit ever written by the prolific Reed and Mason.

It was the last waltz for a revolutionary, too. Che Guevara was killed by anti-guerilla forces in Bolivia on 9 October 1967. On the other hand, it was the first waltz for the Cunard liner, the *Queen Elizabeth II*, which was launched at the Clydebank shipyard on 20 September.

An international pop hit for ENGELBERT HUMPERDINCK in 1967, 'Release Me' was originally a 1954 country smash for Jimmy Heap with Perk Williams. (Pictorial Press)

238

MASSACHUSETTS

THE BEE GEES

11 October 1967, for 4 weeks

●●●●

POLYDOR 56 192

Writers: Barry, Robin and Maurice Gibb
Producers: Robert Stigwood and the Bee Gees

The quite remarkable career of the Bee Gees first kicked into top gear with their third British and fourth American hit single, 'Massachusetts'. The Bee Gees are the three brothers Gibb whose parents must have foreseen future royalties, as they had the presence of mind to be in residence in the tax haven Isle Of Man when the boys were born, Barry on 1 September 1947 and the twins Robin and

Maurice on 22 September 1949. There was little money around in Gibb circles in those days, however, and the family emigrated to Australia in 1958 just after the birth of their fourth son, Andy. Down Under the boys' musical abilities soon surfaced, and as the Gibbs, then as the BGs, and finally as the Bee Gees, they became well known. They first recorded in 1963 and had several Aussie chart entries before deciding to return to Britain in early 1967.

Back home they approached the London-based Australian impresario/manager Robert Stigwood, who was, at the time, linked to Brian Epstein's NEMS organization which, of course, included the Beatles among its clients. Stigwood was impressed, and the Bee Gees' second British release, 'New York Mining Disaster 1941 (Have You Seen My Wife Mr. Jones)', became a Top 20 hit in both Britain and America.

'Massachusetts', like every Bee Gees hit of the past three decades, was written by all or some of the Gibb brothers, in this case by all three. They had never actually been to the state in question when they wrote the song, but liked the sound of the name. They even confessed they could not spell the title of this, their first of five number ones, when they recorded the song. At this early stage of their career, the Bee Gees were actually five strong, the Gibbs being supported in performance by guitarist Vince Melouney and drummer Colin Petersen.

239

BABY NOW THAT I'VE FOUND YOU

THE FOUNDATIONS

8 November 1967, for 2 weeks

●●

PYE 7N 17366

Writers: Tony Macaulay and John McLeod
Producer: Tony Macaulay

The Foundations produced six chart hits in two years from September 1967 to September 1969, but none was as big as the first of them all, 'Baby Now That I've Found You', which also gave Tony Macaulay the first of four number one hit productions. The Foundations were Clem Curtis (born 28 November 1940) on vocals, Eric Allandale (born 4 March 1936) on trombone, Pat Burke (born 9 October 1937) on flute, Mike Elliott (born 6 August 1929) on tenor sax, Sri Lankan Tony Gomez (born 13 December 1948), who played organ, Tim 'Sticks' Harris (born 14 January 1948) on drums, Peter Macbeth (born 2 February 1943) on bass and Alan Warner (born 21 April 1941), who played lead guitar. Their second biggest hit came a year later, with a song by Macaulay and Mike d'Abo, the lead singer of Manfred Mann, called 'Build Me Up Buttercup'. It reached number two in Britain and number three in America, but became one of that unfortunate group of highly successful songs (including 'My Sweet Lord', 'Fire' and 'Hello Dolly') which have become the victims of successful plagiarism suits by disgruntled writers of earlier, less successful but very similar songs.

While the Foundations were on top of the British charts, a major force in rock journalism was born. The first edition of *Rolling Stone* was launched by editor/publisher Jann Wenner in San Francisco on 18 November 1967.

240

LET THE HEARTACHES BEGIN

LONG JOHN BALDRY

22 November 1967, for 2 weeks

●●

PYE 7N 17385

Writers: Tony Macaulay and John McLeod
Producer: Tony Macaulay

It was perhaps apt that this song was at number one when the first heart transplant was performed by Dr. Christiaan Barnard at the Groote Schuur Hospital in Cape Town, South Africa, on 3 December 1967. However, this record has more claims to fame than just that. For a start, it was one of the few occasions when writers have ousted another of their songs from the top. Macaulay and McLeod joined Bacharach and David, Lennon and

'Let The Heartaches Begin' was the big British hit for LONG JOHN BALDRY, but it was a minor hit in the States, where its performance was bettered by the Rod Stewart-produced 'Don't Try To Lay No Boogie-Woogie On The King Of Rock And Roll'. (Pictorial Press)

McCartney and Bruce Welch as writers who have achieved consecutive number ones. Tony Macaulay, as producer of both hits, also joined the ranks of producers who have ousted themselves from the top, a list that at that time consisted of Mitch Miller, Dick Rowe, Lee Gillette, Norrie Paramor and George Martin, but which would also include Mike Smith within a few more weeks (see nos. 242 and 243).

Long John Baldry himself, born on 12 January 1941, is probably the tallest act ever to make number one, although Mr. Blobby in full costume must run close. Baldry's height is variously listed as between 6'6" and 6'9", but even the former height is about double that of Little Jimmy Osmond when 'Long Haired Lover From Liverpool' ruled (see. no. 324).

Baldry sang with various blues groups in the 60s, including the Hoochie Coochie Men, Steampacket (a touring R&B revue that at various times included Julie Driscoll, Elkie Brooks, Brian Auger and Rod Stewart) and Bluesology, whose pianist Elton John took his second name from Baldry's first. None of Baldry's blues recordings made the charts and it was a switch to tear-jerking ballads such as 'Let The Heartaches Begin' that brought him to national attention. He was never really happy with his new role as MOR emoter and he eventually returned to his musical roots. No more chart records, but no more having to wear the bow ties either.

241

HELLO GOODBYE

THE BEATLES

6 December 1967, for 7 weeks

●●●●●●●

PARLOPHONE R 5655

Writers: John Lennon and Paul McCartney
Producer: George Martin

Between 'All You Need Is Love' and 'Hello Goodbye' the Beatles' world changed. Brian Epstein, the rich man of 'Baby, You're A Rich Man' (the flip-side of 'All You Need Is Love'), died in August 1967, and the complete domination of the world's record shops achieved by *Sgt. Pepper* meant that the world was looking forward to the Beatles' next record with all the anticipation that was there in 1963 and '64. But with Epstein dead, the Beatles had nobody to direct them, and therein lay the seeds of their disintegration.

'Hello Goodbye' was probably their most straightforward single since 'Help!' (see no. 200). It was nowhere near as inventive as 'Strawberry Fields Forever' or 'Eleanor Rigby', but it stayed at number one for seven weeks, the longest run by any Beatles single since 'From Me To You'. Originality was expressed on the B-side, 'I Am The Walrus', a track from their TV film *Magical Mystery Tour*, which hit the screens on Boxing Day 1967. *Magical Mystery Tour* was panned by the critics and the leadership that Paul McCartney had assumed after the death of Brian Epstein took its first knock.

242

THE BALLAD OF BONNIE AND CLYDE

GEORGIE FAME

24 January 1968, for 1 week

●

CBS 3124

Writers: Mitch Murray and Peter Callender
Producer: Mike Smith

Georgie Fame's record career with CBS was not quite as memorable as his days from 1964-66 had been with Columbia, but while there he did add his name to the still short (and then ever shorter) list of acts who have managed to go all the way to number one three times. Fame was the 17th to do it.

'The Ballad Of Bonnie And Clyde' was inspired by the film *Bonnie And Clyde*, which was a movie sensation of 1967. The Arthur Penn film starred Warren Beatty and Faye Dunaway as a glamorous pair of 1930s bankrobbers and was a huge box-office success around the world. British writers Mitch Murray (see nos. 152 and 152) and Peter Callender wrote a witty, jazz-flavoured pop song that gave away most of the film's plot in three minutes and it proved ideal for the Fame vocal style. It was also his biggest hit to date in the United States, reaching number seven. In both Britain and America it did considerably better on record than the music that was actually in the film, 'Foggy Mountain Breakdown', a guitar/banjo instrumental by bluegrass masters Lester Flatt and Earl Scruggs.

Since his third chart-topper, Fame's biggest single has been a 1971 duet with Alan Price, 'Rosetta'. He has become a highly regarded jazz and sophisticated pop vocalist, whose interpretation of the works of composers such as George Gershwin forms a major part of his contemporary stage act. He made a brief return to the pop charts in 1986 as a guest vocalist on 'New York Afternoon' by Mondo Kane.

243

EVERLASTING LOVE

THE LOVE AFFAIR

31 January 1968, for 2 weeks

●●

CBS 3125

Writers: Buzz Cason and Mac Gayden
Producer: Mike Smith

To cover this Robert Knight American hit, producer Mike Smith saw no reason to use the members of the teeny bop group Love Affair on the record. So, apart from lead singer Steve Ellis, Mike Smith used session musicians rather than the members of the group whose instrumental talents at the time were charitably described as limited. The roster of major hits whose credited performers were nowhere near the studio at the time is long and legendary, but to admit the practice in 1968 was daring. It made no difference, however, as the record made it all the way to the top. What was more amazing was that Love Affair, by now using a higher percentage of their membership on record, managed four more Top 20 hits before breaking up and fading further into the recesses of the pop archives.

Not that 'Everlasting Love' was a bad record. Far from it. Ellis had a powerful and expressive voice. Producer Mike Smith was enjoying his second consecutive number one, while CBS joined Philips, RCA and MGM in having consecutive catalogue numbers (CBS 3124 and 3125) at number one. CBS obviously liked the song. They reissued the Robert Knight original on their Monument label in 1974 and made the Top 20 with it. In 1981 a third CBS version of the song, this time by Rex Smith and Rachel Sweet, also hit the charts. This is the only time that there

have been as many as three chart versions of a song all from the same record company.

244

MIGHTY QUINN

MANFRED MANN

14 February 1968, for 2 weeks

●●

FONTANA TF 897

Writer: Bob Dylan
Producer: Mike Hurst

With the arrival of new vocalist, Old Harrovian and ex-Band Of Angels member Mike D'Abo, Manfred Mann changed record labels and began working with producer Mike Hurst, late of the Springfields. After three vocal Top 10ers and an instrumental hit, 'Sweet Pea', the group returned to the top for their third number one. Mann had already had hits with two other Dylan songs, 'If You Gotta Go Go Now' and 'Just Like A Woman', but 'Mighty Quinn' had lain incomplete on tape for months before Manfred could convince both producer and band that the song would make a hit single.

By now bassist Jack Bruce had left to form Cream, his replacement being Klaus Voorman, the longtime Beatles' friend and designer of their *Revolver* LP sleeve. But by 1969, after 17 hit singles, Manfred decided to dissolve the group and return to his first love, jazz. With Mike Hugg he created Emanon, which evolved into Manfred Mann Chapter Three. Then came a move into heavy rock via Manfred Mann's Earth Band and, between 1973 and 1979, five more Top 50 singles with Chris Thompson on vocals. One of these, a cover version of Bruce Springsteen's 'Blinded By The Light', gave the group something which the Boss has never had, a US number one.

'Hello Goodbye' – the BEATLES come in and out of view in a psychedelic way. (JVH)

245

CINDERELLA ROCKEFELLA

ESTHER AND ABI OFARIM

28 February 1968, for 3 weeks

●●●

PHILIPS BF 1640

Writer: Mason Williams
Producers: Abi Ofarim and Chaim Semel

Only two husband and wife teams have ever topped the charts, and such is the transitory nature of life that both couples are now divorced. Sonny and Cher split up amidst vast publicity, but Esther and Abi Ofarim managed to go their own ways comparatively quietly, some years after their big success.

Esther Ofarim was born Esther Zaled in Safed, Israel, on 13 June 1943, and her husband Abraham Reichstadt was born in Tel Aviv on 5 October 1939. Their marriage entitled Esther to leave the Israeli Army after serving only four months of her national service, and enabled the pair to concentrate on a musical career. By 1963 they were a top attraction in Israel and, rather confusingly, that year Esther represented Switzerland in the Eurovision Song Contest. Their reputation throughout Europe grew as they recorded in French, German and English as well as Hebrew, and by mid-1967 they were frequently appearing on television programmes throughout Europe. It was one such appearance on the *Eamonn Andrews Show* that brought 'Cinderella Rockefella' to the attention of the British public. The song had been written by Mason Williams, an American composer and guitarist who hit in Britain with his 'Classical Gas' later in 1968, and had been recorded by Esther and Abi in 1967. It was not issued as a single until early 1968, when public demand created the hit.

246

THE LEGEND OF XANADU

DAVE DEE, DOZY, BEAKY, MICK AND TICH

20 March 1968, for 1 week

•

FONTANA TF 903

Writers: Ken Howard and Alan Blaikley
Producer: Steve Rowland

Ken Howard and Alan Blaikely, whose knack for writing instantly memorable and entertainingly original pop songs brought them their first chart-topper in 1964 with the Honeycombs (see no. 176), had their greatest and longest-lasting run of pop success with a manically monikered group from Wiltshire previously named Dave Dee and the Bostons. Using the band's existing nicknames, Howard and Blaikley rechristened the group, who were ex-policeman Dave Dee (born David Harman, 17 December 1943), Dozy (born Trevor Davies, 27 November 1944), Beaky (born John Dymond, 10 July 1944), Mick (born Michael Wilson, 4 March 1944) and Tich (born Ian Amey, 15 May 1944).

Their first hit, 'You Make It Move', was followed by a similar sounding Top 10er, 'Hold Tight'. The early DD, D, B, M and T style consisted of shouted vocals and a heavy beat, which gradually evolved into a series of more intricate mini-epics of which 'Legend' was the masterpeice. They'd come close to the top before and surprised no one when 'Legend' went all the way. However, within a year their fortune changed, and by 1970 Dave Dee had split to have one solo hit, 'My Woman's Man', while D, B, M and T soldiered on, also scoring one hit, 'Mr President'. Dave Dee has been a recording executive with several companies, and the rest of the group, with a new Mick, are now based in their own club in Marbella, Spain.

247

LADY MADONNA

THE BEATLES

27 March 1968, for 2 weeks

••

PARLOPHONE R 5675

Writers: John Lennon and Paul McCartney
Producer: George Martin

The Beatles' final number one on the Parlophone label, their 14th number one in all, was by no means their most successful single. Certainly it reached the top, one place higher than Beatles' classics like 'Penny Lane'/'Strawberry Fields Forever' and 'Let It Be', but 'Lady Madonna' stayed on the chart for a total of only eight weeks, the shortest-lived Beatles single ever. At the time, only three other number one hits had stayed on the charts for eight weeks or less. Two of those were Christmas hits - Dickie Valentine's 'Christmas Alphabet' (see no. 40), which lasted only seven weeks on the chart, and Winifred Atwell's 'Let's Have Another Party' (see no. 26), which stuck around for eight weeks. The other short-running chart-topper was Frankie Laine's 'Hey Joe' (see no. 13), which hit the top when the chart was only a Top 12. So 'Lady Madonna' was, in reality, the least impressive, in chart terms, of all number one hits to that time. It is ironic that when finally a non-Christmas chart-topper lasted only seven weeks in the Top 75, it should have been Ferry Aid's version of a Beatles song that did not hit number one by the Fab Four, 'Let It Be' (see no. 588).

'Lady Madonna' did at least give the Beatles a second hat-trick of number ones, and three more were to follow on the Apple label. Between 'Hello Goodbye' and 'Lady Madonna', the double EP 'Magical Mystery Tour' had been released and climbed to number two. The set included one of the Beatles' most covered songs, 'Fool On The Hill', as well as their only instrumental release, 'Flying'. The critical reception of the *Magical Mystery Tour* TV film (it was panned), followed by the mediocre chart performance of 'Lady Madonna', made late 1967 and early '68 the low point of the Beatles' amazing career. For the Beatles, even a low point was a number one hit.

248

CONGRATULATIONS

CLIFF RICHARD

10 April 1968, for 2 weeks

●●

COLUMBIA DB 8376

Writers: Bill Martin and Phil Coulter
Producer: Norrie Paramor

Cliff Richard's first attempt to win the Eurovision Song Contest resulted in his first number one hit for three years, but not in a second consecutive Eurovision victory for Britain. The winner of the 1968 contest, held in London's Albert Hall on 6 April, was the Spanish songstress Massiel, whose 'La La La' pipped Cliff to the post amidst cries of protest from the British press about the tactical voting of some of the foreign delegations.

Not that it really mattered. 'Congratulations' was easily the biggest hit in Europe of all the Eurovision songs of 1968. Cliff eventually recorded 30 different versions of the song for release around the world. Eurovision beamed the contest to only 17 countries in 1968, despite this apparent overkill of languages. 'Congratulations' very quickly rolled to its first million sales. It was Cliff's 41st British single, and it proved to be his biggest worldwide seller to date, even reaching number 99 in the American Hot 100. In later years, both 'Devil Woman' and 'We Don't Talk Anymore' (see no. 441) overhauled the sales figures of 'Congratulations', but all the same it remains one of the biggest hits in the history of the Eurovision Song Contest.

249

WHAT A WONDERFUL WORLD/CABARET

LOUIS ARMSTRONG

24 April 1968, for 4 weeks

●●●●

HMV POP 1615

Writers: 'What A Wonderful World' – George David Weiss and George Douglas; 'Cabaret' – John Kander and Fred Ebb
Producer: Bob Thiele

Despite a remarkably strong rumour to the contrary, Armstrong's biographer James Lincoln Collier maintains that it is 'almost certainly untrue' that Daniel Louis Armstrong was born neatly on 4 July 1900. Collier maintains 'Satchmo' was born in 1898 on an unknown date (many Americans without an official birthday choose 4 July as a date of con venience). If, as seems likely, Collier is correct, then Armstrong was in fact just over 69 years old when he had his first number one, making him the oldest-ever artist to reach the top. It took Armstrong 15 years 127 days after his initial singles chart entry with 'Takes Two To Tango' to make the top. His American 1964 number one, 'Hello Dolly', peaked in Britian at number four.

Armstrong the musician and the man achieved far more than mere chart success, as an American at a time when the

USA was moving to the front of world events, as a black man who, during a period of increased black consciousness and liberation, rose from the background of poverty and a family of history of slavery to become an unofficial ambassador for his country, but more than anything as a magnificent jazz trumpeter and vocalist whose genius gave pleasure to millions for decades. Armstrong stands as a shining light in the cultural history of the 20th century.

'What A Wonderful World' received fresh exposure in America in 1988 through the movie *Good Morning Vietnam*.

250

YOUNG GIRL

THE UNION GAP featuring GARY PUCKETT

22 May 1968, for 4 weeks

●●●●

CBS 3365

Writer: Jerry Fuller
Producer: Jerry Fuller, with arrangement by Al Capps

The group that sold more singles than the Beatles in America in 1968 were led by a man who spent his childhood in Hibbing, Minnesota, the same town that was home to the young Bob Zimmermann, aka Bob Dylan. The group were billed as Union Gap on their first chart hit, 'Woman Woman', but, like the Supremes and the First Edition, they subsequently changed the billing on the record label to feature their lead singer more prominently as their success grew. 'Young Girl' was their second hit, and by the time they hit the charts for a third time, the outfit was known as Gary Puckett and the Union Gap.

Whatever the billing, the line-up was the same for all the singles. Gary Puckett was the vocalist, Dwight Bement played bass, Canadian Kerry Chater handled rhythm guitar duties, Paul Whitbread was the drummer and Gary Withem played keyboards. They wore American Civil War uniforms and gave themselves military ranks (from General Puckett down to Privates Whitbread and Withem) to remind their more erudite fans that they had taken their name from the site of a famous Civil War battle.

The group got together in San Diego, California, in 1967, and through producer and songwriter Jerry Fuller, who auditioned them one night in a bowling alley, they landed a recording contract almost immediately. Within a few months of formation they had received their first gold disc, for 'Woman Woman', and throughout 1968 their bandwagon rolled unstoppably along. It all ground to a halt in 1969.

251

JUMPING JACK FLASH

THE ROLLING STONES

19 June 1968, for 2 weeks

●●

DECCA F 12782

Writers: Mick Jagger and Keith Richard
Producer: Jimmy Miller

This was the Stones' first number one for two years, but what a record! To get the summer parties of 1968 going (in those pre-disco days) all you needed were copies of 'Simon Says' by the 1910 Fruitgum Co., 'Son Of Hickory Holler's Tramp' by O.C. Smith, and this one. Thirteen years later, 'Jumping Jack Flash' was still the number used by the Stones to close the show on their American tour, still the number the fans were waiting for.

The first batch of the Rolling Stones drug problems were over by now, certainly for Mick Jagger and Keith Richard, whose jail sentences of one year and three months respectively (imposed in June 1967) had been overturned on appeal. Brian Jones also had a nine-month jail sentence reduced on appeal to merely a fine, but the strain of the court appearances told on him, an asthmatic, more than on the others. He spent much of the early part of 1968 in hospitals trying to recover his fitness, both mental and physical, but in May 1968, just a few days before the release of 'Jumping Jack Flash', he was arrested once again on drugs charges. Exactly a year after the single dropped from the top he drowned in his swimming pool. By that time he had already

From humble beginnings as a Butlin's Red Coat in the early 50s, DES O'CONNOR went on to top the hit parade in July 1968. (Pictorial Press)

left the Stones, but had shown few signs of sorting out his problems.

252

BABY COME BACK

THE EQUALS

3 July 1968, for 3 weeks

●●●

PRESIDENT PT 135

Writer: Eddy Grant
Producer: Ed Kassner

If anyone could be dubbed the 'leader' of a group called the Equals then it was vocalist Derv Gordon who, with his guitarist twin brother Lincoln, was born in Kingston, Jamaica, on 29 June 1948. The other Equals were guitarist Eddie Grant (born Guyana, 5 March 1948), drummer John Hall (born London, England, 25 October 1947) and guitarist Pat Lloyd (born London, England, 17 March 1948).

The Equals had spent two years recording ska/pop tunes for President Records with some European success when an old song, 'I Get So Excited', became a minor UK hit. Then 'Baby Come Back' was re-released, providing the label with its only number one to date. Other hits followed, including 'Viva Bobby Joe' and 'Black Skinned Blue Eyed Boys'. The group then became embroiled in a long legal dispute with President, making it impossible for them to release any records. After an out-of-court settlement the group resumed work, but the damage had been done. The Equals had been forgotten, but one member, Eddie Grant, eventually more than matched the band's achievements with his own pop/reggae material (see no. 510).

253

I PRETEND

DES O'CONNOR

24 July 1968, for 1 week

●

COLUMBIA DB 8397

Writers: Les Reed and Barry Mason
Producer: Norman Newell

The talents of songwriters Reed and Mason had already assisted the careers of Tom Jones and Engelbert Humperdinck before lifting comedian and compere Des O'Connor (born Stepney, London, January 1932) to the top.

O'Connor was an all-round entertainer who made his show business debut in October 1953 at the Palace Theatre, Newcastle, after a spell working as a Butlin's Red Coat. He played a minor part in the history of rock'n'roll by virtue of the fact that in 1958 he was the linkman on the only British tour undertaken by Buddy Holly. In the early 60s he was the compere of TV's *Sunday Night At The London Palladium*, one of the most popular variety shows of the era. By 1963 he'd been given his own TV series, an excellent vehicle for promoting his vocal prowess, but it wasn't until the final weeks of 1967 that his records began to sell. In a hitmaking career of just over three years he managed seven Top 30 hits, including the unforgettable 'Dick-A-Dum-Dum' and the nostalgic '1-2-3 O'Leary', in which the world 'O'Leary' is made to rhyme with 'Mary'. The ballad 'I Pretend' stayed on the charts for 36 weeks, a total bettered by only five other number one singles. It was the seventh and final number one production by Norman Newell.

254

MONY MONY

TOMMY JAMES AND THE SHONDELLS

31 July 1968, for 2 weeks

••

and 21 August 1968, for 1 week

•

MAJOR MINOR MM 567

Writers: Bobby Bloom, Bo Gentry, Tommy James and Richie Cordell
Producers: Bo Gentry and Richie Cordell

Tommy James (born Tommy Jackson, 29 April 1946, Dayton, Ohio) and the Shondells first graced the UK charts in 1966 with their US number one, 'Hanky Panky', which climbed to a more modest 38 while the English football team were winning the World Cup. 'Mony Mony' was their only other British chart entry, but it was a big hit. In America they were vastly more popular, with 19 hit singles between 'Hanky Panky' in 1966 and 'Come To Me' in 1970.

The Shondells, originally named the Raconteurs, were from Pittsburgh. They were Mike Vale (bass), Pete Lucia (drums), Eddie Gray (not the Leeds United footballer) (guitar) and Ronnie Rosman (organ). James and the group parted company in 1969 and that was the last the charts anywhere heard of the Shondells. James has had 13 solo US hits since 1970, but only one, 'Draggin' The Line', made the Top 10.

'Mony Mony' lives on as a standard rock'n'roll dance number, and Billy Idol brought it back to the Top 10 in 1987. Other James/Shondells hits have been given new leases of life over the years, such as 'I Think We're Alone Now' by Tiffany in 1987/88 and 'Crimson & Clover' by Joan Jett and the Blackhearts in 1982.

255

FIRE

THE CRAZY WORLD OF ARTHUR BROWN

14 August 1968, for 1 week

•

TRACK 604022

Writers: Vincent Crane, Arthur Brown, Peter Ker and Michael Finesilver
Producer: Kit Lambert

When Arthur Brown (born 24 June 1944) and his manager Vincent Crane wrote 'Fire' and built a stage act featuring facial make-up, a burning hat and many stage effects which later lived on through Alice Cooper and others, they hoped they were creating a hit and launching Brown on a successful chart career. On both points they were wrong. Yes, the song was a hit, but two other writers, Peter Ker and Michael Finesilver, sued successfully to show that 'Fire' was not an original creation but a variation of their song 'Fire'. Furthermore, the song was Brown's only hit, and he never really set the world alight as successfully as he had his hat. The *New Statesman*, no less, thought that, "Arthur Brown could easily be the first genuine artist to come out of our local underground. He's disconcerting, even faintly perverse, but distinctly original and very, very English." But once again the *New Statesman* merely showed that its finger was not really on the pulse of British popular music, not even at their local underground.

The record was produced by the late Kit Lambert, manager of the Who. On Arthur Brown's LP, associate producer credits went to Pete Townshend of the Who, but the official producer of the single was Lambert, who owned the Track label.

256

DO IT AGAIN

THE BEACH BOYS

28 August 1968, for 1 week

•

CAPITOL CL 15554

Writers: Brian Wilson and Mike Love
Producer: Brian Wilson

The LP *Sergeant Pepper's Lonely Hearts Club Band* may have been the peak of the Beatles' recording career but it played a part in the downfall of the Beach Boys. Brian Wilson, who had seen the Beatles as rivals, suffered a mental breakdown following the relative commerical failure of his group's *Pet Sounds* album in America. Under his direction the Beach Boys had drifted away from their surfing image into more esoteric and less commercial

The BEACH BOYS had one number one in both Britain and America after 'Good Vibrations' topped both charts, but the later successes, 'Do It Again' and 'Kokomo' were 20 years apart. (Pictorial Press)

waters. This proved too much for some fans to swallow, and the band's popularity waned in the USA after their number one hit 'Good Vibrations'.

Support held up well in the UK, however. A track taken from their 1966 *Summer Days* album, 'Then She Kissed Me', went Top 10 in 1967, as did the rather muddled Brian Wilson creation 'Heroes and Villians'. Three more medium-sized hits followed before 'Do It Again', a nostalgic look back at days of sun and surf, surprised even Beach Boy fans by snatching seven days of chart heaven.

In the late summer of 1987, the Beach Boys climbed back up to number two as guest artists on the Fat Boys' rap version of the Surfaris' 1963 instrumental hit, 'Wipe Out'. Always a major concert attraction, the Beach Boys have continued as living legends to this day, both home and away, although this is sadly not true in the case of Dennis, who drowned off Marina Del Rey, California, in 1983.

257

I'VE GOTTA GET A MESSAGE TO YOU

THE BEE GEES

4 September 1968, for 1 week

•

POLYDOR 56 273

Writers: Barry, Robin and Maurice Gibb
Producers: Robert Stigwood and the Bee Gees

A critic once observed that the Bee Gees of the late 60s were a gloomy bunch. When asked by Barry Gibb what songs could be cited to justify this remark, he replied, "'New York Mining Disaster 1941' ...'I've Gotta Get A Message To You..." And that's it!" Barry concluded.

The critic could be forgiven for having been overly affected by the two singles. They both concerned personal dilemmas of a desperate nature, the first that of a miner trapped below the surface and the second that of a killer who is about to be executed. At least the Gibbs were romantic to the end: both men facing death wanted to communicate with their women.

'I've Gotta Get A Message To You' came at a crucial time for the Bee Gees. After hitting the American Top 20 with their first five singles there and the British equivalent with four out of the first five UK releases, they had suffered their first international miss, 'Jumbo'. 'Message' proved them more than one-year wonders, marking their breakthrough to the US Top 10 and their return to the number one spot in Britain.

258

HEY JUDE

THE BEATLES

11 September 1968, for 2 weeks

••

APPLE R 5722

Writers: John Lennon and Paul McCartney
Producer: George Martin

This song was inspired by Paul McCartney's fondness for Julian Lennon, son of John and Cynthia. While driving to Cynthia's house for a visit after she and John had broken up, he started singing 'Hey Jules'. He changed the title to 'Hey Jude', thinking Jude a name with a more singable flavour than Jules. Paul was uncertain about some of the lyric's obscure lines, such as 'the movement you need is on your shoulder', but John and Yoko Ono considered them marvellously avant garde.

The Beatles' 15th number one, 'Hey Jude' was the longest chart-topper ever, at approximately seven minutes and ten seconds. It ruled the roost for nine weeks in the US, the Beatles' longest run at number one, but was cut short after two weeks in the UK by McCartney's own production, 'Those Were The Days' by Mary Hopkin.

'Hey Jude' was the initial offering on the Beatles' Apple label, part of a debut issue of four. Despite being the first single for the company, it retained Parlophone's numbering system. Wilson Pickett scored a Top 20 hit with his soulful cover version mere months later, and 'Hey Jude' became the title track of an American anthology of Beatles singles.

259

THOSE WERE THE DAYS

MARY HOPKIN

25 September 1968, for 6 weeks

●●●●●●

APPLE 2

Writers: Gene Raskin and Alexander Vertinski
Producer: Paul McCartney

Mary Hopkin (born 3 May 1950, Pontardawe, Wales) was one of a number of acts who found fame following an appearance on a TV talent show. Sixties model and future chart star Twiggy telephoned Paul McCartney after seeing Hopkin win a round of *Opportunity Knocks*. She was immediately signed to the Beatles' Apple label.

It was McCartney who chose to record 'Those Were The Days', a Russian folk song entitled 'Darogoi Dlimmoyo (Dear For Me)' written by Alexander Vertinski with English lyrics by American Gene Raskin. After its release on 16 August, it climbed the charts and toppled her mentor's single, 'Hey Jude', from the summit. Technically, this cannot be included on the list of those instances where consecutive label catalogue numbers have appeared at number one because in June EMI and Apple and agreed that all future Beatles discs would appear on the Apple label with Parlophone numbers. Nonethless 'Hey Jude' was definitely Apple 1 in all but number.

'Those Were The Days' sold four million worldwide and was Hopkin's biggest success. Her follow up was a McCartney composition, 'Goodbye', but this time the Beatles' own 'Get Back' won out, keeping Hopkin in second place. Her debut album, *Postcard*, contained neither of these tracks but did include a version of Ray Noble's 'Love Is The Sweetest Thing', which Peter Skellern took to number 60 in 1978. After a number of years out of the limelight, Hopkin was telephoned by Skellern in 1983 and asked to join his group Oasis, which also comprised Julian Lloyd Webber, Mitch Dalton, and Bill Lovelady. Despite the impressive line-up they produced no hit singles.

260

WITH A LITTLE HELP FROM MY FRIENDS

JOE COCKER

6 November 1968, for 1 week

●

REGAL ZONOPHONE RZ 3013

Writers: John Lennon and Paul McCartney
Producer: Denny Cordell

Ex-gas fitter Joe Cocker (born John Cocker, Sheffield, 20 May 1944) is respected as one of the world's greatest rock vocalists. Few could have so successfully turned this singalong track of the Beatles' *Sergeant Pepper* LP into a soulful ballad.

Cocker had formed his first band, an R&B combo called Vance Arnold and the Avengers, in 1963. The following year he cut his first single, a version of the Beatles' 'I'll Cry Instead', using the name Joe Cocker. Working with numerous musicians he became well known on the London club circuit, gaining the attention of Eric Clapton and Jimi Hendrix. Having recorded 'Marjorine', a mildly successful single, with Procol Harum's producer Denny Cordell, Cocker decided to record the stage favourite 'With A Little Help From My Friends'. The musicians who can be heard on this track are guitarist Jimmy Page, drummer B.J. Wilson, plus bassist Chris Stainton and keyboard player Tom Eyre of Cocker's Grease Band. The backing singers were Madeline Bell, Rosetta Hightower and Sunny Wheetman.

Top 40 hits 'Delta Lady' and 'The Letter' followed, and a memorable appearance at the 1969 Woodstock Festival confirmed Cocker as a major talent. For a while he seemed destined for superstardom, but the singer hid himself away for most of 1970, unhappy with the pressures of fame.

He returned to record with the likes of Albert Lee and Leon Russell, but was not to have another UK hit single until he teamed up with Jennifer Warnes to sing 'Up Where We Belong', the theme to the 1982 film *An Officer And A Gentleman*. This duet reached the Top 10 in 1983.

In 1987 his revival of Ray Charles' 'Unchain My Heart' began a new sequence of solo hits.

261

THE GOOD THE BAD AND THE UGLY

HUGO MONTENEGRO AND HIS ORCHESTRA AND CHORUS

13 November 1968, for 4 weeks

●●●●

RCA 1727

Writer: Ennio Morricone
Producer: Hugo Montenegro

'The Good The Bad And The Ugly' was the first instrumental number one since 3 April 1963, when the Shadows' 'Foot Tapper' gave way four weeks before the Beatles had their first chart-topper. It had as its unlikley birthplace a spaghetti western starring Clint Eastwood. Montenegro himself was born in New York in 1925, but moved to California after serving in the US Navy and became known for the scores to films such as *Hurry Sundown* and TV series like *The Man From U.N.C.L.E.* He also acted as arranger and conductor for label mate Harry Belafonte.

'The Good The Bad And The Ugly' featured Elliott Fisher on electric violin, Manny Klein on piccolo trumpet, Tommy Morgan on electronic harmonica and Arthur Smith on ocarina, the instrument that produced the haunting introduction to the record. The grunting noises were by Ron Hicklin, who led the chorus. Whistler Muzzy Marcellino also featured on the record.

Hugo Montenegro managed to avoid the stigma of being a one-hit wonder on 8 January 1969, when his theme to Clint Eastwood's next spaghetti western, 'Hang 'Em High', reached number 50, only to disappear from the charts the next week.

262

LILY THE PINK

THE SCAFFOLD

11 December 1968, for 3 weeks

●●●

and 8 January 1969, for 1 week

●

PARLOPHONE R 5734

Writers: John Gorman, Mike McGear and Roger McGough
Producer: Norrie Paramor

The Scaffold were Liverpudlians John Gorman, poet Roger McGough and Paul McCartney's younger brother Michael, who called himself Mike McGear. They first hit the charts with 'Thank U Very Much', a Top 5 hit at Christmas 1967 with the enigmatic first line, "Thank U very much for the Aintree Iron". Other equally unusual singles, like 'Today's Monday', failed completely, but at Christmas in 1968 they achieved their only number one, the saga of Lily The Pink and her medicinal compound.

It was the late Norrie Paramor's final number one production, his 27th, a total which is still the record today. At the time it meant that he had produced slightly more than one in ten number one hits, a phenomenal achievement. It was Paramor's only number one as an independent producer after years as a staff producer at EMI. Uncredited vocals in the background in the verse about Jennifer Eccles and her terrible freckles were by Graham Nash of the Hollies, whose single 'Jennifer Eccles' had been a Top 10 hit earlier that year. Also on background vocals was Norrie Paramor's production assistant, Tim Rice. The production had been completed, ready to be pressed, when Mike McGear decided that what it really needed was a bass drum. The drum was added, the tape remixed and the single sold a million. Without that bass drum, would it have hit the charts quite so hard? Nobody will ever know.

263

OB-LA-DI OB-LA-DA

MARMALADE

1 January 1969, for 1 week

•

and 15 January 1969, for 2 weeks

••

CBS 3892

Writers: John Lennon and Paul McCartney
Producer: Mike Smith

The Beatles had released five singles and an EP since February 1967, none of which appeared on a UK album. Three tracks on side one of *The Beatles* double album, released in 1968, would have made good singles: 'While My Guitar Gently Weeps', 'Back In The USSR' (which eventually made the Top 20 when released in 1976) and the reggae-tinged 'Ob-La-Di Ob-La-Da'. It was left to this Scottish group to take the latter tune to the top of the pile.

Marmalade grew out of the band Dean Ford and the Gaylords, formed in 1961. The line-up in 1968 was vocalist Dean Ford (born Tom McAleese, 5 September 1946), guitarists Junior Campbell (born 31 May 1947) and Pat Fairley (born 14 April 1946), bassist Graham Knight (born 8 December 1946) and drummer Alan Whitehead (born 24 July 1946). This quintet had eight Top 30 hits, including 'Reflections Of My Life' and 'Rainbow', both of which hit number three. The group became the toast of Thailand following the Bangkok Music Festival in 1971, before songwriter Campbell left for a mildy successful solo career. Fellow Scot Hughie Nicholson was brought in and three more hits ensued, but by 1974 only Dean Ford remained from the original Marmalade line-up.

Graham Knight returned in 1976 to help the group to one more success with the Macaulay/Greenway song 'Falling Apart At The Seams', by which time even Ford had left. With various personnel the group continued into the 80s, at one point attempting a comeback with a medley of their old hits called 'Golden Shreds'.

264

ALBATROSS

FLEETWOOD MAC

29 January 1969, for 1 week

•

BLUE HORIZON 57 3145

Writer: Peter Green
Producer: Mike Vernon

When guitar virtuoso Peter Green left John Mayall's Bluesbreakers in 1967 (he had originally been recruited to replace Eric Clapton), he invited drummer Mick Fleetwood (who had played a very brief stint with Mayall), bassist John McVie, and guitarists Jeremy Spencer and Danny Kirwan to join him in a group which was originally known as Peter Green's Fleetwood Mac. The hits followed, including this beautiful instrumental which has twice been a massive UK seller. It returned to the charts in 1975, failing by just one place to become the first re-issued chart-topper to make number one again. Then, in 1970, Green left the group in a whirl of religious, moral and personal dilemmas. In 1971 Spencer, an avid New Testament reader who had once got the group banned from the Marquee club by going on stage with a wooden dildo hanging from his fly, disappeared a couple of hours before a gig in LA and was found later in the week with the Children Of God religious sect.

Fleetwood and McVie brought in vocalist Christine Perfect, who became John McVie's wife. After more personnel changes they enlisted the American duo Lindsay Buckingham and Stevie Nicks.

Massive success followed, with the zenith being the huge-selling album *Rumours* in 1977. In 1987 Lindsay Buckingham left the group to go solo.

265

BLACKBERRY WAY

THE MOVE

5 February 1969, for 1 week

●

REGAL ZONOPHONE RZ 3015

Writer: Roy Wood
Producer: Jimmy Miller

In the mid-60s the Cedar Club was the favourite haunt of all the local groups from the Birmingham area. It was here that the Move was formed. Roy Wood (born 8 November 1948), Carl Wayne (born 18 August 1944), Curtis 'Ace' Kefford (born 24 November 1946), Bev Bevan (born 24 November 1944) and Trevor Burton (born 9 March 1949) had all appeared in various Birmingham outfits, but none had gained national fame.

The group moved to London, became a regular act at the Marquee and signed with manager Tony Secunda. Their new-wave sound and sensational TV appearances, in which they smashed TVs, cars and effigies of Hitler, brought attention to their early singles, and the first four all made the Top 10. One of them, 'Flowers In The Rain', gained immortality as the first record ever played on Radio One. In spring 1968, Kefford left, suffering from nervous exhaustion, but the group decided against bringing in a new member. Instead Burton switched from guitar to bass. 'Wild Tiger Woman' became their first flop in the summer, and the band threatened to call it a day if their next single didn't fare any better.

The next release was 'Blackberry Way'. Written – like all their previous hits – by Roy Wood, and with Richard Tandy joining the band for this one record playing keyboards, the song gave the Move their only number one.

Early in 1970, Wayne left following a disagreement over whether or not the group should continue a season of cabaret. He was replaced by Jeff Lynne. By 1972, the Move's final year, the group consisted of Wood, Bevan and Lynne. Their final LP, *Message From The Country*, featuring oboes, violins and flutes, underlined their new and experimental direction. This trio formed the nucleus of the Electric Light Orchestra, and in July 1972 the Move's last single was slipping down the charts as ELO's first single climbed them.

266

(IF PARADISE IS) HALF AS NICE

AMEN CORNER

12 February 1969, for 2 weeks

●●

IMMEDIATE IM 073

Writers: Lucio Battisti; English lyrics by Jack Fishman
Producer: Shel Talmy

Amen Corner were under the control of Welshman Andy Fairweather-Low and comprised Dennis Byron (drums), Alan Jones and Mike Smith (saxophones), Neil Jones (guitar), Clive Taylor (bass) and Blue Weaver (keyboards). Their producer Shel Talmy worked with the Who, the Kinks, the Easybeats and Manfred Mann before leaving the record industry in the early 70s to write a novel, *The Ichabod Deception*.

Based in Cardiff, the band first sprang to prominence with the blues-based hit 'Gin House', which climbed to number 12 in 1967. Their style changed to bubblegum pop and they made numbers three and six in 1968 with 'Bend Me Shape Me' and 'High In The Sky' respectively. The following year, after changing labels from the Decca subsidiary Deram to Immediate, they scored their only number one.

The follow-up single, 'Hello Suzie', made number four in June of the same year, but there were no more hits, although a reissue of their chart-topper staggered to number 34 in 1976. Fairweather-Low had solo success in the 70s with the Top 10 singles 'Wide Eyed And Legless' and 'Natural Sinner'.

267

WHERE DO YOU GO TO, MY LOVELY?

PETER SARSTEDT

26 February 1969, for 4 weeks

●●●●

UNITED ARTISTS UP 2262

Writer: Peter Sarstedt
Producer: Ray Singer

Peter Sarstedt's elder brother Richard had already had a number one hit, 'Well I Ask You' (see no. 122), in 1961, when he sang under the name Eden Kane. Seven and a half years later, Sarstedt was perfectly acceptable as a rock star's surname, especially one who sang so wistfully of the jet set and the meaning of life, so Peter resisted the temptation to become Peter Kane. All the same, he and Richard established a record that has only once been equalled. They were the first brothers to have separate solo number ones in Britain, a record that was equalled by Donny and Little Jimmy Osmond at the end of 1972. Paul McCartney and his brother Mike McGear have also had separate number one hits, but McGear's was as part of a group. The same thing goes for Michael Jackson and his many brothers.

In 1976, the third Sarstedt brother, Clive (for some reason calling himself Robin for recording purposes), reached number three with his version of Hoagy Carmichael's 'My Resistance Is Low', enabling the Sarstedt clan to become the only three brothers in British chart history to rack up separate solo hits. The Osmonds and the Jacksons (two brothers and a sister each with solo hits) come close to the Sarstedt record, as do the Gibbs, of whom Andy and Robin have hit as soloists, while Barry has charted in partnership with Barbra Streisand. But no family has yet quite matched the Sarstedt achievement.

268

I HEARD IT THROUGH THE GRAPEVINE

MARVIN GAYE

26 March 1969, for 3 weeks

●●●

TAMLA MOTOWN TMG 686

Writers: Norman Whitfield and Barrett Strong
Producer: Norman Whitfield

Marvin Gaye (born Marvin Pentz Gay, 2 April 1939) was not the only Motown act to record 'Grapevine'. The Miracles and the Isley Brothers both attempted it before him, the Temptations and the Undisputed Truth after him. It was Gladys Knight and the Pips, however, who produced the first hit version in 1967 when their gospel-flavoured interpretation gave them a minor UK chart entry and a US number two smash. Though not a *Billboard* number one, it was Motown's biggest American seller at that time.

The strength of the song was proved by Gaye's deeply soulful rendition on his *In The Groove* LP, producing a classic single whose US sales surpassed even Knight's record. Gaye had been an underrated artist in the UK, where his greatest success had been a 1967 Top 20 duet with Kim Weston, 'It Takes Two'. In America he'd been charting regularly since 1962, with songs such as 'Stubborn Kind Of Fellow' and 'How Sweet It Is'. Then came 'Grapevine' and other successes, including his only UK Top 10 hit after splitting from Motown, 1982's 'Sexual Healing'. His 1973 winner, 'Let's Get It On', replaced his 'Grapevine' as Motown's best seller in America.

During an argument on 1 April 1984, Marvin Gaye Sr shot his son dead, one day before the singer's 45th birthday. 'Grapevine' returned to the British Top 10 in 1986, revitalized by its use in a Levi's jeans commercial.

269

THE ISRAELITES

DESMOND DEKKER AND THE ACES

16 April 1969, for 1 week

•

PYRAMID PYR 6058

Writers: Desmond Dekker and Leslie Kong
Producer: Leslie Kong

Discounting Marmalade's version of Lennon and McCartney's 'Ob-La-Di Ob-La-Da', 'The Israelites' was reggae's first number one and Desmond Dekker was the genre's first international star.

This New York portrait of MARVIN GAYE wound up on the sleeve of his posthumous 1985 CD, *Marvin Gaye And His Women*. (Pictorial Press)

Dekker, born Desmond Dacres in Kingston, Jamaica, on 16 July 1941, was a former welder who joined Jamaican studio group the Aces in the mid-60s. Their 1967 debut UK hit, '007 (Shanty Town)', was produced by Dekker's musical mentor, the Chinese/Jamaican Leslie Kong. The Aces scored a string of successes in their homeland from 1967 to '69, while in Britain it looked as if '007 (Shanty Town)' would be a one-off hit. Then came 'The Israelites', which also achieved Top 10 status in the USA, a rare achievement for a reggae song at that time.

Dekker came close to topping the chart again in 1970 when his song 'You Can Get It If You Really Want', from the film *The Harder They Come*, went to number two, denied the ultimate glory by Freda Payne. In 1971, Leslie Kong died of a heart attack, an event which sent Dekker's career into decline. Despite two Top 20 hits in 1975, 'Sing A Little Song' and a reissue of his number one, Dekker had by then been replaced as the king of reggae by fellow Jamaican Bob Marley. However, 'The Israelites' continued to earn Dekker a lot of money well into the 90s as the tune behind the Vitalite margarine television advertisement.

270

GET BACK

THE BEATLES with BILLY PRESTON

23 April 1969, for 6 weeks

●●●●●●

APPLE R 5777

Writers: John Lennon and Paul McCartney
Producer: George Martin

After 13 consecutive number ones that reached the top in their second week on the charts, the Beatles finally came straight into the chart at number one with a song performed live on the roof of the Apple offices in London in February 1969. The version which was released was not recorded on the roof: it was produced, as usual, by George Martin at Abbey Road.

Billy Preston, who joined Tony Sheridan as the only individuals to have a performing credit on a Beatles' single, was born in Houston, Texas, on 9 September 1946. He had, by 1969, established a reputation as a brilliant session keyboards man, and it was George Harrison who brought him into the Beatles empire. John Lennon said of Billy Preston, "We might have had him in the group," but the group was already breaking up.

Preston put out a brilliant single on Apple in mid-1969, 'That's The Way God Planned It', which made number 11. Despite vocal and instrumental number ones in America in the early 70s, he faded chartwise in Britain until the beginning of 1980 when the born-again Christian reached number two in duet with Stevie Wonder's ex-wife, Syreeta, with the aptly titled 'With You I'm Born Again'.

271

DIZZY

TOMMY ROE

4 June 1969, for 1 week

●

STATESIDE SS 2143

Writers: Tommy Roe and Freddy Weller
Producer: Steve Barri

Thomas David Roe, born in Atlanta, Georgia, on 9 May 1942, was one of the rank of pop stars who admit that their biggest influence was Buddy Holly. 'Dizzy' was a brilliant piece of bubblegum pop, but early Tommy Roe hits, especially his first, 'Sheila', were virtual duplications of Buddy Holly's phrasing, arrangements and sound. His first break came when, like Bobby Vee, he was asked to stand in on a date which Buddy Holly had been booked for, and a year later Roe recorded and released 'Sheila' on the tiny Judd label in Georgia. The record failed to attract any interest, but within two years Roe had signed with ABC-Paramount, who re-recorded and re-

After his pop success ended, TOMMY ROE had country hits through the 80s. (Pictorial Press)

released 'Sheila'. This time it was a hit and Roe was on his way.

His career was not very consistent after that; there were some big hits, like 'The Folk Singer' in 1963 in Britain, and 'Sweet Pea' and 'Hooray For Hazel' in 1966 in the States, but a lot of failures until Roe and Freddie Weller wrote 'Dizzy'. Roe thus had his first number one seven years after his first hit. Co-writer Weller is now a country singer after a spell as one of Paul Revere's Raiders.

272

THE BALLAD OF JOHN AND YOKO

THE BEATLES

11 June 1969, for 3 weeks

●●●

APPLE R 5786

Writers: John Lennon and Paul McCartney
Producers: George Martin and the Beatles

The last number one hit by the Fab Four in fact featured a Fab Two, as only John and Paul actually played on 'The Ballad Of John And Yoko', a hastily concocted, but irresistibly catchy, paean to some of the then recent events of John Lennon's life, the principal one being his marriage to the avant-garde Japanese artist Yoko Ono.

The chorus had lines like "Christ, you know it ain't easy" and "The way things are going/They're going to crucify me", which immediately caused the media to criticize the increasingly erratic Lennon, and to raise again the furore caused by his "We're bigger than Jesus" remark in America a few years earlier. Not that this bothered the Beatles. By the time this record was released they had all but split up. The later singles 'Something' and 'Let It Be' were both recorded before 'The Ballad Of John And Yoko', which, incidentally, was the 14th of the Beatles' 17 number ones to reach the top in its second week on the chart.

And so the Beatles' reign of unprecedented success was over. John and Yoko climbed into their bag, Paul married Linda, George dug deeper into Indian music and Ringo went into films. Despite the brilliance and phenomenal success of many of their individual records since 1969, nothing has recreated the magic that 'the new Beatles single' always did.

273

SOMETHING IN THE AIR

THUNDERCLAP NEWMAN

2 July 1969, for 3 weeks

●●●

TRACK 604 031

Writer: Speedy Keen
Producer: Pete Townshend

This hit made Pete Townshend the only member of the original Who to have any connection with a number one single. The nearest his group ever came was number two with their 1965 song 'My Generation'.

"Before I met Peter I knew nothing," admitted the former pub pianist and Bix Beiderbecke fan Andy 'Thunderclap' Newman. Vocalist and drummer Speedy Keen had first met the Who in Ealing, London, when they were known as the High Numbers. They had remained firm friends and a Keen composition, 'Armenia, City In The Sky', even appeared on the 1968 *The Who Sell Out* album. The third member of Thunderclap Newman was guitarist Jimmy McCulloch, who later joined Wings. He died in 1979.

Townshend also produced 'Accidents', the follow-up to 'Something In The Air',

which lasted just one week in the Top 50. The group split up soon after. Keen released an interesting, though unsuccessful, album, *Previous Convictions*, and Newman took up the saxophone and returned to the pub circuit.

274

HONKY TONK WOMEN

THE ROLLING STONES

23 July 1969, for 5 weeks

●●●●●

DECCA F 12952

Writers: Mick Jagger and Keith Richard
Producer: Jimmy Miller

Just three weeks afer the last Beatles chart-topper slid from the number one position, the last Rolling Stones number

The members of THUNDERCLAP NEWMAN (left to right: Speedy Keen, Jimmy McCulloch and Andy 'Thunderclap' Newman) broke all records for looking incongruous together. (Pictorial Press)

one (so far) took over. They went out with a bang, at least, as five weeks was their longest-ever run at number one.

The Stones' chart career is amazing in its consistency. Eight number ones put them fifth on the all-time list, but their unbeaten record is that over a period of 14 years and 8 months, every single official release by the Rolling Stones made the Top 10. When 'Respectable' peaked at number 23 in late 1978, it marked the first time that the Stones had missed the Top 10 since 'I Wanna Be Your Man' peaked at number 12 at the end of 1963. It was also the lowest chart placing they had ever had, apart from a Decca cash-in single of 'Out Of Time', in a 15-year career. But they were still making Top 10 hits in the 1980s.

'Honky Tonk Women' was the only Stones number one after Brian Jones left the group, 20 days before 'Honky Tonk Women' reached the top. The replacement Stone on this record is Mick Taylor (born 17 January 1941), who came from John Mayall's Bluesbreakers. Taylor left the Stones at the end of 1974, and his replacement was, and still is, Ronnie Wood from the Faces.

275

IN THE YEAR 2525 (EXORDIUM AND TERMINUS)

ZAGER AND EVANS

30 August 1969, for 3 weeks

●●●

RCA 1860

Writer: Rick Evans
Producers: Denny Zager and Rick Evans

The record that gave way to the Rolling Stones at the top of the American charts also took over from them in Britain. One of the weirdest and therefore best-known one-hit-wonder records in British pop history, 'In The Year 2525' was a bleak vision of man's future written by Evans in half an hour one day in Lincoln, Nebraska. Denny Zager (born 1944) and Rick Evans (born 1943) had originally been part of a group called the Eccentrics, a country outfit from Nebraska, but had been performing as a duo for some years before the success of 'In The Year 2525'. In November 1968, they borrowed $500 to record the song in Texas. They formed their own company, and hawked the initial pressing of 1000 copies around record shops and local radio stations. They sent copies of the record to all the major record companies as well, but it was RCA in New York that took the bait, and signed Zager and Evans to a national deal.

The result was a national release in June 1969 and a number one hit in America by July. In the UK, it also hit the top very quickly, but the duo disappeared just as fast, to join the growing list of one-hit wonders. Exordium and Terminus.

276

BAD MOON RISING

CREEDENCE CLEARWATER REVIVAL

20 September 1969, for 3 weeks

●●●

LIBERTY LBF 15230

Writer: John Fogerty
Producer: John Fogerty

At the time of 'Bad Moon Rising', Creedence Clearwater Revival consisted of John Fogerty (born 28 May 1945), brother Tom (born 9 November 1941), Doug Clifford (born 24 April 1945) and Stu Cook (born 25 April 1945). Their debut UK hit had been 'Proud Mary', the saga of a Mississippi paddlesteamer. It had climbed to number eight and would eventually become their best-known composition, partly through inclusion in Elvis Presley's stage repertoire and a successful reworking by Ike and Tina Turner which cracked the US Top 5 in 1971.

Creedence were at their best live and had appeared at the Denver Pop Festival, the Atlanta Pop Festival and the Atlantic City Pop Festival within the space of five weeks during the summer of 1969. Then came 'Bad Moon Rising', the second of three consecutive number two hits in their native USA, where they never enjoyed a number one single. All the same, for a few months in 1970 they were probably the most popular active rock band in the world. Eight more chart hits by mid-1971 completed Creedence's rise in Britian. In October 1972 the group issued a press statement announcing that they would be working on solo projects for a while, but the band was never revived.

Twelve years after its initial success, 'Bad Moon Rising' was used imaginatively during an horrific yet hilarious scene of metamorphosis in the film *An American Werewolf in London*.

John Fogerty, the driving force and major talent of CCR, has enjoyed considerable solo success since his group's demise, most notably via his 1985 album, *Centerfield*.

277

JE T'AIME....MOI NON PLUS

JANE BIRKIN AND SERGE GAINSBOURG

11 October 1969, for 1 week

•

MAJOR MINOR MM 645

Writer: Serge Gainsbourg
Producer: Jack Baverstock

In the week ending Saturday 11 October 1969, two events occurred that persuaded the older generation in Britain that the country was going to the dogs. Firstly, the 50p piece was introduced, to highlight the inflation that decimalization of coinage would cause, and secondly this obscene record reached the top of the charts.

Mind you, it had everything going for it: a very strong tune (which charted under the title 'Love At First Sight' by a group called Sounds Nice when the BBC banned the original), a beautiful English girl, last seen romping naked with David Hemmings in the Antonioni film *Blow Up*, and for the first, but not the last, time on record, grunts and groans sounding remarkably like a lady and gentleman getting to know each other very well indeed. Of course, it sold like hot cakes, and the only surprising thing is that Fontana, who originally issued the record, were overcome by a fit of morality and deleted it when it was at number two in the charts. Major Minor, who had no such scruples, took over the master and were rewarded by a number one hit in the record's second week on their label.

Birkin and Gainsbourg, who were not married but who were enjoying a long-lasting relationship at the time, never repeated their chart success, and go down in the books as one-hit wonders. The record was, however, reissued in 1974 on the Antic label and enjoyed a further chart run. This makes 'Je T'Aime...Moi Non Plus' not just the only French language chart-topper but also the only number one to hit the chart on three different labels. In racking up a total of 34 weeks on the chart, Birkin and Gainsbourg achieved the longest total chart run of any one-hit wonder.

Jane Birkin, who married James Bond composer John Barry before meeting Serge Gainsbourg, is still based in France and pursues a successful acting career. Serge Gainsbourg died on 2 March 1991.

278

I'LL NEVER FALL IN LOVE AGAIN

BOBBIE GENTRY

18 October 1969, for 1 week

•

CAPITOL CL 15606

Writers: Burt Bacharach and Hal David
Producer: Kelso Herston

With this song from their musical *Promises Promises* Bacharach and David notched up their sixth number one composition, maintaining their third position in the league of most successful number one songwriting partnerships.

Bobbie Gentry (born Roberta Lee Streeter, 27 July 1944) began playing piano at the age of seven, going on to study music at the Los Angeles Conservatory Of Music. After seeing the film *Ruby Gentry*, she decided to jettison her own surname in favour of Ruby's and by 1966 she was singing and writing songs for her own song and dance group.

Bobbie had approached Capitol Records with an eye to selling songs to other artists. Instead they asked her to sing them herself. Her first hit was the mysterious 'Ode To Billy Joe', a UK Top 20 smash and US number one in 1967. There were no more British hits until this one, a song of disillusionment whose listeners felt sure that the singer would one day change the view expressed in the title. A cover of the Everlys' 'All I Have To Do Is Dream' (see no. 73) with Glen Campbell put Gentry back in the Top 10 in December but, apart from a minor hit in 1970, that was it.

Bobbie did fall in love again. After divorcing millionaire Bill Harrah she married singer Jim Stafford in 1978.

279

SUGAR SUGAR

THE ARCHIES

25 October 1969, for 8 weeks

●●●●●●●●

RCA 1872

Writers: Jeff Barry and Andy Kim
Producer: Jeff Barry

The Archies, a cartoon TV series featuring the adventures of comic-book teenager Archie and his friends, was an ideal project for musical supervisor Don Kirshner. He'd been responsible for the early Monkees shows (see no. 22) and had found real-life musicians difficult to manipulate. Two-dimensional characters proved far less troublesome. Session singers Ron Dante and Toni Wine were hired to be the singing voices of the Archies, and when the fictional group sang 'Sugar Sugar' in their series it rocketed to number one in both the US and the UK. The Archies had other hits in America but not in Britain.

Ron Dante achieved the rare chart honour of appearing in the same Top 10 with two different groups, the Archies and the Cufflinks, whose single 'Tracy' peaked at number four. Dante's talents also stretched to production, and in partnership with Barry Manilow he produced 'Mandy', Manilow's first US chart-topper and a UK number five hit in 1975. Canadian Andy Kim, who co-wrote 'Sugar Sugar', also returned to the top of the US charts when his self-penned 'Rock Me Gently' went all the way in 1974. Kim just missed out in Britain. The single stalled at number two.

Only 12 discs have enjoyed a longer run of consecutive weeks at number one than 'Sugar Sugar', and the Archies' eight-week stay at the top is the longest of any one-hit wonder to date.

280

TWO LITTLE BOYS

ROLF HARRIS

20 December 1969, for 6 weeks

●●●●●●

COLUMBIA DB 8630

Writers: Theodore F. Morse and Edward Madden
Producer: Martin Clarke

Rolf Harris' recording of the 1903 song of the two boys, Joe and Jack, who share horses at all possible moments in their lives, from nursery to battlefield, was a perfect Christmas number one. The bearded Australian has always been considered something of a joke by pop fans, which is really a little unfair. Although music has never been his only interest, nor even his principle reason for his continuing success today, Rolf Harris (born 30 March 1930) has always been good at putting unusual songs across. Not even Rolf would claim that he has a magnificent voice, but his skill at finding good songs and making them memorably commercial should not be underestimated.

His first hit, which also reached number three in the American charts, was 'Tie Me Kangaroo Down, Sport', a piece of Aussie nonsense to rank with Slim Dusty's 'A Pub With No Beer'. 'Sun Arise', a number three hit in 1962, was an Aboriginal chant made very commercial, and is still remembered as the archetypical Australian song, almost as much a national anthem as 'Waltzing Matilda'. 'Two Little Boys' was Harris' only major hit to that time that did not have an Australian background. After his chart-topper, Rolf forsook the charts for many years (apart from joining Gerry Marsden and company as part of the Crowd, see no. 551), but finally followed up his number one in 1993 with his strange Top 10 version of Led Zeppelin's 'Stairway To Heaven'.

281

LOVE GROWS (WHERE MY ROSEMARY GOES)

EDISON LIGHTHOUSE

31 January 1970, for 5 weeks

●●●●●

BELL 1091

Writers: Barry Mason and Tony Macaulay
Producer: Tony Macaulay

In 1970, if you wanted a hit record you got Tony Burrows to sing lead. The king of the session singers, Burrows sang with the hastily assembled group Edison Lighthouse, as well as on the Pipkins' Top 10 hit of the spring, 'Gimme Dat Ding', and various other singles. 'Love Grows' raced to the number one position in its second week on the chart, which was, at the time, the quickest rise to the charts by an act. Bearing in mind that Edison Lighthouse existed only in the studio, it was a tribute to the song itself and to the usual faultless Tony Macaulay production that it climbed so quickly. It was, in brief, a perfect light pop song, and it sold accordingly. A group of four anonymous-looking people, none of them Tony Burrows, was put together and given the name Edison Lighthouse to cash in on the success of 'Love Grows'. However, the ploy failed because the voice was wrong. One week at number 49 with a song called 'It's Up To You Petula' at the beginning of 1971 is all that stands between Edison Lighthouse and the paradoxical immortality of being a one-hit wonder.

282

WAND'RIN' STAR

LEE MARVIN

7 March 1970, for 3 weeks

●●●

PARAMOUNT PARA 3004

Writers: Alan Jay Lerner and Frederick Loewe
Producer: Tom Mack

Lerner and Loewe set out to write hit musicals, not hit singles, yet they managed two number ones. The first came in 1958, via Vic Damone (see no. 72). The second was from the soundtrack of *Paint Your Wagon* as performed by Lee Marvin. It was common film practice for an actor who could act but couldn't sing to mime to the vocal track of a more talented singer. However, Marvin's gruff drawl was perfect for the singing voice of the character that he played, and the adage that, 'it ain't what you do, it's the way that you do it', was proved correct once more.

Marvin had often been cast as a tough guy, his most famous role at that time having been Frank Ballinger in the TV cop series *M Squad*. The B-side of 'Wand'rin' Star' featured Marvin's *Paint Your Wagon* co-star, Clint Eastwood, making a rare appearance on disc with 'I Talk To The Trees'. This title was listed on the chart along with the A-side for two weeks, but had been removed by the time the single reached the top. Thus, the star of 'The Good The Bad And The Ugly' (see no. 261) was prevented from becoming a number one hit-maker. Undaunted, Eastwood continued his acting career and in 1986 became Mayor of Carmel, California.

Marvin died on 29 August 1987.

283

BRIDGE OVER TROUBLED WATER

SIMON AND GARFUNKEL

28 March 1970, for 3 weeks

●●●

CBS 4790

Writer: Paul Simon
Producers: Paul Simon, Art Garfunkel and Roy Halee

The song most regularly voted into the Top 10 of Favourite Records Of All Time by magazine readers and radio listeners is Paul Simon's 'Bridge Over Troubled Water'. Paul Simon (born 13 October 1942) and Arthur Garfunkel (born 5

Right: LEE MARVIN and his B-side vocalist Clint Eastwood join Jean Seberg in this line-up from *Paint Your Wagon*. (Pictorial Press)

November 1942) had worked together since they were kids growing up together in New York, and they even had a pop hit in America, 'Hey Schoolgirl', under the names of Tom & Jerry, which reached number 54 on the *Billboard* charts in 1957.

Their first hit as Simon and Garfunkel in America was 'Sound Of Silence', which topped the charts there, but it failed to hit the British charts because it was covered by the Bachelors. The Simon & Garfunkel soundtrack for the film *The Graduate* was a landmark in the use of rock in the movies, and their final studio album, *Bridge Over Troubled Water*, was the biggest-selling album in Britain in the 70s.

The title track, featuring Art Garfunkel's voice at its very best, gave them the biggest single hit of their careers. The inspiration for the song was a New York doo-wop gospel recording, 'Oh Mary Don't You Weep', performed by the Swan Silvertones. That song contained the line, "I'll be your bridge over deep water if you trust in me".

After the LP, the pair went their separate ways, Art Garfunkel into films (*Catch 22*, *Carnal Knowledge*) and on to solo recording successes (see nos. 379 and 436). Paul Simon recorded a series of high quality solo albums, culminating in 1986 in the number one album *Graceland*, which featured one of the biggest-selling singles of Simon's solo career, 'You Can Call Me Al'. In 1981, they reunited briefly for a brilliantly successful concert in New York's Central Park in front of a reputed 500,000 people, but the duo did not get back together on a permanent basis.

284

ALL KINDS OF EVERYTHING

DANA

18 April 1970, for 2 weeks

●●

REX R 11054

Writers: Denny Lindsay and Jackie Smith
Producer: Ray Horricks

'All Kinds of Everything' was the second Eurovision Song Contest winner to top the UK charts (see no. 232) and was the first by a foreign entrant to do so. Before Dana's success on behalf of Ireland, the highest position that any foreign Eurovision song had achieved was number 17 when Italy's Gigliola Cinquetti struck lucky with 'Non Ho L'Eta Per Amarti' in 1964.

Dana (born Rosemary Brown, Belfast, Northern Ireland, 30 August 1951) was still at school when she was chosen to represent the Irish Republic in the 1970 contest held in Amsterdam. She charmed the judges with 'All Kinds Of Everything', a pretty 'list' song about the objects and emotions which reminded her of a loved one. The UK entry that year, 'Knock Knock Who's There' by Mary Hopkin (see no. 259), was beaten into second place, whereas the year before Lulu's 'Boom Bang A Bang' had tied for victory with the Spanish, Dutch and French entries. Among the other performer of songs beaten by 'All Kinds Of Everything' was Spain's Julio Iglesias.

Dana followed up her number one with another Top 20 hit, 'Who Put The Lights Out?', after which four years of silence ensued. She then signed with Dick Leahy's GTO label, leading to further hits, such as 'Fairy Tale' in 1976.

285

SPIRIT IN THE SKY

NORMAN GREENBAUM

2 May 1970, for 2 weeks

●●

REPRISE RS 20885

Writer: Norman Greenbaum
Producer: Eric Jacobson

A song by an unknown New England Jew, with possibly the least romantic name among all the number one hitmakers (except Spitting Image and Mr. Blobby, of course), praising Jesus and telling the world he was "gonna recommend you to the Spirit In The Sky", was one of the most unlikely number ones of all time.

Norman Greenbaum (born in Malden, Massachusetts, on 20 November 1942) moved to Los Angeles in 1966 and put together a good-time jug band, one step beyond Lovin' Spoonful, called Dr. West's Medicine Show and Junk Band, which astonished America with the most unlikely hit of 1966, 'The Eggplant That Ate Chicago', which peaked at number 52. The group split up in 1967, but three years later Greenbaum came up with a solo album, *Spirit In The Sky*, whose title track, with its reverberating fuzz guitar riff, stormed to number three in America, and all the way to the top in Britain. The record was, accidentally, the start of the 'God Rock' boom, which included shows such as 'Godspell' and 'Jesus Christ Superstar' as well as singles like 'Put Your Hand In The Hand' and 'Amazing Grace' (see no. 312). 'Jesus Christ Superstar' even featured the guitar effect on some tracks, consciously borrowed from 'Spirit In The Sky'.

Norman Greenbaum, whose second album was, coincidentally, given the same title as the song that knocked him off the top in Britain - 'Back Home', proved to be a one-hit wonder, but the song did not. Dr. & the Medics (see no. 571) revived the song and took it back to number one in the summer of 1986.

286

BACK HOME

THE ENGLAND WORLD CUP SQUAD '70

16 May 1970, for 3 weeks

●●●

PYE 7N 17920

Writers: Bill Martin and Phil Coulter
Producers: Bill Martin and Phil Coulter

'Back Home' was the song with which England's finest proved that having a number one single was easier than defending a two-goal lead against West Germany. In their delicate illustration of the art of voice control on those awkward high notes, Bobby Moore and the lads showed themselves marginally defter with a 4/4 arrangement than a 4-4-2, even if the former was engineered by two Scotsmen in Martin and Coulter. In Mexico the 1970 squad was plagued by an unhappy list of misfortunes including the Ramsey substitutions against West Germany, Moore and a missing bracelet, stomach troubles, and Peter Bonetti, and was ultimately unable to repeat the success of the 1966 team who lifted the Jules Rimet trophy with the aid of a Russian linesman and Geoff Hurst.

After many flops the group re-formed for the 1982 finals in Spain, this time sporting entirely new personnel, and led by the permed (and ultimately unfit) Kevin Keegan (he later made an extremely ill-advised bid for solo glory but was mercifully brought down outside the Top 40). Keegan, supported by the likes of Paul Mariner (who borrowed Rod Stewart's hairstyle for the occasion), Mick Mills and Peter Shilton, took 'This Time' ('We'll Get It Right') up to the number two spot, where they stalled, as they did on the pitch, due to a lack of fire power when it counted. Their 1986 comeback single, 'We've Got The Whole World At Our Feet', raised serious doubts about the act's long-term musical future, as it peaked at a position that painfully reminded fans of the truly great days – 66.

287

YELLOW RIVER

CHRISTIE

6 June 1970, for 1 week

●

CBS 4911

Writer: Jeff Christie
Producer: Mike Smith

'Yellow River' was written for the Tremeloes, who turned it down, so Jeff Christie decided that the only way he could get the song recorded was to do it himself. He put together a three-piece group consisting of himself, Mike Blakely, a brother of a Trem, and Chris Elms, and managed to persuade Mike Smith, the Tremeloes' producer (see no. 233), to record them. This was a good move as Smith had already produced five number ones, including the only four UK-produced CBS number ones to date (see nos. 233, 242, 243 and 263). The success of 'Yellow River' meant that from the

The wonderfully besuited CHRISTIE, who made the top spot, then enlarged their number to include drummer Paul Fenton. (Pictorial Press)

middle of 1967 until the beginning of 1972, Mike Smith was the only British producer to come up with a number one for CBS, and he did it five times.

Perhaps it is not surprising that a group put together so hurriedly to record rather than to perform did not last long. The follow-up to 'Yellow River' was 'San Bernadino', a song very similar to its chart-topping predecessor. It reached number seven. But that was the end of the story, apart from one week at number 47 over a year later with a song called 'Iron Horse'. All the same, it might have given Christie some satisfaction that this last week on the charts was some eight months after the last Tremeloes hit had dropped off the list. They should never have turned down 'Yellow River'.

288

IN THE SUMMERTIME

MUNGO JERRY

13 June 1970, for 7 weeks

●●●●●●●

DAWN DNX 2502

Writer: Ray Dorset
Producer: Barry Murray

Mungo Jerry were Colin Earl on piano, Paul King on banjo and jugg, Mike Cole on bass and leader Ray Dorset supplying vocals and guitar. As there was no drummer, Dorset was also the group 'stomper'.

Dorset had been doing live shows since the age of 14, and his band the Good Earth were a popular live attraction, able to do shows anywhere in the UK at short notice, with a set that ranged from rockabilly to blues and skiffle. Dorset learnt his songwriting skills when the band backed Jackie Edwards, the man who supplied Spencer Davis with their two number ones. In 1969 he wrote 'In The Summertime', coming up with the riff on his guitar one night and producing the words the following day at work.

Early in 1970 the group went into the Pye recording studios and cut several songs with Barry Murray, one of their early managers. Both he and the record company thought that 'Summertime' was a hit, and it was released just as the group, still called the Good Earth, stole the show at June's Hollywood Festival in Newcastle, playing on a bill that included Traffic, Black Sabbath, Free and the Grateful Dead. Their Saturday performance went down so well that they were quickly added to the Sunday line-up.

After the festival, with the acetate of the single already pressed, the band held a ballot and changed their name to Mungo Jerry, one of the cats in the T.S. Eliot verses. Widespread radio exposure, plus news of their Hollywood performance, helped the song to debut at 13. It quickly rose to the top spot and Dorset, who had a job as a laboratory researcher, had to ask for time off work to record *Top Of The Pops*. The song became the best-selling single in the UK that year and it topped the charts in 26 countries, enabling Dorset to give up his job and concentrate on his passion for music.

289

THE WONDER OF YOU

ELVIS PRESLEY

1 August 1970, for 6 weeks

●●●●●●

RCA 1974

Writer: Baker Knight
Producers: Elvis Presley and Felton Jarvis, arranged by Glen D. Hardin

Elvis' penultimate UK number one (his 16th) took place five years after his previous chart-topper, 'Crying In The Chapel' (see no. 197). Much had happened in those five years. Elvis' career had slipped to its lowest point (1967), with the quality of his output on both wax and celluloid mediocre at best. Then, in 1968, he began a major comeback that was to continue until his death in 1977. He recorded songs that were not featured in abysmal films, and, more importantly, gave up making abysmal films. He starred in his own excellent TV spectacular and returned to live concerts in Las Vegas in 1969. In June 1969 'In The Ghetto' made number two in Britain – his first single to get higher than number 13 for three years. In November he was very unlucky to miss number one with 'Suspicious Minds', one of the best singles of his entire career, although this track did bring him back to the US top spot for the first time since 'Good Luck Charm' in 1962.

'The Wonder Of You' was the single that did the trick for Elvis in Britain and it did so in style, staying at the top for no less than six weeks. It was recorded live at the International Hotel, Las Vegas, as part of four days of recording Presley concerts there from 16-19 February 1970. The Joe Guercio Orchestra, the Sweet Inspirations (a black girl vocal group), the Imperials Quartet (a white vocal group) and Millie Kirkham (vocals) were all with Elvis during these shows, and key rhythm-section players were James Burton (guitar), Glen D. Hardin (piano), Jerry Scheff (bass) and Ronnie Tutt (drums).

'The Wonder Of You' was written by Baker Knight and was originally a hit in 1959 and again in 1964 for Ray Peterson in the US, and for Ronnie Hilton and Peterson in the UK in 1959. On Elvis' version Glen D. Hardin (a former Cricket) is credited with the arrangement of the track.

290

TEARS OF A CLOWN

SMOKEY ROBINSON AND THE MIRACLES

12 September 1970, for 1 week

●

TAMLA MOTOWN TMG 745

Writers: Henry Cosby, William Robinson and Stevie Wonder. Producers: Henry Cosby and William Robinson

The Miracles were the first group to be signed to Berry Gordy Jr's Tammie

Records in 1958, yet they had to wait over a decade to score their first number one in both the UK and the USA.

William 'Smokey' Robinson (born Detroit, Michigan, 19 February 1940) had been singing with high-school group the Matadors for three years before meeting Gordy, then an independent producer. The group, had contained Robinson's wife, Claudette, changed their name in 1958, and at the time of 'Tear Of A Clown' consisted of tenor Bobby Rogers, baritone Ronnie White and bass Warren 'Pete' Moore, with Smokey taking lead vocals.

By 1970, Robinson, an exceptional songwriter and producer, had become vice president of Tamla Motown. In fact he was set to quit singing to concentrate on his other work when UK Motown executive John Marshall, having already revitalized a 1965 Miracles recording, 'Tracks Of My Tears', pulled this song from their 1967 *Make It Happen* album with even greater success, pushing it to number one within six weeks and doing the same in the USA two months later Robinson eventually left the group in 1972, his replacement being Billy Griffin. 'Tears Of A Clown' provided co-writer Stevie Wonder with his first number one credit of any kind, his 'Yester-Me, Yester-You, Yesterday' having peaked at number two nine months before. Both Wonder and Robinson would see their names credited as the writers of number one songs again, but not until the 1980s (see nos. 480 and 538). Wonder had imagined a fairground calliope in composing 'The Tears Of A Clown's' famous introduction; Robinson thought of the heartbroken clown Pagliacci when penning the lyrics.

291

BAND OF GOLD

FREDA PAYNE

19 September 1970, for 6 weeks

●●●●●●

INVICTUS INV 502

Writers: Ron Dunbar and Edith Wayne. Producers: Brian Holland, Lamont Dozier and Eddie Holland

Freda Payne's only number one, indeed only Top 30 single, was put out on the label formed by the record's famous ex-Motown producers Holland-Dozier-Holland. The label had several successes, notably 'Band Of Gold' and the Chairman Of The Board's 'Give Me Just A Little More Time', but was unable to keep on producing the necessary goods through the 1970s and folded. While still with Invictus, Payne achieved a number 33 with 'Deeper And Deeper'. The next year 'Cherish What Is Dear To You' crept up to number 46, and was to prove to be the last of Payne's appearances on the British singles chart. In America she had one of the major protest hits of the Vietnamese war, 'Bring The Boys Home', and by the mid-70s she had returned to the stage, where she had originally started her career.

'Band Of Gold' had a comparatively unusual lyric concerning the failure of a couple to consummate their marriage on their wedding night, and the ultimate failure of the marriage itself. The song was covered by Bonnie Tyler in 1986 with a thumping hi-NRG interpretation by Jim Steinman; it failed to dent the charts. Belinda Carlisle's version also flopped.

292

WOODSTOCK

MATTHEWS' SOUTHERN COMFORT

31 October 1970, for 3 weeks

●●●

UNI UNS 526

Writer: Joni Mitchell
Producer: Ian Matthews

'Woodstock' is the story in song of the Woodstock Music Festival, which ran for three days from 15 August 1969 on a farm belonging to one Max Yasgur, near Woodstock in upper New York State. The festival attracted about 400,000 fans, who had come to see acts such as Jimi Hendrix, the Who, Joe Cocker, Jefferson Airplane, Santana, Country Joe and the Fish and the newly formed Crosby Stills Nash and Young. At the time, Joni Mitchell was close to the 'supergroup', and was originally scheduled to be at Woodstock with them. However, other commitments kept her away from the festival, and she had to be content with watching it on television in her hotel room in New York City. This nevertheless inspired her to write the song, which Crosby Stills Nash and Young duly recorded as a single (peaking at number 11 on the Billboard chart), before the Matthews Southern Comfort version made the top spot some months later in the UK.

Ian Matthews (born Ian MacDonald in June 1946) left the folk-rock band Fairport Convention in 1969, and his first solo album, released at the beginning of 1970, was called *Matthews Southern Comfort*. His band took the name of the album, and on this single the line-up was Matthews on vocals, Gordon Huntley, Ramon Duffy, Andy Leigh, Carl Barnwell and Mark Griffiths. It was to be their only hit, making them, at the time, the 15th member of that exclusive one-hit wonder group and the fourth act to qualify during 1970.

By 1971, Ian Matthews had dissolved his band to go solo and without setting the world on fire with his music, has remained a respected performer on both sides of the Atlantic. Few people will remember that 'Woodstock' was at number one when Charles de Gaulle died, on 9 November 1970, at a place which has been less often celebrated in song than Woodstock, Colombey-les-deux-Eglises.

293

VOODOO CHILE

JIMI HENDRIX

21 November 1970, for 1 week

●

TRACK 2095 001

Writer: Jimi Hendrix
Producer: Jimi Hendrix

Like Otis Redding, Jim Reeves and Laurel and Hardy, Jimi Hendrix had his biggest British singles chart hit posthumously. James Marshall Hendrix was born in Seattle, Washington, on 27 November 1942 (the sleeve notes of his debut album erroneously give his year of birth as 1947), and apart from a brief two-year residence in the US paratroppers, which ended for medical reasons in 1963, he went immediately into music. He played tours of the South, backing acts like B.B. King, Little Richard, Jackie Wilson, the Isley Brothers and Wilson Pickett. In the mid-60s Hendrix, then operating under the name Jimmy James, met Chas Chandler at the Cafe Wha in Greenwich Village. Chandler was impressed and took the young guitar virtuoso to England, where they quickly formed the Experience, who backed Hendrix during his breakthrough in Britain.

Although not primarily a singles artist, Hendrix had four Top 10 singles in 1967 and 1968. He met an untimely death on 18 September 1970 in the London apartment of his girlfriend, Monika Danneman, where he choked on his own barbiturate-induced vomit. He was 27.

Time has not erased his reputation as one of the most skilled and original performers of the electric guitar.

294

I HEAR YOU KNOCKIN'

DAVE EDMUNDS

28 November 1970, for 6 weeks

●●●●●●

MAM 1

Writers: Dave Bartholomew and Pearl King
Producer: Dave Edmunds

Dave Edmunds (born 15 April 1944) first tasted chart success as one-third of the Cardiff-based trio Love Sculpture. Their version of Khachaturyan's 'Sabre Dance', featuring some breakneck guitarwork by Edmunds, made the Top 10 in 1968. The band's short career established Edmunds as one of the country's top musicians.

Between 1968 and '70 Edmunds spent a great deal of time in his own Rockfield studios in South Wales, learning and perfecting his production skills. He taught himself how to recreate the sounds of his heroes, idols such as the Everly Brothers, Phil Spector and the Beach Boys. One of the first productions at the studio was his own version of the Smiley Lewis 1955 soul hit 'I Hear You Knockin'', written by Fats Domino's co-writer, Dave Bartholomew, and Pearl King. When released the song wasted no time at all moving to the top. It smashed in at number 16, then pole-vaulted to number one. Two years later, Edmunds returned to the Top 10 with the Spector-sounding 'Baby I Love You' and 'Born To Be With You'.

Dave's occasional collaborations with Nick Lowe were formalized in 1980, when they formed Rockpile with Billy Bremner and Terry Williams. This line-up had played on most of Lowe's and Edmunds' solo work for some time and was widely acclaimed as a fine live band. Unfortunately, the band split after one LP, a sad loss to all rock fans.

Afterwards Edmunds became one of the world's leading producers, helping to break the Stray Cats and working with the Fabulous Thunderbirds, the Everlys, Chet Atkins, Carl Perkins and others. In 1986 he returned to number one as the producer of Shakin' Stevens' 'Merry Christmas Everyone'.

It was Tennessee Ernie Ford who heard Gale Storm knocking at number two in the American charts and the Platters who kept Smiley Lewis waiting at two in the R&B list the first year 'I Hear You Knocking' was a major hit, 1955, DAVE EDMUNDS finally took the song that last place higher in the British chart in 1970. (Pictorial Press)

295

GRANDAD

CLIVE DUNN

9 January 1971, for 3 weeks

●●●

COLUMBIA DB 8726

Writers: Herbie Flowers and Kenny Pickett
Producers: John Cameron and Clive Dunn

Clive Dunn, born in 1919, was a good deal younger than Louis Armstrong (see no. 249) when he achieved his number one, but his popular image of a bumbling senior citizen may have fooled many into thinking he really was a grandad.

Dunn became known to TV viewers in the early 60s through appearances in the situation comedy *Bootsie and Snudge*. In 1965 he landed the role of Lance-Corporal Jones in *Dad's Army*, the long-running BBC wartime sitcom. For ten years he played the butcher and eager member of the Home Guard whose catch phrase, "They don't like it up 'em", became

known to millions. Dunn certainly knew about the reality of warfare – he had served in the 4th Hussars during the Second World War and was unfortunate enough to be captured in Greece. *Grandad* was written for him by Kenny Pickett and guitarist Herbie Flowers, at that time a member of Blue Mink and a future member of Sky. Coming at the height of *Dad's Army's* popularity, the song used Dunn's image to perfection and climbed to the top after six weeks.

When *Dad's Army* ended, the BBC gave Dunn his own children's series, also called *Grandad*, and in 1978 he was awarded an OBE for his services to TV and the theatre. Clive Dunn the pop star remains a one-hit wonder.

296

MY SWEET LORD

GEORGE HARRISON

30 January 1971, for 5 weeks

●●●●●

APPLE R 5884

Writer: George Harrison
Producers: Phil Spector and George Harrison

George Harrison's first solo effort after the break-up of the Beatles was a triple album, *All Things Must Pass*. The first single from the album was 'My Sweet Lord', which took Harrison to number one in only his second week on the chart as a solo performer. The album was undoubtedly Harrison's masterpiece, although he was certainly helped by the musicians on the album, who included Ringo Starr, Klaus Voorman (who also played on John Lennon's 'Imagine' and Nilson's 'Without You'), Billy Preston, Eric Clapton, Dave Mason, Gary Brooker, Bobby Keyes and Carl Radle among others.

However, the vast success of 'My Sweet Lord' was soured by the fact that the estate representing the deceased writer of the Chiffons' hit 'He's So Fine' successfully sued Harrison for breach of copyright, and what is more, Bill Martin and Phil Coulter rightfully demanded and got royalties for the track 'It's Johnny's Birthday' on the *Apple Jam* third LP of the three-record set, which was to the tune of Cliff Richard's 1968 chart-topper, 'Congratulations'. A track on a later Harrison album, 'This Song', wryly commented on the dangers of breach of another writer's copyright.

In 1987 George made a strong chart comeback. 'Got My Mind Set On You', on which he teamed up with ELO's Jeff Lynne, became an American number one, but at home was kept at number two for four weeks by T'Pau (see no. 600). During the 80s he became a major independent film producer with his company Handmade Films, responsible for many major features, including Monty Python and Madonna vehicles.

297

BABY JUMP

MUNGO JERRY

6 March 1971, for 2 weeks

●●

DAWN DNX 2505

Writer: Ray Dorset
Producer: Barry Murray

Mungo Jerry decided to wait until the massive international sales of 'In The Summertime' had died down before releasing the follow-up, which explains the long gap between these two singles. 'Baby Jump' had been written in 1968/9 and was a concert favourite under a different title. When the band agreed that this would be the follow-up, Dorset re-wrote the lyrics and came up with the new title, 'Baby Jump'.

It was recorded at Pye, originally in a 16-track studio, but the band weren't happy with the sound and they re-recorded it at the 8-track studio where they had cut 'Summertime'. When it rose to number one they became one of the few acts whose first two releases both topped the charts. At the time, only Gerry and the Pacemakers had achieved this feat. However, the band's third single, 'Lady Rose', climbed only to number five.

After an Australian tour, arguments over whether or not they should hire a drummer led to King and Earl leaving. Dorset retained the name Mungo Jerry and in 1973 scored with 'Alright Alright Alright', the group's fourth and final Top 10 entry. Since the hits stopped in April 1974, Dorset has remained involved in the industry. He has continued to sell in Europe and had a big smash with 'It's A Secret', a number one in South Africa. In 1980 he provided Kelly Marie with her breakthrough UK hit (see no. 466). He wrote the theme tune to the TV series *Prospects* and also *Wizbit*, the Paul Daniels show. His diverse songwriting talents have also spread to the field of sport: he has written theme songs used by the Wigan football and rugby teams when they run on to the pitch.

298

HOT LOVE

T. REX

20 March 1971, for 6 weeks

●●●●●●

FLY BUG 6

Writer: Marc Bolan
Producer: Tony Visconti

Marc Bolan was born in Hackney, London, on 30 September 1947, and he grew up around Soho, where his mother ran a market stall. He left school in his early teens and did various casual jobs, including work as a model. His first taste of fame was when his photo appeared in *Town* magazine as an example of the 'mod look'.

One of his early influences was Donovan, and, using the name Toby Tyler, he sang in the London folk clubs. In late 1965 he was signed to Decca under the name Marc Bolan, but after two flop singles in seven months he was dropped. In 1967 he joined John's Children, staying only three months. Bolan left in the summer, initially to form a five-piece rock 'n' roll outfit, but funds wouldn't stretch that far so he ended up with Tyrannosaurus Rex, an acoustic duo, with percussionist Steve Peregrine-Took. This line-up became a fashionable act, often appearing at London's hippie hang-out, the Middle Earth. For the first time Bolan made inroads into the chart, 'Deborah' and 'One Inch Rock' making the Top 40 and the LP *Unicorn* just falling short of the Top 10. Part of this success was due to Radio One's John Peel, a staunch supporter of the band. After 'Unicorn' Took left and was replaced by Mickey Finn.

By 1970 Tony Visconti had become their producer. After the *Beard Of Stars* LP Bolan realised that his acoustic approach was probably limiting his audience. As he always intended to made trends and not follow them, he decided to return to an electric guitar. Under the shorter name of T. Rex, and on the Regal Zonophone spin-off label Fly, the first single release was 'Ride A White Swan'. It climbed the charts to number six, slipped out of the Top 10, then rose once more, peaking at number two. With one fell swoop T. Rex had achieved their long-expected breakthrough. The record company wisely released the follow-up while 'Ride A White Swan' was still on its 20-week chart run. 'Hot Love', which its catchy singalong chorus, not only made number one but stayed there for six weeks, becoming the fifth best-selling single of the year and creating mass interest in T. Rex.

299

DOUBLE BARREL

DAVE AND ANSIL COLLINS

1 May 1971, for 2 weeks

●●

TECHNIQUE TE 901

Writer: Winston Riley
Producer: Winston Riley

The Jamaican duo of Dave and Ansil Collins came from nowhere in the spring of 1971 to hit with only the second West Indian reggae record to top the British charts, two years after the first – Desmond Dekker's 'Israelites' (see no. 269). There was considerable confusion about who they were and how to spell Ansil (Ansel? Ansell? Ansill?), but their anonymity made no difference to the record's success. Apart from its British sales, 'Double Barrel' also climbed to number 22 in the American charts, to become one of the first reggae hits there.

The early success of reggae in Britian in

the first years of the 1970s was helped by the popularity of the music among a growing section of white youth – the skinheads. But, of course, the music in its basic form is primarily appreciated by its creators, the Jamaican people. The Jamaican population in Britain is not large enough to ensure national chart success for most reggae hits, and the few that do break into other sections of the market tend to be light on some of the rougher and deeper aspects of the music. This did not appear to be the case with the Collins hit.

300

KNOCK THREE TIMES

DAWN

15 May 1971, for 5 weeks

●●●●●

BELL 1146

Writers: Irwin Levine and L. Russell Brown
Producers: Dave Appell and the Tokens

Dawn were Tony Orlando (born Michael Anthony Orlando Cassavitis, 3 April 1944) and backing singers Joyce Vincent (born 14 December 1946) and Thelma Hopkins (born 28 October 1948).

Orlando was only 17 when his song 'Bless You' made the Top 10 in late 1961. The song was his second hit single in America, the first, the Goffin/King composition 'Halfway to Paradise', having been covered for the UK market by Billy Fury. One more minor hit followed but by 1963 Orlando had quit his recording career to work for music publishers Robins, Feist and Miller. Early 1970 found him working for a subsidiary of Columbia Records, April Blackwood.

Here Hank Medress of the Tokens ('The Lion Sleeps Tonight') and Dave Appell were working as producers for Bell Records. They had a demo of a song called 'Candida' written by Irwin Levine and Toni Wine, performed by a group called Dawn. The record company liked the song but not the lead vocals. The producers persuaded Orlando to sing lead, which he did merely as a favour, not expecting any long commitment. The tape was then sent to California, where Vincent and Hopkins added their background vocals.

When released, Bell had a massive international hit even they could not have expected. The follow-up single, another Irwin Levine tune, this time in collaboration with L. Russell Brown, was recorded in the same informal manner but, once it had topped the charts in both America and the UK, Bell realized the trio would have to become a 'real' group, if only to stop the endless succession of fake Dawns springing up on either side of the Atlantic. The trio, who still had not met when 'Knock Three Times' was recorded, agreed, and so Dawn was properly born.

301

CHIRPY CHIRPY CHEEP CHEEP

MIDDLE OF THE ROAD

19 June 1971, for 5 weeks

●●●●●

RCA 2047

Writer: Lally Scott
Producers: Giacomo Tosti and Ignacio Greco

Middle Of The Road travelled hundreds of miles to find a song they could have heard down the motorway. The group consisted of four Scots (Ken Andrew, Sally Carr, and brothers Eric and Ian Campbell Lewis). After beginning in Glasgow as Part Four, the part-time quartet concentrated on Latin-American music as Los Caracas. On April Fools Day 1970 they went full time under the name Middle Of The Road, which was a music-business euphemism for easy listening.

The foursome sailed to Italy and were working in Rome when it came to the attention of producer Giacomo Tosti. He had the band record 'Chirpy Chirpy Cheep Cheep' by the Liverpudlian singer/songwriter Lally Scott. Their version was released in Italy in the autumn of 1970 and became a hit in Belgium, spreading across the Continent. It then topped the UK chart, but it didn't manage to cross the ocean. Mac and Katie Kissoon, a Trinidadian couple living in England, got to the US Top 20 first.

'Chirpy Chirpy Cheep Cheep' was, at the time, a rare example of a single selling ten million copies (one million in Germany alone) without registering at all in America. The follow-up, 'Tweedle Dee Tweedle Dum', did one-fifth as well, shifting two million internationally. It just missed inclusion in this book, peaking at number two in Britain. Their third hit, 'Soley Soley', continued the downward trend, stopping at five in the UK and moving one million discs worldwide. One can only hope Middle Of The Road had good accountants, because all this success occurred in one tax year and they had only two minor hits in the second year. After 1972 they never charted again.

302

GET IT ON

T. REX

24 July 1971, for 4 weeks

●●●●

FLY BUG 10

Writer: Marc Bolan
Producer: Tony Visconti

The line-up for this song had been together as T. Rex since December 1970. The members were Marc Bolan and Mickey Finn (who was described as adding 'vocal percussion' to this track) with Steve Collins and Bill Legend, who both joined the group following a *Melody Maker* ad and auditions.

'Get It On' was an early taster of the LP *Electric Warrior*. Its rapid ascent to the top of the charts confirmed Bolan's status as the UK's most popular star. In December T. Rex claimed two of the year's Top 10 best-selling singles: 'Get It On' was at ten and 'Hot Love' five places higher. In the same month the band claimed its first LP chart-topper when *Electric Warrior* forced *Led Zeppelin IV* to move aside and settled in for a lengthy six-week run.

This single was Bolan's only Stateside hit, but the song reached the American Top 10 twice. The T. Rex original halted at ten; in 1985 the Power Station, featuring Robert Palmer as lead vocalist, took it to a new peak of nine.

During this record's four-week supremacy George Harrison held the precursor to Live Aid. His Concert For Bangladesh took place at Madison Square Garden in New York on 1 August.

303

I'M STILL WAITING

DIANA ROSS

21 August 1971, for 4 weeks

●●●●

Writer: Deke Richards
Producers: Deke Richards and Hal Davis

When Diana Ross and the Supremes parted company at the turn of the decade, Motown hoped it would have two star attractions instead of one, but faced the prospect that both might fade. Ross' debut disc, 'Reach Out And Touch', was not a good start. Intended to entreat parents of drug addicts to be understanding to their children, it was too vague to inspire the mass audience and was only a minor hit. It was Diana's extended reading of Marvin Gaye and Tammi Terrell's 1967 classic, 'Ain't No Mountain High Enough', that provided her with the smash she needed. It topped the American chart for three weeks and reached the British Top 10. But after the next hit, 'Remember Me', there was no obvious follow-up and nothing new awaiting release.

BBC Radio 1 breakfast show DJ and self-confessed Diana Ross freak Tony Blackburn told Tamla Motown he would make the album track 'I'm Still Waiting' his Record Of The Week, playing it every morning for five days, if the company would release it as a single. The label did, Blackburn kept his word, and the result was Tamla Motown's biggest UK seller to date.

The record was not a major hit in the United States, and when Ross performed it in her British act by request she was baffled, though pleased, by the standing ovations greeting it. She had unknowingly found a personal anthem.

Right: Marc Bolan and Mickey Finn were the mainstays of T. REX. (Pictorial Press)

Though never considered a major chart act, the TAMS had a quarter-of-a-century span of hits, from 'What Kind Of Fool (Do You Think I Am), in the US, beginning late 1963, to 'There Ain't Nothing Like Shaggin'' in the UK, finishing early 1988. (Pictorial Press)

304

HEY GIRL DON'T BOTHER ME

THE TAMS

18 September 1971, for 3 weeks

●●●

PROBE PRO 532

Writer: Ray Whitley
Producer: Rick Hall

The Tams' chart career in their home country of the United States lasted a fairly healthy six years. Bizarrely, it was over before their British trio of hits even began. In 1970 Stateside Records re-issued the 1968 single 'Be Young Be Foolish Be Happy' and it reached number 32. Floyd Ashton (born 15 August 1933), Horace Key (born 13 April 1934), Charles Pope (born 7 August 1936), his brother and lead singer Joseph Pope (born 6 November 1933) and Robert Smith (born 18 March 1936) were now stars in Britain, too.

In 1971 'Hey Girl Don't Bother Me' was re-issued on the Probe label and soared to the very top. Britain didn't bother with the Tams again until 1987. In that year their harmless dance disc 'Ain't Nothing Like Shagging', a reference to a dance popular on the Atlantic seaboard, became a hit due to the idiomatic British use of the word "shag" and the resultant BBC radio ban.

If you asked someone what group featuring Robert Smith had achieved a number one single, at least 99% would probably answer the Cure. They would be wrong. This British band had, during the period covered by this book, peaked at two in the US and five in the UK, so the correct answer to this party-stopping question is in fact the Tams.

305

MAGGIE MAY

ROD STEWART

9 October 1971, for 5 weeks

●●●●●

MERCURY 6058 097

Writers: Rod Stewart and Martin Quittenton
Producer: Rod Stewart

Professional Scotsman Roderick Stewart was in fact born in London on 10 January 1945, to parents who owned a newsagents on the Archway Road. Stewart attended the same secondary school as Ray Davies of the Kinks. On leaving he tried his hand at professions like fence-erecting and grave-digging. He also had a successful trial at Brentford FC, but left after becoming disillusioned with the wages.

All this time Rod was performing in various situations in England and in Spain. His first performance on a hit record is his disputed appearance (disputed if only because it sounds so unlikely) playing harmonica on Millie's 1964 hit 'My Boy Lollipop'.

One evening at Twickenham Station he was overheard singing loudly by Long John Baldry, who recruited him as a vocalist for the Hoochie Coochie Men. After stints with Steampacket and Shotgun Express, Stewart joined forces with Jeff Beck to make his mark in the guitarist's group. *The Rod Stewart Album* and *Gasoline Alley* were moderate American hit LPs that between them earned only one lowly week on the British list, that for the second disc.

Nothing had prepared the music business for the phenomenon of 'Maggie May'. It was originally issued as the B-side of a cover version of Tim Hardin's 'Reason To Believe', which was charting on both sides of the Atlantic, before overwhelming public enthusiasm for the new tune. Stewart occupied the number one spot on both the singles and album charts in America and Britain at the same time.

306

COZ I LOVE YOU

SLADE

13 November 1971, for 4 weeks

●●●●

POLYDOR 2058 155

Writers: Noddy Holder and Jim Lea
Producer: Chas Chandler

Slade were Noddy Holder (born Walsall, Staffordshire, on 15 June 1950) on lead vocals and guitar, Jimmy Lea (born Wolverhampton, Staffs, on 14 June 1952) on bass and piano, Dave Hill (born Castle Fleet, Devon, on 4 April 1952) on guitar and Don Powell (born Bilston, Staffs, on 10 September 1950). The four came together in the late 1960s and formed the 'N Betweens, their penchant for grammatical tomfoolery already apparent. They were a covers group working with obvious club material, including Beatles and Motown numbers. After changing their name to Ambrose Slade they were spotted at Rasputin's Club in Bond Street in February 1969 by Chas Chandler. The former member of the Animals was searching for someone to follow his recent client Jimi Hendrix. Chandler became their manager and producer, and it was his ear for a commercial sound that was a vital ingredient to their success.

'Get Down And Get With It', an old Little Richard song written by Bobby Marchan, gave them their first chart action, rising to number 16. It established the boot-stomping routine that was to become one of their trademarks. Then Holder and Lea's 'Coz I Love You' brazenly thundered to the top and the 70s were blown wide open for Noddy and the Boyz (sic).

307

ERNIE (THE FASTEST MILKMAN IN THE WEST)

BENNY HILL

11 December 1971, for 4 weeks

●●●●

COLUMBIA DB 8833

Writer: Benny Hill
Producer: Walter Ridley

Benny Hill was born Alfred Hawthorne Hill in Southampton on 25 January 1925. After leaving school he found work as a milkman, so he was well qualified to sing about the profession in later years.

After the war Hill built his reputation as a troop comedian by touring Britain's variety halls. He soon realized that his style of comedy, a mixture of slapstick, madcap characters and eccentric songs, was well suited to the medium of television. After many guest appearances he was given his own BBC TV series, *The Benny Hill Show*. This switched to Thames Television in 1969, the year in which he was named ITV Entertainer Of The Year by the Variety Club Of Great Britain. It was likely that many had forgotten that he had a sprinkling of hit singles in the early 60s, including such titles as 'Gather In the Mushrooms' and 'Transistor Radio'. With Hill now at the peak of his popularity, a new single was likely to do well, but even so 'Ernie', a comedy song full of bawdy innuendos, surprised most people by getting to number one.

As the years progressed Hill began to ration his eagerly awaited TV appearances to just one or two special programmes every year. By the 80s he'd become a cult figure in America through reruns of his old shows. Hill died in April 1992, and EMI re-issued 'Ernie (The Fastest Milkman In The West)' as a form of tribute.

308

I'D LIKE TO TEACH THE WORLD TO SING

THE NEW SEEKERS

8 January 1972, for 4 weeks

●●●●

POLYDOR 2058 184

Writers: Roger Cook, Roger Greenaway, William Backer, and Billy Davis
Producer: David Mackay for Leon Henry Productions

The most successful advertising jingle in history began as 'I'd Like To Buy The World A Coke', was transmogrified into 'I'd Like To Teach The World To Sing' and gave the original jingle artists, the Hillside Singers, a big hit in America. It also gave the New Seekers their biggest hit on both sides of the Atlantic.

Advertising jingles had succeeded before. Georgie Fame's 'Get Away' (see no. 219) was based on an advertisement for petrol. Cliff Adams' 'Lonely Man Theme' in 1960 was probably the first chart hit advertising theme tune. It was the background music for the Strand cigarette advertisement whose punch line, "You're never alone with a Strand", became a national catchphrase, so much so that the commercial featured in Cliff Richard's first starring movie, *The Young Ones*. The advertisement also turned off the customers in such vast numbers that the Strand cigarette disappeared before cigarette advertising on TV went the same way.

The New Seekers were formed on the break-up of the Seekers (see nos. 188 and 206) by Seeker Keith Potger. They were Eve Graham (born 13 April 1943), Lyn Paul (born 16 February 1949), Peter Doyle (born 28 July 1949), Marty Kristian (born 27 May 1947) and Paul Layton (born 4 August 1947). The girls had been in an unsuccessful group called The Nocturnes before Potger created the New Seekers. The men, an Australian, a German, and a Briton, took very much a back seat to the girls, on whose charms the group sold records by the bucketful. 'I'd Like To Teach The World To Sing' was their third hit, and to follow up the overt commerciality of a Coke jingle, only one option was possible - they sang 1972's song for Europe, 'Beg, Steal, Or Borrow'.

309

TELEGRAM SAM

T. REX

5 February 1972, for 2 weeks

●●

T REX 101

Writer: Marc Bolan
Producer: Tony Visconti

T. Rex's third consecutive number one came after a label change from Fly to EMI, where for this single only they were on the T. Rex label. During the switchover period Fly put out another track from the *Electric Warrior* album, 'Jeepster', as an unauthorised single. Despite no promotion at all by the band, it went to number two. After 'Telegram Sam' went to the top spot, Fly delved into the band's back catalogue for further material to release. This proved an excellent idea as 'Deborah/ One Inch Rock', by now four years old, made the Top 10 . On the album lists they claim two number ones. The first was the double album of re-issued material, *Prophets, Seers And Sages And The Angels Of The Ages/My People Were Fair And Had Sky In Their Hair But Now They're Content To Wear Stars On Their Brows*. After Deep Purple took over for seven days, the hits LP *Bolan Boogie* put the group back on top, this time for three weeks.

'Telegram Sam' was the first single from *Slider*, EMI's album of new material that emerged in August. It contained the same line-up as *Electric Warrior*, but it wasn't as successful either artistically of commercially, perhaps because it was the third T Rex LP in five months. 'Telegram Sam' made a brief encore in the lower regions of the chart in 1982.

310

SON OF MY FATHER

CHICORY TIP

19 February 1972, for 3 weeks

●●●

CBS 7737

Writers: Giorgio Moroder, Peter Bellotte, and Michael Holm
Producers: Roger Easterby and Des Champ

The first UK-produced CBS number one not originated by Mike Smith was a record co-written by a man destined to become one of the world's most successful producers, Giorgio Moroder (see nos. 409, 456 and 579). 'Son Of My Father', a Top 50 hit in the USA when recorded by Moroder himself, was covered for the British market by a group of unknowns from Maidstone, Kent.

Chicory Tip vocalist Peter Hewson, guitarist Rick Foster and bassist Barry Mayger had been playing together for seven years. They were joined by drummer Brian Shearer 18 months before the success of 'Son Of My Father'. The single is notable as the first chart-topper to feature a synthesizer, an instrument which first came to public attention when a primitive model was featured on the Beatles' *Abbey Road* album. It was exploited by Moroder on hits he produced for Sparks, the Three Degrees, Donna Summer, Blondie and others. The Moog synthesizer featured on this disc was played, not by a member of Chicory Tip, but by engineer and soon-to-be producer Chris Thomas (see no 449).

'Son Of My Father' sold a million, but after two more Top 20 hits over the next 18 months Chicory Tip disappeared from the charts.

311

WITHOUT YOU

NILSSON

11 March 1972 for 5 weeks

●●●●●

RCA 2165

Writers: Pete Ham and Tom Evans
Producer: Richard Perry

Harry Nilsson, known officially merely as Nilsson, was born in Brooklyn, New York City, on 15 June 1941. He was, in the late 60s and early 70s, a respected and much-covered singer-songwriter, but, ironically, neither of the two songs for which he is best known were written by him.

His first hit, both in America and the UK, was the theme song of the Dustin Hoffman-Jon Voigt movie *Midnight Cowboy*. The song, written by Fred Neil, was called 'Everybody's Talking ', and it stayed 15 weeks on the British charts without ever climbing higher than number 23.

'Without You' is track one on side two of Nilsson's best album, *Nilsson Schmilsson*, recorded in London in June 1971. It was written by two members of the Apple group Badfinger who had played on George Harrison's *All Things Must Pass* album and had scored the first of their own three Top 10 hits with the theme tune from the Peter Sellers-Ringo Starr film, *The Magic Christian*. Also playing bass on 'Without You' is Klaus Voorman, who designed the *Revolver* album cover. But it was not the Beatles connection that made the hit. Nilsson's 'Without You' is quite simply one of the great pop records of the 1970s. It reappeared briefly in the chart in 1994, shortly before a new version of the song by Mariah Carey went to number one. This attention came in tragic circumstances, however. Nilsson died of a heart attack on 15 January of that year.

312

AMAZING GRACE

THE PIPES AND DRUMS AND MILITARY BAND OF THE ROYAL SCOTS DRAGOON GUARDS

15 April 1972, for 5 weeks

●●●●●

RCA 2191

Traditional
Producer: Peter Kerr

The act with the longest name ever to reach number one did so with the first chart-topper to feature the traditional instrument of Scotland, the Scottish bagpipe. The hymn, 'Amazing Grace' had become known to record buyers through Judy Collins' vocal version, which clocked up 67 weeks on the chart between December 1970 and January 1973, but climbed only as high as number five.

The Royal Scots' instrumental version first appeared on the album *Farewell To The Greys*. The LP was a tribute to the Royal Scots Greys (2nd Dragoon) which on 2 July 1971 had amalgamated with the 35th Caribiniers (Prince Of Wales Dragoon Guards) to form a new regiment. At the time of their success the band was stationed in West Germany and so was unaware that a track from its album was gaining tremendous radio-listener reaction, beginning on BBC Radio Two. Public demand forced RCA to release the cut as a single and within three weeks it marched to the top of the chart.

'Amazing Grace', in both its vocal and instrumental versions, was on the charts for 94 weeks, making it the second most popular chart melody next to 'My Way'.

313

METAL GURU

T. REX

20 May 1972, for 4 weeks

●●●●

EMI MARC 1

Writer: Marc Bolan
Producer: Tony Visconti

This was T. Rex's fourth consecutive number one, discounting the two unofficial releases put out by the band's former record company Fly. As it was released on EMI instead of the T. Rex label, it gave the band the obscure record of having three successive number ones on three different labels, all within the space of ten months. Rod Stewart matched this unlikely record in 1977, but it took him almost five years and his number ones were not with consecutive issues.

T. Rex leader Marc Bolan seemed secure as the UK's major star, but when he and producer Tony Visconti split in 1974 his success began to falter. In December that year Micky Finn quit and, despite new line-ups, Bolan entered the Top 20 only twice more, once in 1975 and once the following year with 'I Love To Boogie'.

1977 looked as if it was going to be Bolan's comeback year. He did a UK tour with the Damned as support and moved into television, hosting a six-week series with stars like David Bowie and newcomers including the Jam and the Stranglers. However, Bolan died on 16 September when the car in which he was travelling hit a tree. He was just 30 years old. Since then his records have continued to sell. Every few years a single reaches the chart, a reissue of '20th Century Boy' even making it to number 13 in 1991.

314

VINCENT

DON MCLEAN

17 June 1972, for 2 weeks

●●

UNITED ARTISTS UP 35259

Writer: Don McLean
Producer: Ed Freeman

Don McLean (born 2 October 1945, New Rochelle, New York) had taken to making music when ill health precluded him from outdoor activities. His boyhood idol had been Buddy Holly (see nos. 64 and 84) and McLean's memories of hearing of his hero's death in 1959 moved him to write 'American Pie'. This anthem, a UK number two and a US chart-topper, is the song by which he is best-known.

However, it was the next track to be lifted from his *American Pie* album that gave him his first UK number one. McLean himself thought that 'Vincent', written about the 19th-century artist Van Gogh, drew too detailed a picture and left little to the listener's imagination. Amsterdam's Van Gogh museum disagreed and played the disc daily.

The 1973 *Don McLean* album included a few songs about the singer's reaction to fame. The press and music business disliked his cynicism and the singer/songwriter's popularity took a dip until 1980 (see no. 460). In the meantime Perry Como's version of McLean's 'And I Love Her So' became a Top 10 hit. Don was also the inspiration for Roberta Flack's US number one, 'Killing Me Softly With His Song'. Lori Lieberman had seen McLean perform 'American Pie' at the Troubadour, Los Angeles, and asked Charles Fox and Norman Gimbel to write a song to fit her feelings.

315

TAKE ME BACK 'OME

SLADE

1 July 1972, for 1 week

●

POLYDOR

Writers: Noddy Holder and Jim Lea
Producer: Chas Chandler

By the time 'Take Me Back 'Ome' became the second Slade single to reach the top within eight months (the two number ones had been separated by a number four called 'Look Wot You Dun'), the Wolverhampton boys' style was firmly established. In an attempt to grab a slice of the adolescent market, manager Chas Chandler had first abbreviated the group's name to Slade and then emphasized their skinhead bovver-boy image with closely cropped hair, Doc Martens and Ben Shermans.

The crunching rock Slade played was in good company at the top of the chart in 1973, with other ear-bashers like Suzi Quatro, Sweet, Gary Glitter and Wizzard all making it to the number one spot. Of all these acts, it was Slade who maintained greatest dominance until the end of 1974. With Noddy Holder's rasping vocals and the calculated lack of subtlety in their arrangements and song titles, they bulldozed their way to fourth place in the league table of acts with a dozen consecutive Top 5 releases, behind such luminaries as the Beatles (22), Elvis Presley (20) and Cliff Richard (19), but ahead of such acts as the Rolling Stones (10).

316

PUPPY LOVE

DONNY OSMOND

8 July 1972, for 5 weeks

●●●●●

MGM 2006 104

Writer: Paul Anka
Producers: Mike Curb and Ray Ruff

Paul Anka had dropped to number 15

after his nine-week run at number one with 'Diana' (see no. 63) when Olive Osmond gave birth to her seventh son, Donald, in Salt Lake City, Utah, on 9 December 1957. Donny's first number one was an Anka song which the Canadian had taken to number two in the USA and 33 in the UK in 1960.

Donny was the youngest of the brothers who had been singing as the Osmonds since 1960, although he had to wait until he was six before he was allowed to join Alan, Wayne, Merrill and Jay on stage. Encouraged by parents Olive and George, the boys performed at various Mormon functions, which led to a residency at Disneyland. Regular appearances on the Andy Williams and Jerry Lewis TV shows made the Osmonds household names by the end of the 60s. Yet it was not until 1971, having signed a recording contract with MGM, that they scored their first hit, 'One Bad Apple', featuring a lead vocal from Donny which sounded remarkably like Michael Jackson. A US number one, the single failed to register in the UK charts. Donny also scored three solo Top 10 hits in America during 1971, including the number one 'Go Away Little Girl'. The Goffin-King song was the first composition in the rock era to be number one in America for two different artists, having previously been a success for Steve Lawrence. The wave of Osmondmania took 12 months to cross the Atlantic, but when it did it swept 'Puppy Love' all the way to the top.

317

SCHOOL'S OUT

ALICE COOPER

12 August 1972, for 3 weeks

●●●

WARNER BROTHERS K 16188

Writers: Alice Cooper and Michael Bruce
Producer: Bob Ezrin

Vincent Furnier, the minister's son from Detroit, became Alice Cooper, his group took his name and the world was outraged. Members of Parliament teamed up with ordinary mothers to prevent Alice Cooper from touring Britain, and 'School's Out' shot to the top, the free publicity tailor-made for a number one hit.

Furnier, born on Christmas Day 1945, formed a group called the Earwigs in 1965, who proved to be a rather less commercial bunch of insects than the Crickets or the Beatles. It is alleged that they became Alice Cooper after a session with a Ouija board when a spirit named Alice Cooper told them that she was Vincent Furnier. The group was discovered by Frank Zappa in Los Angeles at a Lenny Bruce memorial gig when the entire audience, except Zappa and Shep Gordon, who became the group's manager, walked out. With a pedigree like that how could they fail? By killing chickens on stage they established a reputation that began to draw the crowds, and the quality of the music improved to the point where only a small percentage of the audience walked out. By this time they had a recording contract, and life began to look good for the Alice Cooper group - Furnier, Glen Buxton, Dennis Dunaway, Michael Bruce and Neal Smith. But it didn't last. After the fourth of four consecutive Top 10 hits, 'No More Mr. Nice Guy', it was no more big hits until 1989, when 'Poison' vaulted to the runner-up spot. Now a grand old man of metal, Cooper was an idol for a new generation. In a celebrated sequence in the 1992 film *Wayne's World* Wayne and Garth prostrated themselves before him, chanting "We're not worthy."

318

YOU WEAR IT WELL

ROD STEWART

2 September 1972, for 1 week

●

MERCURY 6052 171

Writers: Rod Stewart and Martin Quittenton
Producer: Rod Stewart

'You Wear It Well' was the second consecutive solo number one for the gravelly-voiced rocker who was once so poor that while hitching around Europe some years earlier he had had to be repatriated from Spain because he was destitute. 'You Wear It Well' was the first single issued

SLADE display their characteristic gesture – not thumbs up, not thumbs down, thumbs sideways. (Pictorial Press)

from his album *Never A Dull Moment*, which dominated the album listings at the end of 1972. It was similar to its predecessor, 'Maggie May', both in its Stewart/Quittenton composition and its style. The backing cast of the single reflected Stewart's history in previous bands, featuring Ronnie Wood of the Faces on acoustic guitar and Mickey Waller, from Stewart's days with Steam Packet, on drums.

After 'You Wear It Well' Stewart was absent from the top slot for three years before 'Sailing' glided to the top. In the meantime he notched up an impressive seven appearances in the Top 10 in various guises. There were three solo hits ('Angel'/'What Made Milwaukee Famous' - number four, 'Oh No Not My Baby' - number six, and 'Farewell - Bring It On Home To Me'/'You Send Me' - number seven), a number three hit with 'In A Broken Dream' as lead singer for Python Lee Jackson and a similar role for the Faces. Their three Top 10 hits were all during this period of Stewart's absence from number one, the most successful of which was 'Cindy Incidentally', which made number two.

319

MAMA WEER ALL CRAZEE NOW

SLADE

9 September 1972, for 3 weeks

●●●

POLYDOR 2058 274

Writers: Noddy Holder and Jim Lea
Producer: Chas Chandler

'Mama Weer All Crazee Now' was Slade's second consecutive number one single, following directly on from the equally badly spelled 'Take Me Back 'Ome'. They were never to achieve the elusive hat-trick of consecutive number ones, a feat managed by 13 other acts. The single that followed 'Mama Weer All Crazee Now' into the charts was 'Gudbuy T'Jane', which 'only' reached the number two spot. Had it reached the top spot, it would have given Slade an uninterrupted run of five chart-toppers.

Most of Slade's song titles have either a deliberate misspelling, a grammatical error of a forced colloquialism. (The title of their 1987 album, *You Boyz Make Big Noize*, was coined by the studio tea-lady on hearing Noddy and co. at work.) They seem to share this tendency with Prince, who appears to be the only other chart act to perform surgery on the English language continually and deliberately.

320

HOW CAN I BE SURE

DAVID CASSIDY

30 September 1972, for 2 weeks

●●

BELL 1258

Writers: Felix Cavaliere and Eddie Brigati
Producer: Wes Farrell

After their experience with the Monkees, the television company Screen Gems knew what might happen when they launched the Partridge Family in 1970.

David Cassidy (born 12 April 1950), son of the actor Jack Cassidy, played Keith Partridge, guitarist/vocalist with a fictional family group that included his mother, played by David's real stepmother Shirley Jones. The show ran from 1970 to 1974 in the USA. In Britain it was first broadcast in 1971 by the BBC, who decided to drop it after one series. Clamour from fans, who had already bought the Partridges' US number one single, 'I Think I Love You', and made it number 19 in the UK, caused ITV to buy the series. By the time 'How Can I Be Sure' had become a hit in Britain, David Cassidy's career in the USA was taking a nosedive.

His biggest solo hit had been a cover of the Association's 'Cherish', which made the US Top 10 in 1971. None of his subsequent efforts reached the Top 20. 'How Can I Be Sure', a US hit for the Young Rascals in 1967, had been covered by Dusty Springfield in the UK in 1970. In the US, Cassidy's version got no higher than 25.

Rolling Stone printed an article in March 1972 which not only reported Cassidy's dissatisfaction with his squeaky-clean image but published semi-nude photographs. After *The Partridge Family* ceased production, he continued to work as a musical actor, scored an American Top 30 comeback hit, 'Lyin' To Myself', in 1990 and enjoyed a healthy run on Broadway with his brother Shaun and Petula Clark in *Blood Brothers*.

321

MOULDY OLD DOUGH

LIEUTENANT PIGEON

14 October 1972, for 4 weeks

●●●●

DECCA F 13278

Writers: Nigel Fletcher and Robert Woodward
Producer: Stavely Makepiece

Lieutenant Pigeon was formed in Coventry out of the group Stavely Makepeace. Under this guise three schoolboy friends, drummer Nigel Fletcher, pianist Robert Woodward and bass guitarist Steve Johnson, released one unsuccessful single, 'Edna'. The change of name to Lieutenant Pigeon improved their luck and gave them a number one in their fifth week on the chart.

'Mouldy Old Dough' was indeed old by the time it had climbed to the top, having been released eight months earlier. It contained almost no other vocal content than its title, which the band deny is a corruption of 'vo-de-o-do', the phrase well loved by megaphone-toting band vocalists of the 20s and 30s. Rob Woodward's piano-teacher mum, Hilda, appeared on this hit, which was recorded in the front room of the Woodward's semi-detached home. Lieutenant Pigeon thus became the only number one hit to feature a mother and son.

The group continued their success with 'Desperate Dan', a similar sounding tune which made it to the Top 20, but their album, *Mouldy Old Music*, failed to chart and the following months saw the popularity of Lieutenant Pigeon dropping.

322

CLAIR

GILBERT O'SULLIVAN

11 November 1972, for 2 weeks

●●

MAM 84

Writer: Gilbert O'Sullivan
Producer: Gordon Mills

Gilbert O'Sullivan's first number one single came almost exactly two years after his first chart appearance with 'Nothing Rhymed', which climbed to number 8. In between, O'Sullivan had another three Top 10 hits as well as a Top 20 success. Simultaneous with the success of 'Clair' was the Irishman's only chart-topping album, *Back To Front*, which remained on chart for a fine 64 weeks.

'Clair' was not an obvious love story but was inspired by the young daughter of O'Sullivan's manager Gordon Mills, for whom Gilbert babysat. The angle gave the song a wider audience than it would have received had it been a traditional romance. Chuck Berry with 'Memphis Tennessee' and the Brotherhood Of Man with 'Save All Your Kisses For Me' (see no. 387) have also put a twist involving infants at the end of a musical tale.

Gordon Mills, who managed Tom Jones and Engelbert Humperdinck as well as O'Sullivan, created a large public company on the back of their successes. He died in 1986.

323

MY DING-A-LING

CHUCK BERRY

25 November 1972 , for 4 weeks

●●●●

CHESS 6145 019

Writer: Chuck Berry
Producer: Esmond Edwards

It is a strange twist of fate that Chuck Berry has his only British number one with 'My Ding-A-Ling', a comparatively inconsequential piece of ribaldry that had been in and out of Berry's live set since he turned professional in the 1950s. The song was recorded live at the Lanchester Arts Festival in 1972 and went to the top of the singles listings on both sides of the Atlantic. Berry's previous singles had included many historic recordings but none ever made the very top, although a double A-side combination of 'Memphis Tennessee'/'Let It Rock' had climbed to number six in October 1963, and 'No Particular Place To Go' made number three in May of the following year.

Berry was born Charles Edward Berry in St. Louis, Missouri, on 18 October 1931, and learned guitar through his teens, copying the patterns of the Delta blues players of the 30s. After a spell in reform school, a marriage and brief employment at General Motors, he signed to Chess records in 1955 with the backing of Muddy Waters. From there he helped define rock and roll, influencing artists such as the Beatles and the Rolling Stones with his reshaped boogie. His 'Johnny B. Goode' was one of three examples of Earth music packed into an American spacecraft sent into the far reaches of the galaxy.

324

LONG HAIRED LOVER FROM LIVERPOOL

LITTLE JIMMY OSMOND

23 December 1972, for 5 weeks

●●●●●

MGM 2006 109

Writer: Christopher Kingsley
Producers: Mike Curb and Perry Botkin Jr.

Born on 16 April 1963, Jimmy Osmond was the youngest of Olive and George Osmond's eight sons. By reaching the top at the tender age of nine years, two hundred and fifty one days, he took over the title of Youngest Number One Hitmaker from Frankie Lymon, who'd made his appearance at the top at the advanced age of 13 (see no. 48).

Little Jimmy's triumph came at the end of the first year of Osmondmania. His big brothers had amassed five Top 40 hits in eight months. Two of them, 'Down By The Lazy River' and 'Crazy Horses', featured Alan, Wayne, Merrill, Jay, and Donny Osmond. The other three, 'Puppy Love' (see no. 316), 'Too Young' and 'Why', were credited to Donny alone. The day that Little Jimmy became the second Osmond to make it to the top, Donny's 'Why' stood at number five and the Osmond's 'Crazy Horses' at nine. Never before had a family so dominated the chart. A rush of Christmas spirit also returned 'Puppy Love' and 'Too Young' to the listings so that for three festive weeks five Osmond discs could be found in the Top 50.

Little Jimmy Osmond enjoyed two more Top 20 hits before getting on with the task of becoming big Jimmy Osmond. After a spell as an actor he became a successful TV director in the USA.

325

BLOCKBUSTER

SWEET

27 January, for 5 weeks

●●●●●

RCA 2305

Writers: Nicky Chinn and Mike Chapman
Producer: Phil Wainman

There are only five acts that have spent more than 150 weeks on the singles charts and fewer than ten on the albums charts. Four of that list, Bill Haley, David Whitfield, Johnnie Ray and Guy Mitchell, were all stars before the LP lists began, so they can be honourably excused. The fifth name in this select group is Sweet, whose album success was limited to two weeks in 1974 and a hits retrospective a decade later. On the singles charts, however, they were one of the top acts of the early 70s.

Sweet was formed in 1968 with Brian Connolly on vocals, Steve Priest on bass, Andy Scott on guitar and Mick Tucker on drums. In 1970 they joined forces with the then unknown writers Nicky Chinn and Mike Chapman, who penned all their early hits and provided them with 'Blockbuster', the longest-running number one of the year and a song that used an air-raid siren a decade before one was used on Frankie Goes To Hollywood's 'Relax'. After this number one they had three consecutive singles stall at two. 'Ballroom Blitz' even entered that high and failed to improve, an anomaly that had only ever previously happened to the Beatles with 'Let It Be' (Lee Marvin stayed at number one).

In 1975 the band decided to split from the Chinn/Chapman stable. At first this seemed to be a wise move, as their own composition, 'Fox On The Run', shot to their customary number two slot. However, they lost sales in an effort to find a more musically appreciative audience. Their last Top 10 hit came in 1978 with 'Love Is Like Oxygen', taken from Joan Collins' 'come back' movie *The Bitch*. In their time Sweet were at the forefront of the glam rock movement. Unlike Slade, Gary Glitter and Marc Bolan, they were a big American success, claiming four Top 10 hits, more than all the others put together.

326

CUM ON FEEL THE NOIZE

SLADE

3 March 1973, for 4 weeks

●●●●

POLYDOR 2958 339

Writers: Noddy Holder and Jim Lea
Producer: Chas Chandler

'Cum On Feel The Noize' signalled a new low in Slade's always eccentric spelling but marked the zenith of their action-packed chart career, for they were now in the middle of the most successful post-Beatles run of any group. Their work was remarkable not in its cleverly crafted constitution, mixing heavy metal and a pseudo-rebellious stance, but in that it enjoyed both critical and public acclaim. The latter was obviously reflected in the seal of commercial approval their offerings found from the masses who bought them to number one. But Slade also found themselves blessed with the former, probably because there was no act around at the time who were able to come near their raw energy and eternal enthusiasm.

SWEET are shown blitzing somebody's ballroom. (Pictorial Press)

On stage Slade were as thunderous as on record, and they remained a popular live act long after the chart heroics were memories. In the 1980s they were still being booked to appear at prestigious rock festivals, including Donnington. A sweet chart comeback gave them two more Top 10 hits in 1983-84, one of which, 'Run Runaway', became their first disc to reach the American Top 20.

As 'Cum On Feel The Noize' headed the singles listings on 29 March 1973, the last US soldier left Vietnam.

327

THE TWELFTH OF NEVER

DONNY OSMOND

31 March 1973, for 1 week

•

MGM 2006-199

Writers: Jay Livingston and Paul Francis Webster
Producers: Mike Curb and Don Costa

Donald Clark Osmond's second number one was his fourth solo UK hit. All had been Top 10ers and all had been cover versions of late 60s ballads. Mike Curb planned the release of the remakes to coincide with the seasons in which the originals were popular. To be fair to Donny, most of them will be best remembered in their original versions, the definitive 'The Twelfth Of Never' having been recorded in 1957 by Johnny Mathis. Oddly, his version was never a hit in the UK, though it reached the American Top 10. It had a longer life as a key part of *Johnny's Greatest Hits*, for many years the longest runner in US chart history. Cliff Richard had had the first UK success with the song, making the Top 10 in the autumn of 1964.

Before long Donny recorded with his sister Marie, who had a solo hit in November of 1973 with 'Paper Roses'. Their four hits together were also cover versions. Donny and Marie achieved the fairly interesting feat of successfully covering consecutive US number ones, namely Dale and Grace's 'I'm Leaving It (All) Up To You' and Nino Tempo and April Stevens' 'Deep Purple', both American chart-toppers at the end of 1963.

328

GET DOWN

GILBERT O'SULLIVAN

7 April 1973 for, 2 weeks

●●

MAM 98

Writer: Gilbert O'Sullivan
Producer: Gordon Mills

Gilbert O'Sullivan's second consecutive and final number one was 'Get Down'. Unlike all the other songs with Get Down in the title, such as KC and the Sunshine Band's 'Get Down Tonight' or Kool & The Gang's 'Get Down On It', O'Sullivan's song had nothing to do with dancing at the discotheque. It was a plea to his dog to get down off the furniture.

'Get Down' represented the peak of O'Sullivan's popularity. Only one more Top 10 hit was to follow, and two years later the hits stopped. There then followed a bitter dispute with manager and producer Gordon Mills which resulted in a widely reported court case early in 1982, with claims and counterclaims about how much money O'Sullivan had earned and how much of his earnings he had been able to get his hands on. In May 1982, the law found in favour of Gilbert (real name Ray O'Sullivan), describing him as 'a patently honest and sincere man' who had not received a just proportion of the vast income his songs had generated. Well before the case came to court, O'Sullivan had left MAM and even scored his 15th hit, 'What's In A Kiss' on CBS, at the end of 1980. It was his first hit for over five years and his last for ten, 'So What' grazing the Top 75 in 1990.

Leather-clad SUZI QUATRO made one of the most electrifying debuts in *Top Of The Pops* history, helping 'Can The Can' vault from 34 to five. (Pictorial Press)

329

TIE A YELLOW RIBBON ROUND THE OLD OAK TREE

DAWN FEATURING TONY ORLANDO

21 April 1973, for 4 weeks

●●●●

BELL 1287

Writers: Irwin Levine and L. Russell Brown
Producers: Hank Medress and David Appell

Whilst the pioneers of glam rock were dominating the charts, the song that kept Sweet's 'Hell Raiser' and Gary Glitter's 'Hello Hello I'm Back Again' off the number one spot was the heartrending story of a convicted criminal returning home to his loved one after serving a three-year jail sentence. Songwriters Irwin Levine and L. Russell Brown turned this tale into 'Tie A Yellow Ribbon Round The Old Oak Tree', 1973's best-selling single on both sides of the Atlantic. World sales for the single topped six million but, more importantly for Dawn, it resurrected their US career. By the end of 1975 they had sold over 25 million records worldwide. It became Dawn's biggest-selling single and, according to *The Guinness Book Of Records,* is one of the most recorded songs of all time, with over 1,000 versions.

The task of following up this monster smash proved difficult in the UK, but not in America. One Top 20 entry and a minor Top 40 effort was all the group could muster over here, but in their homeland they enjoyed several big chart hits, including their final number one, 'He Don't Love You (Like I Love You)', written by Calvin Carter, Curtis Mayfield and Jerry Butler.

By the end of their career the group's billing had changed to Tony Orlando and Dawn. It is therefore ironic to reflect that the forgotten singers in the group, Joyce Vincent and Thelma Hopkins, appeared on more number ones than the highlighted Orlando, their backing vocals having graced the Four Tops' 'Reach Out I'll Be There' and 'I Heard It Through The Grapevine' by Marvin Gaye.

330

SEE MY BABY JIVE

WIZZARD

19 May 1973, for 4 weeks

●●●●

HARVEST HAR 5070

Writer: Roy Wood
Producer: Roy Wood

Roy Wood was born in Birmingham on 8 November 1946, attending Mosley College Of Art before being expelled. He then drifted through local bands before joining Birmingham supergroup the Move in 1966. Five years later, with musical differences arising between members of the group, Wood left to found the Electric Light Orchestra. He wished to create on stage the sort of lush orchestral sounds the Beatles were achieving with numbers like 'Strawberry Fields Forever'.

After just one album with ELO in their year of inception, *Message From The Country*, and two Top 10 singles, Wood left the group in the hands of Jeff Lynne and formed Wizzard. The latter was initially a large band sporting a French horn player, an electric cellist and two drummers. After a disappointing first album, Wood refined Wizzard to a more basic combination and immediately scored the group's first number one with 'See My Baby Jive'. This success introduced Roy to a younger audience than that of the Move. With Wood's ear for a commercial melody, Wizzard enjoyed another number one and a Top 5 the same year.

331

CAN THE CAN

SUZI QUATRO

16 June 1973, for 1 week

●

RAK 150

Writers: Nicky Chinn and Mike Chapman
Producers: Nicky Chinn and Mike Chapman

Suzi Quatro (born Detroit, Michigan, 3 June 1950) was the daughter of Art Quatro, leader of a mildly famous jazz band of the 1950s. Suzi made her musical debut aged eight, playing bongos in her dad's band. Assuming the name Suzi Soul she became a TV go-go dancer at 14. A year later she teamed up with sisters Patti and Nancy to form her first group, the Pleasure Seekers. The band stuck together for five years, playing across the USA and overseas, including one trip to entertain the troops in Vietnam.

The group had changed their name to Cradle and were performing in a Detroit club when Suzi was signed by producer Mickie Most to his RAK Records. Leather-clad Suzi hit the road in 1972 as support act to Slade, accompanied by drummer Dave Neal, keyboard player Alistair Mackenzie and guitarist (and future husband) Len Tuckey. Her debut single, 'Rolling Stone', flopped in 1972, and for a year Suzi's self-penned singles sank without trace. Then Most teamed her with writers and producers Chinn and Chapman, who had just written their first number one for Sweet (see no. 325). The result was 'Can The Can'.

332

RUBBER BULLETS

10 C.C.

23 June 1973, for 1 week

●

UK 36

Writers: Kevin Godley, Lol Creme and Graham Gouldman. Producers: 10 C.C. at Strawberry Studios

'Rubber Bullets' represented the first taste

of number one hit-making for the four members of 10 C.C. This must have been particularly gratifying for Eric Stewart, the only member of the group who did not have a writing credit on this song.

Stewart had been a member of Wayne Fontana and the Mindbenders, who reached number two with 'The Game Of Love' in 1965. When the Mindbenders split from their leader, their first solo hit, 'A Groovy Kind Of Love', reached number two in 1966. The Mindbenders later broke up and Eric Stewart formed Hotlegs with Kevin Godley and Lol Creme. Their only hit, 'Neanderthal Man', in 1970, also reached chart-topper.

When 10 C.C.'s first hit, 'Donna', also reached number two, Stewart must have felt doomed never to reach the very top. The week ending 23 June 1973 not only gave him and 10 C.C. their first number one, but it also gave Jonathan King's label, UK, its only number one.

None of Jonathan King's many efforts under other names and on other labels ever reached number one, and this record is his only claim to a number one hit.

333

SKWEEZE ME PLEEZE ME

SLADE

30 June 1973, for 3 weeks

●●●

POLYDOR 2058 377

Writers: Noddy Holder and Jim Lea
Producer: Chas Chandler

Slade's penultimate number one put them in the select club of artists who had two singles enter straight at number one. At the time, only Elvis Presley had previously achieved the feat (with 'Jailhouse Rock' and 'It's Now Or Never'). As with 'Mama Weer All Crazee Now', 'Skweeze Me Pleeze Me' also preceded a follow-up single that stalled at number two, thus again preventing Slade from achieving the elusive hat-trick of chart-toppers with consecutive releases. This time it was 'My Frend Stan' that couldn't quite make it.

While Slade were enjoying unchallenged supremacy in the singles listings, they were also proving themselves no slouches in the long-playing stakes. During the halcyon years of 1972-74 the five albums released by the Wolverhampton group included three consecutive number ones (*Slayed?* in 1972, *Sladest* the following year and then *Old New Borrowed And Blue* in 1974), a number two (*Slade Alive* from 1971) and a number six (*Slade in Flame*, Christmas of 1974).

334

WELCOME HOME

PETERS AND LEE

21 July 1973, for 1 week

●

PHILIPS 60006 307

Writers: Jean-Alphonse Dupre, Stanislas Beldone;
English lyrics by Bryan Blackburn
Producer: Johnny Franz

Until they joined forces in 1970, the blind Lenny Peters had been a pub pianist in London's East End and Di Lee had been half of a dancing duo called the Hailey Twins. In April 1970 they made their first public appearance together as guests on a Rolf Harris stage show in Bournemouth. After three years of touring clubs and theatres they were spotted by TV host Hughie Green, who put them on his ITV *Opportunity Knocks* talent show. Following their first appearance on 12 February 1973, TV viewers voted for them to return time and time again.

'Welcome Home', Peters and Lee's first single, took two months to climb to the top, and was the tenth and final number one production by Philips' resident A&R man Johnny Franz. The production on this ballad bore all his hallmarks, including lush orchestration and a choir of backing singers.

Over the next three years Peters and Lee became stalwarts of television variety shows and scored four more hits, including the 1974 number three smash, 'Don't Stay Away Too Long'.

Lenny Peters died of bone cancer on 10 October 1992.

335

I'M THE LEADER OF THE GANG I AM

GARY GLITTER

28 July, for 4 weeks

●●●●

BELL 1321

Writers: Gary Glitter and Mike Leander
Producer: Mike Leander

Gary Glitter was born Paul Gadd on 8 May 1940. As a youngster he hung out at the Two I's coffee bar in Soho along with all the other fashionable rockers, including Cliff Richard, the Shadows and Marty Wilde. His first single, released in 1959 by Decca, has been critically acclaimed as one of the worst singles of all time, with Glitter himself admitting the disc's lack of artistic credibility. During the 60s he released a succession of flop R&B singles under his real name, despite working with top producers Ron Richards (the Hollies) and George Martin. The closest he came was with 'Walk On Boy', which would have been a hit if the chart had been just a few places bigger.

He was nonetheless never short of work, helping out on *Ready Steady Go!* and spending a five-year period in Germany, working in clubs and learning his skills as a live entertainer. He returned to the UK in 1969 and renewed his partnership with producer Mike Leander, whom he first met in 1964. As Paul Monday he released his falsetto reworking of 'Amazing Grace' and a squatter's anthem entitled 'We're All Living In One Place'. Unfortunately, the public would have nothing of it. As MCA weren't too keen either, he left to join Bell records.

Glitter and Leander decided the best move would be to return to their rock 'n' roll roots. They decided to write audience-participation rock similar to that of their heroes Elvis Presley, Little Richard and Gary US Bonds. They played all the instruments on the early hits, the first of which was 'Rock 'n' Roll Parts 1+2'. This broke after becoming an anthem in the clubs, where it put rock 'n' roll back on the dance floors.

Having at last made the charts, Gary Glitter now found himself competing with Marc Bolan as flavour of the month. His next three singles all made the Top 10, two stalling at the runner-up spot, and he was duly rewarded for all his efforts when 'I'm The Leader Of The Gang (I Am)' smashed in at two and took that final step to the top, where it remained for four weeks. It may not have been the best of all his records, but it is Glitter's favourite "because it was my first (number one)". The song remains the anthem of his followers. When Glitter appears, the whole auditorium erupts into chants of "leader, leader, leader". Indeed a tribute stage show in 1994 was simply called *Leader*.

336

YOUNG LOVE

DONNY OSMOND

25 August 1973, for 4 weeks

●●●●

MGM 2006 300

Writers: Carole Joyner and Ric Cartey
Producers: Mike Curb and Don Costa

Donny Osmond had already revived one former UK number one, 'Why', and successfully hoisted it back into the Top 5. Britain's favourite Mormon was at the peak of his popularity in 1973, so when he covered Tab Hunter's 1957 smash (see no. 56) it raced back to the top. For a tune to have appeared at the top via two different acts was not unique. 'Answer Me', 'Cherry Pink And Apple Blossom White' and 'Singing The Blues' had all been manoeuvred to number one in two versions, but the gap between their appearances at the top had been two weeks at the most. Sixteen years and 136 days separated Tab and Donny.

Donny's final solo hit of the '70s, the fittingly titled 'Where Did All The Good Times Go', fell off the chart in the second week of 1975, although he continued to have success with his brothers and in partnership with his sister Marie until 1976.

Donny and Marie hosted their own variety show on American television until the

GARY GLITTER looks sharp. (Pictorial Press)

end of the 70s. Donny married, had three children and dropped out of the music business to concentrate on TV production. In 1987 a new deal with Virgin generated further hits, including the American number two 'Soldier Of Love'.

337

ANGEL FINGERS

WIZZARD

22 September 1973, for 1 week

•

HARVEST HAR 5076

Writer: Roy Wood
Producer: Roy Wood

'Angel Fingers' was Wizzard's second consecutive number one hit, and it marked the peak of Roy Wood's chart success. 1973 was dominated by the RAK/Bell/Donny Osmond school of teenypop, but Wood managed to introduce subtleties of production into his basically simple pop tunes that make them stand up to the test of time. He also knew that he was not producing great art and was happy to joke about his music. 'I Wish It Could Be Christmas Every Day' (number four at Christmas 1973 and a hit again over the Yuletides of 1981 and 1984) featured Wizzard with "vocal backing by the Suedettes plus the Stockland Green Bilateral School First Year Choir, with additional noises by Miss Snob and Class 3C".

Roy Wood is still active in the recording studios and on television. At the end of 1986 he joined forces with Dr. & The Medics on a remake of Abba's first hit, 'Waterloo', which climbed briefly into the Top 50, and in 1989 he sang on Jive Bunny's third number one, 'Let's Party' (see no. 637).

338

EYE LEVEL

SIMON PARK ORCHESTRA

29 September 1973, for 4 weeks

••••

COLUMBIA DB 8946

Writers: Simon Park and Jack Trombey
Producer: Simon Park

The 50th and final number one for EMI's legendary Columbia label was performed by an orchestra led by a graduate of music at Winchester College, Oxford. Simon Park (born Market Harborough, March 1946) had begun playing the piano at the age of five.

'Eye Level' was the first TV theme to top the chart. The music was used for the ITV series *Van Der Valk*, which was based on the detective thriller novels of Nicholas Freeling. Just as the actor who played Van Der Valk, Barry Foster, pretended to be a Dutchman, the Dutch co-writer of this tune, Jan Stoeckhart, pretended to be an Englishman when he assumed the nom de plume Jack Trombey.

The single was initially released during *Van Der Valk*'s first series and reached number 41 in November 1972. Viewing figures for the second series increased and the theme tune was re-released by public demand. This time the theme climbed all the way to the top. At the time, the 308 days that had elapsed from first chart entry to chart peak placed the single second to 'Rock Around The Clock' on the list of tardiest number ones. Bill Haley's classic had taken 322 days. Park's theme proved to be the final instrumental number one for over 20 years.

339

DAYDREAMER/ PUPPY SONG

DAVID CASSIDY

27 October 1973, for 3 weeks

●●●

BELL 1334

Writers: 'Daydreamer' - Terry Dempsey; 'Puppy Song' - Harry Nilsson
Producer: Rick Jarrard

The BBC broadcast the 500th edition of its long-running pop show *Top Of The Pops* on 4 October 1973. Among those appearing on that special one-hour programme were Gary Glitter, Slade and the Osmonds. It was this last act, and Donny Osmond in particular, who were Cassidy's main rivals in the teen heart-throb stakes so his managers, Screen Gems, used the event for one of pop PR's most cunning stunts.

Cassidy appeared to be jetting in especially for the show. An aeroplane was seen taxiing to a halt and when the doors opened, out jumped David for an apparent live performance of both sides of his new single. But the singer had in fact already been in the UK for several days and had taped the songs the day before they were transmitted. Screen Gems' ploy worked. The double A-side entered the chart at number eight. The following week it was at the top.

However, Cassidy's appeal soon began to diminish. It was expected that after his version of the Beach Boys' 'Darlin'' had fallen off the chart at the end of 1975 that was the last of David Cassidy. But this was a hasty assumption. In 1985 the singer returned to the Top 10 with his own composition, 'The Last Kiss', which featured backing vocals by the teen hero for a later generation, George Michael.

In 1987 Cassidy took over from Cliff Richard in the lead role in the West End musical *Time* from Cliff Richard.

340

I LOVE YOU LOVE ME LOVE

GARY GLITTER

17 November 1973, for 4 weeks

●●●●

BELL 1337

Writers: Gary Glitter and Mike Leander
Producer: Mike Leander

Four songs entered the charts at number one during 1973. Three were by Slade; the fourth, 'I Love You Love Me Love', was Gary Glitter's second consecutive number one.

Many of Glitter's hits were linked to his live shows. Several started out as lines he would speak between songs. He would then team up with Mike Leander to build a song around the phrase. Glitter did say that he was the 'leader of the gang', and when he asked fans, "Do ya wanna touch?", they all shouted "Yeah!" Both writers thought 'I Love You Love Me Love' would make a great song title. When asked what the next single was going to be called they gave this nonsensical title. 250,000 labels were duly printed before the song was actually written.

Glitter and Leander firmly believed this was a number one single, feeling more secure about it than any other hit before or after. What they could not have guessed was its rapid sale. It quickly passed the one-million mark and became a massive international success. It remains in the UK's Top 40 best-selling singles of all time. It was covered in America by Joan Jett, who also took a cover of 'Do You Wanna Touch?' into the Top 20.

341

MERRY XMAS EVERYBODY

SLADE

15 December 1973, for 5 weeks

●●●●●

POLYDOR 2058 422

Writers: Noddy Holder and Jim Lea
Producer: Chas Chandler

Slade's last number one single was produced and written by the same personnel responsible for all of their six chart-topping singles. It was also the first single to come straight in at the top spot directly after the previous number one had also done this, a feat that was not repeated until 1989 (see nos. 628 and 629).

'Merry Xmas Everybody' was the biggest of Slade's successes, selling a million in its original version. It was re-recorded by the Wolverhampton lads and the Reading Choir for a minor hit over Christmas 1980, but during the following six holiday seasons the original returned to the Top 75. This remains a British record for the most consecutive years in which a single has charted, though it should be noted that Bing Crosby's 'White Christmas' visited the American chart for ten straight Yuletides.

'Merry Xmas Everybody' became the biggest-selling Christmas record in Britain, until overtaken by both 'Do They Know It's Christmas' and Wham's 'Last Christmas' in 1984. It also held the record for most weeks on chart by a Christmas single, until it was overtaken by John Lennon's 'Happy Christmas (War Is Over)' in 1988.

342

YOU WON'T FIND ANOTHER FOOL LIKE ME

THE NEW SEEKERS

19 January 1974, for 1 week

●

POLYDOR 2058 421

Writers: Tony Macaulay and Geoff Stephens
Producer: Tommy Oliver

The New Seekers matched the original Seekers by hitting the top twice when the Tony Macaulay/Geoff Stephens song 'You Won't Find Another Fool Like Me' reached number one in its ninth week on the chart.

By this stage, the break-up of the outfit seemed to be inevitable. Earlier releases had billed them first as 'The New Seekers featuring Marty Kristian' and then as 'Eve Graham and the New Seekers'. Lyn Paul was also looking for the opportunity to break out from the confines of membership of a group, so it was not surprising when the follow-up to their second chart-topper, another long-titled hit, called 'I Get A Little Sentimental Over You', became the final single before a split.The solo careers of the individual New Seekers never really took off, with Lyn Paul doing best by barely scraping into the Top 40 in 1975 with the ironically titled 'It Oughta Sell a Million'. In 1976 they re-formed on a new label, CBS, and enjoyed three more Top 50 hits and 18 more weeks on the charts over the next two years. Since then, their only brush with the charts has been as a part of Ferry Aid (see no. 588).

343

TIGER FEET

MUD

26 January 1974, for 4 weeks

●●●●

RAK 166

Writers: Nicky Chinn and Mike Chapman
Producers: Nicky Chinn and Mike Chapman

Mud were the third act taken to the top by the Chinnichap writing team of Nicky Chinn and Mike Chapman. Suzi Quatro and Sweet had already reached number one with the duo's compositions by the time 'Tiger Feet' stomped to the top spot for a month. Mickie Most's record label, RAK, had already had a number one with Quatro, but Mud were to become its biggest success.

'Tiger Feet' was the first number one amongst ten Top 20 hits that the Mud/RAK/Chinnichap alliance produced between March 1973 and July 1975. Mud had first broken into the singles chart in 1973 when 'Crazy' and 'Hypnosis' reached numbers 12 and 16 respectively. 'Dyna-mite' hinted at the greater success that lay ahead for the group when it reached number four near the end of the year. It was the first of eight consecutive Top 10 singles for the group, including three number ones, between October 1973 and June 1975.

344

DEVIL GATE DRIVE

SUZI QUATRO

23 February 1974, for 2 weeks

●●

RAK 167

Writers: Nicky Chinn and Mike Chapman
Producers: Nicky Chinn and Mike Chapman

Suzi Quatro's second chart-topper was Chinn and Chapman's fourth number one composition. It was also the fifth time in chart history that consecutive label numbers had become number one hits. '48 Crash' and 'Daytona Demon' had come between Quatro's 'Can The Can' and 'Devil Gate Drive', all four portraying Quatro as an aggressive rocker.

In the mid-70s the Detroit native took her stage act back to America, but wasn't able to sell her image in the same successful manner as she had done in Britain. At the same time she began to lose touch with her UK audience. For a couple of years it looked like Suzi was sliding off the charts for good in the company of other glam rockers.

But in 1978 she returned with a softer persona and the singles 'If You Can't Give Me Love' and a duet with Smokie's Chris Norman, 'Stumblin' In', the latter providing her with her elusive Top 5 US hit. An acting career followed. Quatro appeared in several episodes of the TV series *Happy Days* in the role of Leather Trocadero. Stage roles since have included the part of Annie Oakley in the West End revival of the musical *Annie Get Your Gun*.

345

JEALOUS MIND

ALVIN STARDUST

9 March 1974, for 1 week

●

MAGNET MAG 5

Writer: Peter Shelley
Producer: Peter Shelley

Born Bernard Jewry on 27 September 1942, Alvin Stardust had first seen chart action in 1961 as Shane Fenton. Although Jewry was the vocalist with Shane Fenton and the Fentones, he was in fact the second singer to bear that name, the first having died suddenly before the group's success. In the summer of 1962 'Cindy's Birthday', the band's biggest hit, dropped out of the chart. From then until the winter of 1973 the world heard nothing from Bernard Jewry.

Producer Peter Shelley had persuaded Michael Levy to start an independent label called Magnet in mid-1973. He had already heard Stardust's demo of 'My Coo-Ca-Choo'. Released as a single and given the catalogue number MAG 1, the song bounded up to the number two position, kept from number one only by Gary Glitter's 'I Love You Love Me Love'. Stardust's black leather clothes and imaginative way of holding the microphone quickly became well-known. 'My Coo-Ca-Choo', which resembled 'Spirit In The Sky' (see no. 285) in melody if not in sentiment, was considered a better song than the follow-up, 'Jealous Mind', but it was the second disc that won Stardust seven days at the top.

Shelley wrote six consecutive Top 20 hits for Stardust before the singer decided to look elsewhere for material, a decision which doomed him to six years of chart obscurity. He renewed his career in 1981 by making a move to the independent label Stiff Records, for whom he recorded a Top 10 version of Nat 'King' Cole's 'Pretend'. Three more hitless years followed until he signed with Chrysalis, with whom he was able to generate two more Top 10ers, 'I Feel Like Buddy Holly' and 'I Won't Run Away'. This gave Jewry/Fenton/Stardust 17 chart singles, seven of them Top 10s, on three labels over a 24-year period.

346

BILLY DON'T BE A HERO

PAPER LACE

16 March 1974, for 3 weeks

●●●

BUS STOP BUS 1014

Writers: Mitch Murray and Peter Callander
Producers: Mitch Murray and Peter Callander

Paper Lace joined Mary Hopkin and Peters and Lee as number one hitmakers who owed their initial success to the TV talent show *Opportunity Knocks*. Like them, the band got to the top with their very first hit. The group, based in the lace-making city of Nottingham, were singer/drummer Phil Wright (born 9 April 1950), bassist Cliff Fish (born 13 August 1949), and guitarists Chris Morris (born 1 November 1954), Michael Vaughan (born 27 July 1950) and Carlo Santanna (born 29 June 1947).

'Billy' was Murray and Callander's second number one composition (see no. 242). Murray had also co-written Gerry and the Pacemaker's first two number ones (see nos. 150 and 152). 'Billy' emulated its UK success in the USA when Bo Donaldson and the Heywoods rushed out a chart-topping cover version. A vengeful Paper Lace quickly released their number three hit, 'The Night Chicago Died', in America. The ploy worked and the group enjoyed seven days atop the *Billboard* Hot 100.

The quintet's fortunes waned in Britain, where they managed to score only one more Top 20 hit before becoming entangled in legal problems with their record label. They kicked the ball into the chart net for the last time with a 1978 version of 'We've Got The Whole World In Our Hands', accompanied by Nottingham Forest FC.

347

SEASONS IN THE SUN

TERRY JACKS

6 April 1974, for 4 weeks

●●●●

BELL 1344

Writer: Jacques Brel; English lyrics by Rod McKuen
Producer: Terry Jacks

Winnipeg-born Terry Jacks was the first Canadian act since Paul Anka to score a British number one. Terry and his wife Susan had already seen chart action as the Poppy Family with the 1970 Top 10 tune 'Which Way You Going Billy', a single that Mrs. Jacks had originally intended to release under her own name, Susan Pesklevits.

The couple were divorced in 1973. While in session that year with the Beach Boys (see nos. 226 and 256), Terry recorded the French song 'Le Moribond (The Dying Man)', adapted into English by the poet Rod McKuen and recorded by the Kingston Trio in 1964. Jacks had wanted the Beach Boys to record the tune, but they were not keen.

A year later, Jacks was persuaded to release the track himself. It gave him a number one hit in Canada, on his own Goldfish label, and bowled over the rest of the world on Bell. It led the American list for three weeks. Another Brel song, the equally mournful 'If You Go Away', provided him with a further Top 10er in 1974, but after two seasons in the chart it was Jacks who went away.

348

WATERLOO

ABBA

4 May 1974, for 2 weeks

●●

EPIC EPC 2240

Writers: Bjorn Ulvaeus, Benny Andersson and Stig Anderson
Producers: Bjorn Ulvaeus and Benny Andersson

Benny Andersson (born in Stockholm on 16 December 1946) began his musical career with a group called the Hep Stars, who were for some years very popular in Sweden. Bjorn Ulvaeus (born in Gothenberg on 25 April 1948) was with an outfit called the Hootenanny Singers. In the late 60s the two combined to form the duo Bjorn and Benny. By the early 70s the duo had achieved considerable popularity in Scandinavia. At this point they brought their girlfriends into the act. The young women were Agnetha Faltskog (born in Janskoping on 5 April 1950) and Annifrid Lyngstad (born in Norway on 15 November 1945). By the original ploy of taking the initial letters of the quartet's first names, the acronym Abba was conceived.

'Waterloo' was Sweden's Eurovision entry for 1974. It won easily and became the biggest international hit of any contest winner in history, although a previous loser, 'Love Is Blue', spent five weeks at number one in America as an instrumental by Paul Mauriat. 'Waterloo' created a new standard for Eurovision acts, which continued in 1981 with Britain's Bucks Fizz, another quartet of two men and two women.

349

SUGAR BABY LOVE

THE RUBETTES

18 May 1974, for 4 weeks

●●●●

POLYDOR 2058 442

Writers: Wayne Bickerton and Tony Waddington
Producer: Wayne Bickerton

When songwriters try to sell their compositions they don't send along pieces of sheet music. They record demonstration tapes on which either they or other musicians have performed their songs. Wayne Bickerton and Tony Waddington had hired six session musicians for this purpose. The artists were singer Paul da Vinci, keyboard players Bill Hurd and Peter Arnisson, guitarist John Thorpe, bassist Mick Clarke and drummer John Richardson. The session men really liked one tune, 'Sugar Baby Love', and approached Polydor to release it as a single. They did, and it became a hit.

The musicians hurriedly formed themselves into a group and adopted the name the Rubettes. Da Vinci had aspirations to become a solo star and declined the offer to join the new band, so guitarist Alan Williams was brought in as the sixth Rubette. After two more hits with Polydor the group moved to State records, owned by Bickerton and Waddington. Their first release there, 'I Can Do It', did indeed reach the Top 10 in 1975. Meanwhile, Paul da Vinci managed a Top 20 entry of his own with 'Your Baby Ain't Your Baby Anymore'. The Rubettes carried their success through to 1977, by which time they had discarded their white stage berets and rock and roll pastiches for casual clothes and a softer, more thoughtful sound. Their final chart appearance came in April 1977 when 'Baby I Know' made the Top 20.

350

THE STREAK

RAY STEVENS

15 June 1974, for 1 week

•

JANUS 6146 201

Writer: Ray Stevens
Producer: Ray Stevens

The eclectic Ray Stevens (born Ray Ragsdale in Clarksdale, Georgia, on 24 January 1939) was a music student from Georgia State University who went on to record in one of the widest ranges of styles of any chart interest.

Even before his first British hit in 1970, the American number one 'Everything is Beautiful', he had charted in the States with both novelty ('Gitarzan') and protest ('Mr. Businessman') material. His very first hit, 'Jeremiah Peabody's Poly-Unsaturated Quick Dissolving Fast Acting Pleasant Tasting Green And Purple Pills', boasted the longest unbracketed title in chart history, while his Top 10 success, 'Ahab the Arab', had the nearly as unlikely distinction of being covered in Britain by Jimmy Savile.

Stevens had nearly matched the number one US status of 'Everything Is Beautiful' in the UK with 'Bridget the Midget (The Queen of the Blues)', a comedy number with applause and sound effects that reached number two in 1971. In 1974 he used the audience participation concept again and went to the head of the hit parade in both countries with 'The Streak'. While on an aeroplane he had read about the new campus fad of running naked in public places, the more observers the better. He wrote, recorded and rush-released his song just days after a television audience of millions saw a spectacular streaker at the Academy Awards.

'The Streak' was Stevens' greatest international hit, but his top honour came a year later when his bluegrass version of 'Misty' won a Grammy for the Best Arrangement Accompanying A Vocalist. The Georgian pushed back the frontiers of fun even further in 1977, when he made the Top 40 imitating a group of chickens clucking Glenn Miller's 'In The Mood'. He continued to have country hits through the 1980s, including one with the immortal title 'Would Jesus Wear A Rolex'.

351

ALWAYS YOURS

GARY GLITTER

22 June 1974, for 1 week

•

BELL 1359

Writers: Mike Leander and Gary Glitter
Producer: Mike Leander

After two highly successful slow songs, 'I Love You Love Me Love' and 'Remember Me This Way', Gary Glitter and writing partner Mike Leander decided an uptempo song was needed. They released 'Always Yours' and claimed their third number one. The song was an ode to Glitter's fans, as had been several of his earlier hits. Gary usually introduced the number in concert, grinning and announcing, "I'm yours, I'm always yours."

This was Glitter's third and final number one. The follow-up, 'Oh Yes! You're Beautiful', peaked at number two, and within a year his run of Top 10 hits had ended. His first 11 hits had all made the Top 10, a record at the time that has since been surpassed by the 13 initial hits of Kylie Minogue.

Years later Gary's financial difficulties were publicised. It wasn't that he had not received his royalties, it was merely that he had somehow managed to spend them. What saved him from financial ruin was his showmanship and mutual love affair with his fans. He became a perennial concert performer, maintained a high television profile and enjoyed occasional hits such as the 1984 Top 10 success 'Another Rock And Roll Christmas'. With two minor hits in 1992, he expanded his span of hits to 20 years.

352

SHE

CHARLES AZNAVOUR

29 June 1974, for 4 weeks

●●●●

BARCLAY BAR 26

Writers: Charles Aznavour and Herbert Kretzmer
Producer: Eddie Barclay ; arranged by Del Newman

The theme from the television series *The Seven Faces Of Woman* gave French superstar Charles Aznavour his biggest international hit. His only other British hit, 'The Old Fashioned Way', only reached number 38 in the chart but gave him 15 weeks of chart glory, one more than 'She' offered.

Aznavour was born in Paris of Armenian parents on 22 May 1924. He was supported in his early career by Edith Piaf, who included him in one of her shows and took him to America for his first live work there. The 5'3" singer/songwriter was already a major concert attraction in the US when one of his compositions, 'Hier Encore', became a Top 20 hit for Roy Clark in the translation 'Yesterday When I Was Young'. The English lyrics for this 1969 success were supplied by British wordsmith and journalist Herbert Kretzmer. It was only natural that Aznavour and Kretzmer should team again on 'She'.

Five years after his compatriot Serge Gainsbourg had partnered Jane Birkin to number one, Aznavour became the only French solo singer to top the British chart. This fact gave particular joy to French music business mogul Eddie Barclay, so influential a figure he even merited his own label in Britain. Although Aznavour never returned to the UK best sellers after 'She', all three principals enjoyed continued success. The singer himself starred in an American TV special with Liza Minnelli this same year and has remained a leading world concert attraction into the 90s. Kretzmer, who had penned the Top 5 Peter Sellers and Sophia Loren duet 'Goodness Gracious Me' in 1960, registered his greatest triumph in the 80s with the English lyrics of the musical *Les Miserables*.

Charles Aznavour affected British music in a roundabout way through starring in the 1960 François Truffaut film *Shoot The Pianist*, which inspired the title of the Elton John album *Don't Shoot Me, I'm Only The Piano Player*.

353

ROCK YOUR BABY

GEORGE MCCRAE

27 July 1974, for 3 weeks

●●●

JAYBOY BOY 85

Writers: Harry W. Casey and Richard Finch
Producers: Harry W. Casey and Richard Finch

Eras in popular music are quite often signalled by individual records. 'Rock Your Baby' clearly began the disco craze of the 70s. The first number one by a black artist since 'My Ding-a-Ling' in 1972, it was followed by five soul and reggae chart toppers by the end of the year.

'Rock Your Baby' was originally intended for McCrae's wife Gwen, but when she couldn't make the session, engineer Harry Casey cut the record with George, allegedly on scrap tape. The unusual production, distinguished by a lengthy instrumental introduction and the vocalist's falsetto delivery, fast found favour in Puerto Rican and gay clubs in New York. Purchases by their clientele forced the record onto WABC, then the nation's most important Top 40 outlet. Other radio stations had to follow suit, and 'Rock Your Baby' became a worldwide smash with total sales estimated in excess of ten million.

McCrae had come a long way from his first group, the Fabulous Stepbrothers. Ironically, his producer and record company went on to more lasting success than he did. Casey won fame as KC of KC and the Sunshine Band, while TK, an American label distributed in Britain by Jayboy, was a leading label of the mid-70s.

George visited the British Top 10 twice more in the year, following 'Rock Your Baby' with 'I Can't Leave You Alone' and 'It's Been So Long', but he never managed to reach the heights of the American chart again. However, his wife Gwen got to the Top 10 in 1975 with 'Rockin' Chair', and she charted long after his final success when she made her British debut in 1988 with 'All This Love That I'm Giving'.

354

WHEN WILL I SEE YOU AGAIN

THE THREE DEGREES

17 August 1974, for 2 weeks

●●

PHILADELPHIA INTERNATIONAL
PIR 2155

Writers: Kenny Gamble and Leon Huff
Producers: Kenny Gamble and Leon Huff

The original members of the Philadelphia trio the Three Degrees were Fayette Pinkney, Linda Turner and Shirley Porter. The latter two were replaced in 1966 by Sheila Ferguson and Valerie Holiday. In 1970 the group enjoyed their first American Top 40 hit with a revival of the Chantels' 1958 wailer 'Maybe', written and produced by their manager Richard Barrett. They were signed to Gamble and Huff's Philadelphia International Records and enjoyed two simultaneous British Top 40 hits in the spring of 1974, although the general public was unaware of the feat. 'Year of Decision' was the group's own hit, but they were also the vocalists who appeared at the end of the MFSB smash 'TSOP (The Sound Of Philadelphia)'. The latter song was the theme to the American television phenomenon *Soul Train*, but since the Three Degrees were singing "Soul Train, Soul Train" from the very beginning of the track their contribution was wiped off the single until the very end to encourage other programmes to play the disc. It went to number one in America under the full billing 'MFSB featuring The Three Degrees'.

Within months the trio had a British number one, 'When Will I See You Again'. It hadn't even been released in the States yet, since PIR was busy promoting the TSOP follow-up 'Love Is The Message', another 'MFSB featuring The Three Degrees' release. When America finally saw 'When Will I See You Again' in the autumn of 1974, it climbed to number two, and the Three Degrees got to relive those 'precious moments' of chart stardom all over again.

Despite the many memorable hits on the Philadelphia International label from artists like the O'Jays and Harold Melvin and the Bluenotes, the Three Degrees were the only act to reach number one in Britain. They enjoyed four more UK Top 10 successes after 'When Will I See You Again'. At least equally important was the reputation they had earned as Prince Charles' favourite pop group, which kept the tabloid press interested in the fortunes of Sheila Ferguson long after she experienced two degrees of separation and brought other singers into her popular club act.

355

LOVE ME FOR A REASON

THE OSMONDS

31 August 1974, for 3 weeks

●●●

MGM 2006 458

Writer: Johnny Bristol
Producer: Mike Curb

The five singing Osmonds were Alan (born 22 July 1949), Wayne (born 28 August 1951), Merrill (born 30 April 1953), Jay (born 2 March 1955) and Donny (born 9 December 1957). Older brothers Virl and Tommy were involved with the Osmonds' management company. The group began as a quartet in 1959, Donny having not yet reached his second birthday, but he was on board when they were regulars on Andy Williams' television series of the mid-60s.

The Osmonds exploded onto the American charts when their first hit, the Jackson Five soundalike 'One Bad Apple', spent five weeks at number one in 1971. It was not until three years later that they led the list in Britain. 'Love Me For a Reason' was written by Johnny Bristol, one of the great Motown writer/producers of the late 60s. Although his was the male voice on the final Diana Ross and the Supremes hit, 'Someday We'll Be Together', he did not have his own hit until he recorded 'Hang On In There Baby', which, like 'Love Me For A Reason', entered the chart on 25 August 1974. It peaked at number three. The career of producer of the Osmonds disc, Mike Curb, did not peak with this single, however. He went on to become Lieutenant Governor of California.

This was the final number one by any of the Osmond configurations. In all the family mustered a handsome 26 hits in just over four and a half years. The last of these, 'I Can't Live A Dream', charted in 1976. To the extent that brothers can break up, the Osmonds did in 1980. The older ones re-formed two years later and became regulars on the country charts under the sequential billings the Osmonds, the Osmond Brothers, and the Osmond Bros.

356

KUNG FU FIGHTING

CARL DOUGLAS

21 September 1974, for 3 weeks

●●●

PYE 7N 45377

Writer: Karl Douglas
Producer: Biddu

'Kung Fu Fighting' was recorded in ten minutes flat, sold nearly ten million copies worldwide and was a number one in both the UK and US. Not bad work for a song that was intended to be a B-side!

Carl Douglas was born in Jamaica but was living in London when he and Indian-born producer Biddu began working together. The pair had previously collaborated on the film *Embassy*; Biddu had written the title song and Douglas supplied the vocals. During a recording session for the singer's single 'I Want To Give You My Everything', Douglas asked his producer if he could write the B-side. Kung Fu, a martial art not unlike karate, was being taught throughout Britain in 1974, having risen to popularity through Bruce Lee films. Douglas had written a song about the fad and presented it, along with a handful of others, to Biddu. The tune was recorded and little else thought about it.

Pye flipped the single to feature 'Kung Fu Fighting' as the A-side and, after a slow start, it began selling. By climbing to the top it gave Biddu the distinction of being the first Asian to produce a number one hit. It came to be an example of records that instantly evoke an era, and in 1994 was prominently featured in the movie *Wayne's World 2*.

357

ANNIE'S SONG

JOHN DENVER

12 October 1974, for 1 week

●

RCA APBO 0295

Writer: John Denver
Producer: Milt Okun

John Denver was born John Deutschendorf in New Mexico on the last day of 1943. He took his name from the capital city of Colorado, an area which gave him great personal peace and inspired the title of his 1972 American hit single and album 'Rocky Mountain High'. By the time of his British breakthrough he had sold more records in the United States than there are people in the city of Denver. He had executed the double of achieving American number ones both as a writer ('Leaving On A Jet Plane' by Peter, Paul and Mary) and artist ('Sunshine On My Shoulders'). 'Annie's Song' was another American number one, denying Elton John's 'Don't Let The Sun Go Down On Me' the top spot, and this time Denver's success crossed the Atlantic.

A tribute to his wife Ann Martell, 'Annie's Song' was written in ten minutes while Denver was a on a ski lift. The name Annie was not mentioned in the lyric, which meant that the tune could still be performed without personal reference after the couple divorced in 1983.

Despite his phenomenal success in the US singles and album charts, in both of which he is rated among the top one hundred artists of all-time, Denver visited the UK Top 75 on only one further occasion, with the 1981 duet with Placido Domingo, 'Perhaps Love'. He had far more success on the album side with five

Top 10 LPs. The highest-placed of all was the local product *Live In London*, which scaled to number two. He continued his either-side-of-the-ocean tradition with two more American number ones that didn't even register in Britain, 'Thank God I'm A Country Boy' and 'I'm Sorry'. The latter was number one the first week one of the co-authors of this book began his American hits series on Radio 1.

John Denver was a major star in the United States, appearing on the cover of *Time* magazine and winning an Emmy for his television special, *An Evening With* John Denver. He continued to play successful concerts in both America and Britain into the 90s. 'Annie's Song' had further life, too, reaching number three in 1978 in the instrumental version by flautist James Galway.

358

SAD SWEET DREAMER

SWEET SENSATION

19 October 1974, for 1 week

●

PYE 7N 45385

Writer: D.E.S. Parton
Producers: D.E.S. Parton and Tony Hatch

Like Showaddywaddy before them, Manchester-based Sweet Sensation were winners of the ITV talent show *New Faces*. One of the panel of judges was Tony Hatch, who took the group under his wing to produce his seventh and final number one to date.

At the time of their success Sweet Sensation was an eight-man outfit comprising four vocalists and four musicians. The singers were Vincent James, Junior Daye, St. Clair Palmer and Marcel King, who, at 16, was the youngest member. The music came from Barry Johnson (bass), Leroy Smith (piano), Roy Flowers (drums) and Gary Shaugnessy (guitar). Producer and writer D.E.S. Parton was in fact David Parton, who would score a Top 10 hit of his own two years later by covering 'Isn't She Lovely'. This was a track from Stevie Wonder's double album, *Songs In The Key Of Life*, that the Motown star himself refused to edit for single purposes, on the grounds that he would have to cut out the voice of his wailing daughter, who inspired the song in the first place.

Sweet Sensation had only one further success, 'Purely By Coincidence', which reached number 11. Indeed it was pure coincidence that Ken Boothe, who replaced Sweet Sensation at number one, enjoyed just one more hit, that at number 11. Although they tried for a third hit, Sweet Sensation's next single release, 'Boom Boom Boom', lived up to its title and bombed.

359

EVERYTHING I OWN

KEN BOOTHE

26 October 1974, for 3 weeks

●●●

TROJAN TR 7920

Writer: David Gates
Producer: Lloyd Chalmers

Ken Boothe was born in Jamaica in 1949. In 1967, he recorded a version of Sandie Shaw's 'Puppet On A String', but the first the British charts knew of him was when his reggae version of Bread's 'Everything I Own' climbed all the way to the summit some seven years later. The song was written by Bread's lead singer David Gates in memory of his grandfather, and had already been a number 32 hit in 1972 for Bread, their third and lowest-placed hit of five between 1970 and 1976. In America the tune had stopped at number five. Gates also wrote Telly Savalas' number one, 'If' (see no. 367).

Throughout his version, Ken Boothe sings "Anything I Own" rather than "Everything I Own", thus making this record one of the few number ones in which the title is never actually sung. There are other examples of this, such as 'Space Oddity', 'The Ballad Of John And Yoko', 'Bohemian Rhapsody' and 'The Chicken Song', but Ken Boothe's record is the only one on which the title should have been sung, but by mistake wasn't.

Ken Boothe seemed to have the makings of a regular chartbuster, with a smoother style than most reggae acts and a choice of material that showed the breadth of his musical tastes. However, after only one more hit, 'Crying Over You', he dropped off the charts at the end of February 1975 for ever. The song, however, came back to life in 1987 when Boy George (see no. 586) took his version - following the Boothe arrangement rather than Bread's original - to the very top, the 11th song to hit number one in two different versions.

Four days after Ken Boothe hit the top for the only time, Muhammad Ali did so for the second time, by knocking out George Foreman in Kinshasa, Zaire, and regaining the heavyweight boxing championship of the world.

360

GONNA MAKE YOU A STAR

DAVID ESSEX

16 November 1974, for 3 weeks

●●●

CBS 2492

Writer: David Essex
Producer: Jeff Wayne

David Cook's first musical occupation was as a jazz drummer in the 60s band the Everons. Derek Bowman, then theatre critic for the *Daily Express*, was told about the group. When he saw them in a pub at Leytonstone he was immediately impressed by the charismatic drummer. When Cook (born 23 July 1947) left the band Bowman became his manager, persuading the youngster to change his surname to Essex, one he felt was more suited to both music and theatre.

Initial releases on Fontana, then Decca, all failed. Somewhat disappointed with his singer's lack of chart success, Bowman turned to the world of theatre in which he himself had more interest. Essex's first role was in a provincial production of the American musical *The Fantasticks*. A part in *Oh Kay* by P.G. Wodehouse/George and Ira Gershwin followed. His first lead was in the American show *Your Own Thing*.

The big break came in October 1971,

David Cook was made a star as DAVID ESSEX. (Pictorial Press)

when Essex landed the role of Jesus in *Godspell* at Chalk Farm's Roundhouse Theatre. The reviews were ecstatic. When film producer David Puttnam saw the show he offered Essex the part of Jim McClain in his forthcoming production, *That'll Be The Day*. Essex took a seven-week break from *Godspell* to shoot the film, and wrote 'Rock On' for the soundtrack. The song was released worldwide by CBS in August 1973 and became a massive international hit, putting Essex in the enviable position of being a star of cinema, theatre and music.

'Lamplight' and 'America' followed 'Rock On' into the UK charts. So did' Stardust', the title song of the film follow-up to *That'll Be The Day*. Essex then concentrated on his career as a pop singer.

'Gonna Make You A Star' was recorded at Advision Studios and featured an infectious bass riff by Herbie Flowers.

The STATUS QUO sound went up the charts again in 1994, thanks to Manchester United. (Pictorial Press)

361

YOU'RE THE FIRST THE LAST MY EVERYTHING

BARRY WHITE

7 December 1974, for 2 weeks

●●

20TH CENTURY BTC 2133

Writers: Barry White, Tony Sepe and Peter Radcliffe
Producer: Barry White

Big Barry is by far the most successful of any of the Whites to appear in the British singles chart. Of the other four (Chris, Snowy, Tam and Tony Joe), only Snowy has had more than one chart entry, and his second and final hit peaked at only number 65.

Barry first appeared in 1973 with 'I'm Gonna Love You Just A Little Bit More Baby', which made number 23 and set the standard for the title length of White's singles. The longer the title, the better White's chances of a hit. His shorter titles (there are three of four words each) tended not to get quite as high as songs like 'You See The Trouble With Me' (number two in 1976) and 'Can't Get Enough Of Your Love Babe' (number eight in 1974), although quite against form 'It's Ecstasy When You Lay Down Next To Me', which ought by rights to have been a surefire number one, stalled at a disappointing number 40.

Barry White was born in Galveston, Texas, in 1944, and between the years of 1973 and '78 notched up a creditable five Top 20s, four Top 10s and a number one. His smash instrumental, 'Love Theme' by the Love Unlimited Orchestra, was another Top 10er. White is also the answer to the bizarre trivia question, "Who had a bigger UK hit with 'Just The Way You Are' than its composer Billy Joel?"

362

LONELY THIS CHRISTMAS

MUD

21 December 1974, for 4 weeks

●●●●

RAK 187

Writers: Nicky Chinn and Mike Chapman
Producers: Nicky Chinn and Mike Chapman

Mud's first two chart-topping singles were separated by two more Top 10 hits, 'The Cat Crept In' (number two) and

'Rocket' (number six). The group were now in the middle of their glorious but short-lived run of success. This spot of delicate Yuletide emotional blackmail, like their first two number ones, came from the combination of the pens of Chapman and Chinn and the presses of Mickie Most's RAK label.

Mud consisted of Les Gray on lead vocals, Rob Davis on guitar, Roy Stiles on bass and Dave Mount on drums. In 1987, long after the glitter of the charts had faded, a re-formed group billed as Les Gray's Mud could be found playing at supper clubs, as well as college dances and Student Union Christmas parties for students with long memories. Like Gary Glitter, the group are able to capitalize on being a nostalgic remnant so that for the next few holiday seasons middle-aged people up and down the country will murmur the chorus of 'Lonely This Christmas'.

363

DOWN DOWN

STATUS QUO

18 January 1975, for 1 week

•

VERTIGO 6059 114

Writers: Francis Rossi and Robert Young
Producers: Status Quo

In 1975 Status Quo were guitarist/vocalist Francis Rossi (born Michael Rossi 29 May 1949), guitarist/vocalist Rick Parfitt (born 12 October 1948), bassist/vocalist Alan Lancaster (born 7 February 1949) and drummer John Coghlan (born 19 September 1946). Rossi met Lancaster at school and formed the Scorpions when the pair were but 13 years old. Coghlan was recruited in 1965 and the name changed to the Spectres. This was followed by three flop singles released through Pye and another change of name - to Traffic Jam. Under this guise they recorded the prophetically titled 'Almost There But Not Quite'. 1967 saw the arrival of Parfitt and a final name change to Status Quo.

The early Quo were purveyors of psychedelic bubble-gum music and scored two Top 10 hits with 'Pictures of Matchstick Men' and 'Ice In The Sun'. But they soon became disenchanted with their pop image and replaced their Carnaby Street clothes with T-shirts and jeans. The band kept a low profile for two years while they perfected their harder, 12-bar-boogie sound. A Top 20 entry, 'Down The Dustpipe', heralded the change which was complete by the time Quo had moved to Vertigo Records in 1972. Their first single for the label, 'Paper Plane', hit the Top 10 and was third in an unbroken run of 32 Top 40 hits, a feat no other group can boast. 'Down Down' was fifth in this sequence.

Lancaster and Coghlan grew tired after years of touring and quite the group in the 80s. After a brief retirement, Rossi and Parfitt revived the Quo with fresh members and returned to the charts in 1986 with 'In The Army Now', a number two hit and their biggest for six years.

364

MS GRACE

THE TYMES

25 January 1975, for 1 week

•

RCA 2493

Writers: John Hall and Johanna Hall
Producer: Billy Jackson

With 'Ms Grace' the Tymes joined the Dave Clark Five, Bobbie Gentry, Paper Lace, the Osmonds and Barry White on the list of acts who have scored only one number one in the UK and one in the USA, but with different singles. The Tymes took longer about it than the others, having topped the American chart back in 1963 with 'So Much In Love', a UK number 21. By remaining at the top for just seven days on both sides of the Atlantic they made the list with the minimum credentials.

Tymes members George Hilliard and Norman Bennett had been singing together since they met at summer camp in 1956. They formed the Latineers with Donald Banks and Albert Berry. In 1960, when George Williams joined as lead vocalist, the group assumed their more familiar moniker. Hits were always sporadic for the Tymes, one of their best known being their 1969 Top 20 uptempo version of 'People', the Barbra Streisand classic from the musical *Funny Girl*. 'You Little Trust Maker' reintroduced the group to the charts in September 1974, to be followed three months later by 'Ms Grace'. The original title had been 'Miss Grace' but was altered in the wake of women's liberation.

365

JANUARY

PILOT

1 February 1975, for 3 weeks

●●●

EMI 2255

Writer: David Paton
Producer: Alan Parsons

With perfect timing 'January' reached number one on 1 February, to give Alan Parsons his first-ever number one production. His second followed immediately, but his third is yet to come. Pilot were David Paton, Ian Bairnson, Billy Lyle and Stuart Tosh. They first hit the charts with 'Magic' at the end of 1974, which spent 11 weeks on the chart without reaching the Top 10 but promised great things for the future. The great things came with 'January', which hit number one in its third week on the charts. It was a major surprise when neither of the next two singles hit the Top 30, and the band died a natural death. The song's arranger, Andrew Powell, went to to record Kate Bush, and both David Paton and Ian Bairnson played on her first LP, which included 'Wuthering Heights' (see no. 420), but as a group Pilot was grounded.

'January' was the first month to appear in a number one title, apart from Rod Stewart's 'Maggie May'. A year later, the Four Seasons took 'December '63' (see no. 385) to number one, but otherwise months have been unsuccessful title subjects.

366

MAKE ME SMILE (COME UP AND SEE ME)

STEVE HARLEY AND COCKNEY REBEL

22 February 1975, for 2 weeks

●●

EMI 2263

Writer: Steve Harley
Producers: Steve Harley and Alan Parsons

Alan Parsons' second consecutive chart-topper as a producer was the only

'Bye Bye Baby', a 1975 number one for the BAY CITY ROLLERS, had originally been a Four Seasons hit in America ten years earlier. (Pictorial Press)

number one by a group who at one time looked set to be very big indeed. The line-up for 'Make Me Smile (Come Up And See Me)' was Steve Harley on vocals, Stuart Elliott on drums, Jim Cregan on guitar, Duncan Mackay on keyboards and George Ford on bass. Tina Charles (see no. 386) sang back-up vocals. Cregan later joined Rod Stewart and played on 'Da Ya Think I'm Sexy?' (see no. 429) and co-produced 'Baby Jane' (see no. 523), while Mackay moved up to Strawberry Studios when Kevin Godley and Lol Creme left 10 C.C., and can be heard on 'Dreadlock Holiday' (see no. 426). If this band had stayed together, they might have lived up to the promise of the first few hits. However, after only one more single taken from their album *The Best Years Of Our Lives*, a Top 20 hit called 'Mr. Raffles (Man It Was Mean)', Cockney Rebel disbanded.

Steve Harley had one more Top 10 hit on his own with the Lennon/McCartney composition 'Here Comes The Sun' in 1976, but it was to be a further decade before he reappeared in the Top 10, in partnership with Sir Andrew Lloyd Webber's second wife, Sarah Brightman, with the title song from the fabulously successful musical *Phantom Of The Opera*, which reached number seven early in 1986.

367

IF

TELLY SAVALAS

6 March 1975, for 2 weeks

●●

MCA 174

Writer: David Gates
Producer: Snuff Garrett

A catch phrase of 'who loves ya, baby?' and a shaven head brought TV policeman Kojak to the public's attention, and it was primarily on the back of Kojak's popularity that actor Telly Savalas had his first and only British number one single. Savalas had first shed his hair for Burt Lancaster's *Birdman Of Alcatraz* (1962), and it became his trademark in a long and varied career, which included *Horror Express*, *A Town Called Bastard* and *Genghis Khan*. He also made an appearance in *On Her Majesty's Secret Service* (1969) and *The Great Muppet Movie* (1979). Although in most of the films Savalas's bald head and stocky build made him an ideal villain, in real life it was a different story.

Telly Savalas (real name Aristotle Savalas) was born on 21 January 1925 in Garden City, New York, from Greek stock. He graduated from Columbia University and went straight into action as a GI in World War II. He was injured in action and thus decorated with the Purple Heart. After the war he joined the Information Services of the State Department and went on to work as a senior director for ABC News. While at ABC he won the Peabody Award for one of his series, *Your Voice Of America*. He was in his late 30s when he turned to acting, first on TV and later in feature films.

Savalas died of prostate cancer on 22 January 1994.

368

BYE BYE BABY

BAY CITY ROLLERS

22 March 1975, for 6 weeks

●●●●●●

BELL 1409

Writers: Bob Gaudio and Bob Crewe
Producer: Phil Wainman

The Bay City Rollers (original name the Saxons) hailed from Edinburgh and were Leslie McKeown (born 12 November 1955) on lead vocals, Eric Faulkner (born 21 October 1955) and Stuart Wood (born 25 February 1957) on guitars, Alan Longmuir (born 20 June 1953) on bass, and his brother Derek (born 19 March 1955) on drums. By the time 'Bye Bye Baby' hit the top the Rollers' first five singles had already been Top 10 hits, four of them in 1974. The Rollers were backed with slick material, mostly from the pens of Bill Martin and Phil Coulter, who had previously written Sandie Shaw's Eurovision winner, 'Puppet On A String', and management from Tam Paton.

Despite accusations that they didn't actually play on their own records, the Bay City Rollers became a group with an hysterical following, their young audience imitating their trademark tartan clothing. At their heady peak the Bay City Rollers were not just a British, but a worldwide, teen sensation.

369

OH BOY

MUD

3 May 1975, for 2 weeks

●●

RAK 201

Writers: Sonny West, Norman Petty and Bill Tilghman
Producers: Nicky Chinn and Mike Chapman

'Oh Boy' was the last of Mud's three number ones and was actually issued after the group had moved away from Chinn and Chapman and RAK to a new home at the Private Stock label. The song also had the distinction of being the only chart-topper that Chinn and Chapman produced but did not write. It was issued by RAK as a follow-up to the number three hit 'The Secrets That You Keep'. This was a comparatively long title for Mud, who would here appear to be the antithesis of Barry White. Ten of their 15 chart singles had either one- or two-word titles. This was the second time 'Oh Boy' had been a major hit. The first time around, in 1958, it climbed to number three for the Crickets.

After 'Oh Boy' Mud did not reascend the heights they had previously reached. They still managed another four Top 10 singles, three on the new label, one an earlier RAK recording, between June 1975 and November 1976. They are able to look back proudly at a career that boasts three number ones, six Top 10s and three Top 20s in three years. Indeed one of their singles in this period failed to make the Top 30.

370

STAND BY YOUR MAN

TAMMY WYNETTE

17 May 1975, for 3 weeks

●●●

EPIC EPC 7137

Writers: Billy Sherill and Tammy Wynette
Producer: Billy Sherrill

Tammy Wynette (born Virginia Wynette Pugh, 5 May 1942) had been divorced from her husband, country singer George Jones, for exactly two months when this song of female devotion became her only number one. It had been recorded seven years earlier. Tammy's chart career is unusal in that each of her three hit singles, 'Stand By Your Man', 'D.I.V.O.R.C.E.' and 'I Don't Want To Play House', were re-releases of American country hits from 1967/68.

Tammy was well qualified to sing about the subject of marriage, having gone through the process five times, beginning at the age of 17. By 20 she had three children. Working as a beautician in Birmingham, Alabama, she supplemented her income by plugging records and singing in local clubs and bars. She then came to the attention of Epic producer Billy Sherrill, who signed her to the label in 1966. Her relationship with George Jones was at first musical, but matrimony followed in 1969.

On 6 July 1978 Tammy decided to stand by yet another man, manager and record producer George Richey. The pair married in the singer's luxury Florida home. Her biography, also called *Stand By Your Man*, was adapted for film in 1982.

Wynette nearly had a second number one in 1992, when she guested on KLF's number two hit 'Justified And Ancient'.

371

WHISPERING GRASS

WINDSOR DAVIES AND DON ESTELLE

7 June 1975, for 3 weeks

●●●

EMI 2290

Writers: Fred and Doris Fisher
Producer: Walter Ridley

TV comedy writers Jimmy Perry and David Croft had a long association with the BBC, responsible as a team, or with other writers, for such series as *Are You Being Served*, *Hi De Hi*, *'Allo 'Allo* and *Dad's Army*. Each of these series spawned one hit: 'Are You Being Served Sir?' by John Inman, 'Hi De Hi (Holiday Rock)' by Paul Shane and the Yellowcoats, 'Je T'Aime (Allo Allo)' by Rene and Yvette and, indirectly, 'Grandad' by Clive Dunn (see no. 295). *It Aint Half Hot Mum*, set in wartime India, starred Windsor Davies and Don Estelle, who respectively played the bullying Battery Sgt Major Williams and the diminutive and cowardly Private 'Lofty' Sugden. They became the most successful of Perry and Croft's creations by scoring two hits. 'Whispering Grass' had been made popular four decades earlier by one of the most successful singing groups of the pre-chart era, the Inkspots. When the cast of *It Ain't Half Hot Mum* was asked to record an album of army-concert party favourites, 'Whispering Grass' was a natural choice, but in this version Estelle's beautiful tenor was juxtaposed with Davies' gruff spoken voice. When released as a single it climbed to the top of the charts within a month. The follow-up, 'Paper Doll', reached number 41 in autumn 1975, but subsequent solo efforts by Don Estelle failed to chart. However, the Davies/Estelle partnership had been formed and the pair continued to appear together in pantomime and cabaret for several years.

372

I'M NOT IN LOVE

10 C.C.

28 June 1975, for 2 weeks

●●

MERCURY 6008 014

Writers: Graham Gouldman and Eric Stewart
Producers: 10 C.C.

'I'm Not In Love' was 10 C.C.'s second number one single, coming two years

After 10 C.C. were no longer in love, Godley and Creme found duo success together, Graham Gouldman joined Andrew Gold in Wax and Eric Stewart briefly worked with Paul McCartney. (Pictorial Press).

after 1973's 'Rubber Bullets'. It was also the second release for their new label, Mercury, who had signed them from Jonathan King's UK label. The track was taken from their *Original Soundtrack* album, a set that had yielded a number seven for the group, in the shape of 'Life Is A Minstrone', and would give them a number five later in the year with 'Art For Art's Sake'.

With hindsight, 'I'm Not In Love' can be seen as one of the outstanding songs of the 1970s and certainly one of the best of 10 C.C.'s influential output. The string of successful singles the group put together between 1972 and 1978 made them the most consistent hitmakers of any British group in the 70s. They can list three number ones and eight Top 10s.

'I'm Not In Love' also enjoyed a further brief spell of chart success in 1987 when two-time Eurovision winner Johnny Logan took his version into the Top 50. Godley and Creme split from Gouldman and Stewart in 1976, creating two hit acts. They were together on 1987's smash compilation album *Changing Faces.*

373

TEARS ON MY PILLOW

JOHNNY NASH

12 July 1975, for 1 week

●

CBS 3220

Writer: Ernie Smith
Producer: Johnny Nash

John Lester Nash Jr, born in Houston, Texas, on 19 August 1940, first hit the British charts in 1968 when his reggae-flavoured 'Hold Me Tight' reached number five in the autumn of that year. He had been a successful recording star in America since the end of 1957 when his first hit, 'A Very Special Love', reached number 46 in the *Billboard* charts. At the end of 1958 he released a single with ABC Paramount stablemates Paul Anka and George Hamilton IV called 'The Teen Commandments', which gave him his biggest hit until 'Hold Me Tight' and which is now a collector's item.

A succession of hits followed 'Hold Me Tight', oddly enough in batches of three every three years. After three hits in 1968/69, and three more in 1972 (including his US number one hit 'I Can See Clearly Now'), 'Tears On My Pillow' was the first of three hits in 1975/6. 1979 passed without Nash's distinctive voice returning to the charts. He remains one of the most successful reggae acts in British chart history, and his early recordings of the late Bob Marley's songs certainly contributed to the subsequent success that came to Marley and the Wailers a little later.

374

GIVE A LITTLE LOVE

THE BAY CITY ROLLERS

19 July 1975, for 3 weeks

●●●

BELL 1425

Writers: Johnny Goodison and Phil Wainman
Producer: Phil Wainman

'Give A Little Love' was the Bay City Rollers' second consecutive number one single. A year later they had the last of their ten consecutive Top 10 singles, 'I Only Wanna Be With You'. By then Alan Longmuir had left because he felt that, at 26, he was too old for the group. He was replaced by 18-year-old Ian Mitchell, who himself left and was replaced by Pat McGlynn. When McGlynn quit in 1977 the group continued as a four-piece. They met with little success when their record company tried to give them a more adult image.

During the last year of their huge British success, they also managed a number one single in the USA, but it was all downhill after this, and after two chart appearances at number 16 and 34 in 1977 they did not appear in the chart again.

375

BARBADOS

TYPICALLY TROPICAL

9 August 1975 , for 1 week

●

GULL GULS 14

Writers: Jeffrey Calvert and Max West
Producers: Jeffrey Calvert and Max West

Jeffrey Calvert and Max West, two recording engineers, used spare studio time to record their own compositions. One of those was a Christmas novelty tune, 'The Ghost Song', which was recorded for Mickie Most's RAK label but was finished too late to be released for the 1974 festive season. Having failed to cash in on the Christmas market, they then made a bid for summer success with a piece of ersatz reggae entitled 'Barbados', featuring spoken vocals by Captain Tobias Wilcock of Coconut Airways.

Although it was far from the genuine article, 'Barbados' had orignally been scheduled for release with legendary reggae label Trojan Records. At the last moment Gull stepped in with a better offer. As perfect for summer as 'In The Summertime' had been in 1970, the single took off as soon as it was released, but had to hold at number two for a couple of weeks before the Rollers lost their grip on the top spot.

Apart from Calvert and West, who aspired to emulate the success of writers/producers Mike Chapman and Nicky Chinn, Typically Tropical was an aggregation of session musicians. Even at the time it seemed unlikely that they could follow up their hit, and plans to revitalize 'The Ghost Song' came to nothing. Typically Tropical remain one-hit wonders to this day.

376

CAN'T GIVE YOU ANYTHING (BUT MY LOVE)

THE STYLISTICS

16 August 1975, for 3 weeks

●●●

AVCO 6105 039

Writers: Hugo Peretti, Luigi Creatore and George David Weiss
Producers: Hugo Peretti and Luigi Creatore

The leftovers of two defunct Philadelphia groups, the Percussions and the Monarchs combined at the beginning of the 1970s to create the Stylistics, a five-man vocal group which built its hits around the falsetto singing of their lead vocalist, Russell Thompkins Jr. The other members of the group, James Dunn, Aaron Love, Herbie Murrell and James Smith, provided a slick backing but the only real distinction of the group sound was Thompkins' lead vocal.

When first they signed for Hugo and Luigi's Avco label, their singles were produced by Thom Bell, and were, in the main, written by Bell and Linda Creed. Records like 'I'm Stone In Love With You' and 'You Make Me Feel Brand New' made the Stylistics one of the hottest groups in the world by the mid-70s, and when Hugo and Luigi themselves (with more than a little help from the late Van McCoy) took over production of Stylistics singles, the hits carried on uninterrupted. 'Can't Give You Anything (But My Love)' was the group's tenth chart single and was co-written by George David Weiss, who had co-written 'Can't Help Falling In Love' for Elvis Presley (see no. 133).

It was no surprise, therefore, that the Stylistics recorded 'Can't Help Falling In Love' in 1976 and made it one of those very rare songs to have been a Top 10 hit three times.

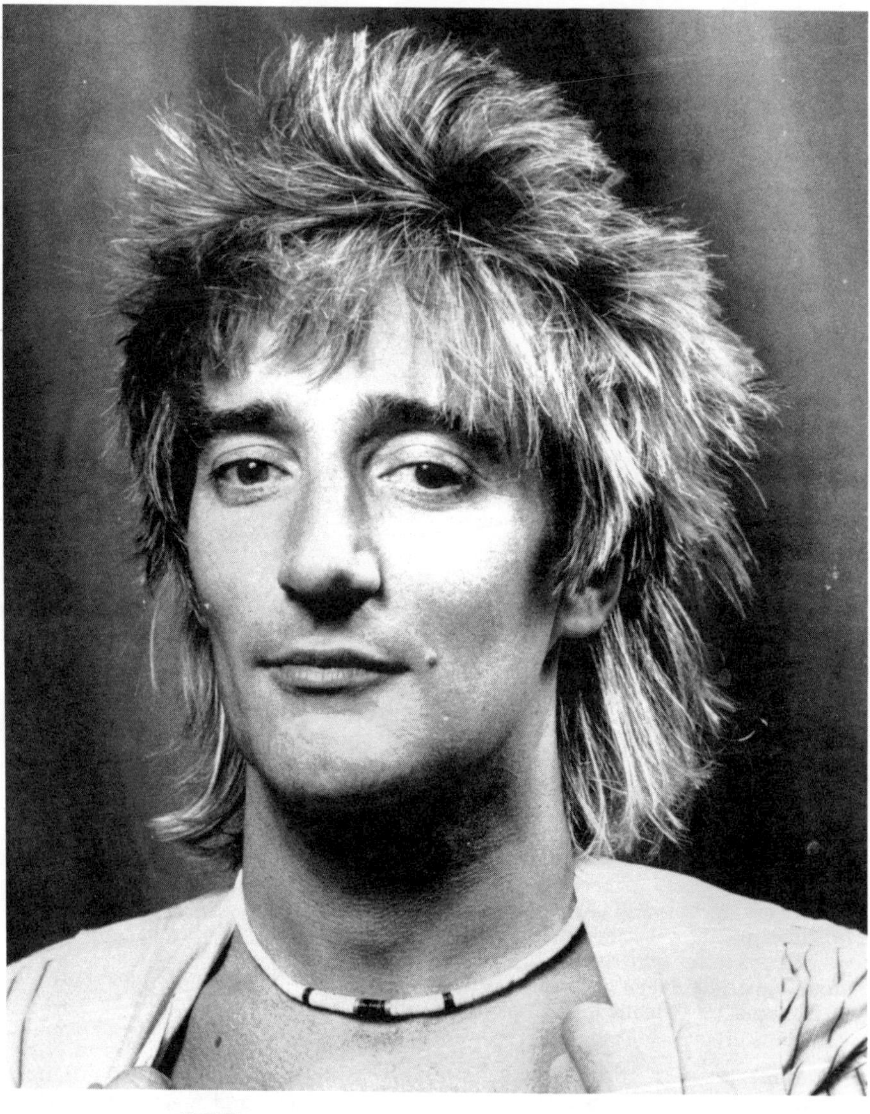

ROD STEWART sailed to number one in September 1975, anchoring there for 4 weeks. (Pictorial Press)

377

SAILING

ROD STEWART

6 September 1975, for 4 weeks

●●●●

WARNER BROTHERS K 16600

Writer: Gavin Sutherland
Producer: Tom Dowd

In the second half of the 70s, 'Sailing' had more weeks on the chart than any record except Boney M's 'Rivers of Babylon'/ 'Brown Girl In The Ring'. It had 11 weeks in its first go, which included four weeks at number one and 20 weeks in the second run the following year, when it crawled back to number three. The come-back was spurred by the use of the record as the theme for a BBC television series about HMS *Ark Royal*.

This song originally appeared on an album by the Sutherland Brothers. Sutherland knew he had penned a catchy tune and used it with joke lyrics for a flimsy single distributed as a Christmas greeting, now a collectable for trivia buffs and Stewart aficionados.

Rod, who realized his recording career needed a shot in the arm, went to record in the United States with legendary producer Tom Dowd. Arriving at the Muscle Shoals Studio he inquired where the famous rhythm section was. Told he was looking them, he blurted out in surprise that they were white men. He had assumed that such soulful players had to be black.

Stewart intended his version of 'Sailing' to be 'one for the terraces', a record whose popularity would be enhanced by its use by football crowds. He was not disappointed; the song was used by supporters up and down the country.

378

HOLD ME CLOSE

DAVID ESSEX

4 October 1975, for 3 weeks

●●●

CBS 3572

Writer: David Essex
Producer: Jeff Wayne

Since 'Gonna Make You A Star' reached the top in 1974, David Essex had finished filming *Stardust* and had twice made the Top 10. 'Hold Me Close' proved to be his final number one.

Essex was involved in Jeff Wayne's massively popular *War Of The Worlds* LP, but he then changed careers once more, returning to the theatre in 1978 to win the Variety Club Personality Of The Year award for his portrayal of Che Guevara in *Evita*. His single 'Oh What A Circus', from *Evita*, reached number three in the autumn of 1978.

In 1980 the theme from his motorcycle movie *Silver Dream Machine* gave him his eighth Top 10 hit. 1982 found him hosting his own TV series, *The David Essex Showcase*, a programme which concentrated on new acts such as Mari Wilson and Philip Jap. Later that same year he appeared as the poet Byron in the Young Vic's production of *Childe Byron*, and he rounded off a hectic 12 months by having one of his biggest hits to date, 'A Winter's Tale', which was kept from the top by only Renée and Renato's immortal love duet. Probably his most ambitious project started in 1983, when he began work on a musical based on 1789's mutiny on HMS *Bounty*. The show opened in London's Piccadilly Theatre in 1984, with Essex as Fletcher Christian and Frank Finlay as Captain Blythe. 'Tahiti', taken from the musical, brought Essex's Top 10 tally into double figures.

379

I ONLY HAVE EYES FOR YOU

ART GARFUNKEL

25 October 1975, for 2 weeks

●●

CBS 3575

Writers: Harry Warren and Al Dubin
Producer: Richard Perry

After splitting with Paul Simon, Art Garfunkel followed a film career, starring in such successes as *Catch 22* and the Jack Nicholson/Ann-Margret/Candice Bergen film *Carnal Knowledge*. He recorded only sporadically, and his first solo hit in Britain came after Paul Simon had already had four solo outings on our charts, including two Top 10 hits. Garfunkel did better than his former partner, however, by reaching the very top with this song from the 1930s which had been an American hit for the Flamingos in 1959.

The writers of the song, Harry Warren and Al Dubin, also wrote such standards as 'September In The Rain' and 'You're Getting To Be A Habit With Me', but 'I Only Have Eyes For You' was their only major success on the British charts. Art Garfunkel's chart career then went into total collapse until his next hit and his next number one in 1979 (see no. 436). Once again, eyes were the secret of his success.

ABBA put their best feet forward in 1976 when they had three number ones. (Pictorial Press)

380

SPACE ODDITY

DAVID BOWIE

8 November 1975, for 2 weeks

●●

RCA 2593

Writer: David Bowie. Producer: Gus Dudgeon

'Space Oddity' was for years the only record to go to number one as a re-issue. As it first charted in 1969, it had the further distinction of being the only single to have taken more than one year to reach number one after its initial appearance in the best sellers, until equalled by John Lennon's 'Imagine'. It was a slower-moving hit than even these statistics suggest. Bowie wrote the number in 1968 for a proposed German television special, *Love You Till Tuesday*.

'Space Oddity' was eventually released to tie in with the 1969 *Apollo* moon landing, but Americans shied away from the terrible tale of Major Tom; they wished Neil Armstrong and company success, not doom. The single finally charted in Britain in the first week of September, but then dropped out. It re-entered later in the month, eventually earning a placing at number five. The song finally made the American Top 10 in 1972. Upon re-issue as part of a series of RCA oldies it made its glorious British flight in 1976. Bowie re-recorded it in sparser style for a 1980 B-side. That year his 'Ashes To Ashes' (see no. 464), continuing the story of Major Tom, became the only sequel to a number one hit to make number one itself.

'Space Oddity' was the only Bowie A-side produced by Gus Dudgeon, who later worked on Elton John's hits, including, ironically, 'Rocket Man'. Rick Wakeman played synthesizer on this Bowie disc.

381

D.I.V.O.R.C.E.

BILLY CONNOLLY

22 November 1975, for 1 week

●

POLYDOR 2058 652

Writers: Billy Connolly, Claude Putnam Jr and Bobby Braddock. Producer: Phil Coulter

Six months after Tammy Wynette hit the

top of the charts with her classic moral clarion call (see no. 370), Scottish comedian Billy Connolly adapted one of her biggest American hits to his own purposes and took it all the way to the top, bleeped language and all. The original song, which went to number 12 as a follow-up to 'Stand By Your Man' in the summer of 1975, is one of the most sickly, yet most compulsive, of all Tammy Wynette's recordings, but the Big Yin transformed the song into the saga of a scruffy Scottish dog breaking up an otherwise happy and civilised Glasgow couple.

Billy Connolly has been so successful as a comedian that his record sales, though considerable, are merely a sideline. He has had only four chart singles, but he has enjoyed greater success as an album artist, including three Top 10 hits on the LP charts. After the success of 'D.I.V.O.R.C.E.', he attacked another Tammy Wynette song which had, in the meantime, reached number one when covered by J.J. Barrie (see no. 389). Connolly's version was called 'No Chance (No Charge)'. After 'In The Brownies' in 1979, a song based in part on the Village People's 'Y.M.C.A.' (the only other initials song to hit number one), he body swerved the singles charts until 1985, when his TV-theme 'Super Gran' reached number 32.

382

BOHEMIAN RHAPSODY

QUEEN

29 November 1975, for 9 weeks

●●●●●●●●●

EMI 2375

Writer: Freddie Mercury
Producers: Roy Thomas Baker and Queen

Only 18 months after their first hit, 'Seven Seas of Rhye', Queen topped the list with a single that was a masterpiece of popular music. Not since 'Rose Marie' by Slim Whitman had dominated the chart for 11 weeks in 1955 had a record remained at the top for so long. Any other group may have been cowed by such early success but for vocalist Freddie Mercury (born Frederick Bulsara, 5 September 1946), guitarist Brian May (born 19 July 1947), bassist John Deacon (born 19 August 1951) and drummer Roger Taylor (born 26 July 1949) it was simply the start of a career that saw them become one of the most popular groups in the world.

Queen grew out of the art-school band Smile, which Mercury formed in the early 1970s. They evolved their sound, characterized by Mercury's dramatic vocals and May's distinctive guitar sound, partly achieved by employing a coin as a plectrum. Whether it was the mock gospel of 'Somebody To Love', the rock and roll pastiche of 'Crazy Little Thing Called Love' or the disco-influenced 'Another One Bites The Dust' (the last two being US number ones), the act was always identifiable as Queen.

A promotional video for television was made for 'Bo Rhap', as the group affectionately referred to the song, and it is generally acknowledged as the first pop video to assist the success of a single. The trend for video production grew until, by the mid-80s, any hit which didn't have an accompanying video was an exception to the rule.

383

MAMMA MIA

ABBA

31 January 1976, for 2 weeks

●●

EPIC EPC 3790

Writers: Stig Anderson, Bjorn Ulvaeus and Benny Andersson
Producers: Bjorn Ulvaeus and Benny Andersson

The record that changed Abba from just another European group into the Superswedes whose sales exceeded those of Volvo was 'Mamma Mia'. Not that 'Mamma Mia' was itself a massive worldwide smash, but by giving Abba their second number one in Britain almost two years after their first, it established a base of international popularity on which they built their incredible sales of the late 70s and early 80s.

Between 'Waterloo' and 'Mamma Mia' there were some flops and three hits. Two of those hits did not even make the Top 30, but 'SOS', the release before 'Mamma Mia', climbed to number six to return Abba to the Top 10 after 18 months' absence. When 'Mamma Mia' hit the top Abba became the first act to have a number one hit after their Eurovision number one, a feat that has since been equalled by Brotherhood Of Man, Cliff Richard and Bucks Fizz but never by a foreign act. Abba changed popular music by making record executives realize that European groups can sell, whether or not they are Abba imitators. Acts like Europe, A-ha and Roxette owe a lot of their international success to the achievements of Abba, which really began with 'Mamma Mia', the 383rd record and 400th different song to reach number one.

384

FOREVER AND EVER

SLIK

14 February 1976, for 1 week

•

BELL 1464

Writers: Bill Martin and Phil Coulter
Producers: Bill Martin and Phil Coulter

Slik, the last of the 70s teen groups were, like the Bay City Rollers, from Scotland. Bill Martin and Phil Coulter wrote and produced them, as they had the Rollers, so - not surprisingly - they also sounded like the Bay City Rollers.

Martin and Coulter had parted company with the Rollers bandwagon some 12 months before their association with Slik and had been looking for another musical vehicle. They'd long been associated with Eurovision, having written the UK entries in 1966 and 1968 (see nos. 232 and 248), and had also masterminded hits for Irish artist Kenny. When Kenny left RAK records, Martin and Coulter simply retained the name, to which they owned the rights, and dumped it on another bunch of young hopefuls, who hit with 'The Bump' and 'Fancy Pants'.

Then came Slik, who were guitarist James 'Midge' Ure, keyboard player Billy McIsaac, drummer Kenny Hyslop and bassist Jim McGinlay. Dressed in smart baseball outfits they were leapt upon by the pop press, who applauded them as the Next Big Thing. However, Slik were not to be stars forever and ever. Their follow-up, 'Requiem', clambered to number 24 and that was it.

Ure, who nearly joined the Sex Pistols, was able to demonstrate his talent later with new wavers the Rich Kids, then with New Romantics Visage and electropoppers Ultravox, who had a massive number two hit with 'Vienna' in 1981. Hyslop also managed to revive his career by joining Simple Minds that same year. Midge Ure was not to be associated with another number one until almost nine years later. It was to be the biggest-selling single in the UK to date (see no. 543).

385

DECEMBER '63 (OH WHAT A NIGHT)

THE FOUR SEASONS

21 February 1976, for 2 weeks

••

WARNER BROTHERS K 16688

Writers: Bob Gaudio and Judy Parker
Producer: Bob Gaudio

The Four Seasons emanated from New Jersey and named themselves after the cocktail lounge in a bowling alley. The original line-up was Frankie Valli (born Francis Castelluccio in Newark, 3 May 1937), Tommy and Nick DeVito, and Hank Megenski. The group achieved huge success in the early 60s with hits like 'Sherry', 'Let's Hang On', and 'Rag Doll', but the line-up that operated by then had changed to Valli, Tommy DeVito, Bob Gaudio (born in the Bronx, New York, on 17 November 1942) and Nick Massi. They achieved considerable credibility, that helped them survive a turbulent period in pop music's history, when the Rolling Stones announced that the Four Seasons was the only American group worth paying any attention to.

In the year before their only British number one single they had two Top 10 hits with 'Night' and 'Who Loves You', but by now the group was really five

Seasons, featuring Valli, Gaudio, Don Ciccone, John Paiva and Gerry Polci, the last-named handling the lead vocal on 'December '63'. The follow-up was 'Silver Star', which made number three in the same year. Valli was not through, however, landing a Top 10 theme tune, 'Grease', in 1978.

386

I LOVE TO LOVE (BUT MY BABY LOVES TO DANCE)

TINA CHARLES

6 March 1976, for 3 weeks

●●●

CBS 3937

Writers: Jack Robinson and James Bolden
Producer: Biddu

With 'I Love To Love' Tina Charles emerged from the legion of studio session singers to become, albeit briefly, Britain's foremost female disco star. Her loud and full-throated voice had anonymously graced many hits, most notably 'I'm On Fire', a Top 5 hit released under the group name 5000 Volts in 1975. At the beginning of 1976 she began working with Indian producer Biddu, who had provided Carl Douglas with a number one hit in both the UK and the USA 18 months earlier (see no. 356). The partnership worked and a star was born.

Tina made the Top 10 on only two further occasions with 'Dr Love' and 'Dance Little Lady Dance', although a remixed version of 'I Love To Love' sold over 600,000 copies across Europe when released in 1986.

Tina's career was held back by a lack of good material and the birth of her first baby in 1977. A friend at the time of her number one was Trevor Horn. Horn had long been a pal of musician and jingle-writer Geoff Downes, whom he recruited to Tina's tour band. Downes and Horn began writing songs with Bruce Wolley, including 'Baby Blue', a minor hit for Dusty Springfield in 1979 (see no. 213). But the Downes-Horn partnership was to produce greater success once they had assumed the group identity of the Buggles (see no. 444).

387

SAVE YOUR KISSES FOR ME

BROTHERHOOD OF MAN

27 March 1976, for 6 weeks

●●●●●●

PYE 7N 45569

Writers: Tony Hiller, Martin Lee and Lee Sheriden
Producer: Tony Hiller

More than 'Waterloo', more than 'Puppet On A String', more than 'Non Ho L'Eta Per Amarti', 'Save Your Kisses For Me' was a runaway Eurovision Song Contest winner even before the voting had started. The coy little song of Daddy going to work and leaving his 3-year-old daughter at home for the day not only smashed through the charts and into the hearts of Europe, but marked an astonishing and surprisingly long-lived comeback for Brotherhood Of Man.

In 1970 Brotherhood Of Man were a two-man, two-girl vocal group rather hurriedly put together around a session hit, 'United We Stand', that reached number ten in Britain. It was used an an anthem of gay liberation in America in the early 70s.

388

FERNANDO

ABBA

8 May 1976, for 4 weeks

●●●●

EPIC EPC 4036

Writers: Stig Anderson, Bjorn Ulvaeus and Benny Andersson
Producers: Bjorn Ulvaeus and Benny Andersson

Abba's third number one, their second in succession, was 'Fernando'. It knocked Brotherhood Of Man off the top, but they retaliated by modelling their style ever closer on Abba, even coming up with two more chart-toppers, 'Angelo' and 'Figaro' (see nos. 410 and 418), whose titles bore a more than coincidental similarity to 'Fernando'.

'Fernando' was a gentle anti-war song, featuring the only mistake in English in Bjorn Ulvaeus' lyrics, when he wrote, "Since many years I haven't seen a rifle in your hand". It may seem churlish to point out the mistakes in English, but it is worth mentioning only because it is unique. How many English writers could write nine number one hits in a foreign language virtually without error? Albert Hammond (writer of 'When I Need You' – see no. 401) speaks fluent Spanish, but even he prefers to write about the rain in Southern California rather than the rain in Spain. Abba had also had hits with song titles in Italian, 'Mamma Mia', and French, 'Voulez-vous', but the nearest they had got to their native Swedish was their ode to Stockholm, 'Summer Night City'.

389

NO CHARGE

J.J. BARRIE

5 June 1976, for 1 week

●

POWER EXCHANGE PX 209

Writer: Harlan Howard
Producer: Bill Amesbury

Canadian J.J. Barrie (born Barrie Authors, 7 July 1933, Ottawa, Ontario) made it to the top with a cover version of a Melba Montgomery country hit which was also a US success for Tammy Wynette and her daughter, Tina. It was only the second song he had ever recorded.

Barrie, a former comedian and manager of Blue Mink, had not intended to become a singer when he released his first single, 'Where's The Reason?', in 1976. He and Terry Britten had written the song for Glen Campbell and had sent him a demonstration tape, but Campbell's producer saw no reason why Barrie shouldn't put the song out himself.

Then came the somewhat sentimental 'No Charge', a version of which Barrie had once included in his comedy routines. The uncredited female vocalist who contributed greatly to the single's success is the late Vicky Brown, the wife of early 60s rocker Joe Brown. Comedian Billy Connolly wasted no time in lampooning the song in the way he had Tammy Wynette's 'D.I.V.O.R.C.E.' (see no. 381). The Scotsman's version, titled 'No Chance (No Charge)', also made the Top 30. Barrie re-released 'Where's The Reason?' as a follow-up but it failed again. Then, in 1977, as a tribute to the late Bing Crosby, Barrie recorded his song 'So Long Bing'. Ten albums and many singles later, J.J. remains a one-hit wonder. Harlan Howard is the writer of many country classics, including 'Busted' and 'The Chokin' Kind'.

390

COMBINE HARVESTER (BRAND NEW KEY)

THE WURZELS

12 June 1976, for 3 weeks

●●●

EMI 2450

Writer: Melanie Safka
Producer: Bob Barratt

While the scorching summer of 1976 created havoc for real farmers, the trio who made their career singing about that industry found it a time of celebration. The Wurzels, who started out in 1966 as Adge Cutler's backing band, were Tommy Banner, Tony Baylis and Pete Budd. They had been managed since the late 60s by John Miles, and they secured a record deal with EMI after Bob Barratt heard a tape of theirs and saw potential in their distinctive brand of entertainment. The group decided to continue after Cutler's death in a car crash in 1974, and it was Barratt who suggested that they put new lyrics to Melanie's US number one and UK Top 5 hit, 'Brand New Key'. The Wurzels totally re-wrote the lyrics, though Melanie still received all the songwriting royalties, and the result was 'Combine Harvester', the saga of a West Country farmer courting his lady love.

The song charted after extensive radio

play. It was one of those few comedy records that can withstand a certain number of repeated plays.

Although the Wurzels had been a popular club act in the south for over ten years, and had even appeared on the Simon Dee and David Frost television shows, the number one hit broke them beyond their native West Country. Their immortal *Top Of The Pops* appearances featured a full-size combine harvester as a prop, and they were quickly signed up to promote farming equipment. They appeared on many television variety shows.

The trio was determined not to become a novelty act and very nearly returned to the top spot with their follow-up, 'I Am A Cider Drinker', based on George Baker's 'Una Paloma Blanca'. Their last hit was in June 1977.

391

YOU TO ME ARE EVERYTHING

THE REAL THING

26 June 1976, for 3 weeks

●●●

PYE INTERNATIONAL 7N 25709

Writers: Ken Gold and Micky Denne
Producer: Ken Gold

The Real Thing, four Liverpool lads, were another of those number one hitmakers who first came to public notice on the Hughie Green talent show, *Opportunity Knocks*.

Success was not immediate for the group even after they had been spotted by the ex-Radio Luxembourg DJ Tony Hall. The Real Thing, who were Chris Amoo and his brother Eddie, Dave Smith and Ray Lake, were signed, unsuccessfully, to a couple of major labels before a move to Pye changed their luck. Linking up with producer Ken Gold, they took one of his songs to the very top as their first chart entry. Eight other hits followed over a three-year period, including 'Can't Get By Without You', which reached number two, and over two years later, 'Can You Feel The Force?', which reached number five. Another label change in 1980 to Calibre resulted in one more minor hit, 'She's A Groovy Freak'.

It was six years before the public heard much more of the Real Thing, although they had toured with David Essex in the interim. In 1986, PRT remixed the group's three biggest hits of ten years earlier, two of which became Top 10 hits all over again. 'You To Me Are Everything (The Decade Remix)' climbed to number five and stayed on the charts for 13 weeks, two weeks more than the chart-topping original. A new release, 'Straight To The Heart', on the Jive label gave the four-some a hit on their fourth different label, but probably the major event of the 80s for the band was when an Afghan hound bred by Chris Amoo emerged as the Cruft's Supreme Champion for 1987.

392

THE ROUSSOS PHENOMENON EP

DEMIS ROUSSOS

17 July 1976, for 1 week

●

PHILIPS DEMIS 001

Writers: 'Forever And Ever' - Stylianos Vlaviano and Robert Costandinos; 'Sing An Ode To Love' - Stylianos Vlaviano, Charalampe Chalkitis and Robert Costandinos; 'So Dreamy' - Stylianos Vlaviano and Robert Costandinos; 'My Friend The Wind' - Stylianos Vlaviano and Robert Costandinos
Producer: Demis Roussos

Demis Roussos (born 15 June 1947 in Alexandria) and Vangelis Papathanassiou were members of Aphrodite's Child, whose million-selling single, 'Rain and Tears', hit the British Top 30 late in 1968. Demis had to wait another eight years to get to number one with an EP of songs he had recorded between 1973 and 1976. Vangelis was patient until 1981, when his solo chart debut was made with the theme to the film *Chariots Of Fire*, a US chart-topper the following year.

At seventeen and a half stones Roussos was possibly the heaviest number one hit-maker. His EP was certainly heavy on playing time, clocking in at 14 minutes and 44 seconds. Britons taking holidays in Greece had been enchanted by his flowing robes and ethereal voice for many years and had been returning home with suitcases full of Roussos albums. Philips decided to market his appeal in the UK, and his chart account was opened with the 1975 Top 10 hit 'Happy To Be On An Island In The Sun'. His number one EP was followed by a number two smash, 'When Forever Has Gone', but it is Roussos who has been gone from the charts since 1977.

His name returned to the headlines in the most dramatic of circumstances in 1985, when he was hijacked along with the passengers and crew of the airliner in which he was travelling. For several days he was held hostage at Beirut airport until he and his fellow prisoners were released unharmed.

393

DON'T GO BREAKING MY HEART

ELTON JOHN AND KIKI DEE

24 July 1976, for 6 weeks

●●●●●●

ROCKET ROKN 512

Writers: Ann Orson and Carte Blanche
(aka Elton John and Bernie Taupin)
Producer: Gus Dudgeon

Elton John was the world's most prominent and best-selling recording artist in the early and mid-70s. But for all his global success he had never reached number one in his home country, coming closest with the 1972 number two 'Rocket Man'. In March of 1976 he recorded his part of the duet at Eastern Sound in Toronto, Canada. The tape was then brought to London where Kiki Dee added her vocal. As usual, Gus Dudgeon produced and Bernie Taupin supplied the lyrics. The difference was the use of the songwriting pseudonyms Anne Orson and Carte Blanche, which Elton and Bernie used sometimes when penning material for Kiki.

Elton's first release on his Rocket label, 'Don't Go Breaking My Heart' exploded in the summer, going to number one in Britain for six weeks and America for four. It penetrated international markets previously closed to Elton as a soloist and was the world number one for 1976.

The pair considered recording the Four Tops' 'Loving You Is The Sweeter Than Ever' but didn't get around to it until 1981. In 1993 they finally issued a follow-up, 'True Love', which surged to number two. The release of 'Don't Go Breaking My Heart' came as Elton entered a period of voluntary retirement, with no original studio material emerging for nearly two years. He has had five solo number ones in America and appeared there on the chart-topping AIDS relief disc, 'That's What Friends Are For' by Dionne and Friends.

394

DANCING QUEEN

ABBA

4 September 1976, for 6 weeks

●●●●●●

EPIC EPC 4499

Writers: Stig Anderson, Benny Andersson
and Bjorn Ulvaeus
Producers: Benny Andersson and Bjorn Ulvaeus

Abba completed their first hat-trick of number ones in Britain with 'Dancing Queen', which also became their only American number one. The group had been quoted as saying that they would never tour America until they had a number one hit there, so the success of 'Dancing Queen' gave them the excuse to sample the delights of motels and fast food in the United States.

The follow-up to 'Dancing Queen' was Abba's only single in three years not to make the top. It was called 'Money Money Money' and reached number three. It confirmed the jinx on 'money' records. The Bay City Rollers followed up two number ones with 'Money Honey', which also reached number three. Elvis Presley's first flop after five consecutive number ones in 1961 and 1962, was 'One Broken Heart For Sale'. At least the Beatles (with 'Can't Buy Me Love') managed to sing about money without a drop in popularity.

395

MISSISSIPPI

PUSSYCAT

11 October 1976, for 4 weeks

●●●●

SONET SON 2077

Writer: Werner Theunissen
Producer: Eddy Hilberts

Pussycat became the third European act to hit number one in Britain in 1976, and the first-ever Dutch stars at the very top of the British charts. The group began life in Limburg, in South Holland, and the song they took to the top was the third number one about an American state, after 'Carolina Moon' (see no. 75) and 'Massachusetts' (see no. 238).

The line-up on 'Mississippi' was Lou Willé, his wife Tony, who sang lead, her two sisters Marianne Hensen and Betty Dragstra, and three men who had begun their rock career as a band called Scum, Theo Wetzels, Theo Coumans and John Theunissen. The three sisters (the most sisters in any number one group, but still below the brothers record, which stands at five for both the Jacksons and the Osmonds) had been telephone operators in Limburg, while Lou Willé played with his brothers in a group called Ricky Rendell and His Centurions, until he married Tony and helped create a band called Sweet Reaction.

When this band signed to EMI-Bovema in the Netherlands and producer Eddy Hilberts took them into the studio, he changed their name to Pussycat and gave them a song written six years earlier by Werner Theunissen, who was guitar tutor to the three sisters and no relation to John Theunissen. The song, 'Mississippi', was their first single and sold a reputed four and a half million copies worldwide, making Pussycat the biggest thing to come out of Limburg since the cheese.

396

IF YOU LEAVE ME NOW

CHICAGO

13 November 1976, for 3 weeks

●●●

CBS 4603

Writer: Peter Cetera
Producer: James Guercio

Chicago began in life in the late 60s as Chicago Transit Authority, which persuaded one co-author of this book to release a couple of singles under the name Huddersfield Transit Authority. For a while it looked as though the two organizations would enjoy equal success in the UK, but then CTA became just plain Chicago, and charted with the Spencer Davis hit, 'I'm A Man'. The follow-up, '25 Or 6 To 4', was another Top 10 hit. Six hitless years followed for both Huddersfield and Chicago. At the end of 1976 'If You Leave Me Now' climbed to the very top.

The prime movers of Chicago were Pete Cetera, the vocalist (born 13 September 1944), Robert Lamn on keyboards (born 13 October 1944) and Terry Kath on guitar (born 31 January 1946, died 23 January 1978 in a shooting accident). The rest of the line-up was Lee Loughnana, Jim Pankow, Walter Parazaider, Dan Seraphine and Laudir Oliviera, a Brazilian who joined in 1974. Most of their album titles consisted of their name and a Roman numeral. 'If You Love Me Now' came from *Chicago X*.

397

UNDER THE MOON OF LOVE

SHOWADDYWADDY

4 December 1976, for 3 weeks

●●●

BELL 1495

Writers: Tommy Boyce and Curtis Lee
Producer: Mike Hurst

In 1973 two rival Leicester bands, the Hammers and the Choice, decided to marry their fortunes to create an eight-piece rock and roll group called Showaddywaddy. This explains why the band had two of everything; vocalists Dave Bartram and Buddy Gask, drummers Romeo Challenger and Malcolm Allured, guitarists Trevor Oakes and Russ Field and bassists Rod Deas and Al James.

Showaddywaddy achieved their big break on ITV's talent show *New Faces*. A recording contract with Bell followed immediately and the band's debut single, the self-penned 'Hey Rock And Roll', leaped to number two in 1974. The group persisted with their own compositions, but with diminishing success. Then, in 1975, they released a version of Eddie Cochran's 'Three Steps To Heaven' (see no. 102). It stopped one step below the original, kept off the top by actors Windsor Davies and Don Estelle, but Showaddywaddy had hit upon the formula which was to provide them with a run of nine Top 10 singles. Each one was a pop version of a rock and roll classic. 'Under The Moon Of Love' had been a hit for writer Curtis Lee, who had also hit the US Top 10 in 1961 with 'Pretty Little Angel Eyes', Showaddywaddy's final Top 10er in 1978. By 1980, however, Shakin' Stevens had replaced the group as Britain's most successful rock and roll revivalist.

398

WHEN A CHILD IS BORN (SOLEADO)

JOHNNY MATHIS

25 December 1976, for 3 weeks

●●●

CBS 4599

Writers: Fred Jay and Di Damicco Ciro
Producer: Jack Gold

Eighteen years and 216 days after the first chart appearance of Johnny Mathis (born in San Francisco on 30 September 1935), he finally hit the number one spot with a million-selling Christmas hit. Eighteen years earlier he had enjoyed another seasonal success, 'Winter Wonderland'.

Mathis racked up nine hits between May 1958 and the end of 1960, including three Top 10 hits. Then the bottom fell out of the Mathis market and, apart from one week at number 49 on 4 April 1963, he was hitless until early 1975, when his remake of the Stylistics' 1972 hit, 'I'm Stone In Love With You', climbed to number ten. However, Johnny always remained a star. His albums never stopped selling. Most noteworthy was *Johnny's Greatest Hits*, which stayed on the American charts for 490 weeks from April 1958.

The German, Michael Holm, had an earlier international hit with 'When A Child Is Born'. In 1981 Mathis popped back at number 74 with a duet version of this song with Gladys Knight.

399

DON'T GIVE UP ON US

DAVID SOUL

15 January 1977, for 4 weeks

●●●●

PRIVATE STOCK PVT 84

Writer: Tony Macaulay
Producer: Tony Macaulay

David Soul (born David Solberg, Chicago, Illinois, 28 August 1943) was known to British TV viewers as Detective Ken Hutchinson, the blond half of *Starsky and Hutch*. Listeners to 'Don't Give Up On Us' may have been startled to learn that David Soul had in fact begun as a singer, not an actor. He'd been cutting folk and pop singles throughout the 70s but without any luck. In desperation he sent a photograph of himself to the famous New York entertainment agency William Morris. His ploy of disguising his face with a ski mask caught their imagination and he was immediately contracted to become the Covered Man, the resident singer on the Merv Griffin TV Show.

Soul completed a series of *Starsky and Hutch* before deciding to try his hand at recording once more. His first album for Private Stock had already been released before he was teamed with prolific hit writer Tony Macaulay (see nos. 239, 240 and 281). 'Don't Give Up On Us' also reached number one in the singer's homeland four months later.

400

DON'T CRY FOR ME ARGENTINA

JULIE COVINGTON

12 February 1977, for 1 week

●

MCA 260

Writers: Tim Rice and Andrew Lloyd Webber
Producers: Tim Rice and Andrew Lloyd Webber

The hit tune from the phenomenally successful musical *Evita* was not given its title, which has now passed into the realms of popular cliché, until almost the final take of the final recording session of the original *Evita* album.

An extensive search for a woman to take the title role on the record ended when the performance of Julie Covington in the TV series *Rock Follies* persuaded Lloyd Webber and Rice that this was the singer they needed for the part. The recording went very well, but for the strongest tune they wanted a title that would make the song a hit out of the context of *Evita*. Covington even recorded the title line as 'It's Only Your Lover Returning'. This just didn't sound right so, with the deadline for completion of the album approaching, it was decided that 'Don't Cry For Me Argentina' would have to do; a good title for the storyline but a rotten one (so everybody thought) for a single release from the album.

Nobody need have worried. The single sold 980,000 copies in the UK alone, which made it the biggest-selling single ever by a female vocalist until it was overtaken in 1985 by Jennifer Rush's 'Power Of Love' (see no 558). Julie Covington did not want the title role when *Evita* was produced in London, and the search for the star ended with Elaine Paige, who went on to become Britain's greatest musical theatre star and to record, with Barbara Dickson, Britain's biggest-selling record ever by a female vocal duo (see no. 545).

401

WHEN I NEED YOU

LEO SAYER

19 February 1977, for 3 weeks

●●●

CHRYSALIS CHS 2127

Writers: Albert Hammond and Carole Bayer Sager
Producer: Richard Perry

Leo Sayer, born in Shoreham, Sussex, on 24 May 1948, first came to the notice of the record-buying public early in 1973. That was when the debut solo LP by Roger Daltrey of the Who was released, featuring songs by Leo Sayer and Dave Courtney. A single culled from the LP, 'Giving It All Away', took Roger Daltrey to number five in the late spring of that year. Leo Sayer, like Sandie Shaw, had been discovered by Adam Faith, but unlike Shaw, Sayer was also managed by Faith, who by the early 70s had given up singing.

At the end of 1973 Leo Sayer's first single, 'The Show Must Go On', was released. He performed the song with a whitened face and a clown's outfit and it shot to number two. In America it was covered by Three Dog Night, who took it to the Top 5. It might have been difficult to throw off the clown image, which, like Gilbert O'Sullivan's short trousers and pudding-basin haircut, was fine for attracting public attention but not much good for sustaining a musical career. However, Sayer followed up with hit after hit - 'One Man Band' (another song originally recorded by Roger Daltrey), 'Long Tall Glasses', 'Moonlighting' and his first American chart-topper, 'You Make Me Feel Like Dancing'. After three number two hits in his first five singles, Sayer must have despaired of ever topping the charts. But on 19 February 1977 his sixth hit (the first he had not co-written) gave the Chrysalis label their first number one.

402

CHANSON D'AMOUR

MANHATTAN TRANSFER

12 March 1977, for 3 weeks

●●●

ATLANTIC K 10886

Writer: Wayne Shanklin
Producer: Richard Perry

Americans Tim Hauser, Janis Siegel, Laurel Masse and Alan Paul had to work hard before charming their way to the top of the charts. Hauser was the most experienced of the group, having begun his career with R&B group the Criterions in the late 50s. As session singers, Siegel and Masse had been heard on hundreds of advertising jingles. Paul specialised in musicals and film work.

Manhattan Transfer first formed in 1969, although only Hauser remained from those days. They honed their kitsch image in New York's gay bars, reviving swing and doo-wop classics of the 40s and early 50s. The group broke through in Britain and France before achieving success in the US singles chart. 'Chanson D'Amour' was originally an American hit for Art and Dotty Todd. The Man Tran version, producer Richard Perry's second consecutive number one, is best remembered for its 'rat tat tat tat tat' hook line. Further hits included ballads such as 'Walk In Love', uptempo numbers like 'Spice of Life' and revivals of such songs as 'On A Little Street In Singapore'. A 1981 reworking of the Ad Lib's classic, 'The Boy From New York City', made the American Top 10, their best US showing. Manhattan Transfer continue today, Cheryl Bentyne having replaced Laurel Masse in 1979.

403

KNOWING ME KNOWING YOU

ABBA

2 April 1977, for 5 weeks

●●●●●

EPIC EPC 4955

Writers: Benny Andersson, Stig Anderson and Bjorn Ulvaeus
Producers: Benny Andersson and Bjorn Ulvaeus

Despite the small hiccup in Abba's stream of chart successes when 'Money Money Money' reached only number three, the quartet from snowy Sweden showed their ability to bounce back when their next single, 'Knowing Me Knowing You', hit the top on 2 April 1977, in its sixth week on the chart. It stayed there for five weeks, and became the first number one in Abba's second hat-trick of chart-toppers. That second threesome took 46 weeks to complete, the third-slowest trio after the Beatle's 'Lady Madonna'/'Hey Jude'/'Get Back' run, which covered 56 weeks, and the Police, who took 52 weeks in 1979 and 1980 over their hat-trick.

The Beatles took 46 weeks over their 'Help'/'Day Tripper'/'Paperback Writer' hat-trick as well, while Frankie Goes To Hollywood took 45 weeks to complete their 1984 trio of chart-toppers. John Lennon completed his posthumous threesome in just seven weeks.

MANHATTAN TRANSFER, pictured performing at the Atlantic Records 40th anniversary concert. Oddly enough, their only UK Top 10 hit wasn't a hit in the US, and their only American Top 10 success, a cover of 'The Boy From New York City', did not chart in Britain. (Atlantic Records)

404

FREE

DENIECE WILLIAMS

7 May 1977, for 2 weeks

●●

CBS 4978

Writers: Deniece Williams, Hank Redd, Nathan Watts and Susaye Green
Producers: Maurice White and Charles Stepney

Deniece Williams (born Deniece Chandler on 3 June 1951 in the Jackson family hometown of Gary, Indiana) never intended to make her living through music, having trained as a nurse in Chicago. To earn some extra cash she took a job in a record shop, where her boss heard her singing. He invited two friends over from a local record label, Toddlin' Town, which led to Williams cutting her first tracks. Stevie Wonder (see nos. 499 and 538) heard them, and for four years she sang with him as a member of his vocal backing group Wonderlove. It was Wonder who convinced Williams she had the potential to become a star. A meeting with Maurice White, leader of soul/funk outfit Earth, Wind and Fire, led to her signing with CBS. White masterminded her debut album, *This Is Niecy*, on which 'Free' was the standout ballad.

'That's What Friends Are For' provided a further Top 10 hit in 1977, and a duet with Johnny Mathis (see no. 398), 'Too Much Too Little Too Late', climbed to number three a year later. Despite some US success there were no hits between 1979 and 1983. Then came a song from the 1984 film *Footloose*, 'Let's Hear It For The Boy', which returned Williams to the top. Both 'Too Much Too Little Too Late' and 'Let's Hear It For The Boy' were American number ones.

405

I DON'T WANT TO TALK ABOUT IT/FIRST CUT IS THE DEEPEST

ROD STEWART

21 May 1977, for 4 weeks

●●●●

RIVA 7

Writers: 'I Don't Want To Talk About It' – Danny Whitten; 'First Cut Is The Deepest' – Cat Stevens
Producer: Tom Dowd

Here was a case where the artist really had to thank his fans for his number one. Without their participation, 'I Don't Want To Talk About It' would never even have been released. It originally appeared on the album *Atlantic Crossing*, leading off the slow side of the set that included 'This Old Heart Of Mine' and concluded with 'Sailing'. The massive success of the latter track tended to obscure the remaining material, and Stewart's new label Riva began issuing singles from the following album, *Night On The Town*, in the summer of 1976.

But at Christmas concerts Rod gave in London that year, he and his associates were startled when fans sang along with the chorus of 'I Don't Want To Talk About It', even continuing when Rod dropped out to watch them. Clearly the artist had a potential hit of which he had been unaware. The track was issued as his next single, and it went to number one for four weeks. Since so many fans already had *Atlantic Crossing*, a track from *Night On The Town*, 'First Cut Is The Deepest', was made part of a double-A disc, but 'Talk' was far and away the lead side.

Sadly, Danny Whitten, a member of Neil Young's Crazy Horse and author of the song, did not live to see it become a hit. He had died of a drug overdose on 18 November 1972.

406

LUCILLE

KENNY ROGERS

18 June 1977, for 1 week

●

UNITED ARTISTS UP 36242

Writers: Roger Bowling and Hal Bynum
Producer: Larry Butler

Kenneth Donald Rogers (born Houston, Texas, 21 August 1938) came close to having a number one with the First Edition in 1969 when 'Ruby Don't Take Your Love To Town', a song about a crippled Vietnam veteran, was kept at bay by first the Archies and then Rolf Harris. The First Edition, a country/pop outfit, had formed themselves in 1967 out of the New Christy Minstrels and were the first group to sign to Frank Sinatra's Reprise label. Rogers' distinctive gravelly voice was always to the fore, propelling them to several hits in the USA. When he left the group in 1973, he found no problem in securing a solo recording contract with United Artists. Minor US country successes followed until 'Lucille' became his first solo smash, winning him the 1977 Grammy Award for Best Country Vocal Performance.

The 'Lucille' referred to in this tear-jerking chart-topper had walked out on her man and their four hungry children at an inconvenient moment. It was a completely different song to the Little Richard rocker of the same title, which was also about a missing lady called Lucille, but who did not have four hungry offspring. In Britain, BBC Radio Two DJ Terry Wogan found Kenny Rogers' sentiment irresistible and played the single at every opportunity, assisting the record's progress and returning the bearded six-foot country star to the UK chart after an absence of seven years.

407

SHOW YOU THE WAY TO GO

THE JACKSONS

25 June 1977, for 1 week

•

EPIC EPC 5266

Writers: Kenny Gamble and Leon Huff
Producers: Kenny Gamble and Leon Huff

Jermaine Jackson married Berry Gordy's daughter and stayed with Motown when his brothers moved to Epic. The remaining quartet of Jackie (born 4 May 1951), Tito (born 15 October 1953), Marlon (born 12 March 1957) and Michael (born 29 August 1958) added their youngest brother Randy (born 29 October 1962) on bongos. A newcomer, Gerald Brown, replaced Jermaine on bass. The new line-up was called the Jacksons since Motown contested ownership of the original name.

Neither the Jackson Five nor the Jacksons had achieved a number one single in Britain before 'Show You The Way To Go' went to the top in 1977, immediately after the group had finished their first UK concerts for five years. Depite the many hits that followed, the Jacksons have not had another British number one single, their highest effort being 'Shake Your Body (Down To The Ground)', a number four hit in 1979.

Legendary Philadelphia writers/producers/executives Kenny Gamble and Leon Huff achieved with this single the UK number one that had eluded them with the O'Jays and Billy Paul. They had previously succeeded with the Three Degrees (see no. 354).

408

SO YOU WIN AGAIN

HOT CHOCOLATE

2 July 1977, for 3 weeks

•••

RAK 259

Writer: Russ Ballard
Producer: Mickie Most

There have been seven 'Hot' groups in the singles chart besides the Chocolate one: Hot Blood, Hot Butter, Hot House, Hot Streak, Hothouse Flowers, Hotlegs and Hotshots, not to mention the Red Hot Chili Peppers. None of them has a record of chart success that can come anywhere near Hot Chocolate's. Although 'So You Win Again' was their only number one, they had 12 Top 10 singles, plus another seven Top 20s and six Top 40s. Hot Chocolate were one of only three acts to put in a chart appearance in every year of the 1970s - the illustrious company they kept in this exclusive club being Diana Ross and Elvis Presley.

Formed by lead singer Errol Brown (born 12 November 1948) in 1970, Hot Chocolate were Patrick Olive (bass, born 22 March 1947), Larry Ferguson (keyboards, born 14 April 1948), Tony Connor (drums, born 6 April 1948) and Harvey Hinsley (guitar). One-time member Tony Wilson, who played bass and composed most of the early material with Brown, left in 1975 to go solo. Among the hits Hot Chocolate had written for other acts were Mary Hopkin's 'Think About Your Children' and Herman's Hermits' 'Bet Yer Life I Do'.

'I Feel Love' by DONNA SUMMER was the artist's only UK number one, but in America she paced with 'MacArthur Park', 'Hot Stuff', 'Bad Girls' and 'No More Tears (Enough Is Enough)'. (Pictorial Press)

In 1987, after a Top 10 remix version of 'You Sexy Thing', Errol Brown embarked on a solo career with a Top 40 hit, 'Personal Touch'.

409

I FEEL LOVE

DONNA SUMMER

23 July 1977, for 4 weeks

●●●●

GTO GT 100

Writers: Giorgio Moroder, Pete Bellotte and Donna Summer
Producers: Giorgio Moroder and Pete Bellotte

Giorgio Moroder was first heard of as the composer and original performer in Italy of the Chicory Tip hit 'Son Of My Father' (see no. 310). Five and a half years later, he re-emerged as the composer and producer of many hits for disco goddess Donna Summer, whose 'Love To Love You Baby' gave her her first British hit at the beginning of 1976. Moroder and Summer have both gone on to even greater heights of success, but this summertime Summer hit remains their only number one collaboration in Britain. It had the mournful honour of being at number one on 16 August 1977, when Elvis Presley died.

By 1992, Donna Summer had racked up a total of 35 hits in Britain, including a duet with Barbra Streisand, the powerful 'No More Tears (Enough Is Enough)'. This climbed to number three in Britain but gave Donna her third number one of the year in America in 1979. Summer was born LaDonna Gaines on the last day of 1948 in Boston, Massachusetts, and thus was already in her late 20s before her chart breakthrough. Her massive success with a string of disco hits has subsequently made her the fourth most successful female vocalist in British chart history, and, although her tally of only nine Top 10 hits (including that duet with Ms Streisand) is not dramatically impressive, her list of chart entries is longer than that of any other woman except Diana Ross. She certainly proved she could succeed in a variety of styles when she enjoyed Top 10 hits with two Stock Aitken Waterman productions in 1989.

410

ANGELO

BROTHERHOOD OF MAN

20 August 1977, for 1 week

●

PYE 7N 45699

Writers: Tony Hiller, Martin Lee and Lee Sheridan
Producer: Tony Hiller

The sad story of the Mexican shepherd boy Angelo gave Brotherhood Of Man their second number one and confirmed their style of music as Abba-inspired. Their Eurovision chart-topper of 1976, 'Save Your Kisses For Me' (see no. 387), was obviously in the style of Abba, but then so were practically all the successful Europop songs of the mid-70s. Brotherhood Of Man's third post-Eurovision single had been an imaginative cover of Diana Trask's big US country hit, 'Oh Boy (The Mood I'm In)', which led fans to assume the Abba influence had waned as far as the Brotherhood were concerned. This proved not to be the case when their next single, 'Angelo', came out. But they answered their critics in the best possible way - the record shot to number one.

Angelo lived high on a mountain in Mexico, and when he and his rich girlfriend ran away together, they ran and ran until they reached the coast, where they chose to die in the sand. The cause of death is not stated, but one must suspect exhaustion.

411

FLOAT ON

THE FLOATERS

27 August 1977, for 1 week

●

ABC 4187

Writers: Arnold Ingram, James Mitchell Jr and Marvin Willis
Producer: Woody Wilson

Led by Larry Cunningham, the Floaters formed in Detroit 13 years before their one and only British hit single. 'Float On' was lifted from their 1977 album *Floaters*, and had originally been composed as an instrumental track. All that could be heard of the group was the occasional chant of 'float on, float on' in the background. They had intended to use the music as a linking device throughout the album, but James Mitchell of Detroit Emeralds heard the melody and persuaded them to record ad lib vocals.

The Floaters now had a song with which they could introduce themselves. Thus, the world learned that Ronnie was an Aquarian who liked 'a woman who can hold her own' and that Charles was a Libran who liked 'a woman who carries herself like Miss Universe'. Paul wasn't so choosy. He was a Leo who liked 'all women of the world'. And finally there was Larry, a Cancerian, who needed 'a woman that loves everything and everybody'. Whether they found their heart's desires we will never know. After 11 weeks on the chart, 'Float On' floated off, leaving the Floaters high and dry as one-hit wonders.

412

WAY DOWN

ELVIS PRESLEY

3 September 1977, for 5 weeks

●●●●●

RCA PB 0998

Writer: Layng Martine Jr
Producers: Elvis Presley and Felton Jarvis

Elvis' 17th and final UK number one was the single that had been issued shortly before his tragic death on 16 August 1977. It had not shown signs of being more than a minor chart entry when the King died. Very quickly it shot to number one.

It was ironic that Elvis' death resulted in him equalling the Beatles' record of 17 number one records. The song was written by Layng Martine Jr and is the only Elvis number one to carry a production credit as follows: 'Executive Producer: Elvis Presley; Associate Producer: Felton Jarvis.' Vocal accompaniment is by J.D. Sumner and the Stamps, Kathy Westmoreland, Sherrill Neilson and Myrna Smith being the other Stamps. The track was recorded at Elvis' home, Graceland, in Memphis, during sessions at the end of October 1976. James Burton is one of the guitarists on the sessions. These were the last studio recordings of Presley's life - all that was to come in 1977 were some indifferent concert tapings of previously recorded material.

Since his death Elvis has had several more hits, two of which made the Top 10. An 18th number one is obviously not impossible but as the years go by, it becomes less and less likely. It is probably right that both Elvis and the Beatles should remain the joint all-time UK number one champions.

413

SILVER LADY

DAVID SOUL

8 October, for 3 weeks

●●●

PRIVATE STOCK PVT 115

Writers: Tony Macaulay and Geoff Stephens
Producer: Tony Macaulay

The co-star, with Paul-Michael Glaser, of the American detective series *Starsky and Hutch*, David Soul is not the only singing policeman to find success in the singles chart - Don Johnson (*Miami Vice*) and Dennis Waterman (*The Sweeney*) have both had hits. Soul is not even the first law-enforcer to get himself a number one, since Telly Savalas (*Kojak*) and Lee Marvin (one-time star of *The Streets Of San Francisco*) had already beaten him to it.

'Silver Lady' was Soul's second chart-topping single. Sandwiched between the two number ones was a number two, 'Going In With My Eyes Open'. Soul thus belongs to a group of chart acts such as Shakin' Stevens who were only prevented from getting that elusive hat-trick of number ones with consecutive releases by the 'failure' at number two of one of the records in the sequence. After 'Silver Lady' Soul had another Top 10 and a Top 20 before he disappeared from the charts. His enviable record of all his singles becoming at least Top 20s not only reflects his background as a singer, it makes him the most successful of the singing detectives.

414

YES SIR I CAN BOOGIE

BACCARA

29 October 1977, for 1 week

●

RCA PB 5526

Writers: Frank Dostal and Rolf Soja
Producer: Rolf Soja

Astonishingly, it took 414 number ones and nearly 25 years for the first female vocal duo, Maria Mendiola and Mayte Mateus, to hit the very top. There have been plenty of male vocal duos at the top, from the Everly Brothers to Typically Tropical, plenty of male/female vocal duos at the top, beginning with Sonny and Cher, and even female vocal trios such as the Supremes and the Three Degrees. But it took two leggy Spanish girls singing a Dutch production in English to make a breakthrough in the British charts. By an extraordinary coincidence one record that their success kept out of the top spot was 'Black Is Black', a song originally recorded by a German/ Spanish vocal group in English but this time revived by La Belle Epoque, a French female duo.

Baccara were also the first Spanish act to hit the top in Britain. They remained the only Spaniards to have a number one until Julio Iglesias actually sang in his native tongue four years later (see no. 490).

415

THE NAME OF THE GAME

ABBA

5 November 1977, for 4 weeks

●●●●

EPIC EPC 5750

Writers: Stig Anderson, Benny Andersson and Bjorn Ulvaeus
Producers: Benny Andersson and Bjorn Ulvaeus

It was perhaps fitting that one of the biggest chart names of all time should be at number one on 14 November 1977, on the 25th birthday of the singles charts in Britain. Abba's sixth number one hit brought them level with Slade in the all-time rankings, behind only Elvis and the Beatles (17 each), Cliff Richard (then nine number ones) and the Rolling Stones (eight). Abba have now overtaken the Stones, but look very unlikely indeed to overtake Cliff for the bronze medal position. While Cliff has gone on to score four more chart-toppers, Abba have split. Another Abba single, let alone another chart-topper, seems more unlikely as each year passes.

Abba's achievements in opening the doors of the British charts to the sounds of the European charts should not be underestimated. Before the Swedish quartet burst onto the scene, hits by European acts in Britain were very rare indeed. Domenico Modugno, Marino Marini, Alice Babs and Nina and Frederick are among the only names that spring to mind, and none of them ever topped the charts.

Another Abba chart achievement is less well known. Apart from their 19 Top 10 hits (peaking at every position between one and seven), Abba never even reached the Top 20 with their other six chart entries. The best of the rest was 'Head Over Heels', which stopped at number 25. (The number 16 placing of 'Dancing Queen' in 1992 is excluded since the disc was a re-issue.) No other act has such a sharply divided chart-success rating.

416

MULL OF KINTYRE/ GIRLS' SCHOOL

WINGS

3 December 1977, for 9 weeks

●●●●●●●●●

CAPITOL R 6018

Writers: Paul McCartney and Denny Laine
Producer: Paul McCartney

Paul McCartney had registered ten post-Beatle Top 10 singles by the end of 1976, but none of them had gone all the way. Three, 'Another Day', 'Silly Love Songs' and 'Let 'Em In', had peaked at number two. To add to this frustration, he had scored five US chart-toppers in the same period, 'Silly Love Songs' being one of the biggest hits of 1976 in America, without crossing over to head the UK lists. The pattern changed drastically with 'Mull Of Kintyre'. McCartney wrote the song because he felt Scotland needed a contemporary anthem and, quite simply, because he loved his home there. Laine helped complete the composition. At the time, the line-up of Wings was undergoing certain changes, and the trio on this record of Paul, Linda and Denny Laine was as small as the group ever got.

McCartney was not certain that 'Mull Of Kintyre' would be a hit, so he made it part of a double A-side with the uptempo 'Girls' School'. In the States, his doubts were justified, as 'Mull Of Kintyre' did not capture the American imagination, and it was left to the other side to peak at a rather lowly number 33. In Britain, it was obvious that 'Mull Of Kintyre' was the popular side. It was the first single to sell more than two million copies in the United Kingdom, surpassing the Beatles' 'She Loves You' to become the nation's all-time number one, at least until Band Aid came along (see no. 543).

417

UPTOWN TOP RANKING

ALTHIA AND DONNA

4 February 1978, for 1 week

●

LIGHTNING LIG 506

Writers: Althia Forest, Donna Reid and Errol Thompson
Producer: Joe Gibson

After the first wave of reggae in 1969/70, chart reggae music had begun to move away from its authentic roots and begun making compromises for the pop market. Bob and Marcia's 1970 'Young Gifted And Black' even included a string section. By 1974 there were two distinct categories of successful reggae: 'lovers' rock' ('Every-thing I Own', 'Tears On My Pillow') and quirky novelties. Althia Forest and Donna Reid's hit, a Jamaican number one, was one of the quirkiest of them all.

Althia was 17 and Donna 18, both just out of school in Kingston, Jamaica, when the record began to take off. Producer Joe Gibson supplied the tune, to which the women added slang words they'd heard on out-of-town trips. The title 'Uptown Top Ranking' actually describes what a non-urban Jamaican does when he goes into the city to show off.

Finding initial radio support from BBC Radio One's John Peel, the song was 'playlisted', that is placed on the list of singles that must be featured on daytime Radio One shows, a rare achievement for a reggae single. The song became a national talking point because no one understood the lyrics. Curiosity value hoisted it to the top after seven weeks on the chart. But Althia and Donna were unable to find a successful follow-up and became one-hit wonders, the novelty having worn off.

418

FIGARO

BROTHERHOOD OF MAN

11 February 1978, for 1 week

●

PYE 7N 46037

Writers: Tony Hiller, Martin Lee and Lee Sheriden
Producer: Tony Hiller

The third number one for Brotherhood Of Man was the third produced by Tony Hiller and the third written by Messrs Hiller, Sheriden and Lee. Coming after 'Angelo', it was their second consecutive number one about a foreign man with a six-letter name ending in o. Despite being a happy, uncontroversial record for discos, immaculately performed and produced, it stayed at the top for only one week before being pushed out by 'Take A Chance On Me' by the group the Brotherhood Of Man so successfully imitated, Abba.

The follow-up to 'Figaro', 'Beautiful Lover', also sang the praises of foreign men, but only just managed to make the Top 20. The next single peaked at 41. Their last listed title, 'Lightning Flash', saw its light go out at number 67 in July 1982, giving them a total chart life of 97 weeks, the fewest by any act that had scored as many as three chart-toppers, until Jive Bunny redefined short-lived chart megasuccess in 1989.

419

TAKE A CHANCE ON ME

ABBA

18 February 1978, for 3 weeks

●●●

Writers: Benny Andersson and Bjorn Ulvaeus
Producers: Benny Andersson and Bjorn Ulvaeus

Abba completed a hat-trick of increasing uncertainty on 18 February 1978. The first record of the three had the positive title 'Knowing Me Knowing You' and stayed at the top for five weeks. The second disc had the less certain but still unworried title 'The Name Of The Game', and stayed on top for four weeks. The third single was much less optimistic, pleading 'Take A Chance On Me', which the British public did for three weeks.

Logically, Abba should have recorded 'Maybe Baby' and 'God Only Knows' as their next two singles, which would have held the top spot for two weeks and one week respectively, but they didn't. They recorded 'Summer Night City', which became the first of six consecutive Abba singles to hit the Top 5 without reaching the very top. It was therefore quite a surprise to chart-watchers, if not to Epic Records executives, when, at the end of 1980, two singles from the *Super Trouper* album hit number one (see nos. 463 and 470), putting Abba back on top after two and a half years.

420

WUTHERING HEIGHTS

KATE BUSH

11 March 1978, for 4 weeks

●●●●

EMI 2719

Writer: Kate Bush. Producer: Andrew Powell

'Wuthering Heights', a musical tribute to the classic Emily Brontë novel, launched the career of Kate Bush (born 30 July 1958, exactly 140 years after Emily Brontë), one of the most original talents to hit popular music in the 1970s. With its weird but haunting chorus of "Heathcliff, it's me, I'm Cathy come home again", it became an airplay favourite almost at once and a number one hit in its fifth week on the charts. It appeared as the final track on the first side of *The Kick Inside*, Kate Bush's debut LP, which also included her second single and second Top 10 hit, 'The Man With The Child In His Eyes'. Dave Gilmour of Pink Floyd had discovered and nurtured the teenage Ms Bush, and played guitar on 'Wuthering Heights'.

Whilst a tally of two dozen hits by mid-1994 is impressive enough, Kate's real strength lies in the LP market, where, in 1980, her third album, *Never For Ever*, became the first by a female singer to hit the top. *Hounds Of Love* and the compilation *The Whole Story* brought her level with Barbra Streisand, who also had three long-playing chart-toppers. Even more impressive is the fact that the singer writes all her own material.

Eight years on from 'Wuthering Heights' Bush received the prestigious BPI award for Best Female Vocalist, while the award for Best Male Vocalist went to Peter Gabriel. Coincidentally, Kate has duetted with Gabriel on two Top 10 hits, 'Don't Give Up', on which she received billing, and 'Games Without Frontiers', on which she did not.

421

MATCHSTALK MEN AND MATCHSTALK CATS AND DOGS

BRIAN AND MICHAEL

8 April 1978, for 3 weeks

●●●

PYE 7N 46035

Writer: Michael Coleman
Producer: Kevin Parrott

The song with the second-longest title to reach number one to date is the saga of the Ancoats painter L.S. Lowry, whose death on 23 February 1976 inspired Mick Coleman to write the song. He took the tune to producer Kevin Parrott and the pair recorded it. Parrott decided that Brian and Michael sounded more commercial than Kevin and Michael, so the chance of a Kevin reaching number one was lost. Up to this point the highest-charting Kevin had been the Australian Kevin Johnson, who climbed to 23 in 1975 with 'Rock 'N Roll (I Gave You The Best Years Of My Life)'.

'Matchstalk Men' (not to be confused with Status Quo's 1968 debut hit, 'Pictures Of Matchstick Men') features the St Winifred's School Choir singing with Brian and Michael. The subsequent careers of both Kevin Parrott and Mick Coleman continued to involve children. All the follow-ups to their own number one were failures, but Kevin produced a hit by the Ramblers from the Abbey Hey Junior School, 'The Sparrow', which reached number 11 at the end of 1979. Mick Coleman also wrote 'Hold My Hand', recorded at Christmas 1981 by both Ken Dodd (who made it a hit) and the St Winifred's School Choir (who flopped).

422

NIGHT FEVER

THE BEE GEES

29 April 1978, for 2 weeks

●●

RSO 002

Writers: Barry, Robin and Maurice Gibb
Producers: Barry, Robin and Maurice Gibb, Karl Richardson and Albhy Galuten

The Bee Gees were at the Chateau d'Herouville in France working on the follow-up to their *Children Of The Universe* album when they received a phone call from manager Robert Stigwood. He was making a film of a Nik Cohn article in *New York* magazine and needed a few songs. He couldn't send them a script but needed the numbers within a fortnight.

The Gibbs worked in the black music-based groove that had recently brought them great success with 'Jive Talkin'' and 'You Should Be Dancing'. Without really knowing how the songs would be used, they presented Stigwood with 'How Deep Is Your Love', 'Staying Alive', 'Night Fever', 'More Than A Woman' and 'If I Can't Have You', the last of which was ultimately given to Yvonne Elliman. Stigwood was unhappy he did not have a title track for the film, which he planned to call *Saturday Night*. The Bee Gees noted they did have a song called 'Night Fever', so the movie became *Saturday Night Fever*.

The double-album soundtrack went on to become the world's biggest-ever seller, nearing the 30 million mark. (It was later eclipsed by Michael Jackson's *Thriller*.) The Gibbs became so associated with the film, many people assumed they had appeared in it, but this was not so.

423

RIVERS OF BABYLON

BONEY M

13 May 1978, for 5 weeks

●●●●●

ATLANTIC/HANSA K11120

A traditional song, arranged by Frank Farian and Hans-Georg Mayer.
Produced by Frank Farian.

German-born Franz Reuther adopted the name Frank Farian in order to improve his chances as a pop singer, but his career did not live up to expectations. Farian fared better with Boney M, a disco hit machine he created. Montserrat-born Maizie Williams, Bobby Farrell from the Antilles and two Jamaicans, Liz Mitchell and Marcia Barrett, began their string of successes with 'Daddy Cool' in 1976.

'Rivers Of Babylon', Boney M's only Top 30 success in America, was fifth in a sequence of nine consecutive UK Top 10 hits the quartet managed between 1976 and 1979. It hit number one in its third week of chart action, the first week that a Top 75 was compiled and published, and had been on the chart for some months before DJs and dancers started to flip the disc to feature the B-side, 'Brown Girl In The Ring'. Suddenly, the single, which had fallen to number 20, began to turn around. Chartwatchers agonized as fresh airplay lifted the disc from six to five, then four, then three and finally to number two, but it was blocked from returning to the number one position by the Commodores' 'Three Times A Lady' (see no. 425). It gradually slid down the charts to depart only after the Christmas parties of 1978 had been forgotten, 40 weeks after entering. This was the second-longest consecutive chart run by a number one (after 'Release Me'; see no. 203). More importantly, 'Rivers Of Babylon'/'Brown Girl In The Ring' became the second biggest-selling disc in the UK at that time. Only 'Mull Of Kintyre' had sold more.

424

YOU'RE THE ONE THAT I WANT

JOHN TRAVOLTA AND OLIVIA NEWTON-JOHN

17 June 1978, for 9 weeks

●●●●●●●●●

RSO 006

Writer: John Farrar
Producer: John Farrar

John Travolta (born 18 February 1954) and Olivia Newton-John (born in Cambridge on 26 September 1948) were partnered for the film version of the long-running Broadway hit rock'n'roll musical *Grease*. Travolta had just appeared in one of the biggest box-office successes of all time, the disco-based *Saturday Night Fever*. He later helped temporarily boost the popularity of country music with his movie *Urban Cowboy*.

Newton-John's acting career was less spectacular, but she more than compensated with her singing achievements. She won three Grammy Awards in 1974 and scored her fifth and final American number one in fabulous fashion, 'Physical' staying on top of the *Billboard* Hot 100 for ten weeks in 1981/82. In the UK her solo offerings have never done quite as well, though this is the country of her origin. She is technically British, having emigrated with her family from the UK to Australia when she was four. Although she now lives mainly in America, her nationality is proved by the fact that she represented Britain in the Eurovision

Song Contest in 1974, and she has also been awarded an OBE.

425

THREE TIMES A LADY

THE COMMODORES

19 August 1978, for 5 weeks

●●●●●

MOTOWN TMG 1113

Writer: Lionel Richie, Jr.
Producers: James Carmichael and the Commodores

The world owes this classic love song to Leo Sayer, who had nothing to do with the writing or making of it. In 1977 the Grammy Award for Best Rhythm And Blues Song went to Sayer and Vini Poncia for the former's worldwide hit, 'You Make Me Feel Like Dancing'. Among the defeated writers were the Commodores. Shaken that white men could defeat him in this category, Commodore Lionel Richie vowed to write pop. It had always been the intention of the Commodores to earn as much as the top rock bands. Now Richie set out to develop his craft as a songwriter for all formats.

'Three Times A Lady' followed 'Sweet Love' and 'Just To Be Close To You', all hit Commodore ballads that originally appeared as the last track on side one of an album. The group figured that after a few uptempo dance numbers, this was wise placement. The tracks were always far too long for single release, and it was left to co-producer James Carmichael to edit them. Richie was only too willing to let him handle the chore, but with the passage of time and the development of his reputation and skills he finally began to write ballads with the proper length in mind.

'Three Times A Lady' replaced 'I'm Still Waiting' as Motown's best UK seller. It was also number one in America.

426

DREADLOCK HOLIDAY

10 C.C.

23 September 1978, for 1 week

●

MERCURY 6008 035

Writers: Eric Stewart and Graham Gouldman
Producers: Eric Stewart and Graham Gouldman

By the time 'Dreadlock Holiday' briefly visited the top of the charts for a week in 1978, 10 C.C. had lost Kevin Godley and Lol Creme, who had gone off to develop their new instrument, the Gizmo. The two remaining members, Stewart and Gouldman, cut the album *Deceptive Bends* in 1977 and then took four new members on board for 1978's *Bloody Tourists*, including 'Dreadlock Holiday', based on an experience of Justin Hayward in Jamaica. As befits the Caribbean, the single enjoyed a laid-back lope to the top of the chart, even including a two-week stopover at number four. Unpredictably, after this big record the group could manage only a number 50 in 1982. 10 C.C. had tallied three number ones and eight Top 10s between 1972 and 1978.

Godley and Creme had two Top 10 singles, 'Under Your Thumb' and 'Wedding Bells', in 1981. In the 80s they became award-winning leaders in video direction. The clip for their own 'Cry' helped the single become both a UK and US success in 1985, and the technique of having one face blending into another was subsequently used in many other artists' videos.

427

SUMMER NIGHTS

JOHN TRAVOLTA AND OLIVIA NEWTON-JOHN

30 September 1978, for 7 weeks

●●●●●●●

RSO 18

Writers: Warren Casey and Jim Jacobs
Producer: Louis St. Louis

The only male/female vocal duo to have two number one hits is John Travolta and Olivia Newton-John. In achieving their second number one, they broke all sorts of chart records. They hit number one with every single record they released, which had never been done by any other act that had released more than one single. They reached number one with their first and last chart hits, equalling the record set by Kay Starr in the 50s, and they found themselves on the short lists of acts (made longer by the 31 letters and a hyphen in their combined names) who hit number one with their first two releases, artists who failed to follow up a number one, and artists with 15 or more weeks on top in one year. Unfortunately, most of these distinctions were lost in the early 90s when Polydor issued two mixes of material from *Grease* under their names. Neither reached number one. Their perfect record had been ruined in the interests of commerce, not art nor chartology.

Olivia Newton-John, who has never climbed higher than number two in Britain as a solo singer, has also achieved one-hit-wonder status in combination with Electric Light Orchestra (see no. 461). John Travolta, a singing movie star in the tradition of Tab Hunter and Lee Marvin, also achieved a number two hit on his own.

The film *Grease*, from which both the duo's chart-toppers came, has also proved to be the most successful film in terms of original hits in the annals of the British charts. Two number ones, two number twos ('Hopelessly Devoted To You' and 'Sandy'), two number threes (Frankie Valli's 'Grease' and the Travolta/Newton-John 'Grease Megamix') and a number 11 ('Greased Lightnin'') give it a list of hits that far outstrips its nearest rivals, *Summer Holiday* and *The Young Ones*.

428

RAT TRAP

THE BOOMTOWN RATS

18 November 1978, for 2 weeks

●●

ENSIGN ENY16

Writer: Bob Geldof
Producer: Mutt Lange

The Boomtown Rats had Top 20 hits with their first four releases, but even this streak did not prepare them for the success of 'Rat Trap'. The third A-side from the Top 10 album *Tonic For The Troops*, it was put out to show that the Irish sextet wasn't just a pop band.

Viewing a videotaped Rats performance at the Hammersmith Odeon months later, lead singer and writer Geldof noticed that even shortly after the release of *Tonic* concert-goers were calling for 'Rat Trap'. At the time, this indication of a possible hit had been missed. Now Geldof revoiced an unpleasant line about pus oozing from sores and the track was released as a single.

When 'Rat Trap' replaced 'Summer Nights' at the top it was hailed as the triumph of local talent over a much-hyped Hollywood hit. Conveniently overlooked was the fact that the Boomtown Rats were, in fact, Irish, though they had come to London specifically for the purpose of making it in the international capital of rock. 'Rat Trap' was the first New Wave number one.

With the success of 'Rat Trap' Geldof, already a proven charismatic figure on *Top Of The Pops*, found himself in great demand with television chat-show hosts, who were relieved to find an articulate representative of, if not spokesman for, New Wave.

Right: Frank Farian, mentor of BONEY M (see page 242), successfully created another hit act in 1988 when he launched Milli Vanilli. (Pictorial Press)

429

DA YA THINK I'M SEXY

ROD STEWART

2 December 1978, for 1 week

•

RIVA 17

Writers: Rod Stewart and Carmen Appice
Producer: Tom Dowd

The question of unintentional plagiarism raised in the 'My Sweet Lord' case surfaced again with Rod Stewart's 1978 disco hit. The artist originally claimed full credit for himself and band member Appice until a complaint was made that the music was clearly borrowed from Jorge Ben's 'Taj Mahal', a tribute to the American blues singer who himself used the name of the Indian monument. The issue never blew up in the media because Stewart donated the song to UNICEF in the historic January 1979 United Nations concert. There was, however, a temporary wrangle over how much of the song's rights he had assigned to the charity.

'Da Ya Think I'm Sexy' was a startling departure for Stewart, placing him directly in the mainstream of the 1978 disco boom, and he enjoyed soul and disco chart success with this multi-million seller. Ironically, it temporarily took his career off the rails. He became broadly typed as a leering stud. In seven years he had missed the Top 10 only once, and then by only one place. For the following three years he fell short, often well short.

430

MARY'S BOY CHILD-OH MY LORD (medley)

BONEY M

9 December 1978, for 4 weeks

••••

ATLANTIC/HANSA K11221

Writers: Jester Hairston, Frank Farian and Fred Jay
Producer: Frank Farian

The fifth tune to top the charts in two versions (see no. 65) was Boney M's second number one. Like their first, it had a religious theme. Between these two divine chart-toppers had come 'Rasputin', a song about the diabolical priest from 19th-century Russia. That 'Rasputin' made it only to number two in the charts didn't necessarily prove that good always triumphs over evil. It helped Boney M spend 54 weeks on the charts of 1978, a feat matched by no other act.

The following year Frank Farian's foursome actually made a concert tour of the USSR, where they briefly rivalled Abba for jukebox popularity. In the UK only two more Top 10 hits followed 'Mary's Boy Child'. Farian led his protégés back to the previously fruitful formula of singalong religion with singles such as 'I'm Born Again' and 'Children Of Paradise', but these failed to impress record buyers in the way 'Mary's Boy Child' or 'Rivers of Babylon' had done. The German mentor found further fame with Far Corporation and, most notoriously, Milli Vanilli. The idea of combining an old hit song with one of the producer's own was used again by Michael Zager in his supervision of the Detroit Spinners (see no. 455).

431

YMCA

VILLAGE PEOPLE

6 January 1979, for 3 weeks

•••

MERCURY 6007 192

Writers: Jacques Morali, Henri Belolo and Victor Willis
Producer: Jacques Morali

When Frenchman Jacques Morali saw Felipe Rose wearing Red Indian dress in a New York gay discotheque, then saw him in a second club a week later with other costumed characters, he got an idea. He told *Rolling Stone,* "I say to myself, 'You know, this is fantastic to see the cowboy, the Indian, the construction worker with other men around.' And also, I think to myself that the gay people have no group, nobody to personalize the gay people, you know?"

What a New Yorker might take for

granted the foreigner saw as an exciting fantasy: a group of young men dressed as stereotypical American males. He recruited an ensemble, mostly models, to front songs about US gay capitals. The name Village People represented the men of Greenwich Village in New York City. When the first album sold 100,000 copies and a single, 'San Francisco (You've Got Me)', made the British charts, Morali quickly found himself Village persons who could sing as well as pose, retaining only Felipe Rose and lead vocalist Victor Willis.

The unpredictable happened. 'Macho Man' became a pop hit in America and 'YMCA' an international smash, selling several million copies, including approximately 150,000 in one day in Britain alone over the 1978 Christmas period. All types of audiences could relate to this ode to the Mecca of Manhood, and the group quickly became a mass-appeal fad. In so doing they lost touch with their original supporters and went the way of all fads, falling out of fashion and, even worse, the charts. Their follow-up, 'In The Navy', cruised all the way to number two, but they then appeared in a famous film flop, *Can't Stop The Music*. Ironically, another movie, *Wayne's World 2*, provided the group and their number one with a brief revival in 1994, when Wayne and Garth, unexpectedly finding themselves in a gay disco, performed a mime of 'YMCA'.

432

HIT ME WITH YOUR RHYTHM STICK

IAN AND THE BLOCKHEADS

27 January 1979, for 1 week

●

STIFF BUY 38

Writers: Ian Dury and Chas Jankel
Producer: Chas Jankel

Before this major hit, Ian Dury (born 12 May 1942) had been best known as the leader of one of the earliest New Wave bands, Kilburn and the High Roads, named after Kilburn College, where Dury had taught art. In 1975 Chas Jankel (born 16 April 1952) joined the outfit. During the next 18 months Ian Dury and the Kilburns built up a huge cult following with their early brand of punk, and in 1977 Dury signed a publishing deal with Blackhill Music and manager Andrew King. Having been rejected by all the majors the group, now called Ian and the Blockheads, signed to the newly formed Stiff Records, run by managing director Dave Robinson, Dury's former manager. The young record company had little money and the group signed for the paltry fee of £5,000, inclusive of studio costs.

University and pub gigs and the infamous Stiff tour paid off when the debut album *New Boots And Panties* charted in October 1977. No singles were taken from the set. In April 1978, the Top 10 45 'What A Waste' created widespread interest in the group, giving the LP long-term sales. Later that year, during a 'jam session' at the Warehouse in Old Kent Road, Jankel produced the strong disco melody which Dury took, added lyrics to, and titled 'Hit Me With Your Rhythm Stick'. Almost anyone you ask will tell you the artist on the disc was Ian Dury and the Blockheads, but the label billing was in fact Ian and the Blockheads. The singer's surname was added for subsequent releases.

With no album imminent, the track was released as a single, and in early 1979 the group spent a week at number one. On their last day at the top Sid Vicious died from a heroin overdose at the age of 21.

433

HEART OF GLASS

BLONDIE

3 February 1979, for 4 weeks

●●●●

CHRYSALIS CHE 2275

Writers: Chris Stein and Deborah Harry
Producer: Mike Chapman

Blondie were lead singer Debbie Harry (born Miami, Florida, 1 July 1945), guitarist Chris Stein (born 5 January 1950), guitarist Frank Infante, keyboard player Jim Destri (born 13 April 1954), bassist Nigel Harrison and drummer Clem Burke (born 24 November 1955). Harry had begun taking the vocal spotlight as early as 1967, when she fronted New York folk/rock band Wind In The Willows. At the end of 1973 she and Stein formed the Stilletos, from which Blondie emerged in 1974.

New Wave music was proving more marketable in the UK than in the US. Having gained a recording deal with the London-based label Chrysalis in 1977, the group quickly produced two albums, *Blondie* and *Plastic Letters*. The latter included their first UK hit, a version of Randy and the Rainbows' 1963 US Top 10 winner, 'Denise'. Retitled 'Denis', it climbed to number two in 1978.

Ex-Mud and Suzi Quatro producer Mike Chapman was brought in for the third album, *Parallel Lines*. Two cuts from the LP had already been released as singles before 'Heart Of Glass', which successfully attracted a new audience of disco fans to make it Blondie's first number one. Its appeal also crossed over to the other side of the Atlantic, where it became not only the group's first US success but a number one.

434

TRAGEDY

THE BEE GEES

3 March 1979, for 2 weeks

●●

RSO 27

Writers: Barry, Maurice and Robin Gibb
Producers: The Bee Gees, Karl Richardson and Albhy Galuten

The Bee Gees dominated the international record business in 1978 as no act had done since the heyday of the Beatles. Not only did *Saturday Night Fever* become the best-selling album of all time (until Michael Jackson unleashed *Thriller*), but several records the brothers wrote and produced in varying combinations with different artists were worldwide hits, and the title song of the film *Grease* allegedly earned writer and co-producer Barry Gibb more money than anyone had yet received from a single song.

The age-old show business question asking what one does for an encore was never more apt. The Bee Gees replied with *Spirits Having Flown*, an album recorded in Florida with Galuten and Richardson. They chose to change pace with the first single from the set, preceding the LP's release with 'Too Much Heaven'. This ballad, its publishing rights donated to UNICEF, reached number three in Britain and one in America.

The second single from the package, 'Tragedy', scaled the summit in both countries. At the time the group was concerned that every single they released should be a potential US number one. In this case they got the top spot at home, too. 'Tragedy' was the last UK smash in the late-70s string of Bee Gees hits. Their first number one of the 80s would come, not with their own voices, but with that of Barbra Streisand.

435

I WILL SURVIVE

GLORIA GAYNOR

17 March 1979, for 4 weeks

●●●●

POLYDOR 2095 017

Writers: Dino Fekaris and Freddie Perren
Producer: Dino Fekaris in association with Freddie Perren

Like 'Kung Fu Fighting' and 'Juliet', 'I Will Survive' was originally intended as the B-side of a single but won through. Gaynor had achieved dance-floor fame via side one of her debut LP, which contained three segued tracks, 'Honey Bee', 'Never Can Say Goodbye' and 'Reach Out I'll Be There'. All were edited for single release, the second climbing to number two.

She assumed the title of Disco Queen in 1975, only to have the crown snatched from her head by the sensuously moaning Donna Summer (see no. 490). Subsequent offerings failed to enrapture disco devotees, causing most fans to believe that she had in fact said goodbye.

'Substitute', a single from her album *Love Tracks*, was released in 1979, but it was the

B-side that gained attention. The Who, Clout and Liquid Gold have all made the Top 10 with songs titled 'Substitute' but none has reached number one, so it was perhaps a wise move to promote 'I Will Survive' instead. The track topped the stack in both the UK and the USA, rekindling the flame of Gaynor's career. However, her follow-up, 'Let Me Know (I Have The Right)' was too similar to make much impact. 'I Am What I Am', a song from the musical *La Cage Aux Folles*, put the singer back into the Top 20 in 1983, but she again made the mistake of trying to repeat the formula by releasing 'Strive'. It sank without a trace and Gloria Gaynor's chart career went under for the third time.

'I Will Survive' survives, though, almost as a parody of itself as the most performed karaoke song of all.

436

BRIGHT EYES

ART GARFUNKEL

14 April 1979, for 6 weeks

●●●●●●

CBS 6947

Writer: Mike Batt
Producer: Mike Batt

This number one hit, which removed Art Garfunkel from the embarrassing list of one-hit wonders where he had been languishing since 1975, represented great personal triumphs for both Garfunkel and Mike Batt, yet the song almost missed being a single. The vocalist, always intensely concerned with his image and craft, did not feel the theme from the animated film *Watership Down* would make a worthy single. He also had no intention of putting it on his new album, *Fate For Breakfast*. It was when CBS executives in the UK showed him photographs of fans queuing to see the film that he relented.

'Bright Eyes' became the biggest-selling single of 1979 and the last hit until Culture Club's 'Karma Chameleon' (see no. 527) to last for as long as 6 weeks at the very top. It also went to number one in several other European countries, but it never made the American Hot 100.

This second solo UK number one gave Garfunkel a 2-0 edge over ex-partner Paul Simon. Even during their glorious partnership, their only British number one was a solo vocal by Art, making the tally 3-0, most odd in view of Simon's esteemed reputation as a writer and great success as an album artist. For Mike Batt it was an even sweeter triumph. His eight hits as the Wombles had typed him as a talented lightweight, despite a few other successes. 'Bright Eyes' established him as a serious songwriter.

437

SUNDAY GIRL

BLONDIE

26 May 1979, for 3 weeks

●●●

CHRYSALIS CHS 2320

Writer: Chris Stein
Producer: Mike Chapman

The fourth track to be taken from the album *Parallel Lines* gave Blondie their second number one. A simple, melodic song, it served to broaden the appeal of the group still further. *Parallel Lines* wound up being the best-selling album of 1979.

A great deal of media attention began to be focused upon photogenic vocalist Debbie Harry, whose previous employment had included stints as a barmaid, a Bunny girl and a BBC New York office worker. Just as Alice Cooper (see no. 317) had originally been the name for a whole group, not simply its lead singer, Blondie strove hard for their title to be used as a reference to the band. But when the general public referred to Blondie they meant just the peroxide blonde Debbie Harry, and pin-ups of her began to appear on thousands of bedroom walls throughout the world.

Blondie spent a total of 43 weeks in the Top 75 in 1979. For the first time in history three acts ended the year with exactly the same tally of weeks on chart. It isn't easy to spend ten months of the year in the charts but in 1979 Abba, Blondie and Chic made it seem as simple as ABC.

438

RING MY BELL

ANITA WARD

16 June 1979, for 2 weeks

●●

TK TKR 7543

Writer: Frederick Knight
Producer: Frederick Knight

Anita Ward was a teenager singing a cappella gospel in a Memphis, Tennessee, church when Chuck Holmes discovered her and got her a recording contract. Very little happened for a long time, as acknowledged by Ward on the liner notes to her *Songs Of Love* album, which included 'Ring My Bell'.

The single was perfect midsummer disco music and it raced to the top of the charts. The hook was the synthesizer of Carl Marsh, which produced a sound - impossible to translate into words but instantly recognizable to the ear - which became almost as copied as Donna Summer's referee's whistle. Writer/producer Frederick Knight had enjoyed his own American Top 30 success with 'I've Been Lonely For So Long'.

After the success of 'Ring My Bell', there was absolutely nothing in the way of chart action for Anita Ward. She is now a member of the one-hit wonder club, with little prospect of releasing herself from it.

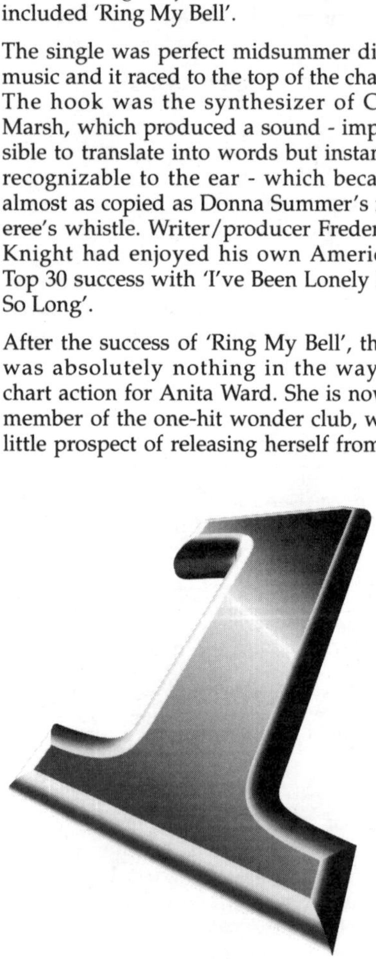

This is a sad fate for a girl who used three studios, four engineers, two remixers and a 'midnight mix by Richie Rivera', as well as a producer, to come up with a number one.

439

ARE 'FRIENDS' ELECTRIC?

TUBEWAY ARMY

30 June 1979, for 4 weeks

●●●●

BEGGARS BANQUET BEG 18

Writer: Gary Numan
Producer: Gary Numan

As a child Gary Numan (born Gary Webb on 8 March 1958) was very interested in gadgets. One of his earliest musical memories was of the Shadows performing on TV, though it was the guitars that intrigued him more than the music. By the age of 15 he had started writing lyrics. In February 1978 he recorded his first song, 'That's Too Bad', at Spacewood Studios in Cambridge. His dad paid for the session, and on the day of release Gary quit his job at W.H. Smith to concentrate fully on a career in music with his group Tubeway Army.

The band consisted of Gary's uncle Jeff Lidyard (born 1 September 1950) on drums and friend Paul Gardiner (born May 1958) on bass. Numan handled vocals, guitar and keyboards. Gardiner heard that local record shop Beggars Banquet were forming their own label, and Numan sent them the punk demo of 'That's Too Bad', not because he favoured that style of music, but simply because he realized it was more likely to secure a deal. His plan worked and the single was released, selling a respectable 7,000 copies.

With Numan Sr once again paying studio fees, the debut LP *Tubeway Army* was recorded in just three days. In early 1979 the follow-up, *Replicas*, was made in a 16-track demo studio in London over a period of five days. The first single from the album, 'Down In The Park', flopped. The second, chosen by Numan, was 'Are

'Friends' Electric?', a merger of two songs, one a ballad with spoken lyrics and one with the basic melody riff.

Sales of 20,000 picture discs put the song in the charts. It shot up the Top 40 and, following a charismatic *Top Of The Pops* performance, reached number one, staying there long enough to be matched by *Replicas* on the LP chart.

440

I DON'T LIKE MONDAYS

BOOMTOWN RATS

28 July 1979, for 4 weeks

●●●●

ENSIGN ENY 30

Writer: Bob Geldof. Producer: Phil Wainman

Bob Geldof had been in Atlanta Georgia, doing an interview at the University, when a story came in over the tickertape news service. A young girl in San Diego, California, called Brenda Spencer, was shooting from her bedroom window at children in the school playground across the street. In mid-massacre, so to speak, she had been telephoned by a journalist, and Miss Spencer paused to answer the phone. The journalist asked her why she was killing people, and her answer was, "Something to do. I don't like Mondays." Geldof turned the tragedy into a dramatic million seller that was chosen as Best Single Of 1979 in the British Rock And Pop Awards, sponsored by Radio One, *Nationwide* and the *Daily Mirror*.

'I Don't Like Mondays' was a worldwide hit, with the glaring exception of the United States. Fear of lawsuits and charges of bad taste as much as any aversion to New Wave kept radio stations from playing the record. The unofficial boycott was front-page news in *Variety*, the only time the Rats earned such prominent coverage in the show business bible.

The Boomtown Rats were Bob Geldof on vocals, Pete Briquette (born Pat Cusack) on bass, Johnny 'Fingers' Maylett on piano, Gary Roberts and Gerry Cott on guitars and Simon Crowe on drums. 'Mondays' was premiered before its release at the 1979 Loch Lomond Festival.

The transformation of Geldof from punk rocker into a major figure in the worldwide politics of poverty has tended to overshadow the musical and innovative importance of his band. They were always an exciting live act. At their best, as with 'I Don't Like Mondays', they were brilliant.

441

WE DON'T TALK ANYMORE

CLIFF RICHARD

25 August 1979, for 4 weeks

●●●●

EMI 2975

Writer: Alan Tarney
Producer: Bruce Welch

Twenty years and 25 days after his first number one hit (see no. 88), Cliff Richard reached the top for the tenth time, with the record that has turned out to be his biggest-selling worldwide hit. It marked a second period of strong resurgence for the ageless Cliff, who came up with seven more Top 10 hits over the next four years. Among those hits was his ninth number two hit, his version of his own favourite song of all time, 'Daddy's Home', which just failed to push Human League off the top at Christmas 1981. The seventh of those comeback Top 10 hits, 'Please Don't Fall In Love', which reached number seven at the end of 1983, was the 50th single featuring Cliff to hit the Top 10, one of which was in duet with Phil Everly. Cliff's 50th solo Top 10 hit came on 4 July 1987, when a song written and produced by Alan Tarney, 'My Pretty One', leapt to number 10. On his 47th birthday, in October 1987, Cliff was enjoying his 51st solo Top 10 hit with another Tarney effort, 'Some People', which climbed as high as number three, his biggest hit since 'Daddy's Home' six years earlier.

In 1986 Cliff's record contract with EMI lapsed, but he still managed to hit the Top 10 twice, in collaboration with firstly the Young Ones (see no. 567), and secondly with Sarah Brightman, with a song from *Phantom Of The Opera*, 'All I Ask Of You'. With that hit he established the bizarre record of hitting the Top 10 with a song from one West End show while actually starring in another - *Time*.

Sadly, during the weeks that 'We Don't Talk Anymore' was at number one, Norrie Paramor, the man who as a producer was most responsible for the recording success of Cliff Richard and the Shadows, died. He was then, and remains now, in a tie with George Martin, the man who has produced the most British number one hits.

442

CARS

GARY NUMAN

22 September 1979, for 1 week

●

BEGGARS BANQUET BEG 23

Writer: Gary Numan
Producer: Gary Numan

Gary Numan was not idle while 'Are 'Friends' Electric?' was in the chart. He found 14 spare days in which to record the LP *The Pleasure Principle*. Tubeway Army had, in reality, been disbanded for several months, so it was no surprise when Numan took solo credit for 'Cars', a song he originally recorded on a bass guitar and which, he claimed, he took as long to write as it did to play. Four weeks after it charted, both the single and the LP were number one.

As a performer Numan had not played live for over a year, and even then only the occasional pub gig, yet in September he started a challenging UK tour, filling theatres such as the Hammersmith Odeon. In the following spring he toured America, where 'Cars' had made the Top 10.

Numan's singles and albums continued to make the Top 10 into the early 1980s. In 1984 he invested all his profits in his own record label, Numa. The only real luxury he has ever afforded himself has been his aeroplane. He remains the only pop star to have flown around the world solo and performed low-level aerobatics displays in a World War II Spitfire.

GARY NUMAN is the only artist to chart with three different versions of a number one, the original 'Cars', a live version on a 1985 EP, and a 1987 remix. (Pictorial Press)

443

MESSAGE IN A BOTTLE

THE POLICE

28 September 1979, for 3 weeks

●●●

A&M AMS 7474

Writer: Sting
Producers: The Police and Nigel Gray

With 'Message In A Bottle' Herb Alpert and Jerry Moss' A&M label scored its first UK number one after 13 years of trying. Just a few months earlier, Deptford group Squeeze had come close with two consecutive number two singles, but it was the Police who finally made the grade.

The line-up of vocalist/bassist Sting (born Gordon Sumner, Newcastle, 2 October 1951), guitarist Andy Summers (born Blackpool, 31 December 1942) and drummer Stewart Copeland (born Alexandria, Virginia, 16 July 1952) had been performing together since the summer of 1977, although the group had been formed by Sting, Copeland and Corsican guitarist Henry Padovani six months before. Before Padovani left in August 1977 the trio recorded one single, 'Fall Out', for Illegal Records, a label set up by Copeland and his brother Miles. It was not a hit at the time but did enter the Top 50 when re-released after the success of 'Message In A Bottle'.

Before reaching the top of the chart each of the Police men had served their musical apprenticeship. Summers had changed his name to Somers in 1964 and joined Zoot Money's Big Roll Band. He played in a variety of groups throughout the 60s and 70s, including Eric Burdon's New Animals. He joined the Police in July 1977. Copeland had been with Curved Air since 1974, and Sting had joined semi-professional Newcastle outfit Last Exit in that year. In 1976 he left his job as a teacher to move to London and concentrate on music. The public soon got the message.

Within a year of their number one, Geoff Downes (left) and Trevor Horn disbanded BUGGLES and joined Yes; within a year that group had temporarily split. Horn produced the relaunched band's 1983 American number one, 'Owner Of A Lonely Heart'. (Pictorial Press)

444

VIDEO KILLED THE RADIO STAR

BUGGLES

20 October 1979, for 1 week

•

ISLAND WIP 6524

Writers: Bruce Wooley, Trevor Horn and Geoff Downes
Producers: Trevor Horn and Geoff Downes

Having worked together briefly in the band of Tina Charles (see no. 386), Trevor Horn and Geoff Downes had gone their separate ways, Downes to become an advertising jingles producer and Horn to become resident bass player at the Hammersmith Palais. In 1978 they began writing songs with Bruce Wooley and conceived the idea of a studio band called the Buggles. No sooner had Wooley left to form his outfit, the Camera Club, than Downes and Horn won a recording contract with Island after label boss Chris Blackwell heard a demo of 'Video Killed The Radio Star'. Three months later the duo was number one.

After one album and three more hit singles the Buggles took part in a seemingly bizarre move, replacing Rick Wakeman and Jon Anderson in Yes, one of the 70s biggest album sellers. It may have appeared crazy but it worked for a while. Following the demise of Yes in 1981, Downes and guitarist Steve Howe joined ex-Family/King Crimson/Uriah Heep bassist John Wetton and ex-ELP dummer Carl Palmer to form the successful supergroup Asia. Horn went on to produce a historic string of hits, including Yes' American number one, 'Owner Of A Lonely Heart', and three British chart-toppers for Frankie Goes To Hollywood.

445

ONE DAY AT A TIME

LENA MARTELL

27 October 1979, for 3 weeks

●●●

PYE 7N 46021

Writer: Kris Kristofferson
Producer: George Elrick

One track from Lena Martell's 13th LP for Pye was the Kris Kristofferson gospel song 'One Day At A Time'. For some years Miss Martell had been a consistent seller in the easy-listening category. Her LPs contained her versions of popular middle-of-the-road hits of the day, all exquisitely performed and painstakingly produced, but none of them seemingly suitable for the singles charts. 'One Day At A Time' proved the one exception. Considerable TV and radio exposure for the song, which had never been a British hit before, created a public demand which suddenly gave Lena Martell her one and only British hit single. Kristofferson had another number one composition in America, but that, too, was a cover version by a female artist, Janis Joplin's posthumous chart-topper 'Me And Bobby McGee'.

LENA MARTELL had one hit single and six hit albums, but her only number one was the single. (Pictorial Press)

The Tim Rice/Andrew Lloyd Webber combination had launched the chart careers of several female vocalists, including Yvonne Elliman, Helen Reddy and Julie Covington. It ended Lena Martell's. Her version of 'Don't Cry For Me Argentina' was the follow-up to 'One Day At A Time', and it missed completely, making Martell a one-hit wonder.

446

WHEN YOU'RE IN LOVE WITH A BEAUTIFUL WOMAN

DR HOOK

17 November 1979, for 3 weeks

●●●

Writer: Even Stevens
Producer: Ron Haffkine

The core of Dr Hook was formed in 1969 when folk guitarist/vocalist Dennis Locorriere (born 13 June 1949) and R&B singer/guitarist Ray Sawyer (born 1 February 1937) began performing together in New Jersey. The act was originally known as Dr Hook and the Medicine Show. Several musicians passed through the group, but the performers on this single were guitarist Rik Elswit, drummer John Wolters, bassist Jance Garfat and keyboard player Billy Francis.

Dr Hook's first hit was 'Sylvia's Mother'. The song, written by the man who had helped gain them their recording contract, *Playboy* cartoonist Shel Silverstein, ascended to number two in 1972. This was followed by a four-year gap until their next British success, another number two hit, 'A Little Bit More'. Their American Top 10 career had continued in the interval with the satirical 'Cover Of *Rolling Stone*' and a version of Sam Cooke's 'Only Sixteen'. The group went on to the odd distinction of achieving six gold singles in America without ever getting higher than number five in a weekly chart; their hit singles were so pleasant to the ear they remained in the *Billboard* Hot 100 for months.

'When You're In Love With A Beautiful Woman' had a bit of premature excitement on 10 November 1979 when Radio 1 DJ Paul Burnett announced it as Britain's new number one. A computing error had occurred, and one hour later Burnett told the nation Lena Martell had been reinstated at the top. However, Dr Hook had their day, and indeed their three weeks, the following Tuesday, when their hit became a true number one.

447

WALKING ON THE MOON

THE POLICE

8 December 1979, for 1 week

●

A&M AMS 7494

Writer: Sting
Producers: The Police and Nigel Gray

The Police's second number one followed hard upon their first. Like its predecessor, it had originally been a track on their number one album *Reggatta De Blanc*. Early Police singles had followed a strange pattern. Three tracks from their debut album, *Outlandos d'Amour*, had been released in 1978. 'Roxanne' and 'So Lonely' had experienced no initial success. In between had come 'Can't Stand Losing You', a minor hit. Both the group and their manager, Miles Copeland, were dismayed by the poor public reaction to their blend of rock and reggae, and for a while Sting laid down his bass guitar and took up acting, appearing on screen in the 'road' movie *Radio On* and the film based on the Who's album *Quadrophenia*. It was during this time that the trio first bleached their hair for a chewing gum TV advert and decided to remain blond.

A successful tour of the USA in 1978 gave the Police new confidence, and the single 'Roxanne' began to sell in America. Repromoted in Britain, it climbed to number 12. 'Can't Stand Losing You' was revitalized and did even better by reaching number two. After a year of giving them the cold shoulder, the music press were now in hot pursuit of the bleach boys and turned Sting into the male equivalent of Debbie Harry in the pin-up stakes. Two number ones followed. A&M then reactivated 'So Lonely', which duly made the Top 10 at the beginning of 1980.

448

ANOTHER BRICK IN THE WALL (PART II)

PINK FLOYD

15 December 1979, for 5 weeks

●●●●●

HARVEST HAR 5194

Writer: Roger Waters
Producers: Roger Waters, Bob Ezrin and Dave Gilmour

Led by the enigmatic Syd Barrett, Pink Floyd had first checked into the charts in 1967 with the psychedelic Top 20 hits 'Arnold Layne' and 'See Emily Play'. Twelve years of singles silence followed until this track from *The Wall* gave the Floyd the biggest surprise of their long career. It also provided Bob Ezrin with his second number one (see no. 317).

In addition to guitarist Barrett (born 4 January 1946), the Floyd of 1967 had been bassist Roger Waters (born 6 September 1944), keyboard player Richard Wright (born 28 July 1945) and drummer Nick Mason (born 27 January 1945). Failing health in late 1967 forced Barrett to be replaced by Dave Gilmour (born 6 March 1944). Like Yes and Led Zeppelin, Pink Floyd built a reputation through the early 70s as an albums-only outfit, with LPs including *Atom Heart Mother* and *Wish You Were Here*, both number ones. In 1973 their classic *Dark Side Of The Moon*, engineered by Alan Parsons, made it to only number two, but it began a 310-week run on the LP charts. In America it lingered in the list for 741 weeks, the longest runner of all time.

'Another Brick In The Wall' unintentionally inspired graffiti along the lines of 'We don't need no education' and 'Teacher leave those kids alone' on school walls throughout the Western world. In 1982 a film version of *The Wall* was produced by Alan Parker, starring Boomtown Rats leader Bob Geldof in the role of Pink. The

name was a reference to the ill-informed question "Which of you is Pink?"

Waters left the group acrimoniously in 1983, but still produced the most spectacular performance of *The Wall* at the Berlin Wall in 1990. An estimated 200,000 people attended the charity concert; millions more saw it on television and video. Just as Genesis confounded pundits who had predicted they would fail after the departure of lead singer Peter Gabriel, Pink Floyd survived the defection of their front man. Most impressively, they enjoyed a world number one album in 1994 with *The Division Bell*.

The students desired neither education nor thought control in Alan Parker's film based on *The Wall* by PINK FLOYD. (Pictorial Press)

449

BRASS IN POCKET

THE PRETENDERS

19 January 1980, for 2 weeks

●●

REAL ARE 11

Writers: Chrissie Hynde and James Honeyman-Scott
Producer: Chris Thomas

The Pretenders that appeared on 'Brass In Pocket' were vocalist/guitarist and ex-*New Musical Express* journalist Chrissie Hynde (born Akron, Ohio), guitarist and keyboard player James Honeyman-Scott, bassist Peter Farndon and drummer Martin Chambers.

The band had previously issued a cover of the Kinks' 'Stop Your Sobbing' and an original song, 'Kid'. Both had nudged into the Top 40 and gained the group critical acclaim. 'Brass In Pocket' was nearly frozen out during the Christmas period but eventually climbed to the top of the tree after ten weeks on the chart.

On 15 June 1982 Farndon announced that he was leaving the band. The following day Honeyman-Scott died of a drug overdose. The tribute single 'Back On The Chain Gang', with Billy Bremner on guitar and Tony Butler on bass, gave the Pretenders their biggest US hit when it climbed to number five. Tragedy struck again when, on 15 April 1983, Farndon was also found dead following an overdose. Martin Chambers stepped down in mid-decade, leaving founder Chrissie Hynde the last remaining original Pretender. She dissolved the group in 1985, only to return in 1986 with three new Pretenders.

450

THE SPECIAL AKA LIVE EP

THE SPECIALS

2 February 1980, for 2 weeks

●●

2 TONE CHSTT 7

Writers: 'Too Much Too Young' – Jerry Dammers and Lloyd Chambers; 'Guns Of Navarone' – Dmitri Tompkin and Paul Francis Webster; 'Long Shot Kick De Bucket' – Sydney Roy Crooks and Jackie Robinson; 'The Liquidator' – Harry Johnson; 'Skinhead Moonstomp' – Monty Naismith and Roy Ellis
Producers: Jerry Dammers and Dave Jordan

'The Special A.K.A. Live' was the only number one for the Coventry-based Chrysalis subsidiary Two Tone Records which, in 1979/80, led a shortlived ska revival. Both Madness (see no. 501) and the Beat achieved their initial success on Two Tone, before moving to Stiff and Go Feet respectively. The Specials had scored their first Top 10 hit in 1979 when 'Gangsters' climbed to number six. This single was unusual because the B-side featured a different act to the A-side, namely the Selecter.

Special A.K.A. had been performing for three years when, in 1980, they adopted the name their loyal fans used for their favourite group, the Specials. The musicians who appeared on this EP were: vocalist Terry Hall, keyboard player Jerry Dammers, vocalist/guitarist Lynval Golding, percussionist/guitarist Neville Staples, drummer John Bradbury, guitarist Roddy Radiation, bassist 'Sir' Horace 'Gentleman' Parker, flugel horn player Dick Cuthell and trombonist Rico Rodriguez, a Jamaican who had played on many of the original ska hits of the late 60s. 'Too Much Too Young' and 'Guns Of Navarone' were recorded at the Lyceum, London, and the other songs at Tiffany's, Coventry.

The group would score three more Top 10 hits before appearing at the very top again just 18 months later.

The SPECIALS recorded the last vinyl EP to get to number one. (Pictorial Press)

451

COWARD OF THE COUNTY

KENNY ROGERS

16 February 1980, for 2 weeks

●●

UNITED ARTISTS UP 614

Writers: Roger Bowling and B.E. Wheeler
Producer: Larry Butler

'Lucille' (see no. 406) had launched Kenny Rogers' solo career in both the UK and his native USA in 1977. In America he had developed into a major artist with a string of country hits to his name. In Britain, where the market for country music is smaller, he was less successful, until 'Coward Of The County' brought him back to the public's attention. Like 'Lucille', 'Coward' was a sentimental 'story song', the variety of country tune most likely to succeed in the UK, and in 1981 Rogers starred in a TV movie based on the lyrics of the song.

At the end of 1980 Rogers scored his first international pop success, 'Lady', penned by Lionel Richie. A US number one and a UK Top 20 hit, it put the singer in the superstar league. Duets with Scotland's Sheena Easton ('We've Got Tonight') and fellow country/MOR superstar Dolly Parton ('Islands In The Stream') continued to broaden his appeal. By 1983 his stature was such that RCA had to pay a reported million dollars to lure him away from UA.

Despite recording an album with ex-Beatles producer George Martin in 1986, Rogers has had no UK chart success since 1983. However, he has made a fortune in the US, donating much of it to fighting famine.

452

ATOMIC

BLONDIE

1 March 1980, for 2 weeks

●●

CHRYSALIS CHS 2410

Writers: Chris Stein and Debbie Harry
Producer: Mike Chapman

Three must have been Blondie's lucky number. 'Atomic', the third track to be lifted from the *Eat To The Beat* album, entered the chart at number three and was their third number one. The single's high chart debut meant that Debbie Harry had entered the list in a higher position than any other female. Needless to say, this was in the days before Madonna altered nearly all the records for achievements by female artists.

Like Blondie's first chart-topper, 'Heart Of Glass' (see no. 433), 'Atomic' was a disco hit. It seemed that the group would always do best with songs you could dance to rather than rock numbers like their two preceding singles, 'Dreaming' and 'Union City Blue'.

In 1980 Debbie Harry appeared in two feature films, Mark Reichert's thriller *Union City*, for which Blondie supplied the theme tune, and Alan Rudolph's *Roadie*, which starred US rocker Meat Loaf (see no. 697) and included guest appearances by Alice Cooper (see no. 317) and Roy Orbison (see nos. 108, 171 and 179).

453

TOGETHER WE ARE BEAUTIFUL

FERN KINNEY

15 March 1980, for 1 week

●

WEA K 79111

Writer: Ken Leray Producers: Carson Whitsett, Wolf Stephenson, Tommy Couch

'Together We Are Beautiful' had been recorded by British vocalist Steve Allan 18 months before Fern Kinney hit the charts, and at the beginning of 1979 he enjoyed two weeks of chart action with his version. A year after Allan dropped out of the charts for ever, Kinney's rendition came on the charts via the discos, and within a month was number one. Six weeks later, she became the 24th current member of the one-hit wonder club, the third consecutive female vocalist to join this exclusive band, and the first of five one-hit wonders of 1980.

In her native land Miss Kinney (born Fern Kinney-Lewis in Jackson, Mississippi) is not quite as obscure as she has been for all but 11 weeks of her life in Britain. She was first noticed when she had a big disco hit in 1979 with her version of King Floyd's 1970 American R&B number one, 'Groove Me'. That record did not break her in Britain, however, and more surprisingly, 'Together We Are Beautiful' missed out in America.

454

GOING UNDER GROUND/DREAMS OF CHILDREN

THE JAM

22 March 1980, for 3 weeks

●●●

POLYDOR POSP 113

Writer: Paul Weller
Producer: Vic Coppersmith-Heaven

The Jam were the most successful English New Wave band. Much of that success was due to the songwriting talents of leader Paul Weller, whose songs combined the articulacy of Ray Davies with the 'Fire And Skill' of Pete Townshend (the motto 'Fire And Skill' was written on the group's bass amp).

The trio from Sheerwater, Surrey, were Weller on guitar and vocals, bassist Bruce Foxton and drummer Rick Buckler. Their very first single, 'In The City', reached number 40 in May 1977. 'Going Underground'/'Dreams Of Children' was their first number one, going straight in at the top on 22 March 1980. Their tenth single, it capitalized on the success of their previous hit, 'The Eton Rifles', and was typically Wellerian in composition, dwelling upon urban alienation and resignation.

The Jam's earlier chart success had been based on a trio of similarly-titled songs which all charted again when they were re-issued in April 1980 - 'All Around The World', 'The Modern World' and 'News Of The World'. They share this titular similarity with the 'world' songs of Ronnie Hilton ('Two Different Worlds', 'Around The World' and 'The World Outside'), although nobody can match the Jam's succession of 'London' songs - 'In The City', 'A-Bomb In Wardour Street', 'Strange Town' and 'Down In The Tube Station At Midnight'.

455

WORKING MY WAY BACK TO YOU-FORGIVE ME GIRL

DETROIT SPINNERS

12 April 1980, for 2 weeks

●●

ATLANTIC K 11432

Writers: Sandy Linzer, Denny Randell and Michael Zager
Producer: Michael Zager

The Spinners were called the Motown Spinners and then the Detroit Spinners in Britain to avoid confusion with the folk singers of the same name. They survived several personnel changes and finally achieved their British number one 25 years after the original group began singing together in high school in Ferndale, Michigan. At that point they went by yet another name, the Dominicos.

Initially protégés of Harvey Fuqua, they scored their first American Top 40 hit in 1961 on his Tri-Phi label with 'That's What Girls Are Made For'. When Fuqua went to Motown so did the Spinners, who hit the 40 again in 1965 with 'I'll Always Love You' and then in 1970 with Stevie Wonder-produced 'It's A Shame'. This disc, also co-written by Wonder, gave the group their first British chart entry. In

1972, now on Atlantic Records, they began a memorable string of hits with producer Thom Bell, including 'Could It Be I'm Falling In Love', 'Ghetto Child' and their US number one with Dionne Warwicke, 'Then Came You'.

Great glory in Britain was reserved for their work with yet another mentor, Michael Zager. He coupled the old Four Seasons hit 'Working My Way Back To You' with his own 'Forgive Me Girl' to reach the top spot, though oddly his own composition was not credited on the original label. A medley of old and new was not only appealing to listeners, it gave Zager a share of the composer's royalties, and he repeated the trick later in 1980 by joining 'Cupid' with 'I've Loved You For A Long Time'.

456

CALL ME

BLONDIE

26 April 1980, for 1 week

•

CHRYSALIS CHS 2414

Writers: Giorgio Moroder and Debbie Harry
Producer: Giorgio Moroder

'Call Me', from the soundtrack of Peter Schrader's *American Gigolo*, saw a temporary divorce between Blondie and producer Mike Chapman, who had master minded their first three number ones. For their fourth they teamed up with the king of disco production, Giorgio Moroder. He shared the writing credits with Debbie Harry, who became the first woman in British chart history to pen three number ones. She nearly didn't make it; Moroder had wanted Stevie Nicks to provide vocals on the track, but Fleetwood Mac's vocalist had declined the offer.

'Call Me' proved to be the most successful of all Blondie singles in their native USA, where it topped the *Billboard* Hot 100 for six weeks and ended the year as the best-selling single of 1980. It bears no connection with the Europop hit of the same title, which the Italian singer Spagna took to number two in 1987.

457

GENO

DEXY'S MIDNIGHT RUNNERS

3 May 1980, for 2 weeks

••

LATE NIGHT FEELINGS R 6033

Writers: Kevin Rowland and Al Archer
Producer: Pete Wingfield

Singer and guitarist Kevin Rowland (born 17 August 1953) was the uncompromising leader of the Birmingham-based Midnight Runners, whose street-gang image was taken from the Martin Scorsese film *Mean Streets*. In addition to Rowland the group line-up in 1980 was trombonist Big Jimmy Patterson, saxophonists Steve Spooner and JB, organist Peter Saunders, bassist Peter Williams and drummer Andy Growcott.

It was Bernie Rhodes, manager of the successful New Wave/punk band the Clash, who steered the Runners' early career by arranging a recording deal with EMI. Their first single, 'Dance Stance', namechecked several Irish authors and grazed the Top 40. Then came their first number one. It was written about one of Rowland's heroes, Geno Washington, who in the mid-60s led the Ram Jam Band, a UK soul outfit whose club reputation was second to none.

Having completed recording their debut album, *Searching For The Young Soul Rebels*, Rowland took charge of the master tapes from producer Pete Wingfield and refused to return them until EMI agreed to provide him with a more favourable contract. Having just scored a number one he was in a strong position and got his own way. After two more Top 20 hits Rowland decided to sack every member of the group save one. Surprisingly, this didn't affect his ability to come up with number one hits (see no. 506).

458

WHAT'S ANOTHER YEAR

JOHNNY LOGAN

17 May 1980, for 2 weeks

●●

EPIC EPC 8572

Writer: Shay Healy
Producers: Bill Whelan and Dave Pennefather

The Irish entry in the 25th Eurovision Song Contest was sung by an Australian, Johnny Logan. There have been many precedents for a country to be represented by an artist of different national origin, though the notion seemed odd in Britain, which traditionally has given the nod to native performers. Logan is now, it should be added, a naturalised Irishman.

The photogenic and personable Logan, real name Sean Sherrard, proved an overnight sensation with his well-made recording of the tune. The single shot in and out of the charts so quickly that it registered only 8 weeks on the chart in all, earning Johnny for the next seven years the dubious distinction of the shortest chart career of any artist with a number one hit to his credit. He might have shed that title earlier, had it not been for legal complications. He had previously contracted to another record company, and with two different labels throwing out material to capitalise on the Eurovision victory, radio programmers and record buyers alike, rarely too excited about follow-ups to Eurovision winners anyway, threw up their hands in despair and ignored them all.

In 1987, things improved. Johnny Logan was once again the Irish entrant for Eurovision, this time with a self-penned song called 'Hold Me Now'. Perhaps it was because of his other well-publicised involvement in European affairs, his engagement to a Turkish belly-dancer, or perhaps it was just the strength of the song, but whatever the reason, 'Hold Me Now' proved an easy winner, making Logan the first act ever to win the contest twice. The recording climbed to number two in Britain, kept off the top by Whitney Houston (see no. 591), but removed Logan's name for ever from the list of one-hit wonders.

459

THEME FROM M*A*S*H* (SUICIDE IS PAINLESS)

MASH

31 May 1980, for 3 weeks

●●●

CBS 8536

Writers: Mike Altman and Johnny Mandel
Producer: Thomas Z. Shepherd

The film **M*A*S*H** (which stands for Mobile Army Surgical Hospital) starred Donald Sutherland. Sutherland also starred in *The Eagle Has Landed* with Michael Caine, the star of *Alfie*, which inspired Burt Bacharach and Hal David to write the song which proved to be a hit for Cilla Black. Another co-star of *The Eagle Has Landed* was Jenny Agutter, who also starred in *The Railway Children*, directed by Lionel Jeffries, who featured in *Chitty Chitty Bang Bang* written by Ian Fleming, whose James Bond books have provided theme-song hits for Nancy Sinatra, Shirley Bassey, John Barry, Sheena Easton, Carly Simon, Wings, Matt Monro, A-Ha, Duran Duran and Gladys Knight among others. Elliot Gould, another star of **M*A*S*H**, was married to Barbra Streisand, who starred in *Hello Dolly*, which provided a hit for Louis Armstrong, who starred in *High Society*, a film which contained the hit song 'Samantha', a hit for Kenny Ball, who also had a hit with 'March Of The Siamese Children' from *The King And I*, which originally starred (in the Broadway production) Gertrude Lawrence, who was portrayed in the biopic *Star* by Julie Andrews, who has never had a hit single. All that proves is that films feature a lot of music, some good, some bad.

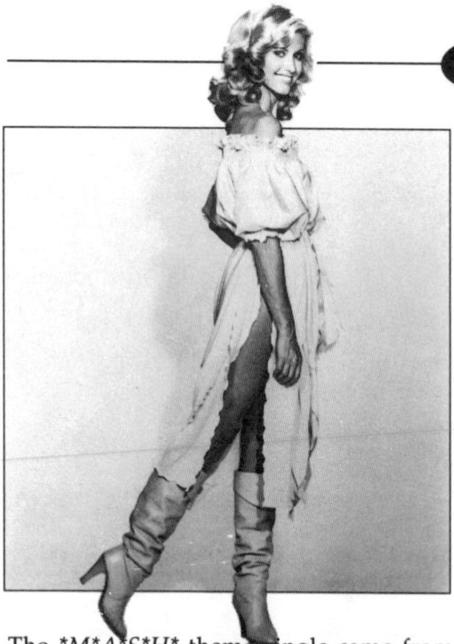

The *M*A*S*H* theme single came from nowhere, via Noel Edmonds' persistent plugging on his Radio One breakfast show, to reach number one a decade after it was recorded. It was co-written by the son of the film's director, Robert Altman.

460

CRYING

DON MCLEAN

21 June 1980, for 3 weeks

●●●

EMI 5051

Writers: Roy Orbison and Joe Melson
Producer: Larry Butler

The odyssey of this track rivals that of Kraftwerk's 'The Model' (see no. 494) as one of the strangest ever. Originally recorded in 1978 as part of the *Chain Lightning* album, it was rejected by McLean's American record company, whose chief executive suggested it be sped up to make it more commercial. McLean resisted, having intentionally dropped the Latin beat of Roy Orbison's 1961 original to create a reflective ballad. He was further resistent to change because he thought 'Crying' was one of his best performances as a singer.

Over a year later, McLean made a personal trip to Israel, stopping over in Northern Europe for a television appearance that would pay for the journey. One of the numbers he performed was 'Crying', which received such viewer reaction the cut was released as a single. When it went Top 5 in a couple of countries, EMI put it out in Britain where it went to number one. With this success McLean made a deal with a new US record company and enjoyed an American Top 5 hit in 1981. American buyers were unaware that 'Crying' had taken three years and an international trek to get there. Always a top concert attraction around the world, McLean was now restored as a media favourite.

The seven years and 357 days that had elapsed between McLean's number one hits was, at the time, the fourth-longest gap in chart history. He had gone to number one in Ireland during the interim with 'Mountains O' Mourne'.

461

XANADU

OLIVIA NEWTON-JOHN AND ELECTRIC LIGHT ORCHESTRA

12 July 1980, for 2 weeks

●●

JET 185

Writer: Jeff Lynne
Producer: Jeff Lynne

"The most dreadful, tasteless movie of the decade. Indeed, probably of all time," Felix Barker wrote in the London *Evening News*, dismissing the Gene Kelly/Olivia Newton-John film *Xanadu*. Barker's criti-

cism was only slightly more severe than the general public's reaction to the musical extravaganza, in which Olivia, a daughter of Zeus, inspires Gene Kelly to open a roller disco in California. The film may have been a folly but the music from it was spectacularly successful. Four tracks became hits in both Britain and the United States, with 'Xanadu' a UK number one and 'Magic' an American chart-topper. But whereas 'Magic' was Olivia's solo, 'Xanadu' was a duet with the Electric Light Orchestra. Indeed, the record was written and produced by ELO leader Jeff Lynne. It was Newton-John's third UK number one, all in tandem with somebody else. For the ELO, who had two hits from the film on their own, it was their first appearance in the number one position in any form. They had previously scored 13 Top 10 hits without going all the way.

Few readers of this book will have seen the box-office disappointment Xanadu, so here are four glimpses of OLIVIA NEWTON-JOHN in action. (The ELECTRIC LIGHT ORCHESTRA did not appear in the movie). (Pictorial Press)

462

USE IT UP AND WEAR IT OUT

ODYSSEY

26 July 1980, for 2 weeks

●●

RCA PB 1962

Writers: Sandy Linzer and L. Russell Brown
Producer: Sandy Linzer

Though it had occasionally happened through the years, in the post-punk era it became commonplace: an American record getting to number one in Britain without even penetrating the Top 100 at home. It was so with three 1980 number ones, 'Together We Are Beautiful' by Fern Kinney, 'Theme From M*A*S*H' by Mash and 'Use It Up And Wear It Out' by Odyssey.

In the last case the clear reason was that the British chart reflected sales and no airplay factor. If a disco record caught on and sold, it made the chart. In the States, the radio-spin element was also important. 'Use It Up And Wear It Out' had in fact done fairly well in the US disco chart but was blocked from spreading to pop because the other side, 'Don't Tell Me, Tell Her', was the stronger deck on black radio. There was no such divided chart action in Britain. 'Use It Up And Wear It Out', which had received heavy disco attention on import, quickly won radio acceptance from programmers fond of the group's 1975 Top 5 hit, 'Native New Yorker'. Odyssey (Tony Reynolds and sisters Louise and Lilian Lopez) were happy to have a number one but slightly dismayed that the side of their work they preferred, the ballad, was not recognized. They need not have worried: the follow-up, the down-tempo 'If You're Looking For A Way Out', was also one of the year's Top 40 sellers.

This triumph was also sweet for co-writer Sandy Linzer. The veteran author had helped pen the Detroit Spinners' number one only three months earlier. His patience had paid off.

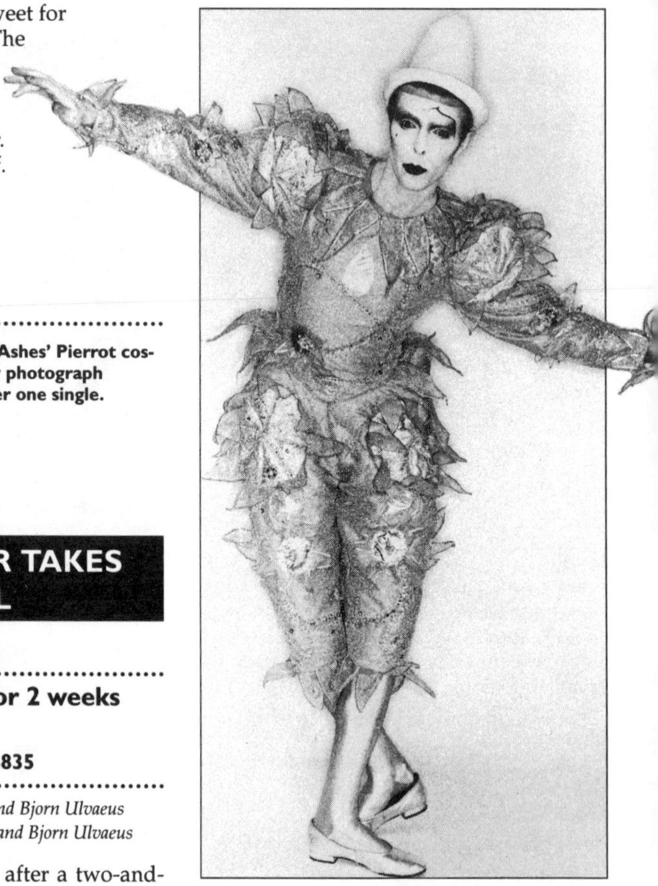

DAVID BOWIE in 'Ashes To Ashes' Pierrot costume from the RCA publicity photograph advertising his second number one single.

463

THE WINNER TAKES IT ALL

ABBA

9 August 1980, for 2 weeks

●●

EPIC EPC 8835

Writers: Benny Anderson and Bjorn Ulvaeus
Producers: Benny Anderson and Bjorn Ulvaeus

Abba's return to the top after a two-and-a-half-year absence was a surprise to chart-form watchers who felt that they would fade slowly into the sunset after a long, hugely successful, but no longer chart-topping, career. The first of two singles taken from Abba's *Super Trouper* album changed all that by leap-frogging to the top in only its second chart week on the chart. The group had come a long way since those far off Hep Stars, Hootenanny Singers and the Anni Frid Four.

By the time the group recorded *Super Trouper,* both romantic partnerships within Abba had come to an end: Benny and Frida, and Bjorn and Agnetha were no longer lovers and/or husband and wife. Yet the quartet seemed to be able to handle the complications of such breakdowns with the skill with which they made records - families had broken up but the hits kept coming. 'The Winner Takes It All' was Abba's eighth number one.

464

ASHES TO ASHES

DAVID BOWIE

23 August 1980, for 2 weeks

●●

RCA BOW 6

Writer: David Bowie
Producers: David Bowie and Tony Visconti

Eleven years after he left Major Tom stranded in 'Space Oddity', David Bowie continued his saga on an even more pessimistic note. Left "floating in my tin can" in 1969, out of radio contact with Ground Control, Major Tom now stood revealed as "a junkie...hitting an all-time low."

The hapless astronaut moaned, "I've never done good things/I've never done bad things/I've never done anything out of the blue." Bowie told the *New Musical Express* the words could be applied to himself, representing a "continuing, returning feeling of inadequacy over what I've done". Reflecting the discontent many thoughtful artists feel he added, "I'm not awfully happy with what I've done in the past." At least he gave himself credit for "the idea that one does not have to exist purely on one defined set of ethics and values, that you can investigate other areas and other avenues of perception and try to apply them to everyday life."

The New Romantic movement, which owed its existence to Bowie's past, was just beginning to exert its influence, and Bowie turned to it for his 'Ashes To Ashes' video. He wore a Pierrot costume and featured the mentor of the movement, Steve Strange.

Unlike 'Space Oddity', 'Ashes To Ashes' was not a great success in the United States, but there Bowie scored an even more important triumph when he successfully took over the title role in the Broadway production of *The Elephant Man*.

465

START

THE JAM

6 September 1980, for 1 week

●

POLYDOR 2059 266

Writer: Paul Weller
Producer: Vic Coppersmith-Heaven

Born on 23 May 1958, Paul Weller's main influence in music has, he says, been Ray Davies of the Kinks, and his favourite record of all time is the Kinks' 'Waterloo Sunset', a song about London, the city that has been the subject of many of the Jam's biggest hits.

Ray Davies and the Kinks emerged from a bleak period in the early 70s to become a very popular live act in America and a big influence on 80s rock. The influence of Davies is sometimes direct, as, for example, with the Pretenders and their versions of his compositions 'Stop Your Sobbing' and 'I Go To Sleep', and sometimes indirect, as through the songs of Paul Weller.

The JAM are shown in 1979, unaware that they are about to have four number ones in a three-year period. (Pictorial Press)

The Jam have a remarkable chart pedigree. It took them nine singles to reach the Top 10, but since the success of 'The Eton Rifles' at the end of 1979 they hit the Top 10 with every single, usually in the first week on the chart. The group hit the very top four times, and their records tended to sell in vast quantities in the week they were released, and sales then tailed off. This also meant they entered the chart at their highest position and just went down from there, a routine event in the 90s, but unusual in the early 80s. None of their four chart-toppers spent more than nine weeks in the Top 75.

466

FEELS LIKE I'M IN LOVE

KELLY MARIE

13 September 1980, for 2 weeks

●●

CALIBRE PLUS 1

Writer: Ray Dorset Producer: Pete Yellowstone

Ray Dorset, former lead singer of Mungo Jerry and composer of their two number ones, decided to write a song for Elvis Presley to record. In the summer of 1977 he came up with 'Feels Like I'm In Love'. Elvis had been one of his idols and Dorset had recorded his favourite Elvis tune, 'Baby Let's Play House', on Mungo Jerry's only hit album. Dorset intended to send the demo of 'Feels Like I'm In Love' to Presley's management. Sadly, the King's untimely death ruled this out and the song ended up as the B-side of a Mungo Jerry single released in France.

Several people wanted to buy the rights to the song from Dorset but he refused. It was Elliott Cowen from publishers Red Bus Music who suggested that the tune would be ideal for Scottish songstress Kelly Marie and would undoubtedly break her in the UK.

Kelly was born Jacqueline McKinnon on 23 October 1957 in Paisley, Scotland. She enjoyed European success when 'Who's That Lady With My Man' won her a French gold disc and made many of the European charts. 'Feels Like I'm In Love' took months to break, selling well in the North before finally charting. When it reached the top it gave the Calibre label a number one with its first single and placed Dorset among the select group of singer/songwriters whose compositions have been number ones for themselves and other performers. Kelly Marie subsequently had two more Top 30 entries and another minor hit.

467

DON'T STAND SO CLOSE TO ME

THE POLICE

27 September 1980, for 4 weeks

●●●●

A&M AMS 7564

Writer: Sting
Producers: The Police and Nigel Gray

1980's best-selling single, a mildly controversial song about the secret love between a teacher and his pupil, entered the chart at number one. It was the third time that the Police had gone to the top of the class, making them the eighth act to achieve this hat-trick. 'Don't Stand So Close To Me' was the first track to be released from *Zenyatta Mondatta*, a set which eventually attained triple-platinum status in the UK. This song also took the Police into the US Top 10 for the first time.

Between 'So Lonely', their previous single, and 'Don't Stand So Close To Me' had come an unusual release known as the 'Six Pack'. It contained each of the group's five hit singles to date plus a new single reworking of a track from *Reggatta De Blanc*, 'The Bed's Too Big Without You'. Issued as a limited edition it was immediately acquired by fans and record collectors alike, who saw that this would eventually become a valuable item. The collection entered the charts at number 17 and sold well for four weeks.

In this year drummer Stewart Copeland released a 10-inch album on the Kryptone label under the name Klark Kent. He had been issuing singles using this pseudonym for two years, and one of them, 'Don't Care', had scraped into the Top 50 in 1978.

468

WOMAN IN LOVE

BARBRA STREISAND

25 October 1980, for 3 weeks

●●●

CBS 8966

Writers: Barry and Robin Gibb
Producers: Barry Gibb, Karl Richardson and Albhy Galuten

At the peak of their success in 1978 the Bee Gees were approached to produce Bob Dylan and Barbra Streisand. Shortly thereafter Dylan began his series of religious albums, but Streisand remained interested. She was in the duet phase of her career, having recently scored with team-ups co-starring Neil Diamond and Donna Summer. Though two tracks from the *Guilty* album featured Barry Gibb and became American hits, the international number one was 'Woman In Love'. Streisand (born 24 April 1942), who had enjoyed a US Top 5 smash in 1964 with 'People', had made her British chart debut in 1966 with 'Second Hand Rose'. The 14-year-279-day interval between her first chart appearance and her first number one was then the fourth-longest wait in UK chart history.

Considered by many to have the finest female voice of her time, Streisand co-operated with other artists so often because she preferred filming to making records, and sometimes had to be lured into the studio. A 20-year fight against stage fright meant that she also avoided live performances until her high-priced comeback at London's Wembley Arena in 1994.

469

THE TIDE IS HIGH

BLONDIE

15 November 1980, for 2 weeks

●●

CHRYSALIS CHS 2465

Writer: John Holt
Producer: Mike Chapman

Blondie were reunited with Mike Chapman, the producer of their first three number ones, for their fifth and final chart-topper. It completed a hat-trick of number ones (see nos. 452 and 456), which together perched on the summit for just five weeks, the shortest-lived threesome to date. A reggae song, it had been written by John Holt, ex-lead singer with the Paragons. He had become a hit-maker in his own right in 1975, when his reggae version of Kris Kristofferson's 'Help Me Make It Through The Night' had made it to number two.

Mike Chapman could now boast nine number ones as a producer, putting him, at the time, behind only George Martin, Norrie Paramor and Johnny Franz on the list of British producers of number one hits.

The follow-up to 'The Tide Is High', 'Rapture', also came from the album *Autoamerican*. It made only number five in the UK but topped the US chart, the first rap record to do so, completing a hat-trick for Blondie in America.

470

SUPER TROUPER

ABBA

29 November 1980, for 3 weeks

●●●

EPIC EPC 9089

Writers: Benny Andersson and Bjorn Ulvaeus
Producers: Benny Andersson and Bjorn Ulvaeus

The second single from the *Super Trouper* album was the title track, which gave Abba their ninth and, in all probability, their final number one. It took a week longer than 'The Winner Takes It All' to climb to the top, but was knocked off the top only by the tragedy of John Lennon's death, which put his otherwise unremarkable '(Just Like) Starting Over' at number one. It was perhaps a fitting reminder to the biggest group in the world since the break-up of the Beatles that the Beatles always were, and always will be, bigger than any other group in popular-music history.

The final Abba album, *The Visitors*, released in 1981, failed to yield a number one single, and by the end of 1982, the group had disbanded in all aspects except a final press announcement. Frida Lyngstad was the first Abba member to have a solo hit, in 1982, and Agnetha Faltskog followed with three small hits in 1983. Bjorn and Benny went on to write, with Tim Rice, the musical *Chess*, which gave them not only their tenth chart-topper as writers (see no. 545), but also a single that sold more copies worldwide than any Abba single, Murray Head's massive smash 'One Night In Bangkok'.

Abba have still not officially disbanded, but it seems unlikely that the four super Swedes (one of whom is Norwegian!) will get back together in the recording studios. Their songs will no doubt return to the charts regularly, though. Already, there have been chart cover versions of their 'Waterloo' (by Dr. and the Medics) and 'The Day Before You Came' (by Blancmange), 'The Winner Takes It All' (by Beverley Craven) and the 'Abba-Esque EP' (by Erasure; see no. 677). The Abba songbook is likely to prove a rich source of hits for many years to come.

471

(JUST LIKE) STARTING OVER

JOHN LENNON

20 December 1980, for 1 week

●

WEA/GEFFEN K 79186

Writer: John Lennon
Producers: John Lennon, Yoko Ono and Jack Douglas

'(Just Like) Starting Over' had peaked at number eight in the British chart and had fallen back to number 21 when the tragic news of Lennon's death broke. The next week the song was number one, to give John Lennon his first British chart-topper since the Beatles split, one week too late.

The long-awaited *Double Fantasy* album had many fine tracks and, all in all, proved that Lennon was in pretty good musical form after his long lay-off. But '(Just Like) Starting Over' was by no means the best track on the album, and its original peak position of number eight was a truer reflection of its real merit as a hit single. Both 'Woman' (see no. 474) and 'Watching The Wheels', the second and third singles from the album, would have been most people's choices for release before '(Just Like) Starting Over'. But what does that matter? The death of John Lennon deprived the world of a man who had made a matchless contribution to 20th-century music and who clearly still had a great deal more to give.

472

THERE'S NO-ONE QUITE LIKE GRANDMA

ST WINIFRED'S SCHOOL CHOIR

27 December 1980, for 2 weeks

●●

MUSIC FOR PLEASURE FP 900

Writer: Gordon Lorenz Producer: Peter Tattersall

One-hit wonders come in all shapes and sizes, but probably the smallest in individual shape but the largest in total size was a girls' school choir whose first single was, at the time, the only single ever released by the budget LP label Music For Pleasure. MFP's 100 per cent success with single releases was not unique, however. The T. Rex label only ever issued one single, 'Telegram Sam' (see no. 309), and that was a number one hit, too.

At Christmas 1981 the girls issued an LP, which sold well, and another single, also on MFP, featuring the song that Ken Dodd turned into a minor hit, 'Hold My Hand', but it flopped completely. MFP's reign as the joint most successful singles label of all time was over. The St Winifred's girls are only just one-hit wonders, though. The children singing on the Brian and Michael hit, 'Matchstalk Men And Matchstalk Cats And Dogs' (see no. 421) are the St Winifred's School Choir, who thus become the only act whose only chart appearances have been on two one-hit wonder singles.

'There's No-Quite Like Grandma' was, incidentally, the 500th track to be listed at number one, thanks to double-sided hits and two EPs which swelled the total above 472.

473

IMAGINE

JOHN LENNON

10 January 1981, for 4 weeks

●●●●

PARLOPHONE R 6009

Writer: John Lennon
Producer: John Lennon, Yoko Ono and Phil Spector

The death of John Lennon created a demand for his records that compares only with the sales of Elvis records in 1977, and one result was that Lennon's masterpiece, 'Imagine', reached number one in Britain.

It was originally recorded in 1971 for the album of which it was the title track, but it was not released as a single in Britain until 1975, when it reached number six. It was released then only because Lennon had gone into retirement until 1980, so

'Imagine' was actually his final single release for five years. Produced by Phil Spector, who had also worked on the Beatles' *Let It Be* album and George Harrison's *All Things Must Pass*, the *Imagine* album featured many of the musicians who were on George's album, including Klaus Voorman and Alan White on the title track.

'Imagine' was the second of three consecutive number ones for John Lennon, and on 7 February 1981 he equalled a record set by the Beatles at the end of 1963 when he took over from himself at the top of the charts.

474

WOMAN

JOHN LENNON

7 February 1981, for 2 weeks

●●

GEFFEN K 79195

Writer: John Lennon
Producer: John Lennon, Yoko Ono and Jack Douglas

Generally accepted as the strongest song on the *Double Fantasy* LP, it is hard to understand why 'Woman' was not released as the first single from the album. When it was released it quickly completed a hat-trick of number ones for John Lennon within a period of seven weeks, which is by far the quickest hat-trick of number ones ever completed.

The sales of Lennon records in the weeks after his death were staggering. On 10 January, in the chart which first reflected immediate post-Christmas sales, three of the Top 5 singles were by Lennon - 'Imagine', 'Happy Christmas (War Is Over)' and '(Just Like) Starting Over'. That same week, the *Double Fantasy* album was at number two in the LP charts (behind Abba), *Imagine* was at number 39 and *The Beatles 1962-1966* was at number 58. By the beginning of February there were five Lennon singles in the Top 40, the extra two being 'Woman' and 'Give Peace A Chance'. There were also three Lennon albums in the Top 15, as well as two Beatles albums in the Top 75. A little later came the Roxy Music single (see no. 476) and even the John Lennon/Elton John live duet single of 'I Saw Her Standing There'. In chart terms it was the most spectacular monopoly of the charts since the Beatles in their heyday - small compensation, however, for the loss of such a musical giant.

475

SHADDUP YOU FACE

JOE DOLCE MUSIC THEATRE

21 February 1981, for 3 weeks

●●●

EPIC EPC 9518

Writer: Joe Dolce
Producer: Joe Dolce and Ian McKenzie

The unlikely one-hit wonder who kept John Lennon songs off the top for three weeks early in 1981 was an Italian-American born in Painesville, Ohio, in 1947. From 1966 he was in a group called Sugarcreek, who recorded an unsuccessful album on the Metromedia label in America in 1969. By 1974, Joe Dolce had formed a 'poetry-music fusion group' and was touring the East Coast of America, 'creating popular songs out of poetry clas-

Photographer Bob Gruen took this portrait of JOHN LENNON in the year of the subject's death, 1980. (Pictorial Press)

sics' by Dylan Thomas, Yeats and Sylvia Plath.

1978 found Dolce in Australia, where he formed the Joe Dolce Music Theatre Show and created the character Giuseppi. As Giuseppi he recorded 'Shaddup You Face', which became a big hit in Australia and was picked up by Epic for the UK market. It became the first comedy record to hit the top since 'D.I.V.O.R.C.E.' (see no. 381) and Joe became the first one-hit wonder of 1981 when all his follow-up singles, including the weird 'Reggae Matilda', missed and Joe Dolce was himself shut up.

476

JEALOUS GUY

ROXY MUSIC

14 March 1981, for 2 weeks

●●

POLYDOR ROXY 2

Writer: John Lennon
Producer: Bryan Ferry and Rhett Davies

The murder of John Lennon moved many artists to write songs about the man and their emotions after his death. Paul McCartney and Ringo Starr joined George Harrison on his tribute single, 'All Those Years Ago', Lennon's close friend Elton John penned 'Empty Garden' and Mike Oldfield released 'Moonlight Shadow'.

The only words printed on the sleeve of this single were the title, the artist and the phrase 'a tribute'. When Lennon was murdered Roxy Music were in Germany, rehearsing for a television show. Like many artists that week they decided to include a Lennon number in their set, and chose 'Jealous Guy' from the *Imagine* album. It was so well received that upon returning to Britain they cut the tune at a studio near Phil Manzanera's home in Chertsey. Three weeks after the release it had climbed to the top, giving Roxy Music their only number one. Within 18 months the group would be no more.

After their first six Top 30 singles Roxy Music were rested while lead singer Bryan Ferry (born 26 September 1945 in Washington, Co. Durham) developed his solo career. In 1979 Ferry reunited with guitarist Phil Manzanera, saxophonist Andy Mackay and drummer Paul Thompson to take up where they had left off. Their new, more sophisticated sound propelled them to ten more Top 40 hits before Ferry slunk off once more. As a solo act, Ferry continues to perform and record successfully, while Roxy Music's back catalogue still sells very strongly.

477

THIS OLE HOUSE

SHAKIN' STEVENS

28 March 1981, for 4 weeks

●●●●

EPIC EPC 9555

Writer: Stuart Hamblen
Producer: Stuart Coleman

Shakin' Stevens was born Michael Barrett in Cardiff on 4 March 1951, so he was not yet four years old when Rosemary Clooney took the song 'This Ole House' to number one (see no. 25). He apparently never heard the song until the end of 1980, by which time he had had two small hits, 'Hot Dog' and 'Marie Marie'. He took the song to his producer Stuart Coleman and the rest is history.

Stevens' first break in the business came in 1969, when he appeared on the same bill (rather lower down) as the Rolling Stones at the Saville Theatre. But he failed to capitalize on that opportunity and found himself trailing up and down the country, playing in thousands of half-empty halls for almost eight years. The second big break came in 1977, when he was one of three artists asked to play the title role in the West End musical *Elvis*. He was very successful and it led to a residency on Jack Good's revamped *Oh Boy* TV show and another series, called *Let's Rock*. This in turn led to an Epic recording contract and a lot of hard work by Stevens, his manager Freya Miller and his record company to turn Shaky into a recording star. It finally paid off with 'This Ole House', which thus became the sixth song in British chart history to hit number one in tw o different versions.

478

MAKING YOUR MIND UP

BUCKS FIZZ

18 April 1981, for 3 weeks

●●●

RCA 56

Writers: Andy Hill and John Danter
Producer: Andy Hill

Bucks Fizz - Bobby Gee, Mike Nolan, Cheryl Baker and Jay Aston - won the Eurovision Song Contest in 1981 with 'Making Your Mind Up'. They became the fourth British winners, after Sandie Shaw, Lulu and Brotherhood Of Man, and the fourth British act to take their Eurovision song to number one (Lulu failed to top the charts with her Eurovision winner, but Cliff topped the charts with the Eurovision runner-up, 'Congratulations'). 'Making Your Mind Up' was in fact the first UK entry to reach the British Top 10 since 1976 and 'Save Your Kisses For Me' (see no. 387). For the first time since 1968, Eurovision provided a number one hit in consecutive years, but unlike 1980's Johnny Logan, Bucks Fizz were conspicuously successful with their follow-up singles.

Perhaps it was the song, far stronger than most Eurovision Europop entries and a runaway winner in Dublin, or perhaps it was the way Cheryl and Jay discarded their skirts as they sang the song, but the most likely reason for their continued success was that they filled a gap in the young teen market which was widening as Abba became more sophisticated and Adam Ant became more aggressive. By the end of 1981, only Shakin' Stevens and Dollar could begin to match Bucks Fizz in the pre-pubescent popularity stakes.

479

STAND AND DELIVER

ADAM AND THE ANTS

9 May 1981, for 5 weeks

●●●●●

CBS CBSA 1065

Writers: Adam Ant and Marco Pirroni
Producer: Chris Hughes

The event that Adam Ant says made him want to become a rock star was a Roxy Music concert at the Rainbow in 1972. It took a while for the then 18-year-old Stuart Goddard to metamorphose into Adam and to find his Ants, but by the start of 1981, "Marco, Merrick, Terry Lee, Gary Tibbs and yours truly" had become Britain's most successful chart act, following in the tradition of Herman's Hermits, T. Rex and the Bay City Rollers as teenybop heroes.

'Stand And Deliver' was the first of Adam's number one hits, and it came in the middle of a year in which his records racked up a total of 91 weeks on the chart (i.e. an average of almost two records on the charts each week throughout the year), a total that has only ever been beaten three times.

Many of the hits of late 1980 and 1981 were recorded a few years earlier, before Marco Pirroni joined the group, when the height of their ambition was, according to some liner notes, to perform in "a very clandestine atmosphere, where Antpeople gather to be entertained". There was nothing very clandestine about Antmania in 1981. Ants records sold in massive quantities and 'Stand And Deliver' went to number one in its first week of chart action, only the third time that an act had gone straight to number one with their first chart-topper. The mania lasted for five years, which says a great deal for the basic talent underlying the media hype of Antmusic.

480

BEING WITH YOU

SMOKEY ROBINSON

13 June 1981, for 2 weeks

●●

MOTOWN TMG 1223

Writer: William 'Smokey' Robinson
Producer: George Tobin in association with Mike Piccirillo

Smokey Robinson's first number one solo single came about as a consequence of a song he had written over a dozen years before. 'More Love' had been a US Top 40 hit for Robinson and the Miracles in 1967. Kim Carnes took it to the Top 10 in 1980 in a version produced by George Tobin, who had overseen Robert John's US number one, 'Sad Eyes'. Robinson always made a point of sending additional songs to artists who had hits with his material. In this case he sent a batch to Tobin, who was well known for the firm control he asserted over his charges. The embarrassed producer had to reply that he was no longer working with Carnes, but he would love to cut the number 'Being With You' with Smokey himself. Robinson, who had liked the Carnes version of 'More Love', consented and enjoyed his biggest success since the 1970 winner 'Tears Of A Clown'.

Ironically, 'Being With You' was held at number two in America by the number one hit of 1981, 'Bette Davis Eyes', by... Kim Carnes. The success of 'Being With You' prompted Motown to celebrate Smokey's 25th anniversary in show business, though literally speaking they were jumping the gun by nearly a year.

481

ONE DAY IN YOUR LIFE

MICHAEL JACKSON

27 June 1981, for 2 weeks

●●

MOTOWN TMG 976

Writers: Sam Brown III and Renée Armand
Producer: Sam Brown III

Michael Jackson was born on 29 August 1958, two weeks before Cliff Richard first hit the charts in Britain. At the age of 11 he sang lead on the first hit (and first American number one) for the Jackson Five, 'I Want You Back'. For several years, even after Michael's voice broke, Motown had the hottest black act in the world with the Jackson family, who hit the charts both as a group and with Michael's solo hits, none of which ever reached number one in Britain.

Michael and his brothers, excluding Jermaine, had moved to Epic in 1976, but Motown still had a lot of old material on file. For no apparent reason a five-year-old single, 'One Day In Your Life', was reactivated and this time hit the very top. For the only time in the label's history, Tamla Motown achieved consecutive number ones in Britain. Both were solo records by lead singers of successful Motown groups, but the Michael Jackson track was so old that over 250 of all Motown singles had been released between the day 'One Day In Your Life' was released and the day it became a hit.

482

GHOST TOWN

THE SPECIALS

11 July 1981, for 3 weeks

●●●

2 TONE CHSTT 17

Writer: Jerry Dammers
Producer: John Collins

A police drugs raid in St Paul's, Bristol, sparked off a series of riots in Britain's decaying inner cities, the like of which had never been seen before in mainland Britain. The Specials second number one, although written before these events, provided a haunting commentary to that troubled summer.

Even before 'Ghost Town' had made it to the top, Neville Staples, Terry Hall and Lynval Golding had announced their departure from the band to form the Fun Boy Three. The trio scored seven hits in 18 months, their biggest being 'It Ain't What You Do It's The Way That You Do It' (in partnership with Bananarama) and a version of 'Our Lips Are Sealed', originally a hit for the American quintet the Go-Gos. The Specials lived on, having reverted to their previous name, the Special AKA. Their first release after the split was 'The Boiler', featuring rap vocals from Rhoda Dakar. The single dealt graphically with the subject of rape and was consequently banned by almost all radio stations. Even so it climbed to number 35. Although in the early days the band's ska style had attracted many skinheads, it had always allied itself with the anti-fascist and anti-apartheid movements, and in 1984 the band came up with one of its finest singles, 'Nelson Mandela'.

483

GREEN DOOR

SHAKIN' STEVENS

1 August 1981, for 4 weeks

●●●●

EPIC EPCA 1354

Writers: Bob Davie and Marvin Moore
Producer: Stuart Colman

Shakin' Stevens' architecture fixation, which had begun with 'This Ole House' (see no. 477), continued with 'Green Door', the second 50s song that the Welsh rocker had resurrected and taken to the top. 'Green Door' had not been a number one the first time round in 1956. Three versions had made the chart, the most successful being by Frankie Vaughan, which gave the high-kicking singer his first Top 10 hit and finally stopped at number two. The original version, by American Jim Lowe, climbed to number eight, and another British cover, by Glen Mason, hit number 24.

'Green Door' was the follow-up to Shaky's own favourite of his recordings, 'You Drive Me Crazy', which he took to number two but couldn't quite push up that final notch. 'Green Door' had arrived on the charts at number 22 the week before, and on 1 August leapt to the summit. At the time, that jump of 21 places was second only to the 26-place climb made by Elvis Presley's 'Surrender' (see no. 119) 20 years earlier. Today there are six records which have jumped from outside the Top 20 straight into the top position, but the 'Green Door' jump remains the fourth biggest of all time.

All this happened a couple of days after one of the authors of this book had told Mr. Stevens that 'Green Door' was a great sound, but did not seem a likely number one. Fortunately, another of the authors had already predicted on radio that it would go all the way, so at least some of the GRR team's blushes were spared.

484

JAPANESE BOY

ANEKA

29 August 1981, for 1 week

●

HANSA HANSA 5

Writer: Bobby Heatlie
Producer: Neil Ross

There was no sense writing to *Jim'll Fix It* asking for a number one record, so Scottish folk singer Mary Sandeman went out and got it for herself. A respected traditional vocalist who sang with the Scottish Fiddle Orchestra, Sandeman felt she'd like the thrill of having a hit record but didn't want to do it under her own name. She had taught herself to sing in Gaelic; pretending she was Japanese for a few minutes was by comparison easy.

Having recorded 'Japanese Boy' Sandeman needed an oriental-sounding pseudonym. She looked through the Edinburgh phone book and found Anika. Rather than risk upsetting the real Anika, she changed the middle vowel and became Aneka. She wore a kimono and Japanese wig on *Top Of The Pops* to further the illusion. Ironically, the Japanese music business wasn't too impressed, thinking the record sounded more like a Chinese effort, but the single was a hit on the European continent as well as in the UK. It was the first number one in Britain by a British artist for Hansa, a large German company.

When her game was over, Sandeman remarked that she found singing to Edinburgh Festival Fringe audiences more frightening than *Top Of The Pops*. She returned to performing Gaelic music.

485

TAINTED LOVE

SOFT CELL

5 September 1981, for 2 weeks

●●

SOME BIZZARE BZS 2

Writer: Ed Cobb
Producer: Mike Thorne

Synthesizer player Dave Ball (born Blackpool, 3 May 1959) and vocalist Marc Almond (born Southport, 9 July 1959) began making music together while students at Leeds Polytechnic. Having released an unsuccessful EP on their own Big Frock label, they signed to Lincoln-based Some Bizzare and recorded two songs, 'The Girl With The Patent Leather Face' and 'Memorabilia', the latter becoming a Top 30 dance hit in the USA.

Gravitating to London as part of the so-called futurist movement, Soft Cell gained much music-press coverage. It was, therefore, not surprising that their next single should do well. What *was* unexpected was its source: northern soul. The pair knew Gloria Jones' version of Ed Cobb's song from their trips to Leeds discotheques and their dramatic reworking stormed the charts after a histrionic performance on BBC TV's *Top Of The Pops*. 'Tainted Love' was 1981's best seller. In the USA it remained on the *Billboard* Hot 100 for a remarkable 43 weeks, the all-time longevity record. There were eight more UK Top 30 hits for Soft Cell. 'Tainted Love' itself returned to the charts on three further occasions. Its third entry was in 1991, with a newly recorded vocal. After the duo split in 1984 Ball concentrated on production, forming his own dance-based outfit the Grid, who hit the Top 5 in 1994 with the banjo-based instrumental 'Swamp Thing'. Almond guested on Bronski Beat's Top 3 medley single of 1985, which contained a reworking of Donna Summer's 1977 number one, 'I Feel Love', and has achieved a healthy string of hits, including another stint at the top of the chart (see no. 622).

486

PRINCE CHARMING

ADAM AND THE ANTS

19 September 1981, for 4 weeks

●●●●

CBS CBSA 1408

Writers: Marco Pirroni and the Ants
Producers: Chris Hughes, Marco Pirroni and the Ants

The songwriting talent of Marco Pirroni, former guitarist with Siouxsie and the Banshees, was once again in evidence on Adam and the Ants' second number one. Both chart-toppers came from Adam and the Ants' third album, *Prince Charming*, which consisted of ten tracks, all written by Pirroni and Ant.

The Ants will be best remembered for their elaborate theatrical image, which was under the control of Adam, a former art student. The promotional videos for both 'Prince Charming' and 'Stand And Deliver' were directed by Mike Mansfield but were based on detailed storyboards drawn by Adam. The fairytale 'Prince Charming' video featured the singer as the Prince, with Stuart Goddard's boyhood heroine, Diana Dors, playing the part of the Fairy Godmother. Lulu starred in the video for the follow-up single, 'Ant Rap', released at the end of 1981. This time the motifs were castles, dungeons and damsels in distress but, unlike Ant's last two efforts, the song had absolutely nothing to do with the pictures that accompanied it. The record stopped short of number one, peaking at three. Within weeks Ants Merrick, Miall and Tibbs had been ousted. Future singles would be credited simply to Adam Ant but Marco Pirroni would remain as his colleague.

487

IT'S MY PARTY

DAVE STEWART WITH BARBARA GASKIN

17 October 1981, for 4 weeks

●●●●

STIFF BROKEN 2

Writer: Herb Wiener, Wally Gold, John Gluck Jnr.
Producer: Dave Stewart

The town of Hatfield is famous for Hatfield House, seat of the Marquess of Salisbury, and for the now closed British Aerospace factory by the A1, where the first flights of such famous aircraft as the *Vampire* and the *Comet* took place. In British chart history it is known as the home town of the Zombies and Scots-born Donovan. It is also featured heavily on the motorway signs known to millions of drivers coming out of London - 'Hatfield and the North'.

The motorway sign became the name of a travelling band in the early 1970s. Hatfield and the North were Richard Sinclair, Phil Miller, Pip Pyle and Dave Stewart, who played piano, organ and tone generator. A female vocal backing group, the Northettes, worked with the band. They were Amanda Parsons, Ann Rosenthal and Barbara Gaskin.

The band broke up, hitless but with a cult following, in the mid-70s. In 1981 Dave Stewart emerged on a new chart version of Jimmy Ruffin's Top 10 hit of 1966 and 1974, 'What Becomes Of The Broken Hearted?', which featured Hatfield-born Colin Blunstone, an ex-Zombie, on vocals. A few months later an extraordinary version of Lesley Gore's 1963 smash, 'It's My Party', climbed right to the top, with vocals by Northette Barbara Gaskin.

488

EVERY LITTLE THING SHE DOES IS MAGIC

THE POLICE

14 November 1981, for 1 week

●

A&M AMS 8174

Writer: Sting
Producer: Hugh Padgham and The Police

The lead-off tracks from the two previous Police albums, *Reggatta De Blanc* and *Zenyatta Mondatta*, had both topped the charts (see nos. 443 and 467). Their 1981 *Ghost In The Machine* album saw the group collaborating with a new producer, but it was not this fact that prevented 'Invisible Sun', the initial release from the set, from getting to number one. The Police always made quality videos to accompany their songs but the footage of riots in Northern Ireland used in the video for 'Invisible Sun' caused the BBC and the IBA to prevent it being shown on British television. The single peaked at number two, kept off the very top by Adam and the Ants' 'Prince Charming'.

A second single, 'Every Little Thing She Does Is Magic', was released with almost embarrassing haste, entering the charts just four weeks after 'Invisible Sun'. With a cheery video shot both in and outside George Martin's recording studio in Montserrat, this happy-go-lucky image proved to be what the fans wanted. The single leapt to number one in the UK and number three in the USA, where 'Invisible Sun' hadn't even been released. The follow-up, 'Spirits In The Material World', made the Top 20 on both sides of the Atlantic.

For a while the band pursued individual projects. Sting acted in the BBC TV drama *Artemis '81* and the feature film *Brimstone And Treacle*, which spawned his Top 20 solo hit, 'Spread A Little Happiness'. Andy Summers teamed up with Robert Fripp for the instrumental album *I Advanced Masked*. It was to be another ten months before the Police enjoyed their final spell at the top.

489

UNDER PRESSURE

QUEEN AND DAVID BOWIE

21 November 1981, for 2 weeks

●●

EMI 5250

Writers: Queen and David Bowie
Producers: Queen and David Bowie

'Under Pressure' marked only the second occasion on which two makers of number one hits came together for the first time to record another number one. The previous case was when Frank Sinatra and daughter Nancy teamed up on 'Something Stupid' (see no. 231). Bowie, like Frank, had scored two prior number ones: Queen, like Nancy, had achieved one.

'Under Pressure' was written and recorded when Bowie and Queen met in a German studio. Since it was an act of on-the-spot inspiration, no album was ever recorded. Indeed, no B-side was made. Since it was Queen's session, one of their tracks went on the flip and they got lead billing on the disc.

Because 'Another One Bites The Dust' had been a long-lived hit in the United States in late 1980, selling over three million copies, the *Queen's Greatest Hits* album planned for Christmas had to be postponed until 1981, even in Britain; imports would otherwise have flooded America. EMI had a long time to plan their UK marketing strategy and pressed hundreds of thousands of *Hits* in anticipation of a television campaign. This meant that initial copies did not include 'Under Pressure': the LP was already sitting in the warehouse. In the States, where no such problem existed, the cut did appear on the set.

490

BEGIN THE BEGUINE (VOLVER A EMPEZAR)

JULIO IGLESIAS

5 December 1981, for 1 week

●

CBS CBSA 1612

Writer: Cole Porter; Spanish lyrics by Julio Iglesias
Producer: Ramon Arousa

On 12 October 1935 the new musical *Jubilee*, with music and lyrics by Cole Porter and book by Moss Hart, opened at the Imperial Theatre, New York. The show was a comparative failure but it has two claims to theatrical immortality. Firstly, it featured Montgomery Clift, one of Adam Ant's heroes, in his first professional role as Prince Peter, and secondly the hit song of the show was 'Begin The Beguine'.

Despite countless versions of the song recorded since 1935, no version appeared on the British charts until a man who had been Real Madrid's reserve-team goalkeeper translated the words rather loosely into Spanish and romped up to number one.

Julio Iglesias, born on 23 September 1943,

had been the idol of Spanish middle-of-the-road fans for some time, filling a melodic niche in Spanish hearts as Charles Aznavour (see no. 352) had with the French. CBS also claimed that by 1980 Iglesias was the top-selling male singer in the world and the 'top-selling artist in the history of CBS Records - ever'. Names on CBS include Michael Jackson, Barbra Streisand, Simon and Garfunkel, Frankie Laine, Guy Mitchell, and Adam and the Ants, but this assertion was before the world-shattering sales of Jackson's *Thriller*.

491

DON'T YOU WANT ME?

HUMAN LEAGUE

12 December 1981, for 5 weeks

●●●●●

VIRGIN VS 466

Writers: Jo Callis, Phil Oakey and Philip Adrian Wright
Producers: Martin Rushent and Human League

It had been a poor year for sales of singles. The synthesizer-based band the Human League scored the only million-seller to be released during 1981 with this unusual love/hate duet between League leader Philip Oakey (born 2 October 1955) and Susanne Sulley (born 22 March 1963). Susanne and her friend Joanne Catherall (born 18 September 1962) had been recruited to the group as dancers after Oakey saw the pair dancing at a nightclub in his native Sheffield. The line-up on 'Don't You Want Me?' included Ian Burden (born 24 December 1957), Jo Callis (born 2 May 1951) and Adrian Wright (born 30 June 1956).

The Human League never quite attained the popularity of Abba, whom Oakey at the time named as his chief musical influence, even though 'Don't You Want Me?' made it to number one in the USA and their next two UK singles, 'Mirror Man' and '(Keep Feeling) Fascination', both climbed to number two. Nor was their success as financially rewarding as it might have been because the group had handed over a percentage of income from record sales to Martyn Ware and Ian Craig Marsh, former group members who were later to find fortune with Glen Gregory as Heaven 17.

After an extended chart absence the Human League returned to the Top 10 in 1986 when they collaborated with prolific US producers Jimmy 'Jam' Harris and Terry Lewis to record the single 'Human'. This semi-eponymous record returned them to the top of the American charts.

492

LAND OF MAKE BELIEVE

BUCKS FIZZ

16 January 1982, for 2 weeks

●●

RCA 163

Writers: Andy Hill and Peter Sinfield
Producer: Andy Hill

The group responsible for bringing the 1982 Eurovision Song Contest to Harrogate managed a second number one early in 1982 with a song which rapidly became a favourite on children's television and radio shows. It was a children's song along the lines of the Seekers' 'Morningtown Ride' (a number two hit 15 years earlier) and even ended with a poem read by 11-year-old Abby Kimber, a member of the Mini-Pops children's group, who had some success with their album over Christmas 1981. To complete the child connections, the wife of Bobby Gee of Bucks Fizz had her first baby a few days before the record hit the top.

The Eurovision Song Contest has proved a mixed blessing for the British contestants. Established acts such as Sandie Shaw, Lulu, Cliff Richard, Olivia Newton-John and Michael Ball all found that Eurovision gave them one hit single but little more. The unknowns like Emma, the Allisons or Prima Donna mostly disappeared back into obscurity once the last television set was switched off. Only Brotherhood Of Man and Bucks Fizz have successfully used Eurovision to launch a career. Dana from Ireland also turned Eurovision success into the basis of a successful career, as did Celine Dion and the quartet from Sweden who won in 1974, Abba.

493

OH JULIE

SHAKIN' STEVENS

30 January 1982, for 1 week

●

EPIC EPCA 1742

Writer: Shakin' Stevens Producer: Stuart Coleman

Elvis Presley's 17th number one, 'Way Down' (see no. 412), was on top when Sir Freddie Laker inaugurated his London to New York Skytrain on 25 September 1977. Shakin' Stevens' third number one, 'Oh Julie', was on top when Laker Airways went bankrupt four years later. Airlines may come and airlines may go, but rock and roll goes on forever.

After the comparative failure of Shaky's follow-up to 'Green Door' (see no. 483), a revival of 'It's Raining' that only just made the Top 10, Epic decided to put out a self-penned song to revive the Shaky fortunes, and it did just that. It was very much in the rock idiom that Shaky had so completely appropriated from the fading Showaddywaddy, and it sneaked a week at the top at a time when outstanding singles were in very short supply.

One unlikely fact about Shakin' Stevens is that his real name at the time 'Oh Julie' reached the top was Clark Kent, a name he had adopted by deed poll a few years earlier.

494

THE MODEL/COMPUTER LOVE

KRAFTWERK

6 February 1982, for 1 week

●

EMI 5207

Writers: Ralf Hutter, Karl Bartos and Emil Schultz
Producers: Ralf Hutter and Florian Schneider

'The Model' is one of the strangest success stories of the 80s. A 1978 track that had received considerable club play, it was placed on the B-side of the new number 'Computer Love' when that title was issued in 1981. As record marketing men were beginning to learn, buyers are more likely to purchase a single if they are partial to the B-side as well as the top deck.

The tactic was only partially successful, as 'Computer Love' was only a minor hit. But it refused to die and featured in sales reports for several months. Clubs still preferred 'The Model'. Finally the picture sleeve was altered, with the colours changed, the title 'Computer Love' taken off the front and the words 'The Model' put in the computer screen. Sufficient sales pushed the record into the Top 75 and subsequent radio plays exploded the disc. Though a double-sided hit, this was never a double-A: 'The Model' was always the official B-side. The group's time had simply come; the synthesizer music long championed by the German ensemble had come to dominate the UK market.

During the first two months of 1982 the BMRB altered its method of chart computation. The traditional Monday-Saturday tally was dropped in favour of Friday-Thursday, on the grounds that the sales diary collectors charged too much for Saturday working. With the impact of weekend sales and *Top Of The Pops* appearances now delayed until a fortnight after they occurred, bizarre yo-yo performances on the chart were observed. 'The Model' went 10-2-3-1, the first single to drop on the chart and then go to number one since the 1981 reappearance of 'Imagine' (see no. 473).

495

A TOWN CALLED MALICE/PRECIOUS

THE JAM

13 February 1982, for 3 weeks

●●●

POLYDOR POSP 400

Writer: Paul Weller
Producers: Pete Wilson and the Jam

This was the second Jam single and the 13th chart single to come straight in at number one. It proved one of the most notable singles ever because of the number of statistics it helped create. Only Slade had bettered the Jam's achievement of two immediate number ones, entering on top with three. Elvis Presley was the only other artist to manage two. As previously stated, the Jam's two instant successes were also among the fastest-moving number ones ever. 'A Town Called Malice'/'Precious' lasted a mere eight weeks on the chart, four of which were in the Top 10, and of that four, three were spent at number one.

This single is also significant for ensuring that nos. 494 and 495 were the only two consecutive number ones to be double-sided hits. Furthermore, this Jam outing caused an industry furore after EMI objected to 'A Town Called Malice'/ 'Precious' being available in a studio-recorded 7-inch version and a live 12-inch version. The feeling was that the Jam's fans were buying both versions of the single and so stopping EMI's big seller of the moment, the Stranglers' 'Golden Brown', from reaching number one. With the growth of CD and cassette singles in the late 80s and early 90s, 'formatting', the simultaneous release of different versions of the same song attracting multi-purchases, was to become a widespread marketing ploy.

496

THE LION SLEEPS TONIGHT

TIGHT FIT

6 March 1982, for 3 weeks

●●●

JIVE 9

Writers: Hugo Peretti, Luigi Creatore, George David Weiss, Solomon Linda, Paul Campbell and Albert Stanton
Producer: Tim Friese-Greene

The Jive label's first number one was a version of a chart stalwart. Based on the Zulu folk tune 'Wimoweh', it had been popularized in pre-rock days by Pete Seeger's quartet the Weavers. Karl Denver first hit the Top 5 with the tune in 1962, pursued up the UK charts by a US number one version with new lyrics by the Tokens, 'The Lion Sleeps Tonight'. Robert John took the song back into the US Top 3 in 1972, and ten years later Tight Fit wailed their own way to success.

Tight Fit was not a new chart name. A group of session musicians had produced two successful medleys of 60s hits using this moniker. Jaap Eggermont's Starsound beat Tight Fit in the medley stakes by grabbing two number two hits, so Jive changed their tactics. 'The Lion Sleeps Tonight' was recorded with vocals by City Boy's Roy Ward and a photogenic group was put together to promote it. The resulting trio comprised model Steve Grant and dancers Julie Harris and Denise Gyngell . The latter had been rejected from the Bucks Fizz auditions. "I'm sure we're going to have at least five hits," dreamed Julie Harris at the time. Yet after just one more Top 5 smash, 'Fantasy Island', Harris and Gyngell were out, replaced by Vicki Pemberton and Carol Stevens. This Tight Fit line-up was completely unsuccessful so Steve Grant moved on to form a high-energy disco troupe called Splash. It sank.

497

SEVEN TEARS

THE GOOMBAY DANCE BAND

27 March 1982, for 3 weeks

●●●

EPIC EPCA 1242

Writers: Wolff-Ekkehardt Stein and Wolfgang Jass
Producer: Jochen Petersen

The Goombay Dance Band, a German-based outfit fronted by the fire-eating 35-year-old Oliver Bendt, took up the mantle of Boney M to top the British charts with a piece of Caribbean Europop. Only a few weeks after Kraftwerk had become the first German act to hit number one in the UK, the Goombay Dance Band became the second. They proved to be another group like Tight Fit, whose line-up in the studios was different to the one on TV and live dates.

The Goombay Dance Band officially comprised Bendt, his wife Alicia, Dorothy Hellings, Wendy Doorsen and Mario

Slijngaard. The Bendt's two children, Danny and Yasmin, often appeared on stage as background vocalists.

Bendt learned his fire-eating and his calypso rhythms on St Lucia in the West Indies, and by 1980 had established his band as one of the most successful acts in Germany. 'Seven Tears' was originally recorded in Germany in mid-1980, and its success soon after its release in January 1982 was the culmination of a long and determined effort by their management and record company to move into the slot that Boney M had begun to vacate. After many flops in Britain their patience was rewarded, albeit briefly.

498

MY CAMERA NEVER LIES

BUCKS FIZZ

17 April 1982, for 1 week

●

RCA 202

Writers: Andy Hill and Nicola Martin
Producer: Andy Hill

'My Camera Never Lies' was the third number one in a 12-month period for Bucks Fizz. They became the first act to achieve three number ones within a year since Shakin' Stevens. Of all the Eurovision winners, only Abba have scored more number ones: Brotherhood Of Man also managed three, but over a two-year period.

The melody of 'My Camera Never Lies' was written by Andy Hill, and the lyrics by Nicola Martin. Hill took Bucks Fizz into the studio and recorded the boys' lines first, since they were the most straightforward. He then cut the girls' part. Finally came the complicated middle sections where the members are chanting "my cam-e-ra" at each other. Hill gave the quartet full credit for mastering this complex sequence without much rehearsal. With the success of this single, Bucks Fizz suddenly found themselves critical as well as commercial favourites, positively reviewed in music papers usually damning of middle-of-the-road pop.

The glory days did not last for long. A highly publicised and messy split in the group when Jay Aston left did not help, but more serious and upsetting was the coach crash the group was involved in when on tour in the North East. Mike Nolan suffered severe brain damage, and it was not known for several months whether he would be able to perform again. However, a Top 10 hit in 1986 with the adventurous 'New Beginning (Mamba Seyra)' proved that Bucks Fizz were not ready to be written off just yet.

499

EBONY AND IVORY

PAUL McCARTNEY WITH STEVIE WONDER

24 April 1982, for 3 weeks

●●●

PARLOPHONE R 6054

Writer: Paul McCartney Producer: George Martin

The final track on the second side of *Tug Of War*, the album that reunited George Martin and Paul McCartney in the recording studio, featured Stevie Wonder (born Steveland Morris Judkins on 13 May 1950, in Saginaw Michigan). When 'Ebony And Ivory' was released as a single, Motown refused to allow Wonder full billing on the label, so Paul McCartney with (rather than and) Stevie Wonder was the name of the act that shot to the top to give McCartney his 24th songwriting credit at number one, and his first such credit on his own.

McCartney and Wonder have between them enjoyed something over 1200 weeks on the British charts, and yet together they remain one-hit wonders. Unlike many other big-name duets, they did at least record the song together, but when it came to making the video, it was impossible to get the two superstars in the same place at the same time. The final video, which features the two of them at the piano keyboard, was put together by technical wizardry and a lot of clever editing, with the end result being a classic example of the promotional pop video, and few people any the wiser that the two stars were actually never together for the filming.

At this stage, neither McCartney nor Wonder had ever had a solo number one hit. Wonder had co-written 'Tears Of A Clown' (see no. 290) for Smokey Robinson and the Miracles, and now had co-sung on a hit he had not written. He had to wait another two and a half years for his solo hit (see no. 538), but when it came, it proved to be one of the biggest-selling singles of all time. Paul McCartney's solo number one (see no. 530) would arrive a few months before Wonder's, again produced by George Martin, but curiously, in sales terms, it was not one of his biggest smashes.

500

A LITTLE PEACE

NICOLE

15 May 1982, for 2 weeks

●●

CBS A 2365

Writers: Ralph Siegal and Bernd Meinunger;
English lyrics by Paul Greedus
Producer: Robert Young

For the third consecutive year the winner of the Eurovision Song Contest also won a place at the top of the British charts. Seventeen-year-old Nicole Hohloch from Saarbrücken was a popular winner for Germany in the contest held in Harrogate on 24 April 1982. She became the sixth winner to top the British charts in the 27 years of the competition and the first of those six performers who didn't sing in English to win. Sweden's Abba won in 1974 with 'Waterloo' (see no. 348), but the Contest rules at that time allowed entrants to sing in languages other than their native tongue, something which was subsequently verboten.

For co-writer Siegel it was a triumph through persistence. He'd composed Germany's Eurovision entry for four years in a row and had come second in 1980 and 1981 before finally providing the winning song in 1982. Siegel thought highly of the work of British songwriter Paul Greedus, which included the 1976 Top 10 hit 'Fairytale' for former Eurovision victor Dana (see no. 284), and asked him to put English lyrics to his song. Greedus continued his connection with Eurovision by producing Britain's 1983 entry, 'I'm Never Giving Up' by Sweet Dreams.

Nicole's chart career is extraordinary. She has had only two hits. Her first, 'A Little Peace', hit the very top and her second, 'Give Me More Time', spent just one week at number 75 in August 1982.

501

HOUSE OF FUN

MADNESS

29 May 1982, for 2 weeks

●●

STIFF BUY 146

Writers: Mike Barson and Lee Thompson
Producers: Clive Langer and Alan Winstanley

The only number one for the North London ska band was written by their keyboard player, Mike Barson, and their saxophonist, Lee Thompson. Six members of Madness emerged from the Camden Town band the Invaders - Barson and Thompson, bassist Mark Bedford, vocalist Graham 'Suggs' McPherson, guitarist Chris Foreman and drummer Daniel Woodgate. By the time of 'House Of Fun' (a celebration of a young man's introduction into the wicked adult world), they had become a seven-piece with the addition of singer/trumpeter/dancer Chas Smash, aka Carl Smyth.

Madness were by far the most popular all-white ska group of their day, enjoying an uninterrupted run of 20 Top 20 hits, 15 of them Top 10, from their first chart entry, 'The Prince', in 1979 to 'Yesterday's Men' in 1985. However, as they abandoned their early 'nutty' image in favour of more sophisticated recordings on their own Zarjazz label, their hits began to make less of an impression on the charts and in 1986 the band announced it would split.

The break was not to be permanent though. They briefly re-formed in 1988 as the Madness, but without Barson, who had left in 1983 and was living in Holland, and Thompson and Woodgate, who had joined Voice Of The Beehive. In

1992 Virgin Records re-released their cover of Labi Siffre's 'It Must Be Love' in time for Valentine's Day, and a compilation album, *Divine Madness*, which quickly shot to the top of the LP listings. A memorable reunion concert in London's Finsbury Park was followed by the band signing to Go! Discs, the label Carl Smyth had been working for during the group's hiatus from the chart.

502

GOODY TWO SHOES

ADAM ANT

12 June 1982, for 2 weeks

●●

CBS A 2367

Writers: Adam Ant and Marco Pirroni
Producers: Adam Ant, Marco Pirroni and Chris Hughes

The third number one to feature the lead vocals of Stuart Goddard (born 3 November 1954), aka Adam Ant, was the only one of the three to be credited to him alone. However, Adam's chief sidekick in the Ants, Marco Pirroni, was still greatly in evidence on 'Goody Two Shoes', and the sound of the third chart-topper was much in the tradition of the first two. As he had with 'Prince Charming' (see no. 486), and as he was to do in 1983 with a number five hit, 'Puss 'N' Boots', Adam drew inspiration for his 1983 number one from the world of pantomime and children's fantasy. The song discussed the clean-living life of its subject - "Don't drink, don't smoke, what do you do?" - a life whose virtues Ant himself often extolled.

It was nearly all downhill after 'Goody Two Shoes' as far as Adam's chart fortunes were concerned. His follow-up, 'Friend Or Foe', reached number nine, and the one after that, 'Desperate But Not Serious', only 33. 'Puss 'N' Boots' restored some honour but it was his last Top 10 success despite a comeback attempt in 1990. However, Ant/Goddard is still a significant talent both visually and vocally. No leader of a group who made an impact achieved by only a score of recording acts in UK music history should be written off. His recent work as an actor supports this positive view.

'Goody Two Shoes' was the only solo number one for ADAM ANT. (Pictorial Press)

503

I'VE NEVER BEEN TO ME

CHARLENE

26 June 1982, for 1 week

●

MOTOWN TMG 1260

Writers: Ron Miller and Ken Hirsch
Producers: Ron Miller, Berry Gordy and Don Costa

Charlene Duncan (born Charlene D'Angelo, 1 June 1950 in Hollywood) is a true UK one-hit wonder, with no other claim to record fame beyond her week of glory with 'I've Never Been To Me'. The disc was originally recorded in 1976 and issued in America on the Prodigal label, a little-known label within the Motown Corporation. It limped to 97 in the US in 1977. Veteran Motown producer Ron Miller must have long consigned Charlene's recording career to the out-tray when, in 1982, a Florida radio station suddenly began playing 'I've Never Been To Me' - to phenomenal audience reaction. Motown re-released the single on the parent label, and this time it went to number three in the States and those vital two places higher in the UK.

It took some time for Motown to rediscover their new hit act, for she had married and settled in England. Charlene was actually working in an Ilford sweetshop when news of her belated triumph reached her. She promoted her hit and went back into the studio in the hope of sustaining her success. Motown even teamed her with Stevie Wonder, and a duet entitled 'Used To Be' made number 46 in America in late 1982.

Charlene's hit is a saga of a woman failing to discover herself and true happiness despite an action-packed lifestyle that included making love to a priest in the sun, visits to the 'Isle of Greece' and being undressed by kings. Halfway through a tear-jerking monologue Charlene points out that the life of a mundane housewife is actually more rewarding. This is probably just as well as Charlene's long-term fortunes in the music world were not improved even by this monster smash.

Two of the men at the controls of this recording had already experienced number one success in Great Britain, Don Costa as producer of Paul Anka (see no. 63) and Donny Osmond (see nos. 327 and 366) and Berry Gordy as writer of no. 158 for Brian Poole.

Charlene's hit took almost six years to reach the top, but another Gordy song, 'Reet Petite', was to take even longer after the original recording date to do so (see no. 582) - a massive 29 years and 42 days. Of course, as the founder of the fabulously successful Tamla Motown group of companies, Gordy has had several other links with the UK top spot.

504

HAPPY TALK

CAPTAIN SENSIBLE

3 July 1982, for 2 weeks

●●

A&M CAP 1

Writers: Richard Rodgers and Oscar Hammerstein II
Producer: Tony Mansfield

Guitarist/bassist/vocalist Captain Sensible began life on 23 April 1955 as Ray Burns, and became part of the important punk band the Damned in 1976 (original line-up: Burns/Sensible, Rat Scabies, Dave Vanian, Brian James). The group made their debut supporting the Sex Pistols at the 100 Club in July of that year. Their early recordings on Stiff were commercial failures and despite their highly praised and explosive stage act, the Damned disbanded in 1978, personality clashes within the group adding to their frustration. However, they soon re-emerged with Algy Ward and then Paul Gray replacing Brian James, and this time around they hit the charts with both singles and albums on Chiswick. The individual members of the band had on several occasions made their own extra-Damned recordings, but none proved to be as overwhelmingly popular as Captain Sensible's version of a Rodgers and Hammerstein standard from *South Pacific*. It outsold every Damned single released before or since and is about as far removed from the Damned as could be.

The Captain signed with A&M for solo projects in 1982, by which time the Damned were with Bronze. He declared his loyalty to the group, stating that they were "the first punk band and they'll be the last whatever happens". Almost immediately his irresistible version of 'Happy Talk' zoomed to number one, making a record leap in its second chart week from 33 to the top. He thus provided Rodgers and Hammerstein with their fifth number one, the legendary pair's first for 19 years (see no. 159).

Sensible remained with the Damned until the end of 1984, but there was a conflict of both interest and style between the two careers. Solo-wise, his only other major

Child actress **IRENE CARA** won an off-Broadway ('Obie') award when she was 11 years old. (Pictorial Press)

hit, 'Glad It's All Over', owed a lot to the 'Damned On 45' flip-side, which consisted of a medley of 15 Damned songs plus 'Happy Talk'. He has advertised Weetabix and appeared on countless pop and children's TV shows as an all-round good egg. Burns has also made cricket records under the name Percy Pavilion.

Minus Sensible, the Damned scored their biggest hit when a revival of Barry Ryan's 1968 winner, 'Eloise', reached number three in 1986.

505

FAME

IRENE CARA

17 July 1982, for 3 weeks

●●●

RSO RSO 90

Writers: Michael Gore and Dean Pitchford
Producer: Michael Gore

Irene Cara broke into the limelight as Coco Hernandez in *Fame*, the hit Alan Parker movie about a New York drama school. She also sang the title song which became her first hit record, reaching number four in the US in the year of the film's release, 1980. It failed to make any impression in Britain at that time but more than made up for this two years later, when the spin-off TV series of *Fame* became an enormous hit, making a chart recording act out of the cast as 'Kids From Fame' and making Irene's original movie song the hit it should have been in the first place. The fast-moving disco winner was written by Lesley Gore's brother Michael and lyricist Dean Pitchford. It was nominated for an Oscar. (Lesley Gore's first hit song, 'It's My Party', a 1963 US number one, was a chart-topper in the UK 18 years later - see no. 487.)

Irene started performing when she was just seven, appearing on Spanish-language radio and TV shows in New York. She made her Broadway debut a year later (playing an orphan in *Maggie Flynn*, starring Jack Cassidy and Shirley Jones - father and stepmother of David Cassidy, see nos. 320 and 330). Already a seasoned concert performer by the age of 12, she began writing songs. By the time the big break of *Fame* came along, she had already appeared in several films, including the musical *Sparkle*, in which she took the lead role, and TV series such as *Roots: The Next Generation*. The soundtrack of *Fame* provided her with a second, lesser, hit single on both sides of the Atlantic, the ballad 'Out Here On My Own', but her second significant hit came from another movie, 1983's *Flashdance*. Irene did not act in this film but her interpretation of 'Flashdance...What A Feeling' gave her an American chart-topper and a number two in Britain. This time around the song sung by Irene Cara won the Oscar.

506

COME ON EILEEN

DEXYS MIDNIGHT RUNNERS AND THE EMERALD EXPRESS

7 August 1982, for 4 weeks

●●●●

MERCURY DEXYS 9

Writers: Kevin Rowland, Jimmy Patterson and Kevin Adams
Producers: Clive Langer and Alan Winstanley

After 'Geno' (see no. 457), his first number one with Dexy's (then sporting an apostrophe), Kevin Rowland's follow-up singles enjoyed only moderate acclaim until the release of this Celtic soul masterpiece. Teamed with a group of fiddlers named the Emerald Express (who received equal billing on the label), a totally new look (gypsy) and nearly all-new personnel, the Runners climbed all the way back to 'Geno' heights with the saga of young love and lust inspired by a girl Rowland grew up with.

The album that contained 'Come On Eileen', *Too-Rye-Ay*, was also a huge success, reaching number two and remaining on the charts for nearly a year. It reflected Rowland's passion at the time for Celtic-influenced folk music allied, on occasion, to a powerful rock beat. Both single and album did very well in America, the former repeating its British chart achievement between Michael Jackson's two *Thriller* number ones in April 1983. Producers Langer and Winstanley's second number one came just three months after their first (see no. 501).

One more Top 10 hit followed 'Come On Eileen', the group's revival of Ulsterman Van Morrison's 'Jackie Wilson Said', but since late 1982 there has not been a great rush to the stores for Dexys product. The group did earn a Top 20 placing at the end of 1986 with 'Because Of You', the theme from *Brush Strokes*, a TV comedy series about a painter/decorator. The decline in their fortunes was not arrested by an extraordinary change of image for the 1985 album *Don't Stand Me Down*. A four-piece line-up was portrayed on the cover in neat, unexciting suits and ties (but no tie for violinist Helen O'Hara).

507

EYE OF THE TIGER

SURVIVOR

4 September 1982, for 4 weeks

●●●●

SCOTTI BROTHERS SCT A 2411

Writers: Frankie Sullivan and Jim Peterik
Producers: Frankie Sullivan and Jim Peterik

The incredible box-office success of Sylvester 'Sly' Stallone's films about the fictitious heavyweight boxer Rocky Balboa spilled over into the record charts on more than one occasion. 'Gonna Fly Now', the theme of the first movie, was a US number one in 1977. The song meant little in England, despite further exposure in *Rocky II*. For *Rocky III*, the saga of Rocky's punch-up with Mr. T. in the guise of Clubber Lang, Stallone commissioned a theme from Chicago band Survivor.

Since 1981, Survivor had consisted of keyboardist Jim Peterik, lead guitarist Frankie Sullivan, vocalist David Bicker, bassist Stephen Ellis and drummer Marc Droubay. They had enjoyed only moderate record sales with one US Top 40 hit to their name, though leader Peterik had been with the Ides Of March in his University Of Illinois days when that group had a number two US success with 'Vehicle'. *Rocky III* ensured Survivor's survival. Peterik and Sullivan came up with a song inspired by a line that cropped up several times in the film's screenplay. It captured the drive, pace and violence of the boxer's life to a (Mr.) T. It became the champ of the American charts in July and scored a second knockout against all-comers in England by September. Survivor (with Jimi Jamieson now lead singer) were retained by Sly for *Rocky IV* in 1985 and their 'Burning Heart' did almost as well (number five in the UK, number two in the US).

508

PASS THE DUTCHIE

MUSICAL YOUTH

2 October 1982, for 3 weeks

●●●

MCA YOU 1

Writers: Jackie Mittoo, Fitzroy Simpson and Lloyd Ferguson
Producer: Peter Collins

The BBC TV News doesn't often feature stories from the record charts, but an exception was made in the first week of October 1982 for five unknown black youths dancing outside the Houses Of Parliament singing a song that would have been totally incomprehensible to the occupants of those buildings. The boys were the Birmingham-based Musical

Youth, and the unusual interest in their success was a fair reflection of the unexpectedness of it.

Musical Youth were all pupils at Duddeston Manor School in Birmingham. The line-up included two sets of brothers, Kelvin and Michael Grant and Junior and Patrick Waite, plus Dennis Seaton. Their ages ranged from 16 down to only 11 and great media interest centred around the fact that the youngest members would be breaking the law were they to work more than a certain number of days, even though they were top of the pops.

The original lead vocalist was Junior and Patrick's father, Fred, who had sung with the Techniques in his native Jamaica. The group appeared in several pubs in and around Birmingham, even though Kelvin was only eight when they started out. They recorded a single, 'Political'/ 'Generals', for Birmingham's 021 Records and secured a session on John Peel's Radio 1 show. In early 1982 Fred backed away from the limelight and Dennis Seaton took over as lead singer. A recording contract was signed with MCA, who thus enjoyed their first number one single since 'Don't Cry For Me Argentina' over five years earlier. The record's leap from 26 to one in its second week was one of the most spectacular and surprising vaults to the top.

The contagious reggae anthem 'Pass The Dutchie' was a re-write of an old Mighty Diamonds tune by Jackie Mittoo. It had

'Do You Really Want To Hurt Me' was the first of seven consecutive Top 5 hits for CULTURE CLUB. (Pictorial Press)

originally been called 'Pass The Kutchie', but the key word was tactfully altered to Dutchie - a Jamaican cooking pot. Kutchie refers to a different kind of pot altogether and was hardly the sort of thing youngsters should have been singing about!

The group enjoyed seven more hits in the following 18 months, but none had the astonishing impact of their debut. 'Pass The Dutchie' went Top 10 in the States and they sang with Donna Summer on her minor hit, 'Unconditional Love'. Since then Musical Youth has floundered and disbanded.

509

DO YOU REALLY WANT TO HURT ME

CULTURE CLUB

23 October 1982, for 3 weeks

●●●

VIRGIN VS 518

Writers: Culture Club
Producer: Steve Levine

George O'Dowd, born 14 June 1961 in South London, was a figure on the glitzy fringe of London's club scene from the end of the 70s before he became professionally involved with music. Thanks solely to his extraordinary appearance, he had become a well-known personality in nightspots such as Billy's and Blitz, where his penchant for make-up, dresses and outlandish headgear made him a centre of attention and a magnet for photographers and gossip. He was eventually spotted by Bow Wow Wow (and ex-Sex Pistols) manager Malcolm McLaren, who asked him to tour with Bow Wow Wow purely because of his visual impact.

It transpired that O'Dowd (who had long called himself Boy George) could actually sing. He formed his own group with bassist Mickey Craig, called In Praise Of Lemmings. They became Sex Gang Children with the addition of John Suede (guitar) and Jon Moss (drums). Suede was eventually replaced by Roy Hay (guitar and keyboards) and George renamed the band Culture Club in 1981.

In early 1982 Culture Club made some demos which impressed Virgin. Two of the tracks became the band's first two A-sides, although neither 'White Boy' nor 'I'm Afraid Of Me' charted. The principal interest in the band was still the look of George himself until they came up with the music to match third time around. 'Do You Really Want To Hurt Me' made the breakthrough, appealing to even those who had not to date clapped eyes on George and Culture Club. When those who bought the gentle, sensitive and unthreatening single, masterfully produced by Steve Levine and dominated by George's excellent white soul vocals, actually saw the outfit that had created it, there was little doubt that an act out of the ordinary was off and running. Sure enough 'Do You Really Want To Hurt Me' became a worldwide best seller, and Boy George was on the way to international superstardom.

510

I DON'T WANNA DANCE

EDDY GRANT

13 November 1982, for 3 weeks

●●●

ICE ICE 56

Writer: Eddy Grant
Producer: Eddy Grant

With his fifth British hit single, ex-Equal Eddy Grant became the 12th member of a number one group to make the top as a solo act. The Equals (see no. 252) had long since gone the way of all flesh by the time Eddy's solo career took shape, and from his initial breakthrough in 1979 with 'Living On The Front Line' Grant built up a substantial list of recording successes whose peak (to date) came in late 1982 and early 1983 with the singles 'I Don't Want To Dance' and 'Electric Avenue'. The second of these reached number two on both sides of the Atlantic.

The Guyana-born Edmond Montague Grant (born 5 March 1948) based himself in Barbados, where he recorded his heavy reggae-rock hits, writing, arranging and producing the material himself for his own label. Among his other noteworthy recordings were 'Living On The Front Line,' which popularized that expression describing ghetto life, 'Gimme Hope Jo'anna', which returned him to the Top 10 in 1988, and 'Walking On Sunshine', taken to the Top 10 in a 1982 cover by Rocker's Revenge. Grant's own version of this song was not released as a single until 1989, when it grazed only the lower end of the Top 75. His theme for the Michael Douglas movie *Romancing The Stone* made the US Top 30 in 1984, despite featuring in the film only for a few seconds.

511

BEAT SURRENDER

THE JAM

4 December 1982, for 2 weeks

●●

POLYDOR POSP 540

Writer: Paul Weller
Producer: Peter Wilson

The fourth and final number one for the Jam was also the last new single release of their five-year recording career. They achieved a mass invasion of the singles charts in early 1983 as 'Beat Surrender' was slipping out of the Top 75, but this was with 13 reissues of previous hits. On 22 January 1983, they made chart history by entering the lists with nine titles simultaneously, adding one more the following week and three more the week after that, giving them, on 5 February, a record 13 hits at once. None got higher than number 21 this time around, but it was an astounding accomplishment bearing in mind that all 13 had been substantial hits at least once before, and not that long before either.

'Beat Surrender' was the Jam's third number one to debut in that position, equalling Slade's achievement (nos. 326, 333 and 341). Jam fans, however, knew that this was the group's swan song because, two months before 'Beat Surrender' came out, the band had amazed the music world by announcing their imminent break-up. A UK chart career of 18 hit singles and eight hit albums was over, spectacular indeed despite the Jam's failure to make any impact in the United States.

Since the Jam's demise Bruce Foxton (three minor solo hit singles) and Rick Buckler (one small hit with the ill-fated Time UK) have not suffered from over-exposure, but Paul Weller has continued to make his presence felt, if not quite at Jam level. From March 1983 to the summer of 1989, his next recording unit, the Style Council, formed with ex-Merton Parka Mick Talbot, consistently hit the singles and albums charts with a series of recordings that owed little to the abrasive and frantic sound of the Jam. In 1990 Weller once again ditched his musical cohort and is now recording as a solo artist, with several hits to his credit. He won an Ivor Novello award in 1994 in recognition of his songwriting talents over almost two decades.

512

SAVE YOUR LOVE

RENEE AND RENATO

18 December 1982, for 4 weeks

●●●●

HOLLYWOOD HWD 003

Writers: John and Sue Edward
Producer: John Edward

Contrary to popular belief, Renée and Renato, the act who gave British music lovers one of the most mind-boggling Christmas number one hits since the inception of the charts, are strictly speaking not one-hit wonders, as a follow-up single by the disparate duo entitled 'Just One More Kiss' lurched up to number 48 in February 1983. It was, however, downhill fast from there.

Roman-born, Birmingham-based Renato Pagliari was a waiter with a powerful set of lungs who was originally only appreciated by his fellow pasta pushers. Legend (or at least the sleevenotes of his album) has it that his break came when he was asked to fill in for a guest singer who had failed to arrive. His reception that night was ecstatic and follow-up appearances in local cabaret venues meant that saltimbocca alla Romana's loss was (among other places) the Winter Gardens,

Margate's gain. There he met Hilary Lefter, who became Renée on Renato's recording of 'Save Your Love'. Unfortunately, Lefter left before the record made its surprise impact upon the Christmas market, so 28-year-old Val Penny and wig were drafted in to mime for the video. 'Just One More Kiss', recorded before the R & R split, featured the original Renée, but after that Renato preferred to continue Renée-less.

513

YOU CAN'T HURRY LOVE

PHIL COLLINS

15 January 1983, for 2 weeks

●●

VIRGIN VS 531

Writers: Brian Holland, Lamont Dozier and Eddie Holland
Producer: Phil Collins, assisted by Hugh Padgham

Phil Collins, drummer and vocalist of Genesis, became one of the biggest international stars of the 80s. He enjoyed his first UK number one with his fifth solo release, the first that was not one of his own compositions. 'You Can't Hurry Love' was one of the many classic Motown hits written by Holland-Dozier-Holland, who, unbelievably, had only two British number ones (see nos. 181 and 225) before Collins' success. The original 1966 version of the song had been a UK Top 3 hit for Diana Ross and the Supremes as well as their seventh US chart-topper.

Phil Collins was born in Chiswick on 30 January 1951. He began drumming at the age of five and at 14 he entered stage school. His brief stage career included the part of the Artful Dodger in the West End production of *Oliver*. By the late 60s he was devoting his creative energies entirely to music, his early bands including the Real Thing (not *the* Real Thing, see no. 391), Hickory and Flaming Youth, a studio aggregation that made one highly acclaimed concept album, entitled *Ark II*, in 1969 . A year later came the vital career move - Phil auditioned for Genesis and became their drummer in September 1970. He made his vocal debut for the band on the *Nursery Cryme* album, released in 1974.

'You Can't Hurry Love' was the first UK number one and first US Top 10 hit for PHIL COLLINS. (Pictorial Press)

Genesis were on the way to becoming a significant international act when front man Peter Gabriel quit in 1975. Many felt that was the end of the group but, after a period of re-thinking, the band re-emerged with Collins as the 'new' lead singer. When guitarist Steve Hackett left in 1977, Genesis continued as a trio of Collins, Mike Rutherford and Tony Banks. It was then that the band matched, and eventually surpassed, the achievements of the Peter Gabriel era. They enjoyed hit singles and albums and sold-out concerts around the world.

The three members of Genesis have all undertaken individual projects while the group continues to prosper. In early 1981, Phil's first solo album, *Face Value*, entered the British album charts at number one in its first week, propelled there, in part, by the number two single 'In The Air Tonight'. His second album, *Hello, I Must Be Going* (November 1992), was nearly as big as the first and included 'You Can't Hurry Love'.

514

DOWN UNDER

MEN AT WORK

29 January 1983, for 3 weeks

●●●

EPIC EPC A 1980

Writers: Colin Hay and Ron Strykert
Producer: Peter Mclan

Men At Work were an Australian quintet formed by lead singer Colin Hay and lead guitarist Ron Strykert at La Trobe University, Melbourne. Joined by keyboard and woodwind player Greg Ham, drummer Jerry Speiser and bassist John Rees, they performed as Men At Work at the Cricketers Arms pub in Melbourne. CBS Australia teamed them up with an American producer, Peter Mclan, and the result was the album *Business As Usual,* which contained two enormous hit singles, 'Who Can It Be Now' and 'Down Under'. A US tour as support to Fleetwood Mac, plus heavy exposure of the video on MTV, enabled the first of these to go all the way to number one in America, although in Britain it could reach only a modest 45 placing at the end of 1982.

The second single more than made up for this quiet UK debut by zipping to the very top in the fifth week after its release. It also became Men At Work's second straight US number one. It was Australia's first visit to the UK summit since Rolf Harris in 1969 (see no. 280), although Joe Dolce's 1981 hit (no. 475) was recorded Down Under and 'semi-Aussies' the Bee Gees and Olivia Newton-John had been at the top more recently. 'Down Under', a reggae-influenced rock number about Australians who travel overseas and then come home, was certainly the first smash to mention Vegemite.

Men At Work never enjoyed such international acclaim again, although their second album, *Cargo,* delivered three medium-sized hit singles. Speiser and Rees left the band in 1984 and Colin Hay issued solo work in 1986.

515

TOO SHY

KAJAGOOGOO

19 February 1983, for 2 weeks

●●

EMI 5359

Writers: Kajagoogoo, lyrics by Limahl and Nick Beggs
Producers: Nick Rhodes and Colin Thurston

Kajagoogoo were a quintet from Leighton Buzzard in Bedfordshire. Originally named Art Nouveau, they consisted of Limahl (lead vocalist), Nick Beggs (bass, vocals), Steve Askew (E Bow and guitar), Stuart Crawford Neale (synthesizers) and Jez Strode (drums, programming). Limahl (real name Chris Hamill - Limahl is an anagram of Hamill) was the last to join, via an advertisement in the music press.

The group had already had demo tapes rejected by EMI when Wigan-born Limahl, working part time as a waiter in London's Embassy Club, spotted Duran Duran's Nick Rhodes. He persuaded Rhodes that he and his band were, at worst, the next sensation but one. EMI showed new interest in the band with the promise of Rhodes and Duran producer Colin Thurston at the recording helm. Kajagoogoo's first single, 'Too Shy', hit the jackpot, achieving something that the well-established Duran Duran had not, at that point, accomplished - the number one singles spot. The song had originally been called 'Shy Shy' after a phrase in the chorus, but was altered to avoid confusion with Duran Duran and Talk Talk.

The group had a further six hit singles in the UK, and 'Too Shy' was a substantial hit in the States, but they were not destined for lasting fame. Limahl left the group in 1984. He subsequently enjoyed worldwide success with the Giorgio Moroder production and composition 'Never Ending Story', while the remaining members of the band soldiered on for a while as Kaja.

516

BILLIE JEAN

MICHAEL JACKSON

5 March 1983, for 1 week

●

EPIC EPC A 3084

Writer: Michael Jackson Producer: Quincy Jones

1983 was the year in which Michael Jackson stopped being a mere superstar and became a phenomenon. This was achieved primarily through his album *Thriller*, which remains the best-selling album in history. Its stupendous success in virtually every country in the world set new commercial standards for all contemporary artists as well as for Jackson's own subsequent releases. *Thriller* is reputed to have sold over 40 million copies.

Michael's previous solo album, *Off The Wall*, also produced immaculately by Quincy Jones, had contained four UK Top 10 hits and a fifth that made number 41. The most successful single, 'Don't Stop Till You Get Enough', had peaked at number three. The first single cut from *Thriller*, a duet between Jackson and Paul McCartney entitled 'The Girl Is Mine', stopped at number eight. 'Billie Jean', however, was the song that kicked *Thriller* into the stratosphere. It told the (fictitious) tale of a woman who attempts to blame Jackson for her illegitimate offspring. The basic rhythm line of the song was laid down by Jackson on a drum machine and enhanced later by drummer Leon Ndugu Chancler, bassist Louis Johnson of the Brothers Johnson, guitarist Dean Parks, Michael Boddiker on emulator, and Greg Smith, Greg Phillinganes and Bill Wolfer on synthesizers. Jerry Hey arranged the strings.

The hits kept coming from *Thriller*. A record-breaking seven titles became US Top 10 items, with five doing so in Britain (a sixth reached number 11). Jackson waited nearly five years before releasing another solo package. In the intervening years he hogged headlines for his personal eccentricities rather than for his music, although he did participate in a Jacksons tour and album in 1984. Tales of oxygen cylinders, plastic surgery, chimpanzees and the remains of the Elephant Man cannot diminish the extraordinary impact of *Thriller*, his masterpiece.

517

TOTAL ECLIPSE OF THE HEART

BONNIE TYLER

12 March 1983, for 2 weeks

●●

CBS TYLER 1

Writer: Jim Steinman Producer: Jim Steinman

Bonnie Tyler was born on 8 June 1953, in Skewen, South Wales, near Swansea. At 17 she won a local talent contest and began singing in Welsh nightclubs, including the Townsman Club in Swansea, where she was seen by Ronnie Scott and Steve Wolfe. They had written a song called 'Lost In France' and asked Bonnie to record it. It became her first hit single, reaching number nine in late 1976. Scott and Wolfe were Bonnie's managers, songwriters and producers from 1976 to '81, but after the debut hit her only major achievement was the 1978 monster 'It's A Heartache', which gave Bonnie her first taste of Stateside success. When Tyler severed connections with her management in 1981, she had been all but forgotten for three years.

Searching for a major producer, Bonnie's new manager, David Aspden, approached Meat Loaf mastermind Jim Steinman (see no. 697). Steinman, based in New York, is a producer who thinks big and who attempts to bring a sense of grand theatre to his work in the recording studio. This he did for Bonnie with 'Total Eclipse Of The Heart'. The six-track extravaganza raced past all opposition to the top, denying none other than Michael Jackson more than a solitary week at the top with 'Billie Jean'. The Steinman-produced album *Faster Than The Speed Of Night* was only the second by a British female to top the album charts since the listings began in 1958 (Kate Bush's *Never For Ever* was the first). The single also went all the way to number one in America.

In early 1984 Bonnie enjoyed a British Top 10 hit with Shakin' Stevens, a revival of the 1960 Brook Benton/Dinah Washington classic 'A Rockin' Good Way'. Over a year after that she was up at number two with a Steinman song from the movie *Footloose*, 'Holding Out For A Hero', which she had recorded in '83. Since then her husky tones have graced only the less glamorous end of the Top 75, via another Steinman epic, 'Loving You's A Dirty Job But Somebody's Gotta Do It', a duet with Todd Rundgren, and the reissue of 'Holding Out For A Hero' at Christmas 1991.

518

IS THERE SOMETHING I SHOULD KNOW?

DURAN DURAN

26 March 1983, for 2 weeks

●●

EMI 5371

Writers: Duran Duran
Producers: Duran Duran and Ian Little

At the height of their popularity, from the end of 1982 until about halfway through 1985, Duran Duran could claim to be as popular with younger rock fans as any other group in the world. 'Is There Something I Should Know?' was their eighth British release and the first to go all the way, topping their previous high of number two with 'Save A Prayer'.

Duran Duran was founded in Birmingham in 1978. Their image was, from the word go, New Romantic, in sharp contrast to the less delicate attitudes portrayed by many of the successful punk groups of the era. Their name was taken from that of the villain in Jane Fonda's 1968 movie *Barbarella*, for Barbarella's in Birmingham was the name of the club in which they performed most in their early days. The line-up that made the first Duran record had evolved by the summer of 1980: Simon Le Bon (vocals), Nick Rhodes (synthesizers and keyboards) and the unrelated Taylors, John (bass), Andy (guitar) and Roger (drums). They began their chart career in early 1981 with 'Planet Earth', which climbed to number 12. Their third single, 'Girls On Film', was the first to take them into the Top 10, helped by a controversial video directed by former 10 C.C. members Godley and Creme (see nos. 332 and 372).

It was videos, particularly those directed by Russell Mulcahy, that broke the band in the States. Duran Duran paid as much attention to their visual appeal as they did to their sound, and the booming MTV channel in America gave hefty exposure to their 1982 Sri Lanka-lensed video, 'Hungry Like The Wolf'. This set them off on a run of big US hits. Alex Sadkin who, before his accidental death in 1987, became a fully-fledged producer of Duran Duran and other major artists, is credited on this track as co-mixer with Ian Little.

519

LET'S DANCE

DAVID BOWIE

9 April 1983, for 3 weeks

●●●

EMI AMERICA EA 152

Writer: David Bowie
Producers: David Bowie and Nile Rodgers

Bowie's third number one was the first not to mention his famous creation Major Tom, who nevertheless made the charts again in 1983 courtesy of German singer/songwriter Peter Schilling's hit, 'Major Tom (Coming Home)'. 'Let's Dance' was lyrically a less complex theme than those of 'Space Oddity' and 'Ashes To Ashes'. It was the title track of his first album for EMI America, and the pairing of Bowie with Chic's Nile Rodgers at the desk resulted in one of the most instantly appealing Bowie albums yet. He promoted it with a mammoth international trek, the Serious Moonlight Tour, that kind of lunar illumination being a line of the 'Let's Dance' lyric. 'Let's Dance' became Bowie's second US number one.

Post-'Let's Dance', Bowie's output has been erratic. He topped the chart once more, in duet with Mick Jagger in 1985 (see no. 556), and in 1986 he scored a number two hit with the theme to a film he appeared in, *Absolute Beginners*, following it with another film theme, 'Underground', from the film *Labyrinth*, in which he also starred.

After only moderate success with his 1987 album, *Never Let Me Down*, Bowie surprised the world by forming a new band, Tin Machine, enlisting Reeves Gabrels on guitar and brothers Tony and Hunt Sales (sons of US comic Soupy Sales) on bass and drums respectively. Critically and commercially panned, the group failed to crack the UK Top 30, despite several single releases. It was not until 1993, when he was reunited with 'Let's Dance' producer Nile Rodgers, that he returned to the singles chart Top 10 via 'Jump They Say' and the album-chart top spot (for the eighth time) with *Black Tie White Noise*.

520

TRUE

SPANDAU BALLET

30 April 1983, for 4 weeks

●●●●

REFORMATION SPANS 1

Writer: Gary Kemp

Producers: Tony Swain, Steve Jolley and Spandau Ballet

Five-man north London group Spandau Ballet made their first live appearance in private in November 1979, before an audience of invited friends, primarily trendsetters of the contemporary fashion scene. They were soon wellestablished as part of the circuit of outrageous West End club life.

Tony Hadley (vocals), the Kemp brothers Martin (bass) and Gary (guitar and keyboards), Steve Norman (sax, percussion) and John Keeble (drums) had a major hit first time out with 'To Cut A Long Story Short'. They had established a run of nine consecutive chart records when their greatest success, the thoughtful Gary Kemp ballad 'True', appeared as both the title track of their third album and a single in spring 1983. Both album and single topped their respective charts.

Spandau were now challenging Duran Duran for the New Romantic/teeny-fan supremacy but, although their next two singles reached numbers two and three respectively in the UK, they never touched their mid-1983 heights again. A further blow to their career came when a drawn-out dispute with Chrysalis prevented the release of any new Spandau product for over a year. It was, therefore, unsurprising that the band were not able to sustain their success after signing to CBS.

Although they have never officially split up, the group have not released any material since 1989. Tony Hadley has pursued a solo career, with only minor success, and the Kemp brothers have pursued acting careers - they portrayed the infamous Kray Twins, and Gary appeared in the box-office smash of 1992, *The Bodyguard*. Thanks to American rappers PM Dawn, Spandau Ballet's music has not been forgotten; a catchy sample from 'True' on PM Dawn's 'Set Adrift On Memory Bliss' in 1991 returned them to the Top 3 in Britain and gave them their first taste of the number one slot in America.

521

CANDY GIRL

NEW EDITION

28 May 1983, for 1 week

●

LONDON LON 21

Writers: Maurice Starr and Michael Jonzun

Producers: Maurice Starr and Michael Jonzun

'Candy Girl' was New Edition's first record, and although it was only a moderate success in their native America, it became one of the more unexpected number one hits in the UK.

The five boys, Ralph Tresvant (lead vocalist), Michael Bivins, Ronald DeVoe, Ricky Bell and Bobby Brown, were all aged between 13 and 15 in 1983. They won a talent contest at their school in Roxbury, Massachusetts, and were spotted by writer/producer Maurice Starr. Michael Bivins' uncle was taken aboard as manager and Starr, working with his brother Michael Jonzun, an established figure on the New York disco scene via his act the Jonzun Crew, gave the boys material to record and worked with them to create a Jackson Five type-stage act.

Streetwise Records of New York snapped up New Edition's first recording and were quickly rewarded when the single broke into the dance charts, and then the black charts, where it scooted all the way to number one. It failed to cross over to the pop charts (a mere number 46) but it paved the way for a substantial four-year chart career in America.

Bobby Brown left to go solo in 1986, replaced by Johnny Gill. Brown's career flourished, and in 1989 the remaining members of New Edition elected amicably to divide and record separately. It was a wise move. Brown, Tresvant, Gill and the trio Bell Biv DeVoe have all had hits climb higher than any New Edition single in America. In Britain, although none of the component parts of the group has repeated the number one success of 'Candy Girl', Bobby Brown has enjoyed a consistent string of hit singles, and in 1992 he married Whitney Houston.

522

EVERY BREATH YOU TAKE

THE POLICE

4 June 1983, for 4 weeks

●●●●

A&M AM 117

Writer: Sting Producers: Hugh Padgham and Police

Police fans had been forced to wait over 18 months for their idols' fifth album, *Synchronicity*. The first track to be stripped from the set, 'Every Breath You Take', charged up the charts to give the band their fifth and final number one. Sting would later affectionately refer to the song's lyrics in his 1985 solo hit 'Love Is The Seventh Wave'.

It was to be the band's swan song. They sold a million copies of a compilation album, also titled 'Every Breath You Take', in 1986 and another greatest hits package made the Top 10 in 1992, but it is unlikely that any new material will be forthcoming from the combined talents of Messers Sumner, Summers and Copeland.

Since the band's demise Sting's solo album sales have remained comparable to his Police days, with his LPs *Nothing Like The Sun* and *Ten Summoner's Tales* picking up plenty of Grammy and BRIT awards, but, despite nearly 20 efforts, Sting's solo singles have failed to grace the Top 10. He seems to have more luck as one third of a male trio. In 1994, in tandem with Bryan Adams and Rod Stewart, he topped the American chart – and narrowly missed repeating the feat in Britain – with 'All For Love', the theme to the film *The Three Musketeers*.

523

BABY JANE

ROD STEWART

2 July 1983, for 3 weeks

●●●

WARNER BROTHERS W 9608

Writers: Rod Stewart and Jay Davis
Producers: Rod Stewart and Tom Dowd; co-produced by Jim Cregan and George Tutko

Rod Stewart records, by his own very high standards, had not been selling at quite the rate of yore after his fifth number one hit, 'Da Ya Think I'm Sexy?' (see no. 429) in 1978. In the following four and a half years he hit the UK Top 10 only once, with 'Tonight I'm Yours (Don't Hurt Me)' in 1981. Thus it was that his sixth number one, 'Baby Jane', was rather unjustly hailed as a comeback for the oft-imitated gravel larynx.

In truth, Rod had never really been away. His status as one of the most photographed personalities of the entertainment business had never faltered, and his tours were never less than massively successful. Two of his early 80s singles, 'Passion' and 'Young Turks', had gone Top 5 Stateside, giving him his first back-to-back Top 10 hits there. But a number one in either Britain or America is a great boost to any act of whatever standing at any time, and Rod's excitement at hitting the top was obvious during his tour to promote the *Body Wishes* album from which the single came.

'Baby Jane' took Stewart's total weeks at number one to 18, level with the Rolling Stones, who had needed eight number one hits to amass their 18 weeks. Besides the Stones, only Elvis, the Beatles, Abba and Cliff now had more number ones, and only Slade the same number. Rod himself has not added to this tally, although he missed out by only one place in summer 1986, with 'Every Beat Of My Heart', and in 1994, with 'All For Love' with Bryan Adams and Sting.

524

WHEREVER I LAY MY HAT (THAT'S MY HOME)

PAUL YOUNG

23 July 1983, for 3 weeks

●●●

CBS A 3371

Writers: Marvin Gaye, Norman Whitfield and Barrett Strong
Producer: Laurie Latham

Paul Young burst into prominence, apparently from nowhere, with his heartfelt rendition of an old Marvin Gaye B-side. The Luton-raised vocalist had, however, been recording for over five years with first Street Band and then the Q-Tips, without ever enjoying the acclaim that 'Wherever I Lay My Hat' brought him with his third solo single.

Street Band were a heavy-metal-meets-R&B-influenced pop band for whom Paul (born 17 January 1956) sang and played harmonica and occasional bass and keyboards. They signed to the small Logo label in 1978 and hit the Top 20 with their first single - but not with the intended A-side. It was the flip, the throwaway novelty item 'Toast', that appealed to

'Wherever I Lay My Hat (That's My Home)' by PAUL YOUNG was the first British number one version of a Marvin Gaye composition. (Pictorial Press)

radio, landing the band with an identity crisis when the music they really wanted to play met with no chart success whatsoever.

The disheartened Street Band had split by the end of 1979, and Young and Mick Pearl (bass) of the group set about forming a new outfit. The result was the Q-Tips, an eight-piece that made its recording debut in March 1980. Their work was principally inspired by and/or featured 60s soul classics, but none of their revivals or original material clicked. Again, a discouraged Paul Young-fronted band broke up.

Paul's fortunes changed completely when he took up a solo deal with CBS. After near misses with 'Iron Out The Rough Spots' and 'Love Of The Common People' (later to become a number two hit for

Paul Young the star), he broke through all the way with the Motown ballad. His solo recording career maintained a good striking rate for the next four years, including a US chart-topper with 'Every Time You Go Away'.

525

GIVE IT UP

KC AND THE SUNSHINE BAND

13 August 1983, for 3 weeks

●●●

EPIC EPC A 3017

Writers: Harry Casey and Debra Carter
Producers: Harry Casey and Richard Finch

Writer/producer Harry Wayne 'KC' Casey began scoring fairly regularly on international charts with his combo KC and the Sunshine Band in the mid-70s. In the United States his efforts led to no less than five number one singles between 1975 and 1980. However, his only British number one to date as a performer was provided by a track from his 1982 album, *All In A Night's Work.*

Casey (vocals and keyboards) and bassist Richard Finch were the founders and constant driving forces behind the band's success. Their made-for-discos recordings swept Europe before they took off in the States, 'Queen Of Clubs' being the song that launched them in Britain and on the Continent some months ahead of their American breakthrough with 'Get Down Tonight'. The band varied in size from seven members to 11, but Casey and Finch were writers and producers of all their major titles, nearly all irresistible dance fodder for the clubs.

On 15 January 1982, Casey was badly injured in a car accident seven blocks from his Hialeah, Florida, home. It took him nearly a year to recuperate and it was during this time that the Irish and British offices of Epic Records decided to push 'Give It Up' as a single. Epic in the US were nonetheless unimpressed and KC released the track on his own label, Meca, making the US Top 20 in early 1984 with the track credited to just KC. With or without the Sunshine Band, KC has not charted on either side of the Atlantic since then, although a cover of his 1979 Top 3 hit, 'Please Don't Go', was a UK number one and US Top 10 hit for KWS in 1992.

526

RED RED WINE

UB40

3 September 1983, for 3 weeks

●●●

DEP INTERNATIONAL DEP 7

Writer: Neil Diamond
Producers: UB40 and Ray 'Pablo' Falconer

Neil Diamond's first British number one as a writer was the January 1967 Monkees monster 'I'm A Believer' (see no. 228). He had to wait over 16 years for his second, again with a song he had written in the 60s. The title was 'Red Red Wine', which had already been a minor hit twice in the UK, by Jimmy James and the Vagabonds in 1968 and by Tony Tribe a year later. Diamond's own version had created just a ripple on the US Hot 100 in 1968.

The team that brought Neil's songwriting back to the heights was the Birmingham octet UB40. The name is taken from the British Government dole registration card, a sad set of digits known only too well to many youngsters when unemployment was at its very worst in Britain in the early 80s. They began their recording career with the small Graduate label but later graduated to their own record company, DEP International. The band's first hit was a double-sider, 'King'/'Food For Thought', and from that excellent start in March 1980 they soon established themselves as one of the most consistent hitmakers of their time. Many of their songs contained a political or social message, their first chart-topper being an exception, unless it is construed as a plea for temperance.

Their canny combination of pop melodies (mainly original) and dub reggae rhythms was the creation of the sons of Scottish folk singer Ian Campbell, Ali (vocals and rhythm guitar) and Robin (lead guitar), and Astro (MC and trumpet), Michael Virtue (keyboards), Brian Travers (sax), Norman Hassan (percussion), Earl Falconer (bass) and Jim Brown (drums).

The hit's producer, Ray 'Pablo' Falconer, was Earl's brother and UB40's sound engineer.

527

KARMA CHAMELEON

CULTURE CLUB

24 September 1983, for 6 weeks

●●●●●●

VIRGIN VS 612

Writers: Culture Club
Producer: Steve Levine

Between their first hit (see no. 509) and their second number one, 'Karma Chameleon', Boy George and Culture Club had rocketed to superstardom, their flamboyant lead singer having one of the most instantly recognizable faces in the western world by late 1983. A succession of outstanding records, of which 'Karma Chameleon' was by some distance the most popular single, coupled with George's dramatic visual appeal, placed the 22 year old and his group briefly on a pinnacle that few personalities in any field achieve in a lifetime.

Problems were looming, yet during the six weeks that Culture Club were back leading the pack, it seemed that the charming Boy George, all innocence wrapped up in drag, was a man totally in control of what had to be a long and colourful career, loved by old and young alike. The band's records sold in every major world market and George's impact on fashion and appearance was sensational.

Culture Club were supported by the powerful larynx of Helen Terry, on this hit and others, as well as for stage appearances. Co-composer of 'Karma Chameleon', Phil Pickett, who had been a member and writer for the three-hit mid-70s pop band Sailor, played keyboards on this smash. Jud Lander supplied harmonica. There were noises made later by the composers of the 1960 Jimmy Jones hit, 'Handy Man', that 'Karma Chameleon' was a little too close to 'Handy Man' for comfort.

528

UPTOWN GIRL

BILLY JOEL

5 November 1983, for 5 weeks

●●●●●

CBS A 3775

Writer: Billy Joel
Producer: Phil Ramone

William Martin Joel (born in Hicksville, Long Island, New York, 9 May 1949) took his first piano lessons at the age of four and formed his first rock and roll band, the Echoes, when he was 14. He underwent serious training for life both by playing piano in all-night bars and by becoming an amateur boxer (22 wins in 28 fights, one broken nose). His first recordings were made as a member of the Hassles and then of heavy rock trio Attila, but these and his first solo album, *Cold Spring Harbor* (1972), did not last the distance. He was saved by the bell, however, when CBS Records spotted him at a Puerto Rican song festival. In 1974 he recorded his *Piano Man* album, and the title song, recalling many of his experiences in those all-night bars, gave him his first single hit in the States.

His 1977 album, *The Stranger,* was his first teaming with ace producer Phil Ramone. This proved to be his passport to international acceptance. One of the album's songs, 'Just The Way You Are', was his first UK hit and has been recorded by scores of other artists, most notably Barry White, becoming a genuine standard.

Joel's first American number one, 1980's 'It's Still Rock And Roll To Me', was his last hit in Britain for nearly three years, until the runaway success of his *An Innocent Man* album lifted his status in Europe to something approaching its American level. The album featured Billy playing and singing in the style of many of his heroes from the 50s and 60s, such as the Drifters, Otis Redding and Little Anthony and the Imperials. His tribute to the Four Seasons, 'Uptown Girl', dedicated to his then girlfriend Christie Brinkley, was the most popular track of all and became the second best-selling single of 1983 in Britain.

Joel, who married model Brinkley aboard a yacht in the middle of New York harbour in 1985, has compiled a substantial list of album and singles hits since this smash. Sadly, his wife is no longer his 'Uptown Girl', the couple having announced their separation in 1994.

529

ONLY YOU

FLYING PICKETS

10 December 1983, for 5 weeks

●●●●●

10 RECORDS TEN 14

Writer: Vince Clarke
Producers: Flying Pickets and John Sherry

The last four months of 1983 contained just three number one singles. Following the long runs at the top of Culture Club and Billy Joel, a cappella vocal sextet the Flying Pickets finished the year in triumphant style with a revival of the not-very-old Yazoo number two hit composed by the male half of that disc, Vince Clarke. The female half was Alison 'Alf' Moyet.

The number one Christmas hit of 1983 was sung by Rick Lloyd, Ken Gregson, Gareth Williams, David Brett, Brian Hibbard and Red Stripe. They met when acting in a touring play about the 1984-5 miners' strike, entitled *One Big Blow,* with the 7.84 theatre company. In the play they were required to sing a cappella. This led to performances in pubs and clubs as an unaccompanied vocal sextet and an album, *Live At The Albany Empire*, in which they gave new life to several pop classics such as 'Not Fade Away', 'To Know Him Is To Love Him' and 'Da Doo Ron Ron'. They were then signed to Virgin's 10 label, where they struck gold.

Not surprisingly, their appeal on record proved to be limited, and apart from the immediate follow-up to 'Only You', which reached the Top 10, they made no significant chart dent thereafter. The band's members have since gone their separate ways, with Hibbard making acting appearances in TV's *Making Out* and *Coronation Street.*

530

PIPES OF PEACE

PAUL McCARTNEY

14 January 1984, for 2 weeks

●●

PARLOPHONE R 6064

Writer: Paul McCartney
Producer: George Martin

Paul McCartney's first UK number one under just his own name completed a unique full house of chart achievements. When 'Pipes Of Peace' made it to the top he became the first performer to have got there as a soloist, as part of a duo (with Stevie Wonder - see no. 499), as part of a trio (with Wings - see no. 416), as part of a quartet (see 16 of the 17 Beatles number ones) and as part of a quintet (the Beatles

FRANKIE GOES TO HOLLYWOOD took their three number ones to the charts again almost exactly a decade later. (Pictorial Press)

with Billy Preston - see no. 270). He later did it with even larger aggregations on charity records such as 'Do They Know It's Christmas?' (see no. 543) and 'Ferry 'Cross The Mersey' (see no. 628).

McCartney also became the third solo Beatle to reach number one, leaving only Ringo out in the cold (though Starr's 'Photograph' and 'You're Sixteen' both went all the way Stateside). This gave the Beatles yet another record in that no other group had seen three ex-members in solitary splendour at the summit.

'Pipes Of Peace' was Paul's 25th number one as a writer, bringing him to within one of John Lennon's record total. It was George Martin's 27th number one as producer, tying him with the late Norrie Paramor as production champ. The single was given a huge boost by its imaginative video, showing Paul in the guise of two soldiers on opposing sides in the trenches of World War I. The album from which the single came, also entitled *Pipes Of Peace*, was the sequel to his highly acclaimed previous effort, *Tug Of War*. It included a US number one duet with Michael Jackson, 'Say Say Say'.

531

RELAX

FRANKIE GOES TO HOLLYWOOD

28 January 1984, for 5 weeks

●●●●●

ZTT ZTAS 1

Writers: Peter Gill, Holly Johnson and Mark O'Toole
Producer: Trevor Horn

The rise and fall of the Liverpool quintet Frankie Goes To Hollywood, their name taken from a headline about the young Sinatra's entry into the music business, is one of the more remarkable stories of recent recording history.

Vocalist Holly (christened William) Johnson spent a year with Scouse band Big In Japan in 1976/77. When Big In Japan became Pink Military, Holly went solo for a while. As just plain Holly he released two singles, both duds. The other four Frankies had even less experience before linking up with Holly to become the sensation of 1984. Paul Rutherford (billed with Frankie as 'vocals and "I came to dance"'), Mark O'Toole (bass), Brian Nash (guitar) and Peter Gill (drums) had all played in local bands of striking anonymity.

The five became one in late 1982 and played their first gig as support to Hambi And The Dance, as obscure a start to a career as it is possible to have. Their break came when they appeared on Channel 4's rock show *The Tube*, where their unsubtle sexual antics made as big an impression as their funk. Ex-Buggle (see no. 444) Trevor Horn, chief of the new Zang Tumb Tumm organization, was watching and wanted them for his label. Horn was by now one of the country's most sought-after producers thanks to work with Dollar, Spandau Ballet, Yes and ABC, and a healthy recording debut seemed a certainty.

Not even Horn could have anticipated just how healthy that debut would be. It took some time for their first single, 'Relax', to emerge, and when it did, in November 1983, its early progress was sluggish. It pottered around the lower regions of the Top 75 until one morning Radio One's breakfast DJ, Mike Read, realized just what the lyrics were saying. He unilaterally declared his disgust and his refusal to play the disc led to an all-out BBC ban. This was just what the record needed. The struggling platter became a huge number one and the Frankie saga was about to begin.

532

99 RED BALLOONS

NENA

3 March 1984, for 3 weeks

●●●

EPIC A 4074

Writers: Joern-Uwe Fahrenkrog-Peterson and Carlo Karges; English lyrics by Kevin McAlea
Producers: Reinhold Heil and Manne Präker

The Nena that gave the world '99 Red Balloons' was a group, not a female singer. Few realized this fact, even when the quintet became the fourth German act to top the British singles charts, following in the footsteps of Kraftwerk (see no. 494), the Goombay Dance Band (see no. 497) and Nicole (see no. 500), all of whom got there in a golden period for Deutschrock between February and May 1982.

Confusingly, Nena was also the professional name of the band's vocalist, Gabriele Kerner. Her male colleagues were Rolf Brendel (drums), Jurgen Dehmel (bass), Joern-Uwe Fahrenkrog-Peterson (keyboards) and Carlo Karges (guitar). The last two were the composers of the number one. The band was formed in Berlin in 1982.

In its original German form, '99 Luftballons', the record became a massive hit in the United States, rising to number two. English fans were deemed too insular and/or ignorant to cope with a German lyric, so Kevin McAlea was drafted in to translate. It is still doubtful whether many Brits who bought it appreciated the anti-nuclear message of what was to most a very catchy pop record. Nena, the group, remained popular in Germany for a while but enjoyed no repetition of their success in English-language markets.

533

HELLO

LIONEL RICHIE

24 March 1984, for 6 weeks

●●●●●●

MOTOWN TMG 1330

Writer: Lionel Richie
Producers: Lionel Richie and James Anthony Carmichael

Lionel Brockman Richie Jr. (born Tuskegee, Alabama, 20 June 1949) found considerable fame and fortune as a member of the Commodores (see no. 425) before establishing himself as America's leading black balladeer and one of the most successful songwriters that vast country has ever produced.

His break with the group came in 1982, but he had broken through as an individual writer and performer before the split. He had written and produced a US number one single for Kenny Rogers in 1980 ('Lady'), and the title song for the Brooke Shields film *Endless Love* in 1981, which he sang sans Commodores but with Diana Ross, had been the longest-running American number one in Motown's history. The solo route beckoned and no one could blame Lionel for taking it when he did.

His solo recording career got off to a hot start with the single 'Truly' and the album *Lionel Richie*. Hotter yet was the monumentally popular second album, *Can't Slow Down*. The collection included several uptempo offerings, but it was the soulful and sentimental 'Hello' that became the favourite track in Britain.

Richie has delighted mantlepiece-manufacturers with the number of awards he has won for his writing and performing (including an Oscar for 'Say You Say Me').

The highlight of his personal career to date, however, was his appearance before a television audience literally measured in billions at the closing ceremony of the 1984 Los Angeles Olympic Games, when he performed an extended version of 'All Night Long' with 200 breakdancers, athletes from all over the world and a spaceship. He was also the driving force behind the American answer to Band Aid, USA For Africa's 'We Are The World' (see no. 548).

534

THE REFLEX

DURAN DURAN

5 May 1984, for 4 weeks

●●●●

EMI DURAN 2

Writers: Duran Duran
Producers: Alex Sadkin, Ian Little and Duran Duran; remixed by Nile Rodgers

After their first number one (see no. 518) Duran Duran had to wait over a year for their second. In between the two peaks their faces became known beyond the confines of the pop world. Simon Le Bon and Nick Rhodes in particular were rarely out of the popular press, the former for

Although they were soon to leave, both Roger Taylor (left) and Andy Taylor (second from right) stayed with DURAN DURAN long enough to enjoy a second number one with 'The Reflex'. The ragged tiger was never part of the group. (Pictorial Press)

his ocean yachting exploits, and all five for various liaisons and/or marriages with members of the opposite sex, mainly models. Duran Duran by mid-1984 meant glamour and jet-setting as well as huge record sales. Their many young admirers were known as Durannies.

'The Reflex' was first heard on their third album, *Seven And The Ragged Tiger*. The first two singles from this album had done well, but the decision to call in Chic genius Nile Rodgers (see no. 519) to remix 'The Reflex' made the third single the biggest of all. It also became their first American number one.

In 1986 the group began to disintegrate, with members recording in two separate units. Andy and John Taylor teamed with Robert Palmer and Chic's Tony Thompson and Bernard Edwards as the Power Station, while the other three recorded as Arcadia. Both new acts had hits, but not in the Duran league.

Duran Duran re-grouped and continued where they had left off with 'View To A Kill' from the James Bond movie of the same name, but the end of Duran Duran Mark I was not long delayed. During the recording of their *Notorious* album, which did not quite measure up to the highest expectations, Andy Taylor left for America, a solo career and eventually to manage metal band Thunder, and Roger Taylor gave up music in favour of the country life.

Le Bon, Rhodes, the sole surviving Taylor and new recruit, American Warren Cuccurullo, continue to this day as a quartet. In 1993 they enjoyed their biggest hit in nearly eight years when 'Ordinary World' made the Top 10 on both sides of the pond.

535

WAKE ME UP BEFORE YOU GO-GO

WHAM!

2 June 1984, for 2 weeks

●●

EPIC A 4440

Writer: George Michael
Producer: George Michael

The George Michael success story shifted into top gear when the sixth Wham! single surpassed all of the duo's previous efforts, rushing to number one in its second week of release. From now until Wham!'s demise the only record to keep a Wham! single from number one was the freak Band Aid mega-seller (see no. 543), which itself included vocals by George Michael.

George Michael (born Georgios Kyriacou Panayiotou on 25 June 1963) and Andrew Ridgeley (born 26 January 1963) met at Bushey Heath Comprehensive school in Hertfordshire when both were in their early teens. They played together in groups and remained friends after leaving school. In 1982 they made a demo of 'Wham! Rap' with George on vocals and bass, and Andrew handling guitar and drum machine. A new label, Innervision, showed interest and released the track, but without much response from the media or public. Next time out they did better. 'Young Guns (Go For It)' entered the Top 10 at the end of 1982. Once the boys' energetic routines and smouldering looks were seen on television, a young following grew quickly. Their first single was re-worked to become their second Top 10er, and by summer 1983 they had made it four out of four. Their debut LP, *Fantastic*, entered the album charts at number one, an outstanding feat at that time for an act's first long-player.

However, problems developed between the duo and their label. Wham! signed with former Marc Bolan manager Simon Napier-Bell, who fought to get them released from Innervision. While the dispute blazed Wham! hit the road for their first tour, the highly theatrical Club Fantastic Tour, featuring, among other side attractions, backing singer/dancers Pepsi and Shirlie, later to score hits as a duo themselves.

When finally free to sign a new deal, Wham! did so with Epic. The first single was the slick and tuneful party item 'Wake Me Up Before You Go-Go'. All at once it was noticed that George Michael was a man of many talents. Speculation about the future of Andrew Ridgeley in such a subordinate role began to surface.

536

TWO TRIBES

FRANKIE GOES TO HOLLYWOOD

16 June 1984, for 9 weeks

●●●●●●●●●

ZTT ZTAS 3

Writers: Peter Gill, Holly Johnson and Mark O'Toole
Producer: Trevor Horn

Frankie Goes To Hollywood's second single and second chart-topper crashed straight in at number one and held down the top spot for a further two months. Its nine-week stretch was the longest since Travolta and Newton-John's glorious summer of '78 (see no. 424).

Where 'Relax' had dealt with sex, 'Two Tribes' tackled politics with about the same depth of intellect and with even greater public approval. The record was a masterpiece of production and marketing. No one saw fit to ban it, although the Godley and Creme video showing Reagan and Chernenko lookalikes fighting hand to hand raised a few hackles. The band's contribution to 'Two Tribes' was merely the first phase of recording. Horn then spent weeks juggling with sound, adding, subtracting, mixing and remixing. Actor Patrick Allen's reading of extracts from government civil defence leaflets became an integral part of the 'song'.

When 'Two Tribes' was released in a blaze of publicity, Frankie mania gave 'Relax' yet another sales boost. There was, after all, nothing else for Frankie fans to buy at that point, on disc anyway. (Frankie merchandising, in particular 'Frankie Say' T-shirts, was shipping nearly as fast as the records). For the weeks of 7 and 14 July FGTH held down both numbers one and two in the singles chart, hitherto a mountain climbed only by the Beatles (for three weeks in 1963 and for three in 1967) and an ex-Beatle (John Lennon, two weeks in 1981). Another factor contributing to the massive and long-running sales of Frankie product was Horn's wheeze of putting out as many as seven different mixes of the singles. Some Frankie nutters bought the lot.

537

CARELESS WHISPER

GEORGE MICHAEL

18 August 1984, for 3 weeks

●●●

EPIC A 4603

Writers: George Michael and Andrew Ridgeley
Producer: George Michael

George Michael's first number one as a writer and producer had been knocked off the top after just two weeks by the explosion of Frankie Goes To Hollywood's 'Two Tribes'. It must have been particularly satisfying for Michael to be the man to bring 'Two Tribes'' nine-week run to a close.

'Careless Whisper' is the only George Michael song for which his Wham! partner gets equal writing credit. Ironically, it was the first released under George's name alone. It was written long before the boys became famous, when they were still Bushey schoolboys. As a bushy adult, George had recorded the sensitive ballad as a solo item in America in 1983, but he did not consider that version good enough to release. His 1984 re-recording in England was obviously of sufficient quality to continue his winning streak.

Naturally, the non-contribution of Ridgeley to the smash fuelled yet more rumours that the days of Wham! were numbered, but, although George himself was now a personality known better to the non-rock public than his group, there was still no official talk of a split. Indeed, in America, where the band broke through in November 1984 with 'Wake Me Up Before You Go-Go' (see no. 535), 'Careless Whisper' was released under the name 'Wham! featuring George Michael' and duplicated its British success with ease in early 1985.

538

I JUST CALLED TO SAY I LOVE YOU

STEVIE WONDER

8 September 1984, for 6 weeks

●●●●●●

MOTOWN TMG 1349

Writer: Stevie Wonder
Producer: Stevie Wonder

Musical giant Stevie Wonder at last achieved one of the few honours to have eluded him - a British number one single - with the ballad 'I Just Called To Say I Love You' from the soundtrack of the film *The Woman In Red*. It did the trick for him 18 years and 218 days after his UK chart debut, at that time the longest wait for a number one hit (see no. 582 for the present record holder).

He had actually written it some seven or eight years before, but it had never made it on to any of his albums. However, it more than made up for its long gestation period when it surfaced as part of Stevie's soundtrack for the Gene Wilder picture. Up against the toughest opposition in years (Phil Collins, Ray Parker Jr., Kenny Loggins and Lee de Carlo, Snow and Pitchford) Stevie won his first Oscar. Save this extraordinary lack of solo number ones, Stevie's UK chart career has been long and loud. 'I Just Called To Say I Love You' was his 15th Top 10 hit and since 1966 he had charted at least once every year, except 1983. He had, of course, shared top-spot honours with Paul McCartney in 1982 (see no. 499), and *The Woman In Red* album was his 11th UK best-seller. 'I Just Called To Say I Love You' sold over a million copies in Britain alone and was his eighth US number one. Impressive though these and other Stevie statistics are, his music sings for itself, and will never need the support of figures to demonstrate its timeless qualities.

539

FREEDOM

WHAM!

20 October 1984, for 2 weeks

●●

EPIC A 4743

Writer: George Michael
Producer: George Michael

When Wham!'s second consecutive number one single peaked, it seemed to some chart observers that George Michael was attempting to establish a personal stranglehold on every alternate chart-topper. 'Freedom', released worldwide under the Wham! monicker, stormed to number one in two weeks flat.

Gimmicky marketing techniques were by now hardly necessary to sell a Wham! or George Michael product, but Epic broke new ground by releasing two different picture discs of 'Freedom', one George-shaped, one Andrew-shaped. The song itself was in the 'Go-Go' mould. The message of the lyric appeared to be that George wanted to tie himself down to one particular lover, but in fact the hook line of the song stated the opposite, viz "I don't want your freedom". This semantic issue never developed into a major issue, or even into a minor one.

Because of Wham!'s long chart runs, their American release dates fell spectacularly behind their British ones. 'Freedom' did not escape there until the following summer. Like the minor confusion in the lyric, this had no detrimental effect on the sales.

540

I FEEL FOR YOU

CHAKA KHAN

10 November 1984, for 3 weeks

●●●

WARNER BROTHERS W 9209

Writer: Prince
Producer: Arif Mardin

American superstar Prince's first connection with a UK number one single came with Chaka Khan's 'I Feel For You'. His second was not to be for a further five years, when shaven-headed Sinead O'Connor covered his composition 'Nothing Compares 2 U'. Despite a prodigious output, Prince did not top the UK's chart as an artist until 1994, with 'The Most Beautiful Girl In The World' (see no. 705), and by then he was no longer known as Prince but by the rather confusing monicker "Symbol".

Khan's triumph ended a barren 20-month spell for female artists at the top. She also brought recent number one debutant Stevie Wonder (see no. 538) back to the summit, for it is he who plays harmonica on the track. Another famous name involved is Grandmaster Melle Mel, whose opening rap around Chaka's name was as striking an intro as you (or Miss Khan) could wish for.

Chaka was born Yvette Marie Stevens on 23 March 1953 in Great Lakes, Illinois. She first came to prominence as the lead singer of soul/funk band Rufus, whose first hit, 'Tell Me Something Good', was a Stevie Wonder song. Chaka's powerful voice and voluptuous appearance were crucial to Rufus' popularity, which took a dive when she left them, not totally amicably, in 1978.

Her debut solo album yielded an international smash single, 'I'm Every Woman', bringing her to the attention of a substantial British audience in early 1979. Rufus had never charted at all in the UK at that point and Chaka had only one modest chart recognition – as vocalist on a Quincy Jones single. Her albums and singles over the next three years were not major sellers, and it took a temporary reunion with Rufus to bring her back into the limelight via 'Ain't Nobody', a number eight hit in spring 1984. This proved to be the prelude to greater things.

The 'I Feel For You' album matched the quality of her best days with Rufus. Chaka's power-packed vocals allied to electronic breakdance rhythms found immediate favour on both sides of the Atlantic. She has had erratic record sales since, and has not always been the most consistent of live performers, but her original and dominating vocal stylings, an influence on many lesser artists, ensure continued interest in her work.

541

I SHOULD HAVE KNOWN BETTER

JIM DIAMOND

1 December 1984, for 1 week

•

A&M AM 220

Writers: Jim Diamond and Graham Lyle
Producer: Pip Williams

Scotsman Jim Diamond (born 28 September 1953) guaranteed himself a permanent place in rock history when he declared, just one week after reaching number one for the first time, that he hoped 'I Should Have Known Better' would not still be there the following week. This rarer-than-rare statement from a newcomer to the hall of fame was not made because Jim disliked his own record, but because the Band Aid single was about to be released. With an admirable display of unselfishness he hoped that 'Do They Know It's Christmas?' would take the minimum time possible to outstrip his sales and thus earn the maximum publicity possible for Bob Geldof's Band Aid campaign.

As things turned out, the Band Aid milestone was not issued in time to make the 8 December chart, and Jim had the less-than-satisfying experience of having to make room at the top for Frankie Goes To Hollywood's third, final and shortest run at number one.

Diamond first made waves as half of PhD, a synthesizer-orientated duo who reached the Top 3 in spring 1982 with 'I Won't Let You Down'. The other 50 per cent was classically trained pianist Tony Hymas. Diamond's high plaintive vocals were the most arresting feature of the hit and for a while the duo enjoyed great acclaim all over Europe. Diamond's voice was heard to equal effect on his first and biggest solo hit, for which he chose a title that the Beatles had used for one of the well-known songs from *A Hard Day's Night*.

Without joining the big league of hefty sellers, Jim came up with three chart entries since 'I Should Have Known Better', including the theme song to the TV series *Boon*, 'Hi Ho Silver', a Top 10 entry.

542

THE POWER OF LOVE

FRANKIE GOES TO HOLLYWOOD

8 December 1984, for 1 week

•

ZTT ZTAS 5

Writers: Peter Gill, Holly Johnson, Brian Nash and Mark O'Toole
Producer: Trevor Horn

Frankie concluded their staggering year by equalling the 21-year-old record – set by fellow Liverpudlians Gerry and the Pacemakers – of making number one with each of their first three single releases. It was, however, a bit of a narrow squeak, and even as 'The Power Of Love' reached number one it was clear that the near-2,000,000 sales of 'Two Tribes' were a thing of their past and that the Frankie bubble was already a little deflated.

Having done their best to offend with sex and politics (see nos. 531 and 536), the quintet attempted to cause a commotion with religion third time out. This was done primarily through their video for the song, which featured an original interpretation of the Nativity. Complaints were virtually nil. There were more about the artwork of their first album, *Welcome To The Pleasuredome*, released with 'The Power Of Love' and an instant number one.

By an extraordinary coincidence, one of the titles on the 12-inch version of 'Relax' was a cover of Gerry's 1964 composition 'Ferry Cross The Mersey'. Great interest centred around Frankie's fourth single. Could they make it four in a row? Gerry's fourth hit had peaked at number two back in 1964 and when FGTH's next, the title track from their double album, did the same, the two bands from the same city but different generations were still locked in a tie for the best-ever start to a singles career. Frankie finally topped the Pacemakers when 'Rage Hard', (released no less than 18 months after 'Pleasuredome') staggered to number four, compared with Gerry's number six fifth time out.

That was about the last major achievement of FGTH's meteoric career (apart from a re-issue campaign in late 1993/ early 1994, when their first four singles all made the Top 20 again). Without Trevor Horn at the controls their recordings had become parodies of their early successes, and Frankie said "That's all folks"!

543

DO THEY KNOW IT'S CHRISTMAS?

BAND AID

15 December 1984, for 5 weeks

●●●●●

PHONOGRAM FEED 1

Writers: Bob Geldof and Midge Ure
Producer: Midge Ure

Bob Geldof's inspired conception and organization of the first and greatest of the all-star charity singles led to the setting of numerous recording achievements that, in many cases, are unlikely ever to be surpassed. The greatest achievement of all, however, remains the skill with which the lead singer of the Boomtown Rats (see nos. 428 and 440) captured the imagination and the hearts of millions for an indisputably worthy cause. Inevitably lesser men followed in his footsteps, with the result that two or three years later it almost seemed that a record whose royalties were not going to charity was an endangered species, but nothing can dim the glory of Bob Geldof, KBE, in creating Band Aid and the Live Aid follow-up concert of 13 July the following year.

Moved by the desperate pictures on TV of the terrifying famine in Ethiopia, Geldof resolved to make some personal effort, however small, to fight the disaster. He had the idea of raising funds through a one-off record featuring many of music's big contemporary names and contacted Midge Ure (see nos. 384 and 557), with whom he wrote a song for the project. In days he assembled a staggering line-up of talent, cut the record (produced by Ure) and began to realize the enormity of what he had set in motion when the sales exceeded his most optimistic forecasts.

'Do They Know It's Christmas?' entered the chart at number one, the first time this had been achieved by a new recording act. It quickly became the biggest-selling single of all time in the UK, with total sales now standing at over 3,500,000. It affected the lives of millions, not least that of Bob Geldof, who dedicated the best part of two years of his life to his new cause. He had always maintained that he was primarily an entertainer who intended to get back to his proper job as soon as he could leave his foundation in safe hands, but the greatness thrust upon him has made it difficult for the public to re-accept him as a rock singer.

The performers credited on the Band Aid single are as follows:

Adam Clayton, Bono (U2); Phil Collins; Bob Geldof, Johnny Fingers, Simon Crowe, Peter Briquette (Boomtown Rats); David Bowie; Paul McCartney; Holly Johnson (Frankie Goes To Hollywood); Midge Ure, Chris Cross (Ultravox); Simon Le Bon, Nick Rhodes, Andy Taylor, John Taylor, Roger Taylor (Duran Duran); Paul Young; Tony Hadley, Martin Kemp, John Keeble, Gary Kemp, Steve Norman (Spandau Ballet); Glenn Gregory, Martyn Ware (Heaven 17); Francis Rossi, Rick Parfitt (Status Quo); Sting; Jon Moss, Boy George (Culture Club); Marilyn; Keren Woodward, Sarah Dallin and Siobhan Fahey (Bananarama); Jody Watley (then Shalamar); Paul Weller (Style Council); Robert 'Kool' Bell, James Taylor, Dennis Thomas (Kool and the Gang); George Michael.

544

I WANT TO KNOW WHAT LOVE IS

FOREIGNER

19 January 1985, for 3 weeks

●●●

ATLANTIC A 9596

Writer: Mick Jones
Producers: Alex Sadkin and Mick Jones

Mick Jones of Foreigner became the first Jones to write a number one hit single when his dramatic gospel-flavoured ballad 'I Want To Know What Love Is' ended the noble Band Aid five-week supremacy. Born 27 December 1944 in London, Mick's first taste of the music business was behind the counter in a Woking record shop. He topped this achievement as a guitarist with Nero and the Gladiators, a group lumbered with a Roman stage costume gimmick, who enjoyed two minor UK chart entries in 1961. From there he went to France where he worked with Johnny Hallyday, then went back to England as part of Spooky Tooth, and then over to the States, where he teamed up with Leslie West for a while.

Foreigner Mark I was formed in New York in 1976. It consisted of Jones, Lou Gramm (vocals), Ian MacDonald (guitar, keyboards), Al Greenwood (keyboards), Ed Gagliardi (bass) and Dennis Elliott (drums). MacDonald and Elliott were Londoners, the other three native New Yorkers. They won a deal with Atlantic and placed four of their first five singles in the American Top 10, but enjoyed only modest success in the UK.

In 1980 the group shrank and re-formed. As a quartet consisting of Jones, Gramm, Elliott and Rick Wills (bass), they broadened their musical horizons, no longer concentrating primarily on heavy rock numbers. 'Waiting For A Girl Like You', a 1981 ballad, broke the all-comers' record by staying at number two for ten consecutive weeks in the US and gave them their first major British hit. 'I Want To Know What Love Is' did even better, going all the way in both countries.

Foreigner were joined on the single by Tom Bailey of the Thompson Twins, Jennifer Holliday and the New Jersey Mass Choir. This hit gave producer Alex Sadkin his second UK number one in eight months (see no. 534).

545

I KNOW HIM SO WELL

ELAINE PAIGE AND BARBARA DICKSON

9 February 1985, for 4 weeks

●●●●

RCA CHESS 3

Writers: Tim Rice, Bjorn Ulvaeus and Benny Andersson
Producers: Tim Rice, Bjorn Ulvaeus and Benny Andersson

The tenth number one single for Abba masterminds Benny and Bjorn was the first not performed by the Swedish supergroup, although – like their other nine – it featured lead vocals by two women. Lennon and McCartney remain the only writers to have hit the top more often than Andersson and Ulvaeus.

This time around, however, Andersson and Ulvaeus had to share the writing limelight with lyricist Tim Rice (see no. 400), with whom they had written the musical *Chess*. The *Chess* album produced two simultaneous hit singles, the other being Murray Head's 'One Night In Bangkok'. Head's track reached only number 12 in the UK, but generally did better than 'I Know Him So Well' around the world and topped the chart in 11 countries, reaching number three in the States.

'I Know Him So Well' became the all-time best-selling single by a female duo in Britain. It was sung by two of the most popular female vocalists in the country, whose principal successes had hitherto been in the theatre (both have won awards for leading West End roles, Barbara in *Blood Brothers* and Elaine in *Evita*), in concert and on album. Both had enjoyed major solo chart singles such as 'January February' and 'Answer Me' (Barbara, born in Dumfermline on 27 September 1947) and 'Memory' (Elaine, born in Barnet on 5 March 1948). 'I Know Him So Well' was recorded in Abba's Polar studios in Stockholm. Because of their hectic schedules, neither singer was present for the other's vocal contribution, but they have twice performed the song together in concert and many times on television around the world. Elaine went on to play the role of Florence for over a year in the West End production of *Chess*.

546

YOU SPIN ME ROUND (LIKE A RECORD)

DEAD OR ALIVE

9 March 1985, for 2 weeks

●●

EPIC A 4861

Writers: Dead Or Alive
Producers: Mike Stock, Matt Aitken and Peter Waterman

'You Spin Me Round (Like A Record)' was not only the first number one to mention the most vital item of music business software ever invented, it made slower uninterrupted progress to the top than any previous hit. It did not get there until its 14th week in the Top 75, having entered the chart before any of the three hits that preceeded it at number one. Peter Burns was once quoted in *Sounds* as saying he would perform an intimate physical act with one of the authors of this book if it would help him to get a hit record, but this unusual promotional offer was neither accepted nor necessary.

Dead Or Alive provided studio genii Stock Aitken Waterman with the first of their many number one successes. The credit 'produced by Stock-Aitken-Waterman' was to become a dominating feature in the industry, but here the single label stated 'directed by Mike Stock and Matt Aitken; a Pete Waterman production'. *Youthquake*, the album that contained 'You Spin Me Round', was, on the other hand, 'produced by Stock Aitken Waterman'.

Formed in Liverpool in 1982, Dead Or Alive consisted of Peter Burns (vocals), Stephen Coy (drums), Tim Lever (keyboards) and Michael Percy (bass). They enjoyed respectable international sales after they spun at the top, making a particularly good impression on the US dance charts, but they have now disbanded.

DEAD OR ALIVE, led by Pete Burns, spun into the charts every year between 1984 and 1989. (Pictorial Press)

547

EASY LOVER

PHILIP BAILEY (DUET WITH PHIL COLLINS)

23 March 1985, for 4 weeks

●●●●

CBS A 4915

Writers: Philip Bailey, Phil Collins and Nathan East
Producer: Phil Collins

Earth Wind and Fire co-lead vocalist and percussionist Philip Bailey (born in Denver, Colorado, on 8 May 1951) launched his solo recording career in late 1984, turning to Phil Collins (see no. 513) for the production duties. Not surprisingly, Phil's contribution to Bailey's album *Chinese Wall* consisted of more than supervision of the sound. He played drums throughout, co-wrote the track that became the album's biggest hit and even sang on it himself. Hitherto, Bailey's greatest UK success had come via the Earth Wind and Fire hits 'September' and 'Let's Groove', both number three hits for the soul/funk band, which usually consisted of nine members.

Philip Bailey joined the Los Angeles-based Earth Wind and Fire in 1972. The band had been founded by Maurice White three years before and was just beginning to take off when Bailey came aboard. His vocal acrobatics were perhaps at their best on the sixth EWF album, *That's The Way Of The World*, from which came the single 'Shining Star', their only US chart-topper to date, which Bailey co-wrote with White and keyboardist Larry Dunn. The single did not even chart in the UK.

'Easy Lover' was actually credited to Bailey with the line 'duet with Phil Collins' in miniscule print on the label. It is remembered as a fully-fledged duet.

548

WE ARE THE WORLD

USA FOR AFRICA

20 April 1985, for 2 weeks

●●

CBS US AID 1

Writers: Michael Jackson and Lionel Richie
Producer: Quincy Jones

The second all-star charity single to reach number one was for the same cause as the first (see no. 543). Bob Geldof's enormous success with 'Do They Know It's Christmas?', which had sold over a million copies in the United States as well as the unparalleled three million-plus in Britain, had started a train of conscience in the music industry which was shortly to lead to the triumph of Live Aid. USA For Africa (United Support of Artists for Africa) was another step on the road to that magnificent event and a direct result of the Geldof/Ure initiative. For once, the music business would not criticize the use by one act of another's idea.

Those who set the music world's battle against Ethiopian famine in motion on the other side of the Atlantic were Harry Belafonte, Ken Kragen (manager of Lionel Richie), Richie himself and Michael Jackson. The latter two wrote the anthemic song, and most of the hottest music names in America came to the A&M studios in Hollywood – under the supervision of Quincy Jones – on the night of 28 January 1985. An inevitable worldwide number one, 'We Are The World' topped the US parade for four weeks and the British for two. (The American charts had not been so kind to the Band Aid record, which, despite its huge sales got no higher than number 13.)

The soloists on the single (in order) are: Lionel Richie, Stevie Wonder, Paul Simon, Kenny Rogers, James Ingram, Tina Turner, Billy Joel, Michael Jackson, Diana Ross, Dionne Warwick, Willie Nelson, Al Jarreau, Bruce Springsteen, Kenny Loggins, Steve Perry, Daryl Hall, Huey Lewis, Cyndi Lauper, Kim Carnes, Bob Dylan, and Ray Charles.

Others credited on the single: Dan Aykroyd, Harry Belafonte, Lindsey Buckingham, Sheila E., Bob Geldof, John Oates, Jackie Jackson, LaToya Jackson, Marlon Jackson, Randy Jackson, Tito Jackson; Waylon Jennings, The News (Huey Lewis and), Bette Midler, Jeffrey Osborne, the Pointer Sisters, Smokey Robinson.

549

MOVE CLOSER

PHYLLIS NELSON

4 May 1985, for 1 week

●

CARRERE CAR 337

Writer: Phyllis Nelson
Producer: Yves Dessca

The fifth Nelson to appear in the British single charts was the first to make number one, Phyllis succeeding where Bill, Ricky, Sandy and Willie have all, to date, failed. 'Move Closer' is, however, Phyllis' only hit in the UK so far, and by the beginning of 1994 she had been on the one-hit wonder list for almost nine years.

Phyllis was born in Jacksonville, Florida,

where she sang with her brothers and sisters in the Nelson Five. Realizing that she would have done better to have been born in Nelsonville and to have sung with the Jackson Five, she moved to Philadelphia where she joined a group called Brown Sugar. She also sang back-up for Major Harris, and after a stint with another act, named Philly Cream, she made her first solo records, 'Don't Stop The Train' becoming a big dance-floor hit.

She began to make a national name for herself when her recording of 'I Like You' came on to the US dance charts in late 1985 and proceeded to climb to number one. It also crossed over – with some success – to the Hot 100. It was however, a ballad, her own composition, that brought her to the attention of British fans. 'Move Closer' made leisurely progress up the UK chart, grabbing just one week in pole position after a ten-week climb. In America the track made little impression, possible because Phyllis was only established as a dance-record act and her supporters in that field found little to jump around to in 'Move Closer'. The song has recently resurfaced in Britain, featuring in an advert for Soft & Gentle antiperspirant.

550

19

PAUL HARDCASTLE

11 May 1985, for 5 weeks

●●●●●

CHRYSALIS CHS 2860

Writers: Paul Hardcastle, William Coutourie and Jonas McCord
Producer: Paul Hardcastle

London-born (on 10 December 1957) producer and keyboard player Paul Hardcastle achieved his first number one production with his own name in the artist slot as well. However, he is not a performer in the conventional sense on this smash, the title of which refers to the average age of American soldiers in the Vietnam war.

To an electro-funk rhythm track, Hardcastle made use of the speaking voices of American commentators and soldiers (and the singing voices of a female chorus) to spell out some of the unpleasant facts of being a soldier in the conflict that tore America apart in the 60s. "In World War II," states the record, "the average age of the combat soldier was 26; in Vietnam he was nineteen - n-n-n-n-nineteen." The electronic stutter that preceded the title word many times during the track became a catch phrase within days of the record's release. '19' inspired a hit parody by impressionist Rory Bremner operating as the Commentators, entitled 'N-N-Nineteen Not Out' (referring to the England cricket team captain's batting average).

Hardcastle has notched up a string of chart records in Britain, under his own name, under a pseudonym (Silent Underdog), and as producer of other artists, but none has yet repeated the phenomenal success of his digitally titled monster, which made the Top 20 in the country where the soldiers of the hit were born.

551

YOU'LL NEVER WALK ALONE

THE CROWD

15 June 1985, for 2 weeks

●●

SPARTAN BRAD 1

Writers: Richard Rodgers and Oscar Hammerstein II
Producers: Graham Gouldman and Ray Levy

The third number one single recorded by a hastily assembled aggregation of stars in aid of a particular cause came about as a result of the fire that destroyed a stand at Bradford City Football Club, killing over 50 people. A fund was set up to provide financial compensation for the relatives of the victims and to help Bradford City to recover from the disaster. One of the principal sources of income for the fund was the Crowd's recording of the song that Gerry and the Pacemakers had taken to number one in 1963, 'You'll Never Walk Alone' (see no. 159).

The line-up for this single was put together by Graham Gouldman of 10 C.C.

(who had been a co-writer of three previous chart-toppers, nos. 332, 372 and 426) and Ray Levy. The cast list was not as distinguished as those of the two Ethiopian famine records, but neither this nor the more parochial nature of the cause seemed to affect the British public's desire to contribute via the Crowd. Naturally, appeal outside the UK was limited.

Over 50 artists (many not really connected with the music business) are credited on the sleeve, with the inclusion of Gerry Marsden as lead vocalist the point of greatest interest. Gerry became the first artist in history to hit number one with each of two different versions of the same song, a feat to be equalled a year later (see no. 567). Rodgers and Hammerstein were each at number one for the sixth time, the fifth as a team, a mere three years since their comeback via Captain Sensible (see no. 504). Zak Starkey, son of Ringo Starr, is also on the record, making him and his dad the first father-son team to feature on number ones, with the older Starr leading 17-1.

The artists credited on the sleeve with helping the Crowd (not all of whom are actually performing in 'You'll Never Walk Alone'), are as follows: Gerry Marsden, Tony Christie, Denny Laine, Tim Healy, Gary Holton, Ed Stewart, Tony Hicks, Kenny Lynch, Colin Blunstone, Chris Robinson, A. Curtis, Phil Lynott, Bernie Winters, Girlschool, Black Lace, John Otway, Rick Wakeman, Barron Knights, Tim Hinkley, Brendan Shine, John Verity, Rolf Harris, Rob Heaton, Patrick McDonald, Smokie, Bruce Forsyth, Johnny Logan, Colbert Hamilton, Dave Lee Travis, Rose Marie, Frank Allen, Jim Diamond, Graham Gouldman, Pete Spencer, Chris Norman, Gerard Kenny, the Nolans, Graham Dene, Suzy Grant, Peter Cook, The Foxes, Jess Conrad, Kim Kelly, Motorhead, John Entwhistle, Jimmy Henney, Joe Fagin, David Shilling, Karen Clark, Gary Hughes, Zak Starkey, Eddie Hardin, Paul McCartney, Kiki Dee and Keith Chegwin.

552

FRANKIE

SISTER SLEDGE

29 June 1985, for 4 weeks

●●●●

ATLANTIC A 9547

Writer: Joy Denny
Producer: Nile Rodgers

North Philadelphia family act Sisters Sledge first recorded in 1971 but by the time they first came to public attention in 1975 with their first US chart record 'Love Don't You Go Through No Changes On Me', they had shortened their name by one letter to Sister Sledge. They are not related to Percy of 'When A Man Loves A Woman' fame, nor is their number one related to Connie Francis' 1959 US Top 10er of the same title.

Their 1975 American charter was hardly a major breakthrough for the girls. It was a Top 40 soul hit but reached only number 92 on the Hot 100. They achieved much greater chart recognition in England when 'Mama Never Told Me' broke out of the clubs and into the Top 20 in the summer of that year, a track that never registered anywhere in their home country. From 1976-79 they had the odd success on the US soul charts but never the pop list.

Then, in 1979, Joni (who sings lead on Frankie), Debbie, Kim and Kathy Sledge burst out of the medium time with their album *We Are Family*. The major factor responsible was the Chic production team of Nile Rodgers (see nos. 519 and 534) and Bernard Edwards. The album went to number three in America, with two of its singles, 'He's The Greatest Dancer' and the title track, making the Top 10. Both were also substantial hits in the UK, as was a third cut, 'Lost In Music'.

Apart from 1984 remixed versions of old hits, the girls failed to capitalize on *We Are Family* until the unexpected rise of 'Frankie', taken from the album *When The Boys Meet The Girls*. Nile Rodgers was back at the helm, but even his wizardry did not help a great deal in the States where 'Frankie', the one track from the package to chart, limped only to position number 75.

553

THERE MUST BE AN ANGEL (PLAYING WITH MY HEART)

EURYTHMICS

27 July 1985, for 1 week

●

RCA PB 40247

Writers: David A. Stewart and Annie Lennox
Producer: David A. Stewart

Waitress Annie Lennox from Aberdeen met itinerant musician David Stewart in a restaurant in his home town of Sunderland. Stewart had at one time been part of Longdancer, the first group signed to Elton John's Rocket Records. The worker/customer relationship developed into a romantic and professional association, the latter beginning with the Tourists in 1977. The group, which also included Stewart's fellow Wearsider Peet Coombes, enjoyed five hit singles and three albums in 1979/80, their most notable waxing being their revival of the Dusty Springfield hit 'I Only Want To Be With You'. The Tourists became the third act to take the song to number four, versions by both Dusty (1963) and the Bay City Rollers (1976) having reached that exact position before them.

A legal bust-up with their label, Logo, and the end of their romance led to the demise of the Tourists, but from these two wreckages Eurythmics (they insist there is no 'The' in their group name) were born in 1981. They were now simply a professional duo starting again. It was a struggle which took its toll on the physical and mental health of both performers in Eurythmics' early days. In 1981 'Never Gonna Cry Again' scraped into the Top 75, and over a year later 'Love Is A Stranger' almost reached the Top 50. 'Sweet Dreams (Are Made Of This)' changed everything. Stark image (Annie) allied to economic electro production (Dave), plus Annie's intense interpretation of their haunting song, took them all the way bar one place in the UK and all the way bar nothing in the States.

Between 1981 and 1990 Eurythmics racked up 24 hits, a total for a duo surpassed only by the Everly Brothers, but by the end of 1990 Dave and Annie had decided to dissolve their partnership. Dave has achieved moderate success with his groups the Spiritual Cowboys and Vegas, but it is Annie who has hogged the limelight with her million-selling debut solo album, *Diva*.

554

INTO THE GROOVE

MADONNA

3 August 1985, for 4 weeks

●●●●

SIRE W 8934

Writers: Madonna and Steve Bray
Producers: Madonna and Steve Bray

The phenomenon that is Madonna reached the top of the British pops for the first time with her seventh consecutive hit single. It featured in the movie in which she starred with Rosanna Arquette, *Desperately Seeking Susan*. During the four weeks that 'Into The Groove' led the pack, Madonna's debut hit from 1984, 'Holiday', re-entered the charts and rose all the way to number two, beating its first-time peak by four places. On 17 August 1985 Madonna became the only female and the fourth act ever to hold down both the number one and two positions in the UK singles chart simultaneously.

The lady who became the biggest female star the music industry has ever known was born Madonna Louise Veronica Ciccone on 16 August 1958 (probably!) in

Detroit, Michigan. She moved to New York in 1977, looking for stardom. She enrolled at a dance theatre and met disco star Patrick Hernandez (who had a big international hit with 'Born To Be Alive' in 1979). He took her to Paris where she sang back-up vocals on various tracks, but she did not feel she was in the right place at the right time to satisfy her ambitions and Madonna soon returned to New York. With a drummer friend from way back, Steve Bray, she produced a series of dance-orientated demo tapes of original songs which in turn led to a deal with Sire Records.

As an unknown aiming for the top she presented herself to, and was accepted by, Michael Jackson's then manager Freddy DeMann. Her first single, 'Everybody', did next to nothing, and the next, 'Burning Up', did little better. Her first album, *Madonna*, appeared in 1983, containing her third single, 'Lucky Star'. Again, little response. It was one of two tracks on the album written by outsiders that got her away. 'Holiday' by Curtis Hudson and Lisa Stephens took her to number six in the UK and to number 16 in the States.

The hits just kept on coming. Second time around 'Lucky Star' scored, as did a second non-Madonna-composed track from the LP, 'Borderline' (by Reggie

'I Got You Babe' by UB40 and guest vocalist CHRISSIE HYNDE was a kind of reunion, since she had welcomed them as support act on the first major Pretenders tour. (Pictorial Press)

Lucas). The first mega-smash was her fourth hit, 'Like A Virgin' (number three in the UK, number one in the US), produced by the ubiquitous Nile Rodgers. In Britain the next three, 'Material Girl', 'Crazy For You' and 'Into The Groove' all did as well – or better – than the one before. Ms. Ciccone's looks excited as much interest as her music. By the middle of 1985 Madonna-mania was an international phenomenon.

555

I GOT YOU BABE

UB40, GUEST VOCALS BY CHRISSIE HYNDE

31 August 1985, for 1 week

•

DEP INTERNATIONAL DEP 20

Writer: Sonny Bono
Producers: UB40 and Ray 'Pablo' Falconer

Exactly 20 years after 'I Got You Babe' topped the charts for its originators,

MIDGE URE waits backstage at the Royal Albert Hall before performing in a Prince's Trust concert. (Pictorial Press)

Sonny and Cher (see no. 201), UB40, with Pretenders leader Chrissie Hynde credited as guest vocalist, took the song back to number one. Sonny Bono's most famous composition thus became the eighth song to lead the list via two different versions. Both UB40 and Hynde had had one previous chart-topper (see nos. 526 and 449).

In the two years since 'Red Red Wine', UB40 had added impressively to their list of hit singles, five more in all, including the Top 10 entries 'Please Don't Make Me Cry' and 'If It Happens Again'. Three of these hits were from *Labour Of Love*, the same LP that had featured 'Red Red Wine', an album that consisted entirely of UB40's versions of songs recorded by reggae artists between 1969 and 1972. They returned to their own writing talents for their next album, *Geffrey Morgan* (sic), a Top 3 item including 'If It Happens Again', apparently a statement of their intentions were Margaret Thatcher to be re-elected.

In 1985 UB40 made three visits to the States, and the video for 'I Got You Babe' was shot during a concert at Jones Beach on Long Island, where Chrissie Hynde joined the band on stage. The record itself was cut at UB40's own studio, the Abattoir in Birmingham.

UB40 have always run themselves as a collective, resisting all attempts to have any one member of the group pushed to the fore or act as a representative for all. They regarded their friends behind the scenes as equal contributors to the band's fortunes. Thus, the tragic death of their co-producer, Ray 'Pablo' Falconer, in a car crash in late 1987 was a tragic blow.

556

DANCING IN THE STREET

DAVID BOWIE AND MICK JAGGER

7 September 1985, for 4 weeks

●●●●

EMI AMERICA EA 204

Writers: Ivy Hunter, William Stevenson and Marvin Gaye
Producers: Clive Langer and Alan Winstanley

Old-timers Mick Jagger and David Bowie proved that a duo with the combined age of an octogenarian could bop with the best of them. Their dynamic collaboration on disc and on video brought in yet more thousands of much-needed dollars, pounds, yen, marks, francs, etc., for the Live Aid appeal via their vibrant revival of the Martha and the Vandellas classic, 'Dancing In The Street'.

The hit came straight into the charts at number one and held off all opposition for a month. Jagger had not been part of such a smash since the eighth and final Stones number one, 'Honky Tonk Women', in 1969 (see no. 274), and even by Bowie's more recent standards (three number ones since 1975), this was a major landmark of his output.

The original version of 'Dancing In The Street' made only number 28 when it was first issued in 1964, but five years later it did better, climbing to fourth place. The 1985 cover gave Marvin Gaye a posthumous number one as a co-composer, and Brits Langer and Winstanley their third as producers (see nos. 501 and 506). Yet again, Nile Rodgers' name appeared on the credits of a chart-topper; this time he was listed under 'additional production' along with Jagger, Steve Thompson and Michael Barbiero (see nos. 519, 534 and 552).

The next Stones single to chart after the Jagger/Bowie smash was, coincidentally, another cover version, this time of the Bob and Earl standard 'Harlem Shuffle'. The two superstars having not reunited for further chart attacks, they remain (as a combo) on the list of one-hit wonders.

557

IF I WAS

MIDGE URE

5 October 1985, for 1 week

●

CHRYSALIS URE 1

Writers: Midge Ure and Danny Mitchell
Producer: Midge Ure

Having been a major force behind two number one records, Ultravox star Midge Ure finally made it to the heights in his own right with a fairly conventional (by his standards) ballad. His love song spent only one week at the top, but it was long overdue personal recognition for the man who had co-written and produced Britain's all-time best-selling single (see no. 543) and been a part of the briefly famous Slik (see no. 384).

Midge was born in Lanarkshire and cast aside an engineering apprenticeship in Glasgow in favour of the gamble of the music business. He joined a band called Salvation, who became Slik, and in the hands of producer/writers Bill Martin and Phil Coulter scored their big hit in 1976. The group collapsed after a year or so and Midge joined up with ex-Sex Pistol Glen Matlock to form the Rich Kids with Steve New and Rusty Egan. They never enjoyed the good fortune their energetic 'power pop' recordings deserved and they split in 1978, having only once reached the Top 30. It was Midge's arrival in the ranks of the re-formed Ultravox, who had just lost their leader John Foxx, that brought the first taste of real success for both him and the electronic band. This came with their 1980 album, *Vienna*, whose title track reached number two early the following year.

A string of Ultravox hits followed, all composed by the four members: Ure, Chris Cross, Billie Currie and Warren Cann. Their 1982 album, *Quartet*, was produced by George Martin in Montserrat. Midge found time to work with Steve Strange in the studio group Visage, who clocked up seven hits from 1980-84. He enjoyed a solo Top 10 hit in 1982 with the Tom Rush song 'No Regrets' (also a 1976 hit for the Walker Brothers), but only resumed his parallel individual recording projects in earnest with his 1985 album *The Gift*, whence came 'If I Was'. The hit features Level 42's Mark King on bass.

558

THE POWER OF LOVE

JENNIFER RUSH

12 October 1985, for 5 weeks

●●●●●

CBS A 5003

Writers: Candy de Rouge, Gunther Mende, Jennifer Rush and Mary Susan Applegate
Producers: Candy de Rouge and Gunther Mende

The only million seller of 1985 outsold Julie Covington's 980,000 for 'Don't Cry For Me Argentina' (see no. 400) to become the largest-selling single ever by a woman in the UK, until Whitney Houston's 1992 smash ('I Will Always Love You'). It also set an all-time record in the slowness of its progress to the top, taking no less than 16 weeks to make it. It charted on 29 June at number 65, and in its 12th chart week had progressed to only number 42, staying for nine consecutive weeks in the 40s. The following week it broke into the all-important Top 40 at number 36, which automatically increased its airplay dramatically. It then accelerated with remarkable zest: 15 to two to one, where it remained for a further month. Its progress on the way down was also extremely dilatory and it chalked up 32 weeks in all before departing. At the end of 1986 it returned for another wander around the lower regions.

The song was the second with the title 'The Power Of Love' to make number one, following only ten months after Frankie Goes To Hollywood's hit of the same name. A third song with the same title, by Huey Lewis and the News, was a number one in America in August 1985, but in the UK it failed to go beyond number 11. There is no explanation for the sudden rush to use this title which had never provided anyone with a British hit before 1984.

Jennifer Rush was a native of Queens, New York, but she recorded her gigantic Euro-smash in Germany. Her passionate reading of a sensual ballad supported by a powerful synthesized programme struck a chord in the hearts of Euro-lovers once trendy radio stations permitted them to hear it, but her heart-rending voice of experience left her fellow Americans less moved. They let her emote her way only to number 57. She at least had the satisfaction of seeing off a rival version by Air Supply, but had reason to feel hard done by when Laura Branigan's version went Top 30 in late 1987 and French Canadian Celine Dion took the track right to the top in 1994.

Not surprisingly, Rush's records since have never quite matched her devastating debut, but she did make the Top 40 in the States with a duet with Elton John entitled 'Flames Of Paradise', and remains an important European act.

559

A GOOD HEART

FEARGAL SHARKEY

16 November 1985, for 2 weeks

●●

VIRGIN VS 808

Writer: Maria McKee
Producer: David A. Stewart

Ex-Undertone Feargal Sharkey outstripped every chart performance of his former band with his third solo hit. In the producer's chair was Eurythmic David A. Stewart (see no. 553), whose masterly work on Lone Justice singer-songwriter Maria McKee's bright philosophical gem brought the Ulsterman a far wider audience than seven years of highly rated work with the Undertones.

The Undertones were formed in the mid-70s in Derry, Northern Ireland. The original line-up was Sharkey (vocals), brothers John (rhythm guitar) and Damian (lead guitar/keyboards) O'Neill, Mickey Bradley (bass) and Billy Doherty (drums). Their first record, 'Teenage Kicks', was released on a Northern Ireland independent label and subsequently nationwide on Sire. It achieved an encouraging 31 placing in late 1978.

Regular chart singles followed, but only 1980's 'My Perfect Cousin' scraped into the Top 10. Success was never quite consistent or substantial enough to hold them together and they split up in 1983. Feargal, who was the only non-composing Undertone, then teamed up with Vince Clarke in the Assembly. The only Assembly single ever released, 'Never Never', reached number four in 1983. They disbanded before most fans had realized who the group was. Feargal moved to Madness' label, Zarjazz, which issued the first single to come out under his own name, 'Listen To Your Father'. Although this was a medium-sized hit, Sharkey released no Zarjazz follow-up. Instead he moved to Virgin, where one more hit in the 20s preceeded 'A Good Heart'. His follow-up, 'You Little Thief', went Top 5 in early 1986. He premiered the track on British TV live from a jumbo jet several miles up in the air.

560

I'M YOUR MAN

WHAM!

30 November 1985, for 2 weeks

●●

EPIC A 6716

Writer: George Michael
Producer: George Michael

By George Michael's standards, there was a long gap between his third and fourth number one singles. His first three number ones (two with Wham! and one solo - see nos. 535, 537 and 539) had all occurred within a four-and-a-half-month period, whereas his next (a Wham! hit) was over a year coming. There had been no dip in his or his group's popularity, however. The late-1984 Wham! single, 'Last Christmas', had been released simultaneously with the Band Aid mega-smash (see no. 543) and was held at number two, becoming the first single to sell a million in the UK without reaching the top. Its royalties went to Band Aid. 'I'm Your Man', the first Wham! release since 'Last Christmas', took only two weeks to overcome all opposition.

During 1985 George appeared at Live Aid with Elton John, singing 'Don't Let The Sun Go Down On Me'. A later live version topped both the British and American charts in 1991.

At the end of 1985 'Last Christmas' made the Top 10 for the second time. The song became the centre of a court battle when Barry Manilow's publishers claimed (unsuccessfully) that the tune was a lift of Barry's 'Can't Smile Without You'. It charted again over Christmas 1986, reaching number 47.

In March 1986, George finally confirmed that months – if not years – of rumours of a Wham! split were now correct. "It's the most amicable split in pop history," he said in one television interview.

561

SAVING ALL MY LOVE FOR YOU

WHITNEY HOUSTON

14 December 1985, for 2 weeks

●●

ARISTA ARIST 640

Writers: Michael Masser and Gerry Goffin
Producer: Michael Masser

Whitney Houston was born in New Jersey on 9 August 1963, the daughter of Cissy Houston, the cousin of Dionne and Dee Dee Warwick. Her mother was the lead singer of the Sweet Inspirations from 1967-70, and their work included backing vocals for Aretha Franklin and Elvis Presley. Cissy went solo in 1970 but, despite the widespread respect her soulful voice earned her within the music industry, she never made a major breakthrough on her own. It was left to her daughter to earn the family fortune.

Whitney began her showbiz career as a fashion model, became a studio vocalist and made her chart debut duetting with Teddy Pendergrass in 1984 on the medium-sized US hit 'Hold Me'. She then progressed to cutting her own album which, thanks to the superb team of writers, musicians and producers assembled around her by Clive Dickens of Arista Records, became the most successful debut LP of all time.

The first American hit single was 'You Give Good Love', a number three. The second, and the first in the UK, was the ballad of a mistress' dilemma, 'Saving All My Love For You', which topped the charts in both countries. The latter originally appeared on a Marilyn McCoo and Billy Davis Jr. album. Two more American number ones, 'How Will I Know' and 'The Greatest Love Of All', emerged. *Whitney Houston* went on to sell in excess of 13 million copies around the world, the all-time number one by a woman.

Michael Masser and Gerry Goffin had teamed for a US number one before. In 1976 their song 'Theme From 'Mahogany' - Do You Know Where You're Going To' had done the trick for Diana Ross. Goffin was most celebrated for his then wife Carole King and had previously been at the top of the UK charts back in 1964, thanks to Herman's Hermits (see no. 178).

562

MERRY CHRISTMAS EVERYONE

SHAKIN' STEVENS

28 December 1985, for 2 weeks

●●

EPIC A 6769

Writer: Bobby Heatlie
Producer: Dave Edmunds

Nearly four years went by between Shakin' Stevens' third and fourth number ones, but during that time he established himself as one of the most consistent hit-makers the British charts had ever seen. Between 'Oh Julie' (see no. 493) and 'Merry Christmas Everyone', Shaky added another 11 consecutive hits to his tally, seven of them Top 10 and two of them Top 2, as well as a Top 5 hit in duet with Bonnie Tyler (see no. 517). One of the biggest in this string had been his 1982 Christmas offering, 'The Shakin' Stevens EP', which featured 'Blue Christmas' as the lead track.

Both producer Dave Edmunds (see no. 294) and writer Bobby Heatlie (see no. 484) had made number one in their 'Merry Christmas Everyone' modes once before. Heatlie had originally written this song (with different lyrics) as a single for his fellow Scot Aneka, but using the well-tried Chuck Berry device of putting a second set of lyrics to the same tune, he eventually pushed it to the summit as a Christmas song produced by Dave Edmunds for his fellow Welshman Shakin' Stevens.

After his fourth chart-topper (only Elvis, Cliff and Rod Stewart of male solo singers have had more), Shaky has managed to hit the Top 10 only once more in 17 outings - in late 1987 with a cover of Emile Ford and the Checkmates' 'What Do You Want To Make Those Eyes At Me For'. He remains, however, a supreme entertainer, combining a sense of humour with an energetic and immaculately executed performance.

563

WEST END GIRLS

PET SHOP BOYS

11 January 1986, for 2 weeks

●●

PARLOPHONE R 6115

Writers: Neil Tennant and Chris Lowe
Producer: Stephen Hague

Neil Tennant and Chris Lowe met in August 1981 in a hi-fi shop in the Kings Road, Chelsea. Neil had once been a member of a Newcastle group Dust, from which he progressed not to another group but to publishing, working for Marvel Comics and winding up as Assistant Editor on the teen-fan mag *Smash Hits*. Chris, five years Neil's junior, was a former trombonist turned keyboard player whose early professional days included a stretch with septet One Under The Eight.

Now calling themselves the Pet Shop Boys, a name that they claim has no significance beyond being inspired by a friend who worked in a pet shop, they worked together on songs and productions when architectural study (Chris) and journalism (Neil) permitted. A 1983 trip to New York gave Neil the chance to meet producer Bobby 'O' Orlando, and in 1984 Orlando and the Pet Shop Boys recorded the first version of 'West End Girls', which did quite well in Europe but nothing in England, where it was released by Epic.

The duo took the decision to devote their energies full time to PSB. Neil wrote a farewell article in *Smash Hits* entitled "Why I Quit Smash Hits To Be A Teen Sensation!". They signed with EMI, with their first Parlophone single, 'Opportunities (Let's Make Lots Of Money)', released in June 1985 but following the Epic effort into oblivion. The choice for the second EMI offering was a re-recording of 'West End Girls' and the reaction from the public could hardly have been in greater contrast to that which had greeted the original version. The single, produced by

The two PET SHOP BOYS had two weeks at number one with version two of 'West End Girls'. (Pictorial Press)

Stephen Hague, was an eerie half-spoken, half-sung portrait of city life into which were poured real street sounds and synthetic electronic sounds. It entered the chart at the end of November 1985, and just under two months later emerged top of the heap during the post-Christmas shakeout.

564

THE SUN ALWAYS SHINES ON T.V.

A-HA

25 January 1986, for 2 weeks

●●

WARNER BROTHERS W 8846

Writer: Pal Waaktaar
Producer: Alan Tarney

Norway's contribution to the history of popular music had, until 1985, consisted mainly of a string of glorious disasters in the Eurovision song contest. That year a female duo named Bobbysocks represented Norway, although one girl was Swedish. They defied precedent and prediction by winning the annual event that everyone loves to hate with 'Let It Swing'. Despite this sensational victory, the Bobbysocks' single made only number 45 in the UK charts and it was left to Pal Waaktaar, Magne 'Mags' Furuholmen and Morten Harket to do for Norway what only Abba and Blue Swede had previously done for Scandanavian pop groups: top the charts in Britain and/or America. A-Ha did this in both countries.

A-Ha emerged from a Norwegian band named Bridges, formed in 1979. Included in the line-up were Pal (vocals/guitar) and Mags (keyboards). Morten was with the awkwardly named soul band Souldier Blue at the time, but when he met Pal and Mags the three musicians decided to try their luck as a new combination. Visits to London in 1982 and 1983 won them management and record contracts, the latter with WEA.

Their first recording sessions in London

went badly, although 'Take On Me' sold well in Norway. It flopped twice in the UK and when even their second single failed to click in Norway, it seemed as if the torch of their nation's pop music was still in the clutch of one Bobbysock. A-Ha's manager, Terry Slater, still had faith in 'Take On Me' and he persuaded Alan Tarney (see no. 441) to re-cut the song with the trio. This version was issued in Britain and the States in May 1985.

The response of the British public was no greater than it had been to the original version, but in America, thanks in part to a stunning video made by Steve Barron, the Tarney-produced 'Take On Me' made number one within three months. The message finally reached the UK, and with persistent re-promotion by WEA 'Take On Me' charted in September, rising to number two during a 19-week run in the best sellers.

The photogenic threesome soon became teen idols whose looks as much as their music guaranteed them enormous sales with their follow-up. 'The Sun Always Shines On T.V.' nipped to number one in the UK in a mere four weeks and since then they have come up with a healthy sequence of Top 10 items, including a James Bond title song, 'The Living Daylights', in 1987. Lead vocalist Morten Harket has even achieved the honour of an entry in *Who's Really Who.*

A-HA topped the British and American charts with different hits. (Pictorial Press)

565

WHEN THE GOING GETS TOUGH, THE TOUGH GET GOING

BILLY OCEAN

8 February 1986, for 4 weeks

●●●●

JIVE JIVE 114

Writers: Wayne Braithwaite, Barry J Eastmond, R.J. 'Mutt' Lange and Billy Ocean
Producer: R. J. 'Mutt' Lange

Billy Ocean was born Leslie Sebastian Charles on 21 January 1950 in Trinidad. He was raised in England and first came to the attention of British record buyers in 1976. A run of disco-influenced hit singles that began with the number two smash 'Love Really Hurts Without You' took him away from the world of sessions as a back-up vocalist or as an imitator of the stars on cheap albums of cover versions of current hits. These successes (all on the GTO label) ground to a halt by early 1980 and nothing was heard of Billy for over four years.

In 1984 he signed a new deal with Jive Records and quickly registered a huge comeback with a composition he co-wrote with producer Keith Diamond, 'Caribbean Queen (No More Love On The Run)'. This single (originally recorded as 'European Queen...') made number six in Britain but, more importantly, number one in America.

Phase two of Billy's recording career now swung into impressive action. The fifth of his Jive hits (all co-written by him), produced by 'Mutt' Lange, whose only previous number one in the UK had been with the Boomtown Rats (see no. 428), proved to be the one that did the ultimate trick for him in the UK, boosted by its inclusion in the Michael Douglas movie *The Jewel Of The Nile*. Douglas sang backing vocals on the record. In the US it made only number two, but Billy was more than compensated by this minor disappointment by the Stateside achievement of his follow-up, 'There'll Be Sad Songs (To Make You Cry)', which went one better, though 11 worse in Britain.

The origin of the saying that inspired Ocean's only British chart-topper to date is not certain, but it has been attributed to Joseph P. Kennedy, father of John F. Kennedy, and one time US Ambassador to Britain. Whoever came up with it, he/she was indirectly responsible for the third-longest title to a UK number one of all time, its 37 letters tying it with Brian and Michael's hit (see no. 421) and placing it behind only the New Seekers' (see no. 308) and Scott McKenzie's (see no. 236), although pedants argue that as many of the letters in these latter two titles are in brackets, Ocean and Brian and Michael should be considered joint holders of this uncoveted honour.

566

CHAIN REACTION

DIANA ROSS

8 March 1986, for 3 weeks

●●●

CAPITOL CL 386

Writers: Barry, Robin and Maurice Gibb
Producers: Barry Gibb, Karl Richardson and Albhy Galuten

'Chain Reaction' had 'Bee Gees' stamped indelibly all over it. Since those halcyon days of the late 70s when *Saturday Night Fever* reached epidemic proportions, the Bee Gees own recording career had gone into a temporary recession, but Bee Gee Barry Gibb was concentrating his efforts on revitalising the careers of female vocalists such as Barbra Streisand and Dionne Warwick. In 1986 he turned his attention to the most charted female vocalist of all time, Diana Ross.

In 1980, Nile Rodgers and Bernard Edwards of Chic had managed a similar boost to the Ross career (and, it must be said, to their own careers as producers) with the album *Diana*, which spawned three Top 20 hits, including 'Upside Down', which peaked at number two. Since the end of 1982, however, Miss Ross had been absent from the British Top 40. The album with Barry Gibb was called *Eaten Alive*, and the first single release from it, the title track, flopped badly, appearing on our charts for only one week at number 71. 'Chain Reaction', released at the very beginning of the new year, brought the album out of the bargain buckets and into the charts, and became the first Ross chart-topper since 'I'm Still Waiting' (see no. 303) 14 years and 172 days earlier. This was, at the time, the longest wait between number one hits ever recorded, and to add to the oddness of the feat, neither of Diana Ross' two British chart-toppers even so much as dented the bottom end of the US charts, which she has topped five times as a soloist, 12 times with the Supremes and once with Lionel Richie.

In 1993, 'Chain Reaction' was reissued to coincide with the release of a complete CD discography of Diana Ross' career, and it climbed back to the Top 20, while the album *One Woman* became her first-ever number one album.

567

LIVING DOLL

CLIFF RICHARD AND THE YOUNG ONES, FEATURING HANK MARVIN

29 March 1986, for 3 weeks

●●●

WEA YZ 65

Writer: Lionel Bart
Producer: Stuart Colman

The most indestructible British pop star of all time, Cliff Richard, OBE, broke yet more new ground in the 29th year of his career when he zoomed up to the top of the charts for the 11th time, accompanied by his colleague from way back, Hank B. Marvin, and the comedy quartet named after one of Cliff's other number ones (see no. 132). Marvin, with five Shadows number ones and seven other Cliff-and-Shads number ones, was actually gracing the summit for the 13th time.

'Living Doll' was unlike any of Cliff's previous successes in that the song had already been a number one single for him

Johann Holzel became better known as FALCO. (Pictorial Press)

(a mere 27 years earlier). Gerry Marsden, in his role as lead singer of the Crowd (see no. 551), had beaten Cliff to the honour of becoming the first to hit the top twice with the same song, but Gerry's wait between successes had been a less staggering 22 years. It is probable, nay certain, that the vast majority of the purchasers of 'Living Doll' mark II were not even born when Cliff and the Drifters (as Hank's group then was) first took it to the top (see no. 88).

The record was the fifth number one made for charity and the fourth that fought famine in Ethiopia (see nos. 543, 548 and 556). The disc was Stuart Coleman's fourth chart-topper as a producer (his other three all being with Shakin' Stevens) and Lionel Bart's third as a writer (once before, obviously, with 'Living Doll' and once with Anthony Newley - see no. 100).

Although the vocal performance on the 1986 version by Cliff and Hank's lead-guitar work were beyond criticism, it has to be said that the anarchic contributions of the Young Ones was the major selling factor. Nigel Planer, Adrian Edmondson, Rik Mayall and Christopher Ryan had established themselves both collectively and individually as leaders of Alternative Comedy and they were at their destructive best on 'Living Doll', both on record and in the video. They reappeared as cod heavy metal act Bad News in 1987, causing great damage to Queen's 'Bohemian Rhapsody'. Planer (who played Che Guevara during the West End run of *Evita*) had a number two in 1984 with 'Hole In My Shoe' in his guise as moronic hippie, neil.

568

A DIFFERENT CORNER

GEORGE MICHAEL

19 April 1986, for 3 weeks

●●●

EPIC A 7033

Writer: George Michael
Producer: George Michael

With this single, the fabulously successful George Michael notched up his fifth number one as a writer and producer, and his second in two solo outings. Like 'Careless Whisper' (see no. 537), this was a reflective ballad, in sharp contrast to the uptempo Wham! hits. 'A Different Corner' took a mere three weeks to reach the summit, banging another nail into the Wham! coffin which had already been assembled via George's March announcement that the duo's days together would end in June.

There was still one more Wham! chart-topper to come (see no. 572), but the success of 'A Different Corner' naturally provided a superb launch-pad for George's official solo career. Much interest centred around the release of the third George Michael single, as he seemed a dead cert to equal the best-ever starts to a singles career by Gerry and the Pacemakers in 1963 and Frankie Goes To Hollywood in 1984, both acts having hit number one with their first three releases. Alas, George narrowly missed this distinction, partly because his next single, 'I Want Your Sex', received only restricted airplay because of its lyrical content. George maintained that it was a plea for safe sex and monogamy, but opposition was just enough to spoil his track record. His next single, 'Faith', released in autumn 1987, also fell just short of the ultimate honour.

'A Different Corner' was the first single to be issued in the United States as a George Michael record. It climbed to number seven.

569

ROCK ME AMADEUS

FALCO

10 May 1986, for 1 week

●

A&M AM 278

Writers: Rob Bolland, Ferdi Bolland and Falco
Producers: Rob Bolland and Ferdi Bolland

Falco, born in Vienna as Johann Holzel, is the most successful pop export Austria has ever produced, in as much as he is the first native of that country to reach number one in both Britain and America. However, mention must be made here of Anton Karas, whose *The Third Man* music ('The Harry Lime Theme') made number one in America in 1950, and probably would have done in Britain had record charts been in operation then.

The song that elevated Falco to worldwide attention was his tribute to another Austrian, whose musical achievements put even Falco and Karas into the shade, viz Wolfgang Amadeus Mozart. The Peter Shaffer play *Amadeus,* about the rivalry between Mozart and fellow composer Salieri, had been an international hit in the early 80s, and by the time Falco's dance smash had broken around the world, there can have been few unaware of the great composer's middle name. Purchasers of Falco's album, *Falco 3*, were treated to a potted history of Mozart during the eight-minute-plus mix of 'Rock Me Amadeus', recited in English by a voice bearing a remarkable resemblance to Kermit the Frog, but the American edit mix that topped the singles lists concentrated on rhythm rather than history.

Falco's first breakthrough outside German-speaking territories came in 1983, when a song he co-wrote and recorded, 'Der Kommissar', went Top 5 in the United States. It was, however, an English act, After The Fire, who had the hit; Falco's own version was a Top 10 dance item, but an English translation by After The Fire leader Andrew Piercy made the difference as far as the pop charts were concerned. Neither version made much impact in the UK. Falco had a second consecutive US dance hit with 'Maschine Brennt', but after that zilch until 'Rock Me Amadeus'.

His immediate follow-up, 'Vienna Calling', was a substantial hit in both Britain and America, but subsequent releases – though often enormous hits in Germany, Austria and Switzerland – have made little impression. Mozart remains internationally popular.

570

THE CHICKEN SONG

SPITTING IMAGE

17 May 1986, for 3 weeks

●●●

VIRGIN SPIT 1

Writers: Philip Pope, Robert Grant and Doug Naylor
Producer: Philip Pope

From the *Economist* magazine to the top of the charts is an unusual progression, but it was the route taken by Peter Fluck and Roger Law, the inventors and designers of the Spitting Image puppets, whose late-night Sunday television show, *Spitting Image,* is compulsory viewing for politicians and other public figures who are the likely targets of the Fluck and Law lampooning. They began with designing models for the front covers of the *Economist* in the early 70s, but progressed into television in the 80s with what they see as the logical development of political cartooning.

The television shows feature a huge cast of writers and impressionists, and the musical contributions are very often the lowlight of the evening. The simply appalling 'Chicken Song' was written by Philip Pope, star of BBC's award-winning show *KYTV*, and by Doug Naylor and Rob Grant, the creators of another BBC comedy show, *Red Dwarf*. It was designed to be a lampoon of songs like Black Lace's longlasting Eurohit 'Agadoo', but either too many or too few people saw the joke, and Spitting Image's first single shot to the number one spot in only its second week of chart life. 'Agadoo' had peaked at number two.

571

SPIRIT IN THE SKY

DOCTOR AND THE MEDICS

7 June 1986, for 3 weeks

●●●

IRS/MCA IAM 113

Writer: Norman Greenbaum
Producer: Craig Leon

The tenth song to make number one in two different versions was Norman Greenbaum's 1970 chart-topper, 'Spirit In The Sky' (see no. 285), which was resurrected by the band who described themselves as "a cross between Valerie Singleton and a slug". Doctor and the Medics consisted of six multi-coloured people, namely Clive Jackson (known professionally as the Doctor), sisters Collette and Wendi (the Anadin Brothers), Steve the guitarist, Vom the drummer and Richard Searle on bass. Their first single was 'The Druids Are Coming,' with the even more paranoid title 'The Goats Are Trying To Kill Me' on the flip-side. If the Druids ever came, it was without the great British public knowing anything about it, as the record failed to get anywhere the charts.

The 6'5" Doctor (a fully qualified St. John's Ambulance Brigade first aider) is one of the tallest people ever to reach the top of the charts, but, despite the ease with which his group accomplished the feat with their first hit, subsequent singles made less rapid headway. The follow-up, also from their first album, *Laughing At The Pieces*, was called 'Burn', but failed to catch fire, and was extinguished at number 29. Their next chart hit was another revival of a previous number one, this time Abba's 'Waterloo' (see no. 348), for which they enlisted the help of another highly painted and flared-trousered number one hitmaker, Roy Wood. It proved to be their Waterloo, their final battle with the charts.

572

THE EDGE OF HEAVEN

WHAM!

28 June 1986, for 2 weeks

●●

EPIC FIN 1

Writer: George Michael
Producer: George Michael

The final official Wham! single release followed the golden route taken by three of the previous four to the top of the pops. It had been over six months since Wham!'s penultimate winner, 'I'm Your Man' (see no. 560), but, hardly a cold spell for George Michael, who had the solo 'A Different Corner' slotted into the number one position almost exactly halfway between the two final Wham! offerings (see no. 568). He was now moving into the very big league indeed, with six number ones under his belt.

The 7-inch version of 'The Edge Of Heaven', which featured Elton John on piano, initially appeared only in double-pack form with the second disc headed by 'Where Did Your Heart Go', a cover of a Was (Not Was) song. Before long the two A-sides were issued on one disc, at which stage 'The Edge Of Heaven' became the A-side of the A-sides, for those who were either too slow or too unenthusiastic to purchase 'Battlestations' and a reworking of 'Wham! Rap' (both Michael songs).

Wham! went out in style at the end of June in front of 72,000 fans at Wembley Stadium for 'The Final' show (Elton John again making a guest appearance). Their farewell album (also called *The Final*) was a compilation of some of their greatest cuts and was available as either a straightfoward double LP or as a super-glamorous boxed set with gold-vinyl discs and items of Wham! memorabilia. Both sold prodigously. That was it for the duo who had gone about as far as they could go in just four years (less than two in America). George Michael continued to be a major force in the music industry (see nos. 671 and 678), Andrew Ridgeley somewhat less so, but both can be proud to have been half of Wham!.

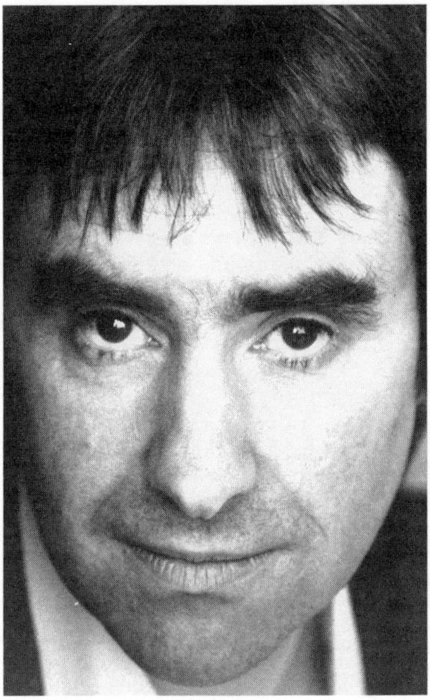

The 1987 single 'The Simple Truth (A Child Is Born)' by CHRIS DE BURGH became the theme song of the 1991 Wembley Arena benefit for Kurdish refugees. (Pictorial Press)

573

PAPA DON'T PREACH

MADONNA

12 July 1986, for 3 weeks

●●●

SIRE W 8636

Writers: Brian Elliott; additional lyrics by Madonna
Producers: Madonna and Stephen Bray

Madonna's second number one was a heart-wrenching song about a girl's plea to her father not to criticize her for becoming pregnant. It was more tuneful and thoughtful than many of her other hits, but still recorded with at least one eye on the dancefloor.

Virtually a year had passed since 'Into The Groove' (see no. 554), but in between her first two number ones Madonna had moved into undisputed worldwide superstardom. She actually had eight Top 5 UK hits in 1985, a record not even matched by Elvis Presley in a calendar year. In that year she also beat, by four chart weeks, Ruby Murray's 30-year-old record of 80 chart weeks in one year by a female artiste (see no. 29). Another major event in her life that took place in 1985 was her marriage to the excitable actor Sean Penn.

True Blue, her third album, featured 'Papa Don't Preach' and indeed two other number one hits. It was itself an instant LP chart-topper when issued in June 1986. The first single from the multi-platinum set was 'Live To Tell' from Penn's film *At Close Range*, in which Madonna did not appear. The 45 narrowly missed repeating its US number one success in the UK. 'Papa Don't Preach', issued just two months later, did not falter at the final hurdle, extending her sequence of consecutive Top 5 hits to 11.

Among the background vocalists on 'Papa Don't Preach' was Siedah Garrett (see no. 596). She warbled on most of the *True Blue* tracks, including all three number one singles (see also nos. 577 and 589).

574

THE LADY IN RED

CHRIS DE BURGH

2 August 1986, for 3 weeks

●●●

A&M AM 331

Writer: Chris de Burgh
Producer: Paul Hardiman

Chris de Burgh, born Christopher John Davidson on 15 October 1950, is an Irishman who spent part of his childhood in Argentina. During the late 1970s and early 80s, he built up an enormous following among album buyers. His first British album chart placing was with his 1981 set, *Best Moves*, and subsequent albums *The Getaway* and *Man On The Line* enjoyed lengthy runs on the charts. With his single releases he was less successful. In Australia, he had a massive smash with 'Don't Pay The Ferryman', which reached only number 48 in Britain, and

'High On Emotion', his only other chart single before 'The Lady In Red', rose higher on foreign emotion than it did on the British stiff upper lip. Still, with the consistent success of his albums (he was the first act to crash into the Swiss album charts at number one) and his worldwide tours, it was only a matter of time before the big hit single arrived in Britain.

In 1986 he released his album *Into The Light*, and the first single from it was the song he wrote for his wife, 'The Lady In Red'. It was undoubtedly the most romantic male vocal since Stevie Wonder's 'I Just Called To Say I Love You', and it crossed over from the mums of Radio Two to the younger singles buyers of Radio One. *Into The Light* became de Burgh's most successful album, and his 1986 British tour was a sellout.

Apart from this one big hit, which hit the Top 10 in America too, it took Chris de Burgh over two years to place another single in the Top 40, when another romantic ballad, 'Missing You', climbed to number three. Chris is not a regular singles hitmaker, but remains a firmly established favourite with his army of album-buying followers.

575

I WANT TO WAKE UP WITH YOU

BORIS GARDINER

23 August 1986, for 3 weeks

●●●

REVUE REV 733

Writer: Mac David
Producer: Willie Lindo

Jamaican Boris Gardiner has had probably the most confusing chart career of any of the number one hitmakers. His first chart hit was in 1970, when an instrumental entitled 'Elizabeth Reggae' crept into the Top 50 (as it then was) for one week and then disappeared. The record was credited to one Byron Lee, whose name was listed as the artist on the labels of the first copies pressed. When the record re-entered the charts a week later, the instrumentalist credited was still Mr. Lee. It was not until the sixth week of its chart life that 'Elizabeth Reggae' was credited to the real performer, Boris Gardiner, but even then his name was spelt Gardner, and it was as Boris Gardner that he was known to British chart freaks until the summer of 1986.

16 years and 87 days after Gardner/Lee fell off the charts, the gentle reggae love ballad 'I Want To Wake Up With You' entered the British charts, and for the first time Boris Gardiner was correctly billed. As if to celebrate, the record quickly swept right to the top, and put Boris at that time third in the list of slowest number one hitmakers, behind Stevie Wonder and Johnny Mathis. Within six months, he had been overtaken by both Jackie Wilson and Ben E. King, but neither of them had hit with both an instrumental and a vocal hit. Of all the number one hitmakers, only Russ Conway, Fleetwood Mac, Manfred Mann, Elton John and the Shadows have had both vocal and instrumental hits, apart from Boris Gardiner.

576

DON'T LEAVE ME THIS WAY

COMMUNARDS WITH SARAH JANE MORRIS

13 September 1986, for 4 weeks

●●●●

LONDON LON 103

Writers: Kenny Gamble, Leon Huff, Carry Gilbert
Producer: Mike Thorne

Bronski Beat's lead singer, James William Horsburgh Somerville, left at the height of his band's success to form the Communards with Richard Coles and an all-girl backing band. After two singles sold disappointingly, it looked as though Jimi had made the wrong commercial move. Then they recruited vocalist Sarah Jane Morris, whose unusually deep voice complemented Somerville's higher-pitched vocal range, and their galloping remake of the Harold Melvin and the Bluenotes Top 5 hit of 1977 climbed to number one and went on to outsell all other singles of 1986. Black soul singer

Thelma Houston had also recorded the song, and, although her Motown version had climbed only to number 13 in Britain, in America she hit the very top, while Harold Melvin's single did not breach the Top 40.

The Communards took their name from the Paris Commune after the Franco-Prussian War, a revolutionary experiment which was proclaimed on 28 March 1871 and crushed exactly two months later. The 1986 Communards were also politically active through their involvement with the Red Wedge, a group of like-minded pop people who toured the country promoting political awareness amongst the young. 'Don't Leave Me This Way' was itself an apolitical song, but was poignantly dedicated to the Greater London Council, which was, at the time, in the process of being abolished.

577

TRUE BLUE

MADONNA

11 October 1986, for 1 week

●

SIRE W 8550

Writers: Madonna and Stephen Bray
Producers: Madonna and Stephen Bray

'True Blue', the title song and third single from Madonna's third album, may only have held down the top spot for one week but it was enough to give Ms. Ciccone a clutch of new chart-history distinctions.

Madonna became the only female recording artist to achieve three number one singles in the UK since Sandie Shaw in 1967. In the 19 years between 'Puppet On A String' (see no. 232) and 'True Blue', only the two young ladies from Abba and Debbie Harry with Blondie had enjoyed nine and five number ones respectively, but throughout that period Sandie's feat had remained unique. Madonna also became only the second female writer to have had a hand in three number ones, equalling Debbie Harry in that respect. Stephen Bray, a mere male, promoted from being plain Steve first time out (see no. 554), achieved his second number one credit with the catchy song with a late-50s feel. 'True Blue' just failed to become Maddie's fifth Stateside number one, but the next single from the album, 'Open Your Heart', which did not go all the way in Britain, did.

In 1986 Madonna starred in a non-musical movie with husband Sean Penn, entitled *Shanghai Surprise*. It was produced by George Harrison's film company, Handmade Films. The main surprise turned out to be that the film flopped. However, this had no effect whatsoever on Madonna's power as a recording star.

578

EVERY LOSER WINS

NICK BERRY

18 October 1986, for 3 weeks

●●●

BBC RESL 204

Writers: Simon May, Stewart James and Bradley James
Producers: Simon May, Stewart James and Bradley James

The soap opera *EastEnders* has proved to be the most successful programme ever shown on BBC television. With audiences just under the 20-million mark, the Tuesday and Thursday episodes regularly took the top two positions in JICTAR ratings throughout 1986, 1987 and 1988. The biggest audiences came in the autumn of 1986, when 17-year-old Michelle, daughter of Arthur and Pauline Fowler and already the mother of 'Dirty Den' Watts' baby, married Lofty Holloway, the asthmatic barman at Den's pub, the Queen Victoria. The saga was spun out over several weeks as first Arthur stole the money to pay for the reception, then Michelle left Lofty standing at the altar but finally decided to go through with the wedding.

Nick Berry played Simon Wicks, fellow barman and best man to Lofty. During the episodes between Michelle jilting Lofty and finally marrying him, Lofty consoled himself by playing again and again 'Every Loser Wins'. The viewers loved it. The record climbed from number 65 to number four in one week, the biggest-ever leap within the charts. It went on to give BBC Records its only number one to date.

Despite the best efforts of Anita Dobson and other *EastEnders* stars, Nick Berry is still the only member of the cast to top the charts since Wendy Richard (aka Pauline Fowler) got there with Mike Sarne back in 1962 (see no. 137). Berry nearly turned the trick a second time in 1992, with a cover of Buddy Holly's 'Heartbeat', the theme to the ITV series of the same name in which he plays a Yorkshire-based policeman in the 1960s.

579

TAKE MY BREATH AWAY

BERLIN

8 November 1986, for 4 weeks

●●●●

CBS A 7320

Writers: Giorgio Moroder and Tom Whitlock
Producer: Giorgio Moroder

Giorgio Moroder's fourth chart-topper as a writer and his third as a producer was the song that won the Academy Award for Best Song at the presentation ceremony in March 1987. 'Take My Breath Away' was the love theme from the Paramount film *Top Gun*, which also featured songs by Kenny Loggins, Teena Marie, Cheap Trick and Harold Faltermeyer. The flip-side of the 7-inch single was credited to "Giorgio Moroder (featuring Joe Pizzulo)", and Berlin themselves were only on CBS by courtesy of Phonogram. All in all, it was not a deliberate part of Berlin's career progression, and yet it gave them their biggest worldwide hit, topping the charts on both sides of the Atlantic.

Berlin, the only chart-topping act named after an European city, are from Los Angeles. They began as a six-piece band, but by the time 'Take My Breath Away' was recorded, they were a three-piece outfit, Terri Nunn on vocals, John Crawford on bass and Rob Brill on drums.

In their second week at number one, the Top 5 singles in Britain all featured female vocalists. Kim Wilde, the Bangles, Mel & Kim and Swing Out Sister were the acts holding onto the positions from two to five, an unprecedented domination of the charts by the fairer sex.

'Take My Breath Away' hit the charts twice more, once in early 1988 and again at the end of 1990, when it climbed back to number three and completed a total of 30 weeks of chart action.

580

THE FINAL COUNT DOWN

EUROPE

6 December 1986, for 2 weeks

●●

EPIC A 7127

Writer: Joey Tempest
Producer: Kevin Elson

The second Swedish act to top the British chart were the five-man rock band Europe. Their music was described by Bjorn Ulvaeus, a member of the first Swedish outfit to take a record to number one in England, as "melodic hard rock... that's the way music should sound today".

Europe arose out of a four-man band formed by Joakim Larsson, called Force. Larsson grew up in the north Stockholm suburb of Upplands Väsby, the fastest-growing industrial and business centre in Sweden. He changed his name to Joey Tempest and in the early 1980s, Force rocked their way through gig after gig, playing mainly Tempest originals based on the sound of 70s bands like Slade and Sweet. In 1982 a Swedish daily newspaper organized a rock band contest, the prize being the chance of a recording contract. Tempest changed the name of his band to Europe, entered the competition and won. From then on, success beckoned ever more strongly.

By 1986 the band had grown to five people - Joey Tempest, Mic Michaeli, Ian Haughland, John Leven and Kee Marcello. Only Tempest survived from the original group Force. 'The Final Countdown' was the band's first big hit outside Sweden. It eventually sold well over two million copies and topped the charts in 13 countries.

581

CARAVAN OF LOVE

HOUSEMARTINS

20 December 1986, for 1 week

•

GO! DISCS GOD 16

Writers: Ernie Isley, Chris Jasper and Marvin Isley
Producer: John Williams

The Isley Brothers spin-off trio Isley Jasper Isley issued their eponymous album in 1985, and one cut from the album, 'Caravan Of Love', brushed the British charts at the end of 1985, climbing to number 52 during its five weeks of chart action. Early in 1986, Hull's most successful four-piece band, the Housemartins, debuted in the charts with the oddly titled 'Sheep', which ran out of support at number 54. Their follow-up, however, was a Top 3 hit, 'Happy Hour'. Norman Cook, Paul Heaton, Stan Cullimore and Hugh Whittaker were suddenly the flavour of the month.

When, at Christmas 1986, the avowedly Christian Housemartins put out an a cappella version of the same song that had proved so mediocre for writers Isley Jasper Isley, nobody was really surprised to see it at the very top of the lists. The only surprise was that it could only hold on for one week before being flattened by the Jackie Wilson phenomenon.

The sleeve notes stated, with great histori-

The HOUSEMARTINS won Best British Newcomer at the BRIT Awards in February 1987, two months after 'Caravan Of Love' reached number one. (Pictorial Press)

cal inaccuracy, that "a cappella is a musical form, using voices alone, which started in the small Northern town of Hull at the beginning of the twentieth century. Suitably shamefaced and apologetic for their dark past involving 'pop' instruments such as the electronic guitar and the electronic bass guitar, the Housemartins now proudly present for your listening pleasure and spiritual regeneration a selection of their favourite a cappella numbers. May they touch your heart. Power to the people. Respect for the steeple". The Housemartins split in 1988, but spawned two more chart-topping bands, Beats International (see no. 642) and Beautiful South (see no. 652).

582

REET PETITE

JACKIE WILSON

27 December 1986, for 4 weeks

●●●●

SMP SKM 3

Writers: Berry Gordy and Tyran Carlo
Producer: Carl Davis

29 years and 42 days after the single first hit the chart at the end of 1957, Jackie Wilson's 'Reet Petite' outsold all other singles in Britain to become the 582nd chart-topper. The 64th number one, 'That'll Be The Day' by the Crickets, was at the top of the charts when 'Reet Petite' originally came into the British Top 30 on 15 November 1957. Its reappearance at the end of 1986 beat all re-issue statistics by several years.

Jack Leroy Wilson was born in Detroit, Michigan, on 9 January 1934, and at first seemed more likely to become a world champion boxer than a million-selling recording star. However, 'Sonny' Wilson's professional welterweight career was less than impressive; he won only two of his ten fights. By 1951, Wilson turned to singing and was soon discovered by Johnny Otis. Billy Ward, then leader of the highly successful Dominoes, also heard and liked Wilson's voice. For five years Wilson was a Domino, firstly singing back-up vocals for lead vocalist Clyde McPhatter, and then, from 1953, singing lead after McPhatter's departure to the Drifters. In 1956, Billy Ward and his Dominoes reached number 13 on the American pop charts with 'St. Therese Of The Roses', the first Jackie Wilson lead vocal to make a national impact. The success of this single encouraged him to go solo, and his very first single was 'Reet Petite', written by Tamla Motown founder Berry Gordy and Jackie Wilson's cousin, Billy Davis, who penned it under the name Tyran Carlo. Although that single was far more successful in Britain, where it reached number six first time out, he was launched on a career that was to bring six American Top 10 hits and 14 other Top 40 hits over the next ten years.

Despite his artistic success, Wilson's life was tragic. On 15 February 1961, he was shot by a fan in New York, and, although he appeared to have made a good recovery, he was never fully fit again. On 29 September 1975, he suffered a massive heart attack while on stage in New Jersey. He fell and hit his head and lapsed into a coma. He eventually regained consciousness, but his health was irreparably damaged. It was almost a mercy when he died, aged 50, on 21 January 1984. Three years later, this great and underrated talent finally hit number one on the charts, with one of the very best of all the British chart-toppers.

583

JACK YOUR BODY

STEVE 'SILK' HURLEY

24 January 1987, for 2 weeks

●●

DJ INTERNATIONAL LON 117

Writer: Steve 'Silk' Hurley
Producer: Steve 'Silk' Hurley

As Sinatra sang, "They do things they don't do on Broadway, in Chicago". The windy city became the birthplace of House Music, a hybrid of Hi-NRG and soul music designed with the feet in mind. House hit the dancefloors of Great Britain in 1986 and the charts via Farley 'Jackmaster' Funk's 'Love Can't Turn Around', a song that borrowed copiously from J.M. Silk's 'I Can't Turn Around'.

J.M. Silk were Keith Nunnally and Steve 'Silk' Hurley, and it was a solo Hurley who took House music to the top of the singles chart for the first time, although officially 'Jack Your Body' should have been an album hit instead. The record sold heavily as a 12-inch, becoming the first number one to register over half its sales in the larger format, but the playing time of the 12-inch disc was over 26 minutes, exceeding Gallup's regulation 25 minutes for a single. The 12-inch record should really have been considered an album, and this being the case, the 7-inch on its own would have peaked at a mere number seven on the singles chart.

Hurley has joined the growing list of one-hit wonders. He nearly added himself to the list of instrumental number ones, which had remained unchanged since Simon Park's 'Eye Level' (see no. 338), but the repetitious chanting of the title words denies 'Jack Your Body' the chance of being considered a true instrumental.

584

I KNEW YOU WERE WAITING (FOR ME)

GEORGE MICHAEL AND ARETHA FRANKLIN

7 February 1987, for 2 weeks

●●

EPIC DUET 2

Writers: Simon Climie and Denis Morgan
Producer: Narada Michael Walden

Aretha Franklin was born on 25 March 1942 in Detroit, one of the five children of the Reverend C.L. Franklin, America's best-selling maker of recorded sermons. Aretha started singing in church before going on to a secular career. Signed to CBS by John Hammond, she broke through on *Aretha* with sides produced by Jerry Wexler. One of these, 'Respect', became a US number one.

However, it took a duet with George Michael to get the Queen Of Soul to the top of the singles chart in Britain, 19 years and 244 days after her solo chart debut. Aretha Franklin's highest placing before 'I Knew You Were Waiting (For Me)' was a number four hit in August 1968, 'I Say A Little Prayer'. For her partner on 'I Knew You Were Waiting (For Me)' the top of the singles chart was not a new position; Michael had visited the peak six times before, four times as half of Wham! and twice as a solo artist in his own right. This was the first of the seven number ones he was involved with which he had neither written nor produced. For producer Narada Michael Walden this was the first of three number ones in 5 months.

585

STAND BY ME

BEN E. KING

21 February 1987, for 3 weeks

●●●

ATLANTIC A9361

Writers: Jerry Lieber, Mike Stoller and Ben E. King
Producers: Jerry Lieber and Mike Stoller

For the second time in two months, a record over 25 years old stood at the very top of the charts. 25 years and 244 days after the record first entered the British lists, 'Stand By Me' peaked at the summit. The reason was that it was featured in the successful Rob Reiner film *Stand By Me*, which gave the late River Phoenix his first major role, and in 1987 rock fans took the chance to give this soul classic a chart placing far more in line with its influence over generations of soul singers than the number 27 slot it had attained in 1961. In the United States, its re-release took the record to number nine, five places lower than it had managed in 1961, but it still became only the third record to hit the American Top 10 on two entirely different occasions - after Chubby Checker's 'The Twist' and Bobby 'Boris' Pickett's 'Monster Mash'.

Ben E. King, born Benjamin Earl Nelson in North Carolina on 28 September 1938, first sang professionally with the New York group the Crowns. In 1959, they were signed to Atlantic as the Drifters, and Ben E. King became the sixth singer in three years to sing lead on a Drifters' single. The new Drifters' first single was 'There Goes My Baby', which failed to chart in Britain despite climbing to number two in America. King's supreme moment with the Drifters was his wonderful lead vocal on 'Save The Last Dance For Me', late in 1960, a record which climbed to number two in Britain and one place higher in their homeland. Even before it reached the top of the charts, King had left the Drifters to go solo, a career he kicked off with the classic soul single 'Spanish Harlem', backed with a lesser tune called 'First Taste Of Love', which was the hit side in England. Then came 'Stand By Me', a record that was covered with remarkable lack of success by Cassius Clay, aka Muhammad Ali, and later taken into the British charts by such diverse talents as Kenny Lynch and John Lennon. King's version was the classic.

586

EVERYTHING I OWN

BOY GEORGE

14 March 1987, for 2 weeks

●●

VIRGIN BOY 100

Writer: David Gates
Producer: Steve Levine

Since his peak of success as lead singer of Culture Club, life had treated George O'Dowd very badly indeed. A very highly publicised and self-destructive involvement with drugs kept Boy George on the front pages of the tabloids for weeks, during which time it seemed not only his career but his life was damaged beyond repair. George had other ideas.

Covering the David Gates song that Ken Boothe had already taken to number one twelve and a half years earlier (see no. 359), Boy George rose very quickly to the top, to make 'Everything I Own' the 11th song to hit number one in two different versions. It was also the first of those 11 songs that did not hit the top at the time it first charted. The original version, by writer Gates' group Bread, peaked at number 32 two years before Ken Boothe's reggae-tinged version climbed to number one. Boy George borrowed the Boothe arrangement rather than a slice of the Bread version.

Culture Club was by now officially dead, but Boy George was launched on a solo career. With 'Everything I Own', he became the first male soloist known professionally only by his first name to top the charts, but none of his next eight hits over a six-year period even reached the Top 10.

587

RESPECTABLE

MEL AND KIM

28 March 1987, for 1 week

●

SUPREME SUPE 111

Writers: Mike Stock, Matt Aitken and Peter Waterman
Producers: Mike Stock, Matt Aitken and Peter Waterman

The first official Stock/Aitken/Waterman production to hit the very top was the second chart single for London-born sisters Mel and Kim Appleby. Kim, born in 1962, was the elder by five years, but both got their start in show business at roughly the same time through modelling assignments. In Mel's case, the most publicised sessions were for *Penthouse* and *Mayfair*, magazines which do not feature a lot of clothing in most of their photographs. Sister Kim was, at the time, working in a clothes factory, which was obviously of

little use to Mel, who preferred the night clubs of London's West End. "We were very streetwise," she says of her life before Stock, Aitken and Waterman.

Their first hit was 'Showing Out (Get Fresh At The Weekend)', which peaked at number three late in 1986. That was followed by 'Respectable', which in turn was followed by their appearance on the Ferry Aid single with which they knocked themselves off the top. Their third single was the title track from their first album, *F.L.M.*, which gave them their third Top 10 hit. Life for Mel and Kim seemed to promise nothing but Fun, Love and Money, but it was not to be. Tragically, Mel Appleby developed cancer and died on 18 January 1990.

588

LET IT BE

FERRY AID

4 April 1987, for 3 weeks

●●●

SUN AID 1

Writers: John Lennon and Paul McCartney
Producers: Mike Stock, Matt Aitken and Peter Waterman

The sixth charity number one was in aid of the relatives and dependents of the victims of the Zeebrugge Ferry disaster. The Townsend Thorensen ship *Herald Of Free Enterprise* capsized on 6 March 1987, killing almost 200 people. Ferry Aid was organized by *The Sun* newspaper, several of whose readers were on board the doomed ship as a result of a cheap travel offer *The Sun* had run. The single contributed over £700,000 to the Fund.

The hit itself created several chart records. It entered at number one, the third charity record to do so, but lasted only seven weeks on the chart in all, equalling the record for the shortest chart run by a number one to that time. It gave Stock, Aitken and Waterman their second consecutive number one as producers, and it gave Lennon his 27th number one as a writer, and McCartney his 26th, placing them even further ahead of the pack. It also became the only song originally released as a single by the Beatles to enjoy a higher chart placing in the cover version. The Beatles' 'Let It Be' had peaked at number two.

Among the number one hitmakers who made up Ferry Aid were Paul McCartney, Mel and Kim (who thus knocked themselves off the top), Kate Bush, Boy George, Suzi Quatro, Alvin Stardust, Bonnie Tyler, Bucks Fizz, Dr and the Medics, Frankie Goes To Hollywood and the New Seekers. Other stars singing along included Kim Wilde, Edwin Starr and Mark Knopfler.

589

LA ISLA BONITA

MADONNA

25 April 1987, for 2 weeks

●●

SIRE W 8378

Writers: Madonna and Patrick Leonard
Producers: Madonna and Patrick Leonard

Madonna's third number one from *True Blue* finally established her as the all-time distaff champ. Her career total of four chart-toppers to this point put her out on her own ahead of Sandie Shaw as far as solo performers were concerned and ahead of Debbie Harry writer-wise. The co-writer and co-producer of 'La Isla Bonita', and keyboard player on the track, was Patrick Leonard, the third male partner for the lady in these two departments in four chart-toppers. Guitarist Bruce Gaitsch was given a writing credit on the album version of 'La Isla Bonita' but not on the single, hence his exclusion from the single's credit (above).

'La Isla Bonita' is a lament for a little island, San Pedro, which appears to be within the tropics and, of course, Spanish or Spanish-speaking. There is no San Pedro island listed in *The Times Atlas Of The World*, which includes some extremely obscure places, so one must assume that the island is either a figment of Madonna's imagination or very small indeed.

Madonna undertook a world tour in 1987 which included concerts in London and

Leeds. The UK press gave her more space and attention than they normally allotted to all the members of the Royal Family combined. Her music received only a small proportion of the coverage, often being ignored by journalists, who were more interested in watching her jog or in her marital problems. Anyone taking time to listen to the *True Blue* album properly would realize that approach to Madonna was unjustified. Underneath all the hoopla was a talented professional very much in control.

590

NOTHING'S GONNA STOP US NOW

STARSHIP

9 May 1987, for 4 weeks

●●●●

GRUNT FB 49757

Writers: Diane Warren and Albert Hammond
Producer: Narada Michael Walden

Narada Michael Walden's production of Starship's 'Nothing's Gonna Stop Us Now', from the hit movie *Mannequin*, marked a remarkable triumph for Starship's lead singer, Grace Slick (born 10 October 1939). Like the Grateful Dead, who achieved their first-ever American Top 10 album in 1987, Slick was at the peak of her fame 20 years earlier as lead singer with Jefferson Airplane, the West Coast hippie band of the late 60s. Jefferson Airplane never had a hit single in Britain, despite a succession of classic releases, two of which ('White Rabbit' and 'Somebody To Love') reached the Top 10 in America. After two massive albums, *Surrealistic Pillow* and *After Bathing At Baxter's*, the band wound down and gradually evolved into Jefferson Starship, led by Slick and Paul Kantner (born 3 March 1941), with former Airplane colleague Marty Balin (born 30 January 1943) back in evidence by the time their 1974 album, *Dragonfly*, was released. In 1975, Balin's composition 'Miracles' took Jefferson Starship to number three in the American singles chart, but there were still no ripples on the other side of the Atlantic.

In 1980, Jefferson Starship finally broke into the British charts with their fifth American hit, 'Jane', which levelled out at number 21. In 1985, they changed their name yet again, to Starship, and kicked off with consecutive American number ones, 'We Built This City' and 'Sara'. Both records were hits in Britain, but neither made the Top 10. In 1987, Starship scored their third American chart-topper and their first in Britain. The title of the song seemed right for Grace Slick and co., 'Nothing's Gonna Stop Us Now'. But in reality seven years later, they still had not had a follow-up hit in Britain.

591

I WANNA DANCE WITH SOMEBODY (WHO LOVES ME)

WHITNEY HOUSTON

6 June 1987, for 2 weeks

●●

ARISTA RIS 1

Writers: George Merrill and Shannon Rubicam
Producer: Narada Michael Walden

To follow her massive album *Whitney Houston*, Miss Houston recorded the album *Whitney* with Narada Michael Walden in the producer's chair for most of the time. The first single from the new album was the 33-letter title 'I Wanna Dance With Somebody (Who Loves Me)', which gave Walden his second consecutive number one production, and his third of the year. When Stock Aitken and Waterman equalled Walden's feat later in the year, 1987 became the first year since 1963 in which two production teams had each produced numbers ones for three different acts.

'I Wanna Dance With Somebody (Who Loves Me)' featured several famous names behind the Houston vocals. Apart from Narada Michael Walden himself, on drums, Michael Jackson's brother Randy played bass synth, and 1975 'Swing Your

Right: WHITNEY HOUSTON strolls across the Wembley Stadium stage at the Nelson Mandela 70th Birthday Party Concert on 11 June 1988. (Pictorial Press)

Daddy' hitmaker Jim Gilstrap sang back-up vocals. Other tracks on the album featured Kenny G on sax, Jellybean in the production booth and Roy Ayers on vibes. Whitney's version of the 545th number one, 'I Know Him So Well', the final track on side two of the album, was in duet with her mother, Cissy Houston.

The singles culled from *Whitney* to follow up her second chart-topper were almost as successful. 'Didn't We Almost Have It All?' hit the Top 20, and 'So Emotional' climbed into the Top 5. Whitney Houston was soon challenging Madonna for the title of the biggest-selling female vocalist in the world.

592

STAR TREKKIN'

THE FIRM

20 June 1987, for 2 weeks

●●

BARK TREK 1

Writers: Grahame Lister and John O'Connor
Producers: Grahame Lister and John O'Connor

The Firm first hit the charts in 1982, with their song in praise of the George Cole character from the TV series *Minder*, 'Arthur Daley ('E's Alright)'. The song was so obviously a one-off hit that no chart fan was surprised when five years went by without further contributions to *British Hit Singles* by the Firm. But, on 6 June 1987, another song based on a long-running television series brought the Firm back into the charts at the lowly position of number 74. The song was a cheerfully lunatic song called 'Star Trekkin'', which put to music the antics of the Starship Enterprise from the television and film series *Star Trek*. All the same, most people would have felt that a song with a tune as subtle as a nursery rhyme and with lyrics about "klingons on the starboard bow" and "life, Jim, but not as we know it" was unlikely to boldly go where only 591 records had gone before - namely to the very top.

But the Firm did just that. The next week, the record had soared to number 13, a rise of 61 places, the second-biggest climb in the history of the charts. One week later, it hit the top spot, becoming only the 20th record to rise from outside the Top 12 straight to the number one spot. It also beat the chart record set by Charlene's 'I've Never Been To Me' (see no. 503), which had entered the charts at number 73, the lowest original chart entry by a number one until the Firm rewrote the record books. Since 'Star Trekkin'' dropped out of orbit, however, their chart career has apparently slipped into a Black Hole.

593

IT'S A SIN

PET SHOP BOYS

4 July 1987, for three weeks

●●●

PARLOPHONE R 6158

Writers: Neil Tennant and Chris Lowe
Producers: Julian Mendelsohn and Stephen Hague

'It's A Sin' was written at the same time as the Pet Shop Boys' previous chart-topper, 'West End Girls' (see no. 563), but was not released until 18 months later. It was the first track released from their album *Actually*, and it stormed to the top in only its second week on the chart. By topping the charts for a second time, the Pet Shop Boys became only the third male duo ever to hit the top more than once, and they eventually caught up with the Everly Brothers and Wham!, each of whom now have four chart-toppers to their credit. Those who wish to count T. Rex as a duo would also add them to that list of quadruple chart-toppers.

Although 'It's A Sin' is an out-and-out disco stomper, it has a serious lyric, inspired by vocalist Neil Tennant's strict Catholic upbringing. His school, St. Cuthbert's Grammar School in Newcastle upon Tyne, may have been a strictly religious one, but it has also become known as something of a breeding ground for pop stars, as Gordon Sumner, aka Sting, was a pupil there a few years before Tennant.

"A real over-the-top Pet Shop Boys record" is how Tennant describes his second chart-topper. "When we were making it, we did not apply any notions of taste." The accompanying video was directed by Derek Jarman in the same vein, with hooded monks, a church consumed by fire and cameos of the seven deadly sins. Their next single, a number two hit featuring Dusty Springfield, was perhaps aptly titled, 'What Have I Done To Deserve This?'.

594

WHO'S THAT GIRL

MADONNA

25 July 1987, for one week

●

SIRE W 8341

Writers: Madonna and Patrick Leonard
Producers: Madonna and Patrick Leonard

Madonna's lead over the field as the all-time female number one champ was extended yet further when the title track from her 1987 movie, *Who's That Girl*, became her fifth British chart-topper, as writer, performer and producer. In all three categories all other solo females trail her.

Who's That Girl was a comedy featuring Griffin Dunne and Sir John Mills. The latter's closest personal links with the hit parade had come in 1962 with his daughter Hayley's transatlantic smash, 'Let's Get Together'. The new film was Madonna's second successive box-office disappointment. Her quite staggering popularity on disc cut no ice with the critics and their lack of enthusiasm was somehow conveyed to the public. Vincent Canby, the film critic of *The New York Times*, wrote a perceptive piece arguing that the essence of Madonna's screen persona had already been captured in her videos, most notably 'Open Your Heart'.

For all that, the single could hardly have been bigger. It kicked off the soundtrack album, which contained three other Madonna titles plus numbers from Duncan Faure, Club Nouveau, Michael Davidson, Scritti Politti and Coati Mundi, and was also a hefty seller.

Right: MADONNA is shown performing on the 'Who's That Girl' tour. (Pictorial Press)

595

LA BAMBA

LOS LOBOS

1 August 1987, for 2 weeks

●●

SLASH/FFRR/LONDON LASH 13

Writer: Traditional, arranged by Ritchie Valens
Producer: Mitchell Froom

Los Lobos were five large Spanish Americans whose revival of the Ritchie Valens classic 'La Bamba' was the first song ever sung completely in Spanish to top the charts. Julio Iglesias' 'Begin The Beguine' (see no. 490) was mainly in Spanish, but 'La Bamba' (Spanish for 'The Goat') was the first chart-topper since the infamous 'Je T'Aime...Moi Non Plus' (see no. 277) to be performed entirely in a foreign language. It was also the title song from the biopic about Ritchie Valens, who died aged 17 in the plane crash that also killed Buddy Holly and the Big Bopper. By taking over at the top from Madonna's 'Who's That Girl', also a film-title song,

MICHAEL JACKSON is shown in action on stage in Tokyo in 1987.

the British charts had consecutive number ones from the movies for the first time since 'Summer Holiday' (see no. 148) was succeeded by 'Foot Tapper' (see no. 149) almost a quarter of a century earlier.

Surprisingly, the song had not been a hit for Valens the first time around, and its only previous appearance on the British charts had been in 1964, when the Crickets took the song to number 21 as what has proved to be their final hit. The Valens version did enjoy a few weeks of chart glory in the summer of 1987, in the wake of Los Lobos' success, and this chart reappearance by the late rock star, 28 years and 142 days after his previous chart entry, created one of the longest gaps between hits ever achieved.

596

I JUST CAN'T STOP LOVING YOU

MICHAEL JACKSON WITH SIEDAH GARRETT

15 August 1987, for two weeks

●●

EPIC 650202

Writer: Michael Jackson
Producers: Quincy Jones and Michael Jackson

Michael Jackson's third solo number one was not a solo hit at all. Taken from *Bad*, the follow-up album to his all-time best seller, *Thriller*, 'I Just Can't Stop Loving You' featured Jacko in duet with Siedah Garrett, a fact that was mentioned on the single's sleeve, but not on the label itself.

Siedah Garrett had earlier sung without credit on Dennis Edwards' 1984 hit, 'Don't Look Any Further', so she was no doubt used to lack of recognition by now. She was also used to the number one spot. Although Michael Jackson had been there four times before (twice solo, once with the Jacksons and once with USA For Africa), so had Siedah. She had sung backing vocals on all of Madonna's chart-toppers except her very first, 'Into The Groove' (see no. 554), and had last been at the top of the charts only 2 weeks earlier, when 'Who's That Girl' (see no. 594) was ruling the roost. Miss Garrett featured on almost all the tracks on Madonna's *True Blue* album, except for 'White Heat', which was the only track on that album to feature Michael's brother Jackie Jackson on background vocals, so it was only by chance that Michael rather than Jackie was the first Jackson she sang with.

Michael Jackson's third number one was rapidly followed by a number three hit when the title track from his album, 'Bad', was released a few weeks later. Sister Janet also hit the Top 10 again in 1987, when her 'Let's Wait Awhile' climbed to number three as one of seven singles from her album, *Control*. The Jackson family have few rivals to the title of Most Charted Family, although at the end of 1987, the leader of their greatest competition in that category, Donny Osmond, was back in the singles chart after a 13-year gap, with 'Groove'.

597

NEVER GONNA GIVE YOU UP

RICK ASTLEY

29 August 1987, for 5 weeks

●●●●●

RCA PB 41447

Writers: Mike Stock, Matt Aitken and Peter Waterman
Producers: Mike Stock, Matt Aitken and Peter Waterman

Rick Astley, born in the Lancashire town of Newton-le-Willows on 6 February 1966, became the third act shaped by the hot production team of Stock Aitken and Waterman to hit the top in 1987. Like the first of those acts, Mel and Kim (see no. 587), Rick Astley also appeared as part of the second act, Ferry Aid (see no. 588), but, being a complete unknown at the time, got little of the publicity. 'Never Gonna Give You Up' was Astley's first-ever solo single and, from the outset, RCA were confident they had a massive hit on their hands. By the time it had kept all competition at bay for five weeks (the longest stay on top since Jennifer Rush's 'The Power Of Love'), the record had out-sold all other singles of 1987 and launched Astley on what promised to be a very successful career. His second single, 'Whenever You Need Somebody', crashed into the chart at number 11, but could climb only to number three. It did, however, help to earn him a slot on the *Miss World* TV show in November 1987, which further boosted his public exposure.

Astley had graduated from playing drums with a band called FBI to singing lead with them - the same progression that Phil Collins made through Genesis - when he was spotted by Peter Waterman in a northern club in 1985. It took two years after that for the single to come to fruition, but the wait was worth it for Astley, Stock, Aitken and Waterman.

598

PUMP UP THE VOLUME/ANITINA (THE FIRST TIME I SEE SHE DANCE)

M/A/R/R/S

3 October 1987, for 2 weeks

●●

4AD AD 707

Writers: 'Pump Up The Volume' – Steven and Martin Young, A.R. Kane, C.J. Mackintosh, John Fryer and Dave Darrell; 'Anitina (The First Time I See She Dance)' – A.R. Kane and Colourbox
Producer: Martin Young

The legal profession looked set to become the prime beneficiary of the dance smash 'Pump Up The Volume' created by members of two groups signed to the avant-garde label 4AD, home of the Cocteau

Twins, the Birthday Party, This Mortal Coil, Colourbox and A.R. Kane, among others. M/A/R/R/S was an amalgamation of the latter two acts plus scratch DJ C.J. Mackintosh, under the supervision of Colourbox producer/leader Martyn Young.

The aspect of the record that excited the lawyers was the fact that 'Pump Up The Volume' sampled sounds from other recordings. This technique, the electronic process of lifting sounds from one record and inserting them into another, had become a common feature of dance records by 1987. The trouble with 'Pump Up The Volume' was that Pete Waterman of the phenomenally successful Stock Aitken Waterman production team felt that Young's use of a second or two of a Stock Aitken Waterman hit (under their own name), 'Roadblock', was a breach of their copyright. When Young in retaliation claimed that SAW had nicked some of 'Pump Up The Volume' on a remix of a dance hit by Sybil, battle was joined. At one point an injunction placed by Waterman on the M/A/R/R/S single prevented 'Pump Up The Volume' from being distributed for five days. This almost certainly kept Stock Aitken Waterman protégé Rick Astley (see no. 597) on top for one more week than might otherwise have been the case, though, of course, this had not been the motive behind Waterman's injunction.

'Anitina (The First Time I See She Dance)' was listed as being at number one together with this controversial slice of sound, but clearly 'Pump Up The Volume' was the side that sold the single.

M/A/R/R/S remain one-hit wonders to this day, although C.J. Mackintosh continues as an in-demand remixer and DJ.

599

YOU WIN AGAIN

BEE GEES

17 October 1987, for 4 weeks

●●●●

WARNER BROTHERS W8351

Writers: Barry, Robin and Maurice Gibb
Producers: Arif Mardin with Barry, Robin and Maurice Gibb; co-produced by Brian Tench

The return of the Bee Gees to the top of the charts, eight years and 215 days after their previous, fourth, number one (see no. 434) established more chart records for the Manx-born brotherhood Gibb. Only five acts had, to that time, ever suffered a lean period of more than seven years between number one hits, and when 'You Win Again' climbed to the top, the Bee Gees joined that list for the second time. The gap between their second and third number ones had been even longer, 9 years and 231 days. 'You Win Again', the first single release from their album *E.S.P.*, finally fell from the top 20 years and 34 days after their first chart-topper, 'Massachusetts' (see no. 238) reached number one, making them only the third act, after Elvis and Cliff, to achieve a 20-year span of number one hits. The record was the seventh number one written by Barry and Robin Gibb (and the sixth for Maurice), putting Barry and Robin behind only Lennon, McCartney, Andersson and Ulvaeus on the all-time list of successful writers. The three brothers in harness, with six co-written number ones, rank just behind the Lennon/McCartney and Jagger/Richard partnerships.

'You Win Again' stayed on top for four weeks, equalling the longest run at number one by any Bee Gees hit, bringing them level with Rod Stewart and T. Rex at the top of the list of acts who have hit number one on the most labels - three.

Left: The BEE GEES harmonize at New York's Radio City Music Hall. (Pictorial Press)

600

CHINA IN YOUR HAND

T'PAU

14 November 1987, for 4 weeks

●●●●

SIREN SRN 64

Writers: Carol Decker and Ron Rogers
Producer: Roy Thomas Baker

Thirty-five years to the day after the British charts were first published in the *New Musical Express*, the Shropshire band T'Pau claimed the sixth hundredth number one with the second release from their debut album, *Bridge Of Spies*. T'Pau (the name is that of Mr. Spock's Vulcan friend in the *Star Trek* TV series) took the tapes of their album to most of the record companies in Britain, and were turned down by most of the record companies in Britain before being signed by Siren, a Virgin company. At first it seemed that most of the record companies in Britain were right to have turned down T'Pau because when their first single, 'Heart And Soul', was released in January 1987, it sank more quickly than the *Titanic*. However, a month or two later, it resurfaced in America, and eventually reached the Top 5 on both sides of the Atlantic. T'Pau were songwriters Carol Decker (vocals) and her boyfriend Ron Rogers (rhythm guitar and some bits), as well as

Tim Burgess (drums and percussion), Michael Chetwood (keyboards), Paul Jackson (bass) and the native Shropshire lad Taj Wyzgowski, who played 'guitar solos and other bits'. When 'China In Your Hand' leapt from number five to number one on 14 November, producer Roy Thomas Baker achieved a chart-topper for the first time since his classic mega-production, 'Bohemian Rhapsody', 12 years earlier.

601

ALWAYS ON MY MIND

PET SHOP BOYS

19 December 1987, for 4 weeks

●●●●

PARLOPHONE R 6171

Writers: Mark James, Johnny Christopher, Wayne Thompson
Producers: Julian Mendelsohn and Pet Shop Boys, with thanks to David Jacob

'Always On My Mind' is the song that links the Pet Shop Boys with Brenda Lee. Although it was earlier associated in Britain with Elvis Presley, it was Little Miss Dynamite who first charted with the song in 1972. Still under 30, and seven years after the last of her 22 British hits, Lee graced the middle reaches of the country chart with her performance just before she rejuvenated her career with a string of six consecutive Top 10 country hits.

Elvis did slightly better, denting the Top 20 of the country list, but the song was not a pop hit in America until Willie Nelson's laid-back interpretation loped to number five in 1982.

In Britain, however, the Presley platter reached number nine in 1973, his only Top 10 hit of that year. Fourteen years later the Pet Shop Boys appeared on a television special called *Love Me Tender* in which contemporary artists were each asked to perform a song associated with Elvis to commemorate the tenth anniversary of his death. The Pets' dance version of the ballad caused such a stir it was released as a single, in advance of its appearance on any album. It entered the chart at four and then lodged at number one for four weeks. It peaked at four in America, where it was the last of the duo's five Top 10 hits.

As for Brenda Lee, who had enjoyed two US number ones in 1960, it was her only vicarious voyage to the top in the UK, where her best position of three was achieved by 'Speak To Me Pretty'.

602

HEAVEN IS A PLACE ON EARTH

BELINDA CARLISLE

16 January 1988, for 2 weeks

●●

VIRGIN VS 1036

Writers: Rick Nowels and Ellen Shipley
Producer: Rick Nowels

Belinda Carlisle's first hit in Britain was her biggest on both sides of the Atlantic. Carlisle, born 17 August 1958, had been a member of the Go-Gos from 1978 until the group split up in 1985, during which time their only UK hit was 'Our Lips Are Sealed', which peaked just outside the Top 40 in 1982.

The following year, the Funboy Three took the song into the Top 10. 'Heaven Is A Place On Earth' was a track from Carlisle's second solo album, and despite the fact that the first one, *Belinda*, missed out completely in Britain, the lead track from the second LP raced to the top of the charts. Since then, her career has continued with great success, including a number one album with *The Best Of Belinda Volume 1* in 1992.

'Heaven Is A Place On Earth' was the first UK chart-topper to be written by Nowels and Shipley, who also sang back up vocals. Helping them out were two other women with more experience of being on top of the charts - Michelle Phillips of the Mamas and Papas, and Diane Warren, co-writer of Starship's 'Nothing's Gonna Stop Us Now'.

603

I THINK WE'RE ALONE NOW

TIFFANY

30 January 1988, for 3 weeks

●●●

MCA 1211

Writer: Ritchie Cordell
Producer: George E. Tobin

American chanteuse Tiffany Darwisch reached the top with the second revival of a late 60s Tommy James & the Shondells song to hit the upper reaches of the British charts within three months. Billy Idol's 'Mony Mony' (number seven at the end of October 1987) was the first.

Growing up in California, Tiffany started singing at the age of eight. By 12 she had met producer George Tobin, responsible for Robert John's 1979 US number one, 'Sad Eyes', and Smokey Robinson's 1981 UK list leader, 'Being With You'. She was the first artist in America to cultivate an audience by singing at large shopping malls. Indeed, her first live appearance in Britain took place at Newcastle's Eldon Square Shopping Centre.

It was George Tobin who introduced Tiffany to 'I Think We're Alone Now'. Although Lene Lovich had managed a perfectly modern new-wave version, the teenager initially thought the song was old fashioned, and was unenthusiastic about recording it. Tobin prevailed, and her update reached number one on both sides of the Atlantic. An album simply titled *Tiffany* sold four million copies in America. When a follow-up from it, 'Could've Been', also topped the *Billboard* Hot 100, Darwisch had become the youngest female artist in American chart history to have two consecutive number ones.

The double header was not to be in Britain, where 'Could've Been' peaked at four. Her next release, 'I Saw Him Standing There', was the first version of the Lennon/McCartney standard to reach the Top 10 in both the US and the UK, albeit with a gender change. The material from Tiffany's second album, *Hold An Old Friend's Hand*, came nowhere near having the same impact as that of the first, and the artist was overtaken by her early support act, New Kids On The Block.

604

I SHOULD BE SO LUCKY

KYLIE MINOGUE

20 February 1988, for 5 weeks

●●●●●

PWL PWL 8

Writers: Mike Stock, Matt Aitken, Pete Waterman
Producers: Mike Stock, Matt Aitken, Pete Waterman

In 1988 a 19-year-old Australian actress took advantage of Madonna's 'year off' to establish herself as the most popular female vocalist in Britain. Kylie Minogue was born on 28 May 1968 in Melbourne, daughter of an Australian accountant father and Welsh mother. By her tenth birthday the precocious Minogue had landed her first acting role as a Dutch girl in the Aussie TV soap opera *The Sullivans*, followed by a stint in two other soaps, *Skyways*, which also featured her future colleague Jason Donovan, and *The Hendersons*.

It was not until she had left school in 1986 that she was offered the part that was to make her famous - Charlene Ramsey in *Neighbours*. The show rapidly became a hit in her native country, topping the ratings and earning Kylie five Logies, the Australian TV industry awards. Her new-found celebrity status led to an invitation to appear at an Australian Rules football game in Sydney where she sang Little Eva's 'The Loco-Motion'. The performance attracted the attention of the Mushroom label, who promptly gave her a contract and rush released the recording. An instant success, it spent seven weeks atop the national charts and became the best-selling single of the 80s in her homeland.

Meanwhile *Neighbours* was being shown in Britain on BBC TV four times a week and was regularly attracting audiences of over 14 million. Aware of her recording success in Australia, the astute Pete Waterman asked Minogue along to his London studios, where he cut 'I Should Be So Lucky'. Turned down by every

Right: KYLIE MINOGUE was lucky enough to be the top chart star of 1988. (Pictorial Press)

major record company, an exasperated Waterman invested in his own record label, PWL (Pete Waterman's Label), and released the disc. The majors ended up with egg on their face as Kylie's debut release moved to the top of the charts for a five-week residency.

605

DON'T TURN AROUND

ASWAD

26 March 1988, for 2 weeks

●●

ISLAND IS 341

Writers: Diane Warren and Albert Hammond
Producer: Chris Porter

Aswad, which means 'black' in Arabic, is one of the greatest examples of hard work and tenacity paying off in British popular music. Formed as a five-piece in 1975, they became a trio in 1986, the members being vocalist Brinsley Forde, guitarist Tony Gad and drummer Angus 'Drummie' Zeb. Forde had been a children's television star in the 1971 BBC series *Here Come The Double Deckers* and had gone on to appear in the 1980 film *Babylon*, to which Aswad supplied music. The movie studied the problems of young blacks living in London, and could be called the first British reggae film. Aswad were certainly the first UK reggae band to be signed by a major label when they briefly appeared on CBS in the early 80s. It was through relentless touring, however, that they solidified their reputation as one of the nation's leading reggae groups. Their live act was so effective that in the second half of the 80s they managed to get audiences standing and singing at events ranging from an Amnesty International benefit at the London Palladium to Cliff Richard's *The Event* show at Wembley Stadium. It was at the Amnesty concert that they met Jackson Browne, who asked them to join him on his song 'When The Stone Begins To Turn' on his *World In Motion* album.

Aswad's own big hit came in 1988, when they issued 'Don't Turn Around'. The song had first appeared as the B-side of Tina Turner's 'Typical Male'. Co-writer Diane Warren was rated America's top songwriter of 1991 and 1993, but several of her hits did not duplicate their success in Britain. It was, therefore, not surprising that 'Don't Turn Around', a UK number one, remained uncharted in the US until 1994, when Ace Of Base followed up their American number one, 'The Sign', with the song.

606

HEART

PET SHOP BOYS

9 April 1988, for 2 weeks

●●

PARLOPHONE R 6177

Writers: Neil Tennant and Chris Lowe
Producers: Andy Richards and Pet Shop Boys

The fourth UK number one for the former students of architecture and politics tied the record held by Wham! and the Everly Brothers for the most number one hits by a male duo. The Pets just missed setting a new mark when 'Go West' peaked at two in 1993. 'Heart' marked the beginning of the end of the pair's sales success in America, though. Always devoted to the cutting edge of dance music, which Neil Tennant considered the most forward-looking popular music, the pair now found themselves going in a different direction from American pop, and 'Heart' was not a hit there.

The noteworthy video for 'Heart' was shot in Yugoslavia with the noted, and later knighted, actor Ian McKellen taking the role of a character similar to Dracula. For stage performances a backing film by the celebrated director Derek Jarman was shown.

'Heart' was written by the Pet Shop Boys with the intention of submitting it to Madonna. Fearing the possible disappointment of rejection, however, they recorded it themselves. They need not have worried. Starting 1988 at number one with 'Always On My Mind' and returning later with 'Heart', the Pet Shop Boys were the only act to have more than one number one during the calendar year. Inactive herself, Madonna had no new hits during that twelve-month period.

607

THEME FROM S EXPRESS

S EXPRESS

30 April 1988, for 2 weeks

●●

RHYTHM KING LEFT 21

Writers: Mark Moore and Pascal Gabriel
Producers: Mark Moore and Pascal Gabriel

If Tony Blackburn, Chris Hill and Dave Lee Travis had been the first wave of the DJ recording stars, then the second wave arrived in the latter half of the 80s. The likes of Dave Dorrell and C.J. Mackintosh's M/A/R/R/S, Tim Simenon's Bomb The Bass and Mark Moore's S Express were at the forefront of turning the record spinners into the hit- makers. Like Dorell and Simenon, Moore honed his career as a DJ behind the decks at London's Wag Club.

A pastiche of Rose Royce's 'Is It Love You're After' and 'Rose Royce Express', the 'Theme From S Express', produced by Moore and the emerging Pascal Gabriel, with its distinctive "enjoy this trip... countdown is progressing" introduction, was an instant radio hit with the capital's network of pirate radio stations prior to its release on the independent Rhythm King label. "I wanted the song to be a disco record with 70s influences but an 80s feel, in the same way that rap records use old riffs but they're still 80s records," Moore remarked at the time. "We revive sounds that have gone and been forgotten. What annoys me is all these records that simply use what everyone else is using... there should be a moral time limit before you can use a sound in a record!"

S Express, the London-based retro-disco outfit comprising Moore, singer Michelle and dancer, percussionist and vocalist Chilo Harlo, took only three weeks to hit the top after debuting at number 25, and in doing so gave Rhythm King their first and, to date, only chart-topper. Subsequent releases from the group included the Top 10 singles 'Superfly Guy' (number five) and 'Hey Music Lover' (number six).

608

PERFECT

FAIRGROUND ATTRACTION

14 May 1988, for 1 week

●

RCA PB 41845

Writer: Mark E. Nevin
Producers: Fairground Attraction and Kevin Moloney

Three Sassenach blokes and a Glaswegian lady, Eddi Reader (born Glasgow, 29

Things weren't 'Perfect' after all, and Eddi Reader left FAIRGROUND ATTRACTION after their first album. (Pictorial Press)

August 1959) appeared from nowhere in the spring of 1988 with 'Perfect', a striking skiffle-flavoured song written by one of their number, guitarist Mark E. Nevin. Simon Edwards on guitaron (a Mexican acoustic bass) and Roy Dodds behind the drum kit completed the quartet. A second Top 10 single, 'Find My Love', followed, but despite a huge-selling album, *The First Of A Million Kisses*, critical approval and a batch of music industry awards, the promise was never fulfilled.

Reader was an art student who had moved to London in 1983. She had sung with Eurythmics and teamed up with Nevin in 1985, after he had begun to establish himself with Jane Aire and the Belvederes and with Sandie Shaw's mid-80s comeback. Fairground Attraction was created around Nevin's quirky, jazzy compositions with the addition of Edwards and Dodds, the latter a jazz drummer of vast experience, including stretches with Terence Trent d'Arby and Working Week.

Reader became pregnant and left the band shortly before the comparative failure of their second album, *Ay Fond Kiss*. She moved into a solo career which included acting opposite Guy Mitchell in the 1990 BBC TV series, *Your Cheatin' Heart*, based around the Scottish country-music scene. Nevin continued to write, play and produce with such artists as Kirsty MacColl, to whose excellent 1994 album, *Titanic Days*, he made several writing and instrumental contributions.

609

WITH A LITTLE HELP FROM MY FRIENDS/ SHE'S LEAVING HOME

WET WET WET/BILLY BRAGG WITH CARA TIVEY

21 May 1988, for 4 weeks

●●●●

CHILDLINE CHILD 1

Writers: (both sides) John Lennon and Paul McCartney
Producers: 'With A Little Help From My Friends' – Wet Wet Wet/'She's Leaving Home' – John Porter and Kenny Jones

The *New Musical Express*, publishers of the first British record chart back in 1952, was instrumental in assembling a powerful line-up of recording stars to reinterpret the songs from the Beatles' 1967 masterpiece, *Sergeant Pepper's Lonely Hearts Club Band*, in aid of Esther Rantzen's anti-child abuse charity Childline. The resulting album, *Sergeant Pepper Knew My Father*, was only a modest success but two tracks out on their own quickly moved to the top of the singles chart. The Housemartins (see no. 581) were originally scheduled to cut 'With A Little Help From My Friends', which had been a number one for Joe Cocker in 1968 (see no. 260), but were unable to meet the recording deadline. Wet Wet Wet stepped in and cleaned up on behalf of the charity.

The four-man band from Clydebank, Marti Pellow (vocals), Graeme Clarke (bass), Tom Cunningham (drums) and Neil Mitchell (keyboards), first made an impact in 1987 with the single 'Wishing I Was Lucky', and within 12 months were one of the country's top pin-up groups. Their musical abilities, notably Pellow's distinctive white soul vocals, entitle them to more than teen worship and to a certain extent they have achieved this in Britain and Europe.

Billy Bragg chose 'She's Leaving Home' because (a) the lyrics were relevant to the cause, and (b) he reckoned he could play it. Born in Barking on 12 December 1957, Bragg has mixed radical politics and acerbic pop to great effect ever since the release of his album *Life's A Riot With Spy*

Vs. Spy early in 1984. 'She's Leaving Home' was by far the biggest singles dent he had made, though he self-deprecatingly refers to it as a 'modest number one', with most TV and radio shows preferring to program the more teen-friendly Wets. Cara Tivey, according to Bragg, made every noise on the track apart from lead vocal, primarily her own piano arrangement, and Billy's leg wiggles on *Top Of The Pops* were not an Elvis tribute but an attempt to waft the dry ice away from his lyric sheet. For once, he must have cursed his resistance to miming.

610

DOCTORIN' THE TARDIS

TIMELORDS

18 June 1988, for 1 week

●

KLF COMMUNICATIONS KLF 003

Writers: Mike Chapman, Nicky Chinn, Ron Grainer, Gary Glitter, Mike Leander, Timelords
Producers: Timelords

The Timelords are, to date, one-hit wonders but their component parts are certainly not. A weird combination of Gary Glitter's 'Rock And Roll Part Two' (which made number two in 1972), with the less-than-complex lyric of that immortal chant changed to an equally taxing "Doctor Who - the Tardis", intermingled with Ron Grainer's familiar theme from the beloved television series and the odd noise sampled from past Chapman-Chinn masterpieces, spirited Bill Drummond and Jim Cauty in their Timelords guise to one week of singles supremacy.

The two have achieved far greater notoriety as the Kopyright Liberation Front - the KLF (see no. 659). Bill Drummond was born William Butterworth on 29 April 1953 in South Africa. He co-founded the important indie label Zoo in the late 70s, and subsequently managed Echo and the Bunnymen and the Teardrop Explodes. Cauty, a year younger, moved from mid-80s chart band Brilliant to work with Drummond, firstly as the JAMMS - Justified Ancients Of Mu Mu, a name lifted from the Shea-Wilson conspiracy novels that dealt with the Illuminati. Their anarchic approach to the pop world, later used to more devastating effect under the KLF banner, was illustrated shortly after the Timelords' success by their book, *How To Have A Number One The Easy Way*. This included the advice to buy a copy of *The Guinness Book Of British Hit Singles* to help choose songs to be cannibalised for the number one.

Gary Glitter's appreciation of their use of his work was illustrated by the fact that he joined the duo on some of the rare occasions they performed the record. The *Doctor Who* theme, in a more conventional setting, was a number 25 hit for Mankind in 1978.

611

I OWE YOU NOTHING

BROS

25 June 1988, for 2 weeks

●●

CBS ATOM 4

Writers: Bros (Matt and Luke Goss and Craig Logan)
Producer: Nicky Graham

Twins Matt and Luke Goss were born in Peckham, south London, on 29 September 1968, and by the time they were 12 years old they had decided to become pop stars. While at school they teamed up with Craig Logan (born 22 April 1969, Fife, Scotland), who played bass guitar, while Luke drummed and Matt sang the slushy love songs they wrote for their first group, Caviar. They persevered until, aged 18, they attracted the attention of manager Tom Watkins whose principal clients were the Pet Shop Boys.

'I Owe You Nothing' was their first release in the summer of 1987. Its chart failure did not stop the band's good looks from attracting the attention of the teenage pop press and the coverage reached saturation point when Bros's second single, the aptly titled 'When Will I Be Famous?', reached number two in February 1988. Bros established themselves as the biggest home-grown teen idols since the break-up of Wham! when their third single, 'Drop The Boy', also reached number two. With the boys attracting ever increasing amounts of hys-

The titles of the first four BROS hits were prophetic. After 'When Will I Be Famous?', they were. After 'Drop The Boy', Matt and Luke soon said goodbye to Craig. As for 'I Owe You Nothing', they didn't after they offered him a golden handshake. As Craig no doubt stated, 'I Quit'. (Pictorial Press)

teria, it was no surprise when a re-released 'I Owe You Nothing' became their first, and only, number one in June 1988.

Their debut album, *Push*, sold over a million copies in the UK and produced two more Top 5 singles but, at the height of their fame, Craig quit the group in early 1989, claiming he was exhausted. A lengthy legal dispute followed, compounded by an acrimonious decision by Matt and Luke to dispense with Watkins' services. The 1989 'comeback' produced a further three Top 10 singles, but the press mercilessly pursued the fact that their heyday as pop idols was over. A change of direction to a more mature style in 1991 produced disappointing results, and Matt and Luke agreed to split in early 1993.

612

NOTHING'S GONNA CHANGE MY LOVE FOR YOU

GLENN MEDEIROS

9 July 1988, for 4 weeks

●●●●

LONDON LON 184

Writers: Michael Masser, Gerry Goffin
Producer: Jay Stone

Glenn Medeiros, born on 24 June 1970, was only just 18 years old when his first record topped the charts, but he had recorded it two years earlier, in May 1986. Medeiros was raised on the Hawaiian island of Kauai, and early in 1986 he entered a local radio talent contest, singing 'Nothing's Gonna Change My Love For You', a song he had first heard on a George Benson album. He won the contest, and recorded the song on a local Hawaiian label. A visiting radio executive from KZZP Phoenix Arizona heard the song and took the record back to Phoenix. The song was as popular in Phoenix as it had been in Hawaii, and at the beginning of 1987, it was released in mainland USA on the Amherst label. It climbed to number 12, but was not released in Britain until over a year later. Then it took just four more weeks to hit the very top, giving veteran Brill Building songwriter Gerry Goffin his first-ever number one hit in Britain.

Medeiros' follow-up just missed the Top 40. It was not until another two years had passed, in June 1990, that Medeiros came back strongly, with a record which mirrored the chart success of 'Nothing's Gonna Change My Love For You'. It was a duet with Bobby Brown called 'She Ain't Worth It', which hit number one in America but stopped at number 12 in Britain.

613

THE ONLY WAY IS UP

YAZZ AND THE PLASTIC POPULATION

6 August 1988, for 5 weeks

●●●●●

BIG LIFE BLR 4

Writers: George Jackson, Johnny Henderson
Producers: Coldcut (Matt Black and Jonathan Moore)

Born 19 May 1963, Yasmin Evans, the distinctive bleached blonde model, first teamed up with the Coldcut production team of Matt Black and Jonathan Moore for 'Doctorin' The House', a number six hit from February 1988. She switched from Coldcut's own Ahead Of Our Time label to the expanding Big Life Records, a label owned by her then beau Jazz Summers. 'The Only Way Is Up', a cover of a song first performed by Otis Clay in the 70s, took only three weeks to reach pole position, where it stayed for a for a further five weeks. "It was suggested that Coldcut do a remake of the track," Yazz explained. "But they weren't keen because they felt they might spoil the original, but I felt it would be perfect for me."

Yazz previously recorded with the dance act the Biz, where she partnered Suzette Smithson and Austin Howard. They were one of the first acts to work with Stock Aitken Waterman, and enjoyed moderate club success with 'Falling' and 'We're Gonna Groove Tonight' in 1983. Boasting that she never wanted to be a singer but a lollipop lady, Yazz – along with the studio -created Plastic Population (in reality Kiss FM pirate DJs Black and Moore) – recorded several more singles for Big Life, including the Top 10 hits 'Stand Up For Your Love Rights' (number two) and the reggae-tinged 'Fine Time' (number nine) before signing, in the early 90s to the Polydor label.

614

A GROOVY KIND OF LOVE

PHIL COLLINS

10 September 1988, for 2 weeks

●●

VIRGIN VS 1117

Writers: Toni Wine end Carole Bayer Sager
Producers: Phil Collins and Anne Dudley

The former child actor Phil Collins had, as a young adult, found good fortune placing songs in films. Both his song for *Against All Odds*, 'Against All Odds (Take A Look At Me Now)', and his ballad for *White Nights*, 'Separate Lives', had been American number ones. He now won the chart championship on both sides of the Atlantic reviving a 60s song for the movie *Buster*, in which he portrayed one of the perpetrators of the Great Train Robbery.

Collins penned three songs for the film in collaboration with the former Motown legend Lamont Dozier. For the rest of the soundtrack he selected hits of the period covered on screen, using *The Guinness Book Of British Hit Singles* as reference. It was in its pages that he found out that 'A Groovy Kind Of Love' by the Mindbenders had reached number two in early 1966. His own version became his third UK number one and started a hat-trick of US number ones that also included 'Two Hearts' and 'Another Day In Paradise'.

Every solo album released by the singing drummer of Genesis had reached either number one or two in the British LP chart, a distinction that continued into the 90s. The 'Buster' collection peaked at six, but it did win the BRIT Award for Best Film Soundtrack. 'Two Hearts', penned with Dozier, won both a Grammy and an Ivor Novello Award. Of his slightly more obscure prizes, Phil Collins earned a Golden Bug in Sweden and a Genie in Canada for his role in *Buster*.

615

HE AIN'T HEAVY HE'S MY BROTHER

HOLLIES

24 September 1988, for 2 weeks

●●

EMI EM74

Writers: Bob Russell and Bobby Scott
Producer: Ron Richards

Twenty three years and 65 days after their only previous number one single (see no. 198), the Hollies returned to the top with a re-issue of one of their most celebrated recordings, itself originally a number three hit for the band in 1969. At the time, this was the longest gap between number ones any act had enjoyed, if enjoyed is the correct word for so weird a feat!

The group's magnificent string of singles hits had more or less run its course by 1974, with 'The Air That I Breathe' being a number two climax to a glorious sequence that had started in 1963, 26 hits before, with 'Just Like Me'. Long before 1974, the Hollies, despite the departure of Graham Nash and the odd internal rupture, had become one of British pop's immortal acts. Their choice of recording material, whether their own compositions or from outside sources, particularly for singles, always combined quality with commerciality, and their distinctive vocal sound, led by the flawless Allan Clarke, ensured that every Hollies record cut through the late 60s/early 70s airwaves like a knife.

When the big hits stopped, the band continued as a major touring attraction. Hollies founders Clarke and Tony Hicks, together with Bobby Elliott, a 'new boy' of a mere 31 years' service by 1994, remain the core of the band. In 1988 they were introduced to the few members of the younger generation who had not heard of them, via the use of 'He Ain't Heavy He's My Brother' in a TV beer advertisement. The powerful song, by Americans Bob Russell (who also composed 'Honey' and 'Little Green Apples') and Bobby Scott, co-writer of 'A Taste Of Honey', was a Top 10 record for the Hollies in the States in 1970 and a Top 20 hit for Neil Diamond there a few months later.

The Hollies remain one of the few 60s groups that have retained the loyalty of millions for over three decades.

616

DESIRE

U2

8 October 1988, for 1 week

●

ISLAND IS 400

Writers: U2, lyrics by Bono
Producer: Jimmy Iovine

After seven years as a major album-chart force, U2 finally topped the singles chart with their 12th UK hit single, the first track taken from their fourth number one album, *Rattle And Hum*.

U2 are, for the record, Bono (Paul Hewson, born 10 May 1960, vocals), the Edge (David Evans, born 8 August 1961, guitar and keyboards), Adam Clayton (born 13 March 1960, bass guitar) and Larry Mullen Jr (born 31 October 1961, drums). The band formed in 1976, as Feedback, after fellow pupils responded to an ad placed by Mullen on the notice board at Mount Temple school, in Dublin. After several name changes, they became U2, after the American spy plane, and recorded their first songs in 1979. Their first date in Britain in December that year, at the Hope And Anchor pub in London, attracted just nine people, but within three years they had become probably the biggest live act in the world. Their live album, *Under A Blood Red Sky*, released in December 1983, spent over 200 weeks on chart, one of only 14 albums to achieve that total. *Rattle And Hum*, which entered the albums charts at number one two weeks after 'Desire' had topped the singles chart, spent only just over a year on the chart. 'Desire' was recorded at STS studios in Dublin, with post-production work undertaken at the A&M studios in Hollywood.

U2 are shown during the filming of the video for 'Desire'. (Pictorial Press)

617

ONE MOMENT IN TIME

WHITNEY HOUSTON

15 October 1988, for 2 weeks

●●

ARISTA 111613

Writers: Albert Hammond and John Bettis
Producer: Narada Michael Walden

The head of Arista Records and Whitney Houston's mentor, Clive Davis, devised a concept album to tie in with the 1988 Olympic Games in Seoul, South Korea. Eleven tracks were recorded, or chosen from previously issued material, to be used in the NBC-TV transmission of the Games. Titled *1988 Summer Olympics Album/One Moment In Time*, it featured tracks from Arista artists including Eric Carmen, Taylor Dayne, the Four Tops and Kashif. Guest acts such as the Bee Gees also appeared. It was Whitney, however, who won the gold. She went all the way to the winner's circle in Britain and to number five in America, where she had recently completed her unprecedented string of seven consecutive number ones. Since 'One Moment In Time' was not from one of her own albums, the B-side of the single was not one of her performances. 'Olympic Joy' by Kashif was used. Of all the artists represented on the album, he was the most appropriate, having produced her 1985 Top 10 Black Music hit, 'Thinking About You', which was never promoted to a wider market.

'One Moment In Time' was the fourth UK number one for producer Narada Michael Walden. Hammond and Bettis were long-time successful songwriters, the Englishman Hammond having even reached the American Top 5 as an artist in 1972 with 'It Never Rains In Southern California'. His most recent success had been the Aswad number one 'Don't Turn Around' (see no. 605). Bettis had reached those heights as a lyricist with his Carpenters hits, 'Yesterday Once More' and 'Top Of The World', the latter an American number one in 1973. Between albums, Whitney did not even attempt to follow 'One Moment In Time' with a solo single for another two years.

618

ORINOCO FLOW (SAIL AWAY)

ENYA

29 October 1988, for 3 weeks

●●●

WEA YZ 312

Writers: Enya Brennan and Roma Ryan
Producer: Nicky Ryan

The Irish folk-rock group Clannad, from

Gweedore in Co. Donegal, first caught the attention of Britain's record-buying public when they wrote and recorded the theme tune of the television series *Harry's Game* in 1982, although they had been well known in Ireland almost since their formation in 1970. 'Clannad' is Gaelic for 'family', and the group was indeed a family affair, initially consisting of three Brennan children and two of their Duggan uncles. Enya, born Eithne Ni Bhraonain on 17 May 1961, joined the group in 1979, and left in 1982 to pursue a solo career. An album recorded for the BBC atttracted some attention in 1987, but her first major solo impact abroad was with her 1988 album, *Watermark*. While containing many links with her folk-music and Irish roots, the recording was an innovative New Age creation of ethereal subtlety and grace. Enya wrote all the music, played keyboards, and whether singing wordless songs, the English lyrics of Roma Ryan, or her own adaptations of the lyrics in Gaelic, captivated an international audience. The bandwagon began rolling when 'Orinoco Flow (Sail Away)' was played by Steve Wright on Radio One to strong reaction, which prompted the release of the track as a single. It gracefully ascended to the very top.

The song contains a reference to the head of the record company that released *Watermark*, Rob Dickins, which may not have done much for the song's prospects of becoming a standard, but certainly ensured enthusiastic WEA Records support. Both the single and the album were huge hits in the United States, with both *Watermark* and Enya's 1991 album, *Shepherd Moons* (a number one in the UK), selling over two million copies there.

619

THE FIRST TIME

ROBIN BECK

19 November 1988, for 3 weeks

●●●

MERCURY MER 270

Writers: Gavin Spencer, Tom Anthony and Terry Boyle
Producers: Gavin Spencer, Tom Anthony

Canadian chanteuse Robin Beck became the 31st one-hit-wonder in British chart history, and the only one of 1988, when her only hit reached number one in its fourth week of chart action. She was the sixth female vocalist among the most recent ten acts to join the one-hit wonder list, and only the seventh of all time - the other solo female one-hit wonder being the very first name on the list, Kitty Kallen (see no. 21). She was also the third consecutive female soloist to top the charts, the second time that year that this had occurred, although it never happened before 1988, and it hasn't happened since.

The song was from an advertisement for Coca-Cola. It was more than a jingle, like David Dundas' 'Jeans On', and more than a song used for commercial purposes, like the Clash's 'Should I Stay Or Should I Go' for Levi's. It was even more of an advertisement than the previous Coca-Cola song to hit number one, 'I'd Like To Teach The World To Sing' (see no. 308), which was a variation on the original 'I'd Like To Buy The World A Coke'. The original sound recording of 'First Time' was made by the Coca-Cola Company, which held the copyright. The single sleeve had Coca-Cola ads on its back and front, and a photo of a model drinking from the familiar bottle. Unfortunately, Miss Beck's chart career proved to be more disposable than the empty bottle.

620

MISTLETOE AND WINE

CLIFF RICHARD

10 December 1988, for 4 weeks

●●●●

EMI EM 78

Writers: Leslie Stewart, Jeremy Paul and Keith Strachan
Producer: Cliff Richard

Cliff's first self-produced number one, the 12th of his staggering career, came less than three years after his last, the manic partnership with the Young Ones (see no. 567). Chart historians will forever argue as to whether that revival of 'Living Doll' should really count as an 80s number one for Cliff, so the success of 'Mistletoe And Wine' was essential to give Cliff an undisputed claim to the honour of being the only act to have number ones in each of four successive decades. He didn't stop there (see no. 655).

'Mistletoe And Wine' was first heard as part of the score of a musical based on the Hans Christian Anderson story, *The Little Match Girl,* with music by Keith Strachan, and book and lyrics by Leslie Stewart and Jeremy Paul. The show premiered in Richmond at Christmas 1977, and has since been performed in other provincial theatres and in schools. A TV production some ten years later, featuring Twiggy and Roger Daltrey, was seen by Peter Gormley, Cliff's former (retired) manager. Gormley spotted the commercial potential of 'Mistletoe And Wine' and brought it to the attention of his erstwhile client. Just too late for Christmas 1987, Cliff waited a year, and his singalong treatment, with a few lyrical alterations, became Britain's best-selling single of 1988, giving him the personal satisfaction of commercial success with what had become a Christian-message song.

Since 'Living Doll' with the Young Ones, Cliff's singles career had continued at full steam. A duet with Sarah Brightman, 'All I Ask Of You', from (*Phantom Of The Opera)* in late 1986, and 'Some People' in autumn 1987 were the most successful until 'Mistletoe And Wine', both peaking at number three. 'Mistletoe And Wine' was no less than his 98th hit on the British singles charts.

621

ESPECIALLY FOR YOU

KYLIE MINOGUE AND JASON DONOVAN

7 January 1989, for 3 weeks

●●●

PWL PWL 24

Writers: Mike Stock, Matt Aitken, Pete Waterman
Producers: Mike Stock, Matt Aitken, Pete Waterman

"A recording career is something I've always felt confident that I could pursue and although it would have been easy to be satisfied with acting, I always knew that the time would come to expand." Kylie had every reason to be so self-

assured. After the triumphant success of her international debut, 'I Should Be So Lucky', which topped the charts in 12 countries, Miss Minogue followed it with a hat-trick of consecutive number two hits that spent a combined total of 10 frustrating weeks in the runner-up position: 'Got To Be Certain', 'Je Ne Sais Pas Pourquoi' and an update of her initial Australian release, 'The Loco-Motion'. The latter also managed to cross over to the American charts, where it peaked at a very respectable number three.

The diminutive singer not only dominated the singles listings in 1988, but also managed to shift an enormous amount of albums as well. It was generally considered that the teen market to which Kylie appealed were predominantly singles buyers, but this proved not to be the case as her debut LP, simply called *Kylie,* sold over two million copies to become one of the ten best-selling albums of all time in Britain.

Her fourth British release was a duet with Jason Donovan, 'Especially For You', and it looked set to repeat the fate of her previous three singles. It spent four weeks behind Cliff Richard's 'Mistletoe And Wine' at the tail end of 1988 before finally taking over in the New Year. The single tied in with the on-screen marriage of Charlene Ramsey and Scott Robinson (Minogue and Donovan's characters) in *Neighbours,* which also marked the end of Kylie's involvement in the TV soap. She left to devote more time to her recording career.

622

SOMETHING'S GOTTEN HOLD OF MY HEART

MARC ALMOND WITH SPECIAL GUEST GENE PITNEY

28 January 1989, for 4 weeks

●●●●

PARLOPHONE R6201

Writers: Roger Cook and Roger Greenaway
Producer: Bob Kraushaar

In every one of the first seven editions of *The Guinness Book Of British Hit Singles* Gene Pitney qualified in the sad category Most Top Ten Hits Without A Number One Hit - sad not for his total of Top 10 hits, which happened to be ten, but because he had been denied the top slot despite so much international success. In Britain his 'I'm Gonna Be Strong' was held at number two by first the Rolling Stones' 'Little Red Rooster' and then the Beatles' 'I Feel Fine', and 'Nobody Needs Your Love' was kept out by the Kinks' 'Sunny Afternoon'. 'Looking Through The Eyes Of Love' peaked at three, behind the Hollies' 'I'm Alive' and Elvis Presley's 'Crying In The Chapel'. The quartet of acts who kept Pitney out of number one could have spared at least one week at the top, since they accounted for 44 different chart-toppers between them. In the United States Pitney experienced an even more bizarre frustration – 'Only Love Can Break A Heart' being blocked by his own composition, 'He's a Rebel', as produced by Phil Spector using Darlene Love but crediting the Crystals. Another of his songs, 'Hello Mary Lou', reached number two in Britain for Ricky Nelson.

Marc Almond might have appreciated Pitney's quandary. After winning first prize on his very first chart outing, Soft Cell's 'Tainted Love' (see no. 485), Almond drifted downwards with first four Top 10s and then four lesser successes by the duo, punctuated and then followed by a dozen entries in various guises.

His return to the top spot came with a remake of Pitney's final Top 10 solo outing, the 1968 hit 'Something's Gotten Hold Of My Heart'. Almond's original intention had been for Pitney to make only a cameo appearance on the track for his album *The Stars We Are*, but the Rockville Rocket's enthusiasm for the arrangement led to a duet. The cross-generational pairing proved a major international hit, with Top 5 placings in Europe and Australia. Frustration in at least one country seemed inevitable, however, bearing in mind Pitney's unusual history, and that nation proved to be the United States. The record company with the rights to the song refused to release it. Pitney was told that, since he had not had a hit at home in 20 years and Marc Almond was unknown as a soloist in America, young audiences hearing these unfamiliar artists would assume the recording was a gay love duet. 'Something's Gotten Hold Of My Heart' could be the first example of a million-selling single by an American artist denied release in the United States.

623

BELFAST CHILD

SIMPLE MINDS

25 February 1989, for 2 weeks

●●

VIRGIN SMX 3

Writers: Traditional; lyrics by Simple Minds
Producers: Trevor Horn and Steve Lipson

Simple Minds had ten hit singles in six years in Britain before they finally broke into the Top 10 with a song which spent 24 weeks on the UK charts and hit number one in America, 'Don't You (Forget About Me)'. Six singles and four more years later, they finally reached number one, a feat they had already achieved three times on the albums chart. Their fourth consecutive chart-topping album, *Street Fighting Years*, contained 'Belfast Child'. Based on the traditional song 'She Moved Through The Fair', it ran for 6 minutes 39 seconds, to become the second-longest-running number one to that time, after the Beatles' 'Hey Jude' (see no. 258).

Simple Minds are Scottish. At the time of

their number one hit they were: Jim Kerr (born 9 July 1959, vocals), Charlie Burchill (born 27 November 1959, guitar), Michael McNeil (born 20 July 1958, keyboards), John Giblin (bass) and Mel Gaynor (born 29 May 1959, drums). 'Belfast Child' was released as a single backed by 'Mandela Day', a song composed for Nelson Mandela's 70th birthday concert on 11 June 1988, and also as one of three tracks on their 'Ballad Of The Streets' EP, with 'Mandela Day' and 'Biko'.

624

TOO MANY BROKEN HEARTS

JASON DONOVAN

11 March 1989, for 2 weeks

●●

PWL PWL 32

Writers: Mike Stock, Matt Aitken, Pete Waterman
Producers: Mike Stock, Matt Aitken, Pete Waterman

Jason Donovan's first trip to the top on his own was, like his only previous solo hit, 'Nothing Can Divide Us', and his duet chart-topper with Kylie Minogue (see no. 621), a product of the writing-and-production team of Stock, Aitken and Waterman. At the very peak of his teen appeal, Donovan had little difficulty in taking his third consecutive statement of youthful devotion on an A-side to number one.

Jason was born on 1 June 1968 in the Melbourne suburb of Malvern, the son of British-born actor Terry Donovan and his then wife Sue McIntosh, a TV presenter. His show business career began as an 11 year old in *Skyways*, a television drama series about an Australian airline. Starring alongside him was a child actress just three days older than he was, Kylie Minogue.

Other TV roles Down Under followed. When still a year away from his final school exams he was asked to test for a new daily soap opera entitled *Neighbours*. He turned down the opportunity, preferring to complete his education, but the producers approached him again a few months later, and this time he succumbed, taking the part of Scott Robinson as soon as he had graduated. He was thus reunited with Kylie, who played Charlene Ramsey, and their on-screen romance captivated Australia. The extraordinary phenomenon of Australian TV soaps breaking out of the southern hemisphere to dominate the world, with *Neighbours* in the vanguard, ensured that Scott/Jason and Charlene/Kylie became international household names. Both rose to the challenge with a spectacular string of hits.

625

LIKE A PRAYER

MADONNA

25 March 1989, for 3 weeks

●●●

SIRE W 7539

Writers: Madonna and Patrick Leonard
Producers: Madonna and Patrick Leonard

After a quiet 1988 in which no new Madonna singles appeared on the British singles chart (among other projects which kept her away from the recording studio was a Broadway appearance in the David Mamet play, *Speed The Plow*), La Ciccone's quite stupendous UK hit singles record resumed normal service with her 16th consecutive Top 10 hit, her sixth number one and the third on the trot written with Patrick Leonard. She thus extended her statistically unmatched British number one writing, production and performing tallies.

The video of 'Like A Prayer' caused a stir as a result of its juxtaposition of symbols of sex and Christianity. Pepsi-Cola severed commercial connections with Madonna, fearing accusations of sacrilege by association. Her two-minute commercial for the soft drink aired for the first and last time on 2 March 1989. Meanwhile, the album *Like A Prayer* contained three further hit singles, 'Express Yourself', 'Cherish' and 'Dear Jessie', all of which made the UK Top 5.

In 1989 Madonna's less-than-conventional marriage to actor Sean Penn finally ran aground. By the end of the 80s, she was probably the best-known female entertainer in the world, as much for her apparent desire and ability to offend as for her undoubted musical abilities. She never appeared concerned that the former kind of celebrity would eclipse the latter.

626

ETERNAL FLAME

BANGLES

15 April 1989, for 4 weeks

●●●●

CBS BANGS 5

Writers: Susanna Hoffs, Billy Steinberg, Tom Kelly
Producer: Davitt Sigerson

The Bangles had already enjoyed eight UK hit singles when 'Eternal Flame' was released early in 1989. Their first hit, three years earlier, had been the Prince song 'Manic Monday', which hit number two, kept off the very top by Diana Ross' 'Chain Reaction'. At the end of 1986, their longest-running chart hit, 'Walk Like An Egyptian', just failed to emulate its chart-topping success in America by stopping at number three, but since then they had not hit the British Top 10. 'Eternal Flame', a title inspired by the eternal flame burning at Elvis Presley's grave in Memphis, was meant to be a cross between the sound of the Beatles and the Byrds. Twenty-five years after those groups' greatest successes, the sound still worked.

The Bangles, comprising lead vocalist Susanna Hoffs (born 17 January 1957), sisters Vicki (born 11 January 1958, guitar) and Debbie Peterson (born 22 August 1961, drums), and the boyishly named bass guitarist Michael Steele (born 2 June 1954), were the first all-girl group to top the British charts since the St. Winifred's School Choir over seven years earlier. But within seven months of their greatest success the Bangles had broken up, saying that they were "going on hiatus", and Susannah Hoffs had embarked on a solo career.

627

HAND ON YOUR HEART

KYLIE MINOGUE

13 May 1989, for 1 week

●

PWL PWL 35

Writers: Mike Stock, Matt Aitken, Pete Waterman
Producers: Mike Stock, Matt Aitken, Pete Waterman

It was during the filming for the video of 'Hand On Your Heart' that Kylie Minogue decided she had had enough. "I am told what to sing, how to have my hair and what to wear," she claimed, and now it was time for the former soap star to have her own way. Under the guidance of the celebrated songwriting-and-production team of Stock Aitken Waterman, Kylie had risen to the top of her profession with an unparalleled string of six Top 2 records. They had expertly marketed her to a legion of adoring pre-pubescent female fans, but Kylie now wanted to mature, to expand her horizons and broaden her appeal. She grew her hair, adopted a raunchier image and insisted that Mike, Matt and Pete come up with some harder-edged dance material rather than the out-and-out pop fodder that she had been performing.

It was a brave move and only partially successful: she alienated many former Kylie-wannabes and failed to appeal to the hardcore dance fans who would always see her as a SAW product. But she did attract a whole new audience of gay men who idolized her new glamorously kitsch image. However, what she gained in credibility, she lost in sales - her first two albums had sold more than three and a half million copies – her third barely made the Top 10. Despite this decline in LP revenue, Kylie's singles continued to sell prodigiously.

628

FERRY 'CROSS THE MERSEY

CHRISTIANS, HOLLY JOHNSON, PAUL McCARTNEY, GERRY MARSDEN AND STOCK AITKEN WATERMAN

20 May 1989, for 3 weeks

●●●

PWL PWL 41

Writer: Gerry Marsden
Producers: Mike Stock, Matt Aitken, Pete Waterman

On April 15, 1989, the F.A. Cup semi-final between Liverpool and Nottingham Forest was scheduled to take place at Hillsborough, the home ground of Sheffield Wednesday F.C. However, the crowd of Liverpool fans at the Leppings Lane end of the ground became too great for the enclosed space into which they had been confined, and what had promised to be a great game turned into the greatest sporting disaster in British history. 95 Liverpool fans died in the crush, and hundreds more were permanently affected by the disaster.

To raise funds for the Hillsborough Disaster Fund to help those affected by the tragedy, several leading Liverpool stars combined in a version of Gerry Marsden's 'Ferry 'Cross The Mersey', the theme from his only starring movie, which had reached number eight early in 1965 as recorded by Gerry and the Pacemakers. Along with Gerry were Holly Johnson, lead vocalist of Frankie Goes To Hollywood, the band that had equalled Gerry's 25-year-old record of a hat-trick of number ones with their first three singles, Paul McCartney (who had been part of a band that once managed 11 number ones in a row), the Christians (who never topped the charts before or since), and ace producers Stock Aitken and Waterman, for whom producing number one hits was something they seemed to do every week. This was not their greatest production, but musical quality was not the point of this record.

629

SEALED WITH A KISS

JASON DONOVAN

10 June 1989, for 2 weeks

●●

PWL PWL 39

Writers: Gary Geld, Peter Udell
Producers: Mike Stock, Matt Aitken, Pete Waterman

The third track from his debut (May 1989) album, *Ten Good Reasons* (which itself topped the album charts and remained in the best sellers for over a year), to be issued as a single gave Jason Donovan his third hit and his second successive solo number one. His previous successes, including his duet with Kylie Minogue, had been written by the SAW production team, but 'Sealed With A Kiss', one of the all-time champs of schoolday miss-you angst, was an oldie written by Americans Gary Geld and Peter Udell, and introduced by Brian Hyland in 1962.

Hyland took the song to number three in both Britain and America, and returned to the Top 10 in the UK (reaching number 7) when it was reissued in 1975. Donovan's success thus made the 80s the song's third hit decade running. Com-poser Geld and lyricist Udell wrote several other pop hits in the 60s and 70s, such as 'Ginny Come Lately' (also for Brian Hyland) and 'Hurting Each Other' (the Carpenters), and later wrote for Broadway, notably the musicals *Purlie* and *Shenandoah.*

Ten Good Reasons provided Donovan with a fifth hit single (the Kylie duet was also on the album) when another SAW original, 'Every Day (I Love You More)', followed the Geld-Udell classic, making number two. Donovan's second album, *Between The Lines*, in June 1990, was not quite as golden a source of smashes, and it took a venture into musical theatre to reinstate him at number one.

630

BACK TO LIFE (HOW EVER DO YOU WANT ME)

SOUL II SOUL FEATURING CARON WHEELER

24 June 1989, for 4 weeks

●●●●

10 TEN 265

Writers: Beresford Romeo, Caron Wheeler, Simon Law, Nellee Hooper
Producers: Jazzie B (Beresford Romeo) and Nellee Hooper

Jazzie B and his Funki Dred collective were a major force in re-establishing British dance music, particularly in America where they enjoyed major R&B and Hot 100 success. Soul II Soul established itself in the late 80s as the premier exponent of street soul. Leader Jazzie B, the writer and producer of many of their ground-breaking singles, also created the distinctive Funki Dred image, which became their hallmark in more than music. They branched out into the high street, launching their own range of clothes, and onto the airwaves of London on the then pirate Kiss FM station. Eventually, Jazzie B's leadership qualities would cross the Atlantic as the Motown Corporation made Funki Dred an imprint of the label.

'Back To Life' was the second single to feature vocalist Caron Wheeler. She followed in the footsteps of Rose Windross and Do'reen, who had sung on earlier singles, and had also sung lead on their first Top 5 hit, 'Keep On Moving'. Both tracks were taken from the ground-breaking number one album *Club Classics Vol. 1* and both crossed the Atlantic to become Black R&B chart-toppers.

'Back To Life' has the honour of being the fastest-selling 12-inch single ever in New York. The track also earned the group a Grammy award for Best R&B Vocal Group (a second Grammy was won the same year for 'African Dance' as Best R&B Instrumental). "I think we've come as a shock to most black Americans," noted Jazzie B. "We don't sound American, act American or look American, so the culture shock has been incredible."

631

YOU'LL NEVER STOP ME LOVING YOU

SONIA

22 July 1989, for 2 weeks

●●

CHRYSALIS CHS 3385

Writers: Mike Stock, Matt Aitken, Pete Waterman
Producers: Mike Stock, Matt Aitken, Pete Waterman

Sonia Evans was born in Liverpool on February 13 1971 and in the late 1980s she became the most notoriously 'Scouse' female vocalist since Cilla Black. After attending drama school as a teenager, Sonia made a brief appearance in the TV sitcom *Bread*, but her destiny lay in singing and once she had introduced herself to a DJ in her hometown she became an overnight success. The DJ she approached was Pete Waterman, one third of the Stock Aitken Waterman hit machine, who in 1988 was hosting a regular local radio show in Liverpool. Impressed by the fact that Sonia already had her Equity card, he allowed her to perform live on his show. She went on to perform on Waterman's *Hitman And Her* TV show which he hosted live from a nightclub on Saturday nights. The crowd reaction convinced Waterman he should sign her to his PWL management company.

Sonia was introduced to the public via the PWL Roadshow, appearing with the label's more established acts, including Hazell Dean, Sinitta and Jason Donovan. Her first single became her only number one hit but the 11th for the SAW production team and their sixth of 1989. Sonia's debut album produced a further five Top 20 hits, but she was – surprisingly – dropped from Chrysalis and the PWL management company in 1991. She has since diversified as an artist, representing the UK in the 1993 Eurovision Song Contest (where she was narrowly beaten into second place by yet another winning Irish entry), and starring in West End stage productions of *A Slice Of Saturday Night* and *Grease*.

632

SWING THE MOOD

JIVE BUNNY AND THE MASTERMIXERS

5 August 1989, for 5 weeks

●●●●●

MUSIC FACTORY DANCE MFD 001

Producers: Andy Pickles and Les Hemstock
Medley of the following songs: 'In The Mood', by Joe Garland; 'Rock Around the Clock', by Jimmy de Knight and Max C .Freedman; 'Tutti Frutti', by Richard Penniman and Dorothy La Bostrie; 'Wake Up Little Susie', by Boudleaux Bryant and Felice Bryant; 'C'Mon Everybody', by Eddie Cochran and Jerry Capehart; 'Hound Dog', by Jerry Lieber and Mike Stoller; 'Shake Rattle And Roll', by Charles Calhoun; 'All Shook Up', by Otis Blackwell and Elvis Presley; 'Jailhouse Rock', by Jerry Lieber and Mike Stoller; and 'At The Hop', by Arthur Singer, John Medora and Dave White

Andy Pickles and his partners at Music Factory Studios in Rotherham had been running a mastermix service for DJs since 1986, producing medleys of familiar tunes to be played in the clubs. Early in 1989, they produced 'Swing The Mood' and, as was their normal practice, they produced about a thousand copies for DJ use. The reaction this time was incredible, and they decided to release the track as a single. Licensing problems, however, were horrendous. Several companies claimed the rights to Bill Haley's 'Shake Rattle And Roll', and the version of 'Jailhouse Rock' they finally used was not the original by the King, but by Elvis impersonator Peter Wilcox. Distribution problems were equally intractable, but after being turned down by several major labels (shades of Decca refusing the Beatles), they formed their own label, distributed by BMG, and the record shot to the top. It charted in almost every country around the world, became Australia's biggest-selling single ever, and heralded the beginning of the biggest chart success by a rabbit since records began.

633

RIDE ON TIME

BLACK BOX

9 September 1989, for 6 weeks

●●●●●●

RCA PB 43055

Writers: Dan Hartman, Daniele Davoli, Marco Limoni, Valerio Semplici
Producer: Groove Groove Melody

Hailing from Italy, the Mediterranean studio production team Groove Groove Melody comprised producer Daniele Davoli (aka DJ Lelewel), keyboard player Marco Limoni and engineer Valerio Semplici. They sampled the powerful vocal line from Loleatta Holloway's disco anthem and subsequently much plagiarised 'Love Sensation'. Loleatta Holloway failed to receive the full credit she deserved on this huge international hit.

In her place Guadeloupe-born and Italian-resident model Katrin Quinol (an ex-girlfriend of Davoli) fronted the group for video and TV appearances. Her obvious inability to mime the lyrics, as viewers of her *Top Of The Pops* performance will testify, soon gave the game away. "I've been out here for years scuffling and trying to get this one hit record," quipped Holloway, "and I've heard that nobody this year has had a record at number one for six weeks apart from Black Box. Knowing that this is my voice and not getting a credit for it, that was like 'Oh man, what is happening to me?' Then to see this woman up there twisting her butt like it's her who sang the song... and then I heard she can't even speak English!" Several weeks into the record's chart run, and after the threat of legal action, the vocal was re-recorded note-for-note by a session singer. Miss Holloway was awarded a fur coat to placate her. With the diva-like accompaniment of ex-Weather Girl Marth Wash, Black Box scored another half a dozen hits for Deconstruction, including two further Top 5 hits ('I Don't Know Anybody Else' and a cover of Earth Wind And Fire's 'Fantasy').

634

THAT'S WHAT I LIKE

JIVE BUNNY AND THE MASTERMIXERS

21 October 1989, for 3 weeks

●●●

MUSIC FACTORY DANCE MFD 002

Producers: Andy Pickles, Les Hemstock and Ian Morgan
Medley of the following songs: 'Hawaii 5-0', by Morton Stevens; 'Let's Twist Again', by Kal Mann and Dave Appell; 'Let's Dance', by Jim Lee; 'Great Balls Of Fire', by Jack Hammer and Otis Blackwell; 'Johnny B. Goode', by Chuck Berry; 'Good Golly Miss Molly', by Richard Penniman; 'The Twist', by Hank Ballard; 'Summertime Blues', by Eddie Cochran and Jerry Capehart; 'Razzle Dazzle', by Charles Calhoun; 'Runaround Sue', by Ernie Maresca and Dion DiMucci; and 'Chantilly Lace', by J.P. Richardson

How do you follow up one of the biggest-selling singles of the decade, and a novelty single at that? Nobody really believed that Jive Bunny could do it again, but he did. The second single was another club mastermix, based around Chubby Checker's 'Let's Twist Again', because it had a good drum track, but the Bunny men needed a strong theme to hold it all together, as Glenn Miller's 'In The Mood' had done with the first hit. Andy Pickles, the main man behind Jive Bunny, was in a club one night when the DJ played 'Hawaii 5-0', the theme to the TV series of the 1970s which starred Jack Lord as detective Steve Garrett. That was the sound he needed. The next day he asked John Anderson to record it, and the single was soon completed.

Jive Bunny's second single was almost as popular as the first, spending three weeks at the top and equalling Gerry and the Pacemakers, not only by hitting number one with their first two releases, but also by having two chart-toppers out of three consecutive number one hits.

635

ALL AROUND THE WORLD

LISA STANSFIELD

11 November 1989, for 2 weeks

●●

ARISTA 112 693

Writers: Lisa Stansfield, Ian Devaney, Andy Morris
Producers: Ian Devaney and Andy Morris

What appeared to be a charismatic new artist was in fact a talented young woman who had been performing and preparing for years. Stansfield, Devaney and Morris formed Blue Zone in their native Rochdale in 1984. Three singles, all with Lisa's lead vocals, were released in Britain, and one of them, 'Jackie', reached 54 in the United States under the billing Blue Zone UK. But neither these recordings nor Stansfield's presentation work on ITV's *Razzamatazz* made a significant impression on the pop population.

The pointer to the future was Lisa's selection by Coldcut members Matt Black and Jonathan Moore to front their 'People Hold On' single. This soulful dance success, credited to 'Coldcut Featuring Lisa Stansfield', created fresh interest in the mystery singer. The Blue Zone trio retired to their own home-town studio and re-emerged with the single 'All Around The World' and the album *Affection*, both issued under Stansfield's name. Both were instant international hits, with Lisa boasting the most-photographed kiss curl since Bill Haley.

'All Around The World' not only reached number three in the *Billboard* Hot 100 but became the first Black Music number one by a white British female. Stansfield wowed the audience at Harlem's Apollo Theater and became a fixture on the Black Music chart. One of her personal

favourite moments came when Barry White walked up to her, embraced her and told her that he recognized the spoken introduction on 'All Around The World' was in his style. He was correct: the intro had in fact been a tribute to White, whom Stansfield, Devaney and Morris had loved since their youth.

Lisa launched a string of hits with this disc, including two important film tunes. 'Someday (I'm Coming Back)' was placed on *The Bodyguard*, the best-selling soundtrack of the early 90s, and 'All The Right Places' did more than decently from *Indecent Proposal*.

636

YOU GOT IT (THE RIGHT STUFF)

NEW KIDS ON THE BLOCK

25 November 1989, for 3 weeks

●●●

CBS BLOCK 2

Writer: Maurice Starr
Producers: Maurice Starr and Michael Jonzun

Maurice Starr wasted little time whinging when his protégés New Edition (see no. 521) dispensed with his services in 1984. He immediately set out to find 'a white New Edition'. Through his friend Mary Alford of the Massachusetts Department Of Education, Starr met high school student Donnie Wahlberg (born 17 August 1970). He introduced Starr to his old friends from William M. Trotter Elementary School in Roxbury, Danny Wood (born 14 May 1971), Jordan Knight (born 17 May 1971) and Jonathan Knight (born 29 November 1969). Together with Pete Fitzgerald, Jamie Kelley and Donnie's brother Mark, they formed Starr's latest group, Nynuk. The last three members named all soon left the ship and Joey McIntyre (born 31 December 1973) came on board. The quintet signed to CBS in 1986, under the name New Kids On The Block.

NEW KIDS ON THE BLOCK pose before their Meadowlands (New Jersey) concert with their organization's Dick Scott (second from left) and Amnesty International American chapter director Jack Healy. (Pictorial Press)

The significance of Roxbury, the location of Trotter Elementary, is that it was Boston's black area. During the days of school busing to achieve racial balance, an era marked by intense controversy in the city, white children such as the future New Kids were taken to schools in black neighbourhoods, and vice versa. The Wahlberg family and friends emerged as genuine musical hybrids with a true grounding in dance and rap music. The sweet soul ballad 'Please Don't Go Girl' became their first American Top 10 success in 1988, with 'You Got It (The Right Stuff)' providing a harder hit and a Top 3 placing in early 1989. By the time Britain caught onto the act late in the year, the quintet had already enjoyed two US number ones, the wistful 'I'll Be Loving You (Forever)' and the uptempo 'Hangin' Tough'.

CBS in Britain gave the New Kids their own catalogue prefix, BLOCK. 'You Got It (The Right Stuff)', originally CBS 653169 7, was re-issued with a different picture sleeve as CBS BLOCK 2. This time around the first-time failure went to number one. BLOCK 1 would dramatically re-emerge as BLOCK 3 in less than two months.

637

LET'S PARTY

JIVE BUNNY AND THE MASTERMIXERS

16 December 1989, for 1 week

•

MUSIC FACTORY DANCE MFD 003

Producers: Andy Pickles and Ian Morgan
Medley of the following songs: 'March Of The Mods', by Don Doherty and John Anderson; 'Merry Christmas Everybody', by Noddy Holder and Jim Lea; 'I Wish It Could Be Christmas Everyday', by Roy Wood; 'Another Rock And Roll Christmas', by Gary Glitter, Mike Leander and Eddie Seago; and 'Christmas Rap', by Chubby Checker

Jive Bunny couldn't do it again, could he? Yes, he could, and sandwiched in between teeny favourites New Kids On The Block and the Christmas charity single, the rabbit's Christmas single just managed a week of supremacy to complete the hat-trick and equal the record of Gerry and the Pacemakers and Frankie Goes To Hollywood by hitting the top with each of its first three singles. "I can't really believe it. It all happened too fast," said Andy Pickles. Three number ones in 20 weeks compares with Gerry's three in 30 weeks and Frankie's three in 46 weeks to make Jive Bunny's the fastest debut hat-trick by some way.

For their Christmas single, Jive Bunny used the 1964 Joe Loss tune, 'March Of The Mods', to hold together several Christmas favourites. Such were the continuing licensing problems in using the original tracks that Roy Wood, Noddy Holder and Chubby Checker, as well as John Anderson, all came to Rotherham to record their own contributions to the single. "Recording with Roy Wood was one of the highlights of the Jive Bunny project," remembers Pickles.

After 'Let's Party', Jive Bunny never topped the charts again, but in a chart career which included ten hit singles over two and a half years, the terminally unhip rabbit reminded us all that pop music is meant to be fun.

638

DO THEY KNOW IT'S CHRISTMAS?

BAND AID II

23 December 1989, for 3 weeks

•••

PWL/POLYDOR FEED 2

Writers: Bob Geldof and Midge Ure
Producers: Mike Stock, Matt Aitken, Pete Waterman

All sorts of chart records were broken by Band Aid II's chart-topping Christmas charity single. Not only did 'Do They Know It's Christmas?' become the 13th song to hit number one in two different versions, it became the only song to go to number one twice for charitable causes, and the first to be recorded by two different one-hit wonder acts. It was yet another Stock Aitken Waterman production, making them the only producers to have produced as many as three charity number ones (see also nos. 588 and 628), but it sold several million fewer copies than the original Band Aid single, which is still the only single to have sold three million copies in Britain alone. Like its immediate predecessor at the top, 'Do They Know It's Christmas?' stayed on the chart for only six weeks, and in the week ending 20 January 1990 it fell from number four to number 32, the biggest fall from the Top 5 ever recorded.

Featured in Band Aid II were Bananarama (of whom two members, Sarah Dallin and Keren Woodward, were the only people who also performed on the original Band Aid single), Big Fun, Bros, Cathy Dennis, D Mob, Jason Donovan, Kevin Godley, Glen Goldsmith, Kylie

Minogue, the Pasadenas, Chris Rea, Cliff Richard, Jimmy Sommerville, Sonia, Lisa Stansfield, Technotronic and Wet Wet Wet. Nine of these acts had been part of previous number ones.

639

HANGIN' TOUGH

NEW KIDS ON THE BLOCK

13 January 1990, for 2 weeks

●●

CBS BLOCK 3

Writer: Maurice Starr
Producer: Maurice Starr

The apotheosis of Maurice Starr's work with New Kids On The Block, the founder serving as sole writer and producer, 'Hangin' Tough' proved the importance of timing in pop music. On its first release as CBS BLOCK 1 it had limped to number 54, but this less-than-dramatic debut proved enough to introduce British audiences to the pleasures of the New Kids. 'You Got It (The Right Stuff)' (see no. 636) followed by going to number one in November 1989, and the re-issued 'Hangin' Tough' followed less than two months later, the first new number one of the 90s.

Between the time the side had topped the American chart in September and achieved its British supremacy in January, New Kids had accumulated three more US Top 10 hits, part of a string of nine consecutive singles to reach that elite part of the chart. They almost duplicated the feat in the UK, putting together eight straight Top 10s, one a double-sided hit. Through the summer of 1990, they were the biggest young act in the music business. *Fortune* magazine placed the group in the top ten earning entertainers in all of show business, with one modest estimate of their income for the year being in excess of $850 million. This was made possible through the merchandising of cartoons, comics, dolls, videos, and a variety of tour merchandise. All five of their albums were on the American chart for Christmas 1990. One, *Step By Step*, had been a British number one album that summer.

The bubble burst cruelly and suddenly as the American hit singles dried up in late 1990, though Britain at least provided three Top 20 placings in 1991. But popular music continues to re-invent itself, and Mark Wahlberg emerged as Marky Mark, Maurice Starr launched US Top 10 teen trio Perfect Gentlemen, and New Kids On The Block took a tough turn and came back as the harder-edged NKOTB.

640

TEARS ON MY PILLOW

KYLIE MINOGUE

27 January 1990, for 1 week

●

PWL PWL 47

Writers: Sylvester Bradford and Al Lewis
Producers: Mike Stock, Matt Aitken, Pete Waterman

Early in 1989, Kylie was offered a role in *The Delinquents*, a film set in the 1950s with Kylie, in her first-ever feature, as the main character Lola Lovell. The film was only a moderate success, but the single extracted from the soundtrack became her fourth number one single in under two years. Previously, Madonna had been the only female soloist to manage a quartet of British chart-toppers – and that had taken her three and a half years to complete.

Never before a hit in Britain, 'Tears On My Pillow' was originally recorded by Little Anthony and the Imperials and was an American number four hit for them in 1958. Kylie was unable to repeat the success of her cover of 'The Loco-Motion' in the States. Her popularity there dwindled after only three singles, but she did achieve astounding popularity in the world's second largest market – Japan. In 1989 she topped the Japanese chart for an incredible 27 weeks and at one time had five singles simultaneously in the Top 40.

In 1993, after a score of hits – the majority Top 10ers – and four number ones, Kylie's contract with Pete Waterman's label expired. She did not renew it. Instead, in keeping with her more sophisticated image, she signed with the Deconstruction label, best known for their upfront, harder-edged dance releases.

641

NOTHING COMPARES 2 U

SINEAD O'CONNOR

3 February 1990, for 4 weeks

●●●●

ENSIGN ENY 630

Writer: Prince
Producer: Sinead O'Connor

'Nothing Compares 2 U' was originally recorded – without success – in 1985 by Prince's Minneapolis protégés The Family. The following year Irishwoman Sinead O'Connor (born 12 December, 1966) moved to London for a deal with Ensign Records. She reached the Top 20 of the UK chart with 'Mandinka' in 1988 and the same area of the *Billboard* Modern chart the same year with 'Jump In The River'.

SINEAD O'CONNOR smiles at New York's China Club. (Pictorial Press)

Her next hit was a worldwide smash. She produced her own version of 'Nothing Compares 2 U' with "strings, drums & piano by Soul II Soul". The ballad with a shuffle beat moved quickly to number one in both Britain and America, with four-week runs at the top in both countries. Making equal impact was its accompanying video, which showed O'Connor shedding a tear and won three trophies at the MTV Awards. On one occasion Sinead explained she felt tearful because of her recent split with manager Fachtna O'Cellaigh, mentor of the Boomtown Rats during their glory days and at one time her boyfriend. He was on the list of those thanked on the cover of the 7-inch single of 'Nothing Compares 2 U', rating a place behind God and Prince, though he missed the crucial credit. "This record is dedicated to Le Pack of Fags," Sinead wrote on the sleeve.

Sinead O'Connor appeared at benefits for so many worthy causes, and managed to cause so many controversies, that it would be misleading to concentrate on one or even a few. Suffice to say she became an artist of international celebrity despite having only one major hit, even though she subsequently covered another number one, 'Don't Cry For Me Argentina' (see no. 400).

642

DUB BE GOOD TO ME

BEATS INTERNATIONAL FEATURING LINDY LAYTON

3 March 1990, for 4 weeks

●●●●

GO! DISCS GOD 39

Writers: Norman Cook, Jimmy Harris III (Jimmy Jam) and Terry Lewis
Producer: Norman Cook

After enjoying nine hits with the clean-cut Housemartins, including their chart-topping interpretation of 'Caravan Of Love' (see no. 581), Norman Cook left the collective to concentrate on his first love - dance music. After moderate chart success, initially with the studio-created Urban All

Stars and then as a soloist with 'Won't Talk About It'/'Blame It On The Bassline' and 'For Spacious Lies', Cook eventually formed Beats International. He was partnered by keyboard player Andy Boucher, drummer Luke Cresswell and vocalists Lester Noel (who had sung on 'For Spacious Lies') and Lindy Layton. 'Dub Be Good To Me', their introductory single, was an amalgamation of the instrumental loop from the Clash's 'Guns Of Brixton' and a reggae-ish interpretation of the song written by the SOS Band's Jimmy Jam and Terry Lewis, 'Just Be Good To Me'.

Credited featured vocalist Lindy Layton was a child actress in *Grange Hill* and star of a Heinz spaghetti TV commercial. She featured on this single only, later recording as a solo artist for several labels, including Debut, PWL and Arista. It was on Arista that she enjoyed her biggest solo hit, with a cover of Janet Kay's lovers-rock favourite, 'Silly Games'. Beats International enjoyed reasonable success over the next 18 months with a re-recorded 'Won't Talk About It' and a cover of Elvis' 'In The Ghetto', before Cook disbanded the group to form Freak Power in 1993.

643

THE POWER

SNAP!

31 March 1990, for 2 weeks

●●

ARISTA 113 133

Writers: Benito Benites, John 'Virgo' Garrett III
Producer: Snap!

"I've got the power," declared Jocelyn Brown on her John 'Jellybean' Benitez-produced single, 'Love's Gonna Get You', in 1986. The track spent only one week at number 70 but went on to inspire one of the biggest hits of 1990.

Snap!, like numerous other dance acts that emerged in the 90s, were a studio-created group. Put together by the Frankfurt-based producers and composers Michael Muenzing and Luca Anzilotti, who performed on the record under the alias of Benito Benites and John 'Virgo' Garrett III, the real group was fronted by vocalist Penny Ford and rapper Turbo B (real name Durron Butler).

Ford, formally a solo artist in the mid-80s as well as being a past member of the SOS Band and girl group Klymaxx, did not meet the German-resident rapper until the single had been number one in three countries. Muenzing and Anzilotti had first asked Chaka Khan to provide vocals for Snap!, but she was busy and suggested they contact Penny.

She remained with the team throughout 1990 and featured on their Top 10 hits 'Oops Up', 'Cult Of Snap', 'Mary Had A Little Boy' and 'Snap Megamix'. In so doing, she helped earn them the accolade of Biggest-selling New Act Of The Year, with worldwide single sales close to five million. All the same, Ford received no credit on these recordings or the parent *World Power* album, and, due to her shyness and unwillingness to meet the press, Jackie Harris was drafted in for TV and radio interviews.

644

VOGUE

MADONNA

14 April 1990, for 4 weeks

●●●●

SIRE W 9851

Writers: Madonna and Shep Pettibone
Producers: Madonna and Shep Pettibone

Madonna's seventh UK number one, her eighth in her homeland, extended her run of successive Top 10 hits to 20. Although not featured in the Disney/Warren Beatty film *Dick Tracy*, which featured Madonna as Breathless Mahoney, 'Vogue' was the lead track of her *I'm Breathless* album, which featured music and songs from the movie as well as others 'inspired' by the picture. However, co-creator Shep Pettibone has stated that 'Vogue' was the one track on the album that had no connection, actually or artistically, with the Warren Beatty (then Madonna's beau) picture.

Three Stephen Sondheim songs, 'Sooner

Or Later' (which won an Oscar), 'More' and 'What Can You Lose', were the only ones actually from the soundtrack. None of these was issued as a single. 'Vogue' and the Madonna/Pat Leonard composition 'Hanky Panky' were the only two titles from the *Breathless* collection to make it onto the A-side of a smaller format.

'Vogue', originally scheduled to be a mere B-side to Madonna's US single 'Keep It Together', was by no means her strongest effort melodically, but the perfomance and the production, in celebration of the immortal style of a roll-call of stars (Bette Davis, Jimmy Dean, etc.) were so striking that the single became one of her biggest ever. Indeed, although she had not returned to the very top of the Britsh singles lists by the middle of 1994, her run of Top 10 hits was still intact.

645

KILLER

ADAMSKI

12 May 1990, for 4 weeks

●●●●

MCA 1400

Writers: Adamski and Seal
Producer: Adamski

One of the original exponents of the 1988 summer-of-love rave scene, synthesizer whizz kid Adamski (aka Adam Tinley), a 22-year-old hippie child of the New Forest, made a name for himself during those carefree warehouse and outdoor raves. He would play at the likes of Energy, Sunrise and World Dance where 15,000 people would meet somewhere within the boundaries of the M25 with the sole intention of having a good time by whatever means available. Adamski, along with his contemporaries Mr Monday, Jimi Polo and Guru Josh, was responsible for the hypnotic, almost monotonous live synth shows accompanying the proceedings.

Adamski's first creative outing came at age 11 when, under the name the Stupid Babies, he and his five-year-old brother released 'The Babysitters', which reached number three in the indie charts. The groups Diskord Datkord and the Legions Of Diskord followed before he hooked up with recording artist Jimi Polo, who taught him how to program a synthesizer.

Signing with MCA in 1989, Adamski's initial totally instrumental recordings, including the crossover single 'N-R-G', met with mixed reactions. For 'Killer' a vocalist was added, the then unknown Seal. The song hit the number one slot in its sixth week of release after debuting at a lowly number 45. It proved to be a greater launching pad for the career of the uncredited vocalist than for Adamski. Seal went on to top the chart with his eponymous debut album and scored Top 10 hits with 'Crazy' and a re-recording of 'Killer'.

646

WORLD IN MOTION...

ENGLANDNEWORDER

9 June 1990, for 2 weeks

●●

FACTORY FAC 293

Writers: New Order and Keith Allen
Producer: Stephen Hague

One of the most successful recording acts of all time in the British singles charts, with two chart-topping singles and a number two hit from only five singles over a 20-year period, are the England World Cup Squad. Despite changes in personnel and management that would have wiped out the chart chances of many less popular bands, the totally unmusical footballers of England scored their first big hit in eight years when they teamed up with New Order (Barney Sumner, born 4 January 1956; Peter Hook, born 13 February 1956; Stephen Morris, born 28 October 1957; and Gillian Gilbert, born 27 January 1961) to create the 1990 masterpiece which helped us cheer the lads on to third place in the finals in Italy.

The vocal talents helping New Order out on 'World In Motion..' were Peter Beardsley, John Barnes, Paul Gascoigne, Steve McMahon, Chris Waddle and Des Walker, with 'thanks also to Craig Johnston', the Australian Liverpool player who had been the mastermind behind his club's 1988 Top 3 hit, 'Anfield Rap'. A total of 309,243 people turned out to watch England playing in the finals, proving that there are rather more who appreciate their football than their music.

A quick follow-up to the hit was ruled out when England failed to qualify for the finals in the USA in 1994.

647

SACRIFICE/HEALING HANDS

ELTON JOHN

23 June 1990, for 5 weeks

●●●●●

ROCKET EJS 22

Writers: Elton John and Bernie Taupin
Producer: Chris Thomas

In 1976, Elton John's 17th hit single was his first number one (see no. 393), but it was a duet with Kiki Dee. As a solo act he remained one of the most distinguished names on the list of those who had not had a UK number one for a further 14 years and 37 hits. By the time he made it, he was so established as one of the entire entertainment world's most stellar practitioners that he could not have needed it less; but Elton himself was thrilled by his inexplicably belated achievement. Two of the 53 hit singles that had preceded his chart-topper were 'Sacrifice' and 'Healing Hands' themselves. 'Healing Hands' was the first single release from *Sleeping With The Past*, Elton's summer 1989 album, which he dedicated to his career-long writing partner - "This album's for you, Bernie..." It reached only number 45, and the follow-up, 'Sacrifice' did even less well, stalling at 55. In the States, both were Top 20 items.

Six months later, Steve Wright, apparently not as tied to strict playlists as many other national DJs, began replaying 'Sacrifice' on his Radio One afternoon programme. He reported the great listener reaction to Rocket Records, who re-issued the two mini-hits as a double A-side. This time, with 95 per cent of the attention being paid to 'Sacrifice', the two titles moved strongly into the Top 40. By mid-summer a solo Elton was at the very top for the first time, and by the end of July the album followed suit to give Reg his first British number one album since 1974.

'Sacrifice', the hit so nearly missed, has become one of Elton and Bernie's standards; a haunting and melancholy warning to married men encapsulated in the succinct and powerful line, "Some things look better baby, just passin' through". Elton John has never been just passin' through.

648

TURTLE POWER

PARTNERS IN KRYME

28 July 1990, for 4 weeks

●●●●

SBK TURTLE 1

Writers: James P. Alpern and Richard A. Usher Jr.
Producer: Partners In Kryme

'Kryme' stands for 'Keeping Rhythm Your Motivating Energy', and Partners In Kryme were James Alpern (alias Keymaster Snow) and Richard Usher (alias MC Golden Voice). They first met in 1983 while studying Speech Communications at Syracuse University. Alpern and Usher formed a small group which opened for Grandmaster Flash, and in 1986 gave this outfit the name Partners In Kryme. Their message was that "people should get into the groove of their positive life forces instead of acting out violent urges and the seven deadly sins".

The duo were asked to write a song for the movie *Teenage Mutant Ninja Turtles* on a Friday and had completed the task by Monday, without seeing the film. This presented few complications, since their tune was played over the end credits. The Turtles had been hatched in 1984 by Kevin Eastman and Peter Laird, independent comic-book creators from New England. Their first edition of 3,000 sold out rapidly and ten years later was valued at $240 a copy. By this time the phenomenon had spread to other media. The movie was a phenomenon, particularly considering it was an independent production, and so was the song. The single sold over two million copies world-

ELTON JOHN performs at Shea Stadium on his 1992 tour with Eric Clapton. (Pictorial Press)

wide and became the first rap number one in Britain. It was also the fastest-selling number one by a new act, although labelmate Vanilla Ice was to do even better shortly afterwards. Alpern and Usher quit their office jobs on the strength of their number one, but Partners In Kryme remain one-hit wonders.

649

ITSY BITSY TEENY WEENY YELLOW POLKA DOT BIKINI

BOMBALURINA

25 August 1990, for 3 weeks

●●●

CARPET CRPT 1

Writers: Lee Pockriss and Paul Vance
Producer: Nigel Wright

Extraordinary to relate, two Brian Hyland revivals topped the British charts within just 14 months of each other. Although Hyland notched up 22 hit singles in the United States from 1960 to 1971, his material, written almost entirely by others, has never been considered a pop canon of significance, only 'Sealed With A Kiss' (see no. 629) of songs he originated having claim to anything approaching standard status.

'Itsy Bitsy...' was the novelty song that launched Hyland as a reasonably desirable teenage idol in 1960. In America it was number one for one week, with 16-year-old Brian still at high school. In Britain it made number eight. It remained little more than a desperate golden oldies programmer's penultimate resort until the most powerful man in the (allegedly) more serious business of musical theatre, Andrew Lloyd Webber, decided that the song, and merchandising spin-offs, could appeal to a whole new indiscriminate generation.

Lloyd Webber approached Nigel Wright to produce a track even before a vocalist had been selected to step into Brian Hyland's mighty shoes; the maestro pronounced the resulting session highly satisfactory and children's TV hero Timmy Mallett drew the short straw to be the song's front man, operating under the name Bombalurina, a feline character from ALW's now and forever *Cats*. The inanely catchy tune allied to a boisterous and humorous production rocketed out of the locker to the top.

Bombalurina actually came out with an album and a second single, a revival of the Paul Evans and the Curls/Avons 1959 novelty, 'Seven Little Girls Sitting In The Back Seat', lurched to number 18, but that was it. Two years later, Andrew Lloyd Webber, credited as executive producer of 'Itsy Bitsy...', was knighted, but it is unlikely that this record formed part of his citation.

650

THE JOKER

STEVE MILLER BAND

15 September 1990, for 2 weeks

●●

CAPITOL CL 583

Writer: Steve Miller Producer: Steve Miller

Steve Miller was born in Milwaukee, Wisconsin, on 5 October 1943, and grew up in Dallas. It was while in high school that he began a band called the Marksmen with his friend Boz Scaggs. Together they attended the University Of Wisconsin, playing in the Ardells, who became known as the Fabulous Night Trains. After graduation, Miller sojourned to Chicago, joining Barry Goldberg in the Goldberg-Miller Blues Band, before journeying to San Francisco in 1966. In a classic case of being in the right place at the right time, he began the Steve Miller Band just as psychedelia was sweeping the city. Scaggs returned from a period of folk singing in Sweden in time to join in on the group's first two albums, *Children Of The Future* and *Sailor*. He then left for what proved to be a distinguished solo career, highlighted by the LP *Silk Degrees* and its singles, 'Lowdown', 'What Can I Say' and 'Lido Shuffle'.

The Steve Miller Band survived his departure and had assembled a run of four consecutive Top 40 albums before fading from favour in the early 70s. The downward trend was rapidly reversed with the release of *The Joker* in 1973. The album sold over a million copies and the title track went to number one in America. The British singles charts remained undented until Miller's two subsequent US number ones, 'Rock 'N Me' and 'Abracadabra', became UK hits, the latter just missing the top spot due to the tenancies of 'Happy Talk' and 'Fame'. 'The Joker' was known only as an airplay favourite until it was used in a Levi's jeans commercial shown on British television in 1990. Miller, who had loved the blues, now joined R&B legends Sam Cooke, Marvin Gaye and Ben E. King as artists who enjoyed major hits as a consequence of being featured in a Levi's ad. 'The Joker' shattered the record of UB40's 'Red Red Wine' as the song with the longest gap between number one appearances in America and Britain, a whopping 16 years.

The real joke is that Miller had never considered the track commercial and was not particularly proud of it, claiming it took only half an hour to write. He had not even wanted it to be the album's title track, preferring 'Sugar Babe', and in later years referred to 'The Joker' as an albatross. As with 'Rockin' Robin' by Bobby Day and later Michael Jackson, 'The Joker' has nothing to do with Batman.

651

SHOW ME HEAVEN

MARIA McKEE

29 September 1990, for 4 weeks

●●●●

EPIC 656303

Writers: Joshua Rifkin, Eric Rackin and Maria McKee Producer: Paul Staveley O'Duffy

Maria McKee (born in Los Angeles on 17 August 1964) is the much younger half-sister of Bryan MacLean of Arthur Lee's band Love, whose 1967 album, *Forever Changes,* is often cited as the best of all the flower-power albums. By the early 1980s,

McKee and Maclean were playing together as firstly the Maria McKee Band and later the Bryan MacLean Band, but it was not until the pair split up and McKee formed the country-rock band Lone Justice in 1985, that she secured a recording contract. The band originally included bass guitarist Tony Gilkyson, son of Terry Gilkyson who co-wrote Dean Martin's number one, 'Memories Are Made Of This' (see no. 42). They managed a few well-received albums and one hit single in Britain, 'I Found Love', which peaked at number 45 in 1987.

In 1985, Feargal Sharkey hit number one with McKee's composition 'A Good Heart' (see no. 559), but when Lone Justice broke up in 1987, McKee's career went into a temporary decline. In 1990, she soared back to the very top, to become the first woman to write a number one hit for herself and for another act, with her emotional ballad from the soundtrack of the Tom Cruise/Robert Duvall/Randy Quaid/ Nicole Kidman film, *Days Of Thunder*. The film created two other Top 40 hits, Guns N' Roses' version of Bob Dylan's 'Knockin' On Heaven's Door', and Elton John's 'You Gotta Love Someone'. After 'Show Me Heaven', McKee took almost three years to climb back into the Top 40, despite some well-reviewed releases. 'I'm Gonna Soothe You', from her album *You Gotta Sin To Be Saved*, hit number 35 in June 1993.

652

A LITTLE TIME

BEAUTIFUL SOUTH

27 October 1990, for 1 week

●

GO! DISCS GOD 47

Writers: Paul Heaton and Dave Rotheray
Producer: Mike Hedges

When ex-Housemartins (see no. 581) vocalist Paul Heaton formed the Beautiful South, he soon proved that his talent for writing hit songs had not deserted him. The socialist themes that were prevalent in his lyrics for the Housemartins were still a feature of his writing, but by teaming up with co-writer and guitarist Dave Rotheray to form the core of the Beautiful South, Heaton broadened his subject matter. 'A Little Time' was a typically sardonic love song coupled with a radio-friendly melody that epitomised the style that the Beautiful South made their own.

Heaton was joined in the Beautiful South by former Housemartins drummer Dave Hemmingway. Hemmingway, who had previously provided backing vocals on the Housemartins' second album, *The People Who Grinned Themselves To Death*, abandoned his drum kit to become co-vocalist with Heaton. Former Housemartins roadie David Stead filled the vacant drummer position, with bassist Sean Welch and female vocalist Briana Corrigan completing the line-up. Vocal duties on much of the political material went to Heaton, while Hemmingway and Corrigan took control of the (generally more successful) songs dealing with relationships. On 'A Little Time' Hemmingway performed the role of a husband feeling trapped in a marriage and asking for breathing space from a bitter wife, played by Corrigan, who decides that the marriage is over. The theme of the song was emphasized by an excellent video that won a BRIT award for Best Music Video of 1990.

653

UNCHAINED MELODY

RIGHTEOUS BROTHERS

3 November 1990, for 4 weeks

●●●●

VERVE/POLYDOR PO 101

Writers: Hy Zaret and Alex North
Producer: Phil Spector

If you want to catch people out on pop trivia, ask them who had the first number one with 'Unchained Melody'. In Britain, the answer would be Jimmy Young (see no. 34), and in America it would be Les Baxter (May 1955). The younger fan might also be caught out if you asked in what year the Righteous Brothers' definitive version was recorded, for far from being cut in the year when it reached the top, it was made in 1965.

Bobby Hatfield had been upset that Bill Medley had been featured as the soloist in the introductory sections of both 'You've Lost That Lovin' Feelin'' (see no. 186) and the follow-up, 'Just Once In My Life', a song which reached the American Top 10 despite missing the British chart completely. Phil Spector tried to please him by recording his solo performance of 'Unchained Melody', which had provided US Top 10 hits for Baxter, Al Hibbler and Roy Hamilton in 1955 and given lesser placings to June Valli and the doo-wop group Vito and the Salutations. The producer/label chief placed the track on the B-side of his third Righteous Brothers single, 'Hung On You', which once again began with a Medley solo. Completely unexpectedly, the A-side floundered. Radio began supporting 'Unchained Melody', and the surprise hit sprinted to number four in the US and 14 in the UK.

Unfortunately, not only was Hatfield upset with Medley, they both were angry at their famous producer, as recounted in Mark Ribowsky's Spector biography, *He's A Rebel*. While 'Unchained Melody' was still in the charts, Bill and Bob sued both Spector and the head of their previous record company. They left Philles to accept a lucrative offer from MGM, which released the Medley production '(You're My) Soul And Inspiration' on Verve, before even reaching a settlement with Spector. Although they enjoyed an immediate number one, the Righteous Brothers proved anything but fraternal, and broke up in late 1967. Medley went solo, while Hatfield briefly teamed up with Jimmy Walker and released an album under the duo's name in 1969.

Thus, though there were never more than two Righteous Brothers at any moment, three men have been Righteous Brothers, and only one of them was singing on 'Unchained Melody'. None of this would interest anyone other than trivia buffs had the 1965 recording not been used prominently and effectively in the 1990 film *Ghost*. Newly interpreted by the younger generation as an anthem of true love that transcend death, the song shot to number one in Britain. The Righteous Brothers moved past the Hollies as the act with the longest gap between number one hits, 25 years and 259 days. In America, 'Unchained Melody' sales in 1990 were shared by two Top 20 versions: the original, which was made available only on vinyl, and a re-recording on Curb Records, which sold over a million cassettes. This type of split was unprecedented.

654

ICE ICE BABY

VANILLA ICE

1 December 1990, for 4 weeks

●●●●

SBK SBK 18

Writers: Vanilla Ice, Earthquake, David Bowie, Brian May, Freddie Mercury, Roger Taylor and John Deacon
Producer: Vanilla Ice

With a bassline borrowed from Queen and David Bowie's 'Under Pressure' (see no. 489), 'Ice Ice Baby' was a huge international success at the end of 1990. Born Robert van Winkle, Vanilla Ice, the 25-year-old blond-haired, blue-eyed rapper from Miami Lakes, Florida, was briefly propelled to stardom, yet still caused one journalist to refer to him as "looking more like the Pat Boone rather than the Elvis Presley of rap". Ice's initial interest laid in motocross where, for team Honda, he won three national championships. Switching to the challenge of rap music, a move to Dallas in 1988 led to him entering in a local rap contest: "The organisers asked me what I needed, I said just a microphone...I walked off the stage and 40 people handed me their business cards."

Entering the chart at number three, 'Ice Ice Baby' became the highest-debuting single in chart history by a previously uncharted act, eclipsing the number four debut of fellow rappers Partners In Kryme's 'Turtle Power' in July. Both went to the top of the pile and both were on EMI's rookie SBK label, which had been in existence for less than eight months.

Like his peer MC Hammer, with whom Ice extensively toured, he turned single success into album sales: in America the pair monopolised the top of the album chart for an incredible 37 weeks with Hammer's *Please Hammer Don't Hurt 'Em* and Ice's *To The Extreme*.

655

SAVIOUR'S DAY

CLIFF RICHARD

29 December 1990, for 1 week

●

EMI XMAS 90

Writer: Chris Eaton
Producers: Cliff Richard and Paul Moessl

Chris Eaton, who had written 'Little Town', a variation on the Christmas hymn 'Oh Little Town Of Bethlehem', for Cliff Richard in 1982 (a number 11 hit), wrote 'Saviour's Day' for Cliff in October 1989. He brought a demo of the song two months later to Cliff's office Christmas party, despite knowing it was already too late for Christmas 1989, and despite having been told by Cliff's secretary that 'From A Distance' was already scheduled as Cliff's 1990 Yuletide smash. Cliff actually enjoyed two 1989 Christmas hits - one a duet with Van Morrison and the other as part of Band Aid II (see no. 638).

Chris managed to drag Cliff out of the knees-up and into his (Cliff's, not Chris') Rolls to hear the demo. Cliff loved it immediately. Fortunately, the writer of 'From A Distance', Julie Gold, was not in the back seat as, from that moment, the plans for Christmas 1990 changed. Cliff's treatment of 'From A Distance' was released in October 1990, reaching only number 11. The song, introduced by American country performer Nanci Griffith, was eventually recorded by several artists, notably Bette Midler, whose less bombastic version made number two in the United States and number six in Britain.

But Cliff did well to clamber into his Rolls because 'Saviour's Day' quickly made up for the comparative disappointment of 'From A Distance'. Although not as big a seller as the less sophisticated 'Mistletoe And Wine' (see no. 620), it was nonetheless top of the tree on Christmas Day, being the evergreen ever-youthful one's 13th number one hit. Counting the Band Aid II appearance, this made three December 25ths running that Cliff had been at number one.

Paul Moessl was a young keyboard player and arranger who first came to Cliff's manager's attention in a Windsor club. From there he graduated to the band for Cliff's West End musical, *Time*, and thence to Cliff's recording sessions.

656

BRING YOUR DAUGHTER...TO THE SLAUGHTER

IRON MAIDEN

5 January 1991, for 2 weeks

●●

EMI EMPD 171

Writer: Bruce Dickinson
Producer: Martin Birch

Iron Maiden, Britain's most successful heavy metal band since Led Zeppelin, were formed in London in the late 1970s, but it was not until vocalist Bruce Dickinson (born 7 August 1958) joined the band in October 1981 that they made the big breakthrough. His first single with Iron Maiden was their first Top 10 hit, 'Run To The Hills', and his first album with them, *The Number Of The Beast*, was their first number one album. By the time 'Bring Your Daughter...To The Slaughter' crashed into the charts at number one, they had already had six Top 10 hits and inspired a huge and loyal fan base. The other members of the band by the beginning of 1991 were: founder Steve Harris (bass, born 12 March 1957), Dave Murray (guitar, born 23 December 1955), Nicko McBrain (drums, born 5 June 1964), and recent recruit Janick Gers on guitar.

'Bring Your Daughter...To The Slaughter', which had originally been written for the 1989 film *Nightmare On Elm Street 5: The Dream Child*, broke all records for a short chart life but a happy one. The record, which was as different from its predecessor, Cliff's Christmas hit, as it is possible to imagine, had only four weeks in the Top 40 (spending two weeks at the top, a week at number nine and a further seven days at 32) and only five weeks in the Top 75, to make it the shortest-lived number one of all time. EMI and Iron Maiden were criticized at the time for what was

considered to be the cynical device of marketing many different formats of the single in the first week of release, in the knowledge that many fans would buy all the different formats at once and thus boost sales artificially. But because this 'cynical' ploy worked, within a year or two it had become standard marketing practice.

657

SADNESS PART ONE

ENIGMA

19 January 1991, for 1 week

•

VIRGIN DINS 101

Writers: Michael Cretu, Franz Gregorian and David Fairstein
Producer: Michael Cretu

Like the act which follows alphabetically among number one hitmakers, Enya, Enigma come under the new-wave banner as a band whose overall sound is as peaceful as Iron Maiden's is abrasive. Romanian Michael Cretu (born 18 May 1957 in Bucharest) came to Germany in 1975 and worked with Vangelis and the Art Of Noise, among many other innovative studio bands, before beginning to issue his own records under the name Enigma. With vocals by his German wife Sandra, Cretu created a wide range of sounds on his debut album, *MCMXC AD*, including a strange song heavily influenced by Gregorian chant, which was

QUEEN are joined in Budapest by a group of Hungarian folk singers. (Pictorial Press)

called 'Sadeness' on the album. For the UK single release, the title was modified to 'Sadness', perhaps because British fans would not understand the original pun, or perhaps because some officious proofreader was determined to correct the spelling mistake.

Three more singles over the next year failed to break into the Top 40, although all of them charted in the lower regions, and it was not until 1994 that the Cretus climbed back into the British Top 10. 'Return To Innocence', the first single release from their second album, *Cross Of Changes*, reached number three in March 1994.

658

INNUENDO

QUEEN

26 January 1991, for 1 week

•

EMI QUEEN 16

Writers: Queen
Producers: Queen and David Richards

Queen's fourth hit, 'Bohemian Rhapsody', in 1975 (see no. 382), had been the track that had established them as a band out of the ordinary, but, apart from a collaboration with David Bowie in 1981 (see no. 489), one of the most popular British recording acts of all time had to wait 16 years for another number one. When it came it lasted only one week. More importantly however, 'Innuendo', a six-and-a-half-minute barnstormer in many ways reminiscent of 'Bohemian Rhapsody', was the title track of Queen's seventh chart-topping album.

Innuendo the album was also the main plank of a campaign to return Queen to best-selling status in the United States where, for some reason, their popularity had waned during the latter half of the 80s. A new deal with the Disney-owned Hollywood Records and a lavish relaunch of their back catalogue on CD for the first time in America went some way towards achieving the campaign's goal, but ironically it was the success second time around of their greatest hit that really put them back on the American map (see no. 672).

The tragedy of Freddie Mercury's terminal illness, though kept from the public, was by now overshadowing Queen's plans. Freddie's response to the situation was to throw himself ever more determinedly into writing and recording, with his vocal, composing and video performance work for *Innuendo* showing that illness had not impaired his creative talents. The clip of Freddie performing 'These Are The Days Of Our Lives' (see no. 672) is unbearably moving, and the album contained such other hits as 'I'm Going Slightly Mad', 'Headlong' and 'The Show Must Go On'.

659

3.A.M. ETERNAL

KLF FEATURING CHILDREN OF THE REVOLUTION

2 February 1991, for 2 weeks

●●

KLF COMMUNICATIONS KLF 005

Writers: Jim Cauty, Bill Drummond and Ricardo Lyte
Producers: KLF

Bill Drummond and Jimmy Cauty's original recording of '3 A.M. Eternal' was first issued, to limited success, in November 1988 and, like 'What Time Is Love' before it, was completely revamped for re-issue at the turn of 1991. Featuring rapper Ricardo and the mournful title-wailing by Maxine Harvey, the single was a surefire hit. It was originally recorded as part of the soundtrack to the feature-length film *The White Room*, a still-unreleased film made by Bill Butt and the KLF.

Cauty had first appeared with June Montana and Youth in Brilliant, one of Stock-Aitken-Waterman's first signings, who enjoyed three minor hit singles in 1985/6. Unhappy with their lack of artistic control, the trio split. Montana joined Misty Oldland in Oldland Montana, Youth formed Blue Pearl, becoming an acclaimed producer/remixer, and Cauty teamed up with Bill Drummond under the guise of the Justified Ancients Of Mu Mu. The 'JAMMS' evolved into Space Disco 2000 and then the Timelords, achieving notable success in 1988 (see no. 610).

After the chart-topping triumph of '3 A.M. Eternal', the duo scored a further three Top 5 singles including 'Justified And Ancient', featuring country star Tammy Wynette. They then announced their retirement at the zenith of their fame, and used their royalties to fund the KLF Foundation, which specialised in poking fun at pretensions in all forms of art.

660

DO THE BARTMAN

SIMPSONS

16 February 1991, for 3 weeks

●●●

GEFFEN GEF 87

Writer: Bryan Loren
Producer: Bryan Loren

The Simpsons were the first cartoon group to reach number one since the Archies. During the 22-year gap between them, the Smurfs had come close when 'The Smurf Song' by Father Abraham and the Smurfs peaked at two in 1978. Spitting Image had gone all the way in 1986 with 'The Chicken Song', but they were puppet non-humans rather than animated characters.

The Simpsons first appeared in April 1987 on the third episode of *The Tracey Ullman Show*, a prime-time half-hour comedy series on the Fox network in the United States. They were the creation of Matt Groening, former music critic and comic-strip writer/artist. The family consisted of Homer, the father with the perpetual five o'clock shadow, blue-haired mother Marge, saxophone virtuoso Lisa, baby Maggie and the most popular character, Bart, whose name was an anagram of brat. Despite his tough exterior and spiky yellow head, Bart was not all that he seemed. His voice was actually that of a woman, Nancy Cartwright. Furthermore, part of the phenomenal merchandising success which led Geffen Records to contemplate a Simpsons disc was that Bart, a non-white, had a great following in urban areas, where he was considered to have a modern African-American teenager's attitude.

Unlike the Archies, the Simpsons managed a UK chart follow-up, with 'Deep Deep Trouble' reaching number seven later in 1991.

661

SHOULD I STAY OR SHOULD I GO

THE CLASH

9 March 1991, for 2 weeks

●●

COLUMBIA 656667

Writers: The Clash
Producer: Mick Jones mixed by Glyn Johns.

Another Levi's jeans advertisement gave punk band the Clash their only Top 10 hit in 14 years of hit singles. Originally released in 1982, 'Should I Stay Or Should I Go' had originally peaked at number 17, but when it was used to promote Levi's nine years later, it hit the very top in only its second week of renewed chart life. By that time, the Clash had broken up.

Guitarist Mick Jones (born 26 June 1953), vocalist Joe Strummer (born John Mellor on 21 August 1952), and bass player Paul Simonon (born 15 December 1955) had formed the Clash in 1976 with drummer Terry Chimes. After backing the Sex Pistols on their December 1976 tour, Chimes left the group, to be replaced by Nicky 'Topper' Headon (born 30 May 1955). This was the line-up that recorded their only number one hit, a track from their most successful album (if not necessarily their best), *Combat Rock*. But by the time 'Rock The Casbah' and 'Should I Stay Or Should I Go' were hits in both the UK and America in 1982, Headon had left and Terry Chimes was back, drumming his way through a major tour of the United States.

The Clash broke up in 1985, and Mick Jones formed Big Audio Dynamite, who proved no more successful than the Clash in coming up with Top 10 singles. However, Jones made sure that the flip-side of the re-issued 'Should I Stay Or Should I Go' was not the original double-sided charter 'Straight To Hell' but a Big Audio Dynamite track, 'Rush'. By this time, Strummer had begun to concentrate on acting, Simonon's new band, Havana 3 a.m., had issued one album (which failed to chart), and Headon had served time in prison for heroin offences.

662

THE STONK

HALE AND PACE AND THE STONKERS

23 March 1991, for 1 week

●

LONDON LON 296

Writers: Joe Griffiths, Gareth Hale and Norman Pace
Producer: Brian May

In late 1990, Brian May of Queen was asked by British comedy double act Hale and Pace to produce for them a charity single in aid of Comic Relief. Comic Relief was a kind of comedians' Band Aid which encouraged people to perform daft or outrageous tasks in order to raise money, initially for famine relief in Africa. The whole enterprise centred around Red Nose Day, for a while an annual event on which date a considerable proportion of the country's population sported red plastic noses to publicise fundraising events.

Gareth Hale and Norman Pace did both

the cause and themselves a power of good when the results of May's studio expertise coupled with a lunatic, not to say disgusting, song propelled 'The Stonk' to number one. Among the Stonkers, a band whose subsequent career has been on the modest side of invisible, was Roger Taylor, May's Queen colleague.

TV and cabaret stars Hale and Pace are also known as the Two Rons, a duo who bear more than a passing resemblance to well-known East End gangsters of the 60s. Fortunately for Gareth and Norman, the models for the Two Rons are currently prevented (and will be for some time) from expressing any face-to-face opinions of this aspect of Hale and Pace's work.

The flip-side of the rib-tickling smash featured the popular comedienne and musicienne Victoria Wood, but for some reason this fact was not promoted. The single could doubtless have been a double A-side and made the multi-talented Ms. Wood a one-hit wonder along with Hale, Pace and the Stonkers.

663

THE ONE AND ONLY

CHESNEY HAWKES

30 March 1991, for 5 weeks

●●●●●

CHRYSALIS CHS 3627

Writer: Nik Kershaw
Producers: Alan Shacklock and Nik Kershaw

In 1967 Chip Hawkes of the Tremeloes sang lead on that group's biggest hit, 'Silence Is Golden' (see no. 233). 24 years on, his son Chesney completed a unique family double via the seventh best-selling single in Britain in 1991, 'The One And Only'. Other than the likes of Zak Starkey (son of Beatle Ringo Starr) performing little more than a session-man role on charity chart-toppers (see no. 551), there had never hitherto been an instance of father and son enjoying separate UK number ones, or even one together come to that.

'The One And Only' was Chesney's first single. It was featured in the film *Buddy's Song*, in which Chesney starred as Roger Daltrey's son, and was also used in the Michael J. Fox movie, *Doc Hollywood*. As a result of the twin film boost, the single was a hit on both sides of the Atlantic, though merely a number nine in America. Since this outstanding debut, Hawkes' career has stumbled a little, with strong follow-ups proving elusive.

Nik Kershaw's first number one in any capacity narrowly bettered his greatest effort as a solo performer when his 'I Won't Let The Sun Go Down On Me' reached number two in 1984.

664

THE SHOOP SHOOP SONG (IT'S IN HIS KISS)

CHER

4 May 1991, for 5 weeks

●●●●●

EPIC 656 673

Writer: Rudy Clark
Producer: Peter Asher

'The Shoop Shoop Song (It's In His Kiss)' was originally recorded by Betty Everett in 1964. The music business was so obsessed with the Beatles' unprecedented achievement of scoring 30 American hits in one year, including six number ones, that only a few fans would have noticed that Everett managed six hits herself that year. The first, 'You're No Good', boasted one of the most unusual accompaniments in chart history, the Dells stomping their feet to the beat in the next room, unaware they were being recorded. The second, 'The Shoop Shoop Song', brought Betty to number six. She got one position higher with her duet with Jerry Butler, 'Let It Be Me', but after the last of her 1964 hits fell off the chart in early '65, when she scraped the British Top 30 with 'Getting Mighty Crowded', she went into a four-year stretch in the wilderness.

Music was changing rapidly, and no one represented that change in 1965 better than Sonny and Cher. But although 'I Got You Babe' (see no. 201) was an international number one and both halves of the duo enjoyed solo success, Cher had to wait years for her own number ones. They finally arrived at home in America in the form of 'Gypsys, Tramps and Thieves' (1971), 'Half-Breed' (1973) and 'Dark Lady' (1974). Although the first found the number four spot in Britain, the second didn't even chart and the third crept to only 36.

If 1964 had been a wonderful year for Betty Everett, 1987 was at least as special for Cher. She won the Best Actress Oscar for her role in *Moonstruck* and began a new string of world hits with 'I Found Someone'. 'The Shoop Shoop Song' combined her two areas of achievement. It appeared over the end credits of her film *Mermaids* and gave her a solo number one, 25 years and 259 days after her individual chart debut with 'All I Really Want To Do'. This was the Slowest Number One for an artist releasing new material, Jackie Wilson and Ben E. King having finally found the top with re-issues.

It was also a comeback for 'The Shoop Shoop Song', which had finally charted in Britain for Betty Everett in 1968 and Linda Lewis in 1975, under its original subtitle, 'It's In His Kiss'. A completely new category of achievement would have to be invented for producer Peter Asher, who enjoyed this number one 27 years after being on top as an artist as half of Peter and Gordon (see no. 167).

665

I WANNA SEX YOU UP

COLOR ME BADD

8 June 1991, for 3 weeks

●●●

GIANT W 0036

Writer: Dr. Freeze
Producer: Dr. Freeze

When 'I Wanna Sex You Up' replaced Cher's 'Shoop Shoop Song' at number one, it was the first time that three consecutive chart-toppers had been specifically recorded for film projects. The song, lifted from the soundtrack to *New Jack City* followed 'The Shoop Shoop Song' from *Mermaids*, and Chesney Hawkes' 'The One And Only' from *Buddy*.

Color Me Badd were four school friends from Oklahoma City who began their career singing doo-wop harmonies in their school's hallway, although their impromptu concerts were often banned as too many students would miss class. Hailing from multi-racial backgrounds, the group comprised native American Bryan Abrams, Mark Calderon of Hispanic descent, Afro-American Kevin 'KT' Thornton and Anglo-American Sam Watters.

They auditioned for support slots for every major artist in town and eventually found themselves as the warm-up for Bon Jovi. They moved to New York after a meeting with Robert 'Kool' Bell of Kool and the Gang, who secured them a deal with Giant Records.

The group's success in the UK was overshadowed by their success in their homeland, where 'I Wanna Sex You Up' was a number two smash and the year's only double-platinum single. 'I Ador Mi Amor' and 'All 4 Love' went all the way and their album, *C.M.B.*, was certified triple platinum and earned them three Grammy nominations.

666

ANY DREAM WILL DO

JASON DONOVAN

29 June 1991, for 2 weeks

●●

REALLY USEFUL RUR 7

Writers: Tim Rice and Andrew Lloyd Webber
Producer: Nigel Wright

After a slight dip in the power of his recording career in 1990 and early 1991, Jason Donovan proved that this decline was more a result of a lapse in the quality of his material than in his intrinsic popularity when he enjoyed a massive personal success starring in Andrew Lloyd Webber's glitzy West End production of *Joseph And The Amazing Technicolor Dreamcoat*, at the London Palladium in the summer of 1991.

Joseph had been written by Tim Rice and Andrew Lloyd Webber in 1967/'68 as a school play and grew in the subsequent quarter century to become one of the most popular theatrical pieces of its time at both adult and child levels. Lloyd Webber acquired the rights for his Really Useful Company in the late 80s and decided to let rip with a no-holds-barred production in the West End. The plan fired and proved (a) that *Joseph* works no matter what you fling into it and (b) Jason Donovan is an excellent performer.

Inevitably, Jason and the cast made an album of the new treatment, and the obvious single was the show's best-known song, 'Any Dream Will Do', though the version issued as a single was not as heard on the Palladium stage. The 24-year-old song had never been a hit single in the UK, despite the fact that by the early 90s almost everyone under 40 knew the song by heart, having been unable to get through their schooldays without being in at least one production of the musical.

667

(EVERYTHING I DO) I DO IT FOR YOU

BRYAN ADAMS

13 July 1991, for 16 weeks

A&M AM 789

Writers: Bryan Adams, Michael Kamen and Robert John 'Mutt' Lange
Producer: Robert John 'Mutt' Lange

It had taken only one year for a single to overtake David Whitfield's 1954 smash, 'Cara Mia', as the disc with the most consecutive weeks at number one. It took three dozen years for a record to do better than that new standard bearer, Slim Whitman's 11-week wonder 'Rose Marie', but when it did so it didn't just break the record, it shattered it. '(Everything I Do) I Do It For You' remained at the top for 16 weeks, a stretch so long that in late September a *Top Of The Pops* presenter jokingly speculated that it could be the Christmas number one.

The song itself was heard over the end credits of the Kevin Costner movie *Robin Hood: Prince Of Thieves*. Kamen originally presented his melody in an early music style, but the participation of hard rock producer Lange ensured that the end product would not be a period piece. Nonetheless, a rock power ballad with a medieval feel was a first, and the single made immediate impact. It also topped the American chart for seven weeks.

BRYAN ADAMS' first important number one was in fact his 1985 American LP success, *Reckless*. (Pictorial Press)

For Adams (born 5 November 1959), a Canadian with English immigrant parents, this success constituted a spectacular comeback. He had accumulated 13 US chart hits between 1982 and '87, including the 1985 number one 'Heaven', and he had managed 11 UK entries in the shorter span 1985-'87. But, despite high-profile appearances at such charity projects as the 1988 Nelson Mandela 70th Birthday Party at Wembley Stadium and Roger Waters' 1990 performance of *The Wall* at the Berlin Wall, the artist was unable to complete an album to his own standards. The world success of '(Everything I Do) I Do It For You' created a large audience for a Bryan Adams album containing it, and *Waking Up The Neighbours* returned him to the multi-platinum ranks. One reason the single may have stayed at number one so long is that the album did not appear until four months after release of the *Robin Hood* theme, giving consumers the option of buying either the one song or a soundtrack album containing almost exclusively instrumentals. For the sake of Bryan Adams and chart history, most of them bought the single.

668

THE FLY

U2

2 November 1991, for 1 week

●

ISLAND IS 500

Writers: U2
Producer: Daniel Lanois

U2's second number one, which crashed straight into the top position, became the only chart-topper between March 1991 and November 1993 to spend just one week at the top. 'The Fly' was the first track from U2's eighth album, *Achtung Baby*, to be released as a single, and it climbed one place higher in the singles chart than its parent did in the albums list. It owed its success not only to the strength of the song and U2's typically powerful performance, but also to the marketing strategy of Island Records, who announced that 'The Fly' would only be available as a single for a very short time. It was deleted so quickly that it spent only five weeks on the charts, to equal Iron Maiden's record for the shortest stay on the charts by a number one, but then, rather bizarrely for a record that was officially no longer available, came back for a further week of chart action, leaving Iron Maiden's epic single as the stand-alone winner in the short-stay category. Island were also distributing Vic Reeves and the Wonder Stuff's single (see no. 669), and rumours abounded that they had held back stocks of 'Dizzy' to ensure that 'The Fly' had a clear run to the top, which showed off the strategic imagination of Island's marketing department to the full.

The flip-side of the 7-inch version of the single was the oddly titled 'Alex Descends Into Hell For A Bottle Of Milk', from the Royal Shakespeare Company's *A Clockwork Orange 2000*, which had opened in London on 6 February 1990, with music by the Edge.

669

DIZZY

VIC REEVES AND THE WONDER STUFF

9 November 1991, for 2 weeks

●●

SENSE SIGH 712

Writers: Tommy Roe and Freddy Weller
Producer: Mick Glossop

The 15th song to hit number one in two different versions was 'Dizzy', which had spent one week at the top in 1969 when performed by its co-writer Tommy Roe (see no. 271). When the popular comedian Vic Reeves (born Jim Moir in Darlington) teamed up with Stourbridge band the Wonder Stuff, their version of the song enjoyed a further two weeks at the top of the charts, sandwiched between singles from the two biggest album sellers of the time, U2 and Michael Jackson.

"It's nice to have a number one," said Reeves. "I can recommend it." Reeves himself, having first charted earlier in 1991 with the only hit version to that time of John Barry's film theme 'Born Free', obviously decided that one number one was enough, as his follow-up, a musically unchallenging version of the Cup Final hymn 'Abide With Me', stopped short of the Top 40, perhaps because it was issued at Christmas, five months before the Cup Final. The Wonder Stuff (Miles Hunt, Malcolm Treece, Martin Gilks, Martin Bell and Paul Clifford) had enjoyed ten hits before teaming up with Reeves for 'Dizzy', but only one had hit the Top 10. This was 'The Size Of A Cow', which on 4 May 1991 was knocked out of the number six position by Vic Reeves' 'Born Free'. After 'Dizzy', they began 1992 with their excellent 'Welcome To The Cheap Seats' EP which gave them another Top 10 hit, and at the end of 1993, their fourth album, *Construction For The Modern Idiot*, became their third Top 10 hit album.

670

BLACK OR WHITE

MICHAEL JACKSON

23 November 1991, for 2 weeks

●●

EPIC 657 598

Writer: Michael Jackson
Producers: Michael Jackson and Bill Bottrell

Anyone reading this book from cover to cover rather than dipping in and out will now be familiar with the exploits of Michael Jackson (see nos. 481, 516 and 596). Imagine the *Mastermind*-level of knowledge that would have been attained by a reader of an American equivalent of this book. 'Black Or White' may have been Jackson's fourth UK number one, but it was his 12th US chart-topper, tying him with the Supremes for third place on the all-time Most Number One Hits table. This was most appropriate, seeing as his very first LP appearance had been on *Diana Ross Presents The Jackson Five* in 1970.

Michael's own albums did not appear very often. Because he had taken more singles off his LPs than any artist before him, he had given the impression of having been prolific in the 80s, when in fact he had only released two new studio sets. 'Black Or White' was the first release from *Dangerous*, a double album issued just in time for Christmas 1991. A great deal was riding on this project, as Michael had earlier that year issued a multimedia deal with Sony estimated to be worth $1,000,000,000. At the pace Jackson released albums, he would be under contract with the Japanese company until the 2010s.

'Black Or White' was a plea for racial tolerance that in fact was reminiscent of 'Black And White', the peace-and-harmony number that had been a UK hit for Greyhound in 1971 and a US winner for Three Dog Night the following year. Something else was familiar about the disc, too. Just as Eddie Van Halen had highlighted Jackson's 1983 smash, 'Beat It', with his blistering guitar solo, Slash of Guns N' Roses guested on this track.

What was new was that Jackson was working without the services of Quincy Jones, who had been at the helm of all of his post-Motown work, including 11 of his 12 US number ones. This time he produced himself in conjunction with Bill Bottrell, who contributed a rap. The accompanying video, a lengthy and expensive piece, featured Jackson's pal Macaulay Culkin, star of the box-office blockbuster *Home Alone*.

671

DON'T LET THE SUN GO DOWN ON ME

GEORGE MICHAEL AND ELTON JOHN

7 December 1991, for 2 weeks

●●

EPIC 657 646

Writers: Elton John and Bernie Taupin
Producer: George Michael

With three chart versions, 'Don't Let The Sun Go Down On Me' briefly became the John/Taupin song with the most hit recordings. (Rod Stewart's cover of 'Your Song' brought that first Elton/Bernie hit tune into a tie the following year.) This was not bad going for a composition that on its initial outing in 1974 was kept off the BBC Radio 1 A-list its first week of release on the grounds that it was too long and slow. The network had to relent when the song charted, ultimately reaching number 16 in Britain and number two in America. Oleta Adams crept into the Top 40 with her version from the John/Taupin tribute album, *Two Rooms*, in the autumn of 1991.

Recorded at Wembley Arena in March of that year, 'Don't Let The Sun Go Down On Me' was a single choice by George Michael, who had begun his policy of not releasing work unless for charity until he managed to get out of his current recording contract with Sony. Proceeds from the sales of this disc went to AIDS charities, and it appropriately reached number one the week of 1-7 December, 1 December being International World AIDS Day. When George called Elton to ask his advice on releasing the live performance as a single, the writer told him it was probably a bad step, since it might flop and make it appear that his career was in decline when what he needed was a hit with one of his own compositions. Elton was delighted to laugh at the inaccuracy of his counsel when it soared to number one on both sides of the Atlantic. It was his third number one and George's fourth, not counting Michael's four further chart-toppers with Wham!, but the first occasion on which either artist had entered at number one. This meant that George Michael and Elton John as a duo joined the select group of acts who have achieved the Fastest Number One, going from nowhere to the top in 0 days. The pair also entered the table of One Hit Wonders, where George already resided in the company of Aretha Franklin, although he and Elton had previously appeared together on disc when he guested, without billing, on John's 1985 charter 'Wrap Her Up'.

Quoted in Elvis Presley's 'Are You Lonesome Tonight', the Bard of Avon returned to number one, although in a deliberately misspelled form, as the inspiration for the name of SHAKESPEARS SISTER. (Jean Baptiste Mondino)

672

BOHEMIAN RHAPSODY/THESE ARE THE DAYS OF OUR LIVES

QUEEN

21 December 1991, for 5 weeks

●●●●●

EMI QUEEN 21

Writers: 'Bohemian Rhapsody' – Freddie Mercury; 'These Are The Days Of Our Lives' – Queen
Producers: 'Bohemian Rhapsody' – Roy Thomas Baker and Queen; 'These Are The Days Of Our Lives' – Queen and David Richards

The death of one of rock music's greatest entertainers, Freddie Mercury, of AIDS on 24 November 1991, inevitably pushed interest in Queen's work old and new to new heights. The band in any case were going through an inspired spell of creativity in terms of both quality and quantity – the single and album 'Innuendo' (see no. 658) had been an artistic and commercial triumph.

The re-issue of Queen's 1975 rock and video classic (see no. 382), perhaps Freddie's greatest solo composition, as a Christmas tribute to him could hardly fail to go all the way again, even had it not been coupled with one of the best songs ever to emerge from the band's collective writing talents. The reflective lyric of 'These Are The Days Of Our Lives' was made doubly poignant by Freddie's masterful vocal and his tragic condition.

All royalties from this recording were donated by the band and their manager, Jim Beach, to the leading AIDS charity, the Terence Higgins Trust. The royalties were huge. Like 'Innuendo' earlier in the year, the single had entered the charts at number one. It sold 1.1 million copies in Britain alone, nearly as many as the staggering 1.3 million that 'Bohemian Rhapsody' had sold in 1975.

'Bohemian Rhapsody' became the first record to be number one over two separate Christmasses. In December 1991 Queen had no fewer than ten albums simultaneously in the UK Top 100. The extremely amusing use of 'Bo Rhap' in the film *Wayne's World* enabled the single to be a hit all over again in America too, a much rarer feat than a repeat smash in the UK charts.

673

GOODNIGHT GIRL

WET WET WET

25 January 1992, for 4 weeks

●●●●

PRECIOUS JEWEL 17

Writers: Graeme Clark, Tommy Cunningham, Neil Mitchell, Marti Pellow
Producers: Wet Wet Wet

Wet Wet Wet's second number one hit owed nothing to charitable causes or the Beatles, and everything to their own talent and staying power. Ten years after the band formed in Glasgow, the same four were still together, and their fourth album, *High On The Happy Side*, provided them with their second number one hits on both singles and albums charts. 'Goodnight Girl' was actually the third single released from the album, after 'Make It Tonight', which had peaked at number 37, and 'Put The Light On', which stopped at number 56. These were the two least successful singles of the Wets' career, so it was rather surprising that 'Goodnight Girl' took off so strongly in the first weeks of the New Year.

The album was released at a time when the teenyboppers were giving up on Wet Wet Wet, to such an extent that drummer Tommy Cunningham was quoted as saying that "*Smash Hits* won't put us on the cover any more", and the older audience had not yet become aware of the more mature Wet Wet Wet sound. The transition from teen sensation to adult appreciation is a tricky one, as practically everybody except Cliff Richard and George Michael has proved, but with 'Goodnight Girl' Wet Wet Wet went some way towards showing that they too could look forward to life after *Smash Hits*.

674

STAY

SHAKESPEARS SISTER

22 February 1992, for 8 weeks

●●●●●●●●

LONDON LON 314

Writers: Siobhan Fahey, Marcella Detroit and Guiot (Dave Stewart)
Producers: Chris Thomas, Alan Moulder and Shakespears Sister

Despite never having a number one single, Bananarama are the most succcessful British all-girl group in chart history. Siobhan Fahey was, therefore, taking a risk when she quit the group in 1988, citing dissatisfaction with the act's lack of artistic control over their own material. Fahey had married Dave Stewart, one half of Eurythmics, in August 1987, and he was instrumental in persuading his wife that she would find success in her second pop incarnation. Marcella Detroit's (born Marcella Levy in Detroit) first professional breakthrough came when she was hired as a backing singer for an Eric Clapton world tour which led to her co-writing Clapton's classic 'Lay Down Sally' in 1977. Detroit and Fahey were introduced in Los Angeles and found that they had a lot in common, including a shared love of the Smiths, whose 1985 single 'Shakespeare's Sister' became the basis for the act's name.

Shakespears Sister's first taste of Top 10 success came in 1989 with their second single, 'You're History', widely interpreted as a reference to Fahey's former colleagues. The first single from the duo's second album, *Hormonally Yours* (both women had been pregnant prior to the recording of the set), failed to make the Top 30. The second single, the hymn-like 'Stay', had no trouble in going where no Banana had gone before - to the top of the charts.

Despite international acclaim, a troubled Fahey dissolved the partnership in 1993, leaving Detroit to launch her solo career after over 20 years in the music business.

675

DEEPLY DIPPY

RIGHT SAID FRED

18 April 1992, for 3 weeks

●●●

TUG SNOG 3

Writers: Richard Fairbrass, Fred Fairbrass and Rob Manzoli
Producer: Tommy D.

Two very different singles became the sounds of the summer of 1991. While Bryan Adams ruled for 16 weeks at number one, an unlikely hit spent five weeks at number two. The song, 'I'm Too Sexy', was, in essence, a novelty hit, a classic example of the humorous off-the-wall songs that surface every few years in the British chart. The artists that perform such hits usually disappear from the charts, never to be heard of again. Such was the fate of Joe Dolce, neil and the Firm, but Right Said Fred (the name taken from Bernard Cribbins' 1962 Top 10 hit of that name) surprised everyone by progressing to enjoy a brief reign as Britain's top pop artists.

Success was a long time coming for Richard Fairbrass (vocals) and his brother Fred. Both had spent over ten years in the background of various acts that had not taken off. Until they approached songwriter Rob Manzoli, the highlight of their careers had been a stint in Bob Dylan's backing band.

The brothers were managing their own gymnasium in Putney, south west London when they met Manzoli rehearsing in a studio down the street. Richard and Fred were impressed enough to suggest that they join forces in a band, and within nine months they were number one in America and all over the world, apart from their homeland, where they had to be content with a number two. They were finally awarded the UK number one accolade with their third single, which actually sold only half the amount of 'I'm Too Sexy', but did not have the Bryan Adams phenomenon to compete with.

676

PLEASE DON'T GO/ GAME BOY

KWS

9 May 1992, for 5 weeks

●●●●●

NETWORK NWK 46

Writers: 'Please Don't Go' – Harry W. Casey, Richard Finch; 'Game Boy'– Chris King, Winston Williams
Producers: Chris King and Winston Williams

In the spring of 1992 an intriguing battle took place in a race to release a cover version of KC and the Sunshine Band's 1979 Top 3 hit, 'Please Don't Go'. The competitors were the UK's KWS and Willie Morales, an Italian vocalist who recorded under the name Double You?. Morales lost out by seven days and the result was the paltry consolation of a number 41 hit, while KWS, the Nottingham-based production duo of Chris King and keyboardist Winston Williams, reaped the rewards of a five-week stay at the chart pinnacle and a Top 5 US hit.

Not surprisingly, ZYX, the label that released the rival version, and Double You?, who had recorded the song with the distinctive dance arrangement first, were not amused. "It's not illegal, but it's unethical," remarked ZYX sales manager Alex Gold. Originally, KWS's record label, Network, had approached ZYX to licence Double You?'s version of the song for UK release, but were turned down. They subsequently released KWS's expeditious version, recorded for the sum of £237 in a Midlands bedroom.

Both in their mid-20s and friends since childhood, King and Williams' first venture into the recording world was as B Line, a techno-influenced group who secured the deal with Network. Although not a permanent fixture in the group, vocal input was provided by Delroy Joseph. Smaller hits followed 'Please Don't Go': 'Rock Your Baby', 'Hold Back The Night' and 'It Seems To Hang On'. All were cover versions of 70s disco classics.

677

ABBA-ESQUE (EP)

ERASURE

13 June 1992, for 5 weeks

●●●●●

MUTE 144

Tracks: 'Lay All Your Love On Me', 'Take A Chance On Me', 'Voulez-Vous', 'S.O.S.'
Writers: 'Lay All Your Love On Me', 'Take A Chance On Me', 'Voulez-Vous'– Benny Andersson, Bjorn Ulvaeus; 'S.O.S.' – Benny Andersson, Bjorn Ulvaeus and Stig Anderson
Producer: Dave Bascombe

As is often the case with successful writer/performers (e.g. Phil Collins, Nilsson, UB40, Wet Wet Wet), some of their biggest hits result when they make a rare excursion into another writer's (or writers') catalogue. This has certainly been true in the case of one of Britain's leading acts of the late 80s and early 90s, Erasure. Seventeen consecutive self-penned hits (including 11 Top 10 entries) from October 1985 through to March 1992 meant consistent and considerable acceptance, but the best showing of any one single had been the number two peak of 'Sometimes', in 1986, and the 'Crackers International EP' (with the lead track 'Stop') of 1988. An inspired collection of songs from the greatest pop-song writers of the 70s, Benny Andersson and Bjorn Ulvaeus (with help from manager Stig Anderson on the odd title), pushed the duo of keyboards-and-synthesizer master Vince Clarke and vocalist Andy Bell all the way for the first time.

Vince Clarke (born 3 July 1961) first hit the charts as a member of Depeche Mode, but departed that band at the end of 1981 to become half of Yazoo with singer Alison Moyet. In that guise his greatest moment was the number two success of 'Only You', a song which was even bigger for the Flying Pickets (see no. 529) in 1983. In 1985, by which time Yazoo had folded, he embarked on an album project which was to have featured ten different singers. When Andy Bell (born 25 April 1964) auditioned, Clarke abandoned this plan and Erasure took shape. The string of hits, and concerts emphasizing the contrast between the low-profile Clarke and the flamboyant Bell, soon followed.

The Erasure EP took Abba's Bjorn and Benny to number one in Britain as writers for the 11th time, and for the second time in non-Abba mode (see no. 545).

678

AIN'T NO DOUBT

JIMMY NAIL

18 July 1992, for 3 weeks

●●●

EASTWEST YZ 686

Writers: Guy Pratt, Danny Schogger, Jimmy Nail and Charlie Dore
Producers: Guy Pratt, Danny Schogger and Jimmy Nail

Actor Jimmy Nail, born James Michael Aloysius Bradford in Newcastle in 1954, came to public notice for his role as Oz in TV's *Auf Wiedersehen Pet*. Nail had always been an R&B fan and had played in several unsuccessful bands in and around Newcastle in his teens and 20s. In 1985 he released his version of Rose Royce's 'Love Don't Live Here Anymore', produced by Roger Taylor of Queen, on the back of his television fame. It hit number three, but after that Nail's recording career stayed in limbo as his acting career developed.

In 1992, he went back into the studios and came up with the album *Growing Up In Public*, which featured several illustrious names backing Nail's abrasive vocals. Gary Moore, George Harrison and Dave Gilmour were all involved, as were keyboardist Danny Schogger and Pink Floyd session man Guy Pratt. Schogger, Pratt and Nail co-wrote 'Ain't No Doubt' with Charlie Dore, whose haunting love song to a radio DJ, 'Pilot Of The Airwaves', had hit number 13 in America early in 1980, 53 places higher than the record's peak position in her native Britain.

After the huge success of 'Ain't No Doubt' and the album (which reached number two), the next single, 'Laura', failed to make even the Top 50, and Nail switched his efforts back to acting. His starring role in *Spender*, a series based around an unconventional Geordie policeman, which Nail had conceived and co-written, ensured that he remained in the forefront of his fans' minds, even if he failed to replace Sting as Newcastle's leading rock star.

679

RHYTHM IS A DANCER

SNAP!

8 August 1992, for 6 weeks

●●●●●●

LOGIC 115309

Writers: Benito Benitez, John 'Virgo' Garrett III, Thea Austin, Durron Butler
Producer: Snap!

Featuring one of the all-time tasteless lyrical lines of pop history - "I'm as serious as cancer, 'cause rhythm is a dancer" - 'Rhythm Is A Dancer' became Snap!'s second number one of the 90s, following in the footsteps of the introductory 'The Power'. Since their previous chart-topper, group member Penny Ford had departed to pursue a solo career with Columbia Records; her replacement Thea Austin's pairing with Turbo B was even shorter lived. This was her only outing with Luca Anzilotti and Michael Muenzing's group.

After the *World Power* album, which yielded five UK Top 10 hits, and following their US tour with MC Hammer, Snap! settled back into the Master Studios in Frankfurt to record a follow-up, *The Madman's Return*. The first track elevated to single status, 'Rhythm Is A Dancer', topped the chart in almost every territory in Europe. The single also marked the last outing with Snap! for rapper Turbo B, the former GI from Pittsburgh, while Austin's role was purely a one-off appointment. Their vacated positions went to Niki Haris who, for the previous eight years, had been recording and touring with Madonna. She kept up the group's impressive chart record, placing their next two singles, 'Exterminate' and 'Do You See The Light', at numbers two and ten respectively.

680

EBENEEZER GOODE

SHAMEN

19 September 1992, for 4 weeks

●●●●

ONE LITTLE INDIAN 78

Writers: Colin Angus, Richard West (Mr. C)
Producer: Shamen

The death in May 1991 of the Shamen's Will Sin in a drowning accident marked a turning point for remaining band member Colin Angus. After four years of limited success on the indie circuit, the duo were poised for chart glory with a remix of their techno/house club favourite, 'Progen'. Retitled 'Move Any Mountain', the single eventually reached number four and opened up the world of the Shamen to a greater audience.

Formed in Aberdeen in 1986 as a predominantly rock-based indie band, the group drew their early influences from late 60s psychedelia, in particular Pink Floyd's Syd Barrett. Moving to London and slimming their line-up to a duo, they signed a deal with One Little Indian.

After Sin's untimely death, Angus and the all-singing, all-rapping Mr. C. (aka Richard West) decided to continue with the band. The hits followed. The irresistibly catchy 'Ebeneezer Goode', their third straight Top 10 hit, dethroned Snap! after a six-week run at the top.

The track, with it's repeated chorus of "Eezer Goode, E's Ebeneezer Goode", was a thinly disguised reference to the use of the illegal drug Ecstacy (or 'E'). It incurred the wrath of the tabloids and received little support from local radio, but Radio One, perhaps wary after the

BOYZ II MEN named themselves after 'Boys To Men', a song by the 1983 UK chart-toppers New Edition. (Motown)

'Relax' (see no. 531) fiasco, championed the song nonetheless.

681

SLEEPING SATELLITE

TASMIN ARCHER

17 October 1992, for 2 weeks

●●

EMI EM 233

Writers: Tasmin Archer, John Beck and John Hughes
Producer: Paul 'Wix' Wickens

'Sleeping Satellite' was Tasmin Archer's first single and it got her recording career off to a dream start, becoming number one in five European countries besides the UK. Born in Bradford, she was first gainfully employed as a sewing machinist and a magistrate's clerk (not at the same time) before starting work as a general factotum at Flexible Response recording studios in her home town. She sang back-up on a few sessions, and it was here that she met her future writing partners, guitarist and former chemical engineer John Hughes and keyboard wizard John Beck.

The trio wrote together for five years, by which time Tasmin had signed to EMI, before coming up with the distinctive ballad 'Sleeping Satellite', which has been interpreted both as a love song and as a lament for man's unfulfilled space ambitions. An album, *Great Expectations*, followed and a second single, 'In Your Care', for the benefit of the children's charity Childline, made number 16.

After that came a few lesser single hits, but in 1993 Tasmin received a BRIT award for 'Sleeping Satellite' and was planning the release of a second album in 1995. She joins a distinguished list of stars who have had number ones about satellites, beginning with the Stargazers in 1954 and including Connie Francis in 1958, the Marcels and Danny Williams in 1961, the Tornados in 1962, Creedence Clearwater Revival in 1969, Showaddy-waddy in 1976 and the Police in 1979.

682

THE END OF THE ROAD

BOYZ II MEN

31 October 1992, for 3 weeks

●●●

MOTOWN TMG 1411

Writers: L.A. Reid, Babyface and Daryl Simmons
Producers: L.A. Reid and Babyface

Boyz II Men are an example of how being true to one's inspirations can lead to one's own success. Wanya Morris, Michael McCary, Shawn Stockman and Nathan Morris were four Philadelphia boys who met at the city's High School Of Creative And Performing Arts. They named themselves after one of their favourite songs, New Edition's 'Boys To Men', and received an enthusiastic reception from their fellow students at a school talent show in 1989. Shortly afterwards, they managed to get backstage after a concert by three New Edition alumni, Bell Biv Devoe, impressing Michael Bivins to the extent that he promised to get in touch with them.

To his credit and profit, he did. Bivins negotiated a production deal with Motown and Boyz II Men recorded their first album, *Cooleyhighharmony*, the title being a tribute to the 1975 film *Cooley High*. This movie had used 60s songs from the Motown catalogue and included a new piece sung by G. C. Cameron, 'It's So

Hard To Say Goodbye To Yesterday'. Boyz II Men's virtually a cappella recording reached number two on the *Billboard* Hot 100 and topped the R&B chart. 'Motownphilly', a tribute to their two cities of musical inspiration, nearly did the same, getting to number three on the pop side. *Cooleyhighharmony* became the best-selling album ever by an R&B group, passing five million in sales by the end of 1992.

Incredibly, the best was yet to come. Producers L.A. Reid and Babyface, who had enjoyed great success, particularly in the American charts, with a variety of artists ranging from Whitney Houston to Sheena Easton, recorded the quartet on a song for the soundtrack of the Eddie Murphy movie *Boomerang*.

'End Of The Road' seemed to have no end to its run at number one on the Hot 100, breaking the 36-year-old mark of 11 weeks set by Elvis Presley's double-sided hit, 'Don't Be Cruel/Hound Dog'. Boyz II Men were finally dethroned after 13 weeks at the top, but they had the consolation of winning the Grammy for Best R&B Group Performance for the second consecutive year, and a crossover to three weeks at the top of the British chart.

683

WOULD I LIE TO YOU

CHARLES AND EDDIE

21 November 1992, for 2 weeks

●●

CAPITOL CL 673

Writers: Mick Leeson and Peter Vale
Producer: Josh Deutsch

Philadelphian Charles Pettigrew and Eddie Chacon, from Oakland California, met on a New York subway and went on to become the first black and white male duo to hit number one since Paul McCartney and Stevie Wonder over ten years before (see no. 499).

The first single released from their first album, *Duophonic*, hit number one in its fourth week of chart life, before having to give up all thoughts of being the Christmas number one as Whitney Houston's megasmash swept everything else aside. All the same, it enjoyed 18 weeks on the chart, an impressive run in the 1990s.

'Would I Lie To You', a title that had already provided Top 40 hits for Whitesnake in 1981 and Eurythmics in 1985, was one of only three tracks on the duo's first album that was not co-written by Eddie Chacon, a Hispanic-American who had recorded two unsuccessful solo albums in Miami before getting together with jazz vocalist Pettigrew. Their meeting is described in song. The second track on their album, 'N.Y.C. (Can You Believe This City?)', which was also their second single, notes that Eddie "Ran into C on the E train/Had a brand new copy of Marvin Gaye's "Trouble Man"'. Surprisingly, after uniformly rave reviews for the album and a monster first hit single, the talented Charles and Eddie failed to consolidate their number one hit start.

684

I WILL ALWAYS LOVE YOU

WHITNEY HOUSTON

5 December 1992, for 10 weeks

●●●●●●●●●●

ARISTA 74321120657

Writer: Dolly Parton
Producer: David Foster

If someone were to ask from which movie 'I Will Always Love You' came, the most frequent response would be *The Bodyguard*. Yet *The Best Little Whorehouse In Texas* would also be a correct answer.

'I Will Always Love You' has been a number one of some sort for three consecutive decades. It first topped the country chart for writer Dolly Parton in 1974. She revisited the country top spot in 1982 with a new version for the saucily-named but family fare film mentioned above. Whitney Houston then adapted the song in her own emotional style for *The Bodyguard*.

The Whitney-Kevin Costner feature was panned by critics but adored by international audiences, climbing to number five on the all-time table of box-office successes outside the United States. 'I Will Always Love You' did even better on the singles charts, spending ten weeks at the summit in Britain to overtake Doris Day's 'Secret Love' as the longest-running number one by a woman. In America it lasted a mighty 14 weeks, adding one to the recent record-breaking total of 13 by Boyz II Men's 'End Of The Road'. The new disc was Houston's ninth American number one, one behind Madonna's total of ten, the most by a woman. But whereas Madonna may have sold more newspapers, Whitney sold more albums. By August of 1993, the Arista star had shifted more than 55 million albums worldwide, including sales of *The Bodyguard* soundtrack.

In the UK 'I Will Always Love You' was the artist's fourth number one, selling over 1.5 million copies and becoming the best-selling CD single to date.

685

NO LIMIT

2 UNLIMITED

13 February 1993, for 5 weeks

●●●●●

MCA PWL 256

Writers: Anita Dels, Ray Slijngaard, Phil Wilde and Jean Paul de Coster
Producers: Phil Wilde and Jean Paul de Coster

Described by one journalist as 'the Elton John and Kiki Dee of rave', Holland's 2 Unlimited, Anita Dels and Ray Slijngaard, hit the high spot after threatening to do so with their previous outings, 'Get Ready For This' and 'Twilight Zone', which between them notched up three weeks at number two. The simply titled 'No Limits', which prompted the TV show *Spitting Image* (see no. 570) to satirize the song as 'No Lyrics', became only the second Dutch recording to reach number one, after Pussycat's 'Mississippi' in 1976.

2 Unlimited was formed in May 1991. Before then, Slijngaard and Dels had both rapped and danced with various local groups, Anita also working as a session singer and model. Teaming up with the Belgian production team of Phil Wilde and Jean Paul de Coster, who had enjoyed European success with Bizz Nizz's 'Don't Miss The Partyline', the duo soon established themselves as the pop radio-friendly face of rave culture. 'No Limits' enjoyed number one positions in no less than 19 countries, whilst their second album, also titled *No Limits*, and also a UK chart-topper, sold over two-and-a-half million copies worldwide.

686

OH CAROLINA

SHAGGY

20 March 1993, for 2 weeks

●●

GREENSLEEVES GRE 361

Writer: John Folkes
Producer: Sting International

Greensleeves Records was formed in 1978, but until 1993 they had failed to place a record in the UK Top 40. That changed in February when Shaggy entered the charts with a song penned by John Folkes and originally recorded with his brothers.

Born Orville Richard Burrell in Kingston, Jamaica, on October 22 1968, Shaggy moved to New York aged 15 and teamed up with friends to form the Brooklyn sound system Sting International Posse. Several years later he joined the US marines, going AWOL to complete recordings. His publicists claimed that this double life earned him three reggae number ones and a commendation from the US government after leading his platoon through a minefield during the Gulf War's 'Operation Desert Storm'.

'Oh Carolina' was his breakthrough. It also set the scene for what was to become a remarkable year for reggae. The previous best showing for Jamaica's greatest export had been in July 1971, when Dave and Ansil Collins, Bob and Marcia, John Kongos and Lobo had all championed reggae, but during the 70s and 80s it had meant little more than the occasional novelty hit. With Shaggy at number one, Snow's 'Informer' at two and 'Mr Loverman' by Shabba Ranks third, reggae dominated the top of the charts as never before.

687

YOUNG AT HEART

THE BLUEBELLS

3 April 1993, for 4 weeks

●●●●

LONDON LON 338

Writers: Bobby Hodgens and Siobhan Fahey
Producers: Colin Fairley and Robert Andrews

The Bluebells of Scotland were formed in 1982, originally comprising David McCluskey (born 13 January 1964, drums) and his brother Ken (born 8 February 1962, vocals and harmonica), Robert 'Bobby Bluebell' Hodgens (born 6 June 1959, vocals and guitar), Russell Irvine (guitar) and Lawrence Donegan (bass). The last two were later replaced by Craig Gannon (born 3 July 1966, guitar) and Neal Baldwin on bass.

The group enjoyed reasonable commercial success as exponents of melodic unelectronic pop, but never to the extent that their talents merited, until it was too late.

Their first chart single, 'Cath', limped to number 62 in the spring of 1983, and the follow-up, 'Sugar Bridge (It Will Stand)', did slightly worse. 'I'm Falling', in March 1984, rose to number 11, paving the way for the irresistible 'Young At Heart' (not Frank Sinatra's first-ever chart song, but an original written by Bananarama diva Siobhan Fahey and 'Bobby Bluebell' when the two were an item), which peaked at number eight in the summer. These hits in turn pushed their album *Sisters* into the Top 30, and a re-issue of 'Cath', this time making the Top 40, wound up the Bluebells' only-ever year of consistent acceptance.

The band had long since split, with the McCluskey brothers established as folkies with their own label, when 'Young At Heart' was used by Volkswagen as the soundtrack to a TV commercial. The nine-year-old track was re-issued, and this time the superb exposure ensured that everybody heard it. Almost everybody bought it. The band got together again for a *Top Of The Pops* performance but there was no permanent reformation. Siobhan Fahey (see no. 674) thus achieved her second number one, neither of them written for Bananarama.

688

FIVE LIVE (EP)

GEORGE MICHAEL AND QUEEN WITH LISA STANSFIELD

1 May 1993, for 3 weeks

●●●

PARLOPHONE R 6340

Tracks: 'Somebody To Love' – George Michael and Queen; 'Killer - Papa Was A Rolling Stone' (medley) – George Michael; 'These Are The Days Of Our Lives' – George Michael and Queen with Lisa Stansfield and 'Calling You' – (George Michael)
Writers: 'Somebody To Love' – Freddie Mercury; 'Killer - Papa Was A Rolling Stone' – Seal, Adam Tinley, Norman Whitfield and Barrett Strong; 'These Are The Days Of Our Lives' Queen and 'Calling You' – Bob Telson
Producers: 'Somebody To Love' and 'These Are The Days Of Our Lives' – George Michael, Queen and David Richards; 'Killer - Papa Was A Rolling Stone' and 'Calling You' – George Michael and Chris Porter

The huge Freddie Mercury tribute concert (in support of AIDS charities), which had been announced by the surviving members of Queen shortly after his death in November 1991, took place at Wembley on 20 April 1992, Easter Monday. Brian, Roger and John opened the show at 6 pm and fellow performers included Metallica, Extreme, Guns N' Roses, Def Leppard, Elizabeth Taylor, Liza Minnelli, George Michael, Elton John and Lisa Stansfield. 80,000 Freddie fans packed the stadium and millions (one estimate even reached a billion) watched worldwide on television. The Mercury Phoenix Trust was established to handle the income from this and other AIDs projects in Freddie's name.

Five songs from the show were issued as an extended single, again in aid of the cause. Thus, two great Queen hits returned to the charts, 'Somebody To Love', previously number two for the band in 1976, and the recent number one, 'These Are The Days Of Our Lives' (see no. 672). George Michael, his official recording career seriously interrupted by a long drawn-out dispute with Sony Records, was spending more time in the courts than in the charts, but must have been delighted on a personal as well as a charitable level to return to the number one slot; and Lisa Stansfield, although she had consolidated her reputation as a major white soul act since 'All Around The World' (see no. 635), had not been back to the very top since. 'Killer', originally in the hands of Adamski (see no. 645), was another song making a second trip to number one, but magnificent though the material was, it was undoubtedly the cause and nostalgia for Freddie Mercury that drove this EP all the way.

689

ALL THAT SHE WANTS

ACE OF BASE

22 May 1993, for 3 weeks

●●●

LONDON/METRONOME 861 270

Writers: Joker and Buddha
Producers: Denniz Pop, Joker and Buddha

The seeds of a flourishing Swedish music industry were sown by Abba in the 70s. In the late 80s and early 90s the seeds came to fruition with worldwide success for Swedish acts Roxette, who scored four American number ones (three more than their palindromic and acronymic predecessors), Dr. Alban and Ace Of Base.

The family team of sisters Jenny and Malin Bergren on vocals and brother Jonas joined forces with childhood friend and programmer Ulf Ekberg in their hometown of Gothenburg, Sweden's second largest city. Hawking demo tapes around various Swedish record companies, they were unanimously turned down until 1991 when Mega Records, a Danish company, signed them. Their debut release, 'Wheel Of Fortune', went unnoticed in their homeland but shot straight to number one in Denmark and Norway in February 1992. It was not until their second single, 'All That She Wants', knocked 'Wheel Of Fortune' from pole position in Denmark, thus providing Ace Of Base with a stranglehold on the top two positions there, that Sweden woke up and took notice. After monopolising the listings on the continent for over a year, 'All That She Wants' was finally released in Britain, repeating its European success and selling over half a million copies. America, too, proved not to be immune to the infuriatingly catchy lyric. The single was a million seller, peaking at number two. Positions were reversed for 'The Sign', their second US release - it went all the way in America but stopped one place short here. In Britain, they were only the third Swedish act to top the charts, after Abba and Europe. In America, they were the fourth, after Blue Swede, Abba and Roxette.

690

(I CAN'T HELP) FALLING IN LOVE WITH YOU

UB40

12 June 1993, for 2 weeks

●●

DEP INTERNATIONAL DEP 40

Writers: Hugo Peretti, Luigi Creatore and George David Weiss
Producers: UB40

UB40 first entered the British charts in 1980 and had reached the survey every year since, a record of consistency by a still-current act eclipsed only by Diana Ross' interminable string of 30 years, the first six as lead singer of the Supremes. Although the Birmingham group wrote most of their material, each of their three number ones had been covers. 'Can't Help Falling In Love' had gone all the way for Elvis Presley in 1962, hit three in 1970 for Andy Williams and reached four for the Stylistics in 1976. A minor hit by Lick The Tins in 1986 gave a Los Angeles oldies station material for a comedy sketch speculating that Elvis had been reincarnated as a Scotswoman.

The first UB40 number one, 'Red Red Wine', had become a US chart-topper five years later, and still held the record for slowest westward crossing over the Atlantic by a mutual number one. (The Steve Miller Band's 'The Joker' took even longer to travel in the opposite direction.)

GABRIELLE found fame with her platinum debut chart album, *Find A Way*. 'Dreams' found its way to the top, giving her an emotional evening at the *Brit Awards* in February 1994. (Martin Gardiner)

This third number one gave its writers number ones in four consecutive decades, including the Elvis original (see no. 133), 'Can't Give You Anything (But My Love)' (see no. 376) by the Stylistics and 'The Lion Sleeps Tonight' by Tight Fit (see no. 496).

UB40's 'Can't Help Falling In Love' was featured conspicuously in the Sharon Stone film *Sliver*, although it had not been recorded for it. The video incorporated footage from the movie.

691

DREAMS

GABRIELLE

26 June 1993, for 3 weeks

●●●

GO! DISCS GOD 99

Writers: Gabrielle and Tim Laws
Producer: Richie Fermie

"Dreams can come true," sang 23-year-old south Londoner Louise Gabrielle Bobb on her debut single, and in the long tradition of pop fairy tales this one was one of the year's best. Originally sampling the distinctive guitar introduction to Tracy Chapman's 'Fast Car', 'Dreams' first appeared as a white-label release on the indie Victim label in 1991. After securing a distribution deal with reggae specialists Jetstar, the single started to sell in 1992. It pottered around the lowest reaches of the chart for over a year, peaking at number 136 in January 1993. Chapman refused to sanction the use of the sample and the record was deleted.

Based on the initial buzz, Go Beat signed Gabrielle and re-recorded the single without the offending introduction. They also commissioned a slew of remixes which were distributed to clubs several weeks before release, generating massive demand for the record. In June the single exploded into the chart at number two, the highest entry to date by a new artist, and the following week gave the label its fourth number one in 99 releases. Gabrielle also became the third artist at number one to wear an eye patch, after Johnny Kidd (see no. 105), and Ray Sawyer of Dr. Hook (see no. 446).

The dream continued with a platinum album, *Find A Way*, and a Top 30 placing for the single in America.

692

PRAY

TAKE THAT

17 July 1993, for 4 weeks

●●●●

RCA 74321 154507

Writer: Gary Barlow
Producers: Steve Jervier, Paul Jervier and Jonathan Wales

Successful Manchester entertainment agency owner Nigel Martin-Smith's ambition was to create a British pop group that would grip the world's imagination, a British answer to the five US heart-throbs New Kids On The Block.

Gary Barlow began writing songs in his teens and formed his first act, the Cutest Rush, with Mark Owen. Howard Donald and Jason Orange had met through their shared interest in breakdancing, and together they formed a duo, Street Beat. By combining Gary and Mark's musical ability with Howard and Jason's athleticism, Martin-Smith moved towards achieving his ambition, but he still wanted a fifth member. After Robbie Williams, a young actor on Martin-Smith's books, performed a rousing rendition of 'Any Dream Will Do' in front of the other four members, he was accepted into the group. The whirlwind of media interest generated by the semi-nude (from the waist up) video for their first single, 'Do What U Like', led to RCA signing the group in 1991. The group's subsequent singles saw Take That's popularity steadily grow. By the time their ninth single, 'Pray', was released in 1993, Take That fever had gripped the nation. The song's predecessor, 'Why Can't I Wake Up With You', had entered the chart at number two, despite being the eighth single to be lifted from the debut *Take That And Party* album, so it wasn't surprising that Gary's first composition from the follow-up album entered the chart at number one.

693

LIVING ON MY OWN

FREDDIE MERCURY

14 August 1993, for 2 weeks

●●

PARLOPHONE R 6355

Writer: Freddie Mercury
Producers: Mack and Freddie Mercury; rearranged, produced and recorded by NMB, Serge Ramaekers, Colin Peter and Carl Ward

Nearly two years after his death, there was still no sign of waning enthusiasm for Freddie Mercury's life and Freddie Mercury memories. His manager Jim Beach responded to the incessant demand for fresh material by inviting the Belgian-based production team No More Brothers of Messrs. Ramaekers, Peter and Ward to re-work one of the songs from Freddie's 1985 album, *Mr. Bad Guy*, for the 1993 singles market. The LP, containing 11 songs written by Freddie, had been his first major extra-Queen activity, although his first solo single hit had been 'Love Kills' in 1984, taken from a new Giorgio Moroder soundtrack to the great Fritz Lang silent movie, *Metropolis*.

Mr. Bad Guy was only a modest triumph, by Queen's standards anyway, with the first of three singles, 'I Was Born To Love You', the most successful, peaking at number 11. 'Living On My Own' was the third single and could do no more than totter up to number 50. However, Beach correctly reasoned that this solo venture had been seriously underrated and that there was gold in them thar grooves.

NMB proved him right in Antwerp in April 1993. Their remix hit big and quick on European radio and Freddie achieved the solo number one smash that he had never enjoyed while alive.

As of the middle of 1994, Brian May, Roger Taylor and John Deacon were working on three or four unreleased Queen tracks recorded during the time of

Innuendo, so there may well be some brand new Mercury vocals yet to storm the airwaves.

694

MR. VAIN

CULTURE BEAT

28 August 1993, for 4 weeks

●●●●

EPIC 659468 2

Writers: Steven Levis, Nosie Katzmann and Jay Supreme
Producer: Torsten Fenslau

Culture Beat first strayed across the British consciousness with their 1990 club hit, '(Cherry Lips) Der Erdbeermund' ('Erdbeermund' actually translates as 'strawberry mouth' rather than 'cherry lips', but why worry?). But three years later, the massive Eurohit of the summer brought the insidious Culture Beat rhythms to the top of the British charts - and to the top of almost every other European chart – to make it the biggest-selling record of the year in Europe. Culture Beat was the brainchild of German producer Torsten Fenslau, but 'Mr. Vain' was actually performed by Tania Evans and rapper Jay Supreme, who were the stage presence of Culture Beat.

The main historical interest in the single, though, was not in its meaningful lyrics or its sales figures. The true significance of 'Mr. Vain' was that it was the first single not issued on 7-inch vinyl to hit number one since the 1950s, before the 7-inch single had been invented. The fact that a single selling only in cassette and CD formats could hit number one was described in the press as heralding the end of the single, but this is, of course, not so. Just as the breakable 78 rpm single died out and was replaced by the 7-inch single, so new technology is replacing vinyl with CDs. But the single is here to stay, on whatever format we choose to listen to it.

Sadly, Torsten Fenslau was killed in a car crash near Darmstadt in November 1993, at the age of 29, but this did not bring to an end Culture Beat's success. 'Got To Get It' and 'Anything' followed 'Mr. Vain' into the Top 5, as the band played on.

695

BOOM! SHAKE THE ROOM

JAZZY JEFF AND THE FRESH PRINCE

25 September 1993, for 2 weeks

●●

JIVE R 335

Writers: Will Smith, Lee Haggard, Walter Williams and Ken Mayberry. The song contains a sample of 'Funky Worm', written by Leroy Bonner, Clarence Satchell, Marshall Jones, Jimmy 'Diamond' Williams, Merv Pierce, Billy Beck and Ralph Middlebrook
Producer: Mr. Lee

When, against all expectations, 'Boom! Shake The Room' leapfrogged over the Pet Shop Boys' 'Go West', it gave Philadelphia rappers Jeff Townes (Jazzy Jeff) and Will Smith (Fresh Prince) their first number one after seven years of trying. The hard-edged yet radio-friendly club hit produced by hip-house producer Mr. Lee marked a strong comeback for the duo whose previous outing, 'Ring My Bell', had stalled at an ignominious 53.

The pair first hit the charts in 1986 with the comically worded 'Girls Ain't Nothing But Trouble' from the album *Rock The House*. Their next set, *He's The DJ, I'm The Rapper*, yielded no UK hit singles

but broke them in the States, winning a Grammy and selling nearly three million units. Transatlantic chart success came with the lead-off track from their 1991 set, *Homebase*. 'Summertime', with a sample borrowed from Kool and the Gang's 'Summer Madness', was a Top 10 item in both countries.

A two-year hiatus followed, during which Smith concentrated on his acting career. One of the hottest comedy actors in America, thanks to his starring role in the US sitcom *The Fresh Prince Of Bel Air*, he lined up alongside Whoopi Goldberg and Ted Danson in his first film, *Made in America*. Immediately after filming he was back in the studio recording the album *Code Red*, from which 'Boom! Shake The Room' was lifted.

696

RELIGHT MY FIRE

TAKE THAT featuring LULU

9 October 1993, for 2 weeks

●●

RCA 74321 16772

Writer: Dan Hartman
Producers: Joey Negro and Andrew Livingstone

Take That had come close to giving up their dream when their third single, 'Once You've Tasted Love', failed to make the Top 40 in January 1992. They persevered and undertook an extensive tour of schools and teenage nightclubs to build support in their target audience of young girls. It was agreed that a cover version would provide a greater chance of a hit, and Tavares' 'It Only Takes A Minute' was selected, becoming their first Top 10 hit in May 1992. The second Take That cover version was Barry Manilow's 'Could It Be Magic', which peaked at number three. Their third, 'Relight My Fire', was the most successful yet, entering the charts at number one.

Take That's manager, Nigel Martin-Smith, remembered the Dan Hartman song being a hit in the clubs of the North West in 1979, and felt it would be an ideal song for his protégés to update. The original version featured a raucous female vocal courtesy of Loleatta Holloway, so Martin-Smith contacted his boyhood heroine Lulu to guest on the track.

Lulu, born Marie Lawrie on 3 November 1948 in Glasgow, had enjoyed her first hit in 1964 with the Top 10 item 'Shout'. Although she had topped the chart in America with 'To Sir With Love' in 1967, before any of Take That's members had been born, she had never reached the number one slot in Britain, despite an impressive string of hits. Her wait of 29 years 148 days for a UK chart-topper was the longest ever.

697

I'D DO ANYTHING FOR LOVE (BUT I WON'T DO THAT)

MEATLOAF

23 October 1993, for 7 weeks

●●●●●●●

VIRGIN VS 1443

Writer: Jim Steinman
Producer: Jim Steinman

In one of the most astonishing comebacks in pop history, Meat Loaf, who had not enjoyed a British hit single in seven years and had been absent from the American list since 1981, burst back on the scene with the first release from his album *Bat Out Of Hell II - Back Into Hell*. Born Marvin Aday on 27 September 1947 in Dallas, Meat had issued the original *Bat Out Of Hell* in 1977. The album achieved the bizarre distinctions of selling over seven million copies in the US without ever making the Top 10 and accumulating eight years on the UK chart without climbing higher than number nine. Not only had he never approached a number one placing on the album side, none of his singles ever neared the top. A dozen UK hits yielded only one Top 10 title, the duet with an uncredited Cher, 'Dead Ringer For Love', and Meat never lunched in the US Top 10, despite selling a million copies of the long-running 'Two Out Of Three Ain't Bad'.

The Meat Loaf/Jim Steinman reunion changed all that. Titled *Bat Out Of Hell II - Back Into Hell* for what the artist cheerfully confessed were commercial reasons, it soared to the top of the album charts on both sides of the Atlantic and spawned this massively successful single. 'I'd Do Anything For Love (But I Won't Do That)' stayed at number one in the UK for seven weeks, a long run for a long song. Even edited down from its 11-minute-55-second album length, the track was timed at just under eight minutes. It wrested the title of Longest Number One away from the Beatles' 'Hey Jude', which had held the title for a quarter of a century, and duplicated the feat in the US.

Meat Loaf had long been a part-time actor, appearing as Eddie in *The Rocky Horror Picture Show* and playing in several less noteworthy films. He was also seen in projects ranging from the original Broadway production of *Hair* to *Wayne's World*. The gothic *Beauty and the Beast*-type video that accompanied '...Anything...' allowed him further room to display his acting ability.

Steinman had previously helmed the Bonnie Tyler number one 'Total Eclipse Of The Heart', but this was the first appearance at number one, indeed on any hit record, by the uncredited female vocalist Mrs. Loud of Newcastle duo the Louds.

698

MR. BLOBBY

MR. BLOBBY

11 December 1993, for 1 week

●

and 25 December 1993, for 2 weeks

●●

DESTINY MUSIC DMUS 104

Writers: Paul Shaw and David Rogers
Producers: Paul Shaw and David Rogers

'Gotcha' was a feature of Noel Edmonds' hugely popular BBC-TV programme *Noel's House Party*, which involved

Marvin Lee Aday was just 13 when christened MEAT LOAF by his football coach. A career in football was not to be, but the nickname proved extremely useful in his music life. (Rex Features)

celebrities being taken for a ride on camera. The first series of japes had famous victims believing that they were being filmed for a new children's series. These 'programmes' featured a new juvenile character, Mr. Blobby, who would instruct the tinies how to take up the celebrity's particular skill or interest. Thus, Mr. Blobby learned rugby football with Will Carling and ballet with Wayne Sleep.

Mr. Blobby, devised by the *House Party* producer, the aptly named Mike Leggo, was a huge mound of pink blubber with yellow spots, containing an extremely warm actor. 'Gotcha' began with a fairly serious rehearsal in which it seemed that Mr. Blobby really would master the intricacies of the line-out or *pas de deux*, but come the actual take, Noel Edmonds would nip into the Blobby outfit and chaos would break out. Bewildered stars would watch in a combination of horror and delight as the pink presence pulverised the script and the set in his calamitous attempts to educate the young. Eventually, Noel would reveal himself, celebrity got the joke and 'Gotcha Oscar' statuette, and laughs abounded.

Mr. Blobby became so popular in his own right that he was retained for the third series of *Noel's House Party* in 1993. His cover having been blown, he could no longer participate in the 'Gotchas', so he majored on the destructive aspects of his persona. Now permanently housing actor Barry Killerby, he lumbered around the studio, and indeed many other parts of Britain, wrecking everything in his path.

With the eyesore well on his way to becoming a cult, the *House Party* team were besieged with extracurricular offers, particularly recording ones. Searching for a signature tune for their manic creation, Leggo and co. unearthed a Carlin Music mood tape for children's TV which contained a 20-second item entitled 'Mr. Jellybun', by Paul Shaw and David Rogers, eminently suitable as a musical illustration of the Blobby phenomenon.

It seemed logical to ask the writers to expand their brief masterpiece, and the 'Mr. Blobby' single was the result. With the *House Party* backing Blobby to the hilt, how could it miss? Not only did the single hit number one, it even reclaimed the top spot after being usurped for one week by the only musical act to rival Mr. Blobby in the popularity stakes, so take that, Take That.

699

BABE

TAKE THAT

18 December 1993, for 1 week

•

RCA 74321182137

Writer: Gary Barlow
Producers: Steve and Paul Jervier and Jonathan Wales

Twelve people and a dog had turned up to Take That's first appearance at a Huddersfield nightclub back in 1990. By the time Take That's 11th single was released in 1993, they had just completed a sell-out tour of 21 arenas across Britain, performing to over 200,000 fans. On the eve of the release of 'Babe', Gary, Jason, Howard, Mark and Robbie had appeared at the annual *Smash Hits* Poll Winners Party. They won a record eight awards, as voted by readers of Britain's leading pop magazine. The winner of the all-important 'Most Fanciable Male' category went to Mark Owen and it was he who sang lead on 'Babe', taking over vocal duties from Gary Barlow, who usually crooned the group's tunes.

Seven days after the awards Take That made chart history when 'Babe' crashed into the charts at number one. They

became the first act to have three consecutive singles debut in that position, beating the existing record held by both Slade and the Jam. Take That were expecting to hold on to the position for a further week and so grab the Christmas number one slot, but their marketing strategy was so successfully targetted that the majority of fans bought the disc in its first week of release. Second-week sales generally saw a disappointing decline and so it was that Mr. Blobby (see no. 698) was able to regain the top spot and enjoy the Christmas accolade.

700

TWIST AND SHOUT

CHAKA DEMUS AND PLIERS WITH JACK RADICS AND TAXI GANG

8 January 1994, for 2 weeks

●●

MANGO MNG 814

Writers: Bert Berns and Phil Medley
Producers: Sly Dunbar, Robbie Shakespeare and Lloyd 'Gitsy' Willis

Chaka Demus (born John Taylor in 1964), a Jamaican DJ, teamed up with reggae singer Pliers (born Everton Bonner in 1963) to record an album, *Tease Me*, which was released in the middle of 1993 to very favourable reviews. The first single was the title track, which climbed to number three. This was followed by a 1981 Curtis Mayfield R&B hit in America, 'She Don't Let Nobody', which took the duo to number four. For their third single they chose a track not originally on the album, but it took them to the very top.

The 700th number one was written in 1962 and originally recorded, with no chart success, by the Top Notes. It was the Isley Brothers, however, who had the first big hit with the song, climbing to number 16 in America in 1962. The song did not chart in Britain until Brian Poole and the Tremeloes covered it in the summer of 1963. Their version climbed to number four, while the Isleys enjoyed just one week of chart glory at number 42. The Beatles also recorded the song on a 1963 EP, which would have been a Top 10 hit if EPs had qualified for inclusion on the singles chart at the time. Salt-N-Pepa's unusual version of the song brought it back into the Top 5 a quarter of a century later in 1988, but Chaka Demus and Pliers' version was nevertheless the first to hit number one.

It was producer Sly Dunbar's idea to record the song with the duo, as he had already worked on it with another Jamaican reggae singer, Jack Radics, and thought it would be perfect for Chaka Demus and Pliers' style. With Jack Radics making a guest appearance on the recording, they created the first-ever twist song to hit the top, over 35 years after the dance was invented. When the *Tease Me* album was re-released in the wake of their first three Top 10 hits, 'Twist and Shout' was included and the album shot to the top of the charts.

701

THINGS CAN ONLY GET BETTER

D:REAM

22 January 1994, for 4 weeks

●●●●

MAGNET MAG 1020

Writers: Peter Cunnah and Jamie Petrie
Producer: D:Ream with Tom Frederikse; remixed by Paul Oakenfold

Londonderry's Peter Cunnah gained his first musical experience fronting unsuccessful rock band Ciderboy, but as the 90s began he immersed himself in London's club culture. Al McKenzie, a native of Dundee was deejaying at the fashionable Gardening Club in 1991 when he met Cunnah. A shared interest in dance music led them to form D:Ream, with McKenzie as keyboardist and Cunnah as vocalist. Their first release, 'U R The Best Thing', on the independent FXU label in 1992, became a club anthem and a favourite of influential Radio One DJ Pete Tong, but made only number 72.

The original version of 'Things Can Only Get Better' was the follow-up and became the duo's first Top 40 hit, peaking at number 26. it was accompanied by three further Top 40 hits, including a re-release of 'U R The Best Thing'.

When a support slot with teen idols Take That was offered to D:Ream, it seemed the ideal opportunity but McKenzie, unhappy with the effects of stardom and anxious to return to life as a DJ, declined the proposal and the duo amicably split. The record company were keen to capitalize on the exposure the tour provided so, in the absence of new material following the split, an improved remix of 'Things Can Only Get Better' by top producer Paul Oakenfold was issued as a single. One month later it was number one.

702

WITHOUT YOU

MARIAH CAREY

19 February 1994, for 4 weeks

●●●●

COLUMBIA 6599192

Writers: Pete Ham and Tom Evans
Producer: Walter Afanasieff and Mariah Carey

Mariah Carey was born on 22 March 1970, the third child of Patricia Carey, who used to sing with the New York City Opera, but turned to voice coaching. Her star pupil turned out to be her own daughter. Patricia named her daughter after the Lerner and Loewe song 'They Call The Wind Mariah', from the musical *Paint Your Wagon*. Incidentally, Mariah was born on the day that another song from that musical, Lee Marvin's 'Wand'rin' Star', fell from the number one slot in Britain.

Carey was working as a Manhattan waitress when she managed to get her demo tape to Tommy Mottola, then president of CBS Records. Mottola was impressed, and by the middle of 1990 had released Carey's first single, 'Vision Of Love'. It went to number one in America, and she quickly established herself as the most successful chart performer in American history. When her fifth single, 'Emotions', became her fifth chart-topper, she had broken the record set by the Jackson Five, who had topped the charts with each of their first four singles. But her success did

Long Island lady MARIAH CAREY, has a voice that spans 7 octaves. (Daniela Federici)

not end there, or with her June 1993 marriage to Tommy Mottola. 'Without You', which peaked at number three in America, became her first single not to make the Top 2. Ironically, in Britain it became her first to get to the very top, and the first single by a woman to enter the charts at number one.

Taken from her chart-topping fourth album, *Music Box*, 'Without You' went on to outsell Nilsson's version, which had hit number one in 1972 (see no. 311), over Carey's second birthday. Nilsson did not live to see the song have a second run at number one, as he had died on 15 January 1994.

703

DOOP

DOOP

19 March 1994, for 3 weeks

●●●

CITYBEAT CBE 774

Writers: Frederick Ridderhof
Producers: Peter Garnefski

The first instrumental to hit the top for just over 20 years was a strange concoction of house and Charleston by two studio producers from the Hague in the Netherlands. Ridderhof and Garnefski claimed to have noticed the great similarity between the rhythms of 1990s house music and 1920s jazz, and decided to put the two together. The result was 'Doop', an instrumental (apart from bursts of the title word, repeated by high-kicking, scat-singing flapper girls) which combined the instrumentation of the 1920s with the studio sophistication of the 1990s. Several mixes were released, by Mother, and by Judge Jules and Michael Skins, as well as the Jean Lejeux Orchestra mix, the Sidney Berlin Ragtime Band mix and the Urge 2 Merge mix, which was the A-side of the 7-inch single version.

'Doop' was the second record within a few months to get to number one performed by an act with exactly the same name as the song they performed, 'Mr. Blobby' having been the first. Until these two great talents came along, no truly eponymous single had ever topped the charts, although S'Express and MASH had come close.

TAKE THAT are (left to right), Howard Donald, Gary Barlow, Jason Orange, Robbie Williams and Mark Owen. (RCA)

704

EVERYTHING CHANGES

TAKE THAT

9 April 1994, for 2 weeks

●●

RCA 74321167732

Writers: Gary Barlow, Mike Ward, Eliot Kennedy and Cary Baylis
Producers: Mike Ward and Eliot Kennedy

The British press are often quick to proclaim any act that inspires scenes of mass hysteria among young girls as 'The New Beatles' and Take That have been no exception. Yet the five lads from Manchester have come closest in Britain to matching the achievements of the Fab Four.

The title track and fourth single from their second album stretched their record-breaking achievements still further. Never before had an artist scored four immediate chart-toppers and no artist had ever lifted four winners from one album. The last act to score an uninterrupted quartet of number ones was the Beatles, and so it was appropriate that the B-side to

'Everything Changes' was a medley of Beatles tracks, performed as a tribute by the boys at the 1994 BRIT award ceremony. After the show, Take That were anxious to dismiss comparisons between themselves and the Beatles. Speaking on behalf of the group Gary Barlow stated, "We'll only start comparing ourselves with the Beatles if people are still singing our records 25 years from now." The lead vocal on 'Everything Changes' is performed by the band's joker Robbie Williams, and he typically quipped, "We're not the new Beatles, we're just YTS legends."

705

THE MOST BEAUTIFUL GIRL IN THE WORLD

PRINCE

23 April 1994, for 2 weeks

●●

NPG NPG 60155

Writer: Prince
Producers: Prince and Ricky P

Prince Rogers Nelson, born in Minneapolis on 7 June 1958, has been known as one of rock's most eccentric geniuses since his first UK hit in 1980. Despite performing several of the classic tracks of the 1980s, including 'When Doves Cry', 'Purple Rain', and 'Kiss', and despite writing number one hits for Chaka Khan (see no. 540) and Sinead O'Connor (see no. 641), it was not until his 37th single release in Britain that he topped the charts as a performer. And even then, there was some doubt about his identity, as he insisted on being known by the symbol he had devised rather than by his name.

Nobody who has reached number one has taken as many as 37 attempts before getting there, but Prince has never been an ordinary recording star. His many changes of image, backing musicians, partners and labels (his number one was released on an 'indie' label of his own) cannot disguise the immense musical talent and brilliant songwriting that Prince has always displayed. Many artists, from Tom Jones and Sheena Easton to the Bangles, have had hits with Prince's songs, and many other acts, including Wendy and Lisa and Sheila E, have begun their careers by working with Prince. He may be weird, but he's also possibly the most significant recording star of the 80s and early 90s.

706

THE REAL THING

TONY DI BART

7 May 1994, for 1 week

●

CLEVELAND CITY BLUES CCB 715001

Writers: Lucinda Drayton, Tony di Bart and Andy Blissett
Producers: Rhyme Time Productions; remixed by the Joy Brothers

Slough-born Tony di Bart began singing semi-professionally at the age of 16, performing in gospel choirs. For a suburban white boy to be involved in black church music might seem odd, but young di Bart proved so fine a gospel singer that by the time he decided to turn professional as a solo singer, he had graduated to lead

By the time PRINCE finally got to number one he wasn't even calling himself Prince anymore. **(See p. 397)**

vocalist and had performed with gospel choirs at many major concert halls, including the Royal Albert Hall.

He began in the way that many recording stars have kicked off their studio careers - as a session singer on countless recording sessions for other artists, in both Britain and Italy. 'The Real Thing' began life in 1993, as a demo which di Bart sent to several record companies. Wolverhampton-based Cleveland City signed him up, and 'The Real Thing' was released as a single in September that year. It scored highly on the dance charts, but did not look like crossing over onto the main charts until the remix by the Joy Brothers early in 1994 prompted Cleveland City to re-release the single. It entered the charts just outside the Top 10 and within five weeks climbed to the very top, just edging ahead of a pack of records, all of which were selling similar amounts - hits by Prince, the Crash Test Dummies, C.J. Lewis and Stiltskin.

707

INSIDE

STILTSKIN

14 May 1994, for 1 week

●

WHITEWATER LEVI

Writer: Peter Lawlor
Producer: Peter Lawlor

Few acts which have come from nowhere (or at least, from Scotland) have had the benefit of an £8-million advertising campaign to help them to the top, but Stiltskin were one of the lucky few. When Levi's jeans wanted another song for their next television campaign, advertising agents Bartle Bogle Hegarty persuaded them to go for a new song for the first time, rather than using an oldie. As the policy of using classic recordings had always been successful (see nos. 585, 650, 661), it was a gamble to use an unknown song by an unknown heavy metal band, but it worked. Two other tracks, previously released but hardly yet in the category of oldie, were reportedly in the running for the campaign, but the new boys got the nod. Whether Massive's 'Unfinished Sympathy' or the Breeders' 'Cannonball' would have made the very top with the aid of an £8-million campaign is, therefore, something we shall never know.

Glasgow-based Stiltskin are vocalist Ray Wilson, bass guitarist James Finnigan, drummer Ross McFarlane and lead guitarist Peter Lawlor, who also wrote and produced the single. The choir which gave the song its distinctive intro were the Ambrosian Singers.

For many weeks before the single's release, TV viewers were exposed to the sound of Stiltskin, behind an advertisement featuring two prim young women from the Old West watching a typical Levi's male taking a dip at a swimming hole while they hold what they assume to be his jeans. The advertisement was certainly memorable, as was the music. The world awaited Stiltskin's first album with interest.

708

COME ON YOU REDS

MANCHESTER UNITED FOOTBALL SQUAD

21 May 1994, for 2 weeks

●●

POLYGRAM TV MANU 2

Writers: Francis Rossi, Andy Bown, John Edwards
Producers: Status Quo

By winning the League Championship for the second year in a row, Manchester United joined a list containing only two other clubs, Aston Villa and Liverpool, who have both won the league title two seasons in a row more than once. By also beating Chelsea 4-0 to win the FA Cup, just 24 hours before their number one hit was announced, Manchester United not only equalled their own record for the biggest winning margin in a Cup Final at Wembley, they also equalled Tottenham Hotspur's record tally of eight FA Cup wins and Arsenal's record of 12 FA Cup

Final appearances. More importantly, they became only the sixth club in history, after Preston North End, Aston Villa, Tottenham Hotspur, Arsenal and Liverpool, to perform the Cup and League double, and the third in a row to perform the feat under a Scottish manager.

But none of those other great clubs had ever had a number one hit record. Manchester United became the first club side to complete the League, Cup and charts treble, beating Liverpool's 1988 record football club chart position of three with 'Anfield Rap'. There had, of course, been two number one hits for the England World Cup squad (see nos. 286 and 646), but no club had previously achieved the kind of national fan base required to have a number one hit.

Paul Parker, once of Fulham and QPR but now of Manchester United, was the only man who played in both the England squad of 1990 and the Manchester United 1994 Cup Final team, so officially this was his second number one hit. Bryan Robson, another World Cup 1990 veteran, did not play in the final, but did sing on the hit.

The song, based on Status Quo's 1988 hit, 'Burning Bridges', also gave the eternal rockers their first number one production, and Francis Rossi his first number one as a writer since 1975 (see no. 363).

709

LOVE IS ALL AROUND

WET WET WET

4 June 1994, for 12 weeks

●●●●●●●●●●●●

(Still at number one at time of going to press 13 August 1994)

THE PRECIOUS ORGANISATION
JWL 23

Writer: Reg Presley
Producers: Wet Wet Wet and Graeme Duffin

The first Scottish act to have three number one hits is Wet Wet Wet. Like their first chart-topper (see no. 609), the Wets' third number one, six years and a hundred number ones later, was a revamped version of a hit from the 1960s. The original version reached number five to give the Troggs their final Top 10 hit in 1967.

While the Troggs version, with writer Reg Presley on vocals, was a predatory growl disguised as a love song, the Wet Wet Wet version was much more of a sweet rock balld, and perfectly suited to the context from which it emerged, the soundtrack of the hit film starring Hugh Grant and Andie MacDowell, *Four Weddings And A Funeral.*

By hitting number one as a writer again, 488 chart-toppers after his previous success (see no. 221), Reg Presley became the writer with the third-longest span of number one hits with different songs.

Excluding writers on Jive Bunny's medley hits, only Oscar Hammerstein II, who wrote both no. 36 and no. 551, and Richard Rodgers, who wrote nos. 46 and 551 among others, and who therefore have a writing span of over 500 hits each, are ahead of Reg Presley. Lennon and McCartney's chart-topping songwriting career has spanned a mere 458 hits, from no. 151 to no. 609, putting them immediately below Presley in this particular all-time list. Incidentally, Wet Wet Wet recorded the final chart-topper for them as well.

When the record spent its twelfth consecutive week at number one, it became the second-longest-running chart-topper of all time.

Section Two

Over Seven Hundred Number Ones Listed Alphabetically By Artist

The information given in this part of the book is as follows: the week that the record first reached number one, the title and the number of weeks at number one.

We have also listed acts under the name they used for their number one hits, which is not necessarily their usual styling. For example, Ian Dury is listed under 'Ian And The Blockheads', which is how he was billed for *Hit Me With Your Rhythm Stick*. Cross-reference will also be found under 'Blockheads' and 'Ian Dury'.

ABBA
4 May 74 WATERLOO......2 wks
31 Jan 76 MAMMA MIA......2 wks
8 May 76 FERNANDO......4 wks
4 Sep 76 DANCING QUEEN......6 wks
2 Apr 77 KNOWING ME KNOWING YOU......5 wks
5 Nov 77 THE NAME OF THE GAME......4 wks
18 Feb 78 TAKE A CHANCE ON ME......3 wks
9 Aug 80 THE WINNER TAKES IT ALL......2 wks
29 Nov 80 SUPER TROUPER......3 wks

ACE OF BASE
22 May 93 ALL THAT SHE WANTS .3wks

ACES - see Desmond DEKKER & the ACES

ADAM and the ANTS
9 May 81 STAND AND DELIVER......5 wks
19 Sep 81 PRINCE CHARMING......4 wks
12 Jun 82 GOODY TWO SHOES...2 wks
Final number one billed as Adam Ant

Bryan ADAMS
13 Jul 91 (EVERYTHING I DO) I DO IT FOR YOU......16 wks

ADAMSKI
12 May 90 KILLER......4 wks

A-HA
25 Jan 86 THE SUN ALWAYS SHINES ON T.V. ......2 wks

Marc ALMOND with special guest Gene PITNEY
28 Jan 89 SOMETHING'S GOTTEN HOLD OF MY HEART....4 wks
See also SOFT CELL

ALTHIA and DONNA
4 Feb 78 UP TOWN TOP RANKING......1wk

AMEN CORNER
12 Feb 69 (IF PARADISE IS) HALF AS NICE......2 wks

ANEKA
29 Aug 81 JAPANESE BOY......1 wk

ANIMALS
9 Jul 64 HOUSE OF THE RISING SUN......1 wk

Paul ANKA
30 Aug 57 DIANA......9 wks

ANTS - see ADAM and the ANTS

Tasmin ARCHER
17 Oct 92 SLEEPING SATELLITE......2 wks

ARCHIES
25 Oct 69 SUGAR SUGAR......8 wks

Louis ARMSTRONG
24 Apr 68 WHAT A WONDERFUL WORLD/CABARET......4 wks

Rick ASTLEY
29 Aug 87 NEVER GONNA GIVE YOU UP......5wks

ASWAD
26 Mar 88 DON'T TURN AROUND......2 wks

Winifred ATWELL
3 Dec 54 LET'S HAVE ANOTHER PARTY......5wks
13 Apr 56 POOR PEOPLE OF PARIS......3 wks

Charles AZNAVOUR
29 Jun 74 SHE......4 wks

BACCARA
29 Oct 77 YES SIR, I CAN BOOGIE......1 wk

BACHELORS
20 Feb 64 DIANE......1 wk

Philip BAILEY
23 Mar 85 EASY LOVER......4 wks
Billed "with Phil Collins". See also Phil COLLINS

Long John BALDRY
22 Nov 67 LET THE HEARTACHES BEGIN......5wks

BAND AID/BAND AID II
15 Dec 84 DO THEY KNOW IT'S CHRISTMAS?......5 wks
23 Dec 89 DO THEY KNOW IT'S CHRISTMAS?......3 wks
Second version credited to Band Aid II

BANGLES
15 Apr 89 ETERNAL FLAME......4 wks

J. J. BARRIE
5 Jun 76 NO CHARGE......1 wk

Shirley BASSEY
20 Feb 59 AS I LOVE YOU......4 wks
21 Sep 61 REACH FOR THE STARS/CLIMB EV'RY MOUNTAIN......1 wk

BAY CITY ROLLERS
22 Mar 75 BYE BYE BABY......6 wks
19 Jul 75 GIVE A LITTLE LOVE......3 wks

BEACH BOYS
17 Nov 66 GOOD VIBRATIONS......2 wks
28 Aug 68 DO IT AGAIN......1 wk

BEATLES
2 May 63 FROM ME TO YOU......7 wks
12 Sep 63 SHE LOVES YOU......4 wks
28 Nov 63 SHE LOVES YOU......2 wks
12 Dec 63 I WANT TO HOLD YOUR HAND......5 wks
2 Apr 64 CAN'T BUY ME LOVE......3 wks
23 Jul 64 A HARD DAY'S NIGHT......3 wks
10 Dec 64 I FEEL FINE......5 wks
22 Apr 65 TICKET TO RIDE......3 wks
5 Aug 65 HELP!......3 wks
16 Dec 65 DAY TRIPPER/WE CAN WORK IT OUT......5 wks
23 Jun 66 PAPERBACK WRITER......2 wks
18 Aug 66 YELLOW SUBMARINE/ ELEANOR RIGBY......4 wks
19 Jul 67 ALL YOU NEED IS LOVE......3 wks
6 Dec 67 HELLO GOODBYE......7 wks
27 Mar 68 LADY MADONNA......2 wks
11 Sep 68 HEY JUDE......2 wks
23 Apr 69 GET BACK......6 wks
11 Jun 69 BALLAD OF JOHN AND YOKO......3 wks
Get Back is "with Billy Preston". See also George HARRISON; John LENNON; Paul McCARTNEY

BEATS INTERNATIONAL featuring Lindy LAYTON
3 Mar 90 DUB BE GOOD TO ME......4 wks

BEAUTIFUL SOUTH
27 Oct 90 A LITTLE TIME......1 wk

Robin BECK
19 Nov 88 FIRST TIME......3 wks

BEE GEES
11 Oct 67 MASSACHUSETTS......4 wks
4 Sep 68 I'VE GOTTA GET A MESSAGE TO YOU......1 wk
29 Apr 78 NIGHT FEVER......2 wks
3 Mar 79 TRAGEDY......2 wks
17 Oct 87 YOU WIN AGAIN......4 wks

Harry BELAFONTE
22 Nov 57 MARY'S BOY CHILD......7 wks

Tony BENNETT
13 May 55 STRANGER IN PARADISE......2 wks

BERLIN
8 Nov 86 TAKE MY BREATH AWAY......4 wks

Chuck BERRY
25 Nov 72 MY DING-A-LING......4 wks

Nick BERRY
18 Oct 86 EVERY LOSER WINS......3 wks

Jane BIRKIN and Serge GAINSBOURG
11 Oct 69 JE T'AIME...MOI NON PLUS......1 wk

Cilla BLACK
27 Feb 64 ANYONE WHO HAD A HEART......3 wks
28 May 64 YOU'RE MY WORLD......4 wks

BLACK BOX
9 Sep 89 RIDE ON TIME......6 wks

BLONDIE
3 Feb 79 HEART OF GLASS......4 wks
26 May 79 SUNDAY GIRL......3 wks
1 Mar 80 ATOMIC......2 wks
26 Apr 80 CALL ME......1 wk
15 Nov 80 THE TIDE IS HIGH......2 wks

BLUEBELLS
3 Apr 93 YOUNG AT HEART......4 wks

BLUE FLAMES - see Georgie FAME

BOMBALURINA
25 Aug 90 ITSY BITSY TEENY WEENY YELLOW POLKA DOT BIKINI......3 wks

BONEY M
13 May 78 RIVERS OF BABYLON......5 wks
9 Dec 78 MARY'S BOY CHILD - OH MY LORD (medley)......4 wks

BOOMTOWN RATS
18 Nov 78 RAT TRAP......2 wks
28 Jul 79 I DON'T LIKE MONDAYS......4 wks

Pat BOONE
15 Jun 56 I'LL BE HOME......5 wks

Ken BOOTHE
26 Oct 74 EVERYTHING I OWN....3 wks

David BOWIE
8 Nov 75 SPACE ODDITY................2 wks
23 Aug 80 ASHES TO ASHES............2 wks
9 Apr 83 LET'S DANCE....................3 wks
See also David BOWIE and Mick JAGGER; QUEEN and David BOWIE

David BOWIE and Mick JAGGER
7 Sep 85 DANCING IN THE STREET................................4 wks
See also David BOWIE; ROLLING STONES

BOY GEORGE
14 Mar 87 EVERYTHING I OWN ....2 wks
See also CULTURE CLUB

BOYZ II MEN
31 Oct 92 END OF THE ROAD.......3 wks

Billy BRAGG with Cara TIVEY
21 May 88 SHE'S LEAVING HOME................................4 wks

BRIAN and MICHAEL
8 Apr 78 MATCHSTALK MEN AND MATCHSTALK CATS AND DOGS................................3 wks

BROS
25 Jun 88 I OWE YOU NOTHING ....2 wks

BROTHERHOOD OF MAN
27 Mar 76 SAVE YOUR KISSES FOR ME..6 wks
20 Aug 77 ANGELO.............................1 wk
11 Feb 78 FIGARO...............................1 wk

Crazy World Of Arthur BROWN
14 Aug 68 FIRE..1 wk

BUCK'S FIZZ
18 Apr 81 MAKING YOUR MIND UP..3 wks
16 Jan 82 LAND OF MAKE BELIEVE..............................2 wks
17 Apr 82 MY CAMERA NEVER LIES..1 wk

BUGGLES
20 Oct 79 VIDEO KILLED THE RADIO STAR.......................................1 wk

B. BUMBLE and the STINGERS
17 May 62 NUT ROCKER....................1 wk

Kate BUSH
11 Mar 78 WUTHERING HEIGHTS...........................4 wks

BYRDS
22 Jul 65 MR TAMBOURINE MAN..................................2 wks

Eddie CALVERT
8 Jan 54 OH MEIN PAPA................9 wks
27 May 55 CHERRY PINK AND APPLE BLOSSOM WHITE...........4 wks

CAPTAIN SENSIBLE
3 Jul 82 HAPPY TALK.....................2 wks

Irene CARA
17 Jul 82 FAME...................................3 wks

Mariah CAREY
19 Feb 94 WITHOUT YOU.............4 wks

Belinda CARLISLE
16 Jan 88 HEAVEN IS A PLACE ON EARTH...............................2 wks

David CASSIDY
30 Sep 72 HOW CAN I BE SURE....2 wks
27 Oct 73 DAYDREAMER/THE PUPPY SONG..................................3wks

CHARLENE
26 Jun 82 I'VE NEVER BEEN TO ME . 1 wk

CHARLES and EDDIE
21 Nov 92 WOULD I LIE TO YOU..2 wks

Ray CHARLES
12 Jul 62 I CAN'T STOP LOVING YOU...................................2 wks

Tina CHARLES
6 Mar 76 I LOVE TO LOVE (BUT MY BABY LOVES TO DANCE).............................3 wks

CHECKMATES - see Emile FORD and the CHECKMATES

CHER
4 May 91 THE SHOOP SHOOP SONG.................................5 wks
See also SONNY and CHER

CHICAGO
16 Oct 76 IF YOU LEAVE ME NOW..................................3 wks

CHICORY TIP
19 Feb 72 SON OF MY FATHER .....3 wks

CHRISTIANS, Holly JOHNSON, Paul McCARTNEY, Gerry MARSDEN and STOCK AITKEN WATERMAN
20 May 89 FERRY 'CROSS THE MERSEY...............................3 wks
See also FRANKIE GOES TO HOLLYWOOD; Paul McCARTNEY; GERRY and the PACEMAKERS.

CHRISTIE
6 Jun 70 YELLOW RIVER..................1 wk

Petula CLARK
23 Feb 61 SAILOR ....1 wk
16 Feb 67 THIS IS MY SONG...........2 wks

Dave CLARK FIVE
16 Jan 64 GLAD ALL OVER.............2 wks

CLASH
9 Mar 91 SHOULD I STAY OR SHOULD I GO..................2 wks

Rosemary CLOONEY
26 Nov 54 THIS OLE HOUSE ....1 wk
14 Jan 55 MAMBO ITALIANO ....1 wk
4 Feb 55 MAMBO ITALIANO.........2 wks

Eddie COCHRAN
23 Jun 60 THREE STEPS TO HEAVEN...............................2wks

Joe COCKER
6 Nov 68 WITH A LITTLE HELP FROM MY FRIENDS......................1 wk

COCKNEY REBEL - see Steve HARLEY and COCKNEY REBEL

Alma COGAN
15 Jul 55 DREAMBOAT...................2 wks

Dave and Ansil COLLINS
1 May 71 DOUBLE BARREL............2 wks

Phil COLLINS
15 Jan 83 YOU CAN'T HURRY LOVE..................................2 wks
10 Sep 88 A GROOVY KIND OF LOVE..................................2 wks
See also Philip BAILEY

COLOR ME BADD
8 Jun 91 I WANNA SEX YOU UP..3 wks

COMETS - see Bill HALEY and his COMETS

COMMODORES
19 Aug 78 THREE TIMES A LADY ...5 wks
See also Lionel RICHIE

COMMUNARDS with Sarah Jane MORRIS
13 Sep 86 DON'T LEAVE ME THIS WAY....................................4 wks

Perry COMO
6 Feb 53 DON'T LET THE STARS GET IN YOUR EYES..................5 wks
28 Feb 58 MAGIC MOMENTS..........8 wks

Billy CONNOLLY
22 Nov 75 D.I.V.O.R.C.E. ....1 wk

Russ CONWAY
27 Mar 59 SIDE SADDLE...................4 wks
19 Jun 59 ROULETTE........................2 wks

Alice COOPER
12 Aug 72 SCHOOL'S OUT ....3 wks

Don CORNELL
8 Oct 54 HOLD MY HAND...........4 wks
19 Nov 54 HOLD MY HAND ....1 wk

Julie COVINGTON
12 Feb 77 DON'T CRY FOR ME ARGENTINA.......................1wk

Floyd CRAMER
18 May 61 ON THE REBOUND ....1 wk

CREEDENCE CLEARWATER REVIVAL
20 Sep 69 BAD MOON RISING......3 wks

CRICKETS
1 Nov 57 THAT'LL BE THE DAY....3 wks
See also Buddy HOLLY

CROWD
15 Jun 85 YOU'LL NEVER WALK ALONE...............................2 wks

CULTURE BEAT
28 Aug 93 MR. VAIN ....4 wks

CULTURE CLUB
23 Oct 82 DO YOU REALLY WANT TO HURT ME...........................3 wks
24 Sep 84 KARMA CHAMELEON ....6 wks
See also BOY GEORGE

DAKOTAS - see Billy J. KRAMER and the DAKOTAS

Vic DAMONE
27 Jun 58 ON THE STREET WHERE YOU LIVE ....2 wks

DANA
18 Apr 70 ALL KINDS OF EVERYTHING...................2 wks

Bobby DARIN
3 Jul 59 DREAM LOVER................4 wks
16 Oct 59 MACK THE KNIFE...........2 wks

Windsor DAVIES and Don ESTELLE
7 Jun 75 WHISPERING GRASS.....3 wks

Spencer DAVIS GROUP
20 Jan 66 KEEP ON RUNNING........1 wk
14 Apr 66 SOMEBODY HELP ME....2 wks

DAWN
15 May 71 KNOCK THREE TIMES..................................5 wks
21 Apr 73 TIE A YELLOW RIBBON ROUND THE OLD OAK TREE....................................4 wks

Doris DAY
16 Apr 54 SECRET LOVE.....................1 wk
7 May 54 SECRET LOVE...................8 wks
10 Aug 56 WHATEVER WILL BE WILL BE 6wks

Chris DE BURGH
2 Aug 86 THE LADY IN RED ....3 wks

DEAD OR ALIVE
9 Mar 85 YOU SPIN ME ROUND (LIKE A RECORD)...........2 wks

Dave DEE, DOZY, BEAKY, MICK and TICH
20 Mar 68 THE LEGEND OF XANADU.............................1 wk

Kiki DEE - see Elton JOHN and Kiki DEE

Desmond DEKKER and the ACES
16 Apr 69 THE ISRAELITES.................1 wk

Chaka DEMUS and PLIERS with Jack RADICS and TAXI GANG
8 Jan 94 TWIST AND SHOUT......2 wks

John DENVER
12 Oct 74 ANNIE'S SONG..................1 wk

DETROIT SPINNERS
12 Apr 80 WORKING MY WAY BACK TO YOU - FORGIVE ME GIRL.............................2 wks

DEXY'S MIDNIGHT RUNNERS
3 May 80 GENO.................................2 wks
7 Aug 82 COME ON EILEEN..........4 wks
Come On Eileen with EMERALD EXPRESS.

Toni DI BART
7 May 94 THE REAL THING ....1 wk

Jim DIAMOND
1 Dec 84 I SHOULD HAVE KNOWN BETTER.................................1 wk

Barbara DICKSON - see Elaine PAIGE and Barbara DICKSON

DOCTOR and the MEDICS
7 Jun 86 SPIRIT IN THE SKY..........3 wks

DR. HOOK
17 Nov 79 WHEN YOU'RE IN LOVE WITH A BEAUTIFUL WOMAN...........................3 wks

Ken DODD
30 Sep 65 TEARS.................................5 wks

Joe DOLCE MUSIC THEATRE
21 Feb 81 SHADDUP YOU FACE ...3 wks

Lonnie DONEGAN
12 Apr 57 CUMBERLAND GAP.......5 wks
28 Jun 57 GAMBLIN' MAN/PUTTING ON THE STYLE................2 wks
31 Mar 60 MY OLD MAN'S A DUSTMAN........................4 wks

Jason DONOVAN
11 Mar 89 TOO MANY BROKEN HEARTS..............................2 wks
10 Jun 89 SEALED WITH A KISS....2 wks
29 Jun 91 ANY DREAM WILL DO.2 wks
See also Kylie MINOGUE and Jason DONOVAN

DOOP
19 Mar 94 DOOP ....3 wks

Carl DOUGLAS
21 Sep 74 KUNG FU FIGHTING.....3 wks

Craig DOUGLAS
11 Sep 59 ONLY SIXTEEN ....4 wks

D: REAM
22 Jan 94 THINGS CAN ONLY GET BETTER ....4 wks

DREAMWEAVERS
16 Mar 56 IT'S ALMOST TOMORROW ....2 wks
6 Apr 56 IT'S ALMOST TOMORROW ....1 wk

Clive DUNN
9 Jan 71 GRANDAD ....3 wks

DURAN DURAN
26 Mar 83 IS THERE SOMETHING I SHOULD KNOW ....2 wks
5 May 84 THE REFLEX.....................4 wks

Ian DURY - see IAN and the BLOCKHEADS

EDISON LIGHTHOUSE
31 Jan 70 LOVE GROWS (WHERE MY ROSEMARY GOES)..........5 wks

Dave EDMUNDS
28 Nov 70 I HEAR YOU KNOCKIN' ....6 wks

Tommy EDWARDS
7 Nov 58 IT'S ALL IN THE GAME ....3 wks

ENGLAND WORLD CUP SQUAD
16 May 70 BACK HOME.....................3 wks

ENGLANDNEWORDER
9 Jun 90 WORLD IN MOTION ....2 wks

ENIGMA
19 Jan 91 SADNESS PART ONE ....1 wk

ENYA
29 Oct 88 ORINOCO FLOW (SAIL AWAY) ....3 wks

EQUALS
3 Jul 68 BABY COME BACK ....3 wks
See also Eddy GRANT

ERASURE
13 Jun 92 ABBA-ESQUE (EP) ....5 wks

David ESSEX
16 Nov 74 GONNA MAKE YOU A STAR...............................3 wks
4 Oct 75 HOLD ME CLOSE...........3 wks

Don ESTELLE - see Windsor DAVIES and Don ESTELLE

EUROPE
6 Dec 86 THE FINAL COUNTDOWN...............2 wks

EURYTHMICS
27 Jul 85 THERE MUST BE AN ANGEL (PLAYING WITH MY HEART)...............................1 wk

EVERLY BROTHERS
4 Jul 58 ALL I HAVE TO DO IS DREAM ....7 wks
5 May 60 CATHY'S CLOWN..........7 wks
2 Mar 61 WALK RIGHT BACK ......3 wks
20 Jul 61 TEMPTATION...................2 wks

FAIRGROUND ATTRACTION
14 May 88 PERFECT.............................1 wk

Adam FAITH
4 Dec 59 WHAT DO YOU WANT.................................3 wks
10 Mar 60 POOR ME............................1 wk

FALCO
10 May 86 ROCK ME AMADEUS (THE AMERICAN EDIT) ..1 wk

Georgie FAME
14 Jan 65 YEH YEH............................2 wks
21 Jul 66 GET AWAY ....1 wk
24 Jan 68 THE BALLAD OF BONNIE AND CLYDE.......................1 wk
Yeh Yeh and Get Away credit the BLUE FLAMES.

Chris FARLOWE and the THUNDERBIRDS
28 Jul 66 OUT OF TIME ....1 wk

FERRY AID
4 Apr 87 LET IT BE...........................3 wks

FIRM
20 Jun 87 STAR TREKKIN'................2 wks

Eddie FISHER
30 Jan 53 OUTSIDE OF HEAVEN ....1 wk
26 Jun 53 I'M WALKING BEHIND YOU...1 wk

FLEETWOOD MAC
29 Jan 69 ALBATROSS ....1 wk

FLOATERS
27 Aug 77 FLOAT ON ....1 wk

FLYING PICKETS
10 Dec 83 ONLY YOU.....................15 wks

Emile FORD and the CHECKMATES
18 Dec 59 WHAT DO YOU WANT TO MAKE THOSE EYES AT ME FOR.....................................6 wks

Tennessee Ernie FORD
11 Mar 55 GIVE ME YOUR WORD ....7 wks
20 Jan 56 SIXTEEN TONS................4 wks

FOREIGNER
19 Jan 85 I WANT TO KNOW WHAT LOVE IS ....3 wks

FOUNDATIONS
8 Nov 67 BABY NOW THAT I'VE FOUND YOU...................2 wks

FOUR PENNIES
21 May 64 JULIET...................................1 wk

FOUR SEASONS
21 Feb 76 DECEMBER '63 (OH WHAT A NIGHT)...........2 wks

FOUR TOPS
27 Oct 66 REACH OUT I'LL BE THERE.................................3 wks

Connie FRANCIS
16 May 58 WHO'S SORRY NOW..................................6 wks

26 Sep 58 CAROLINA MOON/STUPID CUPID ....6 wks

FRANKIE GOES TO HOLLYWOOD

28 Jan 84 RELAX! ....5 wks
16 Jun 84 TWO TRIBES ....9 wks
8 Dec 84 THE POWER OF LOVE ....1 wk

See also CHRISTIANS, Holly JOHNSON, Paul McCARTNEY, Gerry MARSDEN and STOCK AITKEN WATERMAN

Aretha FRANKLIN - see George MICHAEL and Aretha FRANKLIN

GABRIELLE

26 Jun 93 DREAMS ....3 wks

Serge GAINSBOURG - see Jane BIRKIN and Serge GAINSBOURG

Boris GARDINER

23 Aug 86 I WANT TO WAKE UP WITH YOU ....3 wks

Art GARFUNKEL

25 Oct 75 I ONLY HAVE EYES FOR YOU ....2 wks
14 Apr 79 BRIGHT EYES ....6 wks

See also SIMON and GARFUNKEL

Siedah GARRETT - see Michael JACKSON

Barbara GASKIN - see Dave STEWART with Barbara GASKIN

Marvin GAYE

26 Mar 69 I HEARD IT THROUGH THE GRAPEVINE ....3 wks

Gloria GAYNOR

17 Mar 79 I WILL SURVIVE ....4 wks

Bobbie GENTRY

18 Oct 69 I'LL NEVER FALL IN LOVE AGAIN ....1 wk

GERRY and the PACEMAKERS

11 Apr 63 HOW DO YOU DO IT? ....3 wks
20 Jun 63 I LIKE IT ....4 wks
31 Oct 63 YOU'LL NEVER WALK ALONE ....4 wks

See also CHRISTIANS, Holly JOHNSON, Paul McCARTNEY, Gerry MARSDEN and STOCK AITKEN WATERMAN

Gary GLITTER

28 Jul 73 I'M THE LEADER OF THE GANG (I AM) ....4 wks
17 Nov 73 I LOVE YOU LOVE ME LOVE ....4 wks
22 Jun 74 ALWAYS YOURS ....1 wk

GOOMBAY DANCE BAND

27 Mar 82 SEVEN TEARS ....3 wks

Eddy GRANT

13 Nov 83 I DON'T WANNA DANCE ....3 wks

See also EQUALS, of which Grant was a member

Norman GREENBAUM

2 May 70 SPIRIT IN THE SKY ....2 wks

HALE and PACE and the STONKERS

23 Mar 91 THE STONK ....1 wk

Bill HALEY and his COMETS

25 Nov 55 ROCK AROUND THE CLOCK ....3 wks
6 Jan 56 ROCK AROUND THE CLOCK ....2 wks

Paul HARDCASTLE

11 May 85 19 ....5 wks

Steve HARLEY and COCKNEY REBEL

22 Feb 75 MAKE ME SMILE (COME UP AND SEE ME) ....2 wks

Jet HARRIS and Tony MEEHAN

31 Jan 63 DIAMONDS ....3 wks

See also SHADOWS, with whom Harris and Meehan started

Rolf HARRIS

20 Dec 69 TWO LITTLE BOYS ....6 wks

George HARRISON

30 Jan 71 MY SWEET LORD ....5 wks

See also BEATLES.

Chesney HAWKES

30 Mar 91 THE ONE AND ONLY ...5 wks

Jimi HENDRIX EXPERIENCE

21 Nov 70 VOODOO CHILE ....1 wk

HERMAN'S HERMITS

24 Sep 64 I'M INTO SOMETHING GOOD ....2 wks

HIGHWAYMEN

12 Oct 61 MICHAEL ....1 wk

Benny HILL

11 Dec 71 ERNIE (THE FASTEST MILK MAN IN THE WEST) ....4 wks

Ronnie HILTON

4 May 56 NO OTHER LOVE ....6 wks

Michael HOLLIDAY

14 Feb 58 THE STORY OF MY LIFE ....2 wks
29 Jan 60 STARRY EYED ....1 wk

HOLLIES

24 Jun 65 I'M ALIVE ....1 wk
8 Jul 65 I'M ALIVE ....2 wks
24 Sep 88 HE AIN'T HEAVY HE'S MY BROTHER ....2 wks

Buddy HOLLY

24 Apr 59 IT DOESN'T MATTER ANYMORE ....3 wks

See also CRICKETS

HONEYCOMBS

27 Aug 64 HAVE I THE RIGHT ....2 wks

Mary HOPKIN

25 Sep 68 THOSE WERE THE DAYS ....6 wks

HOT CHOCOLATE

2 Jul 77 SO YOU WIN AGAIN ....3 wks

HOUSEMARTINS

20 Dec 86 CARAVAN OF LOVE ....1 wk

Whitney HOUSTON

14 Dec 85 SAVING ALL MY LOVE FOR YOU ....2 wks
6 Jun 87 I WANNA DANCE WITH SOMEBODY (WHO LOVES ME) .... 2 wks
15 Oct 88 ONE MOMENT IN TIME ....2 wks
5 Dec 92 I WILL ALWAYS LOVE YOU ....10 wks

HUMAN LEAGUE

12 Dec 81 DON'T YOU WANT ME? ....5 wks

Engelbert HUMPERDINCK

2 Mar 67 RELEASE ME ....6 wks
6 Sep 67 THE LAST WALTZ ....5 wks

Tab HUNTER

22 Feb 57 YOUNG LOVE ....7 wks

Steve 'Silk' HURLEY

22 Jan 87 JACK YOUR BODY ....2 wks

Chrissie HYNDE - see UB40, PRETENDERS

IAN and the BLOCKHEADS

27 Jan 79 HIT ME WITH YOUR RHYTHM STICK ....1 wk

Frank IFIELD

26 Jul 62 I REMEMBER YOU ....7 wks
8 Nov 62 LOVESICK BLUES ....5 wks
21 Feb 63 WAYWARD WIND ....3 wks
18 Jul 63 CONFESSIN' ....2 wks

Julio IGLESIAS

5 Dec 81 BEGIN THE BEGUINE (VOLVER A EMPEZAR) ....1 wk

IRON MAIDEN

5 Jan 91 BRING YOUR DAUGHTER... TO THE SLAUGHTER ....2 wks

Terry JACKS

6 Apr 74 SEASONS IN THE SUN ..4 wks

Michael JACKSON

27 Jun 81 ONE DAY IN YOUR LIFE ....2 wks
5 Mar 83 BILLIE JEAN ....1 wk
15 Aug 87 I JUST CAN'T STOP LOVING YOU ....2 wks
23 Nov 91 BLACK OR WHITE ....2 wks

I Just Can't Stop Loving You with Siedah Garrett.
See also JACKSONS

JACKSONS

25 Jun 77 SHOW YOU THE WAY TO GO ....1 wk

See also Michael JACKSON

Mick JAGGER - see David BOWIE and Mick JAGGER, ROLLING STONES

JAM

22 Mar 80 GOING UNDERGROUND/ DREAMS OF CHILDREN .3 wks
6 Sep 80 START ....1 wk
13 Feb 82 A TOWN CALLED MALICE/ PRECIOUS ....3 wks
4 Dec 82 BEAT SURRENDER ....2 wks

Tommy JAMES and the SHONDELLS

31 Jul 68 MONY MONY ....2 wks
21 Aug 68 MONY MONY ....1 wk

Jazzy JEFF and the FRESH PRINCE

25 Sep 93 BOOM! SHAKE THE ROOM ....2 wks

JIVE BUNNY and the MASTERMIXERS

5 Aug 89 SWING THE MOOD ....5 wks
21 Oct 89 THAT'S WHAT I LIKE ....3 wks
16 Dec 89 LET'S PARTY ....1 wk

Billy JOEL

5 Nov 83 UPTOWN GIRL ....5 wks

Elton JOHN

23 Jun 90 SACRIFICE/HEALING HANDS ....5 wks

See also Elton JOHN and Kiki DEE; George MICHAEL and Elton JOHN

Elton JOHN and Kiki DEE
24 Jul 76 DON'T GO BREAKING MY HEART....6 wks
See also Elton JOHN

JOHNSTON BROTHERS
11 Nov 55 HERNANDO'S HIDEAWAY....2 wks

Jimmy JONES
7 Jul 60 GOOD TIMIN'....3 wks

Tom JONES
11 Mar 65 IT'S NOT UNUSUAL....1 wk
1 Dec 66 GREEN GREEN GRASS OF HOME....7 wks

KAJAGOOGOO
19 Feb 83 TOO SHY....2 wks

KALIN TWINS
22 Aug 58 WHEN....5 wks

Kitty KALLEN
10 Sep 54 LITTLE THINGS MEAN A LOT....1 wk

Eden KANE
3 Aug 61 WELL I ASK YOU....1 wk

KC and the SUNSHINE BAND
13 Aug 83 GIVE IT UP....3 wks

Jerry KELLER
9 Oct 59 HERE COMES SUMMER...1 wk

Chaka KHAN
10 Nov 84 I FEEL FOR YOU....3 wks

Johnny KIDD and the PIRATES
4 Aug 60 SHAKIN' ALL OVER....1 wk

KIM - see MEL and KIM

Ben E. KING
21 Feb 87 STAND BY ME....3 wks

KINKS
10 Sep 64 YOU REALLY GOT ME...2 wks
18 Feb 65 TIRED OF WAITING FOR YOU....1 wk
7 Jul 66 SUNNY AFTERNOON..2 wks

Fern KINNEY
15 Mar 80 TOGETHER WE ARE BEAUTIFUL....1 wk

KLF featuring CHILDREN OF THE REVOLUTION
2 Feb 91 3.A.M. ETERNAL....2 wks

KRAFTWERK
6 Feb 82 THE MODEL/COMPUTER LOVE....1 wk

Billy J. KRAMER and the DAKOTAS
22 Aug 63 BAD TO ME....3 wks
19 Mar 64 LITTLE CHILDREN....2 wks

KWS
9 May 92 PLEASE DON'T GO/GAME BOY....5 wks

Frankie LAINE
24 Apr 53 I BELIEVE....9 wks
3 Jul 53 I BELIEVE....6 wks
21 Aug 53 I BELIEVE....3 wks
23 Oct 53 HEY JOE....2 wks
13 Nov 53 ANSWER ME....8 wks
19 Oct 56 A WOMAN IN LOVE....4 wks

Lindy LAYTON - see BEATS INTERNATIONAL featuring Lindy LAYTON

John LENNON
20 Dec 80 (JUST LIKE) STARTING OVER....1 wk
10 Jan 81 IMAGINE....4 wks
7 Feb 81 WOMAN....2 wks
See also BEATLES

Jerry LEE LEWIS
10 Jan 58 GREAT BALLS OF FIRE....2 wks

John LEYTON
31 Aug 61 JOHNNY REMEMBER ME....3wks
28 Sep 61 JOHNNY REMEMBER ME....1 wk

LIEUTENANT PIGEON
14 Oct 72 MOULDY OLD DOUGH....4 wks

Los LOBOS
1 Aug 87 LA BAMBA....2 wks

Johnny LOGAN
3 May 80 WHAT'S ANOTHER YEAR....2 wks

LOVE AFFAIR
31 Jan 68 EVERLASTING LOVE....2 wks

Frankie LYMON - see TEENAGERS featuring Frankie LYMON

Vera LYNN
5 Nov 54 MY SON MY SON....2 wks

Paul McCARTNEY
14 Jan 84 PIPES OF PEACE....2 wks
See also Paul McCARTNEY with Stevie WONDER; BEATLES; WINGS; CHRISTIANS, Holly JOHNSON, Paul McCARTNEY, Gerry MARSDEN and STOCK AITKEN WATERMAN

Paul McCARTNEY with Stevie WONDER
24 Apr 82 EBONY AND IVORY....3 wks
See also Paul McCARTNEY; Stevie WONDER

George McCRAE
27 Jul 74 ROCK YOUR BABY....3 wks

Maria McKEE
29 Sep 90 SHOW ME HEAVEN....4 wks

Scott McKENZIE
9 Aug 67 SAN FRANCISCO (BE SURE TO WEAR SOME FLOWERS IN YOUR HAIR)....4 wks

Don McLEAN
17 Jun 72 VINCENT....2 wks
21 Jun 80 CRYING....3 wks

MADNESS
29 May 82 HOUSE OF FUN....2 wks

MADONNA
3 Aug 85 INTO THE GROOVE....4 wks
12 Jul 86 PAPA DON'T PREACH...3 wks
11 Oct 86 TRUE BLUE....1 wk
25 Apr 87 LA ISLA BONITA....2 wks
25 Jul 87 WHO'S THAT GIRL....1 wk
25 Mar 89 LIKE A PRAYER....3 wks
14 Apr 90 VOGUE....4 wks

MANCHESTER UNITED FOOTBALL CLUB
21 MAY 94 COME ON YOU REDS.2 WKS

MANFRED MANN
13 Aug 64 DO WAH DIDDY DIDDY....2 wks
5 May 66 PRETTY FLAMINGO....3 wks
14 Feb 68 MIGHTY QUINN....2 wks

MANHATTAN TRANSFER
12 Mar 77 CHANSON D'AMOUR....3 wks

MANTOVANI
14 Aug 53 MOULIN ROUGE....1 wk
See also David WHITFIELD

MARCELS
4 May 61 BLUE MOON....2 wks

Kelly MARIE
13 Sep 80 FEELS LIKE I'M IN LOVE.2 wks

MARMALADE
1 Jan 69 OB-LA-DI OB-LA-DA....1 wk
15 Jan 69 OB-LA-DI OB-LA-DA....2 wks

M/A/R/R/S
3 Oct 87 PUMP UP THE VOLUME....2 wks

Lena MARTELL
27 Oct 79 ONE DAY AT A TIME....3 wks

Dean MARTIN
17 Feb 56 MEMORIES ARE MADE OF THIS....4 wks

Al MARTINO
14 Nov 52 HERE IN MY HEART....9 wks

Lee MARVIN
7 Mar 70 WAND'RIN' STAR....3 wks

MASH
31 May 80 THEME FROM "M*A*S*H" (SUICIDE IS PAINLESS)...3 wks

Johnny MATHIS
25 Dec 76 WHEN A CHILD IS BORN (SOLEADO)....3 wks

MATTHEWS SOUTHERN COMFORT
31 Oct 70 WOODSTOCK....3 wks

MEATLOAF
23 Oct 93 I'D DO ANYTHING FOR LOVE (BUT I WON'T DO THAT)....7 wks

Glenn MEDEIROS
9 Jul 88 NOTHING'S GONNA CHANGE MY LOVE FOR YOU....4 wks

MEDICS - see DR. and the MEDICS

Tony MEEHAN - see Jet HARRIS and Tony MEEHAN

MEL and KIM
28 Mar 87 RESPECTABLE....1 wk

MEN AT WORK
29 Jan 83 DOWN UNDER....3 wks

Freddie MERCURY
14 Aug 93 LIVING ON MY OWN...2 wks

George MICHAEL
18 Aug 84 CARELESS WHISPER....3 wks
19 Apr 86 A DIFFERENT CORNER....3 wks
See also George MICHAEL and Aretha FRANKLIN; George MICHAEL and Elton JOHN; George MICHAEL and QUEEN with Lisa STANSFIELD; WHAM!

George MICHAEL and Aretha FRANKLIN
7 Feb 87 I KNEW YOU WERE WAITING (FOR ME)....2 wks
See also George MICHAEL

George MICHAEL and Elton JOHN
7 Dec 91 DON'T LET THE SUN GO DOWN ON ME................2 wks
See also George MICHAEL; Elton JOHN

George MICHAEL and QUEEN with Lisa STANSFIELD
1 May 93 FIVE LIVE (EP)....................3 wks
See also George MICHAEL; QUEEN; Lisa STANSFIELD

MIDDLE OF THE ROAD
19 Jun 71 CHIRPY CHIRPY CHEEP CHEEP................................5 wks

Roger MILLER
13 May 65 KING OF THE ROAD.......1 wk

Steve MILLER BAND
15 Sep 90 THE JOKER.......................2 wks

Kylie MINOGUE
20 Feb 88 I SHOULD BE SO LUCKY...............................5 wks
13 May 89 HAND ON YOUR HEART..................................1 wk
27 Jan 90 TEARS ON MY PILLOW...............................1 wk
See also Kylie MINOGUE and Jason DONOVAN

Kylie MINOGUE and Jason DONOVAN
7 Jan 89 ESPECIALLY FOR YOU...3 wks
See also Kylie MINOGUE; Jason DONOVAN

MIRACLES - see Smokey ROBINSON and the MIRACLES

Guy MITCHELL
13 Mar 53 SHE WEARS RED FEATHERS.........................4 wks
11 Sep 53 LOOK AT THAT GIRL....6 wks
4 Jan 57 SINGING THE BLUES.......1 wk
18 Jan 57 SINGING THE BLUES.......1 wk
1 Feb 57 SINGING THE BLUES.......1 wk
17 May 57 ROCK-A-BILLY ....1 wk

MONKEES
19 Jan 67 I'M A BELIEVER................4 wks

Hugo MONTENEGRO
13 Nov 68 THE GOOD THE BAD AND THE UGLY.........................4 wks

MOODY BLUES
28 Jan 65 GO NOW...........................1 wk

Jane MORGAN
23 Jan 59 THE DAY THE RAINS CAME...................................1 wk

Sarah Jane MORRIS - see COMMUNARDS

MOVE
5 Feb 69 BLACKBERRY WAY..........1 wk

MR BLOBBY
11 Dec 93 MR BLOBBY........................1 wk

MUD
26 Jan 74 TIGER FEET.......................4 wks
21 Dec 74 LONELY THIS CHRISTMAS......................4 wks
3 May 75 OH BOY ....2 wks

MUNGO JERRY
13 Jun 70 IN THE SUMMERTIME....7 wks
6 Mar 71 BABY JUMP.......................2 wks

Ruby MURRAY
18 Feb 55 SOFTLY SOFTLY..............3 wks

MUSICAL YOUTH
2 Oct 82 PASS THE DUTCHIE.......3 wks

Jimmy NAIL
18 Jul 92 AIN'T NO DOUBT ....3 wks

Johnny NASH
12 Jul 75 TEARS ON MY PILLOW..1 wk

Phyllis NELSON
4 May 85 MOVE CLOSER..................1 wk

NENA
3 Mar 84 99 RED BALLOONS........3 wks

NEW EDITION
28 May 83 CANDY GIRL.....................1 wk

NEW KIDS ON THE BLOCK
25 Nov 89 YOU GOT IT (THE RIGHT STUFF)...............................3 wks
13 Jan 90 HANGIN' TOUGH..........2 wks

NEW SEEKERS
8 Jan 72 I'D LIKE TO TEACH THE WORLD TO SING (IN PERFECT HARMONY) ...4 wks
19 Jan 74 YOU WON'T FIND ANOTHER FOOL LIKE ME ....1 wk

Anthony NEWLEY
5 Feb 60 WHY...................................4 wks
28 Apr 60 DO YOU MIND.................1 wk

Olivia NEWTON-JOHN and ELECTRIC LIGHT ORCHESTRA
12 Jul 80 XANADU 2wks
See also John TRAVOLTA and Olivia NEWTON-JOHN

NICOLE
15 May 82 A LITTLE PEACE...............2 wks

NILSSON
11 Mar 72 WITHOUT YOU ....5 wks

Gary NUMAN
30 Jun 79 ARE 'FRIENDS' ELECTRIC? ....4 wks
22 Sep 79 CARS ....1 wk
Are 'Friends' Electric? by Gary Numan under the name TUBEWAY ARMY

Billy OCEAN
8 Feb 86 WHEN THE GOING GETS TOUGH, THE TOUGH GET GOING ....4 wks

Des O'CONNOR
24 Jul 68 I PRETEND.........................1 wk

Sinead O'CONNOR
3 Feb 90 NOTHING COMPARES 2 U...4 wks

ODYSSEY
26 Jul 80 USE IT UP AND WEAR IT OUT....................................2 wks

Esther and Abi OFARIM
28 Feb 68 CINDERELLA ROCKEFELLA...................3 wks

Roy ORBISON
20 Oct 60 ONLY THE LONELY........2 wks
25 Jun 64 IT'S OVER..........................2 wks
8 Oct 64 OH PRETTY WOMAN...2 wks
12 Nov 64 OH PRETTY WOMAN.....1 wk

Tony ORLANDO - see DAWN

Donny OSMOND
8 Jul 72 PUPPY LOVE ....5 wks
31 Mar 73 THE TWELFTH OF NEVER..................................1 wk
25 Aug 73 YOUNG LOVE..................4 wks
See also OSMONDS

Little Jimmy OSMOND
23 Dec 72 LONG HAIRED LOVER FROM LIVERPOOL ....5 wks

OSMONDS
31 Aug 74 LOVE ME FOR A REASON............................3 wks
See also Donny OSMOND

Gilbert O'SULLIVAN
11 Nov 72 CLAIR.................................2 wks
7 Apr 73 GET DOWN.....................2 wks

OVERLANDERS
27 Jan 66 MICHELLE ....3 wks

PACEMAKERS - see GERRY and the PACEMAKERS

Elaine PAIGE and Barbara DICKSON
9 Feb 85 I KNOW HIM SO WELL..................................4 wks

PAPER LACE
16 Mar 74 BILLY DON'T BE A HERO..................................3 wks

Simon PARK ORCHESTRA
29 Sep 73 EYE LEVEL.........................4 wks

PARTNERS IN KRYME
28 Jul 90 TURTLE POWER.............4 wks

Freda PAYNE
19 Sep 70 BAND OF GOLD............6 wks

PET SHOP BOYS
11 Jan 86 WEST END GIRLS...........2 wks
4 Jul 87 IT'S A SIN ....3 wks
19 Dec 87 ALWAYS ON MY MIND.................................4 wks
9 Apr 88 HEART...............................3 wks

PETER and GORDON
23 Apr 64 A WORLD WITHOUT LOVE..................................2 wks

PETERS and LEE
21 Jul 73 WELCOME HOME...........1 wk

PILOT
1 Feb 75 JANUARY..........................3 wks

PINK FLOYD
15 Dec 79 ANOTHER BRICK IN THE WALL (PART II)................5 wks

PIRATES - see Johnny KIDD and the PIRATES

Gene PITNEY - see Marc ALMOND with special guest Gene PITNEY

PLATTERS
20 Mar 59 SMOKE GETS IN YOUR EYES.......................................1 wk

POLICE
29 Sep 79 MESSAGE IN A BOTTLE ....3 wks
8 Dec 79 WALKING ON THE MOON...............................1 wk
27 Sep 80 DON'T STAND SO CLOSE TO ME ....4 wks

14 Nov 81 EVERY LITTLE THING SHE DOES IS MAGIC.................1 wk
4 Jun 83 EVERY BREATH YOU TAKE....................................4 wks

Brian POOLE and the TREMELOES

10 Oct 63 DO YOU LOVE ME ....3 wks

See also TREMELOES

Perez PRADO

29 Apr 55 CHERRY PINK AND APPLE BLOSSOM WHITE...........2 wks

Elvis PRESLEY

12 Jul 57 ALL SHOOK UP...............7 wks
24 Jan 58 JAILHOUSE ROCK...........3 wks
30 Jan 59 ONE NIGHT/I GOT STUNG...............................3 wks
15 May 59 A FOOL SUCH AS I/I NEED YOUR LOVE TONIGHT ....5 wks
3 Nov 60 IT'S NOW OR NEVER....8 wks
26 Jan 61 ARE YOU LONESOME TONIGHT ....4 wks
23 Mar 61 WOODEN HEART ....6 wks
1 Jun 61 SURRENDER ....4 wks
9 Nov 61 HIS LATEST FLAME/LITTLE SISTER ....4 wks
22 Feb 62 ROCK-A-HULA BABY/CAN'T HELP FALLING IN LOVE..................................4 wks
24 May 62 GOOD LUCK CHARM..5 wks
13 Sep 62 SHE'S NOT YOU.............3 wks
13 Dec 62 RETURN TO SENDER....3 wks
1 Aug 63 (YOU'RE THE) DEVIL IN DISGUISE.............................1 wk
17 Jun 65 CRYING IN THE CHAPEL...............................1 wk
1 Jul 65 CRYING IN THE CHAPEL...............................1 wk
1 Aug 70 THE WONDER OF YOU ....6 wks
3 Sep 77 WAY DOWN ....3 wks

Billy PRESTON - see BEATLES

Johnny PRESTON

17 Mar 60 RUNNING BEAR..............2 wks

PRETENDERS

19 Jan 80 BRASS IN POCKET ....2 wks

See also UB40

PRINCE

23 Apr 94 THE MOST BEAUTIFUL GIRL IN THE WORLD...............2 wks

PROCOL HARUM

8 Jun 67 A WHITER SHADE OF PALE.......................................6 wks

Gary PUCKETT - see UNION GAP featuring Gary PUCKETT

PUSSYCAT

4 Sep 76 MISSISSIPPI ....4 wks

Suzi QUATRO

16 Jun 73 CAN THE CAN.................1 wk
23 Feb 74 DEVIL GATE DRIVE.........2 wks

QUEEN

29 Nov 75 BOHEMIAN RHAPSODY 9 wks
26 Jan 91 INNUENDO.......................1 wk
21 Dec 91 BOHEMIAN RHAPSODY/ THESE ARE THE DAYS OF OUR LIVES........................5 wks

See also QUEEN and David BOWIE; George MICHAEL and QUEEN with Lisa STANSFIELD

QUEEN and David BOWIE

21 Nov 81 UNDER PRESSURE ....2 wks

See also QUEEN; David BOWIE

Marvin RAINWATER

25 Apr 58 WHOLE LOTTA WOMAN...........................3 wks

Johnnie RAY

30 Apr 54 SUCH A NIGHT.................1 wk
16 Nov 56 JUST WALKIN' IN THE RAIN......................................7 wks
7 Jun 57 YES TONIGHT JOSEPHINE........................3 wks

REAL THING

26 Jun 76 YOU TO ME ARE EVERYTHING....................3 wks

Jim REEVES

22 Sep 66 DISTANT DRUMS........... 5 wks

Vic REEVES and the WONDER STUFF

9 Nov 91 DIZZY ....2 wks

RENEE and RENATO

18 Dec 82 SAVE YOUR LOVE ....4 wks

Cliff RICHARD

31 Jul 59 LIVING DOLL ....6 wks
30 Oct 59 TRAVELLIN' LIGHT ....5 wks
28 Jul 60 PLEASE DON'T TEASE.....1 wk
11 Aug 60 PLEASE DON'T TEASE...2 wks
29 Dec 60 I LOVE YOU......................2 wks
11 Jan 62 THE YOUNG ONES........6 wks
3 Jan 63 THE NEXT TIME/ BACHELOR BOY ....3 wks
14 Mar 63 SUMMER HOLIDAY.........2 wks
4 Apr 63 SUMMER HOLIDAY...........1 wk
15 Apr 65 THE MINUTE YOU'RE GONE ....1 wk
10 Apr 68 CONGRATULATIONS...2 wks
25 Aug 79 WE DON'T TALK ANYMORE.........................4 wks
10 Dec 88 MISTLETOE AND WINE ....4 wks
29 Dec 90 SAVIOUR'S DAY ....1 wk

See also Cliff RICHARD and the YOUNG ONES. The SHADOWS appear on all Cliff's number ones up to and including Summer Holiday. See also SHADOWS.

Cliff RICHARD and the YOUNG ONES

29 Mar 86 LIVING DOLL ....3 wks

See also Cliff RICHARD

Wendy RICHARD - see Mike SARNE with Wendy RICHARD

Lionel RICHIE

24 Mar 84 HELLO................................6 wks

See also COMMODORES

RIGHT SAID FRED

18 Apr 92 DEEPLY DIPPY..................3 wks

RIGHTEOUS BROTHERS

4 Feb 65 YOU'VE LOST THAT LOVIN' FEELIN'..............................2 wks
3 Nov 90 UNCHAINED MELODY ....4 wks

Smokey ROBINSON

13 Jun 81 BEING WITH YOU..........2 wks

See also Smokey ROBINSON and the MIRACLES

Smokey ROBINSON and the MIRACLES

12 Sep 70 TEARS OF A CLOWN .....1 wk

See also Smokey ROBINSON

Lord ROCKINGHAM'S XI

28 Nov 58 HOOTS MON ....3 wks

Tommy ROE

4 Jun 69 DIZZY ....1 wk

Kenny ROGERS

18 Jun 77 LUCILLE................................1 wk
16 Feb 80 COWARD OF THE COUNTY ....2 wks

ROLLING STONES

16 Jul 64 IT'S ALL OVER NOW.......1 wk
3 Dec 64 LITTLE RED ROOSTER....1 wk
18 Mar 65 THE LAST TIME................3 wks
9 Sep 65 (I CAN'T GET NO) SATISFACTION.................2 wks
4 Nov 65 GET OFF OF MY CLOUD..............................3 wks
26 May 66 PAINT IT, BLACK ....1 wk
19 Jun 68 JUMPING JACK FLASH...2 wks
23 Jul 69 HONKY TONK WOMEN.............................5 wks

See also David BOWIE and Mick JAGGER

Diana ROSS

21 Aug 71 I'M STILL WAITING ....4 wks
8 Mar 86 CHAIN REACTION.........3 wks

See also SUPREMES

Demis ROUSSOS

17 Jul 76 THE ROUSSOS PHENOMENON (EP) ....1 wk

ROXY MUSIC

14 Mar 81 JEALOUS GUY ....2 wks

Pipes and Drums and Military Band of the ROYAL SCOTS DRAGOON GUARDS

15 Apr 72 AMAZING GRACE..........5 wks

Lita ROZA

17 Apr 53 (HOW MUCH IS) THAT DOGGIE IN THE WINDOW ....1 wk

RUBETTES

18 May 74 SUGAR BABY LOVE........4 wks

Jennifer RUSH

12 Oct 85 THE POWER OF LOVE..5 wks

S-EXPRESS

30 Apr 88 THEME FROM S-EXPRESS.........................2 wks

ST. WINIFRED'S SCHOOL CHOIR

27 Dec 80 THERE'S NO-ONE QUITE LIKE GRANDMA..............2 wks

Mike SARNE with Wendy RICHARD

28 Jun 62 COME OUTSIDE..............2 wks

Peter SARSTEDT

26 Feb 69 WHERE DO YOU GO TO, MY LOVELY?......................4 wks

Telly SAVALAS

8 Mar 75 IF ....2 wks

Leo SAYER

19 Feb 77 WHEN I NEED YOU.......3 wks

SCAFFOLD

11 Dec 68 LILY THE PINK..................3 wks
8 Jan 69 LILY THE PINK.....................1 wk

SEARCHERS

8 Aug 63 SWEETS FOR MY SWEET ....2 wks
30 Jan 64 NEEDLES AND PINS.......3 wks

7 May 64 DON'T THROW YOUR LOVE AWAY ....2 wks

SEEKERS

25 Feb 65 I'LL NEVER FIND ANOTHER YOU ....2 wks
25 Nov 65 THE CARNIVAL IS OVER ....3 wks

SHADOWS

25 Aug 60 APACHE ....5 wks
5 Oct 61 KON-TIKI ....1 wk
22 Mar 62 WONDERFUL LAND .....8 wks
24 Jan 63 DANCE ON! ....1 wk
28 Mar 63 FOOT TAPPER ....1 wk
See also Cliff RICHARD; Jet HARRIS and Tony MEEHAN

SHAGGY

20 Mar 93 OH CAROLINA ....2 wks

SHAKESPEARS SISTER

22 Feb 92 STAY ....8 wks

SHAMEN

19 Sep 92 EBENEEZER GOODE .....4 wks

Del SHANNON

29 Jun 61 RUNAWAY ....3 wks

Helen SHAPIRO

10 Aug 61 YOU DON'T KNOW .....3 wks
19 Oct 61 WALKIN' BACK TO HAPPINESS ....3 wks

Feargal SHARKEY

16 Nov 85 A GOOD HEART ....2 wks

Sandie SHAW

22 Oct 64 (THERE'S) ALWAYS SOME THING THERE TO REMIND ME ....3 wks
27 May 65 LONG LIVE LOVE ....3 wks
27 Apr 67 PUPPET ON A STRING .3 wks

Anne SHELTON

21 Sep 56 LAY DOWN YOUR ARMS ....4 wks

SHONDELLS - see Tommy JAMES and the SHONDELLS

SHOWADDYWADDY

4 Dec 76 UNDER THE MOON OF LOVE ....3 wks

SIMON and GARFUNKEL

28 Mar 70 BRIDGE OVER TROUBLED WATER ....3 wks
See also Art GARFUNKEL

SIMPLE MINDS

25 Feb 89 BELFAST CHILD ....2 wks

SIMPSONS

16 Feb 91 DO THE BARTMAN ....3 wks

Frank SINATRA

17 Feb 54 THREE COINS IN THE FOUNTAIN ....3 wks
2 Jun 66 STRANGERS IN THE NIGHT ....3 wks
See also Nancy SINATRA and Frank SINATRA.........

Nancy SINATRA

17 Feb 66 THESE BOOTS ARE MADE FOR WALKIN' ....4 wks
See also Nancy SINATRA and Frank SINATRA

Nancy SINATRA and Frank SINATRA

13 Apr 67 SOMETHING STUPID ....2 wks
See also Nancy SINATRA, Frank SINATRA

SISTER SLEDGE

29 Jun 85 FRANKIE ....4 wks

SLADE

13 Nov 71 COZ I LUV YOU ....4 wks
1 Jul 72 TAKE ME BAK 'OME ....1 wk
9 Sep 72 MAMA WEER ALL CRAZEE NOW ....3 wks
3 Mar 73 CUM ON FEEL THE NOIZE ....4 wks
30 Jun 73 SKWEEZE ME PLEEZE ME ....3 wks
15 Dec 73 MERRY XMAS EVERYBODY ....5 wks

SLIK

14 Feb 76 FOREVER AND EVER ....1 wk
See also Midge URE

SMALL FACES

15 Sep 66 ALL OR NOTHING ....1 wk

SNAP!

31 Mar 90 THE POWER ....2 wks
8 Aug 92 RHYTHM IS A DANCER ....6 wks

SOFT CELL

5 Sep 81 TAINTED LOVE ....2 wks
See also Marc ALMOND

SONIA

22 Jul 89 YOU'LL NEVER STOP ME LOVING YOU ....2 wks

SONNY and CHER

26 Aug 65 I GOT YOU BABE ....2 wks
See also CHER

David SOUL

15 Jan 77 DON'T GIVE UP ON US ....4 wks
8 Oct 77 SILVER LADY ....3 wks

SOUL II SOUL featuring Caron WHEELER

24 Jun 89 BACK TO LIFE (HOWEVER DO YOU WANT ME) .....4 wks

SPANDAU BALLET

30 Apr 85 TRUE ....4 wks

SPECIALS

2 Feb 80 THE SPECIAL A.K.A. LIVE (EP) ....2 wks
11 Jul 81 GHOST TOWN ....3 wks

SPINNERS - see DETROIT SPINNERS

SPITTING IMAGE

17 May 86 THE CHICKEN SONG ...3 wks

Dusty SPRINGFIELD

28 Apr 66 YOU DON'T HAVE TO SAY YOU LOVE ME ....1 wk

Jo STAFFORD

16 Jan 53 YOU BELONG TO ME .....1 wk

Lisa STANSFIELD

11 Nov 89 ALL AROUND THE WORLD ....2 wks
See also George MICHAEL and QUEEN with Lisa STANSFIELD

Alvin STARDUST

9 Mar 74 JEALOUS MIND ....1 wk

STARGAZERS

10 Apr 53 BROKEN WINGS ....1 wk
12 Mar 54 I SEE THE MOON ....5 wks
23 Apr 54 I SEE THE MOON ....1 wk

Kay STARR

23 Jan 53 COMES A-LONG A-LOVE ....1 wk
30 Mar 56 ROCK AND ROLL WALTZ ....1 wk

STARSHIP

9 May 87 NOTHING'S GONNA STOP US NOW ....4 wks

STATUS QUO

18 Jan 75 DOWN DOWN ....1 wk

Tommy STEELE

11 Jan 57 SINGING THE BLUES ....1 wk

Ray STEVENS

15 Jun 74 THE STREAK ....1 wk

Shakin' STEVENS

28 Mar 81 THIS OLE HOUSE ....3 wks
1 Aug 81 GREEN DOOR ....4 wks
30 Jan 82 OH JULIE ....1 wk
28 Dec 85 MERRY CHRISTMAS EVERY ONE ....2 wks

Dave STEWART with Barbara GASKIN

17 Oct 81 IT'S MY PARTY ....4 wks

Rod STEWART

9 Oct 71 MAGGIE MAY ....5 wks
2 Sep 72 YOU WEAR IT WELL ....1 wk
6 Sep 75 SAILING ....4 wks
21 May 77 I DON'T WANT TO TALK ABOUT IT/FIRST CUT IS THE DEEPEST ....4 wks
2 Dec 78 DA YA THINK I'M SEXY ....1 wk
2 Jul 83 BABY JANE ....3 wks

STINGERS - see B.BUMBLE and the STINGERS

STILTSKIN

14 May 94 INSIDE ....1 wk

Barbra STREISAND

25 Oct 80 WOMAN IN LOVE ....3 wks

STYLISTICS

16 Aug 75 CAN'T GIVE YOU ANY THING (BUT MY LOVE) ....3 wks

Donna SUMMER

23 Jul 77 I FEEL LOVE ....4 wks

SUNSHINE BAND - see K.C. and the SUNSHINE BAND

SUPREMES

19 Nov 64 BABY LOVE ....2 wks
See also Diana ROSS

SURVIVOR

4 Sep 82 EYE OF THE TIGER ....4 wks

SWEET

27 Jan 73 BLOCKBUSTER ....5 wks

SWEET SENSATION

19 Oct 74 SAD SWEET DREAMER ...1 wk

T.REX

20 Mar 71 HOT LOVE ....6 wks
24 Jul 71 GET IT ON ....4 wks
5 Feb 72 TELEGRAM SAM ....2 wks
20 May 72 METAL GURU ....4 wks

TAKE THAT

17 Jul 93 PRAY ....4 wks

9 Oct 93 RELIGHT MY FIRE ....2 wks
18 Dec 93 BABE ....1 wk
9 Apr 94 EVERYTHING CHANGES ....2 wks
Relight My Fire featured LULU

TAMS
8 Sep 71 HEY GIRL DON'T BOTHER ME ....3 wks

TEENAGERS featuring Frankie LYMON
20 Jul 56 WHY DO FOOLS FALL IN LOVE ....3 wks

TEMPERANCE SEVEN
25 May 61 YOU'RE DRIVING ME CRAZY ....1 wk

10 C.C.
23 Jun 73 RUBBER BULLETS ....1 wk
28 Jun 75 I'M NOT IN LOVE ....2 wks
23 Sep 78 DREADLOCK HOLIDAY ..1 wk
On Dreadlock Holiday, 10 CC were a vocal/instrumental duo

THREE DEGREES
17 Aug 74 WHEN WILL I SEE YOU AGAIN ....2 wks

THUNDERBIRDS - see Chris FARLOWE and the THUNDERBIRDS

THUNDERCLAP NEWMAN
2 Jul 69 SOMETHING IN THE AIR ....3 wks

TIFFANY
30 Jan 88 I THINK WE'RE ALONE NOW ....3 wks

TIGHT FIT
6 Mar 82 THE LION SLEEPS TONIGHT ....3 wks

Johnny TILLOTSON
12 Jan 61 POETRY IN MOTION .....2 wks

TIMELORDS
18 Jun 88 DOCTORIN' THE TARDIS ....1 wk

TORNADOS
4 Oct 62 TELSTAR ....5 wks

T'PAU
14 Nov 87 CHINA IN YOUR HAND ....5 wks

John TRAVOLTA and Olivia NEWTON-JOHN
17 Jun 78 YOU'RE THE ONE THAT I WANT ....9 wks
30 Sep 78 SUMMER NIGHTS ....7 wks
See also Olivia NEWTON-JOHN and ELECTRIC LIGHT ORCHESTRA

TREMELOES
18 May 67 SILENCE IS GOLDEN .....3 wks
See also Brian POOLE and the TREMELOES

Jackie TRENT
20 May 65 WHERE ARE YOU NOW (MY LOVE) ....1 wk

TROGGS
4 Aug 66 WITH A GIRL LIKE YOU ....2 wks

TUBEWAY ARMY - see Gary NUMAN

Conway TWITTY
19 Dec 58 IT'S ONLY MAKE BELIEVE ....5 wks

2 UNLIMITED
13 Feb 93 NO LIMIT ....5 wks

Bonnie TYLER
12 Mar 83 TOTAL ECLIPSE OF THE HEART ....2 wks

TYMES
25 Jan 75 MS. GRACE ....1 wk

TYPICALLY TROPICAL
9 Aug 75 BARBADOS ....1 wk

UB40
3 Sep 83 RED RED WINE ....3 wks
31 Aug 85 I GOT YOU BABE ....1 wk
12 Jun 93 (I CAN'T HELP) FALLING IN LOVE WITH YOU ....2 wks
I Got You Babe featured guest vocals by Chrissie HYNDE. See also PRETENDERS.

UNION GAP featuring Gary PUCKETT
22 May 68 YOUNG GIRL .... 4 wks

UNIT FOUR PLUS TWO
8 Apr 65 CONCRETE AND CLAY .1 wk

Midge URE
5 Oct 85 IF I WAS ....1 wk
See also SLIK

USA FOR AFRICA
20 Apr 85 WE ARE THE WORLD...2 wks

U2
8 Oct 88 DESIRE ....1 wk
2 Nov 91 THE FLY ....1 wk

Ricky VALANCE
29 Sep 60 TELL LAURA I LOVE HER ....3 wks

Dickie VALENTINE
7 Jan 55 FINGER OF SUSPICION ..1 wk
21 Jan 55 FINGER OF SUSPICION ....2 wks
16 Dec 55 CHRISTMAS ALPHABET ....3 wks

VANILLA ICE
1 Dec 90 ICE ICE BABY ....4 wks

Frankie VAUGHAN
25 Jan 57 GARDEN OF EDEN ....4 wks
7 Dec 61 TOWER OF STRENGTH ....3 wks

VILLAGE PEOPLE
6 Jan 79 Y.M.C.A. ....3 wks

WALKER BROTHERS
23 Sep 65 MAKE IT EASY ON YOURSELF ....1 wk
17 Mar 66 THE SUN AIN'T GONNA SHINE ANYMORE ....4 wks

Anita WARD
16 Jun 79 RING MY BELL ....2 wks

WET WET WET
21 May 88 WITH A LITTLE HELP FROM MY FRIENDS ....4 wks
25 Jan 92 GOODNIGHT GIRL ....4 wks
4 Jun 94* LOVE IS ALL AROUND .12 wks
* Still at number one at time of going to press 13 August 94

WHAM!
2 Jun 84 WAKE ME UP BEFORE YOU GO GO ....2 wks
20 Oct 84 FREEDOM ....3 wks
30 Nov 85 I'M YOUR MAN ....2 wks
28 Jun 86 THE EDGE OF HEAVEN ....2 wks
See also George MICHAEL

Caron WHEELER - see SOUL II SOUL featuring Caron WHEELER

Barry WHITE
7 Dec 74 YOU'RE THE FIRST THE LAST MY EVERYTHING ....2 wks

David WHITFIELD
6 Nov 53 ANSWER ME ....1 wk
11 Dec 53 ANSWER ME ....1 wk
2 Jul 54 CARA MIA ....10 wks
Cara Mia is by David WHITFIELD with the MANTOVANI ORCHESTRA. See also MANTOVANI

Slim WHITMAN
29 Jul 55 ROSE MARIE ....11 wks

Andy WILLIAMS
24 May 57 BUTTERFLY ....2 wks

Danny WILLIAMS
28 Dec 61 MOON RIVER ....2 wks

Deniece WILLIAMS
7 May 77 FREE ....2 wks

Jackie WILSON
27 Dec 86 REET PETITE ....4 wks

WINGS
3 Dec 77 MULL OF KINTYRE/GIRLS' SCHOOL ....9 wks
See also Paul McCARTNEY

WIZZARD
19 May 73 SEE MY BABY JIVE ....4 wks
22 Sep 73 ANGEL FINGERS ....1 wk

Stevie WONDER
8 Sep 84 I JUST CALLED TO SAY I LOVE YOU .... 6 wks
See also Paul McCARTNEY with Stevie WONDER.

WONDER STUFF - see Vic REEVES and the WONDER STUFF

WURZELS
12 Jun 76 COMBINE HARVESTER (BRAND NEW KEY) ....2 wks

Tammy WYNETTE
17 May 75 STAND BY YOUR MAN ....3 wks

YAZZ and the PLASTIC POPULATION
6 Aug 88 THE ONLY WAY IS UP ....5 wks

Jimmy YOUNG
24 Jun 55 UNCHAINED MELODY ....3 wks
14 Oct 55 THE MAN FROM LARAMIE ....4 wks

Paul YOUNG
23 Jul 83 WHEREVER I LAY MY HAT (THAT'S MY HOME) ....3 wks

ZAGER and EVANS
30 Aug 69 IN THE YEAR 2525 (EXORDIUM AND TERMINUS) ....3 wks

Section Three

Over Seven Hundred Number Ones Listed Alphabetically by Title

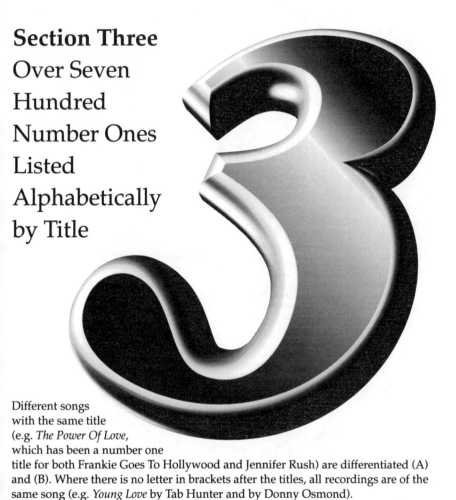

Different songs with the same title (e.g. *The Power Of Love,* which has been a number one title for both Frankie Goes To Hollywood and Jennifer Rush) are differentiated (A) and (B). Where there is no letter in brackets after the titles, all recordings are of the same song (e.g. *Young Love* by Tab Hunter and by Donny Osmond).